CONTENTS

think
PINK
CROCHET FOR THE CURE

General Information

Many of the products used in this pattern book can be purchased from local craft, fabric and variety stores, or from the Annie's Attic Needlecraft Catalog (see Customer Service information on page 64).

When we came up with the idea to publish a book of crocheted projects intended to promote breast cancer awareness, we never dreamed of the response we would receive. Our call for designs brought in not only dozens of wonderful crocheted items, but touching personal stories from many of the designers as well. We heard from survivors as well as friends and family members; it seems everyone had a story to share. So many lives have been touched by the challenge of breast cancer; so many hearts carry love and pride for the survivors, as well as for the brave souls who are survivors in spirit.

introduction

As our contribution, DRG Publishing is pleased to donate a portion of the proceeds of this book to breast cancer research. This book has become a labor of love for everyone involved. It is our hope these items will encourage the recipients to keep a positive and optimistic attitude, and to always "Think Pink!" And, remember getting tested regularly for breast cancer is the best way for women to lower their risk, as screening tests can find cancer early, when it's most treatable.

It is with much love that we dedicate this book to women everywhere who face life's most difficult challenges with optimism, courage and faith.

PIGTAIL HAT *by Darla Sims*

SKILL LEVEL

INTERMEDIATE

FINISHED SIZE

One size fits most

MATERIALS

- Red Heart Soft Yarn medium (worsted) weight yarn (5 oz/256 yds/140g per skein):
    1 skein each color #6768 pink and #4614 black
- Sizes G/6/4mm and I/9/5.5mm crochet hooks or size needed to obtain gauge
- Tapestry needle
- 1½-inch wide checkered ribbon: 48 inches
- Stitch marker

GAUGE

Size I hook: 12 dc = 4 inches

PATTERN NOTES

Chain-3 at beginning of row or round counts as first double crochet unless otherwise stated.

Join with slip stitch as indicated unless otherwise stated.

Work in continuous rounds, do not join or turn unless otherwise stated.

Mark first stitch of each round.

INSTRUCTIONS

HAT

Crown

Rnd 1: With size I hook and pink, ch 2, 8 sc in 2nd ch from hook, **do not join** (see Pattern Notes). (8 sc)

Rnd 2: 2 sc in each st around. (16 sc)

Rnd 3: [Sc in next st, 2 sc in next st] around. (24 sc)

Rnd 4: [Sc in each of next 2 sts, 2 sc in next st] around. (32 sc)

Rnd 5: [Sc in each of next 3 sts, 2 sc in next st] around. (40 sc)

Rnd 6: [Sc in each of next 4 sts, 2 sc in next st] around. (48 sc)

Rnd 7: [Sc in each of next 5 sts, 2 sc in next st] around. (56 sc)

Rnd 8: [Sc in each of next 6 sts, 2 sc in next st] around, **join** (see Pattern Notes) in beg sc. (64 sc)

Side

Rnd 9: Ch 1, sc in first st, tr in next st, [sc in next st, tr in next st] around, join in beg sc.

Rnds 10 & 11: Ch 3 (see Pattern Notes), dc in each st around, join in 3rd ch of beg ch-3.

Rnd 12: Ch 1, sc in first st, tr in next st, [sc in next st, tr in next st] around, join in beg sc.

Rnds 13 & 14: Ch 3, dc in each st around, join in 3rd ch of beg ch-3.

Rnd 15: Ch 1, sc in first st, tr in next st, [sc in next st, tr in next st] around, join in beg sc.

Band

Rnds 1–5: With size G hook, ch 1, sc in each st around, join in beg sc. At end of last rnd, fasten off.

Curly Bangs

With size G hook, join black with sl st in any sc, *ch 6, 3 sc in 2nd ch from hook and in each of next 4 chs, sc in next st on Band, sl st in next st, rep from * 5 times, ch 6, 3 sc in 2nd ch from hook and in each of next 4 chs, sc in next st on Band. Fasten off.

Braid
Make 2.

Cut 21 strands black, each 36 inches in length. Holding all strands tog, fold in half and tie knot in center of strands.

Divide strands into 3 groups of 7 strands in each group. Loosely braid. Wrap end of Braid tightly with black. Trim ends.

Cut ribbon in half. Tie 1 piece of ribbon around end of each Braid. Sew Braids to inside of Band, 2 inches on each side of Curly Bangs. ●

Recently, a friend of mine underwent a double mastectomy and had just begun chemotherapy which was due to last for many long months. I wanted to do something to let her know of my concern and care for her and to cheer her up if possible. The end result was a box filled with nine different crocheted chemo caps I designed just for her, ranging from the traditional pink chemo cap to the whimsical Pigtail Hat (her favorite) featured here.

Darla Sims

pink

FABRIC BASKET *by Susan Lowman*

THINK PINK Crochet for the Cure • Annie's Attic • Berne, IN 46711 • DRGnetwork.com

SKILL LEVEL

INTERMEDIATE

FINISHED SIZE

5 inches high x 8 inches square, excluding Handle

MATERIALS

- 44-inch wide print cotton fabric:
  2¼ yds off-white
  1½ yds pink
- Size K/10½/6.5mm crochet hook or size needed to obtain gauge
- Stitch marker

GAUGE

8 sc = 3¾ inches; 8 rows = 3½ inches

PATTERN NOTE

Join with slip stitch as indicated unless otherwise stated.

FABRIC PREPARATION

Pre-shrink fabric in laundry.
To cut fabric, carefully follow these steps:

1. Cut fabric into 1-yard pieces. Work on only 1 1-yard piece at a time.
2. Fold 1-yard piece in half lengthwise with WS facing.
3. Sew the selvage edges tog twice with sewing machine, creating a tube.
4. Fold the fabric in half lengthwise again, leaving 1-inch selvage at top *(see Fig. 1)*.

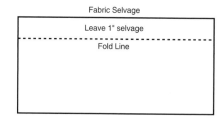

Fig. 1
Fabric Preparation
Folding Diagram

5. Using a pair of scissors, or rotary cutter *(recommended)*, cut 1-inch strips of fabric up to the folding line *(see Fig. 2)*.

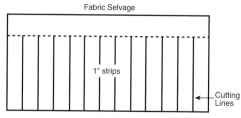

Fig. 2
Fabric Preparation
Cutting Diagram

6. Open both folds and cut the selvage in slants, from 1 end of 1 strip to the end of the other *(see Fig. 3)*.

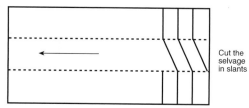

Fig. 3
Fabric Preparation
Cutting at Slant Diagram

7. You will now have a long strip of fabric. Make a ball and begin crocheting.

INSTRUCTIONS

BASKET
Bottom
Row 1 (RS): With pink, ch 17, sc in 2nd ch from hook and in each ch across, turn. *(16 sc)*
Rows 2–16: Ch 1, sc in each st across, turn.
Rnd 17: Working around outer edge, ch 1, 2 sc in first st, sc in each st across with 3 sc in last st, working in ends of rows, sc in end of each row across, working in starting ch opposite side of row 1, 3 sc in first ch, sc in each ch across with 3 sc in last ch, working in ends of rows, sc in end of each row across, sc in same st as beg sc, **join** *(see Pattern Note)* in beg sc. Fasten off.

Side
Rnd 1: With WS of Bottom facing, join off-white in **back lp** *(see Stitch Guide)* of center corner sc, working in back lps, sc in each st around, **do not join**. Mark first st.
Rnds 2–9: Sc in each st around. At end of rnd 9, join in beg sc. Fasten off.
Rnd 10: With RS facing, join pink with sc in center sc on any side of rnd 9, sc in each st around, join in beg sc. Fasten off.

Handle
With off-white, ch 36, sc in 2nd ch from hook and in each ch across. Fasten off.

Sew Handle ends to inside edge of Basket as shown in photo.

Ribbon
Make 2.
With pink, ch 20. Fasten off.

Fold Ribbon in loop as shown in photo and sew 1 to each Side of Basket below Handle. •

FILET BOOK BAG

by Susan Lowman

SKILL LEVEL

INTERMEDIATE

FINISHED SIZE

10 inches wide x 14½ inches high, excluding Handles

MATERIALS

- Aunt Lydia's "Baby Denim" Quick Crochet worsted crochet cotton (400 yds per ball):
    1 ball #1032 baby pink
- Size H/8/5mm crochet hook or size needed to obtain gauge
- Tapestry needle
- Sewing needle
- Sewing thread
- Dark pink fabric:
    11 x 30 inch: 1
    1½ x 14 inches: 2
- Stitch marker

GAUGE

6 mesh = 4 inches; 6 mesh rows = 3 inches

PATTERN NOTE

Chain-3 at beginning of rows or rounds counts as first double crochet unless otherwise stated.

SPECIAL STITCHES

Mesh: Ch 2, sk next 2 sts or ch sp, dc in next st.

Beginning block (beg block): Ch 3, dc in each of next 3 sts.

Block: Dc in each of next 3 sts or 2 dc in next ch sp, dc in next st.

Extended double crochet (extended dc): Yo, insert in place indicated, yo, pull lp through, yo, pull through 1 lp on hook, [yo, pull through 2 lps on hook] twice.

INSTRUCTIONS

BAG
Side
Make 2.

Row 1 (RS): Ch 48, dc in **back bar** (see Fig. 1) of 4th ch from hook (first 3 chs count as first dc), dc in back bar of each ch across, turn. (46 dc)

Fig. 1
Back Bar of Chain

Row 2: Ch 3 (see Pattern Note), dc in each of next 3 sts, [ch 2, sk next 2 sts, dc in next st] 13 times, dc in each of last 3 sts, turn.

Rows 3–27: Using Special Stitches as needed, work according to chart (see Fig. 2) across, turn.

Row 28: Ch 1, sc in each st across, turn.

Row 29: Sl st in first st, [sk next st, (hdc, dc, **extended dc**—see Special Stitches) in next st, (extended dc, dc, hdc) in next st, sk next st, sl st in next st] across. Fasten off on 1 Side only.

Joining

With RS of Side pieces held tog, working through both thicknesses, ch 1, evenly sl st Sides tog down side, working in starting chs on opposite side of rows 1, sl st in each ch across, evenly sl st up side. Fasten off. Turn RS out.

Handle
Make 2.

Row 1 (RS): Ch 56, sc in back bar of 2nd ch from hook and in back bar of each st across, turn. (55 sc)

Row 2: Ch 1, sc in each st across, turn.

Row 3: Ch 5 (counts as first dc and ch-2), sk next 2 sts, dc in next st, [ch 2, sk next 2 sts, dc in next st] across, turn. (18 ch sps, 19 dc)

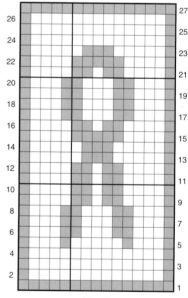

Fig. 2
Filet Book Bag
Chart

STITCH KEY
▨ Beg block/block
☐ Mesh

Row 4: Ch 1, sc in first st, [2 sc in next ch sp, sc in next st] across, turn. *(55 sc)*

Row 5: Ch 1, sc in each st across. Fasten off.

Sew 1 Handle to each Side of Bag as shown in photo.

Lining

Fold large piece of fabric in half with RS tog to form 11 x 15-inch piece. Sew long edges tog with ½-inch seam allowance. Turn RS out.

Turn top edge down ½ inch to WS, turn down once more. Sew close to edge.

Fold long edges of 1 short piece in 3rds, sew down center. Weave through ch sps on 1 Handle.

Rep with rem piece of fabric and Handle.

Place Lining inside Bag, tuck ends of fabric on Handles between Lining and Bag. Sew top edge of Lining to top of Bag below row 29. •

SKILL LEVEL

INTERMEDIATE

FINISHED SIZE

6½ x 13 inches

MATERIALS

- Red Heart Soft Yarn medium (worsted) weight yarn (5 oz/256 yds/140g per skein):
    1 skein each #4600 white and #6768 pink
- Size J/10/6mm crochet hook or size needed to obtain gauge
- Tapestry needle
- Sewing needle
- Sewing thread
- White fabric:
    11 x 7½ inches: 2 pieces
- 2 pound bag long grain rice
- Stitch marker

GAUGE

15 sc = 4 inches; 15 sc rnds = 4 inches

PATTERN NOTE

Join with slip stitch as indicated unless otherwise stated.

INSTRUCTIONS

PACK
Cover

Rnd 1: With white, ch 48, sl st in first ch to form ring, being careful not to twist ch, ch 1, sc in each ch around, join (see Pattern Note) in beg sc. (48 sc)

Rnd 2: Ch 1, sc in first st, sc in **back lp** (see Stitch Guide) of next st, [sc in both lps of next st, sc in back lp of next st] around, join in beg sc.

Rnd 3: Ch 3 (counts as first hdc and ch-1), sk next st, [hdc in next st, ch 1, sk next st] around, join in 2nd ch of beg ch-3.

Rnd 4: Ch 1, sc in first st, sc in next ch sp, [sc in next st, sc in next ch sp] around, sc in same ch sp as last sc, **do not join**. Mark first st. (49 sc)

Rnd 5: [Sc in both lps of next st, sc in back lp of next st] around, with sc in last st.

Rnd 6: [Sc in back lp of next st, sc in both lps of next st] around, sc in back lp of last st.

Rnds 7–40: [Rep rnds 5 and 6 alternately] 17 times or until piece measures 10½ inches from beg. At end of last rnd, [sc in both lps of next st, sc in back lp of next sc] twice, sc in next sc, **sc dec** (see Stitch Guide) in next 2 sts. Rnds will now beg here. (48 sc)

Rnd 41: Ch 3, sk next st, [hdc in next st, ch 1, sk next st] around, join in 2nd ch of beg ch-3.

Rnd 42: Ch 1, sc in first st, sc in next ch sp, [sc in next st, sc in next ch sp] around, join in beg sc.

Rnd 43: Ch 1, sc in first st, sc in back lp of next st, [sc in both lps of next st, sc in back lp of next st] around, join in beg sc. Fasten off.

Ties

Join pink with **fpsl st** (see Stitch Guide) around first st on rnd 3, ch 40, sl st in 2nd ch from hook and in each ch across, fpsl st around same st on rnd 3. Fasten off.

Join pink with fpsl st around 13th st on rnd 3, ch 40, sl st in 2nd ch from hook and in each ch across, sl st in same st on rnd 3. Fasten off.

Join pink with fpsl st around first st on rnd 41, ch 40, sl st in 2nd ch from hook and in each ch across, sl st in same st on rnd 41. Fasten off.

Join pink with fpsl st around 13th st on rnd 41, ch 40, sl st in 2nd ch from hook and in each ch across, sl st in same st on rnd 41. Fasten off.

Edging

Rnd 1: Working in starting ch on opposite side of row 1, with RS facing, join pink with sc in first ch, sc in each ch around, join in beg sc.

Rnd 2: Ch 4 (counts as first dc and ch-1), dc in same st, ch 1, (dc, ch 1) twice in each st around, join in 3rd ch of beg ch-4. Fasten off.

Rep Edging on rnd 43.

Ribbon
Make 2.

With pink, leaving 18-inch end, ch 40, working in **back bar** of chs (see Fig. 1), sl st in 2nd ch from hook, sc in next ch, hdc in each of next 15 chs, 2 hdc in each of next 5 chs, hdc in each of next 15 chs, sc in next ch, sl st in last ch. Leaving 18-inch end, fasten off.

Sew 1 Ribbon to each side of Cover.

Fig. 1
Back Bar of Chain

Rice Pack

With RS tog, sew fabric pieces tog across both long edges and 1 short end with ½-inch seam allowance. Trim bottom corners, turn RS out.

Fill with rice.

Turn top edges down ½ inch to inside and sew edge closed.

Assembly

On 1 end of Cover, weave Ties to center and tie in bow, closing end.

Place Rice Pack in Cover.

Weave Ties to center and tie in bow, closing end.

Rice Pack may be removed for washing by opening 1 end of Cover.

Do not wash Rice Pack. •

FREE-FORM HAT
by Margaret Hubert

SKILL LEVEL

INTERMEDIATE

FINISHED SIZE

One size fits most

MATERIALS

- Plymouth Baby Alpaca DK (light) weight yarn (1¾ oz/125 yds/50g per ball:
    1 ball #3425 (A)
- Plymouth Baby Alpaca Brush bulky (chunky) weight yarn (1¾ oz/110 yds/50g per ball:
    1 ball #567 (C)
- Plymouth Buckingham fine (sport) weight yarn (1¾ oz/218 yds/50g per skein):
    1 skein each #5293 (B) and #9210 (D)
- Size G/6/4mm crochet hook or size needed to obtain gauge
- Tapestry needle

PATTERN NOTES

This amount of yarn actually makes 2 Hats.

The yarn was chosen in order to get different colors and textures, which contribute to the great look of the Hat.

Each skein of Buckingham yarn should be divided in 2 as it is wound, as it is used with 2 strands held together.

Chain-3 at beginning of row or round counts as first double crochet unless otherwise stated.

Join with slip stitch as indicated unless otherwise stated.

SPECIAL STITCH

Bullion stitch (bullion st): Yo 10 times, insert hook in place indicated, yo, pull up lp, yo, pull through all lps on hook, leaving last lp on hook, yo and pull through all lps on hook.

INSTRUCTIONS

HAT
Top

Rnd 1: With A, make a lp, (sc, hdc, dc) in lp, pull up long lp, drop A, join B with sc in lp, (hdc, dc) in lp, pull up long lp, drop B, join C with sc in lp, (hdc, dc) in lp, pull up long lp, drop C, join D with sc in lp, (hdc, dc) in lp, tighten lp, forming circle with 4 segments, each in a different color, mark beg st of rnd, you will continue working with the last color worked each around until you reach the end of the next color. *(12 sts)*

Rnd 2: With D, 2 dc in each st of color A, drop D, pick up A, 2 dc in each st of color B, drop A, pick up B, 2 dc in each st of color C, drop B, continue in this manner with each color, working 2 sts in each st, until you reach the next color, work across to marker. *(24 dc)*

Rnd 3: Continue with last color worked, [dc in next st, 2 dc in next st] around to marker, working each color segment as you come to it. *(36 dc)*

Rnd 4: Continue with last color worked, [dc in each of next 2 sts, 2 dc in next st] around until first 3 colors are worked, with last color, [**bullion st** *(see Special Stitch)* in each of next 2 sts, 2 bullion sts in next st] around to marker. *(48 sts)*

Rnd 5: Continue with last color and bullion sts, [bullion st in each of next 3 sts, 2 bullion st in next st] 3 times, continue this rnd with [dc in each of next 3 sts, 2 dc in next st] around, following colors as before. *(60 sts)*

Rnd 6: Continue as established, inc every 5th st, at end of every color segment, work last 2 sts in hdc and sc. Fasten off all colors, **do not remove marker.**

Rnd 7: Join *(see Pattern Notes)* A by marker, **ch 3** *(see Pattern Notes)*, dc in each st around, join in 3rd ch of beg ch-3.

Rnd 8: Ch 3, dc in each st around, join in 3rd ch of beg ch-3. Drop A, **do not fasten off.**

Rnd 9: Join C in first st, ch 3, dc in each st around, join in 3rd ch of beg ch-3.

Rnd 10: Ch 3, dc in each st around, join in 3rd ch of beg ch-3. Drop C, pick up A.

Rnds 11–14: Rep rnds 7–10.

Rnds 15–17: Rep rnds 7–9.

Rnd 18: Holding 1 strand of A and C tog, ch 1, sc in each st around, join in beg sc.

Rnd 19: Ch 1, working from left to right, **reverse sc** *(see Fig. 1 on page 14)* in each st around, join in beg reverse sc. Fasten off.

Shells

Rnd 1: With A and RS facing, join with sc in sp between any sts 2 rnds

As a breast cancer survivor myself, I was really pleased to be able to contribute to this book. Twelve years ago, I was diagnosed with breast cancer. At first, like everyone else who faces this, I was devastated. Ten months before, my husband was also diagnosed with cancer. I felt that I had really reached a very low point in my life and started preparing myself for the worst. I sought a second opinion, went to the Breast Institute in New

Continued on page 14

pink

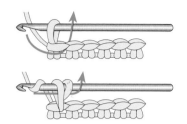

Fig. 1
Reverse Single Crochet

below bullion sts, sk next 2 sts, 5 dc in sp between next 2 sts, [sk next sts, sc in sp between next sts, sk next 3 sts, 5 dc in sp next sts] until 7 shells have been made, sk next 2 sts, 2 sc in sp between next sts, **fasten off A**, join C in center front where Shells began, dc in sp between dc until you meet Shell, **do not turn**.

Rnd 2: Ch 1, working from left to right, reverse sc in dc just worked only. Fasten off.

Leaf
Make 6.

Row 1: With B, ch 13, sc in 2nd ch from hook and in each of next 10 chs, 3 sc in last ch, working on opposite side of ch, sc in each of next 7 chs, leaving rem chs unworked, turn.

Row 2: Working in **front lps** *(see Stitch Guide)*, sc in each of first 7 sts, 2 sc in each of next 3 sts, sc in each of next 7 sts, leaving rem sts unworked. Fasten off.

Flower
Make 4 of each A, C and D.

Rnd 1: Ch 4, sl st in first ch to form ring, ch 1, 10 sc in ring, join in beg sc.

Rnd 2: *Ch 2, 3 dc in next st, ch 2**, sl st in next st, rep from * around, ending last rep at **, join in joining sl st of last rnd. Fasten off.

Assembly

Pin Leaves and Flowers in place with shells facing toward crown, dc row should be facing toward brim. Sew Flowers and Leaves in place. Using **French knot** *(see Fig. 2)* and B, embroider French knots in Flower centers and at random between Flowers and Leaves as shown in photo. •

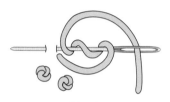

Fig. 2
French Knot

Continued from page 13

York City, and was given such hope and encouragement. I was one of the lucky ones— my cancer was small and found early. I have been told many times that the doctor who read my mammogram saved my life. I have also been told that the only reason that he detected it so early was the fact that he had 10 previous mammograms of mine on file for comparison. With excellent treatment, great support of family and friends and a very strong faith, I got through it.

I would like to encourage every woman to get a yearly mammogram, and, if at all possible, go to the same facility each time. If this is not possible, ask for copies of previous mammograms to be sent to current facilities. Early detection saves lives.

Margaret Hubert

RIBBON PIN *by Susan Lowman*

SKILL LEVEL

INTERMEDIATE

FINISHED SIZE

2 x 3 inches

MATERIALS

- J.&P. Coats Royale Classic Crochet Thread size 10 crochet cotton (white: 400 yds per ball; solids: 350 yds per ball):
  - 10 yds #201 white
  - 5 yds #401 orchid pink
  - 1 yd #493 French rose
- Size 7/1.65mm steel crochet hook or size needed to obtain gauge
- Beading needle
- Size 8 glass beads by Mill Hill: 30 #18010 ice
- 1-inch pin back
- Craft glue

GAUGE

Ribbon: 4 sts = ½ inch; 8 rows = 2 inches

Backing: Rnds 1–3 = 1⅜ inches in diameter

PATTERN NOTES

Chain-3 at beginning of row or round counts as first double crochet unless otherwise stated.

Join with slip stitch as indicated unless otherwise stated.

INSTRUCTIONS

RIBBON

Row 1: With pink, ch 6, dc in 4th ch from hook *(first 3 chs count as first dc)*, hdc in next ch, sc in last ch, turn.

Row 2: Ch 1, sc in first st, hdc in next st, dc in each of last 2 sts, turn.

Rows 3–26: Ch 3 *(see Pattern Notes)*, dc in each st across, turn.

Row 27: Ch 3, dc in next st, hdc in next st, sc in last st, turn.

Row 28: Ch 1, sc in first st, hdc in next st, dc in each of last 2 sts. Fasten off.

Backing

Rnd 1: With white, ch 4, sl st in first ch to form ring, ch 1, 8 sc in ring, **join** *(see Pattern Notes)* in beg sc. *(8 sc)*

Rnd 2: Ch 4 *(count as first dc and ch-1)*, dc in same st, (dc, ch 1, dc) in each st around, join in 3rd ch of beg ch-4.

Rnd 3: Sl st in first ch sp, ch 5 *(counts as first dc and ch-2)*, dc in same ch sp, ch 1, [(dc, ch 2, dc) in next ch sp, ch 1] around, join in 3rd ch of beg ch-5. *(16 ch sps)*

Rnd 4: Sl st in first ch sp, ch 1, sc in same ch sp, [ch 3, sc in next ch sp] around, ch 1, join with hdc in beg sc, forming last ch sp.

Rnd 5: Ch 1, sc in this ch sp, *(dc, {ch 1, dc} 3 times) in next ch sp**, sc in next ch sp, rep from * around, ending last rep at **, join in beg sc. Fasten off.

Beads

Sew 1 bead in each ch-1 sp between dc on rnd 5 of Backing.

Finishing

Fold Ribbon as shown in photo. Place Ribbon on Backing with center of overlapped Ribbon in center of Backing.

Bow

Insert rose thread through center of Ribbon and Backing from front to back and from back to front. Tie center of thread into knot on front.

Make slip knot next to tied knot and ch 30 on each end of thread.

Tie chs in bow. Shorten 1 ch if necessary. String 3 beads onto end of each ch. Tie end in knot to secure bead. Trim ends.

Sew or glue pin back to back of Backing just above center. •

BERRY STITCH HAT & SCARF
by Diane Simpson

SKILL LEVEL

INTERMEDIATE

FINISHED SIZES

Hat: Fits most adults
Scarf: 3 x 57 inches, excluding ends

MATERIALS

- Red Heart Super Saver medium (worsted) weight yarn (7 oz/384 yds/198g per skein):
    1 skein #373 petal pink
- TLC Amoré medium (worsted) weight yarn (6 oz/278 yds/170g per skein):
    1 skein #3001 white
- Size K/10½/6.5mm crochet hook or size needed to obtain gauge
- Tapestry needle

GAUGE

3 cls and 3 sc = 4 inches; 9 sc = 3 inches; 9 pattern rows = 4¼ inches

PATTERN NOTES

Join with slip stitch as indicated unless otherwise stated.
Chain-3 at beginning of row or round counts as first double crochet unless otherwise stated.

SPECIAL STITCHES

Cluster (cl): Holding back last lp of each st on hook, 3 dc in place indicated, yo, pull through all lps on hook.
Beginning cluster (beg cl): Ch 2, holding back last lp of each st on hook, 2 dc in same place, yo, pull through all lps on hook.
Berry stitch (berry st): (Sl st, ch 3, sc) in place indicated.

INSTRUCTIONS

HAT

Rnd 1 (RS): With pink, ch 2, 6 sc in 2nd ch from hook, **join** *(see Pattern Notes)* in beg sc. *(6 sc)*
Rnd 2: Ch 1, sc in first st, **cl** *(see Special Stitches)* in same st, (sc, cl) in each st around, join in beg sc. *(12 sts)*
Rnd 3: Ch 1, sc in first st, 2 sc in next st, [sc in next st, 2 sc in next st] around, join in beg sc. *(18 sc)*
Rnd 4: Ch 1, sc in first st, cl in next st, (sc, cl) in next st, [sc in next st, cl in next st, (sc, cl) in next st] around, join in beg sc. *(24 sts)*
Rnd 5: Ch 1, sc in first sc, 2 sc in next cl, [sc in next sc, 2 sc in next cl] around, join in beg sc. *(36 sc)*
Rnd 6: Ch 1, sc in first st, cl in next st, [sc in next st, cl in next st] around, join in beg sc.
Rnd 7: Beg cl *(see Special Stitches)*, sc in next cl, [cl in next sc, sc in next cl] around, join in beg cl. *(18 cl, 18 sc)*
Rnd 8: Ch 1, sc in first cl, cl in next sc, [sc in next cl, cl in next sc] around, join in beg sc.
Rnds 9–13: [Rep rnds 7 and 8 alternately] 3 times, ending last rep with rnd 7. At end of last row, fasten off.
Rnd 14: With WS facing, join white with sc in first st, ch 1, **berry st** *(see Special Stitches)* in next st, [sc in next st, berry st in next st] around, join in beg sc.
Rnd 15: Ch 1, berry st in first st, sc in next berry st, [berry st in next sc, sc in next berry st] around, join in beg sc.
Rnd 16: Ch 1, sc in first st, berry st in next st, [sc in next st, berry st in next st] around, join in beg sc.
Rnds 17–19: [Rep rnds 15 and 16 alternately] twice, ending last rep with rnd 15. At end of last rnd, fasten off.

Ribbon

With pink, ch 23, working in **back bar of ch** *(see Fig. 1)*, sc in 2nd ch from hook and in each ch across. Fasten off.

Fig. 1
Back Bar of Chain

Fold Ribbon as shown in photo. Sew to Hat.

SCARF
First Ruffle

Row 1: With pink, ch 10, sc in 2nd ch from hook, [**cl** *(see Special Stitches)* in next ch, sc in next ch] across, turn. *(9 sts)*
Row 2: Ch 1, sc in each st across, turn.
Row 3: Ch 1, sc in first st, [cl in next st, sc in next st] across, turn.
Rows 4–8: [Rep rows 2 and 3 alternately] 3 times, ending last rep with row 2.

Row 9: Fold piece in half with row 1 and row 8 tog, working through both thicknesses, ch 1, sc in each st across. Fasten off.

Center

Row 10: Join white with sc in first st, sc in each st across, turn.

Rows 11 & 12: Ch 1, sc in each st across, turn.

Row 13: Ch 3 *(see Pattern Notes)*, dc in each st across, turn.

Rows 14–16: Ch 1, sc in each st across, turn.

Rows 17–129 or to desired length: [Rep rows 13–16 consecutively] 29 times, ending last rep with row 13. At end of last row, fasten off.

2nd Ruffle

Row 1: With pink, ch 10, sc in 2nd ch from hook, [cl in next ch, sc in next ch] across, turn.

Row 2: Ch 1, sc in each st across, turn. *(9 sc)*

Row 3: Ch 1, sc in first st, [cl in next st, sc in next st] across, turn.

Rows 4–8: [Rep rows 2 and 3 alternately] 3 times, ending last rep with row 2.

Row 9: Fold piece in half with row 1 and row 8 tog, working through both thicknesses, ch 1, sc in each st across. Fasten off.
Sew to last row.
Sew ends of rows on both edges of Ruffles tog. •

POST-STITCH SCARF
by Lisa Naskrent

FINISHED SIZE

5½ x 63 inches

MATERIALS

- Bernat Satin medium (worsted) weight yarn (3½ oz/163 yds/100g per skein):
  3 skeins #04420 sea shell
- Size I/9/5.5mm crochet hook or size needed to obtain gauge

GAUGE

20 sc = 4½ inches; 20 sc rows = 5¼ inches

PATTERN NOTES

The purpose of the marked stitches on row 1 and row 25 are to mark the position where to work the first post of each leg when beginning a new ribbon working 2 rows below. Join with slip stitch as indicated unless otherwise stated.

SPECIAL STITCH

Cable: Sk next 2 fpdc, **fptr** *(see Stitch Guide)* around each of next 2 fpdc, working over fptr just made, fptr around first skipped st, fptr around 2nd skipped st.

INSTRUCTIONS

SCARF

Row 1 (RS): Ch 21, sc in 2nd ch from hook and in each of next 5 chs, mark last st for first leg of ribbon, sc in each of next 8 chs, mark last st for 2nd leg of ribbon, sc in each of last 6 chs, turn. *(20 sc)*

Row 2: Ch 1, sc in first st, working in **back lps** *(see Stitch Guide)*, sc in each st across to last st, sc in both lps of last st, turn.

Row 3: Ch 1, sc in first st, working in **front lps** *(see Stitch Guide)*, sc in each of next 4 sts, **fpdc** *(see Stitch Guide)* around marked sc 2 rows below, sk st behind fpdc on this row, fpdc around next sc 2 rows below, sk st behind fpdc on this row, working in front lps, sc in each of next 6 sts, fpdc around next marked sc 2 rows below, sk st behind fpdc on this row, fpdc around next st 2 rows below, sk st behind fpdc on this row, working in front lps, sc in each of next 4 sts, sc in both lps of last st, turn.

Row 4: Rep row 2.

Row 5: Ch 1, sc in first st, working in front lps, sc in each of next 5 sts, fpdc around each of next 2 fpdc below, sk st behind each fpdc on this row, working in front lps, sc in each of next 4 sts, fpdc around each of next 2 fpdc below, sk st behind each fpdc on this row, working in front lps, sc in each of next 5 sts, sc in both lps of last st, turn.

Row 6: Rep row 2.

Row 7: Ch 1, sc in first st, working in front lps, sc in each of next 6 sts, fpdc around each of next 2 fpdc below, sk st behind each fpdc on this row, working in front lps, sc in each of next 2 sts, fpdc around each of next 2 fpdc below, sk st behind each fpdc on this row, working in front lps, sc in each of next 6 sts, sc in both lps of last st, turn.

Row 8: Rep row 2.

Row 9: Ch 1, sc in first st, working in front lps, sc in each of next 7 sts, fpdc around each of next 4 fpdc below, sk st behind each fpdc on this row, working in front lps, sc in each of next 7 sts, sc in both lps of last st, turn.

Row 10: Rep row 2.

Row 11: Ch 1, sc in first st, working in front lps, sc in each of next 7 sts, **cable** *(see Special Stitch)* around each of next 4 fpdc below, sk st behind each fpdc on this row, working in front lps, sc in each of next 7 sts, sc in both lps of last st, turn.

Row 12: Rep row 2.

Row 13: Ch 1, sc in first st, working in front lps, sc in each of next 6 sts, fpdc around each of next 2 fpdc below, sk st behind each fpdc on this row, working in front lps, sc in each of next 2 sts, fpdc around each of next 2 fpdc below, sk st behind each fpdc on this row, working in front lps, sc in each of next 6 sts, sc in both lps of last st, turn.

Row 14: Rep row 2.

Row 15: Ch 1, sc in first st, working in front lps, sc in each of next 5 sts, fpdc around each of next 2 fpdc below, sk st behind each fpdc on this row, working in front lps, sc in each of next 4 sts, fpdc around each of next 2 fpdc below, sk st behind each fpdc on this row, working in front lps, sc in each of next 5 sts, sc in both lps of last st, turn.

Row 16: Rep row 2.

Row 17: Ch 1, sc in first st, working in front lps, sc in each of next 6 sts, fpdc around each of next 2 fpdc below, sk st behind each fpdc on this row, working in front lps, sc in each of next 2 sts, fpdc around each of next 2 fpdc below, sk st behind each fpdc on this row, working in front lps, sc in each of next 6 sts, sc in both lps of last st, turn.

Row 18: Rep row 2.

Row 19: Ch 1, sc in first st, working in front lps, sc in each of next 7 sts, cable around next 4 fpdc below, sk st behind each fpdc on this row, working in front lps, sc in each of next 7 sts, sc in both lps of last st, turn.

Row 20: Rep row 2.

Row 21: Ch 1, sc in first st, working in front lps, sc in each st across to last st, sc in both lps of last st, turn.

Row 22: Rep row 2.

Rows 23 & 24: Rep rows 21 and 22.

Row 25: Ch 1, sc in first st, working in front lps, sc in each of next 5 sts, mark last st for first leg of ribbon, sc in each of next 8 sts, mark last st for 2nd leg of ribbon, sc in each of next 5 sts, sc in both lps of last st, turn.

Row 26: Rep row 2.

Next rows: [Rep rows 3–26 consecutively] until 10 ribbon cables are complete, ending last rep with row 21. At end of last row, **do not turn or fasten off**.

Edging

Rnd 1: Now working in rnds and in ends of rows, ch 1, sc in first row and in each row across with **sc dec** *(see Stitch Guide)* as needed to keep work

flat, working in starting ch on opposite side of row 1, 3 sc in first ch *(corner)*, sc in each ch across with 3 sc in last ch *(corner)*, working in ends of rows, sc in first row and in each row across with sc dec as needed to keep work

flat, 3 sc in first st *(corner)*, sc in each st across with 3 sc in last st *(corner)*, **join** *(see Pattern Notes)* in beg sc.

Rnd 2: Ch 1, sc in each st around with 3 sc in center corner st, join in beg sc. Fasten off. •

CROSS-STITCH LAPGHAN

by Carolyn Pfeifer

SKILL LEVEL

EASY

FINISHED SIZE

34 x 42 inches, excluding Fringe

MATERIALS

- Red Heart Super Saver medium (worsted) weight yarn (5 oz/244 yds/140g per skein):

  5 skeins #972 pink camo
- Size I/9/5.5mm crochet hook or size needed to obtain gauge

GAUGE

17 sts = 5 inches; 7 cross-st rows = 4 inches; 4 sc rows = 1¼ inches

PATTERN NOTE

Chain-3 at beginning of row or round counts as first double crochet unless otherwise stated.

SPECIAL STITCH

Cross-stitch (cross-st): Sk next st, dc in next st, dc in st just sk.

INSTRUCTIONS

LAPGHAN

Row 1: Ch 113, sc in 2nd ch from hook and in each ch across, turn. *(112 sc)*

Row 2: Ch 1, sc in both lps of first st, sc in **front lps** *(see Stitch Guide)* of each st across to last st, sc in both lps of last st, turn.

Rows 3 & 4: Ch 1, sc in both lps of first st, sc in front lps of each st across to last st, sc in both lps of last st, turn.

Row 5: Ch 3 *(see Pattern Note)*, **cross-st** *(see Special Stitch)* across to last st, dc in last st, turn.

Row 6: Ch 3, dc in next st, cross st in each st across to last 2 sts, dc in each of last 2 sts, turn.

Row 7: Ch 3, cross-st across to last st, dc in last st, turn.

Row 8: Ch 3, dc in next st, cross st in each st across to last 2 sts, dc in each of last 2 sts, turn.

Rows 9–16: [Rep rows 7 and 8 alternately] 4 times.

Rows 17–20: Ch 1, sc in both lps of first st, sc in front lp of each st across to last st, sc in both lps of last st, turn.

Next rows: [Rep rows 5–20 consecutively] 4 times.

Last rnd: Working around outer edge in sts, ends of rows and in starting ch on opposite side of row 1, sc in each st and in end of each row and ch around with 2 sc in each corner, join with sl st in beg sc. Fasten off.

Fringe

Cut 3 strands, each 5 inches long. Holding all strands tog, fold in half. Pull fold through st, pull ends through fold. Pull to tighten.

Attach Fringe in every other st around entire outer edge. Trim ends. •

When I was diagnosed with breast cancer last year, two wonderful friends showed up at my door with a handmade item. Each time I covered myself with it, I was reminded of their concern and it brought me comfort. With that in mind, I was delighted to create this simple lapghan that is quick and easy to crochet. I chose the color pink camo not only because pink is the color symbolic of breast cancer, but because it is mixed in with other colors that are still a part of my life. I am especially drawn to the green because for me it is a sign of hope and new life. In spite of all my trials, there is life after treatment. My hope is that someone will make the lapghan with love to give to another in need of comfort.

Carolyn Pfeifer

pink

PINK HANKY EDGING
by Rose Pirrone

FINISHED SIZE
½-inch wide

MATERIALS
- DMC Brilliant Tatting Cotton size 80 (106 yds per ball):
    1 ball each #818 baby pink and #604 pink
- Size 12/1.00mm steel crochet hook or size needed to obtain gauge
- 12-inch rolled-edge hanky

GAUGE
12 sc = 1 inch

PATTERN NOTES
Join with slip stitch as indicated unless otherwise stated.

For ease in crocheting edging, choose a hanky that already has pierced edge.

SPECIAL STITCHES
Shell: (Dc, ch 2, tr, ch 2, dc) in indicated st.

Picot: Ch 4, sc in first ch of ch-4.

INSTRUCTIONS

EDGING
Rnd 1: Join light pink with sc in any corner, 4 sc in same corner, *evenly sp sc across to next corner **, 5 sc in corner, rep from * around, ending last rep at **, **join** *(see Pattern Notes)* in beg sc.

Rnd 2: Ch 5 *(counts as first dc and ch-2)*, (tr, ch 2, dc) in same st, ch 2, sc in next st, ch 2, *sk next 2 sts, **shell** *(see Special Stitches)* in next st, ch 2, sk next 2 sts, sc in next st, ch 2, rep from * around, join in 3rd ch of beg ch-5.

Rnd 3: Sl st in next tr, ch 1, sc in same tr, *ch 2, shell in next sc, ch 2**, sc in next tr, rep from * around, ending last

rep at **, join in beg sc. Fasten off.

Rnd 4: Join medium rose pink in first sc of previous rnd, ch 1, (sc, **picot**— *see Special Stitches*, sc) in same sc, *ch 3, (sc, picot, sc) in next tr, ch 3**, (sc, picot, sc) in next sc, rep from * around, ending last rep at **, join in beg sc. Fasten off.

Steam press Edging with damp cloth. ●

BOUQUET OF HOPE
by Lisa Naskrent

SKILL LEVEL

INTERMEDIATE

FINISHED SIZE
1¾ inches

MATERIALS
- Aunt Lydia's Classic Crochet Thread size 10 crochet cotton (350 yds per ball):
    1 ball #401 orchid pink
- Size 6/1.80mm steel crochet hook or size needed to obtain gauge
- Ribbon:
    ¼-inch wide metallic: ¼ yd
    ⅛-inch wide pink satin: ¼ yd
- Mini bud vase
- Small amount white sand
- 1-inch pink mini rosebuds with wire: 7
- Stitch marker

GAUGE
5 dc = ½ inch

INSTRUCTIONS

RIBBON MOTIF
Make 3.

Loosely ch 31, dc in 4th ch from hook *(first 3 chs count as first dc)* and in each of next 8 chs, mark rem lp of last ch worked in, dc in each of next 2 chs, 3 dc in each of next 7 chs, dc in each of next 2 chs, drop lp from hook, insert hook from front to back in marked ch, pull rem unworked chs through ch, *(8 unworked chs should now be lying on top of first leg of Motif)*, pick up dropped lp, working in rem 8 unworked chs, making sure unworked lp of ch is snug against last dc and working over it, dc in each of next 3 chs, **dc dec** *(see Stitch Guide)* in next ch and dc worked in marked ch, dc in each ch across with (dc, ch 3, sl st) in last ch. Fasten off.

Assembly

Gently slide 1 Motif onto 1 rosebud and push down until snug against leaves. Rep with rem Motifs.
Fill vase with sand.
Arrange rosebuds in sand.
Holding both ribbon pieces tog, tie in bow around neck of vase. Trim ends. ●

RIBBON TRIM AFGHAN
by Lisa Naskrent

SKILL LEVEL

INTERMEDIATE

FINISHED SIZE
36 x 45 inches

MATERIALS
- Bernat Softee Baby light (light worsted) weight yarn (5 oz/468 yds/140g per ball):
  5 balls #02001 pink
- Size G/6/4mm crochet hook or size needed to obtain gauge
- Stitch marker

GAUGE
15 ch-3 sps = 3½ inches; 9 rows = 3½ inches

PATTERN NOTES
Chain-3 at beginning of rows or rounds does not count as first double crochet unless otherwise stated.

Join with slip stitch as indicated unless otherwise stated.

INSTRUCTIONS

AFGHAN
Ribbon Motif
Make 52.
Loosely ch 25, dc in 4th ch from hook *(first 3 chs do not count as dc)* and in each of next 6 chs, mark ch just worked in, dc in each of next 2 chs, 3 dc in each of next 2 chs, 5 dc in next ch, 3 dc in each of next 2 chs, dc in each of next 2 sts, drop lp from hook, insert hook from front to back in marked ch, pull rem unworked chs through ch, *(6 unworked chs should now be laying on top of first leg of Motif)*, pick up dropped lp, working in rem 6 unworked chs, making sure unworked lp of ch is snug against last dc and working over it, dc in each of next 2 chs, **dc dec** *(see Stitch Guide)* in next ch and dc worked in marked ch, dc in each of next 2 chs, (dc, ch 3, sl st) in last ch. Fasten off.

The 3 center dc of 5-dc group at top of Motif will be used when connecting Motifs to Afghan.

Ch-3 at bottom of each leg of Motif will be used when working Edging around Motifs.

Center
Row 1 (RS): Ch 146, (sc, {ch 3, sc} 3 times) in 2nd ch from hook, [sk next 3 chs, (sc, {ch 3, sc} 3 times) in next ch] across, turn. *(111 ch-3 sps)*

Row 2: Ch 3 *(see Pattern Notes)*, sk first ch-3 sp, (sc, {ch 3, sc} 3 times) in next ch-3 sp, [sk next 2 ch-3 sps, (sc, {ch 3, sc} 3 times) in next ch-3 sp] across leaving last ch-3 sp unworked, turn.

Rows 3–92: Rep row 2.

Edging
Rnd 1: Now working in rnds and in ends of rows and in sts, sl st in first ch-3 sp, ch 1, 3 sc in same ch sp *(corner)*, sc in each ch-3 sp across with 3 sc in last ch-3 sp *(corner)*, working in ends of rows, sc in end of next row, 2 sc in end of each row across to last row, 3 sc in last row *(corner)*, working in starting ch on opposite side of row 1 into same ch that sts of row 1 is worked, 2 sc in next ch, 3 sc in each of next 35 chs, 2 sc in last ch, working in ends of rows, 3 sc in end of first row *(corner)*, 2 sc in end of each row across with 3 sc in last row, **join** *(see Pattern Notes)* in beg sc. *(592 sc)*

Rnd 2: *Match WS of next 3 sc on Center to WS of center 3 dc of 5-dc group on 1 Ribbon Motif, working through both thicknesses, ch 1, sc in first st, 3 sc in next st, sc in next st*, ◊sc in each of next 5 sc on Center, rep between * once to connect next Ribbon Motif, [sc in each of next 9 sts on Center, rep between * once to connect next Ribbon Motif] 8 times, [sc in each of next 5 sts on Center, rep between * once to connect next Ribbon Motif] twice, [sc in each of next 9 sts on Center, rep between * once to connect next Ribbon Motif] 14 times, sc in each of next 5 sts◊, rep between * once to connect next Ribbon Motif, rep between ◊ once, join in beg sc. Fasten off.

Rnd 3: With RS facing, join in ch-3 sp at bottom of first leg of first Ribbon Motif on any side, do not join to a corner Ribbon Motif, ch 1, 2 sc in same ch sp, ch 5, 2 sc in next ch-3 sp at bottom of 2nd leg of same Ribbon Motif, *[ch 3, 2 sc in ch-3 sp at bottom of first leg of next Ribbon Motif, ch 5,

2 sc in ch-3 sp at bottom of 2nd leg on same Ribbon Motif] across to corner, ch 11, 2 sc in ch-3 sp at bottom of first leg of next Ribbon Motif, ch 7, 2 sc in ch-3 sp at bottom of 2nd leg on same Ribbon Motif, ch 11**, 2 sc in ch-3 sp at bottom of first leg of next Ribbon Motif, ch 5, 2 sc in ch-3 sp at bottom of 2nd leg on same Ribbon Motif, rep from * around, ending last rep at **, join in beg sc. *(4 ch-7 sps, 8 ch-11 sps, 44 ch-3 sps, 48 ch-5 sps, 208 sc)*

Rnd 4: Ch 1, sc in each st and ch around with 3 sc in center corner ch, join in beg sc. *(704 sc)*

Rnd 5: Ch 1, sc in each st around with 3 sc in each center corner st, join in beg sc. *(712 sc)*

Rnd 6: Ch 1, sc in each of first 5 sts, sk next st, (sc, {ch 3, sc} 3 times) in next st, sk next st, [sc in each of next 5 sts, sk next st, (sc, {ch 3, sc} 3 times) in next sc, sk next st] around, join in beg sc. Fasten off. *(267 ch-3 sps, 445 sc)* •

PINK RIBBON BOOKMARK
by Susan Lowman

FINISHED SIZE

1¾ x 6¼ inches, excluding Ribbon

MATERIALS

- J.&P. Coats Royale Classic Crochet Thread size 10 crochet cotton (white: 400 yds per ball; solids: 350 yds per ball):
  - 25 yds #401 orchid pink
  - 5 yds #493 French rose
  - 1 yd #201 white
- Size 7/1.65mm steel crochet hook or size needed to obtain gauge
- Tapestry needle
- Stitch marker

GAUGE

6 cross-sts = 1¼ inches; 8 cross-st and 7 sc rows = 2½ inches

PATTERN NOTE

Chain-3 at beginning of row or round counts as first double crochet unless otherwise stated.

SPECIAL STITCH

Cross-stitch (cross-st): Sk next st, dc in next st, dc in st just sk.

INSTRUCTIONS

BOOKMARK

Row 1 (WS): With pink, ch 15, sc in 2nd ch from hook and in each ch across, turn. *(14 sc)*

Row 2: Ch 3 *(see Pattern Note)*, **cross-st** *(see Special Stitch)* across with dc in last st, turn.

Row 3: Ch 1, sc in each st across, turn. *(14 sc)*

Rows 4–35: [Rep rows 2 and 3 alternately] 16 times.

Edging

Working around outer edge in ends of rows and in sts, ch 1, sc in first st, [ch 3, **sc dec** *(see Stitch Guide)* in next 3 sts] 4 times, ch 3, (sc, ch 3, sc) in last st, [ch 3, sc dec in ends of next 2 rows] 17 times, working in starting ch on opposite side of row 1, ch 3, sc in first ch, [ch 3, sc dec in next 3 chs] 4 times, ch 3, sc in last ch, [ch 3, sc dec in ends of next 2 rows] 17 times, ch 3, sc in end of last row, ch 3, join with sl st in beg sc. Fasten off.

Ribbon

Row 1: With rose, ch 6, dc in 4th ch from hook *(first 3 chs count as first dc)*, hdc in next ch, sc in last ch, turn. *(4 sts)*

Row 2: Ch 1, sc in first st, hdc in next st, dc in each of last 2 sts, turn.

Rows 3–26: Ch 3, dc in each st across, turn.

Row 27: Ch 3, dc in next st, hdc in next st, sc in last st, turn.

Row 28: Ch 1, sc in first st, hdc in next st, dc in each of last 2 sts. Fasten off.

Finishing

Fold Ribbon as shown in photo. Place at top edge of Bookmark with center of Ribbon ¾ inch down from edge.

Bow

Cut 36-inch length of white, insert through center of crossed Ribbon and Bookmark from front to back to front. Tie center of thread into knot at front. Make slip knot next to tied knot and ch 30 on each end of thread. Fasten off. Tie chs into bow. Shorten 1 ch if necessary. Trim ends to ¼ inch from knot. •

HOODED SCARF *by Elaine Bartlett*

SKILL LEVEL

EASY

FINISHED SIZE

3½ x 67 inches

MATERIALS

- Lion Brand Homespun bulky (chunky) weight yarn (6 oz/185 yds/170g per skein):
  - 2 skeins #392 cotton candy
  - 1 skein #309 deco
- Sizes N/13/9mm crochet hook or size needed to obtain gauge

GAUGE

7 sts = 3¾ inches; 7 pattern rows = 2¾ inches

INSTRUCTIONS

SCARF

Row 1: With cotton candy, ch 125, sc in 2nd ch from hook, dc in next ch, [sc in next ch, dc in next ch] across, turn. *(62 sc, 62 dc)*

Rows 2–7: Ch 1, sc in first st, dc in next st, [sc in next st, dc in next st] across, turn. At end of last row, fasten off.

Hood

Row 8: With WS facing, sk first 44 sts, join with sc in next st, dc in next st, [sc in next st, dc in next st] 17

Continued on page 60

PINK PILLOW & TABLE RUNNER
by Lucille LaFlamme

PILLOW

SKILL LEVEL

INTERMEDIATE

FINISHED SIZE

14½ inches square, excluding Ruffle

MATERIALS

- J.&P. Coats Royale Classic Crochet size 10 crochet cotton (350 yds per ball):
    1 ball each #401 orchid pink and #493 French rose
- Size 6/1.80mm steel crochet hook or size needed to obtain gauge
- Sewing needle
- Sewing thread
- 14-inch pillow form

GAUGE

10 sts = 4 inches

PATTERN NOTES

Chain-3 at beginning of row or round counts as first double crochet unless otherwise stated.

Join with slip stitch as indicated unless otherwise stated.

SPECIAL STITCHES

V-stitch (V-st): (Dc, ch 1, dc) in place indicated.

Shell: (2 dc, ch 3, 2 dc) in place indicated.

Cluster (cl): Holding back last lp of each st on hook, 3 dc in place indicated, yo, pull through all lps on hook

INSTRUCTIONS

PILLOW TOP
Center
Row 1: Ch 113, dc in 4th ch from hook *(first 3 chs count as first dc)*, sk next ch, [**V-st** *(see Special Stitches)* in next ch, sk next 2 chs] across to last 3 chs, sk next ch, dc in each of last 2 chs, turn. *(4 dc, 35 V-sts)*

Row 2: Ch 3 *(see Pattern Notes)*, dc in next st, V-st in ch sp of each V-st across, dc in each of last 2 sts, turn.

Rows 3–40: Rep row 2. At end of last row, **do not turn.**

Edging
Rnd 1: Now working in rnds, ch 6 *(counts as first dc and ch-3)*, (dc, ch 3, dc) in last st, working in ends of rows, ch 3, sk first row, sc in end of next row, [ch 3, V-st in bottom of st at end of next row, ch 3, sk next row, sc in end of next row] across to corner, sk last 2 rows, working in starting ch on opposite side of row 1, (dc, {ch 3, dc} twice) in ch sp at corner, [ch 3, sk next 3 chs, sc in next ch, ch 3, sk next 3 chs, V-st in next ch] 12 times, sk next 3 chs, sc in next ch, sk next 5 chs, (dc, {ch 3, 3 dc} twice) in corner, working in ends of rows, ch 3, sk first row, sc in end of next row, [ch 3, V-st in bottom of st at end of next row, ch 3, sk next row, sc in end of next row] across to corner, sk last 2 rows, (dc, {ch 3, dc} twice) in corner, [ch 3, sk next 3 sts or chs, sc in next st or ch, ch 3, sk next 3 sts or ch, V-st in next st or ch] 13 times, ch 3, sk next ch, sc in next ch, ch 3, sk next ch, **join** *(see Pattern Notes)* in 3rd ch of beg ch-3. *(4 corners, 50 V-sts)*

Rnd 2: Sl st in first ch sp, ch 3, (dc, ch 3, 2 dc) in same ch sp, *ch 1, dc in next dc, ch 1, **shell** *(see Special Stitches)* in next ch-3 sp, ch 3, [shell in ch sp of next V-st, ch 3] across** to corner, shell in next ch-3 sp, rep from * around, ending last rep at **, join in 3rd ch of beg ch-3.

Rnd 3: Sl st in next st, sl st in next ch sp, ch 3, (dc, ch 3, 2 dc) in same ch sp, *ch 3, dc in next ch sp, ch 5, dc in next ch sp, ch 3, [shell in next ch sp, ch 3, sc in next ch sp, ch 3] across** to next corner, shell in next ch sp, rep from * around, ending last rep at **, join in 3rd ch of beg ch-3.

Rnd 4: Sl st in next st, sl st in next ch sp, ch 3, (dc, ch 3, 2 dc) in same ch sp, *ch 3, sc in next ch sp, ch 3, (3 dc, ch 3, 3 dc) in next ch-5 sp, ch 3, sc in next ch sp, [ch 3, shell in ch sp of next shell] 14 times, ch 3, sc in next ch sp, ch 3, (3 dc, ch 3, 3 dc) in next ch-5 sp, ch 3, sc in next ch sp**, [ch 3, shell in ch sp of next shell] 15 times, rep from * around, ending last rep at **, [ch 3, shell in ch sp of next shell] 4 times, ch 3, join in 3rd ch of beg ch-3.

Rnd 5: Ch 1, sc in first st, sc in each st around with 3 sc in each ch sp, join in beg sc. *(660 sc)*

Ruffle
Rnd 6: Ch 1, sc in first st, [ch 3, sk next st, sc in next st] around, ch 3, sk last st, join in beg sc.

Rnd 7: Sl st in first ch of first ch-3, sc in next ch, [ch 4, sc in next ch sp] around, ch 2, join with hdc in beg sc forming last ch sp.

Rnd 8: Ch 1, sc in this ch sp, [ch 4, sc in next ch sp] around, ch 2, join with hdc in beg sc, forming last ch sp.

Rnd 9: Ch 1, sc in this ch sp, [ch 5, sc in next ch sp] around, ch 2, join with dc in beg sc, forming last ch sp.

Rnds 10–13: Ch 1, sc in this ch sp, [ch 6, sc in next ch sp] around, ch 3, join with dc in beg sc, forming last ch sp. At end of last rnd, fasten off.

Ribbon Emblem

Row 1: Ch 9, dc in 4th ch from hook and in each ch across, turn. *(7 dc)*

Row 2: Ch 3, dc in next st, ch 1, sk next st, **cl** *(see Special Stitches)* in next ch, ch 1, sk next st, dc in each of last 2 sts, turn.

Row 3: Ch 3, [dc in next st, ch 1] twice, dc in each of next 2 sts, turn.

Rows 4–54: [Rep rows 2 and 3 alternately] 26 times ending last rep with row 2.

Row 55: Ch 3, dc in each st and in each ch across. Fasten off.

Finishing

With sewing thread and needle, sew Ribbon Emblem to center of Pillow Top as shown in photo.

Sew Pillow Top to 1 side of pillow form.

SKILL LEVEL

INTERMEDIATE

FINISHED SIZE

15½ x 35½ inches

MATERIALS

- J.&P. Coats Royale Classic Crochet size 10 crochet cotton (350 yds per ball):
    2 balls #401 orchid pink
    1 ball #493 French rose
- Size 6/1.80mm steel crochet hook or size needed to obtain gauge
- Sewing needle
- Sewing thread

GAUGE

7 dc dec and 7 ch sps = 3 inches; 6 pattern rows = 1½ inches

PATTERN NOTES

Chain-3 at beginning of row or round counts as first double crochet unless otherwise stated.

Chain-5 at beginning of row or round counts as first double crochet and chain-2 unless otherwise stated

Join with slip stitch as indicated unless otherwise stated.

INSTRUCTIONS

TABLE RUNNER
Center

Row 1: Ch 127, dc in 4th ch from hook and in each ch across, turn. *(125 dc)*

Row 2: Ch 1, sc in first st, [ch 5, sk next 3 sts, sc in next st] across, turn. *(31 ch-5 sps)*

Row 3: Ch 4 *(counts as first tr)*, [3 dc in next ch sp, ch 1] across, ending with 3 dc in last ch sp, tr in last st, turn. *(2 tr, 93 dc)*

Row 4: Ch 3 *(see Pattern Notes)* [dc in each of next 3 sts, ch 2] across to last dc group, dc in each of next 3 sts, dc in last st, turn. *(95 dc)*

Row 5: Ch 5 *(see Pattern Notes)*, *dc dec *(see Stitch Guide)* in next 3 sts**, ch 5, rep from * across, ending last rep at **, ch 2, dc in last st, turn. *(2 ch-2 sps, 30 ch-5 sps, 33 dc)*

Row 6: Ch 1, sc in first st, ch 5, sk next ch-2 sp, sc in next ch-5 sp, [ch 5, sc in next ch-5 sp] across, ch 5, sk next ch-2 sp, sc in last st, turn. *(2 sc, 31 ch sps)*

Row 7: Ch 5, sc in next ch sp, [ch 5, sc in next ch sp] across, ending with ch 2, dc in last st, turn.

Row 8: Ch 1, sc in first st, ch 5, sk next ch-2 sp, sc in next ch-5 sp, [ch 5, sc in next ch sp across, ending with ch 5, sk next ch-2 sp, sc in last st, turn. *(31 ch-5 sps)*

Rows 9–89: [Rep rows 3–8 consecutively] 14 times, ending last rep at row 5.

Row 90: Ch 3, dc in next ch-2 sp, dc in next st, [3 dc in next ch-5 sp, dc in next st] across ending with sk next ch-2 sp, dc in last st, turn. *(124 dc)*

First End Section

Row 1: Ch 1, sc in first st, [ch 3, sk next 2 sts, sc in next st] across, turn. *(41 ch sps)*

Row 2: Sl st in first ch sp, ch 1, sc in same ch sp, [ch 3, sc in next ch sp] across to last ch sp, ch 1, hdc in last ch sp, forming ch sp, turn.

Row 3: Ch 1, sc in this ch sp, [ch 3, sc in next ch sp] across, to last ch sp, ch 1, hdc in last ch sp, forming ch sp, turn. *(39 ch sps)*

Rows 4–38: Ch 1, sc in this ch sp, [ch 3, sc in next ch sp] across to last ch sp, ch 1, hdc in last ch sp, forming ch sp, turn. *(4 ch sps at end of last row)*

Row 39: Ch 1, sc in this ch sp, [ch 3, sc in next ch sp] 3 times. Fasten off.

2nd End Section

Row 1: Working in starting ch on opposite side of row 1, join with sc in first ch, [ch 3, sk next 2 chs, sc in next ch] across to last 4 chs, ch 3, sk next 3 chs, sc in last ch, turn.

Row 2: Sl st in first ch sp, ch 1, sc in same ch sp, [ch 3, sc in next ch sp] across to last ch sp, ch 1, hdc in last ch sp forming ch sp, turn.

Row 3: Ch 1, sc in this ch sp, [ch 3, sc in next ch sp] across, to last ch sp, ch 1, hdc in last ch sp, forming ch sp, turn. *(39 ch sps)*

Rows 4–38: Ch 1, sc in this ch sp, [ch 3, sc in next ch sp] across to last ch sp, ch 1, hdc in last ch sp, forming ch sp, turn. *(4 ch sps at end of last row)*

Row 39: Ch 1, sc in this ch sp, [ch 3, sc in next ch sp] 3 times, **do not turn or fasten off**.

Edging

Rnd 1: Now working in rnds, in ends of rows and in sts in multiples of 4, ch 3, *2 dc in each row across to row 1 of Center, dc in bottom of row 1, 2 dc in end of row 1, dc in top of row 1, dc in end of next row, evenly sp [2 dc in end of dc rows, 3 dc in end of ch-5 rows, dc in end of sc rows] across to First End Section, 2 dc in each row across, 3 dc in each ch sp across row 39, rep from * around in multiples of 4, **join** *(see Pattern Notes)* in 3rd ch of beg ch-3.

Rnd 2: (Sc, ch 6, sl st in 4th ch from hook, 3 dc) in first st, sk next 3 sts, [(sc, ch 6, sl st in 4th ch from hook, 3 dc, ch 3, 3 dc) in next st, sk next 3 sts] around, join in beg sc. Fasten off.

Ribbon Emblem
Make 2.

Row 1: Ch 9, dc in 4th ch from hook, dc in each of next 5 chs, turn. *(7 dc)*

Row 2: Ch 1, sc in each of first 2 sts, ch 5, sk next 3 sts, sc in each of last 2 sts, turn.

Row 3: Ch 3, dc in next st, ch 1, 3 dc in next ch sp, ch 1, dc in each of last 2 sts, turn.

Row 4: Ch 3, dc in next st, ch 1, dc in each of next 3 sts, ch 1, dc in each of last 2 sts, turn.

Row 5: Ch 3, dc in next st, ch 2, dc dec in next 3 sts, ch 2, dc in each of last 2 sts, turn.

Row 6: Ch 1, sc in each of first 2 sts, ch 5, sk next st, sc in each of last 2 sts, turn.

Row 7: Ch 3, dc in next st, ch 3, sc in next ch sp, ch 3, dc in each of last 2 sts, turn.

Row 8: Ch 1, sc in each of first 2 sts, ch 5, sc in each of last 2 sts, turn.

Rows 9–54: [Rep rows 3–8 consecutively] 8 times, ending last rep with row 6.

Row 55: Ch 3, dc in next st, 5 dc in next ch sp, dc in each of last 2 sts. Fasten off.

Sew 1 Ribbon Emblem to each End Section as shown in photo. •

HAT & SCARF FOR ROSE
by Nicholette Purich

SKILL LEVEL

INTERMEDIATE

FINISHED SIZES

Hat: One size fits most
Scarf: 2½ x 56 inches long

MATERIALS

- Caron Simply Soft medium (worsted) weight yarn (6 oz/330 yds/170g per skein):
    1 skein each #9721 Victorian rose and #9723 raspberry
- Size G/6/4mm crochet hook or size needed to obtain gauge
- Tapestry needle

GAUGE

6 shells = 4 inches

PATTERN NOTE

Join with slip stitch as indicated unless otherwise stated.

SPECIAL STITCH

Shell: (Sc, ch 2, sc) in place indicated.

INSTRUCTIONS

HAT

Rnd 1: With rose, ch 4, sl st in first ch to form ring, ch 1, 12 sc in ring, **join** (see Pattern Note) in beg sc. (12 sc)

Rnd 2: Ch 1, **shell** (see Special Stitch) in first st, [sk next st, shell in next st] around, sk last st, join in beg sc. (6 shells)

Rnd 3: Ch 1, shell in ch sp of first shell, shell in next st, [shell in ch sp of next shell, shell in next sc] around, join in beg sc. (12 shells)

Rnd 4: Ch 1, shell in ch sp of first shell, shell in next st, [shell in ch sp of each of next 2 shells, shell in next st] around, join in beg sc. (18 shells)

Rnd 5: Ch 1, shell in ch sp of each of first 3 shells, shell in next st, [shell in ch sp of each of next 3 shells, shell in next st] around, join in beg sc. (24 shells)

Rnd 6: Ch 1, shell in ch sp of each of first 4 shells, shell in next st, [shell in ch sp of each of next 4 shells, shell in next st] around, join in beg sc. (30 shells)

Rnd 7: Ch 1, shell in ch sp of each of first 10 shells, shell in next st, [shell in ch sp of each of next 10 shells, shell in next st] around, join in beg sc. (33 shells)

Rnd 8: Ch 1, shell in ch sp of each of first 10 shells, shell in next st, [shell in ch sp of each of next 10 shells, shell in next st] twice, shell in ch sp of each shell around, join in beg sc. (36 shells)

Rnds 9–24: Ch 1, shell in ch sp of each shell around, join in beg sc.

Rnd 25: Ch 1, sc in each st and in each ch sp around, join in beg sc. (108 sc)

Rnd 26: Ch 3 (counts as first dc), (2 dc, ch 2, 3 dc) in same st, *sk next 2 sts, sc in next st, sk next 2 sts**, (3 dc, ch 2, 3 dc) in next st, rep from * around, ending last rep at **, join in 3rd ch of beg ch-3. Fasten off.

SCARF

Row 1: With rose, ch 12, **shell** (see Special Stitch) in 2nd ch from hook, [sk next 2 chs, shell in next ch] across, turn. (4 shells)

Row 2: Ch 1, shell in ch sp of each shell across, turn.

Next rows: Rep row 2 until piece measures 55 inches or desired length.

Next row (inc): Ch 1, shell in ch sp of first shell, shell in next st, shell in ch sp of each shell across, turn. (5 shells)

Next rows: Rep row 2 until piece measures 62 inches or desired length. At end of last row, fasten off.

Fold inc end over 3 inches and sew to WS to make loop.

Rose
Make 2.

Rnd 1: With raspberry, ch 2, 10 sc in 2nd ch from hook, join in beg sc. (10 sc)

Rnd 2: Working in **front lps** (see Stitch Guide), ch 1, (sc, hdc, dc, hdc, sc) in first st (petal), sk next st, [(sc, hdc, dc, hdc, sc) in next st (petal), sk next st] around, join in beg sc. (5 petals)

Rnd 3: Working in rem lps of rnd 1, [(sc, 2 hdc, 2 dc, tr, 2 dc, 2 hdc, sc) in next st (petal), sk next st] around, join in beg sc.

Rnd 4: Ch 5, [sl st in first sc of next petal, ch 5] around, join in joining sl st on last rnd.

Rnd 5: Ch 1, (sc, 2 hdc, 2 dc, tr, 2 dc, 2 hdc, sc) twice in first ch sp and in each ch sp around, join in beg sc. Fasten off. Sew 1 Rose to Hat and 1 Rose to rem end of Scarf. •

My husband's mother, Rose, battled breast cancer off and on for five years and eventually lost her battle. I designed this hat and scarf as a tribute to her struggle in hopes that something beautiful would be created out of her pain. My husband says his mother's nature was to look for beauty in all things and always try to bring a smile to another's face despite her own pain. We think she would have been proud and happy to see someone going through the same struggle that she did with a smile and a rose.

Nicholette Purich

LACY LAPGHAN *by Darla Sims*

SKILL LEVEL

INTERMEDIATE

FINISHED SIZE

38 x 49 inches

MATERIALS

- Bernat Satin medium (worsted) weight yarn (3½ oz/163 yds/100g per ball): 9 balls #04420 sea shell
- Sizes H/8/5mm crochet hook or size needed to obtain gauge
- Tapestry needle

GAUGE

Motif = 6 inches square

PATTERN NOTES

Chain-3 at beginning of row or round counts as first double crochet unless otherwise stated.

Join with slip stitch as indicated unless otherwise stated.

SPECIAL STITCHES

Beginning cluster (beg cl): Ch 3, holding back last lp of each st on hook, 2 dc in 3rd ch from hook, yo, pull through all lps on hook.

Cluster (cl): Holding back last lp of each st on hook, 3 dc in place indicated, yo, pull through all lps on hook.

INSTRUCTIONS

LAPGHAN

Motif
Make 30.

Rnd 1: Ch 6, sl st in first ch to form ring, ch 5 *(counts as first dc and ch-2)*, [dc in ring, ch 2] 7 times, **join** *(see Pattern Notes)* in 3rd ch of beg ch-5. *(8 dc, 8 ch sps)*

Rnd 2: Ch 3 *(see Pattern Notes)*, **beg cl** *(see Special Stitches)*, [dc in next st, beg cl] 7 times, join in 3rd ch of beg ch-3.

Rnd 3: Ch 1, sc in first st, *ch 3, (**cl**—*see Special Stitches*, ch 3) 3 times in next dc *(corner)*, ch 3**, sc in next dc, rep from * around, ending last rep at **, join in beg sc.

Rnd 4: Ch 3, *3 dc in each of next 2 ch-3 sps, (2 dc, ch 2, 2 dc) in center corner cl, 3 dc in each of next 2 ch-3 sps**, dc in next sc, rep from * around, ending last rep at **, join in 3rd ch of beg ch-3.

Rnd 5: Ch 1, sc in each of first 9 sts, *3 sc in corner ch-2 sp**, sc in each of next 17 sts, rep from * around, ending last rep at **, sc in each st across, join in beg sc. Fasten off.

Assembly

Working in **back lps** *(see Stitch Guide)*, sew Motifs tog, making 5 rows of 6 Motifs in each row.

Border

Rnd 1: Join in center corner st of upper edge, ch 4 *(counts as first dc and ch-1)*, 2 dc in same st, *evenly sp 105 dc across to next corner, (2 dc, ch 1, 2 dc) in corner, evenly sp 137 dc across to next corner**, (2 dc, ch 1, 2 dc) in corner, rep from * around, ending last rep at **, dc in same st as beg ch-3, join in 3rd ch of beg ch-4. *(4 corners, 500 dc)*

Rnd 2: Sl st in next ch sp, ch 4, 2 dc in same ch sp, dc in each st around with (2 dc, ch 1, 2 dc) in each corner ch sp, ending with dc in same ch sp as beg ch-4, join in 3rd ch of beg ch-4.

Rnd 3: Sl st in next ch sp, ch 4, 2 dc in same ch sp, *dc in next st, [beg cl, sk next 2 sts, cl in next st, sk next st, cl in next st, beg cl, sk next 2 sts, dc in next st] 14 times, (2 dc, ch 1, 2 dc) in next corner ch sp, dc in next st, [beg cl, sk next 2 sts, cl in next st, sk next st, cl in next st, beg cl, sk next 2 sts, dc in next st] 18 times**, (2 dc, ch 1, 2 dc) in next corner, rep from * around, ending last rep at **, dc in same ch sp as beg ch-3, join in 3rd ch of beg ch-4.

Rnd 4: Sl st in next ch sp, ch 4, 2 dc in same ch sp, dc in each of next 3 sts, *[ch 3, (cl, ch 1, cl) in next sp between cls, ch 3, dc in next dc] across to last 2 dc before next corner, dc in each of next 2 sts**, (2 dc, ch 1, 2 dc) in corner ch sp, rep from * around, ending last rep at **, dc in same ch sp as beg ch-4, join in 3rd ch of beg ch-4.

Rnd 5: Sl st in next ch sp, ch 4, 2 dc in same ch sp, dc in each st and in each ch-1 sp and 2 dc in each ch-3 sp around with (2 dc, ch 1, 2 dc) in each corner ch sp, dc in same ch sp as beg ch-4, join

with sl st in 3rd ch of beg ch-4.
Rnd 6: Sl st in first ch sp, ch 4, 2 dc in same ch sp, dc in each st around with (2 dc, ch 1, 2 dc) in each corner ch sp, dc in same ch sp as beg ch-4, join in 3rd ch of beg ch-4. Fasten off. •

HOPE BEAR *by Sheila Leslie*

FINISHED SIZE
11 inches high sitting

MATERIALS
- Red Heart Super Saver medium (worsted) weight yarn (7 oz/364 yds/198g per skein):
    - 1 skein #373 petal pink
    - 10 yds #312 black
- Circulo Anne super fine (fingering) weight cotton yarn (5 oz/547 yds/147g per ball):
    - 1 ball #8001 white
- Sizes E/4/3.5mm and H/8/5mm crochet hooks or size needed to obtain gauge
- Tapestry needle
- 12mm flat black shank buttons: 2
- ¼-inch wide pink ribbon: 38 inches
- Fiberfill
- Stitch marker

GAUGE
Size H hook: 4 sc = 1 inch; 4 sc rnds = 1 inch

PATTERN NOTES
If used as toy, you may want to embroider the eyes instead of using buttons that can be pulled off.

Use size H hook unless otherwise stated.

Work in continuous rounds, do not join or turn unless otherwise stated.

Mark first stitch of each round.

SPECIAL STITCHES
Beginning shell (beg shell): Ch 3 (counts as first dc), (2 dc, ch 2, 3 dc) in same place.

Shell: (3 dc, ch 2, 3 dc) in place indicated.

INSTRUCTIONS

BEAR
Head
Rnd 1: Beg at snout, with size H hook and pink, ch 2, 6 sc in 2nd ch from hook, **do not join** (*see Pattern Notes*). *(6 sc)*

Rnd 2: Sc in each st around.

Rnd 3: [Sc in next st, 2 sc in next st] around. *(9 sc)*

Rnd 4: [Sc in each of next 2 sts, 2 sc in next st] around. *(12 sc)*

Rnd 5: [2 sc in next st, sc in each of next 3 sts] around. *(15 sc)*

Rnd 6: [Sc in each of next 4 sts, 2 sc in next st] around. *(18 sc)*

Rnd 7: [Sc in each of next 5 sts, 2 sc in next st] around. *(21 sc)*

Rnd 8: [2 sc in next st, sc in each of next 6 sts] around. *(24 sc)*

Rnd 9: [Sc in each of next 5 sts, 2 sc in next st] around. *(28 sc)*

Rnd 10: Sc in each of first 11 sts, 2 sc in each of next 6 sts, sc in each of last 11 sts. *(34 sc)*

Rnd 11: Sc in each of first 11 sts, [sc in next st, 2 sc in next st] 6 times, sc in each of last 11 sts. *(40 sc)*

Rnd 12: Sc in each st around.

Rnd 13: [Sc in each of next 4 sts, 2 sc in next st] around. *(48 sc)*

Rnds 14–22: Sc in each st around.

Rnd 23: [Sc in each of next 6 sts, **sc dec** *(see Stitch Guide)* in next 2 sts] around. *(42 sc)*

Rnd 24: [Sc in each of next 5 sts sc dec in next 2 sts] around. *(36 sc)*

Rnd 25: [Sc in each of next 4 sts sc dec in next 2 sts] around. *(30 sc)*

Rnd 26: [Sc in each of next 3 sts sc dec in next 2 sts] around. Stuff Head. *(24 sc)*

Rnd 27: [Sc in each of next 2 sts sc dec in next 2 sts] around. *(18 sc)*

Rnd 28: [Sc in next st, sc dec in next 2 sts] around. *(12 sc)*

Rnd 29: [Sc dec in next 2 sts] around. Leaving long end, fasten off. *(6 sc)* Stuff. Weave long end through top of sts on last rnd, pull to close. Secure end.

Finishing
Using **satin stitch** *(see Fig. 1)*, with black, embroider nose as shown in photo. Using **straight stitch** *(see Fig. 2)*, with black, embroider mouth as shown in photo.

Continued on page 60

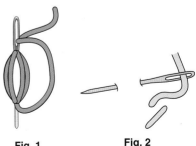

Fig. 1
Satin Stitch

Fig. 2
Straight Stitch

PRAYER SHAWL *by Diane Simpson*

SKILL LEVEL

INTERMEDIATE

FINISHED SIZE

11 x 66 inches

MATERIALS

- Red Heart Super Saver medium (worsted) weight yarn (7 oz/384 yds/198g per skein):
    1 skein #373 petal pink
- Sizes K/10½/6.5mm and P/15/10mm crochet hooks or size needed to obtain gauge

GAUGE

Size K hook: 10 sc = 4 inches; 9 pattern rows = 4 inches

PATTERN NOTE

Gauge is not extremely important but will change the length and width of Shawl if different.

INSTRUCTIONS

SHAWL

Row 1 (RS): With size K hook, ch 164, sc in 2nd ch from hook and in each ch across, turn. *(163 sc)*

Row 2: Working in **front lps** *(see Stitch Guide)*, with size P hook, ch 1, sc in first st, [ch 1, sk next st, sc in next st] across, turn.

Row 3: Working this row in **back lps** *(see Stitch Guide)*, with size K hook, ch 1, sc in each st and in each ch across, turn. *(163 sc)*

Row 4: Working in front lps, with size P hook, ch 1, sc in first st, [ch 1, sk next st, sc in next st] across, turn.

Row 5: Working in front lps, with size P hook, ch 1, sc in first st, [ch 1, sk next ch sp, sc in next st] across, turn.

Row 6: Working in back lps, with size P hook, ch 1, sc in first st, [ch 1, sk next ch sp, sc in next st] across, turn.

Row 7: Working this row in back lps, with size K hook, ch 1, sc in each st and in each ch across, turn. *(163 sc)*

Row 8: Working in front lps, with size P hook, ch 1, sc in first st, [ch 1, sk next st, sc in next st] across, turn.

Row 9: Working this row in back lps, with size K hook, ch 1, sc in each st and in each ch across, turn. *(163 sc)*

Rows 10–25 or to desired width: [Rep rows 2–9 consecutively for pattern] twice or as many times as needed.

Row 26: Working in ends of rows, with size K hook, ch 1, evenly sp sc across. Fasten off.

Row 27: Working in ends of rows on opposite end of Shawl with size K hook, join with sc in end of first row, evenly sp sc across. Fasten off. •

BIT OF WHIMSY HAT

by Margaret Hubert

SKILL LEVEL

INTERMEDIATE

FINISHED SIZE

One size fits most

MATERIALS

- Patons Decor medium (worsted) weight yarn (3½ oz/210 yds/100g per ball):
  1 skein color #01645 pale country pink
- Sizes I/9/5.5mm and J/10/6mm crochet hooks or size needed to obtain gauge
- Tapestry needle

GAUGE

Size J hook: 11 sc = 4 inches

PATTERN NOTES

Chain-1 at beginning of row or round counts as first single crochet unless otherwise stated.

Join with slip stitch as indicated unless otherwise stated.

INSTRUCTIONS

HAT

Row 1: Ch 39, 2 sc in 2nd ch from hook and in each of next 17 chs *(curl)*, sc in each of last 20 chs, turn.

Row 2: Ch 1 *(see Pattern Notes)*, working in **back lps** *(see Stitch Guide)*, sc in each of next 14 sts, leaving rem sts unworked, turn. *(15 sc)*

Row 3: Ch 1, sc in each st across, turn.

Row 4: Ch 1, sc in each st across, sc in each unworked sts on row 1, ch 19 *(curl)*, turn.

Row 5: 2 sc in 2nd ch from hook and in each ch across *(curl)*, working in back lps, sc in each st across, turn.

Rows 6–81: [Rep rows 2–5 consecutively] 19 times. At end of last row, leave long end. Fasten off.
With long end, sew first and last rows

tog, make knot, weave through ribs at base of curls, pull up tightly, wrap yarn around again and secure end.

Bottom Band

Rnd 1: Working in ends of rows, with size I hook, join with sc in seam, sc in end of each row around, **join** *(see Pattern Notes)* in beg sc.

Rnds 2–3: Ch 1, sc in each st around, join in beg sc.

Rnd 4: Ch 1, working from left to right, **reverse sc** *(see Fig. 1)* in each st around, join in beg reverse sc. Fasten off. ●

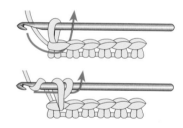

Fig. 1
Reverse Single Crochet

CROSS BOOKMARK

by Patricia Kristoffersen

SKILL LEVEL

INTERMEDIATE

FINISHED SIZE

4½ x 7¾ inches

MATERIALS

- Size 10 crochet cotton:
    25 yds each light pink and dark pink
- Size 7/1.65mm steel crochet hook or size needed to obtain gauge
- Tapestry needle
- Craft glue

GAUGE

7 sc = 1 inch

INSTRUCTIONS

CROSS

Row 1: With either color, ch 385, sc in 2nd ch from hook and in each ch across, turn. Fasten off. *(384 sc)*

Row 2: Join next color with sc in first st, sc in each of next 16 sts, work the following steps to complete row:

A. 2 sc in each of next 4 sts, sc in each of next 10 sts, sk next st;

B. Sc in each of next 3 sts, sk next 3 sts, sc in each of next 3 sts, sk next st;

C. Sc in each of next 7 sts, 2 sc in next st, sc in each of next 3 sts, (sc, ch 2, sc) in next st;

D. Sc in each of next 3 sts, 2 sc in next st, sc in each of next 25 sts, 2 sc in next st;

E. Sc in each of next 3 sts, (sc, ch 2, sc) in next st, sc in each of next 3 sts, 2 sc in next st;

F. Sc in each of next 7 sts, sk next st, sc in each of next 3 sts, sk next 3 sts, sc in next 3 sts, sk next st;

G. Sc in each of next 7 sts, 2 sc in next st, sc in each of next 3 sts, (sc, ch 2, sc) in next st, sc in each of next 3 sts, 2 sc in next st, sc in each of next 33 sts;

H. *[Sk next st, sc in each of next 2 sts] 3 times, sc in each of next 5 sts, rep from * twice;

I. Sc in each of next 26 sts, 2 sc in next st, sc in each of next 3 sts, (sc, ch 2, sc) in next st, sc in each of next 3 sts, 2 sc in next st;

J. Sc in each of next 7 sts, sk next st, sc in each of next 3 sts, sk next 3 sts, sc in each of next 3 sts, sk next st;

K. Sc in each of next 7 sts, 2 sc in next st, sc in each of next 3 sts, (sc, ch 2, sc) in next st, sc in each of next 3 sts, 2 sc in next st;

L. Sc in each of next 25 sts, 2 sc in next st, sc in each of next 3 sts, (sc, ch 2, sc) in next st, sc in each of

Continued on page 61

BEDDY-BYE BOOTIES
by Sharon Phillips

SKILL LEVEL

BEGINNER

FINISHED SIZE

One size fits most

MATERIALS

- Lion Brand Wool-Ease medium (worsted) weight cotton yarn (3 oz/197 yds/85g per skein): 1 skein #140 rose heather
- Size I/9/5.5mm crochet hook or size needed to obtain gauge
- Tapestry needle
- Sewing needle
- Sewing thread
- Ribbon bows: 2

GAUGE

4 dc = 1 inch; 2 dc rnds = 1 inch

PATTERN NOTES

Join with slip stitch as indicated unless otherwise stated.

Chain-3 at beginning of row or round counts as first double crochet unless otherwise stated.

INSTRUCTIONS

BOOTIE
Make 2.

Rnd 1: Ch 4, 11 dc in 4th ch from hook *(first 3 chs counts as first dc)*, **join** *(see Pattern Notes)* in 4th ch of beg ch-4. *(12 dc)*

Rnd 2: Ch 3 *(see Pattern Notes)*, dc in same st, 2 dc in each dc around, join in 3rd ch of beg ch-3. *(24 dc)*

Rnd 3: Ch 3, dc in same st, dc in each of next 3 dc, [2 dc in next dc, dc in each of next 3 dc] around, join in 3rd ch of beg ch-3. *(30 dc)*

Rnd 4: Ch 3, dc in each dc around, join in 3rd ch of beg ch-3.

Rnds 5–12 or to desired length from toe to heel: Rep rnd 4.

Rnd 13: Ch 3, dc in same dc, dc in next dc, [2 dc in next dc, dc in next dc] 3 times, hdc in each of next 5 dc, sc in each of next 5 dc, hdc in each of next 5 dc, [2 dc in next dc, dc in next dc] 3 times, 2 dc in next dc, join in 3rd ch of beg ch-3. *(38 sts)*

Rnds 14–19: Ch 3, dc in each of next 11 sts, hdc in each of next 5 sts, sc in each of next 5 sts, hdc in each of next 5 sts, dc in each of next 11 sts, join in 3rd ch of beg ch-3.

Rnd 20: Ch 3, **dc dec** *(see Stitch Guide)* in next 2 sts, [dc in next st, dc dec in next 2 sts] 3 times, hdc in each of next 5 sts, sc in each of next 5 sts, hdc in each of next 5 sts, dc dec in next 2 sts, [dc in next st, dc dec in next 2 sts] 3 times, join in 3rd ch of beg ch-3. *(30 sts)*

Rnd 21: Ch 3, dc in each st around, join in 3rd ch of beg ch-3.

Rnd 22: Ch 3, [**fpdc** *(see Stitch Guide)* around next st, **bpdc** *(see Stitch Guide)* around next st] around, join in 3rd ch of beg ch-3.

Rnds 23–28: Ch 3, [fpdc around fpdc, bpdc around bpdc] around, join in 3rd ch of beg ch-3. At end of last rnd, fasten off. Sew white ribbon bow to center front of Bootie over rnd 20. ●

LACY BOOKMARK

by Shirley Brown

SKILL LEVEL

INTERMEDIATE

FINISHED SIZE

8½ inches long

MATERIALS

- J.&P. Coats Royale Classic Crochet size 10 crochet cotton (350 yds per ball):
    75 yds #15 shaded pinks
- Size C/2/2.75mm crochet hook

GAUGE

Gauge is not important for this project.

SPECIAL STITCHES

Cluster (cl): Ch 4, dc in 4th ch from hook.

Picot: Ch 3, hdc in 3rd ch from hook.

INSTRUCTIONS

BOOKMARK

Row 1: Cl *(see Special Stitches)* 10 times. *(10 cls)*

Rnd 2: Now working in rnds, down side of cls, **picot** *(see Special Stitches)* 3 times, sl st in top of last cl worked, [cl, sl st between next 2 cls] 9 times, cl, sl st in bottom of last cl, sl st in bottom of last cl, picot 3 times, sl st in last sl st worked, [cl, sl st in between next 2 cls] 9 times, cl, join with sl st in top of last cl on row 1.

Rnd 3: Sl st in first picot, *picot twice, (sl st, picot 3 times, sl st) in next picot, picot twice, sl st in next picot, [cl, picot, sl st in top of last cl, cl, sl st between next 2 cls] 9 times, cl, picot, sl st in top of last cl, cl*, sl st in next picot at end, rep between *, join with sl st in beg sl st. Fasten off. •

SOFT SLIPPERS
by Kathleen Stuart

FINISHED SIZE
Fit up to 11-inch sole

MATERIALS
- Red Heart Baby Clouds super bulky (super chunky) weight cotton yarn (6 oz/140 yds/170g per skein): 1 skein #9724 pink lemonade
- Lion Brand Babysoft light (light worsted) weight yarn (5 oz/459 yds/141g per ball): 1 ball #103 bubblegum
- Sizes G/6/4mm and N/13/9mm crochet hooks or size needed to obtain gauge

GAUGE
Size N hook: 9 sc = 4 inches; 9 sc rows = 4 inches

PATTERN NOTE
If you need a Slipper smaller than the given size, just crochet a few less chains for either the ankle opening or the instep.

If you need a Slipper larger than the given size, just crochet a few more chains for either the ankle opening or the instep.

INSTRUCTIONS

BOOTIE
Row 1: With size N hook and pink, ch 25 *(ankle opening)*, sl st in first ch to form ring, ch 15 *(instep)*, sc in 2nd ch from hook and in each of next 13 chs across instep and 25 chs around ankle, working on opposite side of instep ch, sc in each ch across, turn. *(53 sc)*

Rows 2–12: Ch 1, sc in each st across, turn.

Row 13: Fold piece in half lengthwise, working through both thicknesses, ch 1, sl st in each st across. Fasten off.

Toe
Rnd 1: Turn Slipper to WS, working in end of rows, join with sc in end of any row, [**sc dec** *(see Stitch Guide)* in end of next 2 rows] around opening, ending with last sc dec in last row and first row worked in, **do not join**. *(13 sc)*

Rnd 2: [Sc dec in next 2 sts] around, ending last sc dec in last st and first st worked in. Leaving long end, fasten off. Weave end through top of sts on last rnd. Pull to close. Secure end. Turn Slipper RS out.

Continued on page 61

LACY READERS WRAP

by Elizabeth Ann White

SKILL LEVEL

INTERMEDIATE

FINISHED SIZE

16 x 60 inches

MATERIALS

- Vanna's Choice medium (worsted) weight yarn (3½ oz/170 yds/100g per ball):
    4 balls #101 pink
- Size I/9/5.5mm crochet hook or size needed to obtain gauge
- Tapestry needle

GAUGE

4 shells = 3 inches; 5 shell rows = 2 inches

SPECIAL STITCH

Shell: (Sc, ch 3, sc) in place indicated.

INSTRUCTIONS

WRAP

Row 1: Ch 106, **shell** *(see Special Stitch)* in 2nd ch from hook, [sk next 3 chs, shell in next ch] across, turn. *(27 shells)*

Row 2: Ch 3, shell in ch sp of each shell across, turn.

Next rows: Rep row 2 until piece measures 60 inches or desired length. At end of last row, fasten off.

Pocket
Make 2.

Row 1: Ch 29, shell in 2nd ch from hook, [sk next 2 chs, shell in next ch] across, turn. *(10 shells)*

Rows 2–20: Ch 3, shell in ch sp of each shell across, turn. At end of last row, fasten off.

Finishing

Fold 4 inches of 1 long edge over and tack in place to form collar.

Fold last 5 rows of 1 Pocket over and sew Pocket to Wrap, centered between collar and rem edge as shown in photo.

Fold last 5 rows of last Pocket over and sew Pocket to opposite end of Wrap, centered between collar and rem edge as shown in photo. •

CELIA'S SCARF

by Andrea Lyn Van Benschoten

SKILL LEVEL

INTERMEDIATE

FINISHED SIZE

3½ x 67 inches

MATERIALS

- Bernat Alpaca bulky (chunky) weight yarn (3½ oz/120 yds/100g per ball):
  2 balls #93420 peony
  1 ball #93007 natural
- Size I/9/5.5mm crochet hook or size needed to obtain gauge

GAUGE

3 sts = 1 inch; 8 rows = 3½ inches

INSTRUCTIONS

SCARF

Row 1: With peony, ch 201, sc in 2nd ch from hook, dc in next ch, [sc in next ch, dc in next ch] across, turn.

Row 2: Ch 1, sc in first dc, dc in next sc, [sc in each dc and dc in each sc] across, turn.

Row 3: Ch 1, sc in first dc, dc in next sc, [sc in each dc and dc in each sc] across, turn. Fasten off.

Row 4: Join natural with sc in first dc, dc in next sc, [sc in each dc and dc in each sc] across, turn.

Row 5: Ch 1, sc in first dc, dc in next sc, [sc in each dc and dc in each sc] across, turn.

Row 6: Ch 1, sc in first dc, dc in next sc, [sc in each dc and dc in each sc] across, turn. Fasten off.

Row 7: Join peony with sc in first dc, dc in next sc, [sc in each dc and dc in each sc] across, turn.

Row 8: Ch 1, sc in first dc, dc in next sc, [sc in each dc and dc in each sc] across, turn.

Row 9: Ch 1, sc in first dc, dc in next sc, [sc in each dc and dc in each sc] across. Fasten off. •

I designed this scarf in honor of
my mother-in-law, who ended her
battle with breast cancer in the
early summer of 1992. I am truly
honored to have this design in such
an important book supporting breast
cancer awareness, honoring the
survivors and remembering those who
have gone before us.

*Andrea Lyn
Van Benschoten*

PINEAPPLE SCARF
by Joyce Nordstrom

SKILL LEVEL

INTERMEDIATE

FINISHED SIZE

8 x 54 inches

MATERIALS

- Lion Brand Microspun light (light worsted) weight yarn (2½ oz/168 yds/70g per ball):
    2 balls #102 blush
- Size G/6/4mm crochet hook or size needed to obtain gauge

GAUGE

19 sts = 4 inches; 5 rows = 4½ inches

PATTERN NOTE

Chain-3 at beginning of row or round counts as first double crochet unless otherwise stated.

SPECIAL STITCHES

Shell: (2 dc, ch 1, 2 dc) in place indicated

Beginning shell (beg shell): Ch 3, (dc, ch 1, 2 dc) in same place.

INSTRUCTIONS

SCARF

Row 1: Ch 38, sc in 2nd ch from hook and in next ch, [ch 3, sc in each of next 3 chs] across to last 2 sts, ch 3, sc in each of last 2 sts, turn. *(12 ch sps, 37 sc)*

Row 2: Ch 5 *(counts as first dc and ch-2)*, *sk next 2 sts and next ch sp, dc in next st**, ch 2, rep from * across, ending last rep at **, turn. *(12 ch sps, 13 dc)*

Row 3: Ch 1, sc in first st, [2 sc in next ch sp, sc in next st] across, turn. *(37 sc)*

Row 4: Ch 1, sc in first st, ch 32, [sc in each of next 3 sts, ch 32] across to last 3 sts, sc in each of last 3 sts, turn. *(12 ch sps, 37 sc)*

Row 5: Ch 17, sc in 2nd ch from hook, [ch 2, sc in center of next ch-32] across, turn.

Row 6: Ch 1, sc in first st, [(sc, ch 3, sc) in next ch sp, sc in next st] across, turn.

Next rows: [Rep rows 2–6 consecutively] 9 times.

Next rows: Rep rows 2 and 3.

First End

Row 1 (WS): Ch 1, sc in first st, ch 1, sk next st, sc in next st, ch 2, sk next 2 sts, sc in next st, [ch 3, sk next 3 sts, sc in next st] twice, ch 2, sk next 2 sts, sc in next st, ch 3, sk next 3 sts, sc in next st, ch 2, sk next 2 sts, sc in next st, [ch 3, sk next 3 sts, sc in next st] twice, ch 2, sk next 2 sts, sc in next st, ch 1, sk next st, sc in last st, turn. *(11 ch sps, 12 sc)*

Row 2: Ch 1, sc in first st, ch 1, sk next ch sp, sc in next st, *ch 2, sk next ch sp, sc in next st, ch 1, sk next ch sp, 9 dc in next st, ch 1, sk next ch sp, sc in next st, ch 2, sk next ch sp, sc in next st*, ch 3, sk next ch sp, sc in next st, rep between * once, ch 1, sk next ch sp, sc in last st, turn. *(10 sc, 11 ch sps, 18 dc)*

Row 3: Ch 2, sk next st and next ch sp, *shell (see Special Stitches)* in next st, ch 1, sk next 2 ch sps and next sc, [dc in next dc, ch 1] 9 times, sk next 2 ch sps and next st, shell in next st*, sk next ch sp, rep between * once, sk next ch sp, hdc in last st, turn.

Row 4: Ch 3 *(see Pattern Note)*, *2 dc in ch sp of next shell, ch 3, sk next ch sp, [sk next st, sc in next ch sp, ch 3] 7 times, sc in next ch-1 sp, ch 3, sk next ch sp, 2 dc in ch sp of next shell*, ch 1, rep between * once, turn.

Row 5: Ch 3, 2 dc in same st, *ch 3, sc in next ch-3 sp, [ch 3, sk next st, sc in next ch-3 sp] 6 times, ch 3, sk next ch-3 and next 2 sts*, shell in next ch-1 sp, rep between * once, 3 dc in last st, turn.

Row 6: Ch 3, 2 dc in same st, *ch 3, sk next ch sp, sc in next ch-3 sp, [ch 3, sk next st, sc in next ch-3 sp] 5 times, ch 3, sk next ch sp*, shell in ch sp of next shell, rep between * once, 3 dc in last st, turn.

Row 7: Beg shell *(see Special Stitches)* in first st, *ch 3, sk next ch sp, sc in next ch sp, [ch 3, sk next st, sc in next ch-3 sp] 4 times, ch 3, sk next ch sp*, (shell, ch 1, 2 dc) in ch sp of next shell, rep between * once, shell in last st, turn.

Row 8: Sl st across to ch sp of first shell, beg shell in same ch sp, *ch 3, sk next ch sp, sc in next ch-3 sp, [ch 3, sk next st, sc in next ch-3 sp] 3 times, ch 3, sk next ch sp*, shell in each of next 2 ch sps, rep between * once, shell in ch sp of last shell, turn.

Continued on page 62

SIMPLICITY LAPGHAN
by Glenda Winkleman

FINISHED SIZE

32 x 42 inches

MATERIALS

- Medium (worsted) weight yarn: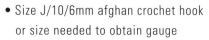
  21 oz/1,050 yds/595g pink **4 MEDIUM**
- Size J/10/6mm afghan crochet hook or size needed to obtain gauge
- Size G/6/4mm crochet hook
- Sewing needle
- Pink sewing thread
- ¾-inch pink ribbon roses: 16

GAUGE

Afghan hook: 15 sts = 4 inches; 19 rows = 4 inches

Size G hook: 6 rows = 2 inches

PATTERN NOTE

Join with slip stitch as indicated unless otherwise stated.

SPECIAL STITCHES

Work loops off hook: Yo, pull through 1 lp on hook *(see Fig. 1)*, [yo, pull through 2 lps on hook] across leaving 1 lp on hook at end of row *(see Fig. 2)*.

Knit stitch (knit st): With yarn in back, insert hook from front to back between both vertical strands of next st, yo, pull yarn through st, hold lp on hook.

Fig. 1

Fig. 2

Work Loops off Hook

INSTRUCTIONS

LAPGHAN

Row 1: With afghan hook, ch 105, insert hook in 2nd ch from hook, yo, pull through ch, [insert hook in next ch, yo, pull up lp] across, holding all lps on hook, **work lps off hook** *(see Special Stitches)* across.

Rows 2–23: Work **knit st** *(see Special Stitches)* across, work lps off hook.

Row 24: [With yarn in front of hook, insert hook under next vertical bar, yo, pull up lp, with yarn in back of hook, insert hook under next vertical bar, yo, pull up lp] across, work lps off.

Row 25: With yarn in back of hook, insert hook under next vertical bar, yo, pull up lp, [with yarn in front of hook, insert hook under next vertical bar, yo, pull up lp, with yarn in back of hook, insert hook under next vertical bar, yo, pull up lp] across, work lps off hook.

Row 26: [With yarn in front of hook, insert hook under next vertical bar, yo, pull up lp, with yarn in back of hook, insert hook under next vertical bar, yo, pull up lp] across, work lps off.

Rows 27–49: Work knit st across,

work lps off hook.

Rows 50–179: [Rep rows 24–49 consecutively] 5 times.

Row 180: [With yarn in back, insert hook from front to back between both vertical strands of next st, yo, pull through st and lp on hook] across. Fasten off.

Border

Rnd 1: Now working in rnds, with RS facing, with size G hook, join with sc in top right-hand corner, sc in each st across to next corner, ch 2, working in ends of rows, sc in end of each row across to next corner, ch 2, working in starting ch on opposite side of row 1, sc in each ch across to next corner, ch 2, working in ends of rows, sc in end of each row across to next corner, ch 2, **join** *(see Pattern Note)* in beg sc. *(4 corners, 570 sc)*

Rnd 2: Ch 1, hdc in each st around with (hdc, ch 2, hdc) in each corner ch-2 sp, join in beg hdc. *(4 corners, 578 sc)*

Rnd 3: Ch 1, hdc in each st around with (hdc, ch 2, hdc) in each corner ch-2 sp, join in beg hdc. *(4 corners, 586 sc)*

Rnd 4: Ch 1, sc in each of first 5 sts, **sc dec** *(see Stitch Guide)* in next 2 sts, *[sc in each of next 5 sts, sc dec in next 2 sts] 14 times, sc in each of last 4 sts, (sc, ch 2, sc) in corner ch sp, sc in each of next 3 sts, [sc dec in next 2 sts, sc in each of next 3 sts] 36 times, sc in next st, (sc, ch 2, sc) in corner ch sp, rep from * around, join

Continued on page 62

POCKET PILLOW
by Elaine Bartlett

SKILL LEVEL

EASY

FINISHED SIZE

14 inches square, excluding Edging

MATERIALS

- Red Heart Super Saver medium (worsted) weight yarn (7 oz/364 yds/198g per skein):
    1 skein each #373 petal pink and #311 white
- Sizes I/9/5.5mm crochet hook or size needed to obtain gauge
- Tapestry needle
- 14-inch pillow form

GAUGE

12 hdc = 4 inches; 11 hdc rows = 4 inches

INSTRUCTIONS

PILLOW

Front

Row 1: With white, ch 44, hdc in 3rd ch from hook *(first 2 chs count as first hdc)* and in each ch across, turn. *(43 hdc)*

Rows 2–5: Ch 1, hdc in first st and in each st across, turn.

Rows 6–33: Ch 1, **changing colors** *(see Stitch Guide)* in last st made according to **chart** *(see Fig. 1)*, hdc in each st across, turn.

Rows 34–37: Ch 1, hdc in first st and

in each st across, turn. At end of last row, fasten off.

Back

Row 1 (WS): With pink, ch 44, hdc in 3rd ch from hook *(first 2 chs count as first hdc)* and in each ch across, turn. *(43 hdc)*

Rows 2–9: Ch 1, hdc in first st and in each st across, turn.

Row 10: Ch 1, hdc in first st and in each of next 10 sts, working in **back lps** *(see Stitch Guide)*, hdc in each of next 21 sts, hdc in both lps of each of last 11 sts, turn.

Rows 11–37: Ch 1, hdc in first st and

in each st across, turn. At end of last row, fasten off.

Pocket

Row 1 (RS): Hold Back with RS facing, join pink with sl st in first rem lp on row 9, ch 1, hdc in each rem lp in each of next 20 sts, turn. *(21 hdc)*

Rows 2–19: Ch 1, hdc in first st and in each st across, turn. At end of last row, fasten off.

Row 20: With WS of Pocket facing, join white with sl st in first st, ch 3 *(counts as first dc)*, dc in each st across, turn.

COLOR KEY	
☐	White
▨	Pink

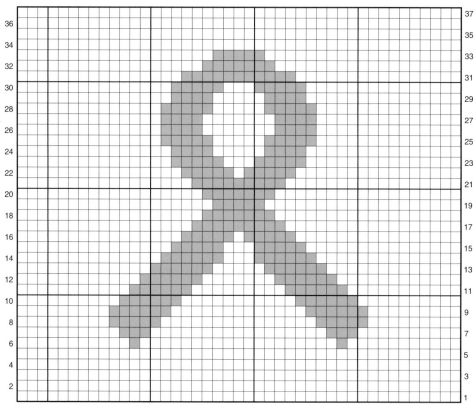

Fig. 1
Pocket Pillow
Chart

Row 21: Ch 1, sc in first st, [sk next st, 4 dc in next st, sk next st, sc in next st] across. Fasten off.

With pink, sew both sides of Pocket to Back, leaving last 2 rows unsewn.

Edging

Rnd 1: Holding Front and Back WS tog, working in sts and in ends of rows around, working through both thicknesses, join white with sc in 1 corner st, sc in each st across and in end of each row around, insert pillow form before closing, join with sl st in beg sc.

Rnd 2: Ch 1, sc in first st, ch 4, drop white to back, join pink with sc in next st, ch 4, drop pink to back, [pink up white, sc in next st, ch 4, drop white to back, pick up pink, sc in next st, ch 4, drop pink to back] around, join white with sl st in beg white sc and join pink with sl st in beg pink sc. Fasten off both colors. •

EASY STITCH HAT
by Mickie Akins

SKILL LEVEL

EASY

FINISHED SIZE
One size fits most

MATERIALS
- Elmore-Pisgah Peaches & Crème medium (worsted) weight yarn (2½ oz/122 yds/71g per ball):
    2 balls #45 pastel pink
- Size G/6/4mm crochet hook or size needed to obtain gauge
- Stitch marker

GAUGE
4 sc = 1 inch; 4 sc rnds = 1 inch

PATTERN NOTES
Work in continuous rounds, do not turn or join rounds unless otherwise stated.

Mark first stitch of each round.

INSTRUCTIONS

HAT
Rnd 1: Ch 2, 6 sc in 2nd ch from hook, **do not join** *(see Pattern Notes)*. *(6 sc)*

Rnd 2: 2 sc in each st around. *(12 sc)*

Rnd 3: [Sc in next st, 2 sc in next st] around. *(18 sc)*

Rnd 4: [Sc in each of next 2 sts, 2 sc in next st] around. *(24 sc)*

Rnd 5: [Sc in each of next 3 sts, 2 sc in next st] around. *(30 sc)*

Rnd 6: [Sc in each of next 4 sts, 2 sc in next st] around. *(36 sc)*

Rnd 7: [Sc in each of next 5 sts, 2 sc in next st] around. *(42 sc)*

Rnd 8: [Sc in each of next 6 sts, 2 sc in next st] around. *(48 sc)*

Rnd 9: [2 sc in next st, sc in each of next 7 sts] around. *(54 sc)*

Rnd 10: Ch 1, sc in each of first 4 sts, [2 sc in next st, sc in each of next 8 sts] around to last 5 sts, 2 sc in next st, sc in each of last 4 sts. *(60 sc)*

Rnd 11: Sc in each st around.

Rnd 12: [2 sc in next st, sc in each of next 9 sts] around. *(66 sc)*

Rnd 13: Ch 1, sc in each of first 5 sts, [2 sc in next st, sc in each of next 10 sts] around to last 6 sts, 2 sc in next st, sc in each of last 5 sts. *(72 sc)*

Rnd 14: [2 sc in next st, sc in each of next 11 sts] around. *(78 sc)*

Rnd 15: Ch 1, sc in each of first 6 sts, [2 sc in next st, sc in each of next 12 sts] around to last 7 sts, 2 sc in next st, sc in each of last 6 sts, join in beg sc. *(84 sc)*

Rnd 16: [Sc in each of next 13 sts, 2 sc in next st] around. *(90 sc)*

Rnd 17: Ch 1, sc in each of first 7 sts, [2 sc in next st, sc in each of next 14 sts] around to last 8 sts, 2 sc in next st, sc in each of last 7 sts, join in beg sc. *(84 sc)*

Rnds 18–29: Sc in each st around.

Rnd 30: Working in **front lps** *(see Stitch Guide)*, [sc in each of next 3 sts, 2 sc in next st] around. *(105 sc)*

Rnds 31 & 32: Working in both lps, sc in each st around.

Rnd 33: [Sc in each of next 4 sts, 2 sc in next st] around. *(126 sc)*

Rnds 34–39: Sc in each st around.

Rnd 40: Sl st in each st around. Fasten off. ●

SUGAR & CREAM SCARF
by Mickie Akins

FINISHED SIZE

3 x 60½ inches

MATERIALS

- Light (light worsted) weight yarn:
  18 oz/1,000 yds/510g pink
- Size 0/2.50mm steel crochet hook or size needed to obtain gauge

GAUGE

22 dc = 4¼ inches; 7 dc rows = 2½ inches

PATTERN NOTES

Chain-3 at beginning of row or round counts as first double crochet unless otherwise stated.

Join with slip stitch as indicated unless otherwise stated.

SPECIAL STITCH

V-stitch (V-st): (Dc, ch 2, dc) in place indicated.

INSTRUCTIONS

SCARF

Row 1: Ch 302, dc in 4th ch from hook and in each ch across, **do not turn**. *(300 dc)*

Rnd 2: Now working in rnds, **ch 3** *(see Pattern Notes)*, working around last st (dc, ch 2, 2 dc), working in starting ch on opposite side of row 1, sk next ch, [**V-st** *(see Special Stitch)* in next ch, sk next 2 chs] across to last 2 chs, V-st in next ch, sk last ch, (2 dc, ch 2, 2 dc) around side of last st, sk next st, [V-st in next st, sk next 2 sts] across to last st, V-st in last st, **join** *(see Pattern Notes)* in 3rd ch of beg ch-3. *(2 ch-2 sps, 8 dc, 200 V-sts)*

Rnd 3: Sl st in next st, ch 5, dc in same st *(V-st)*, sk next ch sp, V-st in next st, V-st in sp between next dc and V-st, working in sp between sts, V-st in each sp between V-sts across to end, V-st in sp between last V-st and next dc, sk next st, V-st in next st, sk next ch sp, V-st in next st, V-st in sp between next dc and V-st, V-st in sp between V-sts across, V-st in sp between last V-st of last row and first st, join in 3rd ch of beg ch-5. *(208 V-sts)*

Rnd 4: Ch 3, dc in same st, [ch 2, sk next ch sp, 2 dc in each of next 2 sts] 3 times, [ch 2, sk next ch sp, dc in each of next 2 sts] 98 times, ch 2, sk next ch sp, 2 dc in each of next 2 sts] 5 times, [ch 2, sk next ch sp, dc in each of next 2 sts] 98 times, ch 2, sk next ch sp, 2 dc in each of next 2 sts, ch 2, sk next ch sp, 2 dc in last st, join in 3rd ch of beg ch-3. *(206 ch sps, 432 dc)*

Rnd 5: Ch 1, sc in first st, *ch 3, dc in 3rd ch from hook, sk next 3 sts or chs**, sc in next st or ch, rep from * around, ending last rep at **, join in beg sc. Fasten off. •

HOODED SCARF

Continued from page 27

times, leaving rem 44 sts unworked, turn. *(18 sc, 18 dc)*

Row 9: Ch 1, sc in first st, dc in next st, [sc in next st, dc in next st] across, turn.

Rows 10–30: Rep row 9. At end of last row, leaving 18-inch end, fasten off. Fold Hood in half. Sew sts of last row tog for top of Hood.

Edging

Hold Scarf so RS is facing, join deco with sc in first st after Hood, sc in each st across this side, (sc, ch 1, sc) in corner, evenly sp 5 sc in ends of rows, (sc, ch 1, sc) in corner, sc in each st to next corner, (sc, ch 1, sc) in corner, evenly sp 5 sc in ends of rows across short edge, (sc, ch 1, sc) in corner, working in starting ch on opposite side of row 1, sc in each ch across, (sc, ch 1, sc) in next corner, evenly sp 5 sc in ends of row across short edge, sc in each st across to Hood, working in ends of rows across front edge of Hood, sl st in end of first row, ch 3, 2 dc in same row, sk next sc row, [sl st in end of next row, ch 3, 2 dc in same dc row, sk next sc row] across, join with sl st in beg sc. Fasten off. •

HOPE BEAR

Continued from page 37

Sew eyes to rnd 10 on Head above nose as shown in photo.

Ear
Make 2.

Row 1: With pink, ch 2, 6 sc in 2nd ch from hook, turn. *(6 sc)*

Row 2: Ch 1, sc in first st, 2 sc in each of next 4 sts, sc in last st, turn. *(10 sc)*

Row 3: Ch 1, sc in each of first 2 sts, hdc in next st, 2 hdc in each of next 4 sts, hdc in next st, sc in each of last 2 sts. Leaving long end, fasten off. With long ends, sew Ears to rnd 17 of Head as shown in photo.

Body

Rnd 1: With pink, leaving long end, ch 30, sl st in first ch to form ring, ch 1, sc in each ch around being careful not to twist ch, **do not join**. *(30 sc)*

Rnd 2: [Sc in each of next 5 sts, 2 sc in next st] around. *(35 sc)*

Rnd 3: Sc in each st around.

Rnd 4: [Sc in each of next 6 sts, 2 sc in next st] around. *(40 sc)*

Rnd 5: Sc in each st around.

Rnd 6: [Sc in each of next 4 sts, 2 sc in next st] around. *(48 sc)*

Rnds 7–10: Sc in each st around.

Rnds 11: [Sc in each of next 11 sts, 2 sts in next st] around. *(52 sc)*

Rnds 12–22: Sc in each st around.

Rnd 23: [Sc in each of next 11 sts, sc dec in next 2 sts] around. *(48 sc)*

Rnd 24: [Sc in each of next 6 sts, sc dec in next 2 sts] around. *(42 sc)*

Rnd 25: [Sc in each of next 5 sts, sc dec in next 2 sts] around. *(36 sc)*

Rnd 26: [Sc in each of next 4 sts, sc dec in next 2 sts] around. *(30 sc)*

Rnd 27: [Sc in each of next 3 sts, sc dec in next 2 sts] around. Stuff Body. *(24 sc)*

Rnd 28: [Sc in each of next 2 sts, sc dec in next 2 sts] around. *(18 sc)*

Rnd 29: [Sc in next st, sc dec in next 2 sts] around. *(12 sc)*

Rnd 30: [Sc dec in next 2 sts] around. Leaving long end, fasten off. *(6 sc)* Stuff.

Weave long end through top of sts on last rnd, pull to close. Secure end. Using long end, sew Head to top of Body.

Leg
Make 2.

Rnd 1: Beg at top of Leg, with pink, ch 24, sl st in first ch to form ring, ch 1, sc in each ch around, **do not join**. *(24 sc)*

Rnds 2–9: Sc in each st around.

Rnd 10: Sc in each of first 8 sts, [hdc in next st, 2 hdc in next st] 4 times, sc in each of last 8 sts. *(28 sts)*

Rnds 11–13: Sc in each of first 10 sts, hdc in each of next 8 sts, sc in each of last 10 sts.

Rnd 14: Sc in each st around. Fasten off.

Sole
Make 2.

Rnd 1: With pink, ch 2, 7 sc in 2nd ch from hook, **do not join**. *(7 sc)*

Rnd 2: 2 sc in each st around. *(14 sc)*

Rnd 3: [Sc in next st, 2 sc in next st] around. *(21 sc)*

Rnd 4: [Sc in each of next 2 sts, 2 sc in next st] around. *(28 sc)*

Rnd 5: Working in **back lps** *(see Stitch Guide)* and through both thicknesses, sl st Sole to last rnd on Leg. Fasten off.

Stuff Leg.
Sew Legs to front of Body as shown in photo.

Arm
Make 2.
Rnd 1: Beg at hand, with pink, ch 2, 7 sc in 2nd ch from hook, **do not join**. *(7 sc)*

Rnd 2: 2 sc in each st around. *(14 sc)*

Rnd 3: [Sc in next st, 2 sc in next st] around. *(21 sc)*

Rnds 4–8: Sc in each st around.

Rnd 9: Sc in each of first 7 sts, [sc dec in next 2 sts] 3 times, sc in each of last 8 sts. *(18 sc)*

Rnds 10–21: Sc in each st around. At end of last rnd, leaving long end,

fasten off.
Stuff Arms, leaving last inch unstuffed.
Fold last rnd tog, sew closed.
Sew Arms to rnds 2–8 of Body, slightly angled toward back.

Collar
Row 1: With size E hook and white, ch 53, dc in 5th ch from hook, [ch 1, dc in next ch] across, turn. *(49 ch sps, 50 dc)*

Row 2: Sl st in first ch sp, **beg shell** *(see Special Stitches)* in same ch sp, [sk next ch sp, **shell** *(see Special Stitches)* in next ch sp] across, turn. *(25 shells)*

Row 3: Ch 1, sl st in each of first 3 sts, sl st in next ch sp, beg shell in

same ch sp, dc in sp between shells, *shell in ch sp of next shell**, dc in sp between shells, rep from * across, ending last rep at **. Fasten off. Thread ribbon through sps of row 1. Place Collar around neck, tie ribbon in bow at front.

Bandage
Make 2.
Row 1: With white and size E hook, ch 10, sc in 2nd ch from hook and in each ch across, turn. *(9 sc)*

Row 2: Ch 1, sc in each st across. Leaving long end, fasten off. Sew Bandages to front of Body as shown in photo. •

CROSS BOOKMARK

Continued from page 42

next 3 sts, 2 sc in next st;
M. Sc in each of next 7 sts, sk next st, sc in each of next 3 sts, sk next 3 sts, sc in each of next 3 sts, sk next sc;
N. Sc in each of next 10 sts, 2 sc in each of next 4 sts, sc in each of next 20 sts, sk next st, sc in each of next 3 sts;
O. Sk next 2 sts, sc in each of next 13

sts, sk next 2 sts, sc in each of next 3 sts, sk next st, sc in each of last 3 sts. Fasten off.
Follow diagram *(see Fig. 1)* for placement. Glue where overlays are located.
Tack center 4 points tog.
Press. •

→ Start Here

Fig. 1
Cross Bookmark
Diagram

SOFT SLIPPERS

Continued from page 45

Ankle Cuff
Row 1: With RS facing, working in starting ch on opposite side of row 1 around ankle opening, join pink with sc in first ch, [ch 1, sk next ch, sc in next st] across, turn. *(12 ch sps, 13 sc)*

Row 2: Ch 2 *(counts as first hdc)*, [hdc in next ch sp, hdc in next sc] across, turn. *(25 hdc)*

Row 3: Ch 2, hdc in each st across. Fasten off.

Ankle Edging
Using bubblegum and size G hook, join with sc in same place as row 1 of Cuff, ch 2, dc in same st, (sc, ch 2, dc) in end of each of next 3 rows, (sc, ch 2, dc) twice in corner st, (sc, ch 2,

dc) in each st around with (sc, ch 2, dc) twice in last st of row 3, working in end of rows of Cuff, (sc, ch 2, dc) 4 times, ending with sc in last ch of starting st. Fasten off.

Ribbon Appliqué
With bubblegum and size G hook, ch 31, hdc in 3rd ch from hook and in each ch across. Leaving long end, fasten off.

Fold Appliqué into ribbon shape and sew to Slipper near center of the top of foot near row 1 as shown in photo. •

PINEAPPLE SCARF
Continued from page 51

First Pineapple
Row 9: Sl st across to ch sp of first shell, beg shell in same ch sp, ch 3, sk next ch sp, sc in next ch-3 sp, [ch 3, sk next st, sc in next ch-3 sp] twice, ch 3, sk next ch sp, shell in ch sp of next shell, leaving rem sts unworked, turn.

Row 10: Sl st across to ch sp of next shell, beg shell in same ch sp, ch 3, sc in next ch-3 sp, ch 3, sk next st, sc in next ch sp, ch 3, shell in ch sp of next shell, turn.

Row 11: Sl st across to ch sp of first shell, beg shell in same ch sp, ch 3, sk next ch sp, sc in next ch-3 sp, ch 3, sk next ch sp, shell in ch sp of last shell, turn.

Row 12: Sl st across to ch sp of first shell, beg shell in same ch sp, sk next 2 ch-3 sps and next st, shell in ch sp of last shell, turn.

Row 13: Sl st across to ch sp of first shell, ch 3, 3 dc in same ch sp, 4 dc in ch sp of last shell, turn.

Row 14: Ch 6, sl st in 3rd ch from hook, ch 3, sl st in last st. Fasten off.

2nd Pineapple
Row 9: With WS facing, join with sl st in ch sp of next shell, beg shell in same ch sp, ch 3, sk next ch sp, sc in next ch sp, [ch 3, sk next st, sc in next ch-3 sp] twice, ch 3, sk next ch sp, shell in ch sp of last shell, turn.

Row 10: Sl st across to ch sp of next shell, beg shell in same ch sp, ch 3, sk next ch sp, sc in next ch-3 sp, ch 3, sk next st, sc in next ch sp, ch 3, sk next ch sp, shell in ch sp of next shell, turn.

Row 11: Sl st across to ch sp of first shell, beg shell in same ch sp, ch 3, sk next ch sp, sc in next ch-3 sp, ch 3, sk next ch sp, shell in ch sp of last shell, turn.

Row 12: Sl st across to ch sp of first shell, beg shell in same ch sp, sk next 2 ch-3 sps and next st, shell in ch sp of last shell, turn.

Row 13: Sl st across to ch sp of first shell, ch 3, 3 dc in same ch sp, 4 dc in ch sp of last shell, turn.

Row 14: Ch 6, sl st in 3rd ch from hook, ch 3, sl st in last st. Fasten off.

2nd End
Row 1: With RS facing, working in starting ch on opposite side of row 1 of Scarf, join with sc in first ch, ch 1, sk next ch, sc in next ch, ch 2, sk next 2 chs, sc in next ch, [ch 3, sk next 3 chs, sc in next ch] twice, ch 2, sk next 2 chs, sc in next ch, ch 3, sk next 3 chs, sc in next ch, ch 2, sk next 2 chs, sc in next ch, [ch 3, sk next 3 chs, sc in next ch] twice, ch 2, sk next 2 chs, sc in next ch, ch 1, sk next ch, sc in last ch, turn.

Rows 2–14: Rep rows 2–14 of First End, First Pineapple and 2nd Pineapple. •

SIMPLICITY LAPGHAN
Continued from page 52

in beg sc. *(4 ch sps, 492 sc)*

Rnd 5: Ch 3 *(counts as first dc)*, dc in each st around with 5 dc in each corner ch sp, join in 3rd ch of beg ch-3. *(512 dc)*

Rnd 6: Ch 1, sc in each of first 2 sts, ch 3, sl st in top of last st, [sc in each of next 2 sts, ch 3, sl st in top of last st] around join in beg sc. Fasten off.

Sew 1 rose to each corner and at each end of the 3 row sections down length on each side at row ends and rnd 1 of Border. •

For more complete information, visit **FreePatterns.com**

ABBREVIATIONS

beg	begin/begins/beginning
bpdc	back post double crochet
bpsc	back post single crochet
bptr	back post treble crochet
CC	contrasting color
ch(s)	chain(s)
ch-	refers to chain or space previously made (i.e. ch-1 space)
ch sp(s)	chain space(s)
cl(s)	cluster(s)
cm	centimeter(s)
dc	double crochet (singular/plural)
dc dec	double crochet 2 or more stitches together, as indicated
dec	decrease/decreases/decreasing
dtr	double treble crochet
ext	extended
fpdc	front post double crochet
fpsc	front post single crochet
fptr	front post treble crochet
g	gram(s)
hdc	half double crochet
hdc dec	half double crochet 2 or more stitches together, as indicated
inc	increase/increases/increasing
lp(s)	loop(s)
MC	main color
mm	millimeter(s)
oz	ounce(s)
pc	popcorn(s)
rem	remain/remains/remaining
rep(s)	repeat(s)
rnd(s)	round(s)
RS	right side
sc	single crochet (singular/plural)
sc dec	single crochet 2 or more stitches together, as indicated
sk	skip/skipped/skipping
sl st(s)	slip stitch(es)
sp(s)	space(s)/spaced
st(s)	stitch(es)
tog	together
tr	treble crochet
trtr	triple treble
WS	wrong side
yd(s)	yard(s)
yo	yarn over

Chain—ch: Yo, pull through lp on hook.

Slip stitch—sl st: Insert hook in st, pull through both lps on hook.

Single crochet—sc: Insert hook in st, yo, pull through st, yo, pull through both lps on hook.

Front post stitch—fp: Back post stitch—bp: When working post st, insert hook from right to left around post st on previous row.

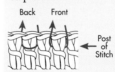

Back   Front   Post of Stitch

Front loop—front lp Back loop— back lp

Front Loop   Back Loop

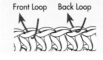

Half double crochet—hdc: Yo, insert hook in st, yo, pull through st, yo, pull through all 3 lps on hook.

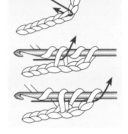

Double crochet—dc: Yo, insert hook in st, yo, pull through st, [yo, pull through 2 lps] twice.

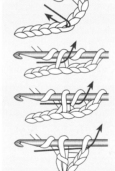

Change colors: Drop first color; with 2nd color, pull through last 2 lps of st.

Treble crochet—tr: Yo twice, insert hook in st, yo, pull through st, [yo, pull through 2 lps] 3 times.

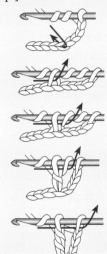

Double treble crochet—dtr: Yo 3 times, insert hook in st, yo, pull through st, [yo, pull through 2 lps] 4 times.

Single crochet decrease (sc dec): (Insert hook, yo, draw lp through) in each of the sts indicated, yo, draw through all lps on hook.

Example of 2-sc dec

Half double crochet decrease (hdc dec): (Yo, insert hook, yo, draw lp through) in each of the sts indicated, yo, draw through all lps on hook.

Example of 2-hdc dec

Double crochet decrease (dc dec): (Yo, insert hook, yo, draw loop through, draw through 2 lps on hook) in each of the sts indicated, yo, draw through all lps on hook.

Example of 2-dc dec

Treble crochet decrease (tr dec): Holding back last lp of each st, tr in each of the sts indicated, yo, pull through all lps on hook.

Example of 2-tr dec

US		UK
sl st (slip stitch)	=	sc (single crochet)
sc (single crochet)	=	dc (double crochet)
hdc (half double crochet)	=	htr (half treble crochet)
dc (double crochet)	=	tr (treble crochet)
tr (treble crochet)	=	dtr (double treble crochet)
dtr (double treble crochet)	=	ttr (triple treble crochet)
skip	=	miss

TOLL-FREE ORDER LINE or to request a free catalog (800) LV-ANNIE (800) 582-6643
Customer Service (800) AT-ANNIE (800) 282-6643, **Fax** (800) 882-6643
Visit anniesattic.com

We have made every effort to ensure the accuracy and completeness of these instructions.
We cannot, however, be responsible for human error, typographical mistakes or variations in individual work.

ISBN: 978-1-59635-220-9

Printed in USA

1 2 3 4 5 6 7 8 9

THE
MACMILLAN
ILLUSTRATED
ENCYCLOPEDIA OF
MYTHS &
LEGENDS

THE
MACMILLAN
ILLUSTRATED
ENCYCLOPEDIA OF
MYTHS &
LEGENDS

ARTHUR
COTTERELL

Macmillan • USA

To Esmor Jones with gratitude

A Marshall Edition
Conceived, edited and designed by
Marshall Editions Ltd
The Orangery
161 New Bond Street
London W1S 2UF

This edition published in 2000 in the UK by Marshall
Publishing LTD for Books Are Fun

Previously published in the UK by Cassell in hardback in
1989 and paperback in 1992

ISBN 1-84028-029-8

Originated by CLG Verona
Printed and bound in Italy by New Interlitho SpA

10 9 8 7 6 5 4 3 2 1

CONTENTS

INTRODUCTION

Why should we know about mythology? The simple answer is that we cannot afford to miss such a rare opportunity to eavesdrop on the innermost thoughts of mankind. For myths and legends are a universal human invention. They have arisen, at different times and in different places, as explanations of the critical problems that always face people. Among their important concerns are the purpose of living, misfortune, success, cruelty, love and fertility, death, the afterlife, family relations, betrayal, old versus new, human versus divine, magic, power, fate, war, accident, chance, madness, creation, and the nature of the universe.

In some traditions the same themes recur – as, for instance, the slaying of demons in the Iranian epics. No less enjoyed during the Middle Ages in Europe were the valiant deeds of the Knights of the Round Table. That their quest for the Holy Grail drew much of its strength from ancient Celtic mythology worried only the Church. The rest of society was simply enchanted by the idea of such a miraculous vessel.

With the rise of philosophy and, more recently, scientific thought, a mythological approach to the reality of daily life has come to seem of little value. Indeed, in modern industrial society myth and legend are almost dead, except as dimly remembered tales of earlier generations. Elsewhere in the world, the mythological faculty thrives, notably in the religious tradition of India, where stories of the great deities, Vishnu, Shiva and Devi are told and retold as a means of reaching a deeper understanding of the Hindu faith.

Nearly all religions have a mythological dimension, which often owes a debt to previous beliefs. Thus in the figure of Satan, the Christian devil, we find an amalgam of ancient Canaanite and Mesopotamian deities. And the name of one of Satan's chief assistants, Baalzebub (lord of the flies), is an obvious distortion of a Canaanite god's name meaning "lord of the house". As a symbol of evil, Satan could hardly be bettered. His spectacular temptation of St Anthony in the Egyptian desert, which sought to undermine the resolution of that austere founder of Christian monasticism, still fascinates writers and painters. And the name of his successor, Antichrist, is still on the lips of both churchmen and laity.

The richness of incident and description in mythology suggests a very deep source in the human psyche. Experts are by no means agreed on an explanation. According to Carl Jung (1876–1961), everyone possesses both a personal and a collective unconscious. The personal one is filled with material peculiar to the experience of the individual, while the collective one holds the mental inheritance of all mankind. Such a common legacy of past experience has, Jung argued, given rise to the archetypes, or primordial images,

Buddha, a vital link between mythology and religion

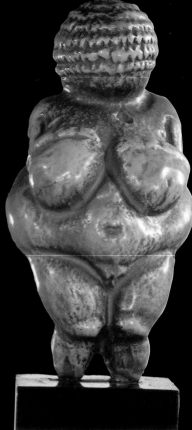

The White Lady, leading hunters to success   *Venus, goddess of love*

"which bring into our consciousness an unknown psychic life belonging to a remote past. This psychic life is the mind of our ancient ancestors, the way in which they conceived of life and the world, of gods and human beings."

Jung's theory – attractive but unproven – suggests that most powerful myths surviving today almost certainly originated in the period immediately prior to the establishment of civilization. The archetypal fertility deity is found, for instance, in prehistoric carvings of the mother goddess. These figurines, with their ballooning breasts, thighs and buttocks leave no doubt as to the purpose of worship. Without fertile women, no primitive band of hunter-gatherers could hope to survive.

Later, another figure appears with this mother goddess – her son and husband. In the ancient cities of Mesopotamia, built from 2600 BC onward, the cult of the fertility goddess and her dying-and-rising consort formed the core of religious observance. Early farmers cultivating fields around the city walls knew about the cycle of germination and growth in plants, and the best time for breeding animals. Their insight and their fears were incorporated in the story of the goddess Inanna and her unfortunate husband Dumuzi. Inanna's descent into the underworld also reveals a profound realization of the paradoxical nature of divinity. The love goddess Inanna and her sister Ereshkigal, the goddess of death, are but the two sides of reality – light and darkness, good and evil, soft flesh and barren dust.

The animal-man, painted on the wall of a cave or carved in stone, is another archetypal figure of prehistory. Images of men crowned with antlers appear in countries as far apart as France and Australia, Canada and China. These spirit masters, or shamans, would have helped the early hunters of wild game. They survive today among the Indian peoples of the American continents, and in northern parts of Asia. Imitating animals is evident in the initiation rites of African peoples, where young men still dress up as lions. Legends of talking animals occur throughout the world although in ancient Greece, Xanthus, the immortal horse of Achilles, was struck dumb by the Erinyes (Fates) because he dared to tell the great warrior of his approaching death.

But it was in the Nile valley that the closest relationships arose between all forms of life. The ancient Egyptians imagined the whole world as a living entity. Every creature shared in a community of being that stretched from the highest deity, Re, the sun god, to the lowest insect, which as Khepra the scarab-beetle could also represent the morning sun. Snake-, dog-, cow- and lion-headed deities filled the Egyptian pantheon. Even the cat was represented, as Bastet, a benevolent deity also associated with the sun. At Bastet's cult town of Bubastis a necropolis even housed mummified cats. However, childbirth was under the protection of the crocodile-headed hippopotamus goddess Tauret.

The planet Saturn, symbol of perfection

The Egyptian cow goddess, Hathor

Cargo cult, a myth of modern times

The antiquity of Egypt so impressed the ancient Greeks that they regarded it as the source of most inventions and ideas. Before 525 BC the first Greek philosopher, Thales of Miletus, visited Egypt to study methods of land measurement. "Perhaps", remarked the historian Herodotus, "this was the way in which geometry was invented, and passed afterwards to Greece." Whatever the truth, the visit was something of a watershed in human consciousness, for Thales had started to reach judgements according to what was observed and to ignore inherited views about the nature of the gods. More critical still was the view of Xenophanes of Colophon. Tilting at the blatant human attributes of the Greek gods, he said that if cattle could draw, they would make their own gods in the likeness of cattle.

Thus the scene was set for coining the word *mythologia*, by which the ancient Greeks meant stories about legendary figures, and nothing more. That is, fiction not fact. Possibly their failure (a rare omission for the knowledge-hungry Greeks) to recognize psychology as a distinct field of study helps to explain the subsequent downgrading of myth and legend. Today we have come to appreciate the insights available from the study of the human mind, including the clues to understanding our own nature to be found in Jung's archetypes.

None of this lessens, of course, the impact of mythological events. The tales in this encyclopedia remain stubbornly capable of speaking for themselves. Nor do the legends about Buddha, for instance, in any way diminish his ministry. The enormous statues of the Enlightened One, carved from living rock in Sri Lanka, bear witness to the continued strength of the Buddhist faith. In the same way, the notion of a golden age, a perfect future, dies hard. It is also ironic that astrology is alive and well in an era that has already seen a spacecraft photograph the rings of Saturn, the planet the Roman diviners associated with perfection.

EGYPT

The critical event in Egyptian history occurred some time before 3200 BC, when Upper and Lower Egypt were united under one ruler. The king's identity remains uncertain, although the name of Menes occurs in several king lists. Because of the lack of written records, the earliest ideas of the ancient Egyptians are equally obscure. However, the first texts carved on royal burial chambers around 2500 BC leave no doubt that a very old system of belief was already in existence.

For centuries, Egypt was almost totally isolated from other ancient West Asian centres of civilization. Surrounded by almost impassable deserts, the Nile valley was secure from all but the most determined invaders. This isolation allowed the remarkable pantheon of the ancient Egyptians to thrive virtually unchallenged by outside beliefs.

Perhaps the most remarkable aspects of the Egyptian pantheon were its size and diversity, from the very beginning of recorded history. Each of the forty-two districts into which the country was divided had its own deity. As even the smallest town maintained a temple for its god, the number of deities worshipped is beyond reckoning.

A fundamental difference between ancient Greek and Egyptian (as well as Mesopotamian) mythology was that the inhabitants of Egypt did not imagine their gods as having a special abode, such as Mount Olympus in northern Greece. There is reference to an island where several deities once met to judge the dispute between Horus and Seth. But the spot seems to have been chosen because it was "in the middle" of the country. Egyptian gods and goddesses tended to reside in the districts they had originally settled. Their ownership of a place was recognized century after century.

Still more amazing than the overwhelming number of Egyptian gods is the variety of forms they take. Instead of thinking about their gods in purely human terms, as did most

Monumental temple complexes such as Karnak (left), on the banks of the Nile, testify to the glory and splendour of ancient Egypt and the dynasties that ruled it.

A sunset over the jutting peaks of the pyramids (far right) encapsulates key aspects of ancient Egyptian life. Countless myths were invented to explain the daily passage of the sun across the sky, and the pyramids commemorate the powerful rulers of Egypt and their obsession with a life after death.

The Nile (below), the lifeline of Egypt, inspired so much of Egyptian mythology. Its annual flood and the fertile silt it left behind, the contrast between its lush margins and the desert, the delta marshes, the animals that lived on the river, and the boats that sailed it, all have a place in what is one of the richest collections of myths in the world.

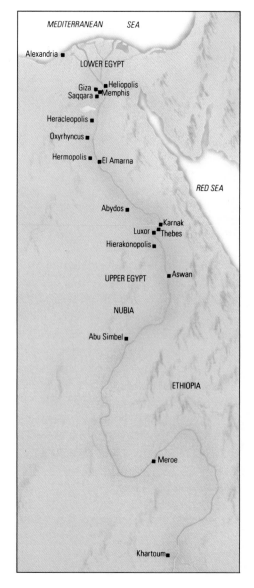

other ancient peoples, the Egyptians were prepared to see the divinity in all living things, and even in inanimate objects.

The ancient Egyptians viewed the world as a living unity, with everything contained therein — men, gods and animals — sharing in its existence. Within this world, the forces of growth and decay, of birth and death, held sway, dominating the Egyptian mind. This fascination with inescapable powers was doubtless inspired by the fierce conditions of the surrounding desert, the annual flooding of the river Nile and the importance of the agricultural cycle. The last two were celebrated in the cult of Osiris.

Perhaps not surprisingly, Osiris, one of the chief deities who took human form, was concerned with the question of survival after death. He may have come to Egypt from abroad, but became so "Egyptianized" as to appear a truly native god. The god of Zedu, a town in the delta of the Nile, his worship was widespread, suggesting that his cult introduced into Egyptian religion an element that was missing from the cults of other deities. This was probably his ability to offer each individual access to an afterlife. Indeed, Osiris was depicted swathed like a mummy, and his struggle against his evil brother Seth focuses on the fate of the individual after death. In the ancient Egyptian *Book of the Dead*, Osiris is the judge of souls and the ruler of the underworld.

Following the decline of Egypt as a state, the mysteries of Osiris spread to other Mediterranean lands. However, Isis, the wife of Osiris, achieved greater popularity outside Egypt. By the time of Julius Caesar (assassinated in 44 BC), she had a temple and an altar on the Capitol Hill in Rome.

In the Old Kingdom (2613–2160 BC), the pharaoh was believed to become Osiris when he died, and his successor was believed to be the son of either Horus or Re, the sun god. Horus and Re, as so often with Egyptian deities, were often

EGYPT/2

indistinguishable, especially when Horus wore the solar disc.

In the New Kingdom (1567–1069 BC), the pharaoh was believed to be the son of Amun, the then ascendant god. In the great temples at Luxor, reliefs show how Amun assumed the form of the reigning pharaoh and united with his queen, giving rise to the new pharaoh's birth. To avoid any rivalry between ram-headed Amun and Re, both gods were assimilated in the form of the composite deity, Amun-Re. The splendid monuments at Luxor and Karnak were raised in honour of Amun-Re and paid for out of the tribute won in the pharaoh's campaigns in Canaan, Syria and northern Sudan.

The harmony of the universe was believed to depend on the well-being of the pharaoh. In theory, he acted as the chief priest of the Egyptian nation, although for practical reasons his office and duties were delegated to high-ranking priests.

In ancient Egypt, as in Mesopotamia, there was a deeply held belief that chaotic forces had existed before the world was created. In the act of creation, these powerful forces had been banished to the outer edges of the world, but they still continued to encroach upon the society of gods and men. Thus, every day, the priests assisted the gods in sustaining the fabric of universal order through the performance of religious rites.

During the Middle Kingdom period (2040–1652 BC), a ceremony was held in the great temple of Re at Thebes to aid the sun god in his daily struggle with the serpent Apophis, or Aapep. The Theban priesthood of Re claimed that Apophis attacked the sun god after sunset, and that the ensuing battle lasted throughout the night.

The ritual enacted by the priests involved the destruction of a magical image. A wax effigy of a serpent or crocodile was inscribed with the name of Apophis, then insulted and hacked into pieces while the chief priest recited a spell. Magic (hike) was looked upon as an effective weapon against the enemies of the gods and the pharaoh. However, the daily harassment suffered by Re pales before the terror caused by Tiamat, the spirit of evil in Mesopotamian religion.

As long as Egypt remained independent, and the pharaoh ruled in partnership with the priesthood, the old ways of the native religion were left almost entirely undisturbed. The one instance of serious religious controversy was brought about by the reforms of the pharaoh Akhenaten. In about 1367 BC, this ruler deserted the cult centre of Amun-Re at Thebes and established a new capital at El Amarna. There he forbade worship of Amun-Re and devoted himself exclusively to the worship of his own god Aton, the sun-disc, a single creator deity who presided over the whole world.

However, after Akhenaten's death, the new capital was deserted and his successor, Tutankhamun, returned the court to Thebes and devotion to Amun-Re. Reaction to the reforms of Akhenaten was so severe that his temples were razed to the ground and his name and that of his god

Egyptians believed that a soul journeyed into the underworld (right), where jackal-headed Anubis weighed it against the feather of truth. The ibis-headed scribe, Thoth, on the far left, recorded the result.

Cats were regarded as sacred by the Egyptians, in honour of the cat-headed goddess Bastet (left), and were often embalmed and mummified. The cat-cemetery at Bubastis, her cult centre, was famous throughout the ancient world.

obliterated. Today, little evidence survives on which to judge the reformer's actual intentions.

Whatever the object of Akhenaten in El Amarna, the main effect of the changes he introduced was a weakening of Egyptian power. By the time the country had recovered from its religious turmoil, Hittite armies had successfully disputed Egypt's control of Syria. The course of Egyptian independence still had six centuries to run, but the days of power abroad were over. Canaan and Sinai were gradually

CHRONOLOGY

3200 BC Unification of country, possibly under Menes.

2650 Construction of the first monumental building in stone, the step pyramid of Zoser at Saqqara.

2575 Great pyramid of Khufu built at Giza.

1652 Hyksos invaders conquer the Nile delta.

1567 Expulsion of the Hyksos.

1467 Tuthmosis III becomes pharaoh and Egyptian power abroad reaches its peak.

1367 Akhenaten's religious reforms plunge the country into turmoil.

1350 Brief reign of Tutankhamun, whose tomb survived virtually intact until discovered in 1922.

1286 Hittites almost defeat the Egyptians at the battle of Kadesh in Syria.

945 Libyan dynasty installed, the first non-Egyptian line.

663 Assyrians attack Egypt, sack Thebes and leave vassal rulers in charge.

525 Persian army occupies Egypt.

332 Alexander the Great conquers Egypt.

305 Ptolemy I Soter becomes King of Egypt.

30 Death of Cleopatra and annexation by Rome.

AD 641 Arab assault on Egypt

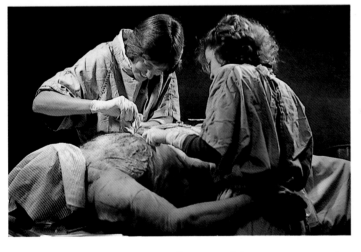

Embalming, a practice that continues today (left), was developed by the ancient Egyptians, for whom it was an important stage in funerary rites. Its invention was incorporated into their mythology, where it was said to have been started by the deities Isis and Anubis.

abandoned, and Egypt was threatened by powers greater than her own. Foreign dynasties soon alternated with native ones, until the Macedonians under their king, Alexander the Great, finally conquered the country in 332 BC.

Never again did an Egyptian monarch sit upon the Egyptian throne, and traditional values began to be undermined. The Macedonian dynasty of the Ptolemies (305–30 BC) treated the Egyptian gods with caution, but the old connection between the ruler and the gods had ended. It was clear that foreign kings paid little heed to the remarkable pantheon of the Egyptian gods, adopting pharaonic titles merely for political purposes.

After the Romans annexed Egypt as a province in 30 BC, the pretence of any continuity with the past was dropped altogether. The old faith faltered and over the next 200 years was replaced by a new belief, Christianity.

The actions of the Egyptian gods were forgotten other than in legendary events connected with the places where their temples once stood. More durable, however, was the ancient skill of the embalmer. St Anthony (AD 251–356) was so worried about Christian use of such a superstitious practice that he made clear his personal desire for an ordinary burial. Deliberately setting his face against traditional Egyptian burial customs, he said, "In the day of the resurrection I shall receive my body incorruptible from the hands of Christ." The days of Osiris were clearly no more.

MESOPOTAMIA

Ancient Mesopotamia comprised the southern end of the plain between the rivers Tigris and Euphrates, roughly the area between modern Baghdad and Basra. The semi-desert land made irrigation vital, while the absence of wood and stone meant that buildings had to be constructed with bricks.

The first settlements appeared around 4500 BC, close to the marshes bordering the Persian Gulf. Their inhabitants were the Sumerians, a culturally creative people who may have arrived from the East.

The complex religion and mythology of ancient Mesopotamia was a Sumerian invention. It took root and flourished in the walled cities that developed out of the early settlements in the third century BC. Many of the cities still had recognizable Sumerian names in later times, which indicates a continuity of population. Similarly, despite being swamped by successive waves of Semites, notably the Babylonians and Assyrians, the cultural tradition of the Sumerians remained virtually intact. The Semites took over the Sumerian philosophy, adding to it features of their own.

Until the conquest of Alexander the Great, King of Macedonia, in the fourth century BC, the religious trend was the evolution of national deities. Both Marduk, the god of Babylon, and the Assyrian war god Ashur came to be looked upon as the supreme powers in the universe, rather than as members of a pantheon that controlled natural forces.

The genesis of Mesopotamian religion was the worship of natural phenomena. At first the Sumerians seem to have imagined some of these forces in animal form, but in later times the human form came to be preferred as a way to represent the gods.

Gradually, the gods drew closer to mankind and moved into the temples that were built for them in every city. Often, these "houses" stood upon ziggurats, huge artificial mounds of sun-dried bricks. According to the Babylonian creation epic, named after its first words *Enuma Elish*, "When on high", men were created only to relieve the gods of the burden of work. The same poem accounts for the flood by saying that Enlil, the Sumerian god of air, could no longer tolerate the din of the city where his own temple was situated. After unsuccessfully trying plague, drought and infertility to silence the people, Enlil sent a huge deluge down upon earth. The sole survivors were the family and animals of a wise man, Atrahasis.

The ultimate supreme authority in the pantheon was An (Sumerian) or Anu (Babylonian), whose name means "sky". The Sumerians probably believed that life arose from the marriage of An (sky) and Ki (earth). However, by the time the population of Mesopotamia was concentrated in cities, Enlil, the city god of Nippur, was the most powerful deity.

Dependence on intensive agriculture led to the belief that the growth of cities was the result of Enlil's gift, the hoe. Because the Sumerians also regarded the city deity as the

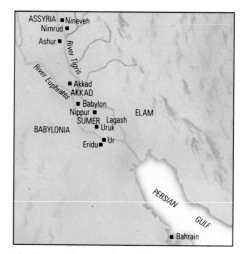

The River Euphrates (right), which formed one of Mesopotamia's boundaries, seemed to produce floods or droughts at whim. This doubtless contributed to the sense of unpredictable powers which shaped the Mesopotamian pantheon.

The hero Gilgamesh (below), was forced to recognize man's helplessness when, despite travelling the world in search of eternal life, he was ultimately unable to discover its secret.

actual owner of the city, the temple possessed and worked most of the irrigated land. The chief duty of the temporal ruler was to safeguard the interests of the city god, for kingship "came down from heaven" as the means of interpreting the divine will to men.

In the great cult ceremonies that took place during the seasonal festivals, the relationship between the deity and the ruler became explicit. At New Year, for example, the king impersonated the god in a holy marriage with the chief priestess, who represented mother earth.

The assembly of the gods, the highest authority in the Mesopotamian universe, met in a corner of the forecourt of Enlil's temple in Nippur. Except on the occasion of his own trial, Enlil usually executed the decisions of the assembly in the shape of a storm. The most dramatic debate of the gods ever recorded is described in *Enuma Elish*. It concerns the

CHRONOLOGY

2750 BC	Appearance of cities in Sumer.
2600	Gilgamesh possibly ruler of Uruk.
2370	Lugal-kinishe-dudu, King of Umna, becomes first overlord of Sumer.
2334	Powerful Semitic-speaking dynasty founded by Sargon at Agade.
2200–2130	Gutians, invaders from the northeastern highlands, dominate most of Mesopotamia.
2130	Utu-hegal, King of Uruk, defeats the Gutians.
2023	Over-irrigation and food shortages eventually weaken Utu-hegal's successors.
2017	The Semitic-speaking Ishi-Erra seizes the throne and establishes the Isin dynasty.
1792	Hammurabi ascends the throne of Babylon and begins to make his city the Mesopotamian capital.
1595	Sack and occupation of Babylon by the Kassites, tribesmen from the Iranian plateau.
1363	Ashur-uballit founds Assyrian power.
689	The Assyrian king, Sennacherib, sacks Babylon.
604	The biblical Nebuchadnezzar revives the fortunes of Babylon, and builds the Hanging Gardens.
539	Cyrus captures Babylon and incorporates the city in the Persian Empire.
323	Alexander the Great dies.

threat posed by the Babylonian chaos-dragon Tiamat. Despairing at the enormity of the forces Tiamat had ranged against them, the gods elected Marduk as their absolute ruler and champion. Marduk's victory in the ensuing struggle gave the leadership of Mesopotamia to the city of Babylon.

The idea of a titanic struggle against evil powers always haunted the inhabitants of ancient Mesopotamia. Unlike the isolated Nile valley of the ancient Egyptians, the historical experience of the Tigris-Euphrates plain was stormy and full of sudden changes. Foreign invasions and internal conflicts combined with the uneven flow of its great rivers to mould a mythological outlook that found significance in cosmic struggle as much as the divine ordering of the universe. Yet the Mesopotamian notion of a conflict between the forces of order and the forces of chaos was moderate in comparison with the strict dualism of neighbouring Iran.

Sumerian	Babylonian	Meaning	Authority
AN	ANU	Sky	Heaven
ENLIL	ELLIL	Lord Wind	Air
NINHURSAGA	—	Lady of the Foothills	Wildlife, fruitfulness
ENKI	EA	Lord Earth	Fresh water, cunning
NANNA	SIN	Moon God	Moon
NINURTA	NINURTA	Lord Plough	Farming, war
NINTUR	NINTUR	Lady Birth, Hut	Womb
INANNA	ISHTAR	Queen of Heaven	Fertility
ERESHKIGAL	ERESHKIGAL	Queen of the Underworld	Death
ISHKUR	ADAD	—	Rainstorm
DUMUZI	TAMMUZ	Faithful Son	Fertility, rebirth
—	MARDUK	Bull Calf of the Sun	Champion of the gods
APSU	APSU	Abyss	Underground fresh waters
TIAMAT	TIAMAT	—	Salt waters of the sea

IRAN

Until the time of the Arab conquest of AD 641, the civilization of Iran falls into four distinct periods: Achaemenid, Macedonian, Parthian and Sassassian. The Achaemenids, whom the Greeks called the Persians, traced their ancestry to a legendary king called Achaemenes. They came to power in 550 BC, conquered West Asia, Egypt and Pakistan, and maintained their authority until they were invaded by Alexander the Great, King of Macedonia, in 334 BC.

Following Alexander's death twelve years later, Iran came under the control of the Seleucids, a Macedonian dynasty based in Mesopotamia. This short-lived period of foreign rule ended in 247 BC when an Iranian provincial governor rebelled and founded the Parthian dynasty, which lasted for nearly five hundred years.

The Parthian era was dominated by an intense struggle with Rome. Following the Romans' sack of the Parthian capital, Ctesiphon, widespread rebellion led to the collapse of Parthian power and the foundation, around AD 226, of the Sassassian kingdom of Iran.

The new dynasty had its origins in the southern Iranian province of Fars, the old seat of the Achaemenids. The lands held by the Sassassians stretched beyond the Iranian plateau to places as remote as Armenia, northern Arabia, Afghanistan and Pakistan. It was during this final period of ancient Iranian history that Zoroastrianism reached its peak.

Zoroaster had preached in northeastern Iran in around 600 BC, shortly before the Achaemenids came to power. Although worship in the Achaemenid court was eclectic, the view of the prophet Zoroaster was accepted: that the world was in the grip of an eternal conflict between the forces of Arta (truth) and Druj (deceit).

The Achaemenids generally tolerated non-Iranian deities, unless they needed to bring a rebel into line. Following the suppression of the Babylonian uprising in 482 BC, Xerxes underlined his authority by removing the statue of Marduk, the city god of Babylon. The Achaemenid kings were not above showing respect for the pronouncements of foreign deities, particularly those of the Greek Apollo.

Shortly after Xerxes' abortive invasion of Greece in 480–479 BC, the Greek historian Herodotus travelled extensively in West Asia and Egypt. He noted that the Achaemenids had neither temples nor altars, but that they conducted sacrifices to the heavenly powers on mountain tops. What Herodotus obviously failed to observe were the numerous towers in which sacred fires were guarded.

Nevertheless, Herodotus was correct in recording that the Achaemenids did not make statues of their gods, considering it foolish to visualize them in human form. Even the greatest of their gods, Ahura Mazdah (wise lord), the guardian of the king, was shown only as a symbol.

The Achaemenid ruler Artaxerxes (475–425 BC) added Mithra to the official Zoroastrian pantheon. Over time, he

The centre of Zoroastrianism today is in Bombay, where it is practised by the Parsees (above). Here, in an initiation ceremony, a boy is being given the symbolic belt, the kusti, which is tied and untied during the ritual; he also wears the sacred white shirt, or sudra.

The impressive entrance staircase to Persepolis (right) proclaims the greatness of the Achaemenids, whom the Greeks called Persians, and whose empire marks the first period of the civilization of Iran. The reliefs on the staircase portray delegates from the many countries of the empire bringing gifts to the king, Darius I (522–486 BC), who founded the city.

became the Iranians' most popular deity and was regarded as the son of Ahura Mazdah.

During the Parthian dynasty a set of mysterious rites, which fascinated people living on both sides of the Euphrates frontier, was added to the cult of Mithra. As Mithras, the warrior god was imported into Europe.

In Sassassian times, the eternal conflict between Ahura Mazdah and Ahriman (the evil one) was the subject of intense speculation, and was complicated by further campaigns against Rome. These wars were intensified when the territory of Armenia came into dispute, since Sassassian antagonism was fuelled by the conversion of the Armenians to Christianity, in about 301. Thus, the Sassassians became militant Zoroastrians and, until a partition was eventually agreed in 387, Armenia was the arena for a religious war.

Militant Zoroastrianism is associated with Kartir, a proselytizing priest who dominated the Sassassian court for sixty years. Within Sassassian lands, it soon became normal

practice to persecute Jews, Buddhists, Hindus, Manichaeans and Christians alike. Kartir himself was responsible for the execution of Mani, who founded Manichaeanism.

In a sense, Kartir's persecution was simply the logical conclusion of Zoroastrianism. For Zoroaster had deliberately cast aside the more usual mythological interpretation of good and evil as effects proceeding from a unique source of being that transcends and reconciles all opposites. Instead, he labelled most other deities as the servants of Ahriman. The fight against the forces of evil was symbolized in the sacred fire, which became the focus of Sassassian worship.

Perhaps the stark contrasts found on the Iranian plateau — steep-sided mountains and flat valleys, bitterly cold winters and boiling hot summers — encouraged this singular rethinking of myth. Certainly, it had an effect on the attitudes of the peoples who came under Iranian domination. It may even be seen to linger on in the outlook of certain Christians and Muslims today.

A tower of silence in the stony desert of central Iran stands sentinel over the dead (below). Ancient Zoroastrians would expose their dead at the top of these towers, since cremation would pollute the sacred fire, and burial would pollute the earth.

CANAAN

The countries that are now Syria, the Lebanon, Jordan and Israel once formed a general cultural area inhabited by Semitic-speaking peoples. That area has been loosely called Canaan (the name comes from *kinahhu*, the word used by the ancient Babylonians to denote a shellfish famous for the dye it produced).

In prehistory, the Semites migrated from a starting point in the Syrian desert. By the middle of the third millennium BC they had founded large settlements in Syria. The city of Ebla, which was discovered only in 1975, dates from this period. It was a prosperous trading centre of about 250,000 inhabitants, administered by a bureaucracy which, according to its archive, numbered more than 1,100 men.

The most common form of government was the city-state. Other great cities included Mari, on the Euphrates, and the port of Ugarit in northern Syria. But the city-state possibly reached its zenith in the great Phoenician trading centres of Tyre, Sidon and Byblos.

Canaan also had links with Egypt. The ancient Egyptians had traded with Byblos from early in the third millennium BC, mainly for the cedarwood from the Lebanese hills, since Egypt had almost no good timber. In later times, Egyptian armies marched overland and brought many of the city-states under the pharaoh's rule, for Canaan was a passageway between the great powers of Egypt, Babylonia, Assyria and the Hittites.

The Hittites are included here because, even though they spoke an Indo-European language related to Greek, their occupation of Syria in the thirteenth century BC brought the full influence of Canaanite religion to bear on their mythology. The other ancient cults from Asia Minor included here are those which focused on the great fertility deities of Phrygia.

Until the discovery of the archive at Ebla, the main source for Canaanite mythology was the information gleaned from clay tablets found in 1929 at Ras Shamra, the site of ancient Ugarit. From them archaeologists have established that the Canaanites believed the home of a god was not a man-made temple, as did the Mesopotamians, but a mountain – Mount Saphon, situated to the north of Ugarit. This mountain was considered to be the home of Baal (which means "lord"), the god who plays the most prominent part in the texts. It was clearly to the Canaanites what Olympus was to the ancient Greeks – not only a dwelling place but also a meeting place for the assembly of the gods. This idea is echoed in the Old Testament, where Zion is placed "on the sides of the north" (Psalms: 48.2).

The nature of the supreme Canaanite deity El (meaning "god") also finds a close parallel in the Bible. El represented omnipotence at one remove, rather like Yahweh, the god of the Hebrews. He would interfere on decisive occasions only and allowed Baal to assume an active role on his behalf. Even

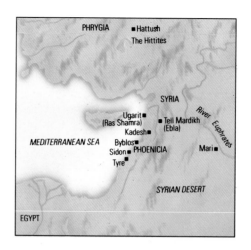

so, it was El who was recognized as the divine father, the creator of all that existed, and the master of time.

The inscriptions from Ugarit also reveal an emphasis on natural phenomena, and a particular interest in fertility and the theme of the disappearing-and-reappearing fertility god. The local title for this god was probably Adon (which also means "lord"). As a result of contact between the Canaanites and the ancient Greeks, who had set up a trading post near Ugarit shortly after 1300 BC, and renewed trading links from 700 BC onward, worship of Adonis was eventually introduced to Greece.

One of the chief Canaanite myths tells of the descent of Baal to the underworld at the bidding of Mot, the god of death. Baal was unable to refuse Mot's invitation, and while in the underworld was also obliged to accept his host's fare and eat mud which was the dreadful food of the dead. In grief, El put on mourning clothes, poured ashes over his head and even mutilated himself. However, Baal's wife Anat (lady of the mountain) was not prepared to lose her husband, and she brought the corpse back to life by killing Mot. She treated him as a field of corn – she cut and winnowed him, and then ground him up.

Anat was known to the Greco-Roman world as Astarte, and this myth was assimilated and adapted by the ancient Greeks. According to them, Adonis was loved by both the love goddess Aphrodite and Persephone, the queen of the

CHRONOLOGY	
2000 BC	Amorite tribes sack Ebla.
1759	King Hammurabi of Babylon destroys the city walls of Mari.
1750	Hittites establish a kingdom in Asia Minor.
1400	Ugarit at its richest.
1350	Hittites at their peak in Asia Minor and Syria.
1286	Drawn battle between the Hittites and the Egyptians at Kadesh in Syria.
1182	"Sea Peoples" overwhelm the Hittites, destroy Ugarit, but are defeated in Egypt by Ramesses III.
922	Death of Solomon, the king of Israel and Judah.
850	Date of earliest Phoenician inscription so far found in Cyprus. Start of colonization movement overseas.
732	Assyrians capture Damascus.
587	Phoenicia under Babylonian control after Nebuchadnezzar captures Tyre. Hebrews taken in captivity to Babylon.
539	Cyrus takes Babylon, releases the Hebrews from captivity, and founds the Persian (Iranian) Empire.
332	Alexander the Great conquers Asia Minor and Canaan.
63	Syria becomes a Roman province.

underworld. When the latter would not let the handsome youth go, Aphrodite descended to the world of the dead to release him. Unlike El, however, Zeus intervened in the dispute and decided that Adonis should spend half the year with each of his admirers. The Greek myth of Adonis not only owes much to the stories told about Baal — it also draws on the dying-and-rising character of Tammuz, the Babylonian version of Dumuzi. Worship of Tammuz, the husband of Ishtar, had spread early into Canaan, even finding a temporary place in Hebrew worship.

A similar concern with fertility is evident in Hittite mythology. Quite often a god disappeared, either in anger or in pursuit of some private occupation, such as hunting, and in consequence a blight afflicted the earth. After an extensive search, and the use of magic, the missing deity would be found and prosperity restored.

The Hittite pantheon also seems to have had an influence on the ancient Greeks. For instance, there is a striking parallel between the Greek Titan Kronos and the king of the Hittite gods, Kumarbi. Instead of emasculating a tyrannous overlord with a sickle, as Kronos did his father Ouranos, Kumarbi performed the deed with a single bite. Another cult involving castration, which also moved westward from Asia Minor, was that of Attis, the lover of the Phrygian mother goddess Cybele. By 204 BC the devotees of Attis in Rome were cutting off their own genitals.

GREECE

The two things above all others that shaped Greek civilization, and the remarkable mythology that arose from it, were landscape and language.

The geography of Greece forced the ancient Greeks to become seafarers; no other country in the Mediterranean was so exposed to the sea. And since Greece's rugged interior virtually closed off its mainland from the European continent, it was dependent on sail and oar for communication.

From earliest times, the Aegean Sea was used by voyagers from the coasts of Europe, Asia and Africa. It is hardly surprising, then, that the large island of Crete, which lies across the southern entrance to the Aegean, should become the site, in about 2000 BC, of the first civilization in Europe comparable with the more ancient traditions of Egypt and West Asia.

Greek legend regarded the Cretan King Minos as the first ruler of the seas, and this underlines the vital role of the sea and ships in the development of civilization on the island. As important is the fact that his mother was a West Asian princess named Europa, who had been forcibly brought to Crete from the Canaanite port of Tyre. The myth of her abduction by Zeus, the chief deity of the Greeks, reveals something of the debt owed by Europe to its more advanced, eastern neighbours. Cadmus, the brother of Europa, searched the islands in vain for her before the oracle of Apollo at Delphi told him to forget his sister and settle on the Greek mainland. This he did, and founded the city of Thebes in Boeotia. Cadmus is credited, moreover, with introducing the alphabet to Greece.

Although the ancient Greeks began by absorbing the myths and legends of older peoples, they soon outgrew what was ready to hand. An example of their creative borrowing is the story of the labours of Heracles. The recent discovery of a Sumerian epic about the similar exploits of Ninurta, son of the air god Enlil, leaves no doubt that there was once a widespread tradition in West Asia about a powerful figure who had a club, a bow and a lion skin. However, the Greeks made the myth their own by allowing the semi-divine Heracles to become a god.

The labours that Heracles undertook reveal a good deal about ancient Greek civilization. Like other heroes, he had to serve a local ruler, the lord of Tiryns, in the Peloponnese. The mountains and broken coastline of Greece divided up the mainland into areas which became small kingdoms, each enclosed by natural barriers. This pattern was followed almost exactly by the city-states that came into being from the eighth century BC onward. The aristocratic families of these city-states constructed genealogies that linked them with the legendary heroes associated with the previous cities, thereby preserving much of Greek mythology.

Landscape, then, had the effect of creating a number of separate myths linked to early settlements. Places such as

With his bare hands, the greatest hero in Greek mythology, Heracles, kills the Nemean lion (above). The many adventures of this popular figure were frequently depicted on Greek vases.

Still standing guard over the city of Athens is the Parthenon (left), the Temple of Athena, goddess of the city that took her name. It was built in the Classical Period of Greece, by Pericles, from 448 to 436 BC.

Scenes from a mosaic in the ruined Greek city of Thugga, in Tunis, reflect the importance to the Greeks of ships and seafaring, bordered as they were by so much coastline (below left).

Sparta, Mycenae, Tiryns, Athens, Thebes, Orchomenus, Corinth and Iolcus appear in story after story.

The second factor that shaped the mythology of the ancient Greeks was the language itself. The subtlety and range of the Greek tongue encouraged speculation about the nature of existence. Poets such as Homer, in the ninth century BC, delighted audiences with tales of the Trojan War and other great adventures. These poems also explained how the gods intervened in human affairs.

Over the centuries, however, there were men who thought that the world should be explained differently. The first was Thales, who came from Miletus in Asia Minor. Instead of drawing on West Asian myth to explain the heavens, Thales used astronomical records compiled by Babylonian priests to predict an eclipse of the sun in 585 BC. His rational outlook eventually led to the emergence of the discipline of philosophy.

The philosopher Plato (429–347 BC) was the first known user of the word *mythologia*. By "myth", he meant the telling of stories that contained only invented figures – they were fiction, and nothing more. By 316 BC, Euhemerus, a Sicilian philosopher at the Macedonian court, could argue that all Greek myths and legends related to historical events, and that the gods were originally men who had distinguished themselves and who, after their death, received divine honours from a grateful people.

Such views had little effect on popular Greek religion and did not stop people retelling marvellous stories about gods and heroes, although the educated were sceptical about the events they claimed to record. Yet as early as the seventh century BC, the poet Hesiod had felt the need to put Greek mythology into some kind of order. His great poem *Theogony* did this by tracing the rise of Zeus to the highest position in the Greek pantheon. It recounts the god's rebellion against his father Kronos and lists the many children that Zeus had with mortal and immortal women. It also refers to the anger of Hera, Zeus's wife, at these liaisons.

Behind the conflict between Hera and her husband's illegitimate children was an historical event only dimly remembered by the ancient Greeks. This was their settlement of the mainland and the Aegean islands. It was recalled that the ancestors of the Athenians had originally spoken another language but, like other pre-Greek peoples, they had adopted the tongue of the Greek settlers, who arrived some time before 2500 BC. What was forgotten by the Greeks, except in the actions preserved in legend, was the extent to which they were themselves influenced by the older inhabitants of their homeland.

There can be no doubt that Hera was a pre-Greek earth goddess, whose cult was so strongly rooted that it had to be absorbed into that of Zeus. Their uneasy marriage was obviously the result of the imposition of a sky father's cult on

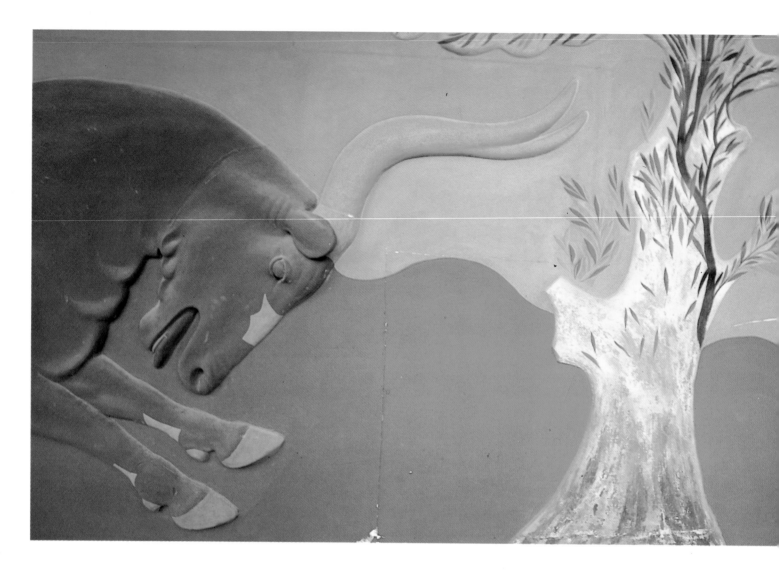

that of a well-established earth mother. Once, when Hera went too far in her persecution of Heracles, Zeus suspended her from heaven, her feet weighed down by an anvil.

Among other places, Zeus and Hera were believed to have married on Crete. It was on this island, almost a thousand years before Homer and Hesiod, that the ancient Greeks met the first and most serious challenge to their own mythological tradition. The Cretan islanders, the Minoans, possessed a religion which had not only an all-powerful mother goddess but also a dying-and-rising god, like the deities of West Asia. When the Greeks conquered Crete, in about 1450 BC, the two mythologies were blended. For example, the birth myth of Zeus was changed to allow for his secret upbringing on Crete, after his mother Rhea had given Kronos a stone wrapped in swaddling clothes to swallow instead of the child. (Kronos ate his children because it was predicted that one of them would depose him.)

But the cult of Zeus was unable to take over the annual death and resurrection of his Cretan counterpart because immortal Zeus could not be touched by death. After the fall

of Kronos, when the universe was divided between Zeus and his two brothers Poseidon and Hades, Zeus was given the sky to rule, Poseidon the sea, and Hades the underworld. Mount Olympus (the seat of the gods in Thessaly) and the earth were regarded as common territory.

A dying-and-rising god whom the ancient Greeks may have inherited from Crete was Dionysus, a deity associated with bulls and wine. The bull games of the Minoans – confused in the legend of the Athenian hero Theseus with the feeding of the monstrous Minotaur – could have been part of a festival in honour of Dionysus.

Greek settlers and traders carried the worship of Dionysus to Italy; by 186 BC the Roman Senate felt it necessary to pass severe laws against the riotous celebrations of the imported god. Several thousand frenzied worshippers (maenads) were executed before Dionysus was merged safely with the Italian wine god Bacchus.

During the expansion of the ancient Greek world between 700 and 500 BC, colonies and trading posts increasingly dotted the shores of the Mediterranean. In eastern waters the

The craggy peaks of Mount Olympus (above) in central Greece were regarded as the seat of the gods in the Greek pantheon.

A reconstructed fresco (left) from the palace at Knossos, on Crete, depicts a charging bull in an olive grove. This represents the Minoan bull cult which gave rise to the Greek myth of Theseus and the Minotaur.

Greek plays such as the Oresteia (right), based on mythology, continue to draw great crowds the world over, such is their timeless appeal.

Apollo's temple at Delphi (below right) held the oracle that determined the fates of so many Greek heroes. Such was its fame and authority that kings travelled from far and wide to consult it.

old relationship was unchanged — the ancient Greeks were the junior partners — but in western waters it was they who brought the fruits of civilization, particularly to Rome. Greek mythology and legend were of especial interest to the Romans. They had not imagined their gods in human form, nor did they have a set of myths associated with them. But gradually Jupiter came to be thought of as Zeus, just as Mars and Minerva were identified with Ares and Athena, and they acquired many of their attributes and myths. The final merging of the Greco-Roman pantheon eventually occurred after the Romans succeeded in annexing the whole of Greece in 148 BC.

In the meantime, the conquests of Alexander the Great (ruled 336–323 BC) had extended Greek influence as far as India. His tolerance of Asian beliefs meant that new cults were soon adopted by the Greeks and spread into Europe. The most powerful were those of Mithras (from Iran), Cybele (from Asia Minor), and Isis (from Egypt). But by then the creative period of ancient Greek mythology was, in any event, largely over.

CELTIC AND CHRISTIAN EUROPE

The Celts relied on the oral transmission of their religious beliefs, and so there is little evidence from which to form a clear picture of the Celtic pantheon. The only written accounts of Celtic myth and legend to have survived from ancient times are those passed down by the Romans. Since Julius Caesar spent ten years conquering the Celtic peoples of Gaul, the area now covered by France, these testimonies are, not surprisingly, unflattering.

Julius Caesar looked upon the Gauls in the same way that eighteenth-century Americans regarded the Indian tribes. He believed them to be a courageous but primitive foe, barring the way to the expansion of the civilized world. "As a nation," he wrote, "they are extremely superstitious. People suffering from diseases, as well as those who are exposed to danger in battle, offer human sacrifices at ceremonies conducted by the druids. They believe that the only way of preserving one man's life is to let another man die in his place. Regular tribal sacrifices are held, at which colossal figures made of wickerwork are filled with living men, and then set alight so that the victims burn to death. They think that the gods prefer the sacrifice of thieves and bandits, but whenever there is a shortage of criminals, they do not hesitate to make up the number with innocent men."

Such descriptions of Celtic practices have been exaggerated by some modern antiquarians as well as by folklore. More trustworthy accounts of Celtic mythology are the legendary tales recorded in Irish and Welsh collections of poetry and prose, dating respectively from the eighth and fourteenth centuries onward. These comprise the epic cycles of medieval Ireland, and the derivative Arthurian tradition in Wales, Brittany and England.

However, even these sources are extremely limited, since they represent only the western areas of the Celtic world. In 387 BC, the Celts defeated the Roman army and set fire to the city of Rome itself. Other groups moved through the Balkans and in 278 BC crossed to Asia Minor, where they gave their name to Galatia.

Fortunately, the mythological cycles of Ireland are extensive and rich in incident. Indeed, only half of the 400 tales known to exist today have been published. Modern scholars have divided these stories into four main cycles.

The first concerns the activities of the Tuatha De Danaan, "the people of the goddess Dana". The chief deity mentioned is Dana's son, Dagda, who owned a magic cauldron which could restore the dead to life. It is possible that this marvellous utensil was the prototype for the Holy Grail, around which grew numerous legends. The Grail was said to be the vessel that Jesus and his disciples drank from at the Last Supper; it also received the blood that flowed from the spear wound in Jesus' side at the Crucifixion.

The second cycle concerns the heroes of Ulster, especially Cuchulainn, the semi-divine warrior and champion of all

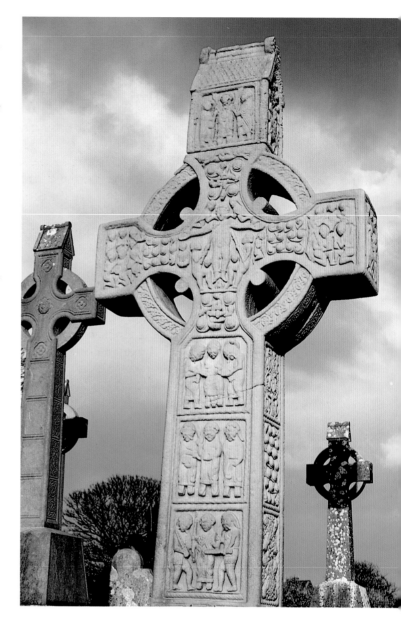

Ireland. The adventures of legendary kings form the third cycle. These rulers frequently fought each other, giving the war goddess Morrigan ample opportunity to litter the battlefield with dead.

Morrigan was imagined as a crow or a raven and embodied all that was savage and perverse among the supernatural powers. But her cruelty has nothing in common with the bleak joy of the Germanic gods of northern Europe.

The Celtic heroes enjoyed pitting themselves against each other in single combat. Many of these tremendous duels are described in the fourth cycle, which centres on adventures of Finn Mac Cumhail, or Finn Mac Cool, who led the Fianna, a group of tried and trusted warriors. One of the present-day Irish political parties recalls this band in its name, Fianna Fail (soldiers of destiny).

Some of the characters and deeds found in the Irish and Welsh legendary cycles carried over into Christian chivalry. The medieval church was always uneasy about the Grail, which Joseph of Arimathea was supposed to have brought to Britain, since it was considered too obvious a descendant of the utensils used in ancient Celtic rites. But there was little that clerics could do to dampen enthusiasm for the legendary tales of the Knights of the Round Table. They even had to accept the story that Sir Galahad alone was granted a vision of the Grail because of his purity, and that afterward the soul of the knight ascended straight to heaven.

Interest in Arthur and his knights was still active when Caxton printed Sir Thomas Malory's *Le Morte d'Arthur*, in the fifteenth century. Introducing it, Caxton declared, "Ye shall see manhood, courtesy and gentleness."

Yet medieval Christianity was itself permeated with legends, particularly concerning the Last Judgement, the Antichrist, and the cult of the Virgin Mary. It seemed as if a host of wizards was only held in check by a blessed troop of saints. Clerics used exorcism as a weapon against the persistent wiles of Satan, but personal anxiety about Hell accounts for the popularity of the apocryphal Gospel of Nicodemus, which narrates the triumphant descent of Jesus to the underworld and the release of many souls held captive there.

Throughout Celtic Europe, it is still possible to find intricately worked Celtic crosses (left). These crosses, examples of the Celts' highly developed culture, have similarities with the Christian crucifix.

Celtic art also appears to have influenced the design of Christian illuminated manuscripts, including the Book of Kells *(below left).*

The Celts excelled at metalwork, as can be seen from the famous Gundesrup cauldron (right).

The Grail legends, with their blend of Celtic and Christian symbolism, continue to hold sway over the imagination of their readers. The work (below) by the painter Burne-Jones depicts the Holy Grail.

CHRONOLOGY	
387 BC	Celtic tribes sack Rome.
228	Galatia, in Asia Minor, is settled by the Celts.
50	Julius Caesar completes the conquest of Gaul.
AD 47	Britain invaded by the Romans.
250	Emperor Decius persecutes Christians.
312	Emperor Constantine has a Christian vision before the battle of the Milvian Bridge.
337	Constantine baptized on his deathbed.
410	Final withdrawal of Roman legions from Britain.
431	Council of Ephesus declares that the Virgin Mary is the Mother of God.
441	Anglo-Saxons start to colonize England.
461	Death of St Patrick, the patron saint of Ireland.
597	Saint Augustine converts the Anglo-Saxons to Christianity, but fails to reach an agreement with the bishops of the Celtic Church.
789	First Viking raid on England at Weymouth, in Dorset.
800	Charlemagne crowned Holy Roman Emperor.
902	Vikings establish a permanent base at Dublin.

NORTH EUROPE

In the winter of AD 406, the river Rhine, which separated the Roman provinces of Germania from the lands of the unconquered peoples of northern Europe, froze over. A Germanic horde seized the opportunity and poured across the river, rampaging through the northwestern provinces of the Roman Empire.

For two years, the unopposed invaders – the Suebi, Vandals and Alans – looted the Roman provinces. Their wanderings took them to the Iberian peninsula, from where, in 429, the Vandals crossed to Africa. Saint Augustine lived long enough to witness their siege of Hippo Regius, the North African city that was his episcopal see. But the saint died before the Vandals made their name a byword for mindless destruction by the sack of Rome in 455.

Saint Augustine was particularly disturbed by the rumour that ascribed the collapse of Roman power to the abandonment of the pagan gods. But another cleric, Salvian of Marseilles, was more pragmatic in his analysis, attributing the barbarian success to the increasing domination of Roman society by a rich and powerful minority. He describes how many people chose to "seek Roman humanity among the barbarians, because they can no longer support barbarian inhumanity among the Romans".

This assessment conflicts with the popular idea of uncouth savages tearing down the fabric of Roman civilization and recognizes that close relations between the peoples living within and without the empire had existed for many years.

Although a few Roman records survive, the chief sources of information on the Germanic deities are the great collections of Viking mythology compiled in the Middle Ages. The *Prose Edda*, by Icelander Snorri Sturluson (1179–1241), is perhaps the most valuable document.

The Viking period lasted from 750 to 1050, during which time a vigorous body of myths developed, revolving around the deeds of Odin, Thor and the brother-sister deities Frey and Freya. Not until the eleventh century were the Vikings finally converted to the Christian faith.

The Vikings – a word which probably means "sudden raiders" – were the Norwegians, Swedes and Danes, who still inhabited the original homeland of the Germanic tribes. They first set out on their raids at the end of the eighth century.

A ready acceptance of danger, and a profound disdain for those who could not endure hardship, characterized the Vikings and was reflected in the fatalism of their myths. Death in battle was a joyous event, since the Valkyries took the gloriously slain to Valhalla, Odin's hall. There, fallen heroes feasted by night and, by day, fought mock battles in preparation for Ragnarok, the final battle which would witness total destruction on the Vigrid plain. According to the *Prose Edda*, a new earth would rise from the ashes of Ragnarok, "green and fresh with fields of corn that grow unsown". Moreover, some of the gods, including Balder and his blind brother Hodr, would return from the underworld and repeople the land.

Both the courage and the cunning of the Vikings are reflected in the adventures of their gods. The unpredictable violence of the Viking world is evident above all in the actions of Loki, the leader of the giants and monsters in the last battle against the gods and heroes. Sturluson describes

this trickster deity as "handsome and good-looking, but his disposition is evil and his mood very changeable. He always cheats and constantly involves the Aesir in great difficulties, although by guile he often helps them out too."

In the myth of Balder, a darker side to Loki's character emerges and he reveals himself as no less evil than his three dreadful children, the serpent Jormungandr, the wolf Fenrir, and the underworld goddess Hel.

Loki was a member of the Aesir, the warrior deities who inhabited Asgard. According to Sturluson, the word "Aesir" derived from "Asia". This led him to believe that Thor was a grandson of Priam of Troy and Odin his descendant in the twentieth generation. Though this seems unlikely, it is possible that the Vanir, a second group of deities led by Frey and Freya, came westward at a later date.

The Aesir and Vanir fought each other until, realizing that neither of them would score a final victory, they joined forces and fought a continuous war against the frost giants, the descendants of Ymir. This primeval being arose from the icy waves and was associated with the numbing cold, which the Vikings knew only too well from their expeditions through freezing waters. The body of Ymir was believed to have provided the raw material from which Odin, together with Vili and Ve, created the world.

High-ranking members of Germanic society were given ship burials and were richly provided with food, ornaments and armour, such as this helmet from the Sutton Hoo burial in East Anglia (above). Such burials emphasized the importance of ships to these peoples.

The North European landscape (far left), frequently frozen and desolate, is reflected in the mythology of this part of the world. In Viking myth, for example, the world was a barren icy waste until the cow Audumla licked a block of salty ice, from which the first man appeared.

The Viking god of thunder, Thor (left), wielding his mighty hammer Mjolnir, still has great appeal, as evidenced in the popularity of the comic-strip adventures that perpetuate his myth.

CHRONOLOGY	
AD 9	Three Roman legions under the command of Publius Quinctilius Varus destroyed by German tribes on the Rhine.
122	Emperor Hadrian builds walls and towers to fortify the northern boundary of Roman Britain and Germany.
253	Devastating Germanic incursion into Gaul cripples the prosperous northwestern provinces.
376	Pressure from the advancing Huns leads to the Visigoths crossing the Danube in strength.
378	Mistreatment of the Visigoth settlers by Roman officials causes an uprising. At the battle of Adrianople, the emperor Valens is killed and his army annihilated.
406	Germanic tribesmen cross the Rhine.
410	Visigoth leader Alaric sacks Rome.
451	Defeat of Attila the Hun at Troyes.
455	Vandals sack Rome in a sea-borne attack from Africa.
476	Romulus Augustulus, the last Roman emperor, is deposed.
568	Lombards invade Italy.
732	Arabs turned back at Poitiers by Charles Martel.
793	Vikings destroy Lindisfarne monastery in Northumberland.
800	Charlemagne crowned as emperor in Rome.
867	Vikings permanently occupy York.
870	King Alfred wins a great victory at Ashdown.
1016	Danish Canute crowned King of England.
1066	Normans (Viking descendants) invade England.

INDIA

The complex nature of religious belief in India is the result of a long historical process of assimilation. Just as the caste system of social organization has grown over the past 3,500 years, by incorporating the customs of newly amalgamated peoples but giving them a low position in the social order, so Indian mythology did not reject many beliefs, but included them in its own developing form, even if they seemed unsuitable at first. The result of this attitude has been the development of a range of myth and legend which is unrivalled anywhere else in the world.

The second significant aspect of Indian belief is the fundamental unity of the universe itself. In Hinduism every part of the cosmos is seen as being a manifestation of an underlying divinity. The gods, demons and heroes of Hindu mythology are merely aspects of an eternal cycle of creation, duration and dissolution. Even Indra, the king of the Hindu gods, finds it hard to grasp the truth when on one occasion the great gods Shiva and Vishnu tell him that an army of Indras has already existed. The deities of the Hindu pantheon recur in each slow-moving cycle, and each time they reappear they repeat their mythological actions.

The vast time scale of Indian thought also distinguishes it from other mythological traditions. The Hindu world is subdivided into ages (*yugas*), not unlike the Greco-Roman ages of gold, silver, brass and iron, which follow each other in an apparently endless stream of time. A *kalpa*, a day and night of the creator god Brahma, is 8,640,000,000 years of human reckoning, and comprises 2,000 world cycles. At the end of one hundred years of Brahma days and nights, the universe dissolves before another Brahma century of rest and a renewed cycle of creation. This cosmic event is currently calculated to be 31,000,000,000,000 years away.

Humankind fits into the vast pattern of the Hindu universe through reincarnation. The goal of Indian ascetics has always been to escape from the wheel of birth, death and rebirth. In release (*moksa*), they will leave behind the distracting sorrows and excitements of ordinary existence and enter a higher realm of consciousness. In fact, all the great religious figures of India have pointed to the way in which the individual can reach this blessed state of being.

One of the greatest of these figures was a north Indian prince who lived in the sixth and fifth centuries BC. He was Buddha, the enlightened one, whose aim, essentially, was to awaken people from the entanglement of illusory experience. It is said, however, that the fear he encountered among people when trying to pass on his vision of universal emptiness (*sunyata*), forced him to alter his teachings. The bodhisattvas (Buddhas-to-be) who followed him, saviours filled with compassion for the sufferings of the world, attempted to lead people gradually toward enlightenment. The supreme example was Avalokitesvara, who in China evolved into the Buddhist goddess of mercy, Kuanyin. When

In Hindu life today, the social order is still dominated by the caste system. A priest (above) belongs to the highest caste, the brahmins. As the sole guardians of the sacred lore of the Rig Veda, and thus of the Vedic tradition, brahmins alone are allowed to perform the most important religious tasks.

Cremation is central to Hindu ceremonial life. In the Rig Veda, the fire god Agni consumes the body at cremation and takes the soul to a blissful existence in the heavens. The ritual often takes place beside a river, preferably the Ganges (right), which the Hindus believe to be the most sacred of all rivers, able to purge all those who bathe in it of their sins.

Avalokitesvara gained enlightenment, he chose not to pass into a state of bliss but to stay behind on earth to provide succour for the afflicted.

Buddhism spread north into Tibet, then to China, Korea and Japan; it also spread south to Sri Lanka, and to Southeast Asia. But in India it was largely reabsorbed into Hinduism, and Buddha himself was accommodated as the ninth incarnation of Vishnu.

The Hindu faith holds that the welfare of Indian society depends on a priestly class, the brahmins. Their closely guarded knowledge of the sacred lore in the *Rig Veda*, the most ancient collection of Hindu hymns, has always been used to justify the power they wield. Buddha himself was not a brahmin but a warrior (*ksatriya*), and therefore indifferent to caste distinctions. Today the revival of Buddhism is not unrelated to its democratic appeal to members of the lowest sections of Indian society.

Another system of belief that has stood outside traditional Hindu practice is Jainism. Its doctrines, especially that of non-violence (*ahimsa*), had a profound influence on Mahatma

Buddha (above) was a north Indian prince who achieved the ultimate Indian aim of enlightenment and inspired the Buddhist religion. Later, he was reassimilated into Hinduism as the ninth incarnation of the great god Vishnu (right) who appears here resting with his wife Lakshmi on a cosmic serpent.

INDIA/2

Gandhi. Through the practice of non-violence and stringent austerities, the followers of Mahavira, the last Jaina saviour, believe that their souls will escape to a heaven near the top of the universe. Mahavira (died 526 BC) was an older contemporary of Buddha, but his teachings never enjoyed the same popularity. They were probably too austere. The rite of fasting until death (*salleknana*) could appeal only to the most dedicated ascetic.

It is tempting to look to the Indus civilization as the source of many of the radical changes that took place in Hindu belief between 900 and 500 BC. The Aryan pastoralists who destroyed the ancient cities of Harappa and Mohenjo-daro, in about 1700 BC, worshipped natural phenomena. Their chief deity was Indra, a storm god whose weapon was the thunderbolt. As Purandara (fort destroyer), he gave them victory over peoples living in walled towns and fortified cities. The character of Indra in the *Rig Veda* is very like that of a war leader. He is portrayed as a great fighter, a slayer of demons, and a lusty drinker of the beverage prepared by the ritual god Soma. Probably a hallucinogen of some kind, the exhilarating qualities of the drink called soma seem to have been appreciated by the gods and their priests, the brahmins.

Another important deity mentioned in the *Rig Veda* is Agni, the god of fire. The hymns addressed to him were clearly composed by poets intoxicated with the juice of the soma plant. Quite possibly the growing interest in the practice of yoga after 900 BC was prompted by a yearning to recapture this ecstasy, which had been lost when the Aryans moved out of the mountains where the plant grew.

While the surviving evidence is not large, the archaeological finds at Harappa and Mohenjo-daro suggest that other deities, such as Devi, the mother goddess, and Shiva as the divine yogi, could have had pre-Aryan origins.

Indra, Agni and Soma all underwent a transformation. Although Indra remained the popular figurehead of the Hindu pantheon, he lost both his power and his dignity. Agni was no longer worshipped at all, and Soma was changed into the moon. Its waxing and waning was said to be due to the gods' taking the heavenly drink from its shore each month. In place of these Vedic deities arose Vishnu, Shiva, Devi, and the shadowy Brahma. In the *Rig Veda* Vishnu appears as a sun god who supports the sky and helps Indra to kill demons. Shiva, in the form of Rudra (howler), is placed on the outer edge of the pantheon, lurking as a sinister force that brings or averts disasters. The goddess Devi and Brahma have no role in the earliest texts at all. The creator deity of the *Rig Veda* is Hiranya-garbha (golden womb). Only toward the close of the first millennium BC was Brahma identified with Hiranya-garbha and the golden egg from which all creation comes.

Since his sole interest is the overall structure of the universe, Brahma has left plenty of scope for Vishnu and Shiva as deities engaged in the struggle against evil. Perhaps

Buddhism spread from India to many other countries including China, Japan, Tibet and Nepal, where this Buddhist temple (above) is situated. But, although Buddhist temples might be highly decorative, the religion's ceremonies have nothing to compare with those of Hinduism for pomp and display.

Processions (right) are very much a part of Hindu life. Here, Shiva appears riding Nandi, the white bull.

Even in a modern Indian laboratory (below) pictures of the gods are kept to hand, showing that science has not been able to suppress their potency.

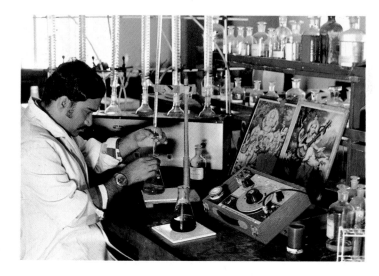

this is most evident in the incarnations (*avatars*) of Vishnu. In one of them, as Krishna, he explains to the warrior Arjuna, "Whenever there is a falling away of goodness and a surge of vice, I take on an earthly body. For the protection of the virtuous, the destruction of the wicked and the restoration of the way of duty, I am born from time to time."

Both Vishnu and Shiva intervene in human affairs when necessary, but on certain occasions neither of them has dared. The first time these powerful gods held back was when a challenge was made by Mahisha, a monster-demon, who through terrific austerities had acquired invincible strength. No deity wished to challenge this colossal water buffalo, except the goddess Devi. On a similar occasion, the Mesopotamian pantheon had elected Marduk as champion against the she-dragon Tiamat; now the Hindu gods passed all their powers to the goddess for the contest. As ten-armed Durga (inaccessible), Devi rode to battle with Mahisha. After a titanic struggle, she overcame the monstrous creature. Thereafter the ascendancy of Devi was guaranteed, and she is now the supreme deity in the Hindu pantheon.

The most remarkable quality of Indian speculation about the nature of existence has been a readiness to accommodate foreign ideas. The attitude on his death in 1885 of the Bengali holy man Sri Ramakrishna, whom many Hindus regarded as an *avatar*, is quite typical. "I have practised all religions, Hinduism, Islam, Christianity," he said, "and I have followed the paths of different Hindu sects. I have found that it is the same God toward whom all are directing their steps, though along different paths. You must try all paths and traverse all the different ways once."

33

CHINA

The present-day Chinese belong to the oldest surviving civilization in the world. Although the Shang kings founded the first state in northern China around 1650 BC, more than a millennium later than the civilizations of Egypt and Mesopotamia were established, their centralized realm formed the basis for all subsequent development. The beliefs of the Shang Chinese are known because it was the custom to keep records when rulers consulted the ancestral spirits.

Divination, which involved interpreting cracks on scorched animal bones and, sometimes, tortoise shells, was used to consult the royal ancestors about future events. Questions were always inscribed, and often the answers were recorded too. The most frequent query addressed to the female ancestral spirts concerned the sex of unborn infants. The word "good" was used to denote a boy and the phrase "not good" to denote a girl. The Shang desire for male descendants survives in the preference of the Chinese today for boys. Although formal ancestor worship has largely disappeared in the People's Republic, respect for one's forebears is still shown, though with flowers rather than by sweeping the ancestral graves.

For the Shang kings, the heavenly powers provided descendants, good harvests and victories on the battlefield. In turn, as the chief worshipper in the ancestral cult, the Shang king was regarded as "the Son of Heaven". Only he possessed the authority to beg for the ancestral blessings, to counter the ancestral curses and to rule on behalf of Shang Di,

the high god of heaven. The unworthiness of a ruler was thought to be reflected in natural phenomena, when "rivers dried up" and "the earth shook". In the philosophy of Confucius (551–479 BC), a harmonious relation between the king and the heavenly powers alone entitled the ruler to enforce political obedience.

In the centuries that followed the Shang dynasty, the mythology associated with the heavenly powers expanded. A list of divine rulers was accepted; twelve heavenly emperors were followed by eleven earthly emperors, then twenty-five sovereigns. After these shadowy monarchs came cultural heroes such as Shennong and Fu Xi. In some representations these two deities have serpent bodies and human heads. The first mortal ruler was the legendary Yu, a hydraulic engineer who, through his great skills, was apparently able to contain the waters of the deluge. As a result of this tremendous service, Yu had the privilege of founding the Xia dynasty; archaeologists in China are presently searching for evidence of this legendary period.

Ordinary people were largely excluded from the ancestor worship practised by the king and his courtiers. They managed instead with male and female sorcerers, who placated bad spirits and invoked aid from those who were more kindly disposed. Details of an ancient rain-making ceremony survive. They reveal that when a sorcerer danced within a circle under the blazing sun, his sweat was expected to induce drops of rain. This magic eventually found a place in Daoism, the native Chinese religion of individual salvation and the opponent of the moral philosophy of Confucianism, which, like imported Buddhism, became popular in the confused years of the third and fourth centuries AD.

Even before this period of disunity, however, the sorcery of Daoist adepts had successfully entered the imperial palace. The superstitious character of Zheng, the first unifier of China in 221 BC, was played upon by several magicians, who promised to obtain the elixir of life for him. Zheng spent a fortune trying to obtain immortality and sent embassies to the tops of mountains to establish relations with the immortals (*hsien*) and overseas to find "the three isles of the blest". Many scholars now believe that the elixir experiments of Daoist alchemists mark the beginnings of what developed into Chinese science.

The other rival faith in China was Buddhism. The earliest reference to the new religion occurs in the first century, but not until the Tang dynasty (AD 618–906) did Buddhism present a serious challenge to official Confucianism. To clear up uncertainties about doctrine, the famous monk Xuan Zhang (also known as Tripitaka) went to India to obtain Buddhist scriptures. Later, the Chinese seized on the story of his journey westward and wove a mass of fantastic detail into it. The exploits of Xuan Zhang's chief companions — the monkey god Hanuman and the piglike Zhu Bajie — have

Buddhism filtered from India to China, where it still thrives. However, whereas Chinese Buddhist priests (above) preach a family-based religion, Indian Buddhism is more concerned with the individual.

enthralled generations of listeners and readers. Even today, *Journey to the West* is probably the most popular book in Chinese literature.

But perhaps the greatest contribution made by China to Buddhist mythology is the goddess of mercy, Kuanyin. She seems to have evolved out of the Indian bodhisattva (Buddha-to-be) Avalokitesvara, toward the close of the Tang dynasty. The addition of female companions for bodhisattvas may have started the process by which Kuanyin became a distinct deity. In Tibet, the spouse of Avalokitesvara was Tara, who was sometimes known as Pandaravasini (clad in white). Since Pai-i Kuanyin is a literal translation of Tara's title into the Chinese language, there is reason to believe that the attributes of Tara combined with Avalokitesvara's all-compassionate character to produce a powerful new mother goddess. As the bestower of children, Kuanyin appealed to a people steeped in ancestor worship.

The Chinese transformation of Avalokitesvara into Kuanyin has proved less attractive to the Japanese, who received their version of Buddhism via China and Korea. In Japan, Avalokitesvara is worshipped in both masculine and feminine forms, as Kwannon.

Because the Chinese believe that mountains lead to the spirit world, monasteries are often built on their slopes (above).

The Chinese Buddhist goddess of mercy Kuanyin (below), is unwilling to enter Nirvana because of her awareness of worldly suffering.

CHRONOLOGY	
2205–2197 BC	Reign of Yu, the first emperor of the legendary Xia dynasty.
1650–1027	Shang dynasty and the emergence of civilization in northern China.
1027–256	Zhou dynasty and feudal age.
551	Birth of Confucius.
221	China united by Zheng, King of Qin.
AD 221–265	The Three Kingdoms, the beginning of an age of disunity.
589–907	Reunification of China under the Sui and Tang emperors.
645	Xuan Zhang (Tripitaka) returns from India with Buddhist scriptures.
960–1279	Song dynasty.
1279–1368	Mongol occupation of China. Marco Polo visits the country.
1368–1644	Ming dynasty and Buddhist revival.
1644–1911	Qing dynasty. End of the empire.

JAPAN

There are no written records on the origins of Shinto, "the way of the gods". Before the introduction of the Chinese script in the sixth century, along with the Buddhist faith, the Japanese were unable to set down their religious beliefs. The well-known creation myth of Izanagi and his sister spouse Izanami, for instance, comes from a late collection of texts and sheds little light on ancient Japanese thought.

Because the influence of China on Japan has been so profound it is very difficult to separate purely Japanese ideas from those imported from China. Some scholars even suggest that the pairing of male and female deities, such as Izanagi and Izanami, may be the result of a Japanese attempt to follow the Chinese notion of the Yin and the Yang. These two interacting forces — female and male — were not regarded as being in conflict but rather as existing together in a precarious balance that if disturbed would bring disasters to mankind.

Shinto is the oldest system of belief in Japan. There can be no doubt that it existed before the arrival of Buddhism and the teachings of Confucius. But it never developed into a unified religion with a mythology of its own. There are several reasons for this. First, Shinto was a mixture of different beliefs. It embraced the shamanism that the Japanese brought from the Northeast Asian continent when they settled the islands, as well as the animistic practices of the Ainu, the first inhabitants. Second, there was a lingering tribalism among the Japanese themselves. The various tribal communities, living in isolated river valleys, maintained their own traditions even after the rise of central government in the seventh century.

Instrumental in establishing a regular system of government, based on the Chinese model, was Shotoku (572–621), a regent prince. Shotoku did more than adopt Chinese methods of organization, however. He was equally concerned about how men should behave. "Punish that which is evil," one of his edicts proclaims, "and encourage that which is good." For Shotoku, the three faiths of Japan were the root, the stem and branches, and the fruit and flowers of a great tree. Shinto was the tap-root, embedded in the rich soil of folk legend. Confucianism served as the sturdy stem and branches of the social order and learning. The blossoming of the spirit was encouraged by the Buddhist faith, whose fruits later included Zen. These three faiths were seen as being mutually supportive right up to the political upheavals of the fourteenth century, when religious strife was a damaging feature of the civil wars.

Shinto has always remained the focus of national worship, for the Imperial Family is supposed to have descended from Amaterasu, the sun goddess. Even today she remains the chief deity in the pantheon, and her worshippers regard her as the dispenser of fertility and of the fortunes of the nation. At some time in the distant past Amaterasu must have

displaced in importance Kunitokotachi, the ancestor of Izanagi and Izanami. This pre-existing god has now become the unseen spirit of the universe, instead of the creator deity he once was.

Although nothing can be known for certain about the earliest Shinto beliefs, the late myth of Izanagi and Izanami does reveal one of its great concerns — death and physical decay. The goddess Izanami died while giving birth to the fire god Kazu-tsuchi, and, grief-stricken, Izanagi went to the underworld to try to bring her back. Izanami met him at the entrance with two requests. He was to wait while she went to arrange her own release, and he was not to look at her too closely. But while she was gone, Izanagi grew impatient, and lit a tooth of his comb to illuminate the passageway beyond the entrance. The sight that greeted his eyes overwhelmed him with horror — maggots swarmed over Izanami's rotting corpse. Outraged and humiliated, Izanami urged the hags of death to tear her husband apart.

Shinto, the country's oldest religion, is still an important part of life in modern Japan. Even today, Shinto priests officiate in household ceremonies (above) to bring health and good fortune to families. The Imperial Family, too, refer to Shinto; they continue to claim descent from the sun goddesss Amaterasu (left). Parallel with Shinto and complementing it is Buddhism, a more philosophical faith centred on one figure, Buddha (below), and based on a body of scripture. Adapted in various forms by the Japanese, it also permeates and colours their lives.

CHRONOLOGY	
57	Japanese envoy received by the Chinese court.
260	Temple of Amaterasu founded in Ise.
552	Introduction of Buddhism to Japan, via China and Korea.
1192	Yoritomo becomes first shogun.
1274–81	Mongol invasions.
1549	St Francis Xavier reaches Japan.
1592	First Korean expedition.
1640	Expulsion of Europeans.
1716	First relaxation of edicts against foreign studies.
1854	United States establishes trade relations.
1868	Meiji Restoration – Japan begins process of modernization.

How different this is from the equivalent Greek myth about the musician Orpheus. When he stole a forbidden glance at his beloved Eurydice on the way out of the underworld, she simply turned into a wraith of mist and vanished forever.

Butsudo, "the way of Buddha", as opposed to Shinto, has developed a separate mythology in Japan. The imported faith introduced ideas from both India and China, but the Japanese added elements of their own. The development of Jizo-bosatsu into a major figure as the consoler of the dead is quite typical. He is depicted as a gentle-faced monk with a shaven head, dressed in a long robe and holding a staff with clattering rings on one end. He is believed to have the power to redeem souls from the underworld and carry them back to heaven. Similarly, the bodhisattva Ksitigarbha (earth womb) was not very popular in India, Buddha's homeland, but his association with the judgement of the dead attracted first Chinese, and then Japanese, Buddhists.

SOUTHEAST ASIA

This vast area of land and sea falls culturally into three parts. First there is Vietnam, which received its civilization from China. The second part comprises the countries and areas that originally came under the influence of Indian culture, although they were not conquered by an Indian state. These are Burma, Thailand, Laos, Cambodia, western Malaysia, and the Indonesian islands of Sumatra, Java and Bali. The remainder of Southeast Asia derives its cultural tradition principally from the more recent arrival of Islam and Christianity. It includes the Philippines, annexed by the Spanish in 1521, the great island of Borneo, and the eastern archipelagos of Indonesia, notably Amboina and the Moluccas, and the Celebes (now Sulawesi).

Only in Vietnam did Chinese political and religious ideas take root firmly, as a result of centuries of occupation. Elsewhere the Chinese emperors were content with nominal recognition from local rulers. The closeness of the Vietnamese relationship with ancient China has stamped itself on Vietnamese myth, and the earliest legends record both the debt owed to the Chinese and the national desire for freedom from their control.

One of these legends recounts that the Lac dragon lord, Lac Long Quan, came from the sea, subdued evil spirits, and taught the people of Vietnam how to grow rice and wear clothes. He then returned to the sea after telling them to call on him if they were ever in need of protection from their enemies. One day a Chinese ruler entered the land, found it without a king, and decided to claim it for himself. The Vietnamese cried out for the return of Lac Long Quan, so he responded, as he had promised, came back from the sea, and captured Au Co, the Chinese ruler's wife. Failing to recover her, the Chinese invader quit the country and Au Co gave birth to the Hung, the first native rulers of northern Vietnam.

The arrival of Indian settlers is similarly recorded in the foundation myth of Cambodia, Vietnam's southern neighbour. According to this tale, an Indian brahmin named Kaundinya appeared one day off the shore of Cambodia. When the local dragon princess paddled out to greet the stranger, he fired an arrow from a magic bow, which struck her boat. As a result of this action, the dragon princess agreed to marry Kaundinya, who in return gave her clothes to wear. Such was the pleasure of Kaundinya's father-in-law that he drained an area of land for the establishment of the Cambodian kingdom.

Like other ancient Southeast Asian states, Cambodia celebrated in this legend more than the marriage of a foreigner and a local fertility goddess. It recognized that its own existence depended on a union between culture and nature. Later Cambodian kings, who were considered to be incarnations of the Hindu god Vishnu, saw their chief duty as the maintenance of irrigation reservoirs and canals. Without such large-scale public works, the enormous temple city of

Since rice is the staple crop of much of Southeast Asia, many villagers feel it is important to make offerings to the rice gods, to keep them happy and ensure a good harvest (above).

Islam has become the predominant religion in much of Southeast Asia, and this splendid mosque in Brunei (right), on the island of Borneo, is now one of many in the region.

Angkor Wat, built in the thirteenth century, could never have been created.

The Cambodians were aided in the construction of Angkor Wat by further immigrants from India, some of whom were Buddhists, for the Buddhist faith had also spread throughout Southeast Asia. The Sailendra kings of Srivijaya were particularly devout Buddhists, and an inscription of AD 778 records the building of a shrine in their territories on Java. The most splendid Sailendra monument is Borobudur, built c.800. Rivalling Angkor Wat in size, this sanctuary portrays in stone every aspect of Buddha's ministry, as well as the legendary deeds of his greatest followers, the bodhisattvas, or "Buddhas-to-be".

The decline of Hindu-Buddhist states in Indonesia resulted from catastrophes such as volcanic eruptions, famine, and war, together with the steady progress of a gradual Muslim infiltration. By 1424, the year in which the great Chinese admiral Zheng He last called at Malacca, the local ruler had already converted to Islam. Thereafter, most of the immigrants from India also professed the same faith. The conversion of the local peoples was largely a peaceful event, but it was nevertheless decisive.

With the tiny exception of Bali, which clung stubbornly to its Hindu culture, the mythology and legends of India were relegated, by the iconoclasm of Islam, to the Indonesian shadow play: Yavadvipa (the great island of barley) became, simply, Java. However, even today scholars are amazed at the underlying strength of pre-Islamic ideas in Indonesia. Only on the eastern Asian continent, in Burma, Thailand,

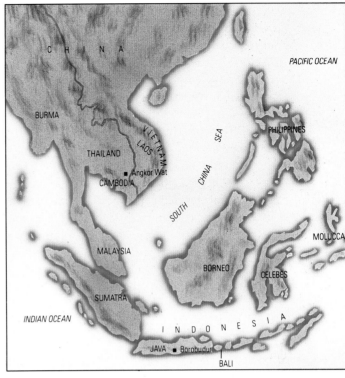

A stone relief from Borob dur, in central Java, depicts a scene from the life of Buddha (left). This monument, a testament to the once-strong Buddhist faith in Java, is one of the finest in the world.

The Hindu practice of cremating the dead has been developed into a lavish and elaborate ritual on the island of Bali. Huge wood and paper sarcophagi (below), which have often been painstakingly modelled into fantastic forms, are built to contain the body, and are then led in a procession to a funeral pyre.

CHRONOLOGY	
214 BC	The first emperor of China sends forces into Vietnam.
111	Direct Chinese rule begins in northern Vietnam.
AD 550	Beginnings of Cambodian power.
860	Borobudur under construction on Java.
906	Collapse of Tang Empire in China finally gives the Vietnamese their freedom.
1044	The warrior king Anoratha ascends the throne of Burma.
1287	Kublai Khan destroys the kingdom of Burma.
1293	Java resists a Mongol expedition sent by Kublai Khan.
1357	Thais capture Angkor Wat, the enormous temple city built in the thirteenth century by the Cambodians.
1405	Admiral Zheng He calls with the Chinese fleet at Java, Sumatra and Malacca.
1513	Javanese kingdom of Majapahit collapses and Islam becomes dominant religion.
1511	Portuguese seize Malacca.
1521	Magellan reaches the Philippines.

Laos, Cambodia and Vietnam, did Buddhism persist as a major religion.

The easternmost part of Southeast Asia was not in contact with the outside world until comparatively recently. Indigenous belief has always been animistic, and where it still survives among the peoples of Borneo, the accompanying mythology is full of ghosts and spirits connected with natural phenomena. One widespread belief is that a series of divine residences once stretched high above a primeval sea, and the gods who lived there threw down rocks to form the islands of the world. The Iban of eastern Malaysia locate their tribal origins in a land near Mecca. From there, the hero Bujang set out on a migration that is still in progress, as groups continue to move through the Borneo jungle searching for land to cultivate.

NORTH AMERICA

Until the beginnings of European settlement in the seventeenth century, the American continents belonged to settlers from the Asian world. The first inhabitants had crossed from Siberia over a temporary land link during the final stages of glaciation. By 9000 BC, their descendants had reached Tierra del Fuego, the southern tip of South America. Migration from East Asia probably ceased when the Ice Age ended and the sea rose, so that the Bering Straits appeared again.

Contact between Asia and America may have continued down the millennia, but the only other large-scale transfer of population for which there is any evidence took place in the thirteenth century AD. Then, a number of nomadic tribes crossed to Alaska from Asia in order to escape the violence of the Mongol leader Genghis Khan. Later, they spread out across Canada and moved southward to Arizona, where they came to form the Apache and Navaho peoples.

Although it was the ferocity of the Mongol horde that brought about this final migration, the American Indians were themselves preoccupied with the prowess of the warrior. Young men prepared for battle by undertaking self-imposed tests. For instance, the Chippewa people of eastern Canada recall how a serpent spirit blessed a brave because he endured a long fast. The young man was promised that he would not die until his old age, and the kindly serpent visited him in his dreams and warned him of impending danger.

The continuity between the nomadic peoples of East Asia and the North American Indians is exemplified in the figure of the shaman. On both sides of the Bering Straits, the medicine-man or medicine-woman is the focus of traditional belief. The shamans act as intermediaries between the spirit world and mankind. In a spirit-possessed trance or frenzy, they raise themselves to the upperworld. Here they can gain control over the spirits of disease in order to exorcize them from sick people. There are even tales in which shamans succeed in bringing the souls of the dead back to earth.

In contrast to a priest, a shaman is not instructed in a body of existing lore; instead, he acquires his own powers. There are contemporary accounts of the final stage of this self-development. In 1968, several Huichol men are known to have "completed themselves" through the use of peyote, a drug derived from a spineless cactus. Anthropologists recorded the impressions of these Mexican Indians on their return from the upperworld.

Among North American Indians today, shamanism is approaching extinction. Of the 2,000 independent tribes known to have existed in the seventeenth century, only 300 remain, and the survivors now live on reserves. The process of concentration and betrayal started in earnest in the nineteenth century, when railroads were built to link the Atlantic and Pacific coasts and immigrant farmers decimated the buffalo herds on the Great Plains. European diseases also took a terrible toll of Indian lives.

Shamans, or medicine-men (above), act as interpreters and intermediaries between people and the spirits, in matters of hunting, the weather, battle and misfortune, and are always key figures in North American Indian societies.

As if tuning in to the spirits that he believes will aid him in his hunting, a lone Eskimo stands still and silent, surveying the Arctic landscape (right). The Eskimo way of life remains one of seasonal hunting and fishing on the ice packs and floes, and spirits associated with hunting are still invoked.

Stories of the origins of maize appear in myths and are symbolized in Indian art, as in this fabric design (below), across the North American continent. Maize cultivation marked the transition from hunting to agriculture for many North American Indians.

The sheer force of European arms put the Indians permanently on the defensive. The fundamental problem was their inability to form a united front against the European settlers. The European powers soon learned how to turn old tribal enmities to their own advantage.

However, some of the early European settlers appreciated the native myths and legends. They were especially impressed by the Haida, Snohomish and Quinault tribes.

The Haida creation story is typical of these myths. It tells how, at the beginning of time, Sha-lana ruled a kingdom which lay high up in the clouds. Below, a vast empty sea stretched in every direction. When Sha-lana's chief servant, Raven, was sacked, he was so horrified that he flapped his wings in despair and, in so doing, stirred up the primeval ocean, causing rocks to grow. Raven then proceeded to create human beings from shells and to introduce the sun and fire. He stole the latter from heaven.

A less benign figure than Raven is Coyote, the trickster god of the Haida and many other western peoples. He was pleased to observe the coming of death, despite the first victim being his own son, poisoned by Rattlesnake.

Mysterious deities such as Raven and Coyote fall into perspective when it is realized that the North American Indians believed that animals were the original inhabitants of the continent, and that they were exactly the same as human beings except that people could put on and take off their furlike clothes. Such a myth seems prophetic now, because the worst victims of European settlement were undoubtedly the wild animals — the beaver, the elk, the buffalo and the bear, to name but a few.

CENTRAL AMERICA

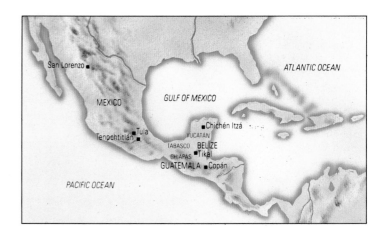

In 1519 when Hernando Cortés and his Spanish soldiers arrived in Central America, the region was dominated by the warlike Aztecs. They had already ruled Mexico for a century and the opulence of Mexico's capital Tenochtitlán deeply impressed the Spanish conquistadors. There the Aztec emperor Montezuma held court and levied tribute from millions of subjects.

Tenochtitlán was a spectacular New World Venice, with palaces and temples lining a network of canals. But the most striking aspect of Aztec city life was the importance placed on religion, and especially ritual practices. Because Cortés understood the Aztec outlook, he was able to overcome Montezuma. Indeed, the swift collapse of the Aztec Empire and the virtual annihilation of its people were attributable as much to fatalism as to firearms.

The Aztecs believed that four eras, or "suns", had preceded the one in which they lived and that, at the end of each era, its people had been destroyed. The Aztec era was expected to end in a cataclysmic earthquake, following the return of the snake-bird god Quetzalcoatl. This complex deity had been the tribal god of the Toltecs, the leading warriors in Mexico before the rise of the Aztecs.

At the beginning of the first era, Quetzalcoatl had created human beings from the bones of the dead which he had brought from the underworld and sprinkled with his blood. He also gave them knowledge of agriculture and handicrafts. But Quetzalcoatl eventually succumbed to a yearning for death and sailed away on a raft of serpents to an enchanted land. The prophecy that, like the Celtic Arthur, he would return one day from the sea was exploited by Cortés. He encouraged the Aztecs to believe that the fair-skinned, bearded deity marched among the Spaniards.

As the successors to the Toltecs, the Aztecs were pleased to acknowledge Quetzalcoatl in order to justify their military power. But the Aztec exaggeration of the Toltec practice of human sacrifice brutalized the cult of the snake-bird god, as well as those of the other deities worshipped alongside him.

In 1598 the official historian of the Indies, Antonio de Herrera, recorded that: "The number of people sacrificed was great." In fact it was believed that the reigning sun god had to be sustained by a constant supply of human hearts and blood. One of the chief purposes of war, therefore, was to take prisoners who could be sacrificed in the temples of Tenochtitlán.

Archaeology has revealed that the roots of Central American civilization go back long before the Aztecs, to at least 1000 BC. The earliest known people are the Olmecs, who flourished on the coastlands facing the Gulf of Mexico. Although their mythology and legends have not survived, the giant stone heads and statues they left behind still fascinate all who see them. The heads, measuring up to three metres (ten feet) high, usually depict fat-faced young men

The rich and complex mythology of the Mayas was recorded on codices (right), many of which were destroyed by Spanish missionaries. Those that remain are still being deciphered.

The plumed serpent Quetzalcoatl, represented on this turquoise and jade inlaid mask (below right), was the principal god of the Aztecs.

Tikal, in the heart of the Guatemalan jungle (below), was a great ceremonial city built by the Maya between AD 300 and 900. Its name means "the place where the spirit voices are heard", which refers to the modern Maya belief that the spirits of their ancestors return there at night.

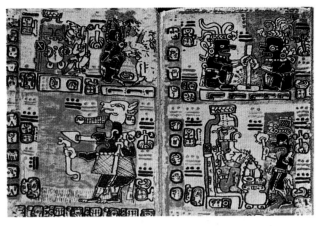

CHRONOLOGY	
1000 BC	Olmecs carve monumental heads and statues in San Lorenzo, Mexico.
AD 600	Beginnings of Maya civilization in western Mexico and Guatemala.
900	City of Tollan founded by the Toltecs.
987	Probable date for Quetzalcoatl's departure from Tollan.
1367	Acamapichtli first Aztec ruler of Tenochtitlán.
1440	Accession of Montezuma, the last Aztec emperor.
1519	Arrival of the Spaniards under the command of Hernando Cortés, who was able to overcome Montezuma because he understood the Aztec outlook.

wearing helmets, and the statues are of animals, such as the jaguar and the serpent, as well as of humans.

The influence of the Olmecs on later peoples is uncertain, although their invention of an alphabet must have assisted the development of civilization. Of the peoples who followed the Olmecs, most is known about the Toltecs, the Mayas, and the Aztecs.

In about AD 900, the Toltecs established their capital at Tollan, modern Tula. Their empire encompassed most of present-day Mexico, and reached as far as northern Yucatán, home of the Mayas, where a Toltec colony was planted at Chichén Itzá. The foundation of the colony, some time before 987, has been linked with Quetzalcoatl, since Maya records note the coming of Kukulkan (the plumed serpent).

It is not unlikely that the Toltec seizure of the Yucatán peninsula hastened the decline of the Mayas, who from the sixth century onward had controlled present-day Guatemala, Belize, and the Mexican provinces of Yucatán, Chiapas and Tabasco. The area is still dotted with their impressive temple platforms and pyramids.

However, there is little to explain the pessimistic outlook of this Central American people, who viewed their existence as a continually precarious balance between life and death. This attitude is reflected in their remote creator deity Hunab, who periodically flooded the world with torrential rains poured from the belly of the sky serpent.

SOUTH AMERICA

The physical geography of South America ranges from tropical rain forests in the north to windswept islands in the south, from high mountains in the west to rolling plains in the east. Despite this diversity, the various tribal traditions have much in common. All take the existence of the world largely for granted, or consider it as the initial act of a remote creator deity; instead, origin myths play an important role.

A typical origin myth is told by the Bakairi Indians of central Brazil. It concerns the twin heroes Keri and Kame, sons of the jaguar spirit Oka. After swallowing two bones, Oka's wife became pregnant, causing her enraged mother-in-law to kill her. However, before she died, Keri and Kame were cut from her womb.

When the heroes grew up, they killed their wicked grandmother by setting fire to the forest, but they themselves were badly hurt in the same blaze. In restoring themselves to perfect health, Keri and Kame decided to change from animal form to a human shape. Then, they pushed the sky away from the earth, set the sun and moon in the heavens, and created fire from a fox's eye and water from a serpent.

According to the Warrau Indians of Guyana, people arrived on earth by accident. Apparently, the sky god Kononatoo (our maker) wanted mankind to live in heaven, but a young hunter discovered a hole in the sky and descended to the ground through the branches of an enormous tree. Out of curiosity, the other human inhabitants of heaven followed him. However, they later found that they were unable to return because a fat woman had become wedged in the sky-hole.

The Warrau also tell of the sadness of Kononatoo, who was deterred from making another entrance to heaven by the misbehaviour of mankind on earth. In particular, the sky god was annoyed at the willingness of girls to mate with water deities. By daring to swim in a sacred lake, the girls gave birth to an evil horde of snakes.

An account of the introduction of disease and death is found among the Arawak Indians, who live to the south of the Warrau in the Orinoco basin. According to Arawak tradition, the creator god Kururumany was displeased to see that mankind had become corrupt and wicked and so took back his gift of eternal life and added to the world such annoyances as snakes and fleas. Beyond Kururumany is the dimly remembered sky god Aluberi, who plays no part in Arawak mythology.

As the myths and legends of the South American Indians become better known, more and more parallels are found with North American Indian beliefs. Trickster gods, animal spirits, and twin heroes are common to both continents. Nonetheless, the beliefs of the Andean peoples of South America were more highly developed than any of those of the North American Indians. As in Central America, the rise

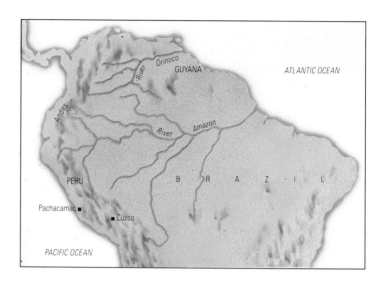

of civilization in the Andes led to an elaborate pantheon and cosmology.

When in 1531 Francisco Pizarro attacked the Incas on behalf of the Spanish crown, he challenged a state comparable in size to the Roman Empire. A century earlier, in about 1438, the city of Cuzco in Peru had been attacked by a rival people. In the desperate defence, a young prince managed to save the Inca throne. The prince was Pachacuti, a descendant of the Ayar brothers who, according to tradition, had founded the Inca dynasty.

Pachacuti ascended the throne, and under his determined direction, the Inca army transformed Cuzco into the capital of a far-flung empire. To swell their ranks, nobles from conquered tribes were recruited as public officials and military commanders — offices traditionally reserved for the Inca nobility. Defeated warriors, on the other hand, were taken into the army.

The Incas acknowledged the gods of subject peoples, as well as those inherited from earlier rulers of Cuzco. But throughout their empire, they built temples dedicated to the worship of Inti, the sun god. Their religion was essentially a form of ancestor worship. Deceased emperors were especially honoured, their mummies being consulted for guidance in all critical matters. Because the Ayar brothers were believed to be the descendants of the sun god, worship of Inti was the peak of the ancestral cult.

The Incas also worshipped a creator deity called Viracocha, who was believed to have made the sun at the beginning of time by giving up part of his own divinity. Yet Viracocha was often subordinated to Inti, and in the Qorikancha, the great temple of the sun at Cuzco, he was regarded as Inti's son. It is possible that the Spanish chroniclers misunderstood the nature of the Inca pantheon by interpreting it in terms of the mythology of Greece and Rome. In fact the Incas probably worshipped a number of gods and goddesses as separate forms of a single deity, Inti himself.

Now in magnificent ruins, the ancient Inca city of Macchu Pichu (above) was a place where the sun god Inti was worshipped.

An Inca drama celebrating the sun is reenacted (left) at the Festival of Inti Raimi in Cuzco, Peru. The Ayar are said to have founded the city of Cuzco.

Several mummies (below), dating from AD 500–1000, found in Eastern Bolivia, demonstrate the importance of an afterlife to the South American Indians.

CHRONOLOGY	
400 AD	End of Chavin civilization in northern Peru.
1200	Rise of the Chimu Empire in Peru.
1438	Pachacuti ascends Inca throne, having successfully defeated a rival people, and commences a policy of conquest, making Cuzco the capital of a vast empire.
1471	Topa Inca, Pachacuti's son, reorganizes the Inca Empire and establishes Quechua, still spoken today, as the official language.
1520	Magellan sails round South America and crosses the Pacific Ocean to the Philippines.
1531	Francisco Pizarro invades the Inca empire on behalf of the Spanish Crown.
1595	Sir Walter Raleigh enters Orinoco in search of El Dorado.

AFRICA

While the ancient period of the African continent north of the Sahara, and especially Egypt, is well documented, little is known of the earliest history of the peoples living to the south of the great desert. Recent discoveries in Olduvai Gorge, in Kenya, have proved that Africa was the first continent to be walked on by our ancestors. From fossil remains of skulls and skeletons that have been recovered there, as well as in Ethiopia and Tanzania, it is apparent that the ancestral line leading to modern human beings stretches back more than four million years. Yet our knowledge of events between these remarkable prehistoric finds and comparatively recent times is very sketchy indeed.

The earliest accounts of Africa come from Arab sources and concern the black Christian states, which opposed the spread of Islam, in what is now Sudan and Ethiopia. These were Dongola, Alwa and Axum. Ethiopian legend claims that Axum was the home of the Ark of the Covenant and that it was brought there by Menelik, the son of Solomon and Sheba. According to the 1955 Revised Constitution of Ethiopia, the emperor Haile Selassie descended "without interruption from the dynasty of Menelik".

Increasing pressure from the Muslim rulers of Egypt after AD 750 gradually wore down the states of Dongola and Alwa, whose territories were much reduced. But it was not until the Turks assumed the leadership of Islam in the early sixteenth century that they were finally destroyed. The inhabitants of Axum had already retreated into the Ethiopian mountains, where their continued independence gave rise to the medieval legend of the Christian king, Prester John.

The influence of Islam was also felt among the peoples of West Africa. Around 1000 the ancient kingdom of Ghana was founded, possibly by Arab or Berber adventurers, although they were soon replaced by a native dynasty. The kingdom collapsed after the Muslim invasion of 1076, but its people were not converted to the conqueror's faith.

In the rest of Africa a string of kingdoms rose and fell, including Great Zimbabwe. Instrumental in these upheavals seems to have been the movement of Bantu-speaking peoples south and east from modern Cameroon. These determined warriors appear to have become dominant by about 1000. The Zulu, who put up such determined opposition to European settlement in southern Africa in the nineteenth century, were their true descendants.

The political fragmentation of Africa, and the movement of its various populations, have prevented the development of a uniform system of belief. Each people possesses its own traditions, and even where languages are shared, the diversity of local belief is surprising. However, there are certain beliefs that are common. Most groups recognize a supreme deity who is all-powerful. The Zulu of South Africa simply call this deity uKqili (the wise one), while the Akan of Ghana refer to him as Brekyirihunuade (he who knows and

The spirit world is frequently celebrated in Africa, in elaborate rituals such as this Dogon funeral ceremony in Mali (above).

Diviners are still consulted to mediate with the spirits, and use a variety of oracles, such as cowrie shells (below).

sees all). When lightning strikes cattle, the Zulu say that uKqili has slaughtered meat for his own table. Also known as Unkulunkulu (chief), the Zulu sky god has always been regarded as the powerful supporter of a warrior nation. He is uMabonga-kutuk-izizwe-zonke (the one who roars so that all the tribes are struck with terror).

Another common African myth is the explanation of mortality. Nearly every tribe has a story which tells of messengers from the supreme deity who deliver the wrong instructions to mankind. In the Zulu version a lizard carrying an announcement of death outpaces a chameleon with the news of eternal life. Arriving late, the chameleon is dismayed to find that the first people have accepted the lizard's words as the truth. An alternative explanation for death places the blame squarely on human beings.

The idea of an underworld is not strong in African mythology. The Zulu traditionally placed the abode of the

African masks, such as this one from the Bapende of Zaire (above), often represent animals' heads, the part of the animal believed to hold its power. The wearer of the mask is protected by this power and enabled by it to dance like the animal.

The vastness of the African continent (left) and its geographical barriers meant that no unified mythology developed among its inhabitants. What they do share, however, is a large number of beliefs in animal spirits and deities.

CHRONOLOGY	
30 BC	Egypt becomes a Roman province.
AD 429	Vandals cross Straits of Gibraltar.
641	Arabs attack Egypt.
750	Muslim Egypt moves against Christian Dongola, Alwa and Axum.
1000	State of Ghana founded.
1076	Muslims invade Ghana.
1350	Mali becomes a black Muslim state.
1371	Dongola and Alwa reduced in size.
1400	Monumental buildings erected at Great Zimbabwe by Bantu-speaking peoples.
1415	Chinese fleet visits East Africa.
1484	The Portuguese reach the Congo river.
1495	Vasco da Gama rounds the Cape of Good Hope.
1517	Spain begins importing African slaves for labour.
1652	Dutch plant a settlement at Cape Town.
1806	The Cape becomes a British Colony.
1841	David Livingstone sets out on his explorations.
1879	The Zulus defeat the British army at the battle of Isandhlwana.
1899	Boer War begins.
1957	Ghana becomes first British colony to gain independence.

dead in the sky. The Bushmen of the Kalahari, also consider that the stars were formerly animals or people. But deceased ancestors could appear on earth in the form of snakes. A traditional character type (*ntoro*) of the Ashanti people of Ghana was even acknowledged to owe its existence to a python. When, long ago, a human couple was unable to have offspring, a python sprayed their bellies with water and uttered a spell. In due course they had children, and their male descendants showed gratitude thereafter by burying a dead python whenever they came across one.

Despite the slave trade, which began seriously in 1517, the impact of Europeans on traditional African society was slight until modern times. Traditional religions are now in retreat, and the African idea of a supreme deity has largely been incorporated in Islam and Christianity. Where medicine-men, or witchdoctors, survive at all, they tend to be associated with still vigorous ancestor cults.

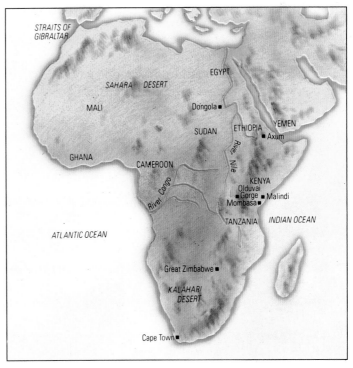

AUSTRALIA

The smallest of the continents, Australia was cut off from the rest of the world until recently. When English and Dutch explorers first reached its shores in the eighteenth century, they were struck by the obvious antiquity of the inhabitants, human and animal. Both appeared to have descended undisturbed from ancient times, so they seemed like "living fossils". There were strange mammals such as the egg-laying duckbilled platypus; marsupials such as the wallaby; and great flightless birds – the emu and the cassowary. The aboriginal population, too, amazed the first European visitors: physically they fitted into none of the categories then in favour. Australian Aborigines still defy analysis and occupy a unique category of the human species – Australoid.

In 1788, when the British annexed Australia, there were probably some 300,000 Aborigines living there, divided into more than 300 separate groups. These people had no knowledge of agriculture or writing, and had no advanced technology; they had no domesticated animals, except for the ferocious and doglike dingo. But they had learned to survive in the inhospitable interior of the continent by adopting a nomadic way of life. They obtained food by hunting and by gathering wild fruits and roots. The first European observers failed to recognize the extent to which the Aborigines compensated for material poverty with a spiritual richness and complex social system.

Only in this century have outsiders come to appreciate the range of their languages and mythology. There is, however, no clue in recorded myths and legends as to the origins of the Aborigines. It is thought that Australia may have been settled at different times by two distinct peoples who crossed from Asia via the Indonesian archipelago. The first group comprised the natives of Tasmania, who were deliberately killed off by European settlers in the nineteenth century. It is assumed that these people were driven from the Australian mainland by the ancestors of the present-day Aborigines. However, such an interpretation of the pre-modern period of Australian history is not conclusive.

Unlike the Pacific Islanders, the Aborigines possess no legendary accounts of ancestors or heroes travelling any distance to their homeland. There is, indeed, nothing in their mythology to suggest that they ever lived outside the continent. Instead, the stories told by each group are characterized by the close relationship they have with their home territory.

Myth and ritual are so closely associated with the movements of clan groups that it seems almost impossible for any change of location to take place without reference to Alchera (Dreamtime). This is the word used by the Aranda people in central Australia to describe the remote era when the ancestral spirits walked the earth. All aboriginal groups believe that during Dreamtime the spirits that sleep beneath the ground rose and travelled about, shaping the landscape, making people and teaching them the arts of survival. Their work done, they subsided once more into sleep.

The Aranda, like many other aboriginal peoples, have a lizard as their tribal ancestor. They have largely forgotten Altjira, their emu-footed sky god, but they look back with nostalgia to the deeds of Mangar-kunger-kunja (flycatcher) during Alchera. This reverence for the lizard is not unusual. Almost everywhere in the world that the lizard is indigenous, people have felt an affinity with it, possibly because of the familiar shape of its "hand". Only in Iran did the prophet Zoroaster curse the lizard as the companion of the damned.

The myths associated with the two lizardmen Wati-kutjara are, fortunately, recorded in full. These stories allow us to grasp something of the meaning for the peoples of central Australia of the ceremonial walkabout. On the journey through the interior, male aboriginal descendants of Wati-kutjara repeat their legendary actions – they dig waterholes, build rock shelters, hunt kangaroos and perform secret rites – and act out the quarrel the two lizardmen had with Kulu, the moon man.

The importance of these legendary pilgrimages cannot be overestimated. Aborigines inhabit land that is intimately associated with their ancestral spirits. Movement into territory that the tribal ancestors have not travelled is seen as foolhardy. Only crazy men are said to abandon the tribal land and forget the traditional lore that instructs them how to live in it safely. Belated recognition by white Australians of this unbreakable tie is behind the current discussions in Australia about the ownership of land in the outback.

Another subject for common concern is the realization that one of the oldest societies in existence is threatened with extinction. As with the North American Indians in the nineteenth century, the effects of alcohol on those Aborigines who drift into towns is often shattering. But the fundamental problem of the aboriginal peoples today is how to reconcile a nomadic way of life with a sedentary modern world that is preoccupied with possessions.

CHRONOLOGY

1768 Captain Cook sets off for the Pacific.

1788 Australia becomes a British colony.

1794 Anxiety over the French Revolution causes the British Government to transport political opponents to the penal colony at Botany Bay.

1834 Tolpuddle martyrs transported to Australia for trades-union activities.

The Aborigines continue to respect the sacred sites (left), where important mythological events are said to have occurred during Alchera (Dreamtime), when the ancestors created the world.

To this day, membership of an aboriginal clan is gained only after an initiation ceremony (below, left)

The mythology of Australia's Aborigines took form when the ancestors walked the land during Alchera (Dreamtime), singing it into existence and dividing the Aborigines into clans. The bark painting (left) shows a clan totem, a kangaroo, with the songlines represented by the broken lines. Sometimes, a clan would have an object rather than an animal as a totem.

The boomerang (right), being vastly important to the Aborigines' survival, was particularly popular. According to one aboriginal group, the ancestor deity Bobbi-bobbi created the boomerang from one of his ribs.

 # OCEANIA

Oceania has three mythological traditions, which almost exactly correspond to the geographical division of the Pacific islands into Polynesia, Melanesia, and Micronesia. Polynesia is the easternmost part of Oceania, stretching in a great triangle from New Zealand to Hawaii and Easter Island; it contains the island groups of Tonga, Samoa, Tahiti and Tuamotu. Melanesia lies west of this area and includes the great island of Papua, the archipelagos of the Admiralty Islands, Solomon Islands, Banks Islands and New Britain, and the outlying Fiji Islands on the western edge of Polynesia. Micronesia is a constellation of tiny islands, which are divided into four main groups – the Gilbert, Marshall, Mariana and Caroline archipelagos.

Polynesian mythology is remarkably homogenous, considering the vast area over which its inhabitants are spread. Memories of the migrations that settled the different islands appear in the legends told of the journeys undertaken by gods and heroes. The favourite figure is Maui, a smaller version of the Greek hero Heracles. His exploits were accomplished more by trickery than by strength, although several stories celebrate his powerful deeds. In one, Maui pulled up the islands from the bottom of the ocean with a jawbone and lassoed the sun with a noose; then, with a poker, he pushed up the sky, leaving behind the dark marks that can still be seen in rainbearing clouds.

Parallels between the mythologies of Polynesia and ancient Greece also occur in the story of creation. According to the Maoris of New Zealand, the sky god Rangi was so enamoured with Papa, mother earth, that his continued lovemaking trapped their children in her womb. The passionate embrace of the Greek deities Gaia and Ouranos had the same effect. Rejecting the suggestion that they should slay both parents, the imprisoned gods and goddesses eventually forced Rangi and Papa apart. (Later Maui forced Rangi up higher still with his poker.) The storm god Tawhiri-ma-tea, who sided with his father Rangi, caused havoc during the initial separation; but the fate of Rangi was mild in comparison with that of the sky god Ouranos. To help her son Kronos deal with his overpassionate father, the earth goddess Gaia conceived a mighty sickle with sharp teeth. Having emasculated Ouranos with this weapon, Kronos liberated his brothers and sisters.

The inhabitants of New Britain explain the advent of evil as the work of To-Karvuvu, the half-witted brother of To-Kabinana. For example, through an act of foolishness, To-Karvuvu gave the shark its terrible teeth. The perpetual rivalry of these twin deities reflects an outlook that considers mishap and misfortune as arising as much from human error as from a hostile environment. For the New Britain Islanders, the only sensible course of action for mankind is to seek a balance between human society and its natural surroundings. Other Melanesian myths develop this idea, though in Papua

The Abelam people of New Guinea have an extremely creative and elaborate ceremonial life which continues to form the foundation of their existence. The highly decorative clan figures (above) indicate the exacting attention they pay to their ritual practices.

The Asaro River people (right), who come from the central highlands of New Guinea, also hold elaborate ceremonies. Here, they have covered themselves with mud and constructed mud masks to reenact an occasion when their ancestors, at the point of being defeated by their enemy, scared them off by emerging from a river so disguised.

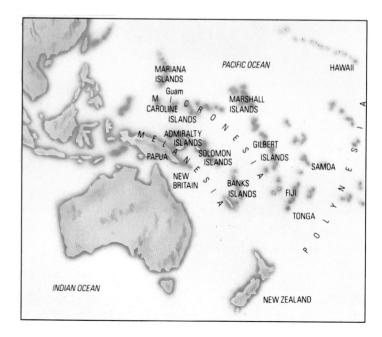

CHRONOLOGY

1405 AD	Chinese fleet under Zheng He explores Micronesia and Melanesia.
1521	Magellan reaches Guam.
1779	Captain Cook killed by natives in Hawaii.
1835	Charles Darwin visits Tahiti and New Zealand.
1894	Robert Louis Stevenson dies on Samoa.
1915	German colonies of Papua and Samoa seized by the Allies.

Canoes (below) are of vital importance to the island-dwelling people of Oceania. Not only are they the chief form of communication between the islands, and thus the means by which myths were transferred, but they are also used for fishing and fighting.

the main emphasis is on the need to secure fertility in man, animals and plants.

Another feature of Papuan belief is the modern cargo cult that first arose in Vailala after the First World War. It consists of ecstatic possession and promises its devotees marvellous gifts from a ship crewed by the ancestral spirits. The founder of the cult, an old man named Evara, later prophesied that an aeroplane would bring the sacred cargo of plenty. Clearly a reaction to the impact of present-day technology, the cargo cult received a powerful boost in the Second World War. The paraphernalia of modern warfare, brought by occupying forces, dazzled peoples who were still using stone tools. They were also fascinated when, after Japan surrendered, the United States Army began to exhume its dead and fly the remains home.

The mythological tradition of Micronesia is the least distinct in Oceania. It seems to have borrowed elements from Melanesian and Polynesian myth, as well as from ideas introduced by European voyagers. (The first European visitor was Magellan, who reached Guam in 1521.) On the Gilbert Islands, for instance, the notion that death came to the world as a consequence of the first people damaging a sacred tree has clearly Christian overtones.

Traditional belief in Micronesia was primarily concerned with ancestor worship. The Gilbert Islanders always distinguished between two kinds of beings whom they propitiated. They were the gods (*anti*) and the divine ancestors (*anti-ma aomata*). Living men (*aomata*) had to perform regular sacrifices for both groups, but they were most anxious to preserve the goodwill of ancestors such as Taburimai. The first human offspring of the original fish gods, Taburimai sailed around the islands, took a wife, and inaugurated civilized living. His son, Te-ariki-n-tarawa, even climbed the sacred tree to heaven, where he married the tree goddess Ne Te-reere. From these adventurous ancestors, the Gilbert Islanders claim, mankind descended.

51

CHARACTERS
and CONCEPTS

This A to Z of major deities relates the fabulous and epic deeds and adventures of characters from mythologies all around the world. Interspersed among them are features concerning the universal concepts in mythology, illustrated with examples from a wide variety of different cultures.

Symbols at the head of each entry denote the cultural geography from which each myth derives, and link with the introductory cultural essays contained in the preceding section. Names indicated in the text in small capital letters refer to other main entries included in this section. Cross-references at the foot of each entry are of two kinds. Those in italics refer to theme boxes. Those in small capitals refer readers to the Micropedia.

ACHILLES

The hero of the *Iliad*, Homer's poetical account of the Greek attack on Troy. Achilles was the son of Peleus, King of Thessaly, and of the sea nymph Thetis.

Even before his birth, it was prophesied that Achilles would be greater than his father. For this reason, neither ZEUS, the king of the gods, nor his brother POSEIDON, dared to pursue the beautiful Thetis, the hero's mother. Instead, the cautious gods arranged for the sea nymph to marry a mortal ruler.

Thetis was not prepared to accept that Achilles would have to die, and so she tried to endow him with immortality by various means. Homer says that she dipped the infant in the river of HADES, the Styx, but since she had to hold him by the heel, this one spot was left unprotected. It was because of this that Paris was able to kill Achilles with a poisoned arrow.

Realizing that Achilles was destined to fall at Troy, Thetis did her utmost to prevent him from learning the arts of war, but she was unable to prevent his prowess as a fighter from becoming well known. As a result, ODYSSEUS brought him to Agamemnon, leader of the Greek expedition against the Trojans. Although Achilles owed Agamemnon no loyalty, he ignored his mother's advice and sailed with Agamemnon, taking with him Patroclus, his squire and lover.

That the southern Greeks needed the presence of Achilles, who was a northern prince, to make a success of their expedition, shows how great his reputation as a fighter must have been. He almost seems an outsider in the *Iliad*: his temper is superhuman; his concern for sacrifice, including that of human beings, is a throwback to earlier times; and his treatment of Hector's corpse was almost barbaric. Yet the Greeks encamped before the strong walls of Troy could do nothing without Achilles.

Achilles and Agamemnon did not get on. Achilles found him high-handed, felt that he was ungrateful for his services as a great warrior, and disagreed with his strategies. Achilles was so stubborn in his opposition to Agamemnon, that he refused all gestures of reconciliation, including the king's apology and an offer of marriage with any of the princesses.

Believing that Achilles' wrath was too unbending, Patroclus put on the armour of his sulking lover and went out to help the Greeks. In the moment of triumph, however, Patroclus was killed by Hector, the bravest son of the Trojan king, PRIAM.

On hearing the news of Patroclus's death, Achilles was overcome by remorse. When Thetis came to mourn with him, he told his mother that he longed for death. He swore to kill Hector and revenge Patroclus. His fate was therefore sealed. Clad in new armour, made at Thetis's request by the smith god HEPHAISTOS, Achilles sought out Hector, who stood his ground only after making the request that if he were killed, his body should be returned to Priam. Beside himself with anger, Achilles slew Hector, defiled his body, and then for twelve days dragged the mutilated corpse behind his chariot round and round Patroclus's grave.

The death of Achilles himself was brought about by the sun god Apollo, when he guided Paris's arrow to the vulnerable heel. The outrageous hero had earned the enmity of Apollo during the siege of Troy, by killing several of his devoted followers, including his own son Tenes, king of the island of Tenedos.

See Heroes, p.55

Achilles slays Hector

SEE ALSO AGAMEMNON, APOLLO, HECTOR, PARIS, PATROCLUS, PELEUS, STYX, TENES, THETIS

ADAPA

In Babylonian myth, the first man on earth; he was also regarded as a sage. Adapa may have been a king of Eridu, a holy city that rose to prominence in Sumerian times.

Adapa was the priest of Ea, the god of water, wisdom and magic, who taught him everything he knew. In this respect, Adapa is like Adam, the first man on earth in Christian myth. But whereas Adam, with his wisdom, named the beasts and fowl, Adapa invented speech and laid the foundations of civilized life.

One day, when Adapa was out fishing in the Persian Gulf, the south wind capsized his boat. In anger, he cursed the wind so effectively that he broke its wings. Alarmed that an ordinary man could be so powerful, the god of heaven, Anu, summoned Adapa to appear before him.

Ea knew that if Adapa went to heaven, he might stay there, and Ea would lose the services of his faithful priest, so he devised a plan to make sure that Adapa returned. Ea dressed him in mourning clothes, and expressly warned him to refuse any food offered there.

On his arrival in heaven, Adapa was greeted by Tammuz, a god who periodically died and was reborn. When Tammuz asked him why he was in mourning, Adapa replied that it was because he regretted Tammuz leaving earth. This pleased Tammuz who put in a good word for Adapa with Anu. As a result, Adapa was treated as a guest rather than a culprit, and was offered food and drink. But Adapa politely declined both and, when asked why, explained Ea's instructions. On hearing them, Anu burst into laughter, for he had actually offered Adapa the food and water of eternal life. Anu had not really wanted to make Adapa immortal, but the sage had been so well behaved that Anu seemed to have no choice.

Adapa thus forfeited his chance to become immortal and was returned to earth; since then mankind has been condemned to mortality.

Ea is the counterpart of the Sumerian water god ENKI, and Anu of the Sumerian chief god AN.

SEE ALSO ADAM, ANU, EA, TAMMUZ

ADONIS

Adonis means "lord", and was originally the title given to the dying-and-rising Babylonian god Tammuz. However, as the cult of Tammuz moved westward to Greece, the title was misinterpreted as the god's name.

Worship of Adonis flourished in Canaan, particularly in the city of Byblos, which boasted his greatest temple. Phoenician settlers took the god's cult to Cyprus where, as part of the cult of the love goddess APHRODITE, his annual death and rebirth passed into Greek mythology.

Despite being transplanted into various local traditions on its journey westward, the story of Adonis remained consistent. It tells how the god resulted from an incestuous relationship between Myrrha and her father, a king. Because Myrrha refused to show respect to her father, Aphrodite punished her with insatiable desire. Twelve nights in a row, Myrrha visited the bed of her father, who did not recognize her in the dark.

When he eventually discovered who he had slept with, the old king sought to slay his daughter. However, the gods heard Myrrha's appeal for divine protection and changed her into a tree, from which comes the gum called myrrh. Ten months later, the tree gave birth to Adonis, who was delivered with a boar's tusk.

The baby was so beautiful that Aphrodite, determined to save him from destruction, hid him in a casket which she gave to PERSEPHONE, goddess of the underworld. When Aphrodite returned to reclaim the casket, she found that Persephone had opened it, seen the beauty of the baby, and decided to keep him herself.

In desperation, Aphrodite appealed to the gods, and ZEUS decided that Adonis should spend half of each year on earth with Aphrodite and half in the underworld with Persephone.

Adonis's annual departure from life was originally the work of a wild boar. Ignoring Aphrodite's advice not to hunt game in the forest, the god was gored by a boar's tusk. Aphrodite, who loved the god to the point of madness, heard his cries and found him dying in a pool of blood.

During Adonis's annual sojourn in the underworld, from late autumn until early spring, Aphrodite disappeared in search of him, leaving the earth infertile. However, each spring the goddess of love recovered the handsome youth. In Cyprus, Adonis was said to return on the blooming of the red anemone, and in Byblos he was supposed to return when the river there ran red with soil brought down from the hills by rain.

When the Greek author Lucian visited the city of Byblos in the second century, he recorded the local belief that Adonis had been killed in a gorge. He also noted that weeping and wailing were involved in the cult rituals and that, at the time of the god's return, pots of plants were kept outside each house and carefully watered to keep pace with the general renewal of the world's vegetation.

Unlike OSIRIS, Adonis was never depicted in mummified form, although the close trading contacts which Byblos maintained with Egypt would almost certainly have allowed the borrowing of cult practices from the great Egyptian saviour.

See Death, p.91 and Afterlife, p.147

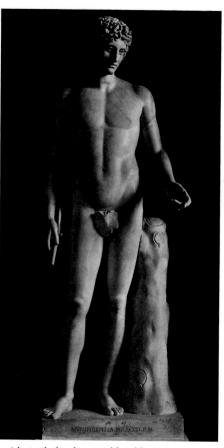

Adonis, the handsome god loved by Aphrodite
SEE ALSO MYRRHA, TAMMUZ

AENEAS

The famous Trojan adopted by the Romans as their national hero. He was the son of Anchises and the Greek love goddess Aphrodite, whom the Romans knew as Venus.

On the fall of Troy, Aeneas was said to have escaped the burning city with his wife Creusa, carrying his father Anchises on his back and leading his son Ascanius by the hand. At first, Anchises refused to abandon Troy, but two signs persuaded him to leave – a gigantic thunderbolt and a halo which appeared about Ascanius's head. During their flight, Creusa became separated from the party and disappeared. Eventually, Aeneas saw her ghost and learned from it that he would found a new state in Italy.

The long and indirect voyage to this final goal took Aeneas and his fellow fugitives to Thrace, Crete, North Africa and Sicily. This zigzag course was caused by disagreement among the gods about whether they should establish a new Troy.

As it was, the refugees from Troy were forced to make for Carthage, where JUNO caused Aeneas to fall in love with Dido, its queen. But despite Dido's legendary beauty, Aeneas obeyed the command of his destiny and set sail for Italy. From his departing vessel, Aeneas saw the flames rising from the pyre on which Dido was cremated – the distraught Carthaginian queen had committed suicide.

Thereafter, Juno's opposition could only slow the approach of Aeneas to his final destination. At Cumae, on the bay of Naples, Aeneas consulted the Sibyl, a revered and ancient prophetess, who directed him to find the entrance to the underworld. There he saw the ghost of his father, who had died on the voyage from Carthage. Learning from the ghost that Rome would eventually dominate the Mediterranean world, Aeneas returned to his followers and moved northward to Latium.

See Heroes, p.55.

SEE ALSO ANCHISES, ASCANIUS, CREUSA, DIDO, NEPTUNE, THE SIBYL

Heroes

The outstanding deeds of extraordinary individuals feature in every mythology. Some heroes are semi-divine. This does not make them immortal, but they usually have superhuman strength. Others are ordinary men who achieve fame through feats of remarkable courage and daring.

The killing of the Erymanthian boar was one of the twelve tasks set for the Greek hero Heracles, to test his courage, ingenuity and stamina. Heracles' semi-divine nature enabled the successful completion of these daunting challenges and earned him immortality.

The Polynesian islands (above) and the islands of New Zealand were formed from land wrenched up from the bottom of the ocean by the Polynesian hero Maui. He accomplished this amazing feat by using the magical jawbone of an ancestress as a hook. Although the Pacific islanders regard all their heroes as deities, they are not immortal, and Maui eventually fell victim to Hine-nui-te-po, the goddess of death.

Sharks have razor-sharp teeth thanks to Olofat's joke, which backfired on mankind, so the Micronesians say. This trickster hero was unusual in Micronesian myth in that he survived death. Although he was killed, in a fight in heaven where he had gone to claim his rights as a god, his father managed to revive him.

Rustem, the Iranian champion, fearlessly conquered all manner of foes, both human and demonic. He is shown (left) despatching a mighty dragon that had attacked his famous steed Rakush. But Rustem's exceptional fame was to prove his downfall. The jealous King of Iran, had him killed.

AGNI

In Hindu mythology, the god of fire and one of the three chief deities of the *Rig Veda*, the oldest religious document surviving in India. His ancient companions were the sky god Indra and Surya the sun god.

Agni was born out of the sacred lotus created by BRAHMA. He is usually shown with two red faces, seven tongues, and four hands. He is clothed in black, carries a flaming spear, and is borne in a chariot with the winds for wheels, which is drawn by fiery horses.

Agni can take on other appearances, however. For example, when INDRA commanded him to destroy a swarming host of flesh-eating goblins (*rakshas*), Agni took on a hideous form with iron tusks and razor-sharp teeth.

Agni symbolizes the vital spark in nature – he consumes so that he can make things live. In the *Mahabharata*, an epic dating from the beginning of the first millennium, he exhausts himself by consuming too many offerings. To recover his strength, he is obliged to burn the Khandava forest, with the assistance of KRISHNA and Arjuna, who guard each end of it so that its inhabitants cannot escape.

Agni is held to be one of the guardian deities of the world (*lokapalas*). Each deity, with the aid of an elephant, presides over one of the eight points of the compass. His point is the southeast, at the place where dawn breaks. In several Vedic hymns he is credited with making the sun and filling the night with stars. In popular belief, to poke a fire disturbs Agni.

Among Agni's powers are the ability to grant immortality and purification from sins after death. He is, therefore, appealed to on all important occasions, especially weddings and funerals. His cult has largely disappeared among Hindus, and today he is called upon only by lovers, to intervene in their affairs, and by men, to increase their virility.

See Fire, p.151

SEE ALSO ARJUNA

AH PUCH

The Maya god of death who presided over the ninth and lowest of the underworlds, a horrible place of torment.

In the few volumes of Maya writings that survive, Ah Puch is portrayed as a skeleton or a horribly bloated corpse. For he is the counterpart of Mictlantecuhtli, the Aztec god of death, who presided over all nine underworlds.

Like the Aztecs, the Mayas were overwhelmed by a sense of the transitoriness of life. Their Spanish conquerors were amazed at the extent of sorrow expressed by the bereaved. It was Maya custom to weep in silence during the day, but at night, when the earth was as dark as Ah Puch's realm, mourners shrieked and howled with such grief that they startled passers-by.

Today the influence of Ah Puch is by no means over. As Yum Cimil (lord of death), he is still feared by the Indians living in Guatemala and the Mexican province of Yucatán. Apparently he prowls the houses of the sick in his endless search for prey, carrying a knife which derives from his insignia.

Because of the scarcity of Maya manuscripts, the relationship of Ah Puch to the other Maya deities of death remains obscure. We do not know if he had authority over Ek Chuah (black war chief). This black-eyed god carried off the souls of warriors who died in battle, as did the hanged goddess Ixtab whose body, like Ah Puch's, was shown in a putrefied state. Ixtab took her favourites in death to a pleasant afterlife beneath the shade of Yaxche, the world-tree.

See Death, p.91

SEE ALSO EK CHUAH, IXTAB, MICTLANTECUHTLI, YAXCHE, YUM CIMIL

AHRIMAN

The principle of evil in ancient Iranian mythology. His name derives from the term Angra Mainya, "destructive thought".

Ahriman was in permanent opposition to AHURA MAZDAH (the wise lord), whose two names fused to become Ormazd. The prophet Zoroaster (*c.*628–551 BC) said: "In the beginning the two spirits were known as the one good and the other evil, in thought, word, and deed. Between them the wise chose rightly, not so fools. And when these spirits met they established life and death so that in the end the followers of deceit should meet with the worst existence, but the followers of truth with the wise lord."

This doctrine of rewards and punishments, of heavenly bliss and infernal woe allotted to good and evil men in a life beyond the grave, had a direct influence on Hebrew, and later Christian, thinking. Indeed, in the Old Testament, the relationship of SATAN and Yahweh is similar to that of Ahriman and Ahura Mazdah.

The Hebrews exiled in Babylon found that their Iranian liberators followed a kindred monotheism. Isaiah, a Hebrew prophet, declared that Cyrus, the first ruler of the Persian Empire, was one of Yahweh's anointed since he saved the Hebrews from captivity.

According to Zoroaster, Ahriman ruined Ormazd's plans for making Iran into an earthly paradise. Initially, creation was wise and free, but soon it was beset with Ahriman's creations: cold in winter, heat in summer, disease, and all manner of other ills that man has to endure. Nothing pleased Ahriman more than a soul which rebelled against Ormazd, rejecting the supreme being's benevolence.

To foster disturbance further, Ahriman created Azhi Dahaka, a three-headed dragon which writhed into the sky like a great snake. In one myth, Ahriman is even credited with killing Geush Urvan, the primeval bull, although in the usual version of the story, MITHRA slays the bull.

According to the standard mythological interpretation, good and evil proceeded from a unique source of being that transcended and reconciled all opposites. However, Zoroaster adopted a strict code of duality, which held that good and evil were perpetually at war on earth.

"Every gift I have given to mankind", Ormazd told the prophet, "has been counterbalanced by an evil present from Ahriman. He is the author of unrest, misfortune and death. It was he who started the unhappy practice of burying or burning the dead."

Under the inspiration of Zoroaster, the Aryan settlers of Iran ignored the local deities and demoted a large number of their own gods to infernal rank. As a result, Ahriman's host of demon supporters included the oldest gods and goddesses in Hindu mythology.

In time, the harsh duality of Iranian mythology was softened. Under the Sassanian kings (226–652) the idea of Zurvan Akarana (infinite time) arose. Zurvan Akarana was a pre-existing primeval being from whom Ormazd and Ahriman both sprang.

Because Zurvan Akarana had promised authority to the firstborn, Ahriman ripped open the womb to claim it. Thus, the principle of evil was allowed to rule for several thousand years, but at a fixed date Ahriman would be destroyed and Ormazd would reign over a resurrected earth. In this Frashkart (final renewal), the principle of good would be aided by SAOSHYANT, a saviour prophet.

The Babylonian chaos dragon TIAMAT and the Hittite dragon Illuyankas were not dissimilar to Ahriman in that they constantly opposed created order.

See Demons, p.126/127

SEE ALSO AZHI DAHAKA, GEUSH URVAN, ILLUYANKAS, YAHWEH, ZURVAN AKARANA

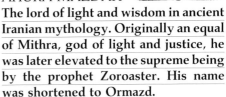

AHSONNUTLI

The chief deity of the Navaho Indians of New Mexico. He closely resembles Awonawilona, the creator god of their neighbours, the Zuni Indians.

Ahsonnutli created heaven and earth, then placed giants at the four cardinal points to support the sky. The North American Indians attach great sanctity to the four quarters of the compass, possibly because they believe that a distinct wind originates from each of them. Indeed, the Navahos think that a great white swan sits at each quarter and conjures up the clouds by agitating its wings. They also associate a colour with each corner: white for the east, blue for the south, yellow for the west, and black for the north. Moreover, they describe the underworld as white or black, while heaven is always blue.

Like most of the North American Indians, the Navaho believe that the deceased's soul has to undertake a long journey before it reaches a final destination. After drinking at a special waterhole, the soul shrinks and passes on to the country of the ghosts, where it lives on a diet of spiritual food and drink. However, the Navaho view the soul as being passive.

Rather than dominating Navaho legend, Ahsonnutli is a somewhat remote deity. His nature seems to have been obscured by later myths, but it is known that he was a hermaphrodite god. He possibly acquired this condition as a result of his association with the Turquoise Woman, a shape-changer who had the power to pass through an endless course of lives, always changing but never dying.

See Creation, p.134

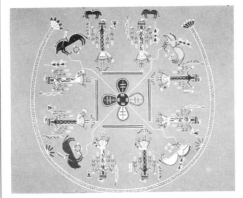

Navaho painting depicting the compass points
SEE ALSO TURQUOISE WOMAN

AHURA MAZDAH

The lord of light and wisdom in ancient Iranian mythology. Originally an equal of Mithra, god of light and justice, he was later elevated to the supreme being by the prophet Zoroaster. His name was shortened to Ormazd.

The Aryan pastoralists who settled on the Iranian plateau derived their gods from the same pantheon as the Aryan invaders of India. But whereas in India the Hindu mind sought a unifying principle within a multiplicity of deities, in Iran this monistic tendency moved toward monotheism, under the guidance of Zoroaster.

Ormazd, the principle of goodness, bestowed fire, the symbol of truth, on his followers whereas those who followed AHRIMAN, the principle of evil, dwelt in darkness.

According to Iranian mythology, Ormazd and Ahriman descended from eternity, known as Zurvan Akarana. Whether through some hesitation on the part of Zurvan Akarana or due to the sheer aggression of Ahriman, the earth passed under the baleful influence of Azhi Dahaka. This evil three-headed dragon, created by Ahriman, burdened mankind with pain, misery and death.

In order to give mankind some respite, Ormazd sent his son Atar, the fire god, to overcome the dragon, and a prolonged contest ensued, during which Azhi Dahaka was harried across land, sea and air. Eventually, Atar overcame the dragon and chained it to a mountain. However, it was destined to escape during Frashkart (final renewal), and destroy a third of mankind, before being slain. Nevertheless, Zurvan Akarana promised that after Frashkart, "Ormazd will reign and will do everything according to his pleasure."

The first man, Gayomart, was born from the sweat of Ormazd. After thirty years he died, but his body gave rise to a human couple, Mashya and Mashyoi. Their seven pairs of children propagated the fifteen peoples into which the ancient Iranians believed mankind was divided.

See Saviours, p.75 and Last Days, p.122

SEE ALSO ATAR, AZHI DAHAKA, GAYOMART, MASHYA, MASHYOI, ZURVAN AKARANA

AJAX

The bulwark of the Greeks in the ten-year siege of Troy, and second only to Achilles in his prowess as a warrior.

Although he commanded only twelve ships in the expedition led by Agamemnon against Troy, Ajax was such a dedicated fighter that his contingent of warriors always stood out on the battlefield. Wherever danger threatened, there fought Ajax and his men. His size certainly helped – he possessed a huge head and shoulders, and towered above everyone else. He may have been slow of speech in the councils of war, but all acknowledged his tremendous courage once battle commenced.

During the war with Troy, Ajax almost killed Hector, the greatest Trojan warrior. However, night intervened before their duel ended, and so the two men gave each other gifts and departed homeward. Ajax saved the life of ODYSSEUS, rallied the Greeks when the Trojans surprised their camp, and brought back the body of ACHILLES when the latter fell victim to a poisoned arrow fired by Paris.

Ajax's own death – and the chief element in his myth – resulted from a competition for the armour of Achilles. It was usual for the personal effects of a hero to be awarded to the winner of a contest, or game, held at the funeral. When Odysseus won the magnificent armour that the smith god HEPHAISTOS had made for Achilles, Ajax became mad with envy and planned a night attack on his own allies. Luckily, the goddess ATHENA deceived him into slaughtering a flock of sheep instead. Aware of his terrible intention in the light of day, and deeply ashamed, Ajax fell on his sword and died. Although there are other accounts of his death, the most potent image is that of the once trusted warrior broken by remorse at the realization of his ungovernable cupidity.

See Heroes, p.55 and War, pp.94/95

SEE ALSO AGAMEMNON, HECTOR, PARIS

AMATERASU

The Japanese sun goddess and the ancestress of the imperial family. The many myths that surround her form the core of the indigenous faith Shinto, "the way of the gods".

Amaterasu was born when IZANAGI, one of the first Japanese gods, washed his right eye. She was given the sky to rule as her domain and her duties also included weaving the robes of the Shinto priestesses. Her brother SUSANOWO was made responsible for populating heaven with a new generation of gods. At his request, Amaterasu broke his sword into three pieces, chewed them, and then breathed out a mist from which three goddesses emerged. Then Susanowo asked her for the five strings of jewels she was wearing; he cracked them between his teeth, breathed on them and produced five gods. The oldest god is considered to be the first of the Japanese emperors.

Susanowo was so elated with his deeds that he lost control. Darkening the sky with storm clouds, he caused untold havoc on the land. In spite of Amaterasu's entreaties, he wrecked rice-fields, uprooted trees and ruined temples. When he tore a hole in the roof of her weaving room, the goddess fled in terror to the cave of heaven, closing the entrance with a great stone. The world was plunged into darkness.

Under cover of the blackness, evil spirits emerged and began to cause widespread destruction. In despair, the gods met to discuss what could be done. Many suggestions were made and at last they agreed that the only way to lure Amaterasu out of her sanctuary would be to arouse her curiosity. So they hung a great mirror and strings of jewels on a tree opposite the cave; cocks were placed nearby and induced to keep up a constant crowing; bonfires were lit to illuminate the entrance of the cave; and the goddess Uzume danced accompanied by loud music. In ecstasy Uzume threw off her clothes and whirled frantically, to the roaring approval of the gods.

From within the cave, Amaterasu heard this merriment and could not resist peering outside. Pulling back the stone door slightly, she asked how it was that the gods could find the heart to laugh in the darkness. With subtle cunning, Uzume replied, "We rejoice and are glad because there is now a more illustrious deity than the sun goddess." While she was speaking, two gods turned the great mirror to face Amaterasu, who saw her own brilliant reflection. As she gazed in astonishment, another god widened the opening and drew her out.

Thus the world was once again bathed in light, evil forces shrank away, and quietness returned. As a punishment, the gods made Susanowo shave off his beard, confiscated his property, and banished him. His subsequent wanderings parallel the exploits of the Greek hero HERACLES, and form a lengendary cycle in themselves.

(The mirror, sword and strings of jewels are still significant symbols of the Japanese imperial family. They are sacred treasures in the imperial household and feature in Shinto rituals today.)

Amaterasu is the counterpart of INANNA, the Sumerian goddess of fertility and love.

Amaterasu emerges from her cave

SEE ALSO IZANAMI, UZUME

AMRITA

The water of eternal life in Hindu mythology (amrita means "non-dead" or "immortal"). As such, it was the prize most desired by gods and demons.

Long ago, the sky god INDRA was cursed by a short-tempered sage called Durvasas (ill-clothed) because Indra had treated a garland, which Durvasas had presented to the gods, with disrespect.

The curse weakened the authority of the gods, and as Indra and the other deities lost their power, they were increasingly threatened by their demonic rivals, the *asuras* (anti-gods). The balance of the whole Hindu cosmos was in jeopardy.

The great god VISHNU came to the aid of the beleaguered deities, incarnated as Kurma the turtle. "I will restore your strength", said Vishnu, "but only if you follow exactly these instructions. Forget about your quarrel with the demons, and seek their assistance in churning from the ocean a precious drink. Collect plants and herbs, cast them into the sea of milk; then, taking the great snake Vasuki as a cord, use

a mountain, which I will support, as the churning-staff."

So a mountain was placed on the back of the turtle and the gods and demons twisted and pulled on Vasuki the snake to turn the mountain and churn the ocean.

But the snake suffered so much that it spurted venom in a deluge which engulfed the earth. In one version of the myth, Vishnu had to summon SHIVA, who swallowed the rivers of poison and saved the world.

At last, the milky sea brought forth its goodness. Out of it emerged the sacred cow Surabhi, who had the power to grant every wish. Then came Varuni, goddess of wine, and Parijata, the tree of paradise, whose fragrant blossoms perfumed the earth. Later appeared Soma as the moon, whose symbol Shiva placed on his forehead, and LAKSHMI, the goddess of good fortune, seated on a lotus flower. Then the divine doctor Dhanvantari appeared, holding the amrita.

At this moment the demon Rahu seized the precious amrita and would have drunk it all had not Vishnu, who was watching, intervened. According to one account, Rahu succeeded in taking a sip, which forced Vishnu to cut off his head in order to prevent the liquid from going any farther into his body and making him totally indestructible. The severed piece of immortality, hideous, horned, with bulging eyes and ravenous jaws, was transformed into a talisman, a protection against evil influences.

Another story recounts how, tipped off by the sun and moon, Vishnu discovered the theft of the amrita after Rahu had drunk enough for it to be absorbed by his whole body. He chopped Rahu into pieces, but because the demon had made himself immortal, Vishnu could not kill him. Instead, the fragments of his body were placed among the stars. There Rahu wreaks his vengeance on the sun and moon by seeking to swallow them.

Amrita is probably identical to a sacred drink of the gods, also known as soma. The ancient Iranians possessed a similar drink called *haoma* which was credited with miraculous healing powers.

SEE ALSO DHANVANTARI, DURVASAS, HAOMA, KURMA, PARIJATA, RAHU, SOMA, SURABHI, VARUNI, VASUKI

AMUN

An Egyptian ram-headed god and the national deity from the sixteenth century BC onward. He is often shown as a man wearing a cap surmounted by two tall plumes. His name possibly means "the complete one".

At the beginning of the second millennium BC Amun was one of the eight deities in the cosmology of Hermopolis, a city in Upper Egypt. The pharaohs of the twelfth dynasty intended him to become their national god, but this promotion was interrupted by the collapse of the dynasty and a period of anarchy in Egypt. During this time Lower Egypt was invaded by the Hyksos, and the country was divided. Amun's ascendancy only began once the pharaohs of the eighteenth dynasty had expelled the West Asian invaders, in about 1576 BC, and mounted a succession of conquests in Palestine and Syria.

Amun may originally have held power over the air or the wind. Later, he acquired the powers of fertility vested in MIN, a god associated with the harvest.

As a national god, Amun was a rival to the sun god RE, the most important member of the Egyptian pantheon. To reconcile the claims of both deities, they were assimilated to form a joint figure, Amun-Re. This new state god was worshipped as being the king of the gods, the creator of the universe, and the father of the pharaohs.

Amun-Re was also looked upon as every pharaoh's guide on the battlefield. At the battle of Kadesh, in 1286 BC, when Hittite chariotry almost routed the Egyptian army of Ramesses II, Amun-Re is supposed to have comforted the hard-pressed pharaoh by saying: "Forward! Your father is with you! My powerful hand will slay an hundred thousand men."

The Greeks identified Amun with ZEUS and consulted his oracle at Siwa, deep in the Libyan desert. The Greek heroes PERSEUS and HERACLES went to the desert shrine, as did Alexander the Great, who endured a dust storm of several days to consult the oracle, in 332 BC. Whatever prediction he may have had, the only information that Alexander was willing to divulge concerned his own parentage. Like the pharaohs of old, he was declared to be the son of Amun, or Zeus.

AN

In Sumerian mythology, the personification of heaven (his name means "sky"). An presided over the assembly of deities, the ultimate court in the universe, and was closely associated with kingship.

An is often depicted as a bull, whose bellowing was said to be the thunder of the overcast sky. He may have been associated with the husband and dying bull of the underworld goddess Ereshkigal (the mistress of death). An's usual wife, however, is Ki, the earth. By him, she gave birth to trees, reeds and other vegetation.

Originally the source of rain and a benevolent vegetation deity, An was "the father who makes the seed sprout". But he was gradually given a wider significance and became the fountainhead of all authority — parental, lordly, royal and divine.

It was An who proclaimed the king, who was thought by the Sumerians to have been chosen by the assembly of gods. This body met to approve political appointments or deal with cases of crime, and gathered in the forecourt of the temple of An's son ENLIL, in the city of Nippur.

The assembled deities would first fortify themselves with food and drink provided by the temple attendants. They would take an oath to abide by the decisions the assembly made, and proposals were then placed before them and voted upon. Enlil saw that the decisions were carried out.

The basic idea of Sumerian kingship was that rulers performed the duties and rites that An determined. The most important were those associated with the calendar.

In later mythology, during the era of Babylon's supremacy, a shadow was cast over An and his son Enlil. MARDUK, the sun god of Babylon, destroyed their powers by flaying An alive, cutting his head off and tearing his heart out, while blinding Enlil. This cruelty presumably reflected the growing violence of the times. The Assyrian king Ashurbanipal (668–627 BC) recorded the soothing of the hearts of the great gods by the "feeding of human flesh to the dogs, pigs, vultures, eagles — the birds of heaven and the fishes of the deep".

An is the counterpart of the Babylonian deity Anu.

SEE ALSO ANU, ERESHKIGAL

ANANSI

The great trickster god of West African mythology, also known as Mr Spider. He is renowned for his cleverness, and has several names. The most widely known, however, is Anansi.

Originally, Anansi was regarded as the creator of the world, and in some traditions this remains his principal role. But in general the spider god is viewed as a crafty and cunning trickster who prospers by his wits. Anansi's exploits form a large cycle of popular stories in West Africa, which has spread to the West Indies (where he is known as Annency) and South America.

Anansi is always duping other animals and even mankind. He is able to outwit men by assuming their shape at will. His greatest asset, however, is the profound knowledge he has of the minds of his victims. As one proverb explains: "The wisdom of the spider is greater than that of all the world put together."

While Anansi finds an easy living in tricking others out of their possessions, or driving them away from the things he wants for himself, there is one person he fears — the Gum Girl, to whom he once stuck fast.

A typical account of Anansi's cunning is the story of his tiger ride. Anansi bragged to the king of the jungle that he often rode a tiger, but the king found that no one believed Anansi's boast. So the king sent the tiger to bring the spider to his court. When the tiger arrived, Anansi told him that he was too weak to make the journey. After much discussion, the tiger was finally persuaded to wear a saddle so that the spider could ride on his back. Thus Anansi rode the tiger.

See Trickster Gods, pp.78/79

SEE ALSO ANNENCY, GUM GIRL

ANTICHRIST

In Christian mythology, the archenemy of Jesus and the merciless despot of the Last Days.

The concept of the Antichrist derives from the idea of absolute evil in Iranian mythology, and may owe something to TIAMAT, the Babylonian chaos dragon.

The first occasion on which an historical figure was called the Antichrist was in 169 BC, when the Greek ruler of Syria pillaged the Hebrew temple in Jerusalem. This was King Antiochus IV Epiphanes, who was opposed to traditional Hebrew worship. The king seems to fit the description of Antichrist given in the Book of Daniel, for he was a mighty ruler, a commander of huge armies, a persecutor of holy men, as well as destroyer of the temple.

Belief in the coming of a false messiah, a corrupt prophet, was taken up by Christianity. In Revelation, the Antichrist is expected to claim absolute power. He will also "make war with the saints, and overcome them". The early Church expected that the Antichrist would appear before the end of the world, and medieval Christians tensely awaited his arrival. Even today, the idea of a tyrant rising up in the Holy Land is by no means dead in some Christian sects.

See Last Days, p.122

The Antichrist, from a medieval manuscript

ANUBIS

A jackal-headed funerary god in Egyptian mythology, sometimes also depicted as a wild black dog. He was associated with the art of embalming, which was considered to be essential for the afterlife. Anubis is the Greek name for the Egyptian god Anpu.

Anubis's mother was Nephthys, who tricked OSIRIS into giving her a son because she had no children by her evil husband SETH (Osiris's brother). However, Seth hated Osiris violently, and would have harmed Anubis when he was born. To protect him, Nephthys hid him in the marshes of the Nile delta. ISIS, Osiris's wife, found and adopted Anubis, a debt he repaid by becoming her protector when he reached adulthood.

When Seth killed Osiris, Anubis embalmed the body and performed the funerary rites. This was regarded as the original burial and became the basis for burial rites thereafter.

Before the rise to prominence of Osiris as the great god of the dead, Anubis was the chief deity to whom prayers at a funeral were made. When Osiris overtook him in importance, Anubis became a guardian of the underworld, guiding the newly arrived dead to the hall of judgement. There he assisted the divine scribe THOTH in using a set of scales to weigh the heart of the deceased against the feather of truth, personified as the goddess Maat, before presenting the dead soul to Osiris.

Other deities connected with the grave who were manifested as dogs included Khenti-Amentiu and Wepwawet.

See Death, p.91, and Afterlife, p.146

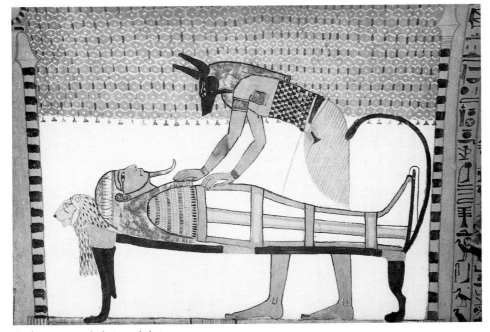

Anubis prepares a body for embalming

SEE ALSO KHENTI-AMENTIU, MAAT, NEPHTHYS, WEPWAWET

APHRODITE

The Greek goddess of love, beauty, and fertility, later identified with the Roman goddess Venus. Her cult was imported from West Asia, probably via the island of Cyprus.

Aphrodite's name is connected with foam (*aphros*), and this may refer to her birth at sea. According to Hesiod, KRONOS cut off the genitals of his father Ouranos and threw them into the sea where they floated amid white foam and produced the beautiful, full-grown Aphrodite.

The unfaithful wife of the smith god HEPHAISTOS, Aphrodite had two children by ARES, the god of war. They were the twins Deimos (fear) and Phobos (panic). When Hephaistos trapped Aphrodite and Ares in bed by means of an invisible net, the other Olympian gods, who witnessed their capture, fell about laughing instead of sympathizing with his shame. ZEUS punished Aphrodite by making her fall in love with a mortal, the Trojan Anchises, and bear him a son, the hero AENEAS.

But Aphrodite's overwhelming passion was for ADONIS. However, she had to share this dying-and-rising god with PERSEPHONE, the queen of the dead. To settle their dispute, Zeus ruled that for one third of the year Adonis was to dwell by himself, for another third with Persephone, and for the remaining third with Aphrodite.

So powerful a goddess was Aphrodite that she was able to revenge herself on Zeus. With unashamed glee, she compelled him to chase nymphs and mortal women, and to neglect his wife HERA. The intense rivalry between Hera and Aphrodite recurs often in Greek mythology.

But the greatest havoc Aphrodite caused was among mankind. For example, when among Hera, ATHENA and Aphrodite, the Trojan prince chose Aphrodite as the greatest beauty, she rewarded him with HELEN, the wife of Menelaus and Queen of Sparta. The elopement of Paris and Helen sparked off the ten-year struggle between the Greeks and the Trojans.

Aphrodite was the Greek equivalent of CYBELE, INANNA, and ISHTAR.

See Love and Fertility, pp.106/107

SEE ALSO ANCHISES, EROS, MENELAUS, OURANOS, PARIS, PHOBOS

ARES

The Greek war god and the only son of Zeus and Hera. He was later equated with the Roman god Mars.

Ares had no wife, although he was constantly under the spell of APHRODITE, the goddess of love. She bore him two children out of wedlock until the scandal of their liaison was ended by almighty ZEUS, king of the gods.

A daughter of Ares, born of a mortal woman, was raped on the slopes of the Acropolis in Athens by Halirrhothius, one of the sons of the sea god POSEIDON. When Ares killed Halirrhothius on the spot, Poseidon, in revenge, had him tried at once for murder by the assembly of gods. Ares was acquitted, and later the Athenians named their homicide court the Areopagus (Hill of Ares).

Ares was an unpopular god and was not generally worshipped by the Greeks, who feared his unbridled joy in violence and cruelty. Nobody felt that they could place their trust in such a vicious deity, and so Ares never received the reverence shown by the Romans to MARS. The exact meaning of the god's name is unknown, although it may be connected with spoils. Certainly there is no suggestion of glory involved.

See War, pp.94/95

Ares, the Greek god of war

SEE ALSO HALIRRHOTHIUS

ARTEMIS

The Greek goddess of the chase, the forest and wild animals. She was probably a hunting goddess of pre-Greek origin.

Although her parentage is uncertain, Artemis was usually regarded as the daughter of ZEUS and the Titaness Leto. She was the sister of Apollo, and shared with him the persecution of the jealous mother goddess HERA, Zeus's wife. Once, at Delphi, Artemis helped Apollo to overcome Python, a terrible serpent belonging to Hera.

Like Apollo, Artemis was associated with death, but whereas Apollo came to be looked upon as the cause of sudden death among men, Artemis was blamed for the death of women. Her fierceness is obvious in a number of myths. For example, when her favourite follower, the nymph Callisto, bore Zeus a child, Artemis was so enraged by Callisto's lost virginity that she changed her into a bear and drove her away with arrows.

The giant hunter Orion also received short shrift on the occasion he dared to approach the goddess. But the fate of Actaeon was the most cruel of all. During a hunt, this mortal had the misfortune of seeing Artemis bathing. The goddess considered herself so insulted by this that she turned Actaeon into a stag. He was immediately devoured by his own hounds. An alternative version has the young man eaten alive as a rebuke for claiming to be a superior hunter to Artemis.

The harshness of Artemis, as well as her association with the wild, made her a dangerous goddess. She was therefore propitiated with great care, and received numerous animal sacrifices. After the battle of Marathon, in 490 BC, the Athenians were very worried because they had promised to sacrifice a number of goats equal to the number of Persians they slew in the battle. So unexpected was the extent of their victory that they decided instead to offer 500 goats each year. Otherwise their flocks would have been severely depleted.

SEE ALSO ACTAEON, APOLLO, CALLISTO, LETO, ORION, PYTHON

ARTHUR

The once-and-future king, Arthur was probably a fifth- or sixth-century Romanized British chieftain around whom a cycle of heroic tales has collected. In the Middle Ages, the exploits of his followers, the Knights of the Round Table, became the standard for chivalry.

Arthur was doubtless based on a legendary Celtic figure, possibly the Welsh priest-king Gwydion. As bard and magician Gwydion was credited with valorous deeds; as cultural hero, he helped to refine civilization. His Irish equivalent was Ogma, the son of DAGDA. Ogma Cermait, "of the honeyed mouth", invented writing and inspired the poets.

The *History of Britain*, written by the ninth-century monk Nennius, states that Arthur was a leader of troops defending the country against foreign invaders. He probably became a popular symbol of Celtic resistance against the Angles, Saxons and Jutes, following the final withdrawal of the Roman legions in AD 410.

Arthur was certainly the focus of late Cornish and Welsh Celtic aspirations. The inscription on his tomb in Glastonbury, in the English county of Somerset, reads: "Here lies Arthur, king that was, king that shall be." As late as 1113 the denial of his undeath, by the servants of French visitors to the Cornish town of Bodmin, provoked a riot.

The son of Uther Pendragon, King of Britain, and Igraine, Duchess of Cornwall, Arthur was conceived out of wedlock and brought up by the wizard MERLIN. While still a child, he revealed himself as the predestined king by pulling the magic sword Excalibur out of a stone from which no one else could extract it.

Crowned in Wales at the age of fifteen, Arthur soon showed his military ability as a commander, even reaching Rome in one campaign. Against Merlin's advice, Arthur married Guinevere, who loved Sir Lancelot and was unfaithful to the king. When Arthur found out about his wife's adultery, Lancelot's position became impossible and the knight removed himself to France.

In Malory's *Le Morte d'Arthur*, published by Caxton in 1485, Lancelot was permitted to see the Grail, the vessel that contained the blood of JESUS, but when he approached he was blasted by a fiery wind because of his sin. The king was reconciled to his queen during his lifetime, although it was through Lancelot's intervention that Guinevere was saved from being burned at the stake. After Arthur's death the two lovers met again, but separated immediately in order to devote themselves to lives of penitence, Guinevere as a nun, Lancelot as a hermit.

The romance between the queen and the knight weakened the unity of the band of knights of the Round Table, which Arthur had caused to be so-shaped to prevent his followers from quarrelling about precedence in the seating arrangements. The Table's final collapse resulted from a civil war rather than an Anglo-Saxon attack. The disastrous quarrel between Arthur and his nephew Modred may well echo an historic conflict.

The final battle took place on a field near Salisbury. Prior to the engagement, Malory tells us, the king had a strange dream in which he saw "a chair, and the chair was fast to a wheel, and thereupon sat King Arthur in the richest cloth of gold that might be made . . . and suddenly the king thought the wheel turned upside down, and he fell among the serpents, and every beast took him by a limb; and the king cried for help as he lay in his bed and slept."

Nevertheless, Arthur went forth to face Modred's "grim host of an hundred thousand men". It was agreed that the king and his nephew would meet between the two armies to discuss the possibility of ending the war but, since neither commander trusted the other, each instructed his troops to attack if they observed anyone draw a sword.

Arthur and Modred came to terms and drank on their agreement but, according to Malory, a knight drew his sword to kill an adder, "and so both hosts dressed themselves". Thus the great battle was fought by accident. Nearly all the Knights of the Round Table were slain, and Arthur, having run Modred through with his spear, "fell in a swoon to the earth and there he swooned many times".

Two surviving knights, Sir Lucan and Sir Bedivere, helped their king to a little chapel by the sea where Arthur asked Bedivere to cast Excalibur into the sea. Eventually, the knight obeyed, whereupon "there came an arm and a hand above the water and caught it, and so shook it thrice, and then vanished away the hand with the sword into the water".

Feeling that his time had come, Arthur asked Bedivere to take him to the beach where three fairies waited in a boat. When Bedivere asked what this meant, Arthur replied: "Comfort thyself, and do all thou mayest, for in me is no trust to trust in. For I must into the vale of Avilion to heal me of my grievous wound. And if thou hear never more of me, pray for my soul."

So Arthur departed for Avalon, which was possibly an island similar to the lands of perfection in Irish mythology. In Cornish, the name has connections with the festival of apples held at the autumn equinox. However, the traditional view holds that Avalon was Glastonbury, on the basis of the legend that both Arthur and Guinevere were buried in the abbey there. Glastonbury is also credited with the guardianship of the Grail.

See Quests, p.64

SEE ALSO AVALON, EXCALIBUR, GRAIL, GUINEVERE, GWYDION, IGRAINE, LANCELOT, LUCAN, MODRED, OGMA, UTHER PENDRAGON

The ruins of the abbey at Glastonbury, Arthur's burial-place

Quests

Heroes in pursuit of an actual or symbolic goal have always gripped the popular imagination. Such quests often involved long voyages, and on the way these brave men encounter all kinds of vicissitudes which enable them to demonstrate their courage, strength and honour.

Many heroes of Celtic legend set sail from the coast of Ireland upon their quests. One such was Bran, whose voyage took centuries to complete.

The epic of Gilgamesh recounts his quest for immortality and celebrates his skill in fighting.

Illustration from the early fifteenth-century French manuscript, Book of Sir Lancelot du Lac, Le Saint Graal. Sir Lancelot pursued the Grail, but, being imperfect, was unable to approach it.

The word odyssey, meaning "a long adventurous wandering", derives from the Greek hero Odysseus's ten-year voyage home after the Trojan war. At one point his sailors, their ears blocked with wax, had to lash him to the mast, lest he succumb to the seductive song of the sirens, who lured sailors onto the rocks.

ASCLEPIUS

The Greek god of healing, and the son of Apollo, he was the principal deity concerned with prophecy and divination.

Asclepius was torn from the dead body of his mother Coronis, daughter of the king of Orchomenus. Coronis was loved by Apollo, but made him angry by being unfaithful when she was carrying Asclepius in her womb. Apollo asked his sister ARTEMIS to slay Coronis but, wishing to save his son, removed the unborn Asclepius from the funeral pyre.

Asclepius was brought up by the wise Chiron, the most gentle of the Centaurs, beastlike monsters who lived in the woods. Chiron was renowned for his wide knowledge, which encompassed all the arts and sciences, and he taught Asclepius the secrets of medicine.

In time, Asclepius reached manhood, married and settled down to family life. But he drew the wrath of ZEUS upon himself, it is said, by daring to bring the dead back to life. Zeus, the king of the gods, struck him down with a thunderbolt and killed him.

Asclepius's father, Apollo, avenged this act by killing, in turn, one of Zeus's sons, the one-eyed giant Cyclops. As a punishment, Apollo was forced to become a slave for a year and serve a mortal king.

The slaying of Asclepius, and indeed the question of his death, remains something of a mystery. He would seem to have been a hero who attained divinity. His cult, like that of Apollo, included prophecy, but was essentially connected with recommended courses of medical treatment. Closely associated with snakes, Asclepius was usually portrayed as a bearded man in early middle age, holding a serpent.

See Seers, pp.82/83

SEE ALSO CENTAURS, CHIRON

ASHUR

The national god of Assyria and god of fertility and war.

Essentially a war god, Ashur was portrayed as a winged disc enclosing a stretched bow ready to let fly an arrow, or armed with lightning. His wife, the love goddess ISHTAR, sometimes identified as Ninlil, responded to his warlike character by sprouting a beard which reached to her ample breasts.

The Assyrian empire subjugated the Babylonian kingdom, which is reflected in Ashur's ascendance over MARDUK, the chief god of the Babylonians. Ashur assumed Marduk's role in the Babylonian creation epic *Enuma Elish* (When on high) as protector of the order of the universe against the powers of chaos.

The antagonism between the two gods mirrors the struggle between the Assyrians and Babylonians on earth. In Assyrian myth, Marduk is credited with misdeeds against Ashur and is treated as a traitor and unworthy rival to Ashur's rule.

See War, pp.94/95
The Assyrian king Ashurbanipal hunting lion

SEE ALSO NINLIL

ASTARTE

The Canaanite mother goddess. In the Ras Shamra texts, clay tablets dating from the fourteenth century BC which were discovered in Syria in 1929, she appears in several forms – as Anat, Athirat and Athtart, the last of which was rendered into Greek as Astarte.

In different guises, Astarte was the wife of the gods BAAL and EL. As Anat (lady of the mountain), she was Baal's sister and wife, possibly his mother as well.

Anat seems to have been responsible for having Baal instated on Mount Saphon, a sacred mountain in "the sides of the north". She achieved this by flattering El grossly.

Baal even owed his continued existence to Anat's bravery. He had been foolish enough to mistreat Mot (death) and refuse him hospitality on earth. As a result, Baal was summoned to the underworld to share the food of the dead, mud.

Anat descended to the underworld in order to recover Baal's corpse and, when there were no immediate signs of his return to life, she attacked and killed Mot. A text relates how, "with a sickle she cut him, with a shovel she winnowed him, with fire she scorched him, with a mill she ground him. She scattered his flesh over the field as food for the birds, so that his fate was fulfilled." By this violence she revived Baal.

Aggressive in her handling of Baal's enemies, Anat was feared and loved by turns. As the slayer of the demon Lotan (LEVIATHAN in Hebrew myth), she rid the world of chaos. But on another occasion she was responsible for causing a drought.

Anat coveted a supernatural bow owned by Aqhat, a renowned king. This fine weapon was a present to Aqhat from the smith god Kothar. Anat offered to give Aqhat silver and then gold for the bow, but he would not part with it. She then offered him immortality, which he also rejected, saying that this was only an illusion for a man already destined to die. Enraged with frustration, Anat killed Aqhat, but in the fray, the bow fell into the sea and was lost. At the same time the rain stopped and vegetation withered. The end of this particular myth is missing, but it is almost certain that Aqhat became a dying-and-rising god connected with the cycle of agriculture. He seems to have journeyed regularly to the land of the dead.

As Athirat (lady of the sea), Astarte was the wife of El. Since El was regarded as the first of the gods, the attributes of Athirat were very impressive: she was the one in whom wisdom resided, the mother of heaven, and the creator of the gods.

Less remote than Athirat, but just as fierce as Anat, was Athtart (lady of heaven). The Hebrews revered her as the queen of heaven and the divine consort of Yahweh, much to the fury of the prophet Jeremiah who was opposed to the influence of West Asian myth.

Astarte is the counterpart of INANNA, in Sumerian mythology, ISHTAR in Babylonian and Assyrian myth, and CYBELE in Phrygian myth.

See Love and Fertility, pp.106/107

The West Asian mother goddess, Astarte

SEE ALSO AQHAT, KOTHAR, LOTAN, MOT, SAPHON, YAHWEH

ATHENA

Daughter of the Greek god Zeus and one of the twelve great Olympian deities. She was the virgin goddess of war and wisdom, and patroness of the arts and crafts.

Athena sprang into being fully formed and fully armed when the smith god HEPHAISTOS clove open the head of ZEUS with an axe. Zeus had been warned about the future power of his child, and fearing it he tricked the pregnant mother, Metis, into changing herself into a fly. He then swallowed her.

Zeus himself had been saved from a similar fate by the cunning of his mother Gaia. Instead of the child, she had given Zeus's father KRONOS a stone wrapped in swaddling clothes, which he ate. Unlike Kronos, Zeus was not content to eat his newborn child; instead he ate Metis while she was still carrying Athena.

In another version of the myth, Zeus desired the knowledge of Metis, whose name means "counsel". The amorous Zeus pursued the reluctant Metis, who was concerned to preserve her virginity. When she disguised herself as a fly, the god swallowed her. As a result, Metis gave birth to Athena in the seat of Zeus's intelligence – his head.

Athena was an active goddess, aiding heroes and adventurers, who included PERSEUS, HERACLES, JASON, and ODYSSEUS. Although she was a virgin, Athena did not hate the presence of men, unlike the goddess ARTEMIS. She enjoyed the bravery and daring of the battlefield but had no time for senseless slaughter, unlike the war god ARES.

Athena's symbol was the owl, a creature associated by the Greeks with the boldness of wisdom. Because Athena protected Athens, an ancient commercial centre, she was considered the patroness of craftsmen.

For Hephaistos, the smith god worshipped at Athens, there is no doubt that Athena represented an attractive rival, and he tried several times to make her his mistress. During one intense struggle his semen fell to the ground, where it became the serpent-king Erichthonius.

Perhaps because it was the nearest Athena ever came to having a son of her own, she took an interest in the welfare of the child. She entrusted the young Erichthonius to the daughters of Cecrops, an early ruler who was said to have been a snake himself. The princesses charged with his care were told by Athena not to look inside the box in which Erichthonius was placed. But they did, and when they saw the serpent child they were driven mad.

Athena took Erichthonius to her temple on the Acropolis and raised him there, until in due time he was made king of the Athenians. In gratitude, Erichthonius promoted the cult of Athena as the city goddess.

It is hardly surprising that Athena was always regarded as the protectress of the Acropolis. From earliest times she was connected with citadels, and only the stronghold of Athens, the Acropolis, would appear to have held out and remained undisturbed in the chaotic period following the fall of the Myceneans.

The Romans identified her with Minerva who, like Athena, was portrayed with a helmet, shield and coat of mail.

See War, pp.94/95

Reconstruction of the statue of Athena

SEE ALSO CECROPS, ERICHTHONIUS, GAIA, METIS

ATTIS

The castrated god of Phrygia. He was the lover of the mother goddess Cybele, whom the Greeks identified with Rhea, the sister and wife of Kronos.

According to the standard tale, Attis was attracted by a nymph, possibly because his relationship with CYBELE was unconsummated. However, Cybele was so incensed by his infidelity that she made Attis lose his mind, whereupon he castrated himself and died. After his death, the god was reborn and united with Cybele.

In another version, Attis is the victim of the monster Agdistis, a hermaphrodite born of heavenly semen dropped to earth. Agdistis fell in love with the hunter Attis and on his wedding day burst into the festivities. As a result of this violent interruption, the bride died of self-inflicted breast-wounds and Attis, driven mad by grief, emasculated himself beneath a pine tree, which became his symbol.

Sometimes, Agdistis is credited with being the father of Attis. The gods feared Agdistis because he was able to procreate endlessly, and lulled him into a deep sleep by adding wine to the pool in which he bathed. While he was sleeping, a god stole up and tied his genitals to a tree. Waking with a start, Agdistis castrated himself.

A tree laden with fruit grew from the blood of Agdistis and, one day, the daughter of a river king or god picked some and gathered them in her lap. Suddenly, one of the fruits disappeared and the girl found herself pregnant. Her father felt himself disgraced and ordered first the death of his daughter and then the exposure of her child, Attis. But on each occasion, Cybele intervened.

All these stories are concerned with the problem of thwarted love. The cult of Attis was introduced to Rome in 204 BC and accounts mention devotees whirling to strident music, slashing themselves with knives to bespatter the altar with blood, and cutting off their genitals.

The relationship of Attis and Cybele is similar to that of the Babylonian deities Tammuz and ISHTAR, and the Canaanite deities ADONIS and ASTARTE.

See Death, p.91
SEE ALSO AGDISTIS, KRONOS, RHEA, TAMMUZ

AVALOKITESVARA

The Buddhist epitome of mercy and compassion. He was the prototype for the Buddhist saviour-saints known as bodhisattvas, who postpone the state of complete enlightenment in order to stay on earth and relieve the sufferings of mankind.

Avalokitesvara is represented as a handsome young man sometimes holding a lotus flower in his left hand, sometimes with his hands joined together. In his hair he often wears a picture of Amitabha, an incarnation of BUDDHA.

In recognition of the extent of his charitable works, and so that he could always help those in need, he was awarded a thousand arms. His innumerable deeds – and Avalokitesvara himself – were soon invested with cosmic significance.

In Tibetan mythology, Avalokitesvara was charged by Sakyamuni with converting Tibet to Buddhism. But when he looked at the land, he saw that it was inhabited only by ogres and animals. So he produced a monkey from the palm of his hand, enlightened it and sent it to meditate in Tibet. An ogress transformed into a beautiful woman approached the monkey and warned that if he did not take her as his consort, she would command all the ogres to devour the world.

The monkey consulted Avalokitesvara, who agreed that the ogress should bear his children, because they would be the descendants of human beings. But the children they bore were covered with hair and had tails. Moreover, they were carnivorous (strict Buddhists are vegetarian). These offspring were sent to a forest to live and mate with other monkeys.

When Avalokitesvara's monkey returned to them a year later, he found that they had multiplied a hundredfold, and were starving. He gave them some food, whereupon their hair fell out and their tails vanished – they had become human beings whom Avalokitesvara could now convert to Buddhism.

See Saviours, p.75
SEE ALSO AMITABHA, SAKYAMUNI

AWONAWILONA

The great father and creator deity of the Zuni Indians, of the southwestern United States. His name means "all-container".

Awonawilona is said to have existed before all else. By his thought he produced the mists that promote growth. His warmth resolved the mists into the primeval sea and then, gradually, from the green scum in the waters, he created earth.

After forming the sky and the land, Awonawilona seeded the world with living things. The seeds seem to have been placed in caverns, or wombs, in the earth. Each womb teemed with unfinished creatures, crawling over one another in the darkness, writhing like reptiles as they endeavoured to reach the warm air above.

Among these potential beings was Poshaiyankaya, the foremost and wisest of men. He found a passage leading from his cavern and followed it upward and onward until, at last, he emerged into the light. There, on the shore of the world ocean, he begged Awonawilona to release creation, and the great god complied. The earth split open, and out streamed animals and men.

Having adapted to life underground, these creatures, including mankind, had scales, short tails, owl-like eyes, huge ears and webbed feet. They greeted the first sunrise by howling, but gradually grew accustomed to life on the surface of the earth. Poshaiyankaya took the lead in all this by founding the Zuni tribe.

The neighbouring Pueblo Indians have a similar culture hero in Poseyemu, the brother of the corn goddess Iyatiku. His birthplace was not a cavern but the inside of a nut. Having fulfilled his duties as the tribal founder, Poseyemu travelled southward from one pueblo to another, before disappearing into the earth. Among Christian Pueblos, he is now identified with the serpent in the garden of Eden.

See Creation, p.135
SEE ALSO POSHAIYANKAYA

The four legendary brothers from whom the Inca rulers of Peru traced their descent. The Incas were overthrown by the Spaniards in 1532.

Inca legend recounts how four brothers and four sisters left caves and proceeded towards the city of Cuzco, looking for somewhere to settle. During the journey Ayar Cachi, the brother with the greatest power, was walled up in a cave by his brothers because they were frightened of his destructiveness.

Ayar Oco then turned himself into a sacred stone and Ayar Ayca became the protector of the fields. The last brother, Ayar Manco, seized Cuzco with his sisters, one of whom he married.

According to one myth, the brothers were the leading gods of the Peruvians, prior to the foundation of the Inca empire. When the Incas came into power, these gods appear to have been drawn into the cult of the sun god INTI. Sometimes they were viewed as Inti's sons or as separate manifestations of him.

See Founders, p.68

A 17th-century illustration of Inca origins

Founders

Founder heroes, who established a city, a country, or a group of people, have been worshipped since the earliest times. Through a sense of obligation to a previous generation, such individuals have often been elevated to divine or semi-divine status.

At Machu Picchu, a centre of Inca civilization, this solar stone (above) is associated with Inti, father of the Ayar, the four brothers who were the founders of Peru.

The legendary founder of Rome (below) was Romulus. Because of a local king, Romulus and his twin brother Remus were left to die, but a she-wolf, a creature sacred to Mars, saved and reared them (left).

Cadmus was a founder hero of immense importance in ancient Greece. On the instructions of the oracle at Delphi, he founded the city of Thebes in Boeotia (in central Greece). There, he introduced the alphabet.

BAAL

Literally "lord", and the title of the god of every Canaanite city. In various regions of the eastern Mediterranean he was addressed differently. Overall, however, he was a rain god who also had the functions of a god of fertility. His arch enemy was Mot, lord of death and infertility.

Originally, Baal may have been married to Baalat, a fertility goddess. But he took on her functions himself, as the storm god Baal-Hadad, appointed by EL to dispense the rain and dew. In most of his myths, Baal's wife was Anat, a ferocious aspect of ASTARTE. Baal is usually shown standing next to a bull and grasping thunderbolts in each hand.

To establish his royal authority and impose order in the face of impending chaos, Baal pitted his strength against the menacing sea god Yamm and all his forces. A hymn from the ancient Syrian city of Ugarit relates how "The mace in the hand of Baal swoops down like a vulture. It falls heavily across the shoulders of the Lord of the Sea and belabours the chest of the River Prince. Then does the great god strike the Sea on the head and the River between the eyes. Both of these lords fall to the ground, broken in strength, their bodies shaking in terror."

Having defeated the sea gods, Baal built a house on Mount Saphon and seized possession of numerous cities. Intoxicated with his success, he announced that he would no longer acknowledge the authority of Mot. So Baal compelled the lord of death and sterility to wander wastelands and denied his presence wherever things grew green.

Mot responded to this mistreatment by requesting Baal to come to his underground abode and eat mud, the food of the dead. Terrified, and unable to disobey the summons to the underworld, Baal mated with a calf to strengthen himself for the impending ordeal and then set out for Mot's home, where he ate mud and died.

El and the other heavenly gods grieved. They put on mourning, poured ashes over their heads, and cut their limbs. But Baal's wife Anat was not prepared to abandon him to the underworld and, aided by the sun goddess Shapash, she brought home his corpse to try to revive him.

Finding that no power in heaven could restore Baal to life, Anat was obliged to ask for Mot's aid, but he refused her request. Outraged by this, Anat assaulted and killed Mot.

In the meantime, El had appointed the irrigation god Athar to Baal's throne, but this deity was soon deposed when Baal returned to Mount Saphon, restored by Anat's bloody deed.

The myth of Baal as a dying-and-rising god suggests an interpretation of the change of seasons: Baal dies, as plants do in the autumn; Anat threshes, winnows and grinds Mot like the harvested corn (over which he was said to preside); and Baal is reborn, like a germinating seed in spring.

Similar ideas surrounded Baal throughout West Asian mythology, with the exception of Hebrew demonology, in which Baal became Baalzebub (lord of the flies), the chief assistant of SATAN.

See Death, p.91

Statue of the god Baal, from Ras Shamra, Syria

SEE ALSO ANAT, BAALZEBUB, MOT, SAPHON, YAMM

BAGADJIMBIRI

The ancestral creator of gods of the Karadjeri peoples of northwestern Australia.

According to Karadjeri tradition, the world was an empty place in the beginning. Then the two Bagadjimbiri brothers rose from the ground, as dingoes. The brothers were unhappy with the featureless landscape, which had no trees, animals, and people. So they made the first waterholes, without which life could not exist. Later, they used a toadstool and a fungus to shape the genitals of the first people, and instituted the rite of circumcision.

All this time, the Bagadjimbiri brothers were growing in size. When at last they became giants and their heads touched the sky, they felt the moment had come to explore the world. They travelled far and wide, until they encountered Ngariman, the cat man. The brothers found this creature so funny that they were paralyzed with laughter. However, Ngariman could not tolerate such an insult and, gathering together his relatives, he attacked and killed the two wanderers.

The earth goddess Dilga was moved by the plight of the Bagadjimbiri brothers. From her ample breasts flowed a torrent of milk, which erupted at the murder spot, drowned the culprits, and revived the two victims.

When the reborn Bagadjimbiri brothers eventually decided that they should leave the world, they dropped down and died. But their corpses turned into water snakes, and their spirits rose into the sky as great clouds. This occurred at the end of Alchera (Dreamtime), the period when the ancestral spirits of the Australian aboriginal tribes walked the earth.

See Gods and Animals, p.103 and Creation, p.135

SEE ALSO ALCHERA

BALDER

The wounded god of Germanic mythology. Renowned for his good looks and wisdom, he was a northern counterpart of the Canaanite Adonis and the Babylonian Tammuz. It was believed that Balder would return from the underworld only in a world made new after Ragnarok (the twilight of the gods).

Balder was the son of one-eyed ODIN and his second wife FRIGG, the goddess of married love. He was the favourite of the gods and married Nanna, an attendant of Freya, Odin's first wife.

At first, Balder led a happy life, but he began to be troubled by ominous dreams. Fearing for his safety, the gods sent Frigg to extract an oath from all things, whether living or inaminate, that they would do the young god no harm.

After this, the gods would amuse themselves by throwing things at Balder, knowing he was invulnerable. However, the trickster god LOKI discovered that Frigg had overlooked one plant, the mistletoe, thinking it was too weak to threaten her son. Out of spite, Loki persuaded Hodr, Balder's blind twin, to throw a shaft of mistletoe at his brother in sport, and guided his hand as he threw.

The dart felled Balder and the gods were thrown into confusion and uncertainty, until Frigg suggested that someone should ride to the underworld and arrange a ransom for her son.

Hermodr, another of Odin's sons, volunteered to visit Helheim (the land of the dead). Mounting Sleipnir, Odin's eight-legged steed, he rode swiftly toward his dreadful destination. For nine days and nights he galloped down ravines ever darker and deeper, meeting no one until he came to a golden bridge stretching across a broad river. There, he learned that Balder had passed over the bridge before him and so he continued to the underworld.

Unafraid, Hermodr rode to the hall of Hel, goddess of death, who allowed him to spend the night in Balder's company. The next morning, Hel told Hermodr that Balder would be released if all heaven shed a tear, and Hermodr returned to Asgard, the heavenly city, with the news.

The gods then dispatched messengers to every part of heaven asking all to weep for Balder, who was described as undead but detained below. However, Loki refused to comply, saying, "Let Hel hold what she has!"

As soon as Balder's body was placed on the burning ship of death, one of the traditional methods of cremation for a chieftain, Nanna joined her dead husband, dying on the same funeral pyre.

Such acts of self-destruction were customary among the Vikings. In 922 the Muslim traveller Ibn Fadlan witnessed a ceremony on the Volga river, down which the Vikings sailed into southern Russia. He recorded that the female slave of a dead chieftain elected to be strangled on the bed where his body lay, after which a flaming torch was applied to the ship in which the deathbed stood.

See Death, p.91 and Last Days, p.122

Mistletoe, the plant used to kill Balder

SEE ALSO ASGARD, FREYA, HEL, HELHEIM, HERMODR, HODR, NANNA, RAGNAROK, SLEIPNIR, TAMMUZ

BATARA GURU

The Malay name under which the Hindu god Shiva was known in southeast Asia, before the arrival of Islam.

Worship of SHIVA, one of the great gods of Hinduism, came to Java, Sumatra, the Malay peninsula and Bali from southern India some time before the fifth century. Inscriptions found in these places refer to the building of temples to Shiva, and often a local ruler is mentioned as a patron.

Whereas monks from India would have tried to maintain the purity of their doctrines about Shiva, the Malay peoples who adopted the god added their own myths. In Sumatra, for instance, the belief developed that Batara Guru created the earth by sending a handful of dust to his daughter, who had jumped from heaven into an immense ocean. When she threw the dust into the ocean, it rapidly formed a huge island, much to the annoyance of the sea serpent Naga Padoha. The sea serpent arched its enormous back and so made the island float away from its home.

So Batara Guru sent down more dust and a hero who placed an iron block on the sea serpent's back. Feeling the great weight bearing down on it, Naga Padoha writhed and twisted powerfully, but to no avail. It could not break free, nor could it move the island. What the movements caused though, were the formation of mountains and valleys. This is the origin of the belief that earthquakes were the result of attempts by Naga Padoha to defy Batara Guru.

Following the creation of the islands of the great southeast Asian archipelago, Batara Guru made animals and plants. His daughter and the hero he sent to pinion Naga Padoha became the parents of the first inhabitants, the Malay peoples.

Prior to his displacement by Allah, when Islam became the main religion, Batara Guru was the all-powerful sky deity. But he was sometimes identified with the ocean as well.

See Creation, p.135

BOBBI-BOBBI

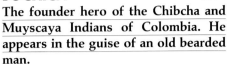

One of the ancestral deities of the Binbinga, a group of aboriginal peoples living in northern Australia.

In Alchera (Dreamtime) the spirits sleeping beneath the ground arose and wandered the earth, shaping the landscape, making man, and teaching the arts of survival. Once their work was done, these ancestral deities sank once more into sleep.

Aboriginal mythology records the actions of the ancestral spirits during this remote period. One aboriginal group, the Binbinga, remember how the snake Bobbi-bobbi once sent a number of flying foxes for men to eat. But these large bats flew high above the ground and escaped capture. To bring down the flying foxes, Bobbi-bobbi sacrificed one of his ribs and thus invented the boomerang. Using this marvellous weapon, which always returned to the thrower, the first members of the Binbinga killed the flying foxes and then cooked them.

This success must have made the early tribesmen rather arrogant, for one day they knocked a hole in the sky with the boomerang. Bobbi-bobbi was so angry at this misuse of his gift that he seized the rib when it fell back to earth. Two tribesmen foolishly tried to save the sacred weapon — and were swallowed by Bobbi-bobbi.

See Gods and Animals, p.103

Bobbi-bobbi is said to have invented the boomerang

SEE ALSO ALCHERA

BOCHICA

The founder hero of the Chibcha and Muyscaya Indians of Colombia. He appears in the guise of an old bearded man.

According to legend, Bochica introduced culture to the tribes living around what is now Bogota. He taught the people how to build houses and gave them laws by which they could live together in peace. However, the moon goddess Chia, Bochica's wife, undermined her husband's good work by leading weak individuals astray. A struggle for domination ensued between the couple, until Chia used her magic to make the rivers flood the homes of the Chibchas and Muyscayas.

Bochica gathered the few survivors of the deluge from the mountain tops and began the process of civilization all over again. To ensure that Chia could not repeat her tricks, he exiled her to the night sky.

Bochica then helped the people to recover from their initial setback and progress materially. After 2,000 years he was satisifed enough to withdraw from human affairs. Leaving his footprint on a rock as a reminder of his work, he disappeared into the west.

The exact nature of Bochica's divinity is hard to determine although he may well have been associated with the sun, which travels in a westerly direction. There can be little doubt that he was a sky god of some kind because at the moment of his victory over Chia's flood he appeared as the rainbow.

Other Chibcha legends suggest that Bochica was challenged by a host of deities, not just his wife. The most formidable of these was Formagata, the storm god, who was portrayed as a wild beast with four eyes, long ears and a tail.

The role of Bochica in his retirement is also obscure, although it is hinted that he might support the sky, like the Greek giant Atlas. Today, the descendants of the ancient Chibchas and Muyscayas say that the earth trembles whenever Bochica moves his shoulders. The Greek god POSEIDON is also associated with earthquakes.

See Founders, p.68 and Natural Phenomena, p.138

SEE ALSO ATLAS

BOR

In Germanic mythology, Bor was the father of Odin, Vili and Ve, the gods who made the world and mankind. His name means "born".

In the beginning there were only two parts to the cosmos: Muspellheim (the land of the fire giants) in the south, and Niflheim, a foggy land of snow and ice in the north. Between them stretched a void, the immense emptiness of Ginnungagap.

Eventually, the warm air blowing from Muspellheim met the cold pouring off the glaciers of Niflheim and formed a sea of rain and melted snow in the void. The first of all living beings, an enormous giant called Ymir, emerged from this warm water.

Under his left arm Ymir grew the first man and woman, both giants, while the family of frost giants came from his two legs. Ymir also looked after the primeval cow Audumla (the nourisher), whose milk sustained him. Audumla started to lick the iceblocks, and by the beginning of the first day, a man's hair appeared at the spot where she had been licking. On the second day a man's head emerged and on the third, an entire man. This was Buri (the born one).

Buri had a son called Bor, who married Bresla, a daughter of the frost giants. The couple had three sons: ODIN was the god of battle, magic, inspiration and the dead; his younger brothers were Vili and Ve, who took over Odin's duties and privileges whenever his wanderings developed into a protracted absence.

These semi-giants immediately declared war on the giants. First they killed Ymir. The tidal wave of blood that rushed from his body drowned all the giants, except Bergelmir and his wife.

The deluge filled Ginnungagap and left enough to form the sea and lakes. Then, from Ymir's body, Bor's sons made the world, called Midgard (middle region), which included Mannheim (the land of men). Ymir's flesh became the ground, his bones the mountains, his teeth and jaws the rocks and stones, his skull the sky. The latter was supported by four dwarfs, rather than by a single supernatural figure such as the Greek giant Atlas. Midgard was protected from the remaining giants by a wall, made from Ymir's eyebrows.

Mankind was created from two trees on the seashore, or from two logs of driftwood, which were whittled into shape. Then each of Bor's sons gave mankind certain gifts: Odin bestowed the soul; Vili, understanding and the emotions; and Ve, the senses and form.

Dwarfs evolved from the maggots in Ymir's corpse. The sons of Bor were content to let them spread underground, just as they allowed mankind to reproduce on the surface of the earth. For their own residence, the sons of Bor built Asgard, the city of the gods.

See Creation, p.135 and Giants, p.159

The wooden prow from a Viking ship

SEE ALSO ASGARD, ATLAS, AUDUMLA, BERGELMIR, BURI, GINNUNGAGAP, MANNHEIM, MIDGARD, MUSPELLHEIM, VE, VILI, YMIR

BRAHMA

The first member of the Hindu triad, which also contains Vishnu the Preserver and Shiva the Destroyer. Brahma is also called Prajapati (lord and father of all creatures), and is regarded as the greatest of all sages. The sages themselves are often called "the mind-born sons of Brahma".

Said to have sprung from a golden egg which floated in the primeval waters, Brahma's creation, as the first god, is explained in terms of an upsurge of consciousness, a welling up of the primeval essence, the unconditioned, self-existent substance (*brahman*).

When he was born, Brahma had one head, but when his wife Saraswati was born, she was so beautiful that he grew four more faces, so that he could see her on every side of him. The fifth face was burned off by the fire of SHIVA's third eye because he spoke disrespectfully to him. In his four hands Brahma holds a sceptre (or a rosary), a bow, an alms-bowl, and the *Rig Veda*, the ancient scriptures.

As Purusha (the cosmic man), Brahma created mankind with Saraswati. Once he had made the world, it remained unaltered for one of his days. During one of his nights there was a steady deterioration which ended in general destruction. A day and night of Brahma is known as a *kalpa*, and is the equivalent of 8,640,000 years.

SEE ALSO SARASWATI

Apart from the gods, the wise and the elements, the world is consumed by fire at each end of a *kalpa*, after which Brahma restores creation. Some Hindu cosmologists say that we are approaching the end of a *kalpa*, although our dark age, the Kali Yuga, has millions of years yet to run.

Now a somewhat remote figure, Brahma has lost his creative powers to Shiva and VISHNU as well as to the great goddess DEVI. A myth that illustrates his displacement by Shiva concerns the origin of the lingam, the phallic stone pillar sacred to Shiva. According to the story, an argument raged between Brahma and Vishnu as to who was the creator of the universe. Their bitter quarrel was finally interrupted when a towering lingam crowned with flame rose from the depths of the cosmic ocean. When Brahma and Vishnu investigated it, the cosmic phallus burst apart, and in a cave-like sanctuary deep within they found the ultimate creator – Shiva.

See Creation, p.135

Brahma, the Creator in the Hindu pantheon

BRAN

The prince of Irish mythology who sailed through incredible adventures before returning home after an absence of centuries. He is the Irish equivalent of the Greek voyager Odysseus.

The Voyage of Bran, an essentially pre-Christian story dated to the eighth century, tells of Bran's strange expedition. The saga begins with a silver branch covered in white blossom, a beautiful woman clad in strange clothes, and her song of the wonders to be found in the lands beyond the sea.

Enticed by the song's promise, Bran and his three foster brothers set sail with 27 warriors. They soon encountered the sea god MANANNAN and shortly afterward reached the Island of Joy.

Bran was particularly delighted with their next port of call, the Land of Women. But, after staying there for what seemed like a year, the crew wanted to return home. In fact, centuries had passed and the voyagers were warned that if they set foot on Ireland again they would age accordingly. Indeed, on their return, one member of the crew leaped ashore and immediately turned to dust.

Realizing that there was no chance of returning to human society, Bran wrote an account of his travels, threw it onto the shore and then cast off for an endless voyage through mysterious islands where sorrow, sickness and death were unknown.

An earlier though less well-known voyage tale was that of Maeldun, the son of a raider and a nun. The purpose of Maeldun's voyage was to find his father's murderers and avenge his death. However, blown off course by a storm, he visited islands occupied by a variety of strange creatures; on other islands he saw strange natural phenomena and his youth was renewed by bathing in a natural lake. Nearing home again, Maeldun caught up with his father's killers but he granted them mercy and made peace.

Maeldun's expedition may have served as the model for the Christian epic, *The Voyage of Brendan*, one of the most popular stories in the Middle Ages.

See Quests, p.64

SEE ALSO MAELDUN

BRIGIT

In Irish mythology, Brigit (or Brigid) was the daughter of Dagda, the father of the gods. She was the goddess of healing, fire, smiths, poetry, wisdom and fertility. In the sixth century, her generosity was inherited by St Brigit.

Above all, Brigit is a goddess of creativity, the protectress of culture and the essentials of civilized life. Her festival, a pastoral celebration, was one of the greatest in the Celtic world. Connected with ewes coming into milk, it reminded her devotees of the continuity and renewal that was necessary for the maintenance of daily life.

In many Irish legends, Brigit seems to be an alternative for her mother, Dana, and it has been suggested that they were different aspects of the same mother goddess.

St Brigit (450–523), one of the three patron saints of Ireland, may originally have been a priestess of the goddess Brigit, and indeed St Brigit's Day is the old festival of spring. The saint's father was a local chieftain who sold her, along with her mother, to a druid.

When the pagan priest was converted to Christianity, Brigit was freed. Returning to her father's house, she became, like her mother before her, a serving girl, looking after the dairy and milking the cows. While there, she is supposed to have invented weaving.

Brigit's cooking soon displayed a miraculous ingenuity, for she was able to feed hungry animals without any reduction in the meals she prepared for the chieftain's table. Her thoughts were full of good wishes and became legendary. She wished for "a great lake of ale for the King of Kings … the family of heaven drinking it through all time", for "Jesus to be among these cheerful folk" and for "vessels full of alms to be given away".

In fact, Brigit fed and gave to the poor so enthusiastically that she was the despair of her father, who endeavoured to marry her off but without success. Eventually, the king recognized the depth of her sincerity and gave her permission to found an order of nuns at Kildare.

The goddess Brigit was associated with the ritual fires of purification, whereas the Christian saint was believed to tend the holy fire along with nineteen nuns. After her death, the nuns kept the fire at the shrine of St Brigit alight.

JESUS's command, "Go and sell that thou hast, and give to the poor, and thou shalt have treasure in heaven: and come and follow me", inspired St Brigit just as it had St Anthony, 300 years earlier in Egypt. However, whereas he retreated to the desert the Irish nun continued the Celtic mother goddess's tradition of largesse by providing the essentials of existence.

St Bride, or St Brigit, as painted by John Duncan

SEE ALSO DANA, ST ANTHONY

BUDDHA

Literally, "the enlightened one". A figure who rose to importance in India and whose doctrines spread to form the basis of a world religion. The central doctrine is that the individual possesses the means to personal salvation. Legend relates that a north Indian prince, Gautama Siddhartha (*c*.563–479 BC), became Buddha.

Buddha never denied the Hindu pantheon and claimed that in earlier lives he had been INDRA, the Hindu sky god.

As the moment approached for the birth of Buddha, earthquakes and miracles testified to his divine ancestry. His mother, Maya, queen of a small kingdom on the modern Indo-Nepalese border, dreamed that she saw Siddhartha, the future Buddha, come down into her womb in the form of a white elephant.

This dream (which amounted to a miraculous conception) and the corresponding natural signs, were interpreted by 64 brahmins, who predicted the birth of a son who would grow up as a world monarch or, if he were made aware of the sufferings of mankind, a world saviour.

According to one legend, Maya died seven days after giving birth to the prince. Having attained supreme knowledge, and out of filial piety, Buddha ascended to heaven and remained there for three months, preaching the law to his mother.

Mindful of the prophecy that the young prince would not become a great ruler if he saw the pain of the world, Siddhartha's father did his utmost to shield him from the outside world. He built a costly palace in which all possible pleasures were offered to beguile the youth, and even the use of words such as "death" and "grief" was forbidden.

When Siddhartha expressed a wish to see the outside world, the king took him to a nearby town, but first ordered the streets to be swept clean, decorated with flowers, and emptied of everything unpleasant. Despite his father's efforts, Siddhartha saw an invalid, an old man and a corpse being carried to the cremation ground, and was shocked to learn that people get sick, grow old and die.

To take his mind off this revelation, the king arranged a marriage for him with a beautiful princess, who bore his son. But the name Siddhartha chose for their son – Rahula, meaning "a bond" – indicated that, despite all his father's efforts to distract him, Siddartha felt a prisoner inside the palace.

One night, while wandering through the palace, he saw dancing girls sleeping off the excesses of the evening, in contrast to their delicate pretty movements while dancing. Siddhartha decided to abandon his throne, family and offspring and seek the real world. He cut off his hair and changed his name to Gautama.

Gautama became a wandering ascetic, bent on discovering the nature of the world. For six years he tried the way of physical suffering, without success. So he went to Bodh Gaya, where there was a fig tree known as the Tree of Wisdom. He resolved to sit in meditation beneath the tree until he completed his quest.

While Gautama meditated, the demon MARA tried to lead him into temptation, like SATAN in Christian myth, who assailed St Anthony while he was meditating in the Egyptian desert. Mara sent his beautiful daughters to seduce Buddha, who resisted them. Mara then threatened Buddha with monstrous devils, but they failed to disturb his concentration. In final desperation at his unassailable calm, Mara hurled the ultimate demonic weapon at him, a fiery discus which had the power of cutting through mountains. But it turned into a canopy of flowers and floated over Gautama's head.

For five weeks the contemplation lasted. Gautama even sat through a world-shaking storm, protected from it by Muchalinda the serpent king, whose massive hood is often shown covering the meditating monk. After the fifth week, Gautama achieved enlightenment – he understood the roots of suffering and saw that to avoid it one had to reach a state of desirelessness. So he became Buddha, the one who is released from all suffering and from the cycle of reincarnation.

Buddha was faced with a choice. Either he could enter *nirvana*, the undisturbed condition of supreme consciousness, and leave the world, or, renouncing personal deliverance for the moment, he could show the way to his fellow humans. Mara urged the first, BRAHMA the second. Finally, Buddha yielded to the creator god's entreaties. He began to travel and teach, founding a monastic order as well as preparing the framework for the Buddhist era of Indian civilization.

After the death of Buddha, the faith was divided and within the competing schools of thought the Buddhist mythology was developed further. Other incarnations of Buddha were worshipped, such as AVALOKITESVARA, a bodhisattva, or Buddha-to-be. In China the bodhisattva Manjusri is believed to lead suffering beings to enlightenment. Like him, in India and east Asia, is the bodhisattva Ksitigarbha who wanders through the realms of hell comforting tortured souls.

Some sects believe in a future Buddha, called Maitreya. In Japan, this final saviour is called Fugen-bosatsu. There is also a primordial, self-existent Buddha called Amitabha, who is known in Japan as Amida-nyorai.

See Saviours, p.75

A fifth-century, rock-cut Buddha, Sri Lanka

SEE ALSO AMIDA-NYORAI, AMITABHA, ST ANTHONY, FUGEN-BOSATSU, MAITREYA, MANJUSRI, MAYA, MUCHALINDA

Saviours

The idea of a bringer of salvation is deeply rooted in human consciousness. Every culture contains a perfect and powerful figure who saves mankind from sin and eternal punishment.

A 15th-century gilt-bronze Buddha. The Buddhist idea of the saviour is the epitome of compassion. Bodhisattvas – Buddhas-to-be – refuse personal salvation and elect to remain in the world, to help suffering humanity along the path to enlightenment and liberation from the wheel of reincarnation.

Devotees place offerings at the feet of a colossal statue of Mahavira, the Jaina saviour who died in about 526 BC.

Zoroastrian priests carried a bull-headed mace representing Mithra, the ally of the saviour Saoshyant.

The Hindu saviour Vishnu, incarnated as a turtle, recovered all the treasures lost in the great flood. He reappears to rescue the world whenever it is in danger.

Cross-bearers leaving a Mexican church at Easter re-enact the Passion of the Christian saviour Jesus Christ.

CADMUS

One of the famous heroes of ancient Greece, and the founder of the city of Thebes in Boeotia, in central Greece.

Cadmus was the son of Agenor, King of Tyre, and brother of EUROPA. When Europa was abducted by ZEUS in the shape of a bull, Cadmus and his four brothers were sent after her. On consulting the oracle at Delphi, Cadmus was told to forget about Europa, who was hidden in a cave on the island of Crete. Instead, he was to find a cow marked with a moon-shaped sign on its flank. He was to follow the cow and found a city on the spot where she settled.

This Cadmus did, and the cow finally stopped in Boeotia, in central Greece. Cadmus decided to sacrifice the cow to ATHENA and sent his followers to collect water from a nearby spring. But the spring was guarded by a dragon, or serpent, sacred to ARES, and it ate the men alive.

Cadmus then killed the creature himself, whereupon Athena appeared and advised him to remove the serpent's teeth and sow half of them in the ground. When he obeyed, armed men sprang up. He overcame them by setting them against each other. The five surviving warriors became the ancestors of the Theban aristocracy.

Cadmus was obliged to serve Ares for eight years as a penance for killing the guardian monster. Once this was over, though, Athena made Cadmus the king of Thebes and gave him splendid gifts.

Because of its bloody foundation, some guilt may have clung to the city, for of all ancient Greek cities Thebes was most troubled by legendary events. One of these occurred when Cadmus's grandson and successor, Pentheus, fell foul of DIONYSUS, whose divinity he refused to recognize. Pentheus attempted to stop the worship of Dionysus, but was torn to pieces by the frenzied worshippers, the maenads – in their hysteria they mistook him for a mountain lion. Among the maenads was his own mother.

A number of stories exist about the end of Cadmus himself. Having abdicated, he may have moved northwestward to Illyria and founded another city there. Or he could have lived in another part of Boeotia.

Ares was thought to have transformed the tottering old Cadmus into a snake, a fitting form for a great hero, according to the ancient Greeks.

The respect accorded to Cadmus reflects his importance as a cultural hero. He was credited with the introduction into Europe of an alphabet of sixteen letters. This gift also indicates how much progress in Greece was due to borrowing from West Asian neighbours.

See Founders, p.68

Cadmus battles with the serpent at the spring

SEE ALSO AGENOR, DELPHI, PENTHEUS

CASSANDRA

The most beautiful of the daughters of the Trojan king and queen, Priam and Hecuba. Cassandra (or Alexandra) was a prophetess who was never believed.

Several foreign leaders fought on the Trojan side during the Greek siege because of Cassandra's beauty. Such were her looks that, even as a child when she slept in his temple, the god Apollo fell deeply in love with her and endowed Cassandra with the gift of prophecy. In the morning, Cassandra was discovered with numerous snakes, whose tongues had passed on secret knowledge by licking her ears.

Later, when Cassandra had grown into a young woman, Apollo tried to claim her as his own. He was shocked to discover that she preferred virginity and denied owing him any gratitude for his gift. She agreed to give Apollo a kiss, whereupon the breath he breathed into her removed the power of belief.

As a result, the trances Cassandra went into before predicting events were regarded as madness. She foretold the harm Paris would bring to Troy by eloping with HELEN, but her words were unheeded. Most dramatic of all was her warning about the wooden horse, the stratagem devised by ODYSSEUS to gain entry into Troy. Even though the armour of the Greek warriors hidden inside its belly was heard to clash aloud, Apollo made sure that Cassandra's warnings were ignored.

After the fall of Troy, the distraught prophetess was raped by Aias, a Greek warrior from Locris. He dared to commit this outrage in the temple of ATHENA. During the struggle, even the statue of the goddess was overturned, a sacrilege for which many Greeks suffered on the journey home.

Cassandra was awarded to Agamemnon, leader of the Greeks, and as a concubine she bore him two sons. He eventually took her back to his home in Mycenae, where she was killed by his wife Clytemnestra. Before this event, however, Cassandra foretold her own fate and that of Agamemnon, who was later also a victim of palace intrigue.

See Seers, pp.82/83

SEE ALSO AGAMEMNON, CLYTEMNESTRA, HECUBA, PARIS

CASTOR

Castor and Polydeuces (Pollux to the Romans) were the heavenly twins, and the brothers of Helen, the cause of the Trojan War.

The two heroes were sons of Leda and were twins. However, they were also half-brothers: Polydeuces was born of ZEUS, and Castor of the Spartan king Tyndareus.

Castor and Polydeuces travelled with JASON and the Argonauts in quest of the golden fleece, and helped Jason to campaign against his enemies at home when the voyagers returned. They were involved, too, in the rescue of their sister HELEN when THESEUS carried her off to Attica.

Their most famous exploit was an attempted abduction. The twins aspired to marry their cousins, Phoebe and Hilaria, who were already betrothed to the princes Idas and Lynceus. Nevertheless, Castor and Polydeuces carried them both off to Sparta, which sparked off a bitter feud. In the final confrontation, Idas and Lynceus were slain, but Castor himself received a fatal spear-thrust.

Polydeuces was so distraught at being parted from Castor that he offered to share his immortality with him. Zeus took pity on them and agreed that Castor should spend one day in the underworld and one day in heaven, by turn.

The Romans were great devotees of Castor and Pollux. They even believed that the divine heroes aided them personally on the battlefield.

See Heroes, p.55

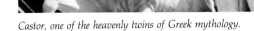

Castor, one of the heavenly twins of Greek mythology.

CHUKU

The supreme deity of the Ibo peoples of eastern Nigeria, Chuku means "great spirit". He is essentially benign.

Another name for Chuku, used in prayer, is Chineke (the creator). The Ibo consider that Chuku created an earthly paradise in which neither evil nor death could harm mankind. Like many African tribes, they explain the advent of death as an accident.

A messenger myth tells the story. Chuku once sent a dog to mankind with the instruction that if anyone died, the body should be placed upon the ground and strewn with ashes. After this, the dead person would come back to life. On his journey, the dog was weakened with hunger and tiredness, and was delayed.

To ensure that the instruction reached men in time, Chuku sent a sheep with the same message. But the sheep stopped to eat, and by the time it came to mankind, it had forgotten the correct wording. It told men to bury the dead, rather than cover a corpse with ashes as it lay on the ground.

When at last the dog arrived with the proper instruction, no one would listen, because the first corpse had already been buried. So death entered the world forever.

Chuku receives offerings and sacrifices beneath trees, in the wild and near dwellings. His daughter Ale, the earth goddess, is also propitiated in the same locations.

See Death, p.91

CIRCE

The divine enchantress of Odysseus on his long journey home to Ithaca, from Troy. She was the daughter of the Greek sun god Helios.

Circe possessed great magical powers which she used to transform her enemies, or those who offended her, into animals. When ODYSSEUS's men arrived at her house, they found wolves and lions wandering around. What the Greek voyagers did not at first realize was that these creatures were the victims of Circe's magic.

As soon as the new arrivals were feasted by Circe, who had introduced a powerful drug into the wine, they lost all memory of their native land and turned into swine. Fortunately, one man from this scouting party saw these events from a distance and reported them to Odysseus, who had remained in his ship anchored on the shore.

Undismayed, Odysseus set off to rescue his men, but on the way was lucky enough to meet HERMES, the deity who protected travellers. In order to strengthen Odysseus against the magic of Circe, the god gave him a herb which had a black root and a white flower. Hermes also warned him to make Circe promise to behave properly toward her guests.

When Circe discovered that Odysseus was immune to the workings of her drug, she was amazed. Under threat, the enchantress agreed to offer Odysseus no harm, and consented to return his men to human shape too. Moreover, Circe gave a banquet for them all and a fair wind as they set sail from her island.

In Homer's *Odyssey*, the account of his voyage home, Odysseus reflects on the enchantress: "Circe of the lovely tresses, human though she seemed, proved her powers as a goddess by furnishing us with a helpful breeze, which arose astern and filled the sail of our blue-prowed ship." Circe also helped Odysseus by giving him instructions for reaching the underworld, the realm of HADES, where Odysseus wanted to consult the spirit of the dead seer Tiresias.

Circe's island was identified with Monte Circeo in Italy. The Romans believed that Odysseus stayed there a number of years and fathered three sons with Circe.

COATLICUE

The earth goddess of the Aztec conquerors of Mexico and the mother of Huitzilopochtli, their tribal war god. Her name means "serpent skirt".

Coatlicue's appearance was particularly horrible. Her skirt was composed of snakes and her necklace of hearts torn from sacrificial victims, severed hands and a skull. Her hands and feet ended in sharp claws and her breasts were flabby.

The devouring goddess of Aztec nightmare, Coatlicue was sated only with human flesh and blood and was thus a deity for whom sacrifice was a pressing necessity. The Aztecs' "flower wars", fought with the intention of taking prisoners for divine sacrifice, ensured she had ample victims.

A wife of Mixcoatl, the cloud serpent and god of the chase, Coatlicue was magically impregnated with HUITZILOPOCHTLI. One day, she was busy sweeping when a feathery ball fell near her. Coatlicue tucked the toy into the top of her dress and later, looking for it, found instead that she was with child. The news of Coatlicue's pregnancy offended her existing offspring, and all 400 sons and daughters resolved that their dishonoured mother must die.

However, the unborn Huitzilopochtli advised his mother to take refuge in a cave. When the 400 children attacked, he emerged from her womb fully armed and slaughtered many of his older brothers and sisters. Eventually, Coatlicue's children accepted Huitzilopochtli's seniority and even the corn god XIPETOTEC gave way to him as lord of the maize harvest.

Xipetotec assisted Coatlicue in ensuring the Aztecs' staple harvest. Their relationship is similar to that of the Greek deities Triptolemus and DEMETER. Coatlicue is even more similar to the Hindu goddess DEVI, because she embodied both the womb and the tomb. Although Coatlicue often dealt benignly with mankind, her savagery knew no bounds. Like Kali, Devi's dark manifestation, she could enjoy a world seething with the blood of sacrificed victims.

See Serpents, p.115

SEE ALSO KALI, MIXCOATL, TRIPTOLEMUS

Trickster Gods

Trickery, dishonesty and deviousness are found in all mythologies. However, cunning is not always used for evil ends – the Indian monkey god, Hanuman, for example, uses his subtle wit to aid the forces of good.

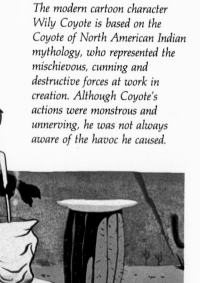

The Norse mischief-maker Loki was finally captured and bound by the gods in order to prevent his causing further chaos. By this time, however, Ragnarok, the twilight of the gods and the end of the world, was upon them all. Although as "the father of lies" Loki was known to be dishonest, the gods had been slow to realize how evil he was in fact.

The modern cartoon character Wily Coyote is based on the Coyote of North American Indian mythology, who represented the mischievous, cunning and destructive forces at work in creation. Although Coyote's actions were monstrous and unnerving, he was not always aware of the havoc he caused.

Hanuman, the trickster god of Hindu and Chinese Buddhist mythology, guided the Chinese pilgrim Tripitaka to India to obtain the Buddhist scriptures. A Chinese TV series Monkey, *based on his adventures, proved highly popular among young western audiences.*

Brer Rabbit, a benign trickster of North American folklore, was introduced to that continent by African slaves.

COYOTE

The trickster god of the North American Indians of the western and southwestern United States. A mischievous, cunning deity, he caused numerous disasters to befall the world.

The North American Indians commonly believed that animals were the original inhabitants of the land. They were thought to have been exactly like their human successors except that they were much bigger and could put on and take off their furlike clothes. However, when mankind was created, these giant animals simply became the ancestors of present-day creatures. Coyote was once such an ancestor.

The Maidu Indians of California believe that even the creator deity Wonomi was pushed aside by Coyote. The trickster god's precedence was due not to his strength but, as Wonomi sadly admitted, because mankind preferred Coyote to himself.

After the creation of the world, Coyote emerged from the ground and watched Wonomi make the first man and woman. He then challenged Wonomi by following suit, but his pair of human beings were blind. Laughingly, the trickster god then watched the easy way of life that Wonomi had given to mankind and decided that it would be much more interesting to introduce sickness, sorrow and death to the scheme of creation.

Coyote was even pleased when the first person to die was his own son, who was bitten by a snake. He may have expected to revive the corpse by submerging it in a lake, a method of rejuvenation which Wonomi had shown to mankind. When the boy remained lifeless, Coyote simply left the corpse to rot.

In despair, Wonomi accepted that Coyote would be a permanent thorn in his side and retired from an active role in the world. But another version of the story tells how Coyote killed himself so that he might roam free as a spirit. The Sioux Indians credit Coyote with introducing the horse to mankind.

See Trickster Gods, pp.78/79, and Creation, p.135

SEE ALSO WONOMI

CUCHULAINN

A semi-divine hero of old Irish sagas. He represents the archetypal warrior, a handsome man who was transformed into an appalling foe when the battle frenzy seized him.

Cuchulainn's parents were the sun god LUGH and Dechtire, the wife of an Ulster chieftain. Lugh appeared before Dechtire in a dream on her wedding night and changed her and fifty of her handmaidens into a flock of birds. He then led them to an enchanted place where they stayed for three years. On her return, Dechtire persuaded her mortal husband to accept her son as his own.

The child was Cuchulainn, who grew into a handsome youth of extraordinary stature and gaiety. However, on the battlefield Cuchulainn's appearance underwent a dreadful change: his body trembled terribly; his heels and calves appeared in front; one eye receded into his head while the other stood out huge and red on his cheek; he could catch an opponent's head between his jaws; his hair bristled like hawthorn, with a drop of blood on the tip of each hair; and a thick column of blood rose from the top of his head like the dark mast of a ship.

Cuchulainn earned his name, which means "the hound of Culann", when a young man. Arriving late at the residence of Culann, the smith god, he was attacked by the great hound that guarded the gates. When Culann discovered that the hero had killed his dog, he was beside himself with anger until Cuchulainn offered to act as his hound while another dog was trained.

The old heroes of Ireland were fierce headhunters, daring cattle rustlers and mighty eaters. Their contests were conducted on a superhuman level, but no one could challenge Cuchulainn, who always took the most heads, the accolade of the warrior. Headhunting may have been connected with the belief that the head was the seat of a person's spirit, and therefore a trophy to preserve in oil and flaunt before one's enemies. There are stories of warriors refusing to part with a head even for its weight in gold.

Between his frequent adventures, Cuchulainn fell in love with Emer, daughter of Forgall, a wily chieftain. Forgall did not want Emer to marry the hero and so sent him away to train under a famous warrior in Scotland.

Having completed his training, and experienced numerous adventures, Cuchulainn returned to claim Emer's hand, but Forgall refused it. The enraged hero killed Forgall and many of his followers before at last Emer became his wife. Although other women still fell in love with Cuchulainn, Emer always succeeded in winning back his affections.

On one occasion, when his enemy was too terrified to face him, women succeeded in cooling Cuchulainn's battle frenzy. The hero was circling the great fortress of Emain Macha in his head-festooned war chariot, crying out for blood and striking terror into the hearts of all who listened. Several naked women were sent out from Emain Macha carrying three vats of cold water. Embarrassed, the hero looked away and at once the women bundled him into the vats. The first exploded, the second boiled, but the third only became very hot. Thus, Cuchulainn was subdued and the fortress was saved.

Cuchulainn was chiefly famous for his single-handed defence of Ulster against the combined forces of the rest of Ireland. Time and again he threw back the invaders, but even the hero's great courage and strength proved insufficient against the war goddess Morrigan. Cuchulainn's indifference to her amorous advances sealed his fate. He was assaulted by innumerable foes and in the final moments of the fight was so exhausted that he had to strap himself to a rock. His enemies cut him down but dared to touch his corpse only after Morrigan settled on it as a crow.

The revenge of Morrigan was a favourite theme of Irish poets. In some versions of the story, Cuchulainn managed to wound the goddess, an unpardonable offence.

The cycle of tales about the hero Cuchulainn greatly influenced the development of the tradition surrounding ARTHUR in Wales, Brittany and England.

See Heroes, p.55

SEE ALSO DECHTIRE, EMER, MORRIGAN

CYBELE

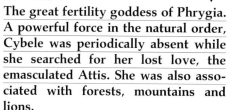

The great fertility goddess of Phrygia. A powerful force in the natural order, Cybele was periodically absent while she searched for her lost love, the emasculated Attis. She was also associated with forests, mountains and lions.

The cult of Cybele, brought to Rome in 204 BC on the advice of the oracle at Delphi, provided an escape from the dour, impersonal character of Roman religion. One of the so-called "mystery" religions which the Romans imported from the eastern Mediterranean, it enabled devotees to recognize their personal aspirations through apparently irrational rites.

Worship of Cybele and her castrated lover ATTIS offered the initiate entry to a state of blessedness that was thought to endure beyond the grave. However, it was not until the reign of the emperor Claudius AD 41–54) that Attis was accorded equal status in the cult.

Cybele's devotees were undoubtedly intrigued by her tempestuous love affair with Attis, and her vengeance on him for his infidelity is an ever-recurring legendary theme. When Cybele discovered Attis's admiration for a nymph, she made him suffer madness, self-emasculation and death, before agreeing to take him back as her consort.

The Romans, unused to West Asian traditions of a eunuch priesthood, were horrified that Cybele's devotees followed the same ritual path. During her festival, held each March, a pine tree was brought to her temple where it was cut, wrapped in bandages, and decorated with flowers and an effigy of Attis. The god's castration and death were celebrated with frantic dances and blood-letting, including self-castration; a carnival was held in honour of his resurrection and the festival closed with the ritual bathing of Cybele's image.

The ceremony of the *taurobolium* or *criobolium*, in which the devotee bathed in the blood of a sacrificed bull or lamb, was a later addition to the cult and became especially popular during the pagan revival toward the end of the fourth century.

See Love and Fertility, pp.106/107

SEE ALSO DELPHI

CYCLOPES

The gigantic one-eyed beings of Greek mythology. Their name means "circle-eyed".

There are two different traditions about the Cyclopes. According to the first, Ouranos (sky) and Gaia (earth) produced, among other children, three giants with one eye in the middle of their forehead: they were Arges (bright), Brontes (thunderer), and Steropes (lightning-maker).

Ouranos imprisoned these three giants, because he feared that they would depose him. He hid them in the abyss of Tartarus, together with other powerful creations. Gaia plotted to avenge this act with the aid of one of her children, KRONOS. Ouranos was overthrown, and Kronos released the Cyclopes for a period of time, but when he feared for his own rule, he cast them into Tartarus again.

When Kronos was overthrown, in turn, by ZEUS, his youngest son, the Cyclopes were freed permanently. In gratitude they became Zeus's servants and the makers of his thunderbolts. They also made wonderful objects for the brothers of Zeus: POSEIDON's trident and HADES' cap of invisibility.

In the second tradition, the Cyclopes were savage and lawless pastoralists. When the wanderer ODYSSEUS visited Sicily, he found the cyclops Polyphemus both inhospitable and cruel – Polyphemus ate six members of his crew, and out of courtesy offered to eat Odysseus last. The resourceful Odysseus got the cyclops drunk and blinded his one eye with the heated point of a stake. He then clung to the underside of a sheep in Polyphemus's cave. The next morning, when the sheep left the cave, Polyphemus passed his hand along only the top of the sheep, and so Odysseus escaped.

The Cyclopes were skilled workers. They were credited by the Greeks with building the massive fortifications at Tiryns and Mycenae in the Peloponnese. The Romans believed that they assisted Vulcan as smiths at his forge, deep in Mount Etna.

See Giants, p.159

SEE ALSO ETNA, GAIA, OURANOS, POLYPHEMUS, STEROPES, VULCAN

DAEDALUS

A legendary Greek craftsman, whose name means "cunning" or "ingenious", Daedalus was looked upon as a great inventor. Among his best-known creations was the Minotaur's labyrinth in Crete. He was also the father of Icarus.

Daedalus's skills included the building of splendid palaces, the construction of impressive machines, and the making of works of art. His statues were so lifelike that they had to be chained in order to stop them from running away.

Despite his renowned talents, the competition from his nephew Talus unsettled Daedalus. When the young apprentice invented the saw, by copying the jaw of a serpent, Daedalus killed him in a fit of jealousy. This quarrel possibly refers to some ancient rivalry over the invention of metal tools. The Greeks, like other ancient peoples, were conscious that they were dependent on such recent advances in technology.

Certainly the services of a talented man like Daedalus were appreciated by ancient rulers. At the command of MINOS, the Cretan king, Daedalus designed and built the labyrinth as a home for the Minotaur. This monstrous creature, half man and half bull, was born of the strange love of Pasiphae, Minos's queen, for a bull.

Minos had asked POSEIDON for a sign when he was seeking the throne, and it happened that a wonderful bull emerged from the sea. Because Minos neglected to sacrifice the bull to the sea god, Pasiphae was cursed with an ungovernable passion for it. So Daedalus made a wooden cow covered with hide, and Pasiphae climbed inside it to entice the bull.

Whether is was due to this piece of cunning handiwork, or because, on another occasion, Daedalus revealed the layout of the labyrinth to THESEUS, Minos was so angered that he threw Daedalus and his son Icarus into prison. They escaped when Daedalus constructed wings for himself and his son.

The wings were made from feathers embedded in wax, so Daedalus cautioned Icarus to fly carefully. They had to beware of the heat of the sun on the wax, and the weight of seaspray on the feathers. But, exhilarated by the experience of flight, Icarus flew too high. The wax melted, his wings fell apart, and he plunged into the sea. After seeing to the burial of his son, Daedalus went and hid in Sicily.

Knowing that the great inventor could not resist a problem, Minos set sail with a shell, and whenever he put into port, promised to reward anyone who could pass a thread through it. When Minos presented the challenge at a Sicilian court, Daedalus rose to it and was thus revealed.

Overawed by the fleet of Minos, the local king agreed to give up the inventor. But first, according to custom, Minos was offered a bath, in which the king's daughters were to bathe him. These princesses were unwilling to lose Daedalus, who made them beautiful toys, and with his help they plotted Minos's death. Inventive as ever, Daedalus laid a pipe through the roof of the bathroom, down which they poured boiling water, or oil, upon the unsuspecting Minos.

The determination of Minos in his pursuit of Daedalus is hardly surprising. As a great architect and engineer, Daedalus was a potentially dangerous man in the court of any rival ruler. This was clearly the case if we accept the version of the legend that says he escaped from Crete by inventing sails, rather than wings, for then Daedalus would have invented the means of adding power to the war galley.

See Craftsmen and Smith Gods, p.154

Daedalus and his son Icarus, by Canova

SEE ALSO ICARUS, MINOTAUR, PASIPHAE, TALUS

DAGDA

In Irish mythology, the father of the gods. A kindly figure, his name means "the good god". He was portrayed as a fat man dressed in simple attire, dragging a gigantic club on wheels.

Dagda was Ruad Ro-fhessa (lord of perfect knowledge), and was therefore patron of the druids. As Ollathair (all-father), he ruled over an already created world. The source of fertility, he sustained mankind, but also apportioned death. He could kill nine men at a time with his club, but with the other end he restored them to life.

Dagda had several typically Celtic magical possessions, including a powerful harp, two marvellous pigs, ever-laden fruit trees and an inexhaustible cauldron which represented material abundance and the restoration of life. A parallel cauldron was that of Annwn, lord of the Welsh underworld.

Dagda, the son of Dana, was the chief of the Tuatha De Danaan, "the peoples of the goddess Dana", who were continually at war against the Fomorii, a race of evil beings. The Fomorii once stole Dagda's harp and the god, together with his son Ogma, the god of eloquence, and LUGH, the sun god, set off in search of it. He found it in the dwelling-place of the Fomorii and, entering their great hall, demanded its return. Before the Fomorii could reply, the harp leapt from the wall, killed those who had put it there and then sang a tune so sad that it put all the Fomorii to sleep.

Accounts of Dagda's actions on the battlefield are contradictory. At the first battle of Magh Tuireadh, "the plain of towers", he slew countless numbers of the enemy, helped by the crowlike form of the war goddess Morrigan, who delighted in the terror of the fray.

At the second battle of Magh Tuireadh, Dagda degenerated into an old man, burdened with excessive weight. Ignoring the battle, he busied himself with the contents of his cauldron which held 80 gallons of milk as well as goats, sheep and pigs. His ladle was so large that a man and woman could easily have slept in it.

See Quests, p.64

SEE ALSO ANNWN, DANA, FOMORII, MORRIGAN, OGMA

DANIEL

The Hebrew "master of magicians", an Old Testament prophet who lived in the sixth century BC, and was exiled from Jerusalem to Babylon.

Although the Book of Daniel, the earliest example of apocalyptic literature, is credited to the prophet, some believe it was written in the second century BC to comfort the Hebrews in Jerusalem. At that time, the policies of the Seleucid ruler Antiochus Epiphanes threatened traditional worship and had driven the Hebrews into open revolt.

The book tells of Daniel comforting the Hebrews, saying, "there shall stand up yet three kings in Persia; and the fourth shall be far richer than them all; and by his strength through his riches he shall stir up all against the realm of Grecia". Some people say that Daniel was here predicting the invasion of Greece in 480 BC by the Persian king, Xerxes.

In 597 BC, Nebuchadnezzar, King of Babylon, seized Jerusalem. Ten years later, the city was sacked and the Hebrews were deported to Babylon where they were held in captivity until the city's fall. Daniel was one such Hebrew exile. His tales of Nebuchadnezzar's discomfiture are straightforward propaganda.

According to the Book of Daniel, the despotic Nebuchadnezzar commanded all his subjects to worship "an image of gold". When Shadrach, Meschach and Abednego refused to do so because of their belief in Yahweh, the Babylonian king cast them "into the midst of a fiery furnace". However, the presence of a companion "like the Son of God" prevented the men from suffering injury – to the astonishment of the king.

By interpreting one of the many dreams that troubled Nebuchadnezzar, Daniel foretold the king's fall from power. To the surprise of the whole court, he said that the people would expel the king from the city of Babylon. "And they shall drive thee from men, and thy dwelling shall be with the beasts of the field, and they shall make thee to eat grass as oxen, and they shall wet thee with the dew of heaven, and seven times shall pass over thee, till thou know that the most High ruleth in the kingdom of men, and giveth it to whomsoever he will."

The prophecy came to pass and the outlawed monarch wandered the countryside "till his hairs were grown like eagles' feathers, and his nails like birds' claws". It is now suggested that this tale of Nebuchadnezzar's madness derives from the voluntary exile of his successor Nabonidus, who spent ten years in a desert fortress.

In Nabonidus's absence, his son Belshazzar ruled Babylon. Belshazzar held a splendid feast, during which mysterious writing appeared on the palace wall. Daniel alone was able to read the message, which told of the kingdom's imminent conquest by the Medes and the Persians.

The last event of the Book of Daniel seems to have occurred when the arrogant Darius, king of the Persians (521–486 BC), ruled over Babylon. Because Daniel's reputation as a magician had risen so high, his enemies, fearful of his power, prepared a trap for him. Darius was persuaded to proscribe all gods but one approved by his royal decree, and to punish those who ignored his command with death. Thus, because he worshipped Yahweh, Daniel was cast into the lions' den. However, Yahweh "sent his angel . . . and shut the lions' mouth", so that he came to no harm.

The book, *Daniel, Bel, and the Snake*, tells how Daniel successfully unmasked the deceitfulness of Babylonian priests. With the aid of ashes sprinkled on the temple floor, he demonstrated to another Persian ruler that the footprints of those who came secretly to eat the food set out for the god Bel belonged to "the priests, with their wives and children".

Daniel also disposed of a sacred serpent by feeding it with cakes made from boiled "pitch and fat and hair" which burst asunder its huge belly. This tale points to the Hebrews' dislike of graven images, not to mention the whole priestly paraphernalia of worship in Mesopotamian temples.

See Seers, pp.82/83

Seers

Wise men and women whose authority and good counsel are never doubted occur in most traditions. In many cases they are held to be divinely inspired. Some, however, are ordinary people endowed with spiritual insight.

The lions' den held no terrors for Daniel. Convinced that his powers of interpretation and prophecy were God-given, he rightly supposed his god would preserve him.

SEE ALSO ABEDNEGO, MESCHACH, SHADRACH, YAHWEH

Merlin, the seer of Arthurian legend, becomes a wizard in this Disney cartoon film. Popular myth now emphasizes his powers of magic rather than of prophecy.

Hiawatha was a North American Indian sage whose vision led to the unification of feuding tribes around the Great Lakes.

Part of the ruins of Delphi (left) in central Greece, the home of the most famous oracle consulted even by rulers from other lands.

DEMETER

An earth goddess in ancient Greece, and specifically the goddess of the fruitfulness of the land. Demeter means "mother earth". She had several consorts, including Zeus and Poseidon.

Demeter was associated with corn, the staple food of the ancient Greeks, and her cult centre was at Eleusis, south of Athens. By ZEUS, her brother, Demeter was mother of PERSEPHONE.

When Persephone was still very young, and without consulting Demeter, Zeus agreed that HADES, the king of the underworld, could marry her. Some years later, Persephone was picking flowers in a meadow with the daughters of Oceanus. As she bent down to pluck a wonderful narcissus the ground split asunder, and Hades, god of death, rode forth in his chariot drawn by dark-blue steeds. In a moment he seized her and carried her back to his gloomy kingdom.

When Demeter learnt that her daughter had vanished, she began a search, wandering the earth, with two burning torches in her hands. She would not eat or wash, nor would Persephone, pining in the underworld. Plants withered, animals languished and mankind died.

At last, Demeter encountered the earth goddess HECATE, who informed her of the abduction. Then Hecate led Demeter to Helios, the sun god, who told her that Persephone was queen of a vast realm. But Demeter was not appeased, until Zeus intervened and persuaded her to accept the marriage.

Persephone was then allowed to return to the earth for part of each year, like the corn itself. The legendary reason for her annual return to the underworld was that while there she had eaten Hades' food, which Zeus had forbidden. The connection of Demeter and her daughter with the underworld is clear: the Athenians referred to their own dead as "Demeter's people".

The Romans identified Demeter with Ceres, but from early times she was also equated with the Phrygian goddess CYBELE and the Egyptian ISIS.

See Love and Fertility, pp.106/107

SEE ALSO CERES, HELIOS, OCEANUS

DEVI

A Hindu goddess and the greatest power in the Hindu pantheon. She is worshipped as a benevolent and a harsh deity, and takes many forms, in all of which she is the wife of Shiva.

There were originally several goddesses acknowledged as the wives of SHIVA. These deities, and other mother goddesses worshipped by different castes in various parts of India, eventually merged in Devi, or Mahadevi, whose womb was said to hold the entire universe.

In the form of Durga, Devi was created as the result of the gods' anxiety over a challenge from the demons. In particular, the buffalo-monster Mahisha had, by subjecting himself to terrible austerities, become so strong that he could overpower the gods. Not even VISHNU or Shiva could stand against the demon. Faced with the loss of their omnipotence, the gods combined their energies to produce the beautiful warrior goddess Durga as the saviour of the world. Seated on a tiger and swinging a weapon from each of her ten hands, Durga went to battle with Mahisha. Repeatedly she avoided his dreadful mace, and at length slew him.

Thereafter, her ascendancy as the great goddess was guaranteed. In times of need, the gods handed her every weapon and power at their disposal.

Devi's influence over daily affairs is not always benevolent. The darkest sides of her existence are manifested in Kali, "the black one". In the myth she is chiefly associated with, Kali engaged in a battle with Raktavija and his army of demons. Having slain the army, she attacked him. But every drop of blood he shed turned into a thousand giants. The only way Kali could overcome Raktavija was by drinking his blood. Intoxicated with her victory, she danced so wildly that the earth shook. Shiva tried to calm her down, but in her delirious state she killed him and trod on his body.

Kali is therefore usually depicted standing on the body of Shiva, who lies on a lotus bed. She is dressed as a dancer and decorated with a girdle of severed arms and a necklace of skulls. Her blood-thirsty tongue lolls from her mouth. One of her left hands grasps a bloody sword, the other dangles a head by the hair; one right hand confers blessing, the other bids her devotees not to fear her.

In this form, Devi is the essential mixture of pleasure and pain, suffering and enlightenment, life and death, the unashamed acceptance of experience that informs Hindu belief.

Devi's gentle aspects include the forms of Uma (light), Gauri (brilliant), Parvati (the mountaineer), Jaganmata (mother of the world) and Jagadgauri (the world's fair one). Her stern side is also represented in Chandi (fierce) and Bhairavi (the terrible).

See Saviours, p.75, and Demons, pp.126/127

Devi, the Great Mother Goddess of Hindu myth

SEE ALSO KALI, MAHISHA, PARVATI, RAKTAVIJA, UMA

DIONYSUS

The Greek god of wine and ecstasy, whose cult promised individual salvation. He was identified with Bacchus, the Roman god of wine.

Dionysus was usually accompanied by woodland spirits: the sileni, who were hairy men with horse's ears, very wise but also very drunk; and the satyrs, goat- or horselike men, who combined drunkenness with lust. These rowdy followers protected fertility, a circumstance which suggests that Dionysus may once, like DEMETER, have been a deity of vegetation and agriculture. His human followers were women known as maenads (frenzied ones).

According to one tradition, the conception of Dionysus occurred at the city of Thebes, where his mother Semele was a princess. This daughter of CADMUS, the city's founder, was loved by ZEUS, who disguised himself as a man. When the goddess HERA heard that Semele was pregnant, she decided to revenge herself on the princess and on Zeus, her wayward husband.

Having disguised herself as Semele's old nurse, Hera refused to believe that Zeus was the father unless the princess could persuade the god to prove it by appearing to her in his true form. So Semele trapped Zeus into granting her the favour of seeing him in his true glory; but the god's unshielded brightness shrivelled Semele to nothing. However, Zeus saved the unborn Dionysus from Semele's womb, and for several months the child stayed inside the thigh of Zeus instead, until he was ready to enter the world.

Another tradition about the birth of Dionysus makes him the son of PERSEPHONE, queen of the underworld.

Although Dionysus was a popular deity, there is a famous Theban legend about the refusal of one of its kings to recognize the god's right to be worshipped. This happened when Dionysus came to the city disguised as a handsome young man. King Pentheus imprisoned the god for stirring up the female citizens, but his jail could not hold Dionysus prisoner. At last, Pentheus decided to investigate the growing frenzy of the women himself. He spied on their worship from a tree, but they saw him, and mistaking him for a mountain lion tore the unfortunate ruler limb from limb. Thus Dionysus was revenged.

There are other tales of Greek cities falling foul of this powerful god, with dreadful consequences. It would seem that the removal of inhibitions in Dionysus's cult, and especially his appeal to women, was a worry to ancient authorities. In 186 BC the Roman Senate had to pass severe laws against the orgiastic rites of the newly arrived god. Several thousand maenads were subsequently executed.

Vineyards in central Crete

SEE ALSO BACCHUS, PENTHEUS, SEMELE

DUDUGERA

In Papuan mythology, the leg-child who became the scorching sun.

Dudugera's conception was a mysterious one. One day, his mother was in a garden near the shore, and saw a great fish sporting in the shallows. Attracted by the brilliance of its scales, she entered the water and played with the fish, which was in reality a god. Some time later, the woman's leg, against which the great fish had rubbed, began to swell and become painful. When her father lanced the swelling, a baby burst forth. This was Dudugera.

As Dudugera grew up, he frightened the other boys with his aggression. They feared playing games with him, and such was his unpopularity that he was violently threatened. To save him from harm, Dudugera's mother decided to send him to his father. Together, Dudugera and his mother went down to the sea, whereupon the fish god appeared, took his son in his mouth, and swam far away to the east.

Before he was carried away, Dudugera warned his mother to take refuge in the shade of a great rock, for he was about to become the sun, the scourge of mankind. His mother and her relatives followed these instructions. From their place of safety, they watched the heat of the sun grow and gradually destroy plants, animals and men. Moved by the sight, Dudugera's mother decided to temper this dreadful revenge. One morning, as the sun rose, she tossed lime into its face. As a result, clouds formed in the sky. Thereafter they protected the earth from the worst of the sun's heat.

In comparison to the sun, the Papuans regard the moon as weak and attribute this characteristic to the premature birth of the moon. The myth relates that a man digging in his garden found a small bright disc and picked it up. Surprised at his find, he let the disc escape from his hands, and it rose into the sky. The implication is that this early discovery prevented the moon from growing properly and acquiring greater strength.

See Natural Phenomena, p.138

DZOAVITS

The ogre of Shoshonean Indian myth. These people dwell in the North American states of Nevada, Utah and Idaho, and include the Comanches.

Monstrous giants frequently occur in North American mythology and seem to have been a particular problem for the Shoshoneans.

One such ogre was Dzoavits, who stole Dove's two children. With the help of Eagle, Dove rescued the children and escaped. Eagle then gave Dove some tallow from a creature he had killed, together with the stomach and some feathers.

Dzoavits chased after Dove and his children, but other animals came to their aid. When Dove and the children came to a river, Crane stretched out his leg and they were able to cross on the bridge it provided. However, when Dzoavits attempted to cross the same bridge, Crane dumped him in the middle of the river. Dove was also helped by Weasel, who dug an underground passage for the fugitives. When Dzoavits attempted to follow, Weasel sent him down the wrong hole.

The ogre again drew near and Dove was forced to throw down Eagle's first magical gift, the tallow, which turned into a ravine and slowed the ogre down. The next time Dzoavits caught up, Dove threw down Eagle's second gift, the stomach, which turned into a cliff so steep that the ogre was unable to climb it. However, before long, Dove again heard the sound of the ogre's approach and so was forced to use the last charm, the feathers. These produced a thick fog which blinded Dzoavits to their movements.

Badger, seeing the plight of the fugitives, dug a hole for them to hide in and hollowed out another one nearby. When the ogre finally arrived, Badger directed him to the wrong hole, threw hot rocks on him and closed the mouth of the hole with a boulder. So it was that Dove and his children escaped.

See Giants, p.159

SEE ALSO BADGER

EL

The first of the Canaanite gods. El literally means "god". He was thought to dwell on the slopes of Mount Saphon, situated to the north of the ancient Syrian city of Ugarit

The father of gods and men, El was remote, very old, all-knowing, and benevolent. He was called Mlk-ab-Anm (master of time). His wife seems to have been Athirat (lady of the sea), one of the forms assumed by ASTARTE.

El represented omnipotence and was always depicted as a seated figure, wearing bull's horns, the symbol of strength. In the Old Testament the supreme deity is mentioned as being both El and Yahweh.

Whatever the similarities between El and Yahweh, the mythology surrounding the Canaanite creator deity is more developed and interesting. Texts unearthed at Ras Shamra, the site of ancient Ugarit, reveal a turbulent world over which El exercised some control. It was he who allowed BAAL, his nearest rival, to assume power over the storm in the form of Hadad (the crasher).

The conflict of Baal and Mot, El's own son who was also the god of death, reflected the agricultural cycle — the authority of Mot extended over the harvest and the dead. That both were stored underground probably accounts for this dual role. Certainly the care taken of the dead in Ugarit suggests a belief in an organized afterlife. In cemeteries, cisterns were built to ensure a regular water supply for the dead.

There is a story that when Anat, a warlike form of Astarte, discovered that she could not revive her husband Baal after she had carried his corpse back from the land of the dead, in her fury she attacked and killed Mot. Eventually, however, Baal recovered and regained his throne.

Two epics closely associated with El concern Keret, his son, and Aqhat, a human ruler. Keret was also a king and ruled over Sidon. There, at El's command, he reluctantly met an attack by the moon god Etrah. At first Keret had no confidence in his ability to defeat Etrah, who had already captured five other cities and was attempting to cut the land of Canaan in half. However, a dream restored his spirits, and after sacrificing silver, honey and animals, he made preparations for war. The decisive encounter took place in the Negeb desert, the wilderness to the south of Palestine. Though Keret repulsed Etrah, he appears to have been dogged with further misfortunes, a fate that was only changed in time by his son.

In the story of Aqhat, a favourite of El, disaster is caused by the jealousy of the goddess Anat. Anat sought the wonderful bow that the smith god Kothar had given to Aqhat in appreciation of his generous hospitality. When Anat offered to give the king immortality in exchange for the weapon, Aqhat refused, on the grounds that the offer could only be an illusion to a man destined to die. For such presumption, and with the consent of El, Anat killed him.

El is closely related to the Hebrew Yahweh, and during the Roman period was identified with SATURN.

SEE ALSO ANAT, AQHAT, KERET, MOT, YAHWEH

ENKI

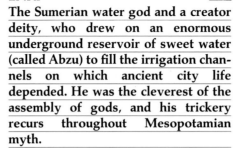

The Sumerian water god and a creator deity, who drew on an enormous underground reservoir of sweet water (called Abzu) to fill the irrigation channels on which ancient city life depended. He was the cleverest of the assembly of gods, and his trickery recurs throughout Mesopotamian myth.

Enki's earthly residence was the city of Eridu, with which he was principally associated, but his life-sustaining waters were believed to feed every field in Sumer. He directed the great rivers Euphrates and Tigris, appointed the god Enbilulu as the guardian of canals, arranged the pattern of the marshes and the coastline, and organized the rain.

Enki's mate NINHURSAGA was an earth goddess associated with the stony margins of the desert and with birth. In the Sumerian myth of paradise they lived together on the island of Dilmun, thought to be present-day Bahrein, in the Persian Gulf. It was an idyllic place, where animals did not harm one another, and neither sickness nor old age were known. At first their marriage was happy, and several children were born. But a bitter quarrel arose as a result of Enki's sexual interest in his own daughters.

As soon as Ninhursaga discovered Enki pursuing their daughters, she took Enki's semen from the body of Uttu, the spider goddess of weaving, whom the god had used and left. These "seeds" grew into eight plants. When Enki dared to eat these plants, Ninhursaga cursed him so severely that he fell ill and a sickness attacked eight

The Euphrates River, associated with Enki

parts of his body. The dismayed gods were powerless to help him. Only a fox managed to persuade Ninhursaga to relent and save Enki. She did this by placing him in her womb, from which he was reborn.

In another version of the myth, Enki was saved by giving birth himself to eight children, to replace the plants he had eaten. All the vegetation in the land was said to originate from the union of Enki and Ninhursaga. Enki's consumption of the plants and subsequent fall from grace is similar to Adam and Eve's banishment from the Garden of Eden after eating the forbidden fruit.

Another myth about Enki with a biblical parallel tells of a flood. The gods were exhausted from the effort of providing their own sustenance, and Enki suggested creating human beings who would work for them. So the four great deities – AN, ENLIL, Ninhursaga (also called Nintur) and Enki – created mankind. At first the gods were pleased, but as the human population increased and cities developed, Enlil became irritated with the noise they made.

Exasperated beyond endurance, Enlil persuaded his peers to wipe out mankind in a great flood. But Enki warned a wise man named Ziusudra, and told him to build a boat in which he, his family, and representative animals, could survive the engulfing waters. (Ziusudra is the Sumerian equivalent of NOAH, and in another version of this story is called Atrahasis.) A similar myth exists in the epic of GILGAMESH, where the hero of the flood is Utanapishtim.

Enki was also the patron of carpenters, stonecutters and goldsmiths. As well as instructing men in handicrafts, he taught them about farming, letters, law, architecture and magic.

In remote times, when men lived like beasts, Enki is said to have appeared from the sea. He is, therefore, represented as part man and part fish, or as a goat with a fish's tail. In reference to this image, Babylonian priests often clothed themselves in a garment shaped like a fish.

Enki is the counterpart of the Babylonian god EA.

See Flood, pp.110/111

SEE ALSO ABZU, ADAM, ATRAHASIS, EVE, UTANAPISHTIM, ZIUSUDRA

ENLIL

Next in rank to the Sumerian sky god An, and sometimes believed to be his son, was Enlil, the god of the air, who embodied energy and force rather than the calm of divine authority. His name means "lord of the wind", and he was regarded as a benevolent as well as destructive god.

The myths of Enlil reflect his complex nature. Best known was the story of his rape of Ninlil, the grain goddess. Enlil had been unable to resist the goddess's beauty when he found her bathing in a canal near the wall of the city of Nippur. For his crime, the assembly of gods banished him from Nippur, where his temple stood, and sentenced him to death.

Enlil left for the land of the dead, but Ninlil decided to follow him, in order to give birth to their son in his presence. This child became the moon god Nanna, a deity associated with cattle. But Nanna would have died in the underworld. In order to save him, Enlil persuaded Ninlil to lie with him so that the outcome of their second union, conceived in the underworld, would be able to survive there and act as a substitute for Nanna. In the event, three underworld deities were born, which more than satisfied the "mistress of death", Ereshkigal. This tale of the condemnation and death of Enlil may be part of a wider cult of a god who dies and is reborn, which is common to ancient West Asia.

Enlil's destructive aspect is revealed in a legend of the deluge. It begins with a rebellion against the god himself. Enlil was responsible for the gods who toiled year after year, digging out the beds of the Tigris and Euphrates rivers. But the regime he imposed on them was too strict, and We-e, one of the worker deities, recommended an uprising. (We-e's name means "had the idea".) So one night they burned their tools and surrounded Enlil's house.

Enlil summoned AN and ENKI the water god to decide what to do. When the rebellious gods announced that their days of work were over, Enlil burst into tears and offered his resignation. As a compromise, Enki suggested that since the labour of the gods was too burdensome, Nintur, the goddess of birth, should create mankind to do the work instead. Nintur mixed some clay with the blood of the ringleader We-e, and mankind was born.

For more than a millennium the solution worked. But the population in the cities of Sumer grew so large that the din kept Enlil awake at night. Thoroughly annoyed, he persuaded the assembly of gods that a plague should be sent down to thin out mankind and reduce the noise.

However, a wise man named Atrahasis (in other versions of this myth he is known as Ziusudra) consulted Enki and learned of this dreadful threat. The people were told to keep quiet, and so many offerings were made to Namtar, the plague god, that he was too embarrassed to appear.

After another thousand years or so, the problem arose again, and this time a drought was promised as punishment. Again, Enki advised Atrahasis about how to deal with the threat, and Enlil enjoyed his sleep in renewed quietness for another millennium. The third time the din became intolerable Enlil had no difficulty in imposing an embargo on fertility. Only the last-minute aid of Enki, who sent shoals of fish along the canals and rivers, saved mankind from starvation.

It was obvious that Enlil would use all the combined power of heaven on the next occasion finally to rid the earth of man's troublesome noise. Enki predicted that a great flood would be sent, so he warned Atrahasis to build a ship.

Enki proved right. For seven days and seven nights the world was lashed by storms and submerged by floodwaters. When the storms passed, the only survivors were Atrahasis, his family, and the animals he had taken on board.

All the gods were horrified by the extent of the destruction, except Enlil, who was enraged only by the fact that Atrahasis had survived the disaster. The gods were also starting to feel hungry, because there was no one left to work the fields. So when, as soon as he landed, Atrahasis made a sacrifice to them, they could not resist it, and sided with Enki against Enlil.

See Flood, pp.110/111

SEE ALSO ATRAHASIS, ERESHKIGAL, NAMTAR, NANNA, NINLIL, NINTUR, WE-E, ZIUSUDRA

EOS

The Greek goddess of the dawn, known to the Romans as Aurora.

Eos was the daughter of the Titan couple Hyperion and Theia. Her brother was Helios, the sun, and her sister was Silene, the moon.

For some unknown reason, Eos was a very amorous goddess, who kidnapped most of her young lovers. One of these was Tithonus, whom she kept until he became helpless with age. This unfortunate situation arose because Eos asked ZEUS to make Tithonus immortal, but forgot to ask that he should be made eternally young as well.

According to Greek myth, each morning Eos was drawn across the sky on a chariot pulled by two fine horses, called Phaeton (shiner) and Lampos (bright). The poet Homer called the dawn goddess "rosy-fingered" and "saffron-robed". Eos herself was usually depicted with wings.

See Love and Fertility, pp.106/107, and Natural Phenomena, p.138

Eos, goddess of the dawn, and her lover Tithonus

SEE ALSO AURORA, HELIOS, HYPERION, PHAETON, TITHONUS

ERINYES

In Greek mythology, three female avengers of wrong, also known as the Furies. In particular, they pursued relentlessly those who were guilty of murder within a family or clan.

Erinyes means "the angry ones". They were usually said to have been born from the blood that fell upon Gaia, when KRONOS castrated his father Ouranos. The first divine pair, Ouranos and Gaia, representing the sky and the earth, could be separated only by this desperate act.

The primeval birth of the Erinyes set them apart from the rest of the immortals. Even their names have an implacable ring: Alecto (the never ending); Tisiphone (voice of revenge); and Megaira (envious anger). The Erinyes were hags, entwined with snakes, brandishing torches and whips, and were looked upon as pitiless pursuers of the guilty.

When ORESTES murdered his mother Clytemnestra, in revenge for her part in the killing of his father Agamemnon, King of Mycenae, the Erinyes tracked him down. Despite the justice of Orestes' act, and the support he received from the god of prophecy Apollo, the Erinyes were determined to avenge the matricide. At Apollo's shrine at Delphi, they demanded blood for blood, and were persuaded to stay their hand only by the gods, who said that the case should be referred to the ancient Athenian court of the Areopagus.

There ATHENA, the protectress of the city of Athens, ensured that Orestes was acquitted, but only on condition that he fulfilled a difficult task as punishment. Afterward, the Erinyes were known as the Eumenides (the soothed ones).

The effect of the Erinyes on their victims was to drive them mad. Their powers were so great that the ancient Greeks never dared to mention the Erinyes by name. When not hounding the guilty on earth, the three avengers tortured wrongdoers in the underworld.

See Fate and Punishment, p.143

SEE ALSO AGAMEMNON, CLYTEMNESTRA, DELPHI, GAIA, OURANOS, RHEA

ERLIK

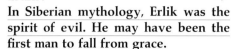

In Siberian mythology, Erlik was the spirit of evil. He may have been the first man to fall from grace.

According to the Altaic Tartars, the god of creation, Ulgan, made the earth by placing a disc on an expanse of water. Three great fish support the disc and their sudden movements cause the earthquakes that still rock parts of Siberia. One day, Ulgan was surprised to find a piece of mud with human features floating in the ocean. The god gave it a spirit and named the creature, the first man, Erlik.

Ulgan then ordered Erlik to bring him a piece of earth from the depths of the primordial ocean. Erlik did so, but hid a portion of the earth in his mouth, thinking he would fashion it into his own world. If Ulgan had not made him spit the earth out, Erlik would have choked because it began to expand. Instead of becoming a world, the mud disgorged by Erlik became marshland.

Other Tartar traditions say that Erlik's spittle was also responsible for the present appearance of mankind. When Ulgan made the people who followed Erlik, he had difficulty in obtaining enough spirits to animate them. Leaving a dog to guard the lifeless people he had created, he went to heaven for assistance.

During Ulgan's absence, Erlik bribed the dog, promising him a golden coat in return for "the soulless ones". The dog agreed, and Erlik defiled the bodies by spitting on them. When Ulgan returned with the spirits and saw Erlik's handiwork, he turned the bodies inside out. This explains why we have spittle in our intestines.

Before long, Erlik's pride annoyed Ulgan so much that he banished him to the underworld. Instead of being downcast by Ulgan's anger, Erlik immediately claimed the dead as his own, contemptuously leaving the smaller number of living people to the god. Ulgan's indifference to the dead was typical of the creator deities of northern Europe and Asia.

Despite Erlik's unpleasant character, the Altaic Tartars never overlooked his parentage of mankind and always referred to him as "the father".

SEE ALSO ULGAN

EUROPA

In Greek mythology, Europa was an important lover of Zeus, by whom she had three sons on the island of Crete. She was the daughter of the Phoenician king, Agenor.

Europa was enticed to Crete by ZEUS, the king of the gods, when he appeared near her home at Tyre in the form of a magnificent white bull.

Europa was playing with her handmaids by the sea when the bull appeared. She found the animal so tame that she dared to climb on its back. Once astride, Europa found herself a prisoner, for Zeus galloped into the sea and then swam to Crete, where he installed her in a cave. There she gave birth to MINOS, Rhadamanthys and Sarpedon.

In gratitude, Zeus presented Europa with three gifts – a self-directed spear, an unbeatable hound, and a bronze man who breathed fire. Europa eventually married Asterius, king of the Cretans, who adopted her semi-divine children. In time Minos succeeded him on the throne.

The legend of Europa may refer to the great Minoan civilization that flourished on the island of Crete up to the fifteenth century BC. Certainly a connection with West Asia is acknowledged. It is even believed that the name of Europa comes from the Semitic verb "to set", which may describe her disappearing into the sunset, travelling westward from Phoenicia on the back of the bull.

Europa astride Zeus in the form of a bull

SEE ALSO RHADAMANTHYS, SARPEDON

FREY

In Scandinavia, and especially Sweden, there were two races of gods at war, the Aesir and the Vanir. After the war, Frey or Freyr, a leading member of the Vanir, was taken hostage by the Aesir.

Frey and Freya were twin deities, the son and daughter of the Vanir sea god Njord and the giantess Skadi. Frey means "lord" and Freya "lady", a circumstance suggesting a parallel to the sacred marriage cult of West Asia.

Frey was possibly a sun god and was also associated with boars, two magnificent specimens of which pulled his chariot. However, his most impressive means of transport was Skidbladnir, a marvellous vessel made by dwarfs, which could travel on land, sea and air and could be folded into his trouser pocket when not in use.

The god also possessed a charger which could gallop through fire and water, and a sword capable of fighting on its own. He gave this wonderful weapon to his servant Skirnir in thanks for his assistance in winning the love of Gerda, a giantess.

As soon as Frey set eyes on Gerda, he was determined to marry her at any cost. At first, Skirnir offered the beautiful giantess innumerable treasures, but it was not until he resorted to threats that she bent to Frey's wishes.

The Vanir subscribed to an ideal beauty. It was therefore not surprising that Frey wanted to marry Gerda as soon as he saw the gleam of her white arms fill the sky and the sea with light. Moreover, the Vanir seem to have been particularly attracted to the race of giants. Not only was Frey's own mother a giantess but also the original quarrel between the Aesir and the Vanir was caused by the Aesir's cruel treatment of a giantess called Gullveig, whom the Vanir had sent to the Aesir on a mission. A long war ensued but finally an understanding was reached and hostages were exchanged, one of whom was Frey.

Frey's Roman counterpart was Priapus, the son of DIONYSUS and APHRODITE.

SEE ALSO AESIR, FREYA, GERDA, NJORD, PRIAPUS, SKADI, SKIRNIR, VANIR

FRIGG

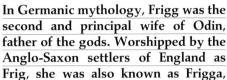

In Germanic mythology, Frigg was the second and principal wife of Odin, father of the gods. Worshipped by the Anglo-Saxon settlers of England as Frig, she was also known as Frigga, Frija and Fri.

Frigg was a goddess of the clouds and sky, but her particular concern was for the household and married love. She protected marriage and bestowed children, over whose destiny she exercised great power.

The giantess Jord, mother of the thunder god THOR, may also have been Frigg's mother. Her father may have been ODIN, whom she later married.

Frigg was depicted as tall and stately, clad in long robes which could be light or dark at her will. A bunch of keys always hung from her belt. Although she was by marriage to Odin the queen of heaven, she chose not to live in her husband's splendid hall but in a modest one of her own called Fensalier (the hall of the sea).

The goddess's companions were eleven handmaidens who helped her to spin golden thread or weave multicoloured clouds. One of these companions was Frigg's sister, Volla, a golden-haired maiden who was associated with abundance and the ripening grain. Her specific duty in Fensalier was to care for the casket in which Frigg kept her jewellery.

Despite protecting marriage, Frigg did not always stay faithful to Odin, who was given to long absences from home. She seems a rather passive deity, for although she knew of events in the present and the future, she had no power to affect them. Gefjon, one of Frigg's handmaidens, shared this clairvoyance.

The one occasion when Frigg endeavoured to alter destiny was when she attempted to protect her son BALDER. Fearing for his life, she extracted an oath from all things in heaven that they would do him no harm. But, like the mother of the Greek hero ACHILLES, she overlooked a small matter, which proved fatal. Thinking that mistletoe was too weak to threaten her son, she ignored it. However, the trickster god LOKI discovered her oversight and conspired to bring about Balder's exile to the underworld.

SEE ALSO FREYA, GEFJON, JORD

GANESA

An elephant-headed god of Hindu myth, who removes obstacles to success and dispenses wisdom. Ganesa is propitiated at the beginning of any important enterprise or business transaction.

Ganesa is represented as a short, yellow, pot-bellied man. He has four hands and a one-tusked elephant head, and is sometimes shown riding on a rat, or attended by one. Ganesa is the son of Parvati and SHIVA, and acts as the guardian at the gate of his mother's house.

There are many myths that account for Ganesa's elephant head. One tells how his mother once asked the god Sani to look after him. Sani was the planet Saturn, and was known as Kruralochana (the evil-eyed one). Parvati had forgotten the danger of the god's glance – when Sani looked at Ganesa, the child's head ignited and was burned to ashes. BRAHMA told the distressed Parvati to replace the head with whatever she could find, which happened to be the head of an elephant.

Another story recounts that Parvati went to have her bath and told Ganesa to guard the door. He did this, even against his father Shiva, who became so angry that he decapitated Ganesa. Parvati was so upset that, to pacify her, Shiva replaced the head with the first he came across – that of an elephant.

The loss of Ganesa's tusk is told in a similar tale. Ganesa stood guarding a doorway – this time the entrance to Shiva's room. When he opposed the entry of Parasurama, VISHNU's sixth incarnation, an argument ensued, which ended in a fight. At first Ganesa had the upper hand – he seized Parasurama with his trunk and swung him off the floor. But when he recovered from his giddiness, Parasurama struggled free and hurled an axe at the elephant-headed god. When Ganesa recognized the weapon as a present from his father to Parasurama, he stood still and received the blow in humility. As a result, one of his tusks was severed.

Ganesa is the Hindu counterpart of the Greek god HERMES and the Roman deity Mercury.

See Gods and Animals, p.103

SEE ALSO MERCURY, PARASURAMA, PARVATI, SANI

GAWAIN

In Arthurian legend, Gawain was the perfect knight and a strict upholder of chivalry. He appears in the cycle of legends about the Knights of the Round Table and is the subject of an alliterative poem, _Sir Gawain and the Green Knight._

Various romances tell how Gawain's strength waxed until midday and waned thereafter. It would, therefore, appear that he was once associated with a Celtic sun god. Indeed, the name of Gawain's father, Loth, is close to the Welsh Lleu and Irish LUGH, both of whom were solar deities.

Gawain also inherited several adventures which originally were associated with the hero CUCHULAINN, Lugh's son. Lugh himself gave rise to Lancelot, Gawain's enemy and the lover of ARTHUR's wife, Guinevere.

Layamon's _Brut_, a poem dating from the late thirteenth century, tells how Arthur had a prophetic dream which foretold the collapse of his kingdom through the machinations of his nephew Modred and Guinevere. The prophecy was not immediately fulfilled but, when Modred's treachery and Guinevere's infidelity came to light, Gawain immediately demanded their punishment. He declared that he would hang Modred with his own hands and tear Guinevere apart with wild horses.

According to Malory's _Le Morte d'Arthur_, published in 1485, Sir Gawain was the perfect knight, the strict upholder of chivalry and the enemy of Sir Lancelot. Guinevere's love for Lancelot weakened the Round Table prior to Modred's rebellion. The Pope's command that Arthur should end his war against Lancelot left the king at a loss to know what to do for, "in nowise Sir Gawain would not suffer the king to accord with Sir Lancelot".

Indeed, it was Gawain who stirred up feeling against Lancelot in the first place for he "made many men to blow upon Sir Lancelot; and all at once they called him false recreant knight". However, the Pope's command was carried out, Guinevere returned to Arthur and Lancelot left for exile abroad. At his departure, "was neither king, duke, earl, baron nor knight, lady nor gentlewoman, but all they wept as people out of their mind, except Sir Gawain".

Gawain's uprightness is also apparent in _Sir Gawain and the Green Knight_, which is at least a hundred years older than Malory's tale. The poem tells of the strange challenge of Bercilak de Hautdesert, the Green Knight, and, in a subtle treatment of Gawain's character, of the perfect knight's failure to live up to his high ideal of knighthood.

The adventure begins when a green giant appears in Arthur's hall on New Year's Eve and challenges the knights to a beheading contest. Gawain accepts the challenge and cuts off the stranger's head with a single blow. To the amazement of all, the giant calmly stoops down, picks up his head and mounts his green charger. The head then commands Gawain to meet the giant at a lonely chapel in a year and a day when he will return the blow.

In the intervening year, Gawain experiences many adventures and meets Morgan le Fay, the half-sister of King Arthur. After a series of temptations, not entirely resisted, Gawain keeps his appointment. However, because Gawain cheats by wearing a magically protective green girdle, the Green Knight wounds him slightly. Thus, the perfect knight returns to court, aware that he is spiritually imperfect, and vows to wear the green girdle for ever as a reminder of his frailty.

See Heroes, p.55 and Quests, p.64

Sir Gawain, a Knight of the Round Table

SEE ALSO GUINEVERE, LANCELOT, LLEU, MODRED, ROUND TABLE

GHEDE

The wise god of death in the Voodoo mythology of Haiti. Like many underworld deities, Ghede is also a fertility god.

Ghede is envisaged as a tall man in a black top hat, long black tail coat and dark glasses. He stands at the eternal crossroads where the souls of the dead pass on their way to the underworld. His wisdom is said to derive from the information he has gleaned from all those who have died.

However, Ghede is the lord of life as well as death and, as a potent fertility god, his phallus is carved alongside gravediggers' tools in the subterranean chamber reserved for his worship. He sustains the living, increases their number and resurrects the dead. He also animates zombies, the recently buried corpses that sorcerers steal from cemeteries to be their slaves. It is believed that if a zombie eats food flavoured with salt, he will either return to the grave or to a previous existence.

The cross of Baron Samedi, as Ghede is sometimes known, is kept in every graveyard in order to guard the dead. Indeed, the symbols of Christianity have fused with Voodoo mythology to a bewildering degree. Ghede's female counterpart, Mama Brigitte, guards the graves. The activities of bodysnatchers have given Baron Samedi and Mama Brigitte a crucial role in Voodoo worship. Both deities are zealously propitiated and implored to protect dead relatives.

Although Ghede seems happiest among the tombs, he sometimes ventures forth into the world at large, often with startling consequences. Once the god has tasted strong rum, nothing can halt his obscenity and recklessness. His possession of worshippers is beyond the control of even the most experienced _hougan_, or medium.

On one occasion in the late 1960s, Ghede entered a group of devotees, all dressed like him in black tail coats, and marched on the palace of Papa Doc, President of Haiti, demanding money for rum. Ogoun is another Haitian god with a penchant for rum.

See Death, p.91

SEE ALSO MAMA BRIGITTE, OGOUN

Death

The only certainty of human existence, death permeates all mythologies. Anxiety about what death itself actually entails has inspired numerous different myths reflecting various attitudes, from abject fear to enlightened and calm acceptance.

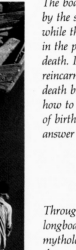

Violent imagery was often employed by the Maya of Central America in their depiction of death, which to them was as horrible as it was unavoidable. Here the god of death, Ah Puch, is shown with a head severed from its body.

The bodies of Hindus are burned by the sacred River Ganges, while their souls are temporarily in the power of Yama, the god of death. In India, the belief in reincarnation mitigates the fear of death but gives rise to a problem: how to escape the endless wheel of birth, death and rebirth. The answer lies in enlightenment.

Through ritual cremation in a longboat, chieftains in Germanic mythology were commended to the care of Odin, king of the gods. The dead heroes then went to live in Valhalla, "the hall of the slain". This ancient ceremony is re-enacted every year at Up-Helly-Aa in the Shetland Islands north of Scotland.

As Baron Samedi, Ghede, the wise god of death in Voodoo belief, protects tombs from bodysnatchers. Ghede guards the eternal crossroads, and his wisdom comes from the news related to him by passing souls.

GILGAMESH

The legendary Sumerian king of Uruk, a city which flourished from around 3000 BC. He is the hero of an epic, based on legends that had existed for centuries in Sumer, which was transcribed on to tablets in the middle of the second millennium BC.

Gilgamesh was an alert, vigorous and strong king and the son of a god. At the start of the Gilgamesh epic he is presented as being so energetic that he wore his people out. They appealed to the gods, who created a companion for him, a man named Enkidu.

This person was enormously strong and hairy, went naked, and lived with wild animals; he ate grass along with them and drank at their waterholes. Enkidu also repeatedly destroyed the traps laid by Gilgamesh's hunters, which is how he came to the attention of the king.

Gilgamesh sent a harlot to the waterhole at which Enkidu drank to try to entice him. Enkidu was, not unnaturally, attracted to her, and for six days and seven nights enjoyed her favours. After the seventh night, satisfied at last, Enkidu tried to go back to the animals, but they fled when they saw him, and he could no longer keep up with them – he had lost his innocence and ceased to be a wild man.

The harlot persuaded Enkidu to travel back to Uruk with her. On the way there he gradually learned more about civilized living, eating cooked food, drinking beer, washing his body, and wearing clothes. She also told him of Gilgamesh's strength, which he relished as a challenge. Arriving in Uruk on the occasion of Gilgamesh's wedding, Enkidu provoked a confrontation by daring to bar the king's way.

In the ensuing fight, Enkidu wrestled Gilgamesh to one knee, much to the amazement of the people gathered around. Even more bewildering was the respect Enkidu then showed the defeated Gilgamesh. But Enkidu also prophesied that Gilgamesh would be a divine favourite, and this was why he showed him deference. The two men became the closest of friends, brothers, and members of the same household.

One day Gilgamesh found Enkidu in tears. Realizing that he was regretting the softening of his muscles by city life,

Gilgamesh suggested that what they both needed was a rigorous expedition packed with testing adventures. Enkidu welcomed the suggestion, but could not agree that their final goal, the destruction of Huwawa, the fire-breathing giant of the cedars, was a very sensible one.

Enkidu had already observed this giant in the wild, but from a safe distance, and a proposed fight to the death seemed to him foolhardy indeed. But Gilgamesh insisted, and they challenged the giant in the cedar forest: Enkidu's spear struck Huwawa the fatal blow.

The heroes returned to Uruk, triumphant and proud. But they had barely refreshed themselves before the love goddess, ISHTAR, threw herself at Gilgamesh. He scorned her passionate advance, reminding her of the indifference and cruelty she had shown to her previous lovers, including Tammuz. Insulted by this rejection, Ishtar rushed to her father Anu and demanded that he allow the bull of heaven to kill Gilgamesh.

When Anu merely tried to appease her, Ishtar became so incensed that she threatened to break down the gates of the underworld and let loose the dead. Anu was forced to loan her the bull. But despite the immense power of the beast, Ishtar was denied her revenge. For while Enkidu grabbed the creature's tail and diverted its attention, Gilgamesh drove his sword into the great neck.

Gilgamesh and Enkidu had triumphed yet again – but the slaying of the bull of heaven had to be answered for, since it personified the will of heaven, which they had opposed. ENLIL, the god of the air, informed the assembly of gods that he would be satisfied only with the deaths of Gilgamesh and Enkidu. After a debate it was agreed that, as a punishment, Gilgamesh would be deprived of his friend Enkidu, who fell sick and died.

Overwhelmed by grief, and stricken to the heart with the realization of mortality, Gilgamesh roamed the wilderness from which Enkidu had come. Day and night the king wept over his companion, and it was not until a maggot crawled from the nose of the corpse that he would allow the burial to take place. Thereafter, Gilgamesh was obsessed with delaying his own end, having realized that, although the son of a

god, as a man born of a woman, he was not truly immortal.

Having heard about his ancestor Utanapishtim, who had been granted eternal life after surviving the flood, Gilgamesh set out to visit him at the end of the world. He got as far as the edge of the encircling sea, and was wondering how to cross it when he met Ishtar, disguised as an innkeeper's wife, who tried to dissuade him from pursuing his quest. But the hero insisted, and so she told him how to get across the sea, by taking a ferry.

Gilgamesh finally reached Utanapishtim's home. There he was told that Utanapishtim and his wife had been allowed to live for ever only because they had saved human and animal life from the flood, which was a unique event. But, Utanapishtim said, Gilgamesh too might gain immortality if he could pass a test, namely to stay awake for seven days and seven nights. He tried, but fell asleep on the sixth night. There could be no hope for the hero if he was unable to resist sleep, the lesser brother of death.

Utanapishtim's wife took pity on Gilgamesh and persuaded her husband to reveal the existence of a magical rejuvenating plant called "Never Grow Old", which grew in the sweet waters underground. Gilgamesh found and gathered the plant with great difficulty, then started the long journey back to Uruk.

The weather was warm, and when Gilgamesh saw an inviting pool, he stopped to bathe in it. While he was in the water, a snake came out of a hole, drawn by the wonderful scent of the precious plant. The creature swallowed the plant and shot back into its hole, where it sloughed its skin and emerged shiny and rejuvenated.

So the quest of Gilgamesh came to nothing. Broken-hearted and in tears, he returned to Uruk, to spend his life waiting inside the great city walls for the unstoppable approach of death.

See Heroes, p.55, Quests, p.64 and Death, p.91

SEE ALSO ANU, ENKIDU, HUWAWA, TAMMUZ, UTANAPISHTIM

GIMOKODAN

The underworld of the Bagobo people of the Philippines.

The Bagobo are one of the hill tribes on the great southern island of Mindanao. They have resisted conversion both to Islam and Christianity, maintaining a belief in a world of spirits linked closely to natural phenomena.

According to Bagobo tradition, the land of the dead, Gimokodan, lies below the earth and is divided into two sections. One is reserved for warriors who die in combat, a parallel of Valhalla, ODIN's hall for the battle casualties in Germanic mythology. The other houses the rest of the dead, whose less exalted status is indicated in its topsy-turvy nature.

In this second section there is a giantess, whose many nipples give succour to the spirits of infants. The other spirits dissolve into dew when the light returns each day, becoming spirits again during the hours of darkness. This is why each spirit is careful to shape for itself a container made from a leaf, in which the dew may hide.

The entrance to Gimokodan is a certain river. The spirit of the deceased (*gimokod*) bathes in it in order to forget its former life. A similar idea existed in Greek mythology, around the River Lethe, although the waters of this underworld river were drunk by the spirits who were about to be reborn.

Death is explained in various ways in the mythologies of the Pacific Islands and Australasia. The New Hebrideans believe that man was originally immortal but, unlike the snake, he forgot how to slough his skin and renew himself. The Dunsun of northern Borneo say that their ancestors would not listen to a god who showed them the way to be immortal, and among the Australian aborigines death is often regarded as a divine punishment for ingratitude.

The Bagobo accept the end of life as a natural event, but they expect their deceased forebears to maintain a lively interest in daily affairs. Gifts are offered regularly to ancestors to ensure good health and harvests.

See Death, p.91 and Afterlife, p.147

GLOOSKAP

Glooskap, Gluskap or Gluskabe means "the liar". In spite of his name, he is regarded as a benevolent culture hero by the Abnaki Indians of the north-eastern forests of the United States.

Glooskap seems to stand for good, while his wolfish brother Malsum is the agent of evil. One tradition suggests that the twins' enmity arose from Malsum's wilfully having chosen to be born in such a way that it killed his mother.

Whereas Glooskap made the sky, earth, animals, fishes and mankind from his mother's body, Malsum made the mountains, valleys, snakes, and everything which he thought would inconvenience the Abnakis.

Each of the brothers could be slain by one particular object only. Malsum asked Glooskap what he was vulnerable to and Glooskap replied that he would die if an owl's feather touched him. Malsum in turn told Glooskap that he was vulnerable to a certain fern.

Taking advantage of his special knowledge, Malsum killed Glooskap. However, like the Germanic BALDER, Glooskap passed into a special state of undeath from which, much to Malsum's disgust, he was able to resurrect himself. The enmity between the two brothers ended when, exasperated, Glooskap struck Malsum with the fern, killing him. However, evil monsters then preyed on Glooskap's creations to avenge their own creator's death.

To protect mankind, Glooskap had to soften the landscape, restrain natural forces and wage a constant war against witches, spirits and sorcerers. Having overcome many evil powers, Glooskap decided that it was time to leave the world. When the appointed day arrived, he gave a great feast for all the animals on the shore of a lake, then drifted away in his canoe. When the animals could no longer see Glooskap, nor hear his wonderful singing, they found that they could no longer understand each other's language.

Glooskap is expected to return one day and save his people.

See Trickster Gods, pp.78/79 and Creation, p.135

SEE ALSO MALSUM

GU

The smith god of the Fon peoples of Dahomey, in West Africa.

Gu is the son of the creator deity MAWU-LIZA. This dual parent (Mawu is female, Liza is male) was responsible for establishing universal order at the beginning of time. On the second day of creation, Mawu-Liza sent Gu down to earth in order to help man cope with his environment.

The Fon imagine Gu as a cutting tool. At birth, his body was said to be a solid stone from which projected a sharp blade. The greatest gifts he gave to the first people were tools and implements. These allowed them to clear and till the land. Later Gu taught them the skills of metalwork, so that never again would man be without strength.

What the smith god may not have foreseen were the warlike purposes to which his gift would soon be put. Metal technology gave the aggressive Fon a considerable advantage over their neighbours. Their spears and swords were much sharper and stronger than those of any other people around them, and gave the Fon the power to subjugate their enemies. Some of the deities of these conquered peoples were eventually assimilated into Fon mythology, one of them possibly being Gu's parent, Mawu-Liza.

An alternative myth makes Gu the divine tool that Mawu-Liza used to shape the first human being out of divine excrement.

Divine gifts of tools occur throughout world mythology. One of the earliest was made to the ancient Sumerians by ENLIL, god of the air. He presented them with the pickaxe, an essential implement for building the temples in which the gods lived and were worshipped.

See also Craftsmen and Smith Gods, p.154

GUAN DI

The unusual Chinese war god, whose chief concern is preventing rather than waging war.

Guan Di remains a popular figure in Chinese folklore, although his role as the deity of war has disappeared in China. His continued popularity arises from the tales told about his life during the troubled times of the third century, when Guan Di was a general. He was in charge of the forces of one of the states into which China was temporarily divided, and was executed as a prisoner-of-war.

Guan Di was officially recognized as a god in 1594, when the Chinese emperor offered sacrifices to him for the first time. In Taiwan this practice was revived after the establishment of the People's Republic of China in 1949.

The size of Guan Di impressed his contemporaries. The general was at least 2.7m (9ft) tall and possessed enormous strength. He is usually shown with a bright red face, a forked beard, powerful eyes and wearing green. Yet what made the Chinese remember Guan Di was not so much his appearance or valour, but his courtesy and faithfulness. In an era of violence his mildness was remarkable.

As a result, Guan Di became the reluctant warrior god. In striking contrast to the Roman MARS, the Chinese god of war was most content when peace prevailed. Guan Di also had nothing in common with the bloodthirsty and fearful ARES, the unpopular Greek war god.

A less well-known feature of Guan Di's cult concerns prophecy. In Chinese temples around the world it is still customary to consult the god about future events. By drawing a number, and then consulting a register of predictions, a worshipper may learn from Guan Di about impending disaster or success.

See War, pp.94/95

War

The organized violence of war is variously explained: for the ancient Greeks it was caused by Ares, the bloody, merciless and cowardly war god; in Germanic belief, however, it celebrated the worship of Odin.

The Roman war god was the righteous Mars, from whom the martial virtues of the Romans were supposed to have descended, and to whom the legionaries paid reverence. The planet Mars was given its name because of its colour – red is the colour of blood and associated with war.

The Chinese deity Guan Di (above) is very different from other war gods. This ex-general has become a god who seeks to prevent conflict and preserve civilized living.

The Aztecs of Central America fed to the sun god the hearts and blood of their captives. Without this sacrifice the universe would, they believed, break down in chaos.

GUINECHEN

The chief deity of the Araucanian Indians, the original inhabitants of Chile. His name means "master of men" and he was also known as Guinemapun, "master of the earth".

Guinechen was an all-embracing deity who had authority over the elements, plants and mankind. However, the thunder god Pillan took a more active role in creation, and Guinechen's chief concern seems to have been fertility.

The Araucanians were fierce warriors who put up a strong resistance to the Incas and Spaniards. When they were hard pressed in battle, Pillan came to their aid, and any warriors who were killed were immediately absorbed into the god. Pillan also gave them their greatest treasure, fire.

But Pillan had an unpleasant side to his divinity which made him the bane of Guinechen's life. He introduced blight, disease and death to the Araucanian Indians. Moreover, his followers, human-headed snakes, were held responsible for all other calamities.

Despite his destructiveness, it would not be Pillan who caused the end of the world. Instead, Guecufu (the wanderer without) would be the source of the deluge. Although this threat of impending doom hung over the Araucanians, they were helped by benevolent deities such as the water god and the wind god.

There is no doubt that Guinechen's remoteness left plenty of scope for the forces of good and evil. Perhaps their free play reflects the helplessness of a nation embattled against superior foes.

The Spaniards record that the Araucanians forecast the effectiveness of their resistance from the direction in which the clouds moved. Southward meant defeat, whereas northward signalled a victory over the invaders.

SEE ALSO GUECUFU, PILLAN

HADES

In Greek mythology, the ruler of the underworld. His name means "the unseen".

Hades was one of the three sons of KRONOS, and the husband of PERSEPHONE. One of his brothers was ZEUS. When Zeus deposed their father Kronos, lots were cast to divide the universe into three realms. Zeus won the sky, the second brother POSEIDON was allotted the water and Hades won the underworld. The earth and Olympus, the mountain of the gods in Thessaly, were shared by all three.

The ancient Greeks considered the name of Hades unlucky. The god of the dead was therefore usually referred to by other titles, among them Pluton (the rich one), Polydegmon (the hospitable) and Klymenos (the renowned). Despite being a grim and ruthless figure, Hades was never looked upon as an evil or unjust deity. Neither was the "House of Hades", the underworld, a hellish abode. Hades did not torment any of its inmates — the task of punishing wrongdoers was left to the ERINYES, the Furies.

The dead arrived in the underworld after being brought to the banks of the river Styx by the god HERMES. There, the spirits of the dead were each expected to give a small coin to the boatman Charon to ferry them across the grey waters. The three-headed dog Cerberus ensured that no one fled back to the world of the living.

The chief myth of Hades concerns Persephone. This daughter of Zeus and DEMETER was exceptionally beautiful, so her mother kept her out of sight for fear of abduction. But Demeter could not counter the desire of Hades: the god simply emerged from beneath the earth and carried Persephone off in his chariot. To placate the outraged Demeter, Zeus arranged that Persephone should spend half the year in the underworld and the other half on earth.

See Death, p.91

SEE ALSO CERBERUS, OLYMPUS, STYX

HAKAWAU

The legendary sorcerer of the Maori people of New Zealand.

Hakawau rose to fame by overcoming the magic head of the rival sorcerers Puarata and Tautohito. This wooden head was able to bewitch anyone who dared to approach the stronghold in which it was kept.

As news of the head's magical powers spread throughout the islands of New Zealand, many sorcerers were tempted to test its strength. All met their death. No longer prepared to tolerate this situation, Hakawau decided to see if he could succeed where others had failed.

With a single companion, he set out on the long journey. His old age made their pace slow, but the care with which they advanced may also have been connected with the magic Hakawau worked as they travelled. At every stage of the journey, the sorcerer cast spells to ward off demons.

Slowly he and his companion picked their way through the rotting corpses of previous challengers of the head. The sight of so many victims would have deterred a lesser magician, but already Hakawau's familiar had ascertained the weakness of Puarata and Tautohito.

When they arrived at the stronghold, Hakawau hurled his magical forces at it and they swiftly seized control. Despite the desperate appeals of the two rival sorcerers, the power of the wooden head was not strong enough to halt Hakawau's progress. The old sorcerer entered the stronghold, looked at its sacred objects, and then left satisfied and unharmed. Having demonstrated his superiority, Hakawau clapped his hands, at which Puarata and Tautohito died.

See Seers pp.82/83

SEE ALSO PUARATA, TAUTOHITO

HANUMAN

The dextrous monkey god of Hindu and Buddhist mythology, and a favourite in India, China and Japan. In the *Ramayana*, an Indian epic, he is the army general and chief adviser to Sugriva, the monkey king.

Hanuman's most notable characteristic is that he is able to change his shape at will. An Indian poet describes how "his form is as vast as a mountain and as tall as a colossal tower, whenever he chooses. His complexion is yellow and glowing like molten gold, a marvellous sight when he dashes from place to place; his enormous tail is so long that the end is hard to find. He roars like thunder, flies among the clouds with a rushing noise, and disturbs the surface of the ocean as he speeds by."

In the *Ramayana*, Hanuman and his army of monkeys come to the aid of Rama, whose wife Sita had been abducted by Ravana, a ten-headed and twenty-armed demon king. The wily Hanuman followed her trail and returned with the news that she was held captive on the nearby island of Sri Lanka.

To help Rama cross the ocean, the monkey army built a bridge linking the island to India. But the agile Hanuman merely leaped across the straits. However, his spectacular action did not go unopposed. As he flew across the water, a female relative of Ravana, named Surasa, seized his shadow and pulled it under the sea, dragging Hanuman with it.

Surasa then tried to swallow him whole. To escape, Hanuman distended his body, forcing Surasa to open her mouth enormously. Then he suddenly shrank to the size of a thumb, shot through her head, and emerged from her right ear.

Having landed safely on Sri Lanka, Rama and Hanuman and his army dealt the forces of Ravana a mortal blow and fired the capital. Rama rewarded Hanuman for his courage and services with the gift of eternal life and youth.

In China an immense collection of tales has grown up around the beguiling exploits of the monkey god, who helped the pilgrim Xuan Zhang obtain the Buddhist scriptures for the Chinese.

See Gods and Animals, p.103

SEE ALSO RAMA, RAVANA, SITA, SUGRIVA, SURASA

HATHOR

The cow goddess, and a goddess of the sky and fertility, in ancient Egypt. She was portrayed as a cow, a woman with the head of a cow, or as a woman with cow's horns and a sun disc on her head, and sometimes took the form of Isis.

Hathor's name means "the house of Horus". HORUS was the son of the underworld god OSIRIS, and Hathor was variously styled as Horus's wife, or, when identified with ISIS, as his mother. Myth relates that Hathor's son once cut off her head in anger, and it was replaced with that of a cow.

Hathor may have been a daughter of the sun god RE. Certainly he seems to have relied on her unquestioning obedience in a number of myths. On one occasion, when people dared to suggest that Re had passed his prime, he summoned a council of gods and announced his intention to destroy those who spoke so impiously. He sent his eye, in the form of Hathor, to wreak destruction on earth. Hathor was so effective that Re saw that unless he did something to halt her depredations, nothing would be spared in the bloodbath.

In order to beguile Hathor, Re flooded the fields with beer dyed with red ochre (in some versions of the myth it is pomegranate juice). Thinking this was blood, Hathor drank it greedily and became intoxicated. Thus mankind was saved.

Hathor's popularity derived mostly from her role as a goddess of love. She was also associated with music and dance, and encouraged her devotees to deck themselves with flowers at her festivals.

In the guise of Isis, Hathor was also a protectress of cemeteries, and held the ladder by which the deserving dead could climb to heaven. It was believed that she would descend from her sacred tree, the sycamore, to feed the dead with bread and water on their arrival.

Hathor's cult spread widely. In Canaan she was equated with Baalat, the wife of BAAL, in Greece with APHRODITE. As Isis she was the equivalent of the Babylonian goddess ISHTAR, the Sumerian goddess INANNA, and the Phrygian deity CYBELE.

See Gods and Animals, p.103

HAYAGRIVA

A gigantic demon in Hindu and Buddhist mythology, Hayagriva was the Indian equivalent of a Titan, a _daitya_. He was an enemy of the gods and spent his time making mischief and threatening world order.

The most daring attack that Hayagriva launched on the gods concerned BRAHMA. Hayagriva stole the four Vedas, the ancient Indian scriptures which are said to have come from Brahma's four heads, while the god was sleeping. (Brahma sleeps for a period of 8,640,000,000 years, after which the world is destroyed. He then wakes up and creates the world anew.) The recovery of the stolen scriptures therefore depended on the intervention of someone else, who happened to be VISHNU. Reincarnated in the form of the fish Matsya, Vishnu killed Hayagriva and retrieved the sacred texts.

In the lore of Tibetan Buddhism, the giant demon escapes to become the lord of wrath, the first of the eight dreadful gods known as Drag-gsshed. For the Mongols, who were converted to Buddhism by Tibetan lamas, Hayagriva (whose name means "horse-necked") was the protector of horses.

See Demons, pp.126/127 and Giants, p.159

The demon Hayagriva emerging from a shell

SEE ALSO MATSYA

HECATE

A Greek goddess of uncertain parentage, who was associated with magic and ghosts. Zeus treated her with great respect.

Hecate means "the distant one". Her authority included the fertility of the earth and the hours of darkness.

The ancient Greeks believed the powers of Hecate to be very great. She could bestow wealth, success and good luck, and could offer sage advice and guidance. But, if Hecate chose, she could show a less generous aspect to mankind. Then she would appear entwined with snakes, as the keeper of the keys of the underworld. Hecate practised black magic, as did her daughter, the enchantress CIRCE.

In later Greek mythology, Hecate became the goddess of the moon. In this guise she was portrayed as a deity with three heads – those of a lion, a horse and a dog. She was also regarded as a companion of ARTEMIS, the goddess of the hunt.

See Seers pp.82/83 and Death, p.91

A Roman engraved gem representing Hecate

HEIMDAL

The Germanic god of the early sun or dawn. Heimdal or Heimdallr, which probably means "he who casts light", was the lone sentinel of heaven. He guarded Bifrost, the rainbow bridge that led to the heavenly city of Asgard.

Like BALDER, Heimdal was a god of light. According to legend, he was born on the horizon, the child of nine giant sisters and the great god ODIN. As a lookout, he corresponds to the Roman god JANUS.

Perhaps Heimdal's sense of duty as a lookout accounts for his being credited with establishing the social order on earth. According to one story, he went to Mannheim following a disaster and created three classes of people: the slaves (_thrall_), the free peasants (_karl_) and the nobles (_jarl_).

First, he visited a hovel by the sea where he ate coarse food and slept for three nights between the husband and wife. Nine months later, the wife gave birth to the horribly ugly Thrall.

Next, Heimdal stayed in a farmhouse. Its industrious owners were hospitable to the god who, during his three-night stay, fathered Karl, a rosy-cheeked, fresh, bright-eyed boy. Finally, Heimdal stayed in a splendid hall where sumptuous food and drink were served. After three nights, the god returned to heaven and in due course Jarl was born, a handsome boy, skilled with sword and spear.

Heimdal was so delighted by the typically Viking raids Jarl led throughout the world that he returned to earth and taught him the secret of the runes. As a result, Jarl's own sons became so skilled in magic that they could cure the sick, prevent storms, and control forest fires.

However, at Ragnarok (the twilight of the gods) Heimdal would sound his horn of warning too late, when the forces of evil were already on the march. He even allowed his sword to be stolen by LOKI, who had instigated Ragnarok. Indeed, Heimdal's only satisfaction in the last battle would be slaying Loki, but he too would die from wounds sustained in the duel.

See Natural Phenomena, p.138

SEE ALSO JARL, KARL, MANNHEIM, RAGNAROK, THRALL

HEITSI-EIBIB

The legendary hero of the Hottentots, a group of pastoralists in southwestern Africa.

In Hottentot mythology, there is a strong emphasis on magic, and sorcerers play a critical role in the ordering of events. So it is not surprising that the chief figure in the Hottentot pantheon combines the skills of war and the chase with the arts of magic. This divinity is called Heitsi-Eibib.

Heitsi-Eibib was the offspring of a cow, an appropriate parent for pastoralists who depend on herding cattle. He is not regarded as a creator deity. Rather, he gave existing creatures their characteristics by means of his spells or curses.

Long ago, Heitsi-Eibib was a warrior against whom none could prevail. He was a superb fighter and knew no fear. Only Heitsi-Eibib could rid the Hottentots of the vicious monster Ga-gorib (thrower-down). This creature used to sit on the edge of a great pit and dare passers-by to throw stones at him. The stones always rebounded and killed the thrower, who then fell into the pit.

When Heitsi-Eibib came to confront Ga-gorib, he refused to take aim until the monster's attention had been distracted and he was looking elsewhere. Heitsi-Eibib's stone struck the monster under the ear and he tumbled into his own trap. In another version of the myth, Heitsi-Eibib succeeded in pushing Ga-gorib into the pit after a wrestling match.

According to legend, Heitsi-Eibib was killed in combat on a number of occasions, but was able to resurrect himself by magical means. Large mounds of stones now mark the places where the hero either performed amazing deeds or chose to return to life. Today Heitsi-Eibib is worshipped as a magician who still uses his expertise for the benefit of the living.

See Heroes, p.55

HELEN

In Greek mythology, Helen was the wife of Menelaus, King of Sparta, who eloped with the Trojan prince Paris and thus caused the ten-year war between the Greeks and the Trojans.

Helen was the daughter of ZEUS and Leda, or of Nemesis, the personification of retribution. She could have been an ancient goddess connected with vegetation, and especially trees. Helen's tree was said to grow in Sparta, and her birth from an egg suggests a connection with birds, in whose shape pre-Greek goddesses were thought to appear. By the time of Homer, in the ninth century BC, she had become a woman whose beauty was such that it brought death and destruction to the mortal world.

With the help of APHRODITE, the goddess of love, Paris persuaded Helen to desert her husband Menelaus and sail away with him to Troy. In the long war that ensued, Helen found herself torn between being the wife of a Trojan prince and the ex-wife of a Greek king. The *Iliad* relates how news of a temporary truce between the two sides filled Helen's heart with tender longing for her former husband, her parents, and the city she had left. After the fall of Troy, Helen and Menelaus were reconciled.

According to PRIAM, the Trojan king, the conflict was the work of the gods. "It is they", he told Helen, "who have made this dreadful war." But Menelaus preferred to blame the arrogance and unscrupulous behaviour of Paris, who had abused the position of an honoured guest.

Something of the sanctity traditionally attached to Helen may have prevented Homer from attaching any personal blame to her in his epic. Evidence of the special status she seems to have enjoyed occurs in a legend about her stay in Egypt. This version of her elopement has the minor sea god Proteus substitute a spirit in her shape as Paris's companion, while Helen remains hidden safely in a cave on the Egyptian shore. After the fall of Troy, Menelaus called to collect her.

See War, pp.94/95

HEPHAISTOS

The Greek god of fire, and especially the smithy. The Romans identified him with Vulcan.

Hephaistos was the son of ZEUS and HERA. Twice he was flung out of Olympus, the mountain home of the gods. The first time was at birth, when his mother took offence at his dwarfish shape; the outcast baby fell into the sea, where he would have drowned had he not been saved by the nymphs.

For nine years the nymphs raised him secretly in a cave and taught him the arts of metalwork. Then the discarded child took his revenge on Hera. He fashioned a magic throne, or, in another version of the myth, shoes, as a gift for his mother. Trapped by their power, the great goddess was helpless, until Hephaistos agreed to release her.

The second ejection occurred when Hephaistos interfered in a quarrel between his parents. Zeus became so angry that he threw his son out of Olympus, and he fell on the island of Lemnos. As a result, the people on the island were taught metalwork, in which they became expert.

Hephaistos was the divine craftsman. He built the palaces in which the gods lived a life of luxury. However, his limp and his sooty face made him a figure of fun. The unfaithfulness of his wife APHRODITE only added to his problems.

Hephaistos was also associated with volcanic fire. Lemnos contained a volcano, and in Italy his cult flourished near Etna and Vesuvius. It is possible that his worship originated in Asia Minor.

See Fire, p.150 and Craftsmen and Smith Gods, p.154

SEE ALSO GA-GORIB

SEE ALSO LEDA, MENELAUS, NEMESIS, PARIS, PROTEUS

SEE ALSO ETNA, OLYMPUS

Sacred Mountains

The exact siting of heaven has always preoccupied mankind. Favourite locations have been the sky or the top of a mountain, but some peoples have chosen to build houses for gods, such as the ziggurats of Mesopotamia, so that heaven was near by.

Zeus, the king of the Greek gods, was said to hold court on Mt Olympus. With its summit frequently enshrouded by cloud, this was considered the natural home for a sky god.

Ziggurats – gigantic manmade mountains of sundried bricks – were built in every city of Sumer. They were built by the people as homes for the city gods.

Chinese pilgrims still make the journey up the steep slopes of Mt Taishan. It was long believed in China that the gods could be reached at the tops of mountains.

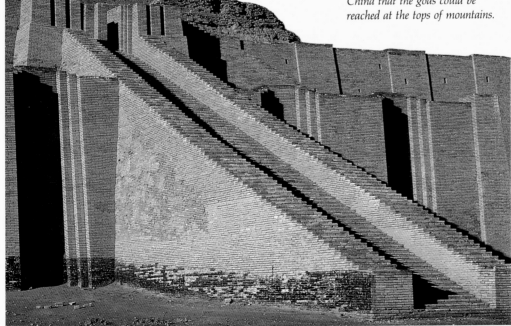

Mt Kailasa is the paradise of the Hindu god Shiva, who is shown seated there with his family. However the Hindu equivalent of Mt Olympus is Mt Meru, home of the sky god Indra.

HERA

The sister and wife of Zeus, the chief god of the ancient Greeks. She was principally a mother goddess.

The daughter of KRONOS and Rhea, Hera was Zeus's older sister and queen of heaven. She was swallowed at birth by her father, who feared that his children would overthrow him. Only Zeus escaped this fate, through the cunning of his mother Rhea and his grandmother Gaia. Having defeated Kronos, and forced him to yield up his swallowed offspring, Zeus decided that Hera should be his wife. Several myths exist about their courtship, and various shrines in Greece commemorate it.

Hera had four children by Zeus: the war god ARES, the smith god HEPHAISTOS, the goddess of childbirth Ilithyia, and Hebe, the cup-bearer of the gods. When the goddess ATHENA, the daughter of Zeus and Metis, emerged from Zeus's head, Hera was so furious at Zeus's adultery that she immediately gave birth to the monster TYPHON. Typhon almost broke the power of Zeus, but eventually the hard-pressed king of the gods managed to imprison the terrible creature under Etna, from which his fiery breath was said to be seen billowing.

Hera was a jealous goddess and spent a great deal of time persecuting the children Zeus had with other goddesses and mortal women. In fact, the quarrels of Zeus and Hera were often so fierce that they shook Olympus, the site of heaven. Once Zeus was so angry about Hera's mistreatment of the hero HERACLES that he suspended her from a pinnacle by her wrists, hanging weights on her feet.

Perhaps the strangest quarrel between the two was their argument about sexual love, a field in which Zeus claimed some knowledge. Hera insisted that the male received most pleasure. When Zeus told his wife it was otherwise, there was no end to the dispute, until they agreed to consult Tiresias, who was both a man and a woman. The answer that a woman has nine times as much pleasure as a man so infuriated Hera that she blinded Tiresias. In compensation for the hurt, Zeus immediately gave him the gift of prophecy.

See Love and Fertility, pp.106/107

SEE ALSO ETNA, HEBE, ILITHYIA, METIS, OLYMPUS, RHEA, TIRESIAS

HERACLES

The great hero of the Greeks, and possibly once lord of Tiryns, an ancient citadel in the Peloponnese. He was known to the Romans as Hercules.

Heracles was the son of ZEUS and Alcmene, the queen of Tiryns. The goddess HERA, the wife of Zeus, tried to frustrate the birth, but succeeded only in stopping Heracles becoming the king of Tiryns, by retarding his birth until another child was born who would inherit the crown. Instead, Heracles was made a slave.

Heracles' semi-divine nature soon showed itself. When Hera sent two snakes to kill him in his cot, the baby Heracles seized one in each hand and strangled them. So he learned early the ways of the warrior.

No one could withstand the spear or arrow of Heracles, who also excelled as a wrestler. But Hera was not to be thwarted and, at the moment of Heracles' greatest triumph, she struck him with a fit of madness. During this terrible derangement, the hero killed his wife and sons.

Unable to find peace of mind after committing this dreadful crime, Heracles consulted the oracle of Apollo at Delphi. There he was told to go to Tiryns and obey the orders of its king, Eurystheus. He did this, and the king set the hero a number of tasks or labours.

The first task Eurystheus imposed was the destruction of the Nemean lion, a fierce beast which terrorized the countryside around Tiryns. When Heracles discovered that the lion could not be harmed even by magic arrows provided by Apollo, he had to resort to using his own bare hands. After a great struggle, Heracles throttled the beast and took the skin for a trophy, using the lion's own sharp claws to skin it. Zeus then turned the dead Nemean lion into the constellation Leo.

The second labour ordered by Eurystheus involved the destruction of the Hydra of Lerna. This nine-headed serpent sacred to Hera proved no less daunting than the Nemean lion. Heracles found that no sooner had he cut off one of the heads than two more sprang up. He called on his nephew Iolaus for help. Immediately after each decapitation Iolaus burned each stump with a torch. When a giant crab came to the rescue of the Hydra, Heracles

dispatched it with a single stamp of his foot. Hera immediately transformed the smashed crab into the constellation Cancer. When at last Heracles was victorious, Eurystheus refused to acknowledge the labour because he had enlisted the help of Iolaus.

The third labour was to capture the Cerynitian hind, a golden-horned creature sacred to ARTEMIS. In one version of the story, the hind was one of the four who pulled her chariot. Heracles captured it in Arcadia, but since Eurystheus had stressed that no harm should come to the creature, the hero set it free again at Tiryns.

Heracles' second adventure in Arcadia, the fourth labour, was the capture of the Erymanthian boar. Heracles shouted outside the boar's lair until it rushed out and became trapped in a snowdrift. He then caught it in a strong net.

The fifth labour was to clean the stables belonging to Augeas, son of Helios the sun god. His vast herds had deposited dung so deep that Heracles could clear it away only by diverting a river. But Eurystheus once again refused to count this as one of the labours.

The sixth labour was the killing of the Stymphalion birds. These vicious creatures created terror in the countryside, where they attacked farmers with their steel-tipped wings. Heracles shot many of them with his arrows and drove off the rest by means of a bronze rattle made by the smith god HEPHAISTOS.

The next labour, the seventh, took Heracles to the island of Crete. There he was ordered to capture the sea-born bull that MINOS had failed to sacrifice to POSEIDON and which had become the object of his wife's desire. Heracles brought the bull back to Tiryns, and then released it.

As the eighth labour, Eurystheus told Heracles to deal with the man-eating horses of Diomedes, a ruler of Thrace. En route, Heracles saved a Thessalian queen by wrestling Thanatos (death) to the ground. At last he reached Thrace and tamed the wild horses, as commanded.

The ninth labour was more difficult. Wanting to please his daughter with a magnificent gift, Eurystheus sent Heracles to get the belt of Hippolyta, queen of the Amazons, a nation of female warriors in

Asia Minor. When Heracles arrived, he was welcomed by Hippolyta, who handed over the belt without demur. But Hera was furious that Heracles should have such luck, and stirred up the Amazons against him. In the desperate fight that followed, Hippolyta was killed by the hero.

The tenth labour took Heracles to Spain. His target there was the herd of oxen belonging to Geryon, a local king with three heads, six hands, and three bodies joined together at the waist. On the voyage the hero set up the twin Pillars of Hercules, as he passed the Straits of Gibraltar. The oxen were driven back to Tiryns overland, where Eurystheus sacrificed them to Hera.

The final two labours had to be performed because Eurystheus had refused to accept the second and fifth ones. Heracles was instructed to fetch the golden apples of the Hesperides, female guardians of the fruit that Gaia gave to Hera on her marriage to Zeus. As the location of the sacred garden where they grew was kept secret, Heracles persuaded the Titan, Atlas, father of the Hesperides, to go on his behalf. In the meantime, Heracles supported the sky for Atlas, with the help of the goddess ATHENA. When Eurystheus received the apples, he returned them at once to Hera, since they were too holy for him to keep.

The twelfth, and last, labour of Heracles was to bring the three-headed dog Cerberus from the underworld. By succeeding in this task, the hero overcame HADES, king of the dead, and so became immortal.

However, Heracles had still to live out the rest of his life and suffer further assaults by Hera. His life as a man was ended by the poisonous blood of Nessus the centaur, whom Heracles had encountered during his second labour. Heracles' second wife, Deianira, was afraid that Heracles would desert her, so when the crafty Nessus told her that his blood had the power to retain Heracles' favour, she readily believed him. Deianira smeared the toxic blood on her husband's tunic and it poisoned him.

See Heroes, p.55

SEE ALSO ALCMENE, AMAZONS, AUGEAS, DELPHI, GERYON, HELIOS, HIPPOLYTA, HYDRA, IPHICLES, MINOTAUR, NESSUS, THANATOS

HERMES

The messenger of the Greek gods and escort of the dead to the realm of Hades. He was known to the Romans as Mercury.

Hermes was the son of ZEUS and the nymph Maia. He was represented as a young man wearing a wide-brimmed hat and winged sandals, and carrying a herald's staff crowned with a pair of snakes. As a god of travellers, and of good luck in general, Hermes was frequently invoked by the ancient Greeks. He appeared to the adventurer ODYSSEUS on CIRCE's island, to warn him of her spells and to advise him how to overcome them.

The young Hermes was precocious and could walk by noon on the day he was born. Soon afterward, he killed a tortoise and, by stretching strings across its shell, invented the lyre. This was a fortunate invention for Hermes, because when he annoyed Apollo by stealing some of his cattle, he was able to offer him the lyre in compensation and so escape punishment.

The nimble fingers of Hermes made him the patron of thieves. He even stole Apollo's quiver and bow during the hearing of the case about the lost cattle. But Zeus made Hermes return them, and soon Apollo forgave him.

A problem for Hermes was HERA, the jealous wife of Zeus, who resented Hermes' birth. In order to divert her anger, he dressed himself in swaddling clothes and deceived her into believing that he was the baby ARES, her own son. Having suckled him, Hera accepted Hermes as a foster-son.

The ploys Hermes used to aid his fellow gods were equally ingenious, and Zeus, too, often relied on his wit. Indeed, Zeus was saved by Hermes in the desperate struggle with the monster TYPHON. This creature had cut out Zeus's sinews and hidden them in a cave, thus incapacitating the king of the gods. Hermes recovered them at great peril.

In Greece today, the verges of country roads are dotted with small Christian pillar shrines. These comforts to the traveller originate from the *hermeia*, square pillars sacred to Hermes.

SEE ALSO MAIA

HINUN

The great thunder spirit of the Iroquois Indians, whose tribes included the Tuscaroras, Susquehannocks, Cherokees, Nottoways, Mohawks and Senecas.

Hinun, the guardian of the sky, is portrayed as a powerful brave armed with a bow and arrows of fire. His wife was Rainbow and his human aid Gunnodoyak, a young warrior who fought the serpent of the Great Lakes which preyed upon the Iroquois Indians. Although Hinun lent Gunnodoyak magical weapons for the combat, the serpent proved so strong and cunning that he swallowed Gunnodoyak whole. Hinun came to Gunnodoyak's rescue and took the wounded warrior to his heavenly abode in the western sky.

In his titanic duel with the water serpent, Hinun used a magic ointment to sharpen his eyesight and improve his aim. When he caught sight of Gunnodoyak's devourer, he sent an arrow whizzing down into the depths of the lake. An awful commotion arose as the great snake writhed in its death agony. Heaven and earth fell silent, terrified by the din, and dared to congratulate Hinun only when the massive bulk of the monster floated inert on the surface of the lake.

The thunder spirit also slew the stone giants, a ferocious people who dwelt in the west. Learning of a threatened attack on the Iroquois, he called up all his powers and struck the giant invaders a devastating blow from which they never recovered. Their shattered bodies fell into an abyss, where they still lie beneath the earth.

Hinun encapsulates the warrior ethic of the Iroquois tribes, whose savagery during the early colonial wars earned them a terrible reputation among European settlers. However, the Iroquois were not simply bloodthirsty warriors. They produced, too, the wise Hiawatha, who advocated peaceful coexistence between the various tribes and organized the Cayugas, Mohawks, Oneidas, Onondagas and Senecas into the league known as the Five Nations.

See Serpents, p.115 and Natural Phenomena, p.138

SEE ALSO GUNNODOYAK, HIAWATHA

HOLAWAKA

The mythical messenger bird of the Galla peoples of Ethiopia. Holawaka brought death to mankind by his treachery.

According to Galla mythology, the first men were not intended to die. But their immortality depended upon receiving instructions from heaven. These were entrusted to the messenger bird Holawaka. The bird was told to tell man, "You shall be immortal, and when you are old and feeble, all you have to do to be young again is to strip off your skins."

On the way to the first men, Holawaka met a snake which was eating a dead animal. Holawaka looked longingly at the snake's meal and offered to let it hear the message in return for sharing the carcass. At first the snake took no interest in this proposal, but the bird persisted, and eventually the snake gave way. Then Holawaka said: "When men grow old they will die, but when you grow old you will change your skin and regain your youth."

The powers in heaven were so angry at this betrayal of mankind that Holawaka was afflicted by a horrible disease. The Galla believe that the bird's cries of pain can still be heard when it calls from the top of a tree.

The connection between the sloughing of a snake's skin and rebirth is a common myth. It occurs, for example, in the story of the Sumerian hero GILGAMESH, when a serpent steals the magic "Never Grow Old" plant from him and gains the power to cast off its skin and emerge rejuvenated. In African mythology, however, snakes are usually regarded as ancestral spirits. They are also commonly held to be ancestral spirits in Aboriginal mythology. BOBBI-BOBBI, the ancestral snake of the Binbinga, invented the boomerang.

See Death, p.91

HORUS

The falcon-headed sun god of Memphis in Egypt. He was believed to be present at the coronation of pharaohs, with whom he was associated during life. After death, Egyptian rulers were said to become Horus's father, the underworld god Osiris.

Horus's mother was ISIS, the sister and wife of OSIRIS. He was conceived by magical means. According to one myth, after SETH killed his brother OSIRIS, Isis went to look for Osiris's body and found it in the delta marshes. She sat on him, warming him enough to awaken his sexual energy and make her pregnant, and thus Horus was conceived.

Horus was raised in the marshes, in the utmost secrecy. But when he reached manhood he determined to avenge the death of his father, and a lengthy series of battles with Seth ensued. By the end of them, Horus had been blinded in one eye by Seth, and had killed Seth (or, in some versions, emasculated him). Horus was judged by the gods to have won an honourable victory, and was given the throne of Egypt. Perhaps to mark this event, Horus gave Osiris the eye he had lost and instead wore a serpent on his head as his second eye. Thereafter the rulers of Egypt always wore the serpent on their crowns, as a symbol of royal authority.

Horus had several forms. As Heru-pa-khret, he was Horus the Child, and was often depicted as an infant wearing a crown or royal headdresss. He was shown sucking his finger or being suckled by his mother Isis.

In this version of his story, Horus appeared before the council of the gods to claim his right to the throne of his father Osiris. But his uncle Seth insisted that he himself should be crowned king because Horus was illegimate (having been mysteriously conceived after Osiris's death).

Finally, the council was swayed by the reasoning (and threats) of Neith, a cow goddess from Lower Egypt. "Give the office of Osiris to his son Horus", she declared, "and do not act wickedly, else I become angry, and send heaven crashing to the ground."

Following this judgement, the sun god RE took offence, Horus was blinded by Seth, and only the persuasion of the cow goddess HATHOR prevented further violence. A resolution was finally reached at the insistence of Osiris, who appeared as a sinister ruler, a source of terror to both men and gods.

Quite separate from Horus, son of Osiris, was the falcon-headed solar god Horus. As Herakhty he was Horus of the Horizon; as Re-Herakhty, he was linked to the great sun god Re himself; and as Horbehudet, he was shown as a solar disc.

See Gods and Animals, p.103

The falcon-headed god Horus at Edfu, Egypt

SEE ALSO HERAKHTY, HERU-PA-KHRET, NEITH, RE-HERAKHTY

Gods and animals

From earliest times, humans have found a special fascination in animals, particularly those with striking features or stunning abilities. Creatures were thought to have acquired their awesome powers through divine intervention. In mythology, many gods take on animal forms.

The shark depicted on this bark painting is an Aboriginal totem, and represents the creature from which one clan believes it is descended.

In an initiation ritual, young men of the Bapende people in Zaire dress up as lions with manes of straw, to imitate the creatures' godlike strength (left).

The Eskimo salmon charm (above) was believed to bring good hunting of this valued food.

Ganesa (right) is the elephant-headed Hindu god of prosperity and good fortune. Still worshipped today, he often appears on the covers of Indian students' notebooks.

Taueret, Egyptian goddess of childbirth, and protectress of infants, often took the form of a pregnant hippopotamus (above).

HUANG DI

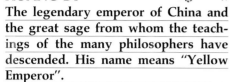

The legendary emperor of China and the great sage from whom the teachings of the many philosophers have descended. His name means "Yellow Emperor".

Huang Di was believed by the ancient Chinese to have been responsible for civilization; before his rule order was unknown on earth. He is credited with founding governmental institutions, inventing the compass, coining the first money, and sponsoring scholarship.

What attracted Qin Shi Huangdi, the first historical Chinese emperor, to the story of Huang Di was not his brilliant reign, however. The unifier of China in 221 BC was more impressed by the fact that, on his abdication, Huang Di rose into the sky as an immortal (*hsien*). Embassies were therefore sent to the tops of mountains in order to contact the immortals, and to find a way for the first emperor to join Huang Di at the end of his own reign.

Belief in an immortal kingdom in the sky, or among distant islands, was fed by the myth of Huang Di's golden age on earth. But the singular appearance of Huang Di, his family, and his attendants was never forgotten. The legendary emperor had four faces so that he could see all that happened. His chariot, pulled by an elephant and six dragons, was driven by a cranelike bird with a human face, a white beak and green plumage. Huang Di's son, Yuhu the sea god, also had the face of a man and the body of a bird, but he had two yellow snakes attached to his ears as well.

See Golden Ages, p.118

HUITZILOPOCHTLI

The chief deity of the Aztecs, who ruled Mexico in the fourteenth and fifteenth centuries. His name means "blue hummingbird on the left".

Huitzilopochtli, the Aztecs' tribal deity, was a god of war. He commanded the fierce warriors to carve out an empire, to fight without mercy, and to gather the captives necessary for sacrifice to the gods.

The characteristic Aztec form of sacrifice was to tear out the heart of a living body and offer it to the sun. This was intended to secure rain, harvests and success in war. Flaying was also a popular form of sacrifice. For some reason, possibly connected with reproduction, Huitzilopochtli's favoured victims were children.

Like most Aztec deities, Huitzilopochtli underwent a nightly death, became bones, and returned to the world in the morning. The god's attributes of the hummingbird and fire are similar to those of Xochipilli, the flayed god of flowers and lord of souls. Both deities were credited with powers over the agricultural cycle. When the corn ripened, the youthful sun god XIPETOTEC was said to merge with Huitzilopochtli.

Huitzilopochtli was depicted as a blue man, fully armed and decorated with hummingbird feathers. The serpent goddess COATLICUE, the Aztec deity of the earth, conceived him when a feathery ball fell from heaven and came into contact with her breast.

The god's numerous elder brothers and sisters, thinking that their mother had disgraced them when she became magically impregnated with Huitzilopochtli, plotted her death. However, the unborn child calmed Coatlicue and, when the children attacked, sprang fully formed out of his mother in her defence, like the Greek goddess ATHENA.

He slew his sister Coyolxauhqui (golden bells) and his other star brothers and sisters, then returned to Coatlicue who said how much she regretted the violence. To distract his mother, the god cut off Coyolxauhqui's head and tossed it up into the heavens to become the moon.

See War, pp.94/95

ICTINIKE

The adventurous trickster god and son of the sun god in the mythology of the North American Sioux or Dakota Indians.

Ictinike is depicted as an Indian brave interested both in warfare and its customs. He is often referred to as the inventor of lies, and the stories surrounding him tell of his cunning and deceit. Eventually, Ictinike's trickery drove his father to expel him from heaven.

During his exile on earth, Ictinike had several disputes with a variety of Sioux totems including the beaver, flying squirrel, rabbit, kingfisher and muskrat. His first encounter was with Rabbit.

After persuading Rabbit to shoot a bird in a tree, Ictinike then asked him to remove his fur in order to climb up and retrieve the game. However, Rabbit was unable to climb down. So Ictinike, laughing, took off his own clothes, put on Rabbit's fur "suit" and left his helper stranded.

Ictinike then went to the nearest village and married one of the chief's beautiful daughters. The other daughter, feeling slighted, wandered into the forest. Hearing Rabbit's complaints, she rescued him and took the skinless creature home. However, no one would believe his story.

When an eagle appeared in the sky both Ictinike and Rabbit tried to shoot it down. Ictinike failed to hit it with his arrow, but Rabbit brought it crashing earthward like a stone. Each morning, a feather from the miraculous eagle became a new bird and the rivals repeated their contest. Rabbit always won, and eventually Ictinike tired of the shooting match.

By now Ictinike had worn out Rabbit's fur and was forced to wear an old piece of tepee hide. Rabbit then gave Ictinike the clothes he had left under the tree where they met and ordered the Indians to beat their drums. Every time they did so, Ictinike was obliged to jump into the air until, at a crescendo of drumming, he jumped so high that when he landed he broke his neck.

See Heroes, p.55 and Trickster Gods, pp.78/79

SEE ALSO COYOLXAUHQUI, XOCHIPILLI

IMANA

The supreme deity of the Banyarwanda people of Ruanda, in central Africa. His name means "almighty".

Even though the ideas about Imana were recorded only relatively recently, they have not been greatly influenced by outside traditions. These myths are therefore very important in understanding traditional African belief.

For the Banyarwanda the invisible world of the spirits has always been a fearful realm. They believe that one section is placed in the sky, one on earth, and another underground. The main task of Imana has been the maintenance of this three-storeyed universe, which is said to be about to collapse.

Imana seems to coexist with the power of death. He keeps the cycle of life going, sustaining fertility and holding the malevolent spirits of the dead at arm's length, while at the same time death raids the earth, carrying away people's souls.

The origin of death is recounted in a story of a chase. At the beginning, Imana hunted death, who appears to have been a wild animal. The god ordered people to stay indoors so that his dangerous quarry should not find a hiding place. But one old woman ignored this instruction and went to her garden, where death persuaded her to let him hide beneath her skirt. Imana was so annoyed by her disobedience that he let death stay on earth.

Another myth also blames the coming of death on women. It relates how there once was a family consisting of a husband, wife and mother-in-law. The wife disliked the mother-in-law greatly and was relieved when she died and was buried. Three days after the funeral she visited the grave, as was the tribal custom, but to her surprise found that it was full of cracks, as if the dead woman were about to emerge. Returning with a heavy pestle, she pounded down the earth and commanded her mother-in-law to stay dead. After repeating this on two subsequent days, the wife was pleased to notice no more cracks. The dead woman had given up the struggle of rebirth and so, Banyarwanda tradition says, the chance of overcoming death was lost for ever.

See Death, p.91

IMHOTEP

An Egyptian scholar and adviser to Zoser, who ruled Egypt in the twenty-sixth century BC. He was a man of great learning, especially in medical science, astronomy and architecture, and was one of the few men to be deified by the Egyptians. His name literally means "he who comes in peace".

Deification of ordinary mortals tended to occur a long time after their deaths: Imhotep acquired divine honours only after more than a millennium had passed, and the period of his greatest popularity was as late as the sixth century BC.

The chief reason for Imhotep's incorporation into the Egyptian pantheon was his design of the pyramid. Rulers had previously been buried in chambers at the bottom of deep rock-cut shafts. Such a habitation for the afterlife would have probably satisfied Zoser, had Imhotep not proposed the building of a "house" above the ground. The Step Pyramid at Saqqara that resulted from the decision was the first monumental building ever built in stone; it rises in six steps to a height of 61m (198ft).

Representations of Imhotep portray him as a priest with a shaven head, seated with an open papyrus-roll on his lap. He was attributed with a treatise on pyramid construction which served as a guide for later architects.

The Greeks identified Imhotep with the god of medicine, ASCLEPIUS.

The Step Pyramid at Saqqara, Egypt

INANNA

The Sumerian goddess of fertility and love, and the most important goddess in the Sumerian pantheon. Her descent into the underworld is the oldest version of the universal myth about the journey of souls from the land of the living to the land of the dead.

In some myths Inanna was the daughter of AN, the god of heaven, and in others her father was the air god ENLIL.

In every city of ancient Sumer there were pairs of temples dedicated to the worship of Inanna and her husband Dumuzi, who among other things was a shepherd. The king of each city impersonated Dumuzi, and the high priestess Inanna herself, in an annual marriage ceremony which was intended to secure prosperity, strength and concord.

The story of Inanna's descent into the land of the dead is fascinating. Inanna suddenly wanted to visit "the land of no return", *kur-nu-gi-a*, a dry, dusty place beneath Abzu, the sweet underground waters of the earth. This wish became an obsession that nothing could shift. There seems to have been no reason for it other than that Inanna may have wanted to test her powers against those of her sister Ereshkigal, "the mistress of death", who lived in the underworld.

Inanna adorned herself with all her finery and left her handmaiden Ninshubur with orders to rescue her should she be detained. At the gate of the land of no return, Inanna was told that she would be admitted only if she shed a garment or ornament at each of the seven portals she encountered. This she did, and at last stood naked before Ereshkigal and the seven judges of the dead.

Undaunted, Inanna pulled her sister from the throne and sat on it herself. But Inanna could not defend herself against the grim judges, who rejected her usurpation and condemned her to death. They hung her from a hook where, like a rotting piece of meat, she turned green with decay.

After three days and three nights, the handmaiden Ninshubur started up a lament for her mistress. Her mourning was so profound that the gods were moved. Even Enlil was touched when Ninshubur told him that his daughter was too precious to be treated as if she were mortal.

But none of these gods could help, because the underworld was outside their domain.

In despair, Ninshubur travelled to Eridu, the home of the water god ENKI, where she found the assistance she needed. Enki created two sexless beings, for whom admission to the land of infertility and death would not be refused. These creatures were instructed as to how they might cunningly ingratiate themselves with Ereshkigal and find a way to revive Inanna. Enki supplied them with water and the grass of life to perform this deed.

Much against her will, Ereshkigal was persuaded to give the creatures Inanna's rotten corpse and was forced to watch the revival of her wilful sister. But the seven judges of the dead intervened a second time, and not until Inanna promised to find a substitute to take her place would they let her leave the underworld.

Inanna was taken back to the land of the living by a ghastly escort of demons. The first person they met on the way was Ninshubur. But Inanna refused to allow her to be the substitute. She did the same for every person they encountered, until they reached her home, the city of Uruk.

There Inanna was stunned by the sight of Dumuzi her husband – he was not dressed in sackcloth and ashes as a bereaved husband ought to be, but instead seemed to be enjoying himself. Outraged, Inanna appointed him her substitute.

According to certain texts, Inanna decided, after some time, to ease Dumuzi's fate. She allowed Geshtinanna, her sister, to alternate with Dumuzi for six-monthly periods in the land of no return.

Interpreting Inanna's descent myth is not easy. It is our misfortune that only portions of it remain. Geshtinanna was the goddess of wine (her name means "leafy grapevine") and Dumuzi himself was responsible for brewing beer, apart from overseeing animal husbandry. So the alternate disappearance of Geshtinanna and Dumuzi could refer to the cycle of manufacture for wine and beer.

In later mythologies, Inanna reappears in the form of ISHTAR, ASTARTE, CYBELE, APHRODITE and VENUS.

See Love and Fertility, pp.106/107

SEE ALSO ABZU, DUMUZI, ERESHKIGAL, NINSHUBUR, TAMMUZ

Love and fertility

The powers of love, and of fertility, assure the future of humanity. Love goddesses are therefore prominent throughout mythology.

Aphrodite, the Greek goddess of love, was unfaithful to her husband and bore the children of the war god Ares. She is shown (below) seeing him off to war.

Radha and Krishna (above), represent the deification of true love. Radha was a milkmaid, Krishna one of the incarnations of the Hindu god Vishnu.

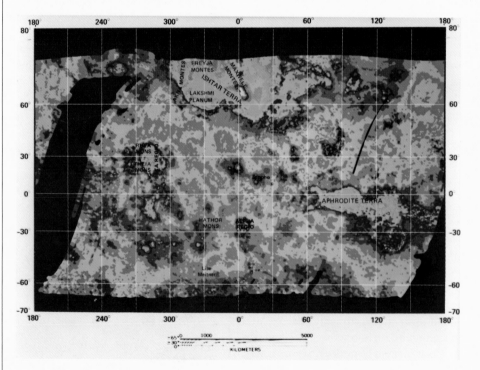

The planet Venus was named after the Greek love goddess. The parts of the planet shown in this topographic map bear the names of love goddesses from other mythologies, including Ishtar, Lakshmi and Aphrodite.

The fertility goddess Nimba is worshipped by the Simo society of women in Guinea.

INARI

The Japanese god of rice, sometimes referred to as the food god. Every Japanese village still contains a shrine dedicated to Inari, as the giver of agricultural wealth, although his patronage now extends to prosperity in international commerce and industry.

Inari is depicted as a bearded old man sitting on a sack of rice, flanked by two foxes, who are his messengers. In some parts of Japan the fox itself has become the divinity of rice. Because rice crops are the basis of all prosperity, Inari is always regarded as a generous god.

Inari's wife was Uke-mochi, the food goddess, who supplied the land with boiled rice, the sea with fishes and the mountains with animals. However the moon god killed Uke-mochi because these gifts had come forth from her mouth. On her death Inari inherited sovereignty over agriculture.

The rice god Inari, flanked by two foxes

SEE ALSO UKE-MOCHI

INDRA

King of the Hindu gods in the *Rig Veda*, an early collection of hymns. Indra had authority over the sky: he could rend the clouds apart with his thunderbolts and make rain.

In the Vedic hymns, Indra is described as a splendid and heroic figure. He rides in a golden chariot drawn by two powerful steeds, which is sometimes seen as a symbol of the sun. He has a ruddy complexion and enormously long arms.

Indra's weapon is the thunderbolt, which he carries in his right hand and employs at his pleasure, to destroy or to revive those slain in battle. He also uses arrows, a cruel hook and a net, in which he entangles his foes. *Soma* juice is his favourite drink and, prior to a battle, he consumes this magical draught in vast quantities.

Indra won his early ascendancy in the Hindu pantheon by slaying Vritra, the serpent of drought, who had swallowed the cosmic waters and lay in coils enveloping the mountains. Indra's decisive thunderbolt split the serpent's stomach, releasing the waters, generating life, and liberating dawn. This victory of a sky god over a snake is an ancient idea which appears in many other myths including those of Greece and Australia.

One of Indra's titles is Purandara (destroyer of cities). He was the war god of the Aryans, who invaded India around 1700 BC, showing little regard for the walled settlements of the country's inhabitants.

By about the fifth century BC, Indra had fallen to the second rank. He was demoted to a god of paradise and his life-sustaining functions on earth were taken over by VISHNU. The lowering of his esteem in Hindu mythology may have been brought about by a resurgence of older beliefs from the Indus civilization which he had helped to destroy. Archaeological evidence suggests that the antecedents of SHIVA and DEVI existed in the great cities that Indra's devotees wiped out.

Indra was a parallel of the Greek sky god ZEUS; he was also identified by the Romans with their sky god JUPITER.

See Natural Phenomena, p. 138

SEE ALSO SOMA, VRITRA

INTI

The sun god from whom the Inca dynasty traced its descent. The Incas ruled Peru from the mid-fifteenth century until 1532, when they were overthrown by the Spaniards.

According to one version of the Inca origin myth, Inti was so distressed by the wretchedness of mankind that he instructed his son Manco Capac and daughter Mama Ocollo in the arts of civilization and sent them down to earth as rulers. They were told to wander from place to place until a golden wedge they carried sank of its own accord into the ground. Wherever this happened, they were to build their capital, which proved to be Cuzco. The Inca dynasty they founded there conquered all the Andean peoples.

The Incas endeavoured to impose a uniform creed throughout their empire. However, it seems that, anxious not to provoke the people they conquered, they did not insist on radical and instant change. Usually, they merely added a sun temple to the principal local cult centre and trusted that future generations would come to recognize Inti's ultimate authority.

One ancient Peruvian deity whom the Incas recognized was VIRACOCHA. He had authority over the storm and light and, according to one tradition, created the stars, moon and even the sun.

The most important shrine in Cuzco, Qorikancha (the sun temple), housed images of Viracocha and all the other important members of the pantheon. Thus, it seems possible that the entire Inca pantheon was seen as various manifestations of a single godhead, namely Inti, the sun itself.

See Founders, p.68

SEE ALSO MAMA OCOLLO, MANCO CAPAC

ISHTAR

The Babylonian goddess of fertility and love, the counterpart of the Sumerian goddess Inanna.

Ishtar was much more aggressive than INANNA and fiercely passionate. She was married to Tammuz, a dying-and-rising deity like Inanna's husband Dumuzi. And like Inanna, Ishtar descended to the underworld domain of her sister Ereshkigal. Here she was so intimidating that even Ereshkigal blanched at her approach.

Eventually, however, Ereshkigal summoned the strength to put a curse on her fearsome sister who was overcome by death. As a result, the springs of fertility on earth ran dry: animals stopped mating and men stopped impregnating women.

Ea, the water god, secured Ishtar's release by enlisting the help of a marvellous eunuch. He so angered Ereshkigal that she exhausted her powers of cursing. This weakened her hold on Ishtar, and the eunuch managed to persuade her to give him Ishtar's body, which he revived with the water of life. But Ishtar had to leave a substitute in the underworld, so she chose her husband, Tammuz.

Ishtar was the protectress of harlots as well as of the alehouse. The evening star was often compared to a harlot soliciting in the sky, its power informing the goddess's sisters below. Tammuz was said to be embodied in any of the men who accepted a harlot's embrace.

As the goddess of love, Ishtar was feared, for those men who fell in love with her died. It was for this reason that GILGAMESH spurned her advances.

The Babylonians developed Ishtar into a grim figure as "the lady of battles". She became the promoter of terror, the violent agony at the very centre of combat. This aspect of her appealed most to the warlike Assyrians, who subjugated the Babylonians. For the Assyrians Ishtar was the perfect wife for their national god ASHUR. In Assyrian myth Ishtar's empathy with Ashur's harsh nature is indicated by her growing a beard and always carrying a bow in her hands.

See War, pp.94/95 and Love and Fertility, pp.106/107

SEE ALSO DUMUZI, ERESHKIGAL, TAMMUZ

ISIS

The mother goddess of Egypt. Isis was often depicted suckling the child Horus. When represented with the solar disc and cow's horns, she was identified with the cow goddess Hathor.

Isis was the daughter of the earth god Geb and the sky goddess NUT; sister and wife of the underworld god OSIRIS; sister of donkey-headed SETH and his wife Nephthys; and mother of the sun god HORUS.

When Osiris succeeded Geb as king of Egypt, Isis taught her subjects how to grind flour, spin, weave and cure illnesses. She is also credited with introducing the custom of marriage. When Osiris travelled, civilizing the rest of the world, Isis remained in Egypt as his regent, ruling the kingdom wisely.

On his return from his travels, Osiris was killed by his jealous brother Seth. Isis grieved, cutting off her hair and tearing her clothes. She set off to look for Osiris's body, which had been hidden in a coffer. When she found it, Isis brought Osiris back to life by magical means for long enough for him to impregnate her. The son born of this union was Horus, whom Isis brought up in the refuge of the delta swamps, where Seth could not find them.

Isis performed the first embalming rites

The Temple of Isis at Philae, Egypt

on Osiris, together with ANUBIS, and so established the burial ritual. The magic of Isis was considered to be very important in gaining entry to the subterranean kingdom of Osiris.

The immense power of the goddess is reflected in a myth about the dotage of RE, the sun god. It was said that when Isis was still his servant, she persuaded him to confide his secret name to her. Taking advantage of Re's senility, Isis collected some of the spittle that dripped from his lips, mixed it with earth and fashioned a snake, which she placed in Re's path. The snake bit and poisoned Re who, being senile, was not able to cure himself. Only Isis could remove the poison and pain. She advised Re to utter his secret name, saying that its divinity bestowed life on whoever spoke it.

As the effects of the snake venom worsened, Re was compelled to speak, and so Isis acquired some of his power and her unmatched skill in the magic arts.

"Isis" is a Greek rendering of the Egyptian name "Ast". Her cult was widespread in the Greco-Roman world where, together with Osiris, she became the focus of a mystery cult that was very popular before the rise of Christianity. The Greeks identified her with DEMETER, HERA and APHRODITE.

See Love and Fertility, pp.106/107

ITHERTHER

The primeval buffalo in the myth of an Algerian people known as the Kalyls, whose traditional lore probably comes down from the ancient Berbers.

In the beginning there was a pair of buffaloes on earth. The male was called Itherther and the female Thamuatz. Both had emerged from a dark place beneath the earth, called Tlam, to which they did not wish to return.

So Itherther and Thamuatz lived on the surface of the earth, and in time they had a son called Achimi. The young buffalo was adventurous: he ran off and came to a village built by the first men, who almost captured him. But Achimi was headstrong and would listen to no one's advice. He even ignored the words of a wise old ant, a creature who, though small, was endowed with great understanding. The ant suggested to Achimi that it was better for an animal to serve man than to run wild, since the reward for such labour was regular meals and protection from lions.

But Achimi was determined to shape his own destiny, and he returned to where his parents grazed with his newly born sister. He violently drove away his father Itherther and mated with both his mother and his sister.

Exiled by Achimi, Itherther wandered the mountains alone. But he could not forget his beloved Thamuatz. Every time the buffalo thought of her, he would pause and deposit his semen on the ground, The sun warmed the semen, which grew and developed into other species of animals, whom Itherther cared for.

The Kalyls believe that all animals were born by this means, except the lion. The king of the beasts was said to be the offspring of a human cannibal.

See Gods and Animals, p.103 and Creation, p.135

ITZAMNA

The chief god in the Maya pantheon. He was lord of medicine and was worshipped as the moon god and the bringer of civilization.

Itzamna was depicted as a toothless old man with sunken cheeks and a prominent nose. Despite his unprepossessing appearance, he was a powerful, benevolent deity.

As lord of medicine, Itzamna was able to banish fatal illnesses and raise the dead. His cult was thus very popular with the death-obsessed Maya peoples, who lived in what today is Guatemala and the Mexican province of Yucatan.

Itzamna also presented the Mayas with the gifts of drawing and writing and the order of religious ceremonies. Moreover, he instructed them in land tenure, showing them how land holdings should be arranged. Unlike the Atzecs, who owned no land and were responsible for driving them from the Mexican plateau, the Mayas seem to have had a complex system of land ownership.

A unique feature of Itzamna's cult in Central America is the fact that the god was never held responsible for any catastrophe. Entirely benign, he saw to the fertility of the fields, even to the extent of ensuring an adequate supply of water.

Possibly fathered by the sun god, Itzamna acted as the all-sustainer in Maya creation and intervened wherever necessary. This contrasts strikingly with the behaviour of Hunab, the aloof creator deity. For some unknown reason, Hunab destroyed the world three times by floods before losing all interest in creation. However, the threat of another flood was not entirely lifted from the Mayas since they believed that the angry goddess IXCHEL still held her jug containing the deluge which she could pour onto them at any moment, and the sky serpent could easily produce a tropical storm.

IXCHEL

The moon goddess in Maya mythology. She was feared, along with the sky serpent, as the sender of disastrous floods and tropical cloudbursts.

Almost all the literature of the Central American Mayas has been lost, so their myths too have largely disappeared. However, from the remaining, poorly understood, codices, a few deities stand out. One of these is the malevolent goddess Ixchel, who is shown as an old woman, crowned with a snake and wearing a skirt decorated with crossed bones.

Sometimes Ixchel appears in the company of a sky serpent. In her clawed hands she holds the vessel of doom which, to show her wrath, she upturns, pouring a torrent of destruction on the earth.

Despite this evil side to her character, Ixchel was regarded as the protective patron of women in childbirth and of weavers. ITZAMNA is often mentioned as her spouse.

No less frightening in her depiction is Ixtab, the goddess of suicide, who hangs from a tree, partially decomposed. The Mayas, who were apparently preoccupied with violent death, seem to have believed that suicide was an honourable way of entering paradise. Ixtab took the souls of those who died by hanging to eternal rest beneath the world-tree Yaxche. There she also gathered the souls of fallen warriors, sacrificial victims, priests and women who died in childbirth.

See Flood, pp.110/111

Flood

Floods are frequently explained as divine punishment for the misdeeds of humankind. In most stories, however, the ultimate survival of the human race is ensured by at least one person being forewarned of the deluge. The Sumerian deluge story dating from 2400 BC is the oldest known myth.

People still search the slopes of Mt Ararat in eastern Turkey for traces of Noah's ark. This is said to be the mountain on which the ark came to rest when the flood subsided.

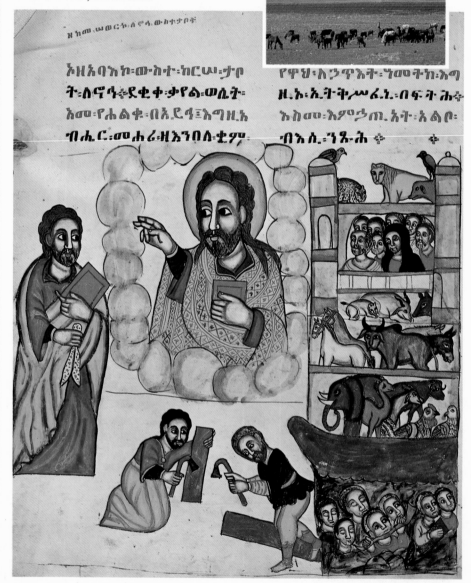

This 10th-century illuminated manuscript shows Noah, his family and some of the animals in the ark. God had instructed him to build the ark when he gave Noah advance warning of his intention to send a deluge to destroy the world because of people's wickedness.

IZANAGI

In Japanese Shinto myth, Izanagi and Izanami were the original ancestors and the first couple. They are credited with much of creation, as well as the realization of death.

For the Maya Indians of Central America, the author of the flood was the goddess Ixchel. It was she who poured the torrential rain of a tropical cloudburst from her great jug. She was assisted by a sky serpent which was said to contain all the waters of the heavens in its belly.

In the Hindu flood myth, the great god Vishnu, incarnated as the fish Matsya, pulled the boat of Manu (the parallel with Noah) to the safety of the Himalayan peaks. When the waters subsided, Matsya gave the survivors religious instruction, so that the world could worship gods properly.

In the beginning, according to Japanese myth, there was only an ocean of chaos. Out of this seething, boiling mass, grew a reed, which was Kunitokotachi (eternal land ruler), and two subordinate deities. The descendants of these two lesser powers were Izanagi and Izanami.

Izanagi and Izanami were sent forth from heaven. Standing on the Floating Bridge of Heaven, they stirred the waters with a lance which the gods had given them. A drop of water fell from its point and turned into an island, upon which the couple made their home and created a sacred column.

The couple walked around this column in opposite directions until they met. Izanami praised Izanagi's beauty and the two consummated their union. But the first child that was born was a monster, and the second was an island. Puzzled, they consulted the gods, who explained that Izanami had addressed Izanagi first, whereas it should have been the god who took the initiative in their sexual union.

Following the gods' advice the couple bore more children, who included the islands of Japan and numerous benevolent deities. However, the last born was Kazu-tsuchi, the god of fire, who burned Izanami so badly while she was giving birth to him that she died. But even in death she was creative, since from her vomit, urine and excrement other gods were born.

Izanagi was so furious with the baby who had caused Izanami's death that he picked up his sword and cut off the child's head. Drops of the baby's blood trickled down the blade and fell on the ground. From these drops, eight gods were created, and from the headless body came eight mountain deities.

Izanagi was inconsolable after his wife's death. He journeyed to "the land of gloom" (yomotsu-kuni) in the hope of bringing Izanami back, because the work of creation was not yet finished on earth.

Izanami met him at the entrance to the underworld and asked him to wait there while she arranged for her release from the powers of death. She warned him not to come in or to look at her closely.

However, when Izanami had been gone for some time, Izanagi broke off the end tooth of a comb that was stuck in his hair, lit it as a torch, and entered the land of gloom. As he looked about him, he was appalled: the darkness was thick with wriggling, crawling maggots and, worse still, Izanami was rotting.

Horrified by this vision of decay, Izanagi fled, pursued by hags. "You have humiliated me!" screamed Izanami, and she urged the ugly women of death to tear him limb from limb. A host of demonic soldiers and thunder gods joined the chase. But Izanagi reached the entrance safely.

As the demons rushed toward him Izanagi pulled three peaches off a tree and hurled them at his pursuers to repulse them. Finally Izanami herself came to the entrance. She accepted a divorce from her husband, retreated into the cave, and the way to the underworld was sealed with a massive boulder.

Izanagi felt sullied by this close encounter with death and went to the sea to cleanse himself. As he cast off his clothes and threw away his personal possessions, they turned into gods and goddesses. The dirt that came off him when he jumped into the sea turned into malevolent gods, so he created benevolent marine deities to counter them.

While Izanagi washed his face, from his left eye the sun goddess AMATERASU was born, from his right eye the moon god Tsuki-yomi, and from his nose came SUSANOWO, the storm god.

The creation of Amaterasu and Tsuki-yomi probably owes something to the Chinese creation myth of PANKU, whose left eye became the sun and right eye the moon. But the chief theme of the myths about Izanagi and Izanami was the Shinto horror of death, decay and dissolution. It was not until Buddhism introduced ideas concerning rewards and punishments after death, and the moral teachings of Confucius emphasized social duties in the here and now, that the Japanese were able to distance themselves from the terrors of the land of gloom.

See Founders, p.68

SEE ALSO IZANAMI, KUNITOKOTACHI, TSUKI-YOMI

JANUS

An ancient Italian deity and the Roman god of beginnings and entrances. His name means "gate" or "barbican".

Janus is represented with two faces, looking in opposite directions. On rare occasions he has four faces. The Romans clearly saw Janus as a deity connected with military success: the double gates of his temple were traditionally closed in times of peace, but they were flung wide open in times of war.

The advantage of Janus's extra face is recounted in a legend concerning the nymph Cara. This teasing beauty liked to lure her admirers into a lonely cave with the promise of her favours; she then slipped quietly away. Because Janus was able to see behind him as well as in front, he foiled her trick and forced the nymph to submit to his passion.

As a guardian deity, one of Janus's exploits involved saving the city of Rome from a surprise attack by the Sabine tribes. At the critical moment, Janus caused a hot spring to flood the threatened gateway. This connection with water is also evident in his family – the river god Tiberinus was his son.

As a god of beginnings, Janus was invoked before all other deities in important undertakings. The first month of the year, January, was sacred to him. It remains a significant time at which people look forward as well as backward, and resolve to start anew. Traditionally, the cult of Janus was instigated by ROMULUS, who built the walls of Rome.

SEE ALSO TIBERINUS

JASON

A legendary Greek hero and leader of the Argonauts. He was probably a Thessalian prince.

Jason was a prince whose father had been dethroned, or denied the succession. Fearing for her son's safety, his mother sent him secretly to the cave of the centaur Chiron. This wise horse-man was the tutor of many of the greatest figures in Greek mythology, such as ASCLEPIUS and ACHILLES. When Jason eventually set off in quest of the Golden Fleece, his crew included several of Chiron's pupils.

The quest came about almost by accident. Because Jason returned home to the city of Iolcus and claimed the throne on a festival day, the usurper Pelias was unable to kill the young contender. Not only would his death have offended the laws of hospitality, but also the gods could have taken grave offence at the violation of their worship. So Pelias pretended that he would step down in Jason's favour in return for the marvellous golden fleece of a ram, which hung from a tree in Colchis, and was guarded by a dragon.

With the support of the Delphic oracle and the goddess HERA, Jason gathered his band of Argonauts, including the great hero HERACLES. After a strenuous voyage they reached Colchis, and with the aid of a local princess, Medea, whom Jason wed, the fleece was gained. When their ship *Argo* hastened away with the prize, pursued by Colchians, Medea suggested that they cut up her brother Apsyrtus and throw him overboard, to slow down the vessels chasing them. The Argonauts did this, forcing their pursuers to gather up the remains for a decent burial.

Medea's interest in dismemberment could also have helped Jason on his return to Iolcus, since she tricked the daughters of Pelias into cutting up and boiling their father the king, in order to restore his youth. But most versions of this myth suggest that Jason did not finally mount the vacant throne; instead he retired voluntarily to the Peloponnese.

The goddess APHRODITE was said to have been responsible for making Medea fall violently in love with Jason. Her purpose was to harm Pelias, whom she hated. The magical skills of Medea were therefore put at Jason's disposal, allowing him to perform the HERACLES-like labours necessary to win the Golden Fleece. Medea means "the cunning one" and she was certainly associated with sorcery.

See Heroes, p.55

Jason and the Argonauts, with Athena

SEE ALSO ARGONAUTS, CHIRON, MEDEA

JESUS

It is hardly surprising that legends were attached to a figure as important as Jesus, but in general these stories have been excluded from the New Testament.

One New Testament story, which is generally accepted as being a myth, and which is paralleled in the stories of Sargon and Moses and is that of the massacre of the children by Herod, the archetypal jealous king. Hearing that a child had been born who was to be ruler of the Jews, Herod, fearing competition, ordered his men to slaughter all young children in the neighbourhood of Bethlehem, where Jesus was born. However, Joseph and Mary fled to Egypt with their son.

Myths about Jesus have free rein in the apocryphal gospels, epistles and acts, which offer a bewildering variety of incident. Because of their dubious authenticity, they were denied entry to the New Testament.

The Gospel of Pseudo-Matthew is a fairly typical example. It tells how the Virgin Mary was fed daily by angels, how she was suspected of adultery by her husband Joseph and how, after she gave birth to Jesus, an ox and an ass adored her newborn child.

The gospel also tells how, on their way to Egypt, the family decided to stop and rest in a cave. When numerous dragons flew from its mouth, the baby Jesus, unperturbed, climbed down from his mother's lap and stood before the dragons, which worshipped him. To calm Mary, Jesus said: "Fear not, neither conceive that I am a child, for I always was and am a perfect man, and it is necessary that all the beasts of the forest should grow tame before me."

The same gospel tells how lions and leopards bowed their heads to Jesus, trees bent to offer Mary fruit, hills moved to ease the family's journey and the statues of Egyptian gods broke at Jesus' approach.

As well as the wonderful stories of Jesus' infancy and boyhood, there are legendary accounts of his ministry and death. Perhaps the Gospel of Nicodemus holds the greatest fascination because it preserves the tradition of the descent of Jesus to the underworld, following his death by crucifixion and his burial.

One of the lost souls there recalls when, "we were holden . . . in darkness and the shadow of death, suddenly there shone upon us a great light, and Hell did tremble, and the gates of death. And there was heard the voice of the Son of the most high Father, as it were the voice of a great thundering, and it proclaimed aloud and began: 'Draw back, O princes, your gates, remove your everlasting doors: Christ the Lord the king of glory approacheth to enter.' "

Thus Jesus strode into the realm of SATAN, prince of death, and overcame the forces of evil ranged against him. No West Asian deity had ever accomplished such a descent without aid, as the deaths of BAAL and INANNA bear witness.

Having thrown Satan into a bottomless pit, Jesus then delivered to the care of the archangel Michael both Adam, the first man God created, and the righteous. He then cast aside the wicked, and set "as a sign of victory, his cross in the midst of Hell".

Although Satan became the snake in Christian demonology, some stories in the apocryphal works seem to be inspired by ancient beliefs in the snake's immortality.

See Saviours, p.75 and Serpents, p.115

Italian wooden crucifix
SEE ALSO ADAM, HEROD, JOSEPH

JUNO

The Roman goddess of women and marriage. In Greek mythology she was identified with Hera, the wife of Zeus.

Juno was the queen of heaven and wife of the sky god JUPITER. She was closely connected with fertility, and particularly with childbirth. It is not unlikely that she began her mythological career as an early Italian moon goddess.

Her chief myth concerns Minerva, the Roman equivalent of ATHENA, the Greek goddess of wisdom and the arts. Like Athena, who sprang from the head of ZEUS, Minerva was born from Jupiter's head without the help of a mother. This event so infuriated Juno that she complained to the goddess Flora, who was responsible for flowering and blossoming plants. At the touch of a magic herb provided by Flora, Juno became pregnant, and bore MARS, the god of war. Juno's counterpart in Greek mythology, Hera, was also the mother of the war god ARES, although Zeus was his father.

As the genius of womanhood, Juno ensured the continuity of the family. The month of June, once called Junonius, was considered to be the most favourable month for weddings.

See Love and Fertility, pp.106/107

Juno, the Roman queen of heaven
SEE ALSO MINERVA

113

JUPITER

The ruler of the sky and the chief god of the Romans. He was also known as Jove.

Jupiter was called Optimum Maximus (best and greatest of the gods), and was regarded as the divine champion of the Romans. After victorious campaigns, generals always made sacrifices to him in his temple on the Capitol Hill, overlooking the centre of Rome.

As a sky god, Jupiter was thought to be responsible for weather of all kinds, especially lightning or rain. From earliest times, he was the protector of vineyards and the harvest. But as Rome developed into a city, Jupiter gradually lost his agricultural associations and became the city god, as MARDUK did before him in ancient Babylon. Eventually, Jupiter became the god who determined all human affairs, whose goodwill was essential to success.

Jupiter's wife was JUNO. Their relations were much less troubled than those of HERA and ZEUS, the supreme goddess and god of the Greeks. But Juno was upset enough by the birth of Minerva (out of Jupiter's head) to bear the war god MARS without a mate. In time, this belligerent son came to rival Jupiter in the affections of the warlike Romans.

The various functions of Jupiter are clear in his titles, such as Tonans (thunderer), Fulgar (wielder of lightning), Imperator (supreme commander), Triumphator triumphant), and Praedator (booty snatcher).

See Natural Phenomena, p.138

Jupiter, the chief god in the Roman pantheon

SEE ALSO MINERVA

KAANG

The remote creator deity of the Bushmen who live in southwestern Africa The god is also called Cagn, Kho and Thora.

The Bushmen say that only the fleet-footed antelope knows exactly where Kaang lives. All they know is that his dwelling is located somewhere in the sky, and when rainstorms occur the Bushmen say that Kaang is tidying his house.

Kaang is an invisible deity whose strength and power are said to reside in one of his teeth. He is thought to work his will through all natural phenomena, but he is particularly manifest in the movements of the mantis and the caterpillar.

Kaang created the world and mankind. At first, relations between the god and human beings were friendly and close. One of Kaang's daughters even married a man. But this friendship did not last long because the first men soon showed the god disrespect. So Kaang sent both destruction and death to earth, and removed his own home to the top of the sky. Even then he did not abandon mankind entirely, for he left two of his sons on earth, and they became the earliest leaders.

Despite this original insult to the creator deity, the exploits of Kaang form the body of Bushmen mythology. From tales of his victories over giants and evil spirits the Bushmen derive strength for their own struggle against Gawama, the leader of the spirits of the dead. Gawama is weaker than Kaang, but his hatred for creation ensures that the lives of the Bushmen are threatened continuously. Their dead are even enlisted by Gawama to harass their living descendants. The two concerns of the Bushmen are therefore the propitiation of Kaang and the exorcism of Gawama.

See Creation, p.135

KAHAUSIBWARE

A female serpent deity worshipped by the Solomon Islanders, who live in the Pacific Ocean.

At the beginning of the world, Kahausibware helped with creation. She made men, pigs and other animals, and trees; she also arranged for fruits to grow without involving human labour.

When the first woman went off to work in her garden, she left the first baby with Kahausibware. But the infant screamed and screamed. Unable to stand the noise, Kahausibware coiled herself around the baby and strangled it, and so introduced death into the world. The mother returned while the serpent's body was still partly wound around her dead child, and seizing an axe, she started to chop the serpent into pieces. Although the serpent goddess was able to rejoin the severed parts of her body, she was so offended that she left the Solomon Islands. The inhabitants say that after her departure things were never the same again.

Another myth about a snake comes from the neighbouring Admiralty Islands. The story recounts how a woman once entered the forest and met a great serpent. After some hesitation, the woman agreed to marry the creature, and she bore a boy and a girl. When these children grew up, their serpent father told them to catch and cook some fish. But they merely heated the fish in the sun's rays, and ate it still raw and bloody.

Seeing this, the serpent said: "Spirits you are, eaters of raw meat. Perhaps you will eat me." He ordered the boy to crawl into his belly and bring out fire. Though the boy was frightened, he did as he had been told, and then, at the serpent's further bidding, he cooked some vegetables on the fire. When the children had eaten, their serpent father asked: "Is my kind of food or yours better?" They answered "Yours! Ours is bad." So it was, according to the Admiralty Islanders, that the rudiments of civilization were first introduced.

See Death, p.91, Serpents, p.115, Creation, p.135 and Fire, p.150

Serpents

As well as its clearly phallic connotations, the serpent embodies a number of different symbolic values. The power to give life – implicit in the fertility symbol – is allied to great knowledge. The power to slough off its skin implied immortality – often represented by a coiled serpent.

Heracles overcomes a sea monster, called Triton, in one of his many adventures. This deity was, however, usually thought of as benevolent, and calmed the waves with a conch-shell.

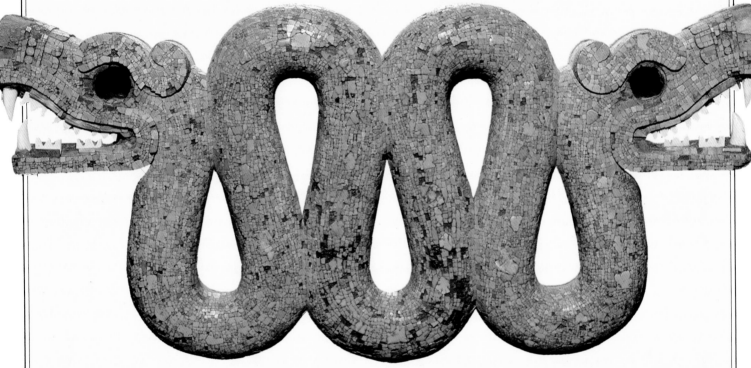

This double-headed serpent was a pendant worn by the high priest of Tlaloc, the Aztec rain god. A sky serpent, with a belly filled with rain, was believed to assist Tlaloc. Infants were regularly sacrificed to the god, who was pleased if they shed tears.

The Murngin of northern Australia worship the great copper serpent Yurlungur as an ancestral spirit. In this bark painting (below), two girls who have broken a taboo by sleeping with men from a forbidden clan are crushed by the snake.

The evil serpent king Kaliya is about to devour some cowherds. Fortunately they are saved by Krishna, who as a child had forced the great snake to acknowledge his divine authority.

KAMAPUA'A

The popular pig god of Hawaiian mythology, whose amorous and war-like nature is the subject of many tales.

Kamapua'a means "hog child" – the deity was born with the face and body of a pig, as well as human hands and feet. He seems to have survived several attempts on his life as an infant, some possibly by his parents. But once he had grown into a strong and energetic god, there were few who could challenge him.

In battle, Kamapua'a would use his snout to throw up mounds or dig trenches; he would wield a huge club in his human hands; and when he charged his enemies, terrifying snorts came from his nostrils. Because of his prowess, Kamapua'a was a welcome ally in the frequent wars of Hawaii.

The pig god was no less determined in the pursuit of love. Once Kamapua'a tried to woo the fire goddess Pele. She spurned him with insults, calling Kamapua'a a filthy pig. Soon the two deities were involved in a slanging match, and their supporters in an all-out fight. While Pele's relations threatened to overwhelm Kamapua'a and his followers with flames, they answered by attacking the volcanic stronghold of the fire goddess with fog and rain. In the end Pele yielded, and the pig god achieved his desire.

The adventures of Kamapua'a are used to explain natural phenomena, such as the occasion when he saw two pretty women and decided to chase them. But they were goddesses and disappeared underground. When Kamapua'a dug into the soil after them, two springs of water emerged, which ever since have been called "the springs of Kamapua'a". His unpredictable behaviour also represents the chaos of human emotions in love and war, for Kamapua'a always acts on impulse, only later considering the consequences of his actions.

See War, pp.94/95 and Natural Phenomena, p.138

SEE ALSO PELE

KANE

In Hawaiian mythology, Kane was the creator deity and chief god of generation.

In Polynesian mythology, the creation of the world is often attributed to TANGAROA, the sea god. However, the immense distances between the Polynesian islands frequently lead to local variations in the area's mythology. Thus, in Hawaii, Kane is the creator god. The direct Hawaiian equivalent of Tangaroa is the squid god Kanaloa, with whom Kane is closely associated. Later Christian missionaries identified Kanaloa with SATAN.

The cult of Kane was bloodless, whereas those of other deities often incorporated human and animal sacrifice.

Kane's creation myth tells how three worlds were made: the upper heaven, the lower heaven and the earth. In the beginning, Kane dwelt in darkness. Then, light was created and Ku, the ancestor god, together with Lono, the god of the heavens, helped Kane to fashion the earth and to furnish its surface with living things.

Eventually these gods created the first human couple but, because they soon showed too much independence, Kane made them subject to death. He then left the earth and retired to the upper heaven.

The Hawaiians remember Kane's original intention to live on earth in their traditional name for the world: Ka-honua-nui-a-Kane (the great earth of Kane). However, few images were made of the god, perhaps because of his remoteness. On the other hand, the Hawaiians may have felt that they should not do anything else to provoke the god's wrath, for Kane's great power is apparent in his titles, such as Kane-hekili (thunder) and Ka-uila-nui-maka-keha'i-i-ka-lani (lightning flashing in the heavens).

See Creation, p.135

SEE ALSO KANALOA, LONO

KRISHNA

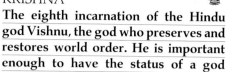

The eighth incarnation of the Hindu god Vishnu, the god who preserves and restores world order. He is important enough to have the status of a god himself.

According to one myth, VISHNU plucked out two of his hairs – one black, the other white – and he placed them in the wombs of two women. The black hair was born as Krishna and the white one as Balarama, his elder brother. Krishna is usually depicted as dark skinned.

Krishna's uncle Kansa, ruler of Mathura and a usurper, had been told that one day he would be deposed by the "Dark One", who would be one of his sister's children. So Kansa killed his nephews as they were born. Krishna therefore was brought up in secrecy, among the cowherds. However, his adoptive mother, Yasoda, was aware of his special powers because one day when she looked down Krishna's throat she was stupefied to see the whole universe there.

On reaching manhood, Krishna left the cowherds and went to Mathura where his tyrannical uncle lived, and killed him.

The *Bhagavad Gita*, or "Song of the Blessed Lord", which forms part of the *Mahabharata*, relates Krishna's conversations with Prince Arjuna prior to and during a great battle between the Pandavas and the Kauravas. Krishna was Arjuna's charioteer and amazed Arjuna when he revealed that he was the "Divine One". He did this by appearing in all his radiant glory. Arjuna was overwhelmed and terrified by the vision and was reassured only when Krishna resumed his earthly shape.

Krishna played an important role on overcoming Arjuna's hesitations about entering a battle which was destined to end with a senseless massacre of friends and foes. He declared that "the hero whose soul is unmoved by circumstance, who accepts pleasure and pain with equanimity, he alone is fit for immortality."

The love of Krishna for Radha the milkmaid comprises the focus of his modern worship. Their relationship is seen as a deification of daily life.

See Love and Fertility, pp.106/107

SEE ALSO ARJUNA, BALARAMA, KANSA, RADHA, YASODA

Krishna subdues the serpent Kaliya

KRONOS

In Greek mythology, Kronos (or Cronos) was the youngest son of Gaia (earth) and Ouranos (sky).

The Titans (giants) were the cleverest offspring of Gaia and Ouranos, the first divine pair. Although Kronos was the youngest Titan, his rebellion against Ouranos led to him becoming king.

All Ouranos's children were imprisoned in Gaia's body. To end this uncomfortable situation, Gaia gave Kronos a sickle and, the next time the couple mated, Kronos attacked Ouranos, castrating him. Thus, Kronos seized control of the world.

When Kronos threw the severed genitals down, the drops of blood became the ERINYES (Furies), giants and nymphs. In another version of the tale, Kronos flung the genitals into the sea, where foam gathered around them and produced the love goddess APHRODITE.

The reign of Kronos soon became as tyrannical as that of Ouranos. He forced the giants, including the CYCLOPES, back underground and, having been warned by Gaia that one of his children would depose him, he swallowed them at birth. Rhea, his wife, bore six children: Hestia, DEMETER, HERA, HADES, POSEIDON, and ZEUS. Kronos ate all of them except Zeus, for whom Rhea substituted a stone wrapped in swaddling clothes.

Zeus was taken away to be reared in secret. Eventually, with the aid of the Titans, he flung Kronos into the abyss of Tartarus, where hundred-armed giants were appointed to guard him. In another version of the myth, Kronos was exiled to an island near Britain, where he slept with his followers.

According to the Greek poet Hesiod, who lived around 700 BC, the first men were contemporaries of Kronos and lived in a Golden Age, free from worry and fatigue. Indeed, Kronos was probably a deity worshipped before the arrival of the Greeks. He would therefore have had to be deposed to allow for the rise of Zeus and the Olympians (the gods who dwelt on Mount Olympus).

See Sacred Mountains, p.99, Golden Ages, p.118 and Giants, p.159

SEE ALSO GAIA, OLYMPUS, RHEA, TARTARUS, TITANS

KUANYIN

The Buddhist goddess of mercy in China. She is known to the Japanese as Kwannon.

The transformation of the Indian AVALOKI-TESVARA, a male bodhisattva, into the goddess of mercy Kuanyin is just one of the many profound adaptations that Chinese Buddhists have made to the faith. Such changes enabled the imported Indian religion of individual salvation to be fitted into a society which placed great emphasis on the family. Thus, Chinese Buddhists believe BUDDHA showed great respect for his parents, whereas he named his own son Rahula (bond).

Similarly, in Chinese legends, Avaloki-tesvara (whose name means "the lord who looks down in pity") became Kuanyin, the all-compassionate, all-sustaining mother goddess who bestows children on the faithful.

Stories of Kuanyin's interventions in human affairs on errands of mercy are found throughout traditional Chinese literature. Indeed, Kuanyin developed into the ultimate bodhisattva, or enlightened being, whose awareness of suffering in the world prevented her from making a personal escape into bliss, and instead caused her to remain in this world to help others achieve salvation. The festivals of Kuanyin's birth and enlightenment are particularly significant for Chinese Buddhists.

In Japan, both a masculine and a feminine form of the bodhisattva exist, but the goddess Kwannon remains the dominant form. Her attributes reveal the extent of her powers and understanding: she is called both Sho (the wise one) and Nyoirin (all-powerful).

SEE ALSO KWANNON

Golden ages

The golden age reflects a past peak of civilization. This high point might imply a state of paradise, in which all was perfection, but could also bring with it a loss of innocence. Myths may embody the hope that a golden age may one day return.

In China, a belief in past perfection was strongly held by the followers of both Confucius and Lao Zi (above).

Dilmun (above), the ancient Mesopotamian paradise, was probably sited at Bahrain. Dilmun belonged to Enki, the Sumerian fresh-water god, and his wife Ninhursaga.

Eden was the biblical garden of earthly delights, probably inspired by Mesopotamian versions of paradise. Here Adam and Eve lost their innocence when they ate from the tree of knowledge. This idea has long fascinated painters, not least Hieronymus Bosch (left).

KUAT

The sun god of the Mamaiurans, an Amazon Indian tribe living along the banks of the Xingu river in Brazil. Kuat obtained light from the king of the birds and illuminated the world.

According to Mamaiuran legend, it was always night at the beginning of time and the Indian tribes were forced to live in perpetual fear of attack from wild animals. Life was so hard that the brothers Kuat and Iae decided that, no matter how dangerous the task, conditions had to be improved.

Eventually, they resolved to steal light from the vulture god, Urubutsin, king of the birds. It would seem that the birds' wings blocked the sky, preventing the light from reaching the Mamaiurans. But how were the brothers to approach the light enjoyed by the inhabitants of the bird kingdom without ending up as Urubutsin's dinner?

The solution, they decided, was to send a swarm of flies with a corpse full of maggots to Urubutsin as a gift. At first, Urubutsin could not understand the flies' message but finally he realized that the multiplying maggots were intended as a delicious titbit and, moreover, that he was invited to a feast at the home of the two brothers.

Urubutsin and his birds shaved their heads and set out for the feast. Meanwhile, Kuat and Iae hid themselves in another corpse. As soon as Urubutsin landed on the corpse to eat the maggots, Kuat grasped the vulture god's leg.

Unable to get away, and deserted by his followers, Urubutsin was obliged to agree that he would share daylight with the two brothers. However, to ensure that light lasted for a long time, Urubutsin insisted that day should alternate with night. As a result, Kuat became associated with the sun and Iae with the moon in Mamaiuran mythology.

SEE ALSO IAE

LAKSHMI

In Hindu mythology, the lotus goddess and wife of Vishnu. She is also the goddess of good fortune, love and beauty.

According to one legend, Lakshmi rose, like APHRODITE, from the froth of the ocean, in radiant beauty, with a lotus in her hand. Lakshmi's birth occurred when the sea was churned by the gods and demons to produce the magical drink AMRITA. This is the source of her name Kshrirabhi-tanaya (daughter of the milk of the sea).

In another legend, she is represented floating on a lotus flower at the time of creation. In yet another, she is born by her own will, in a beautiful field opened up by the plough.

Lotus-eyed, lotus-coloured and decked with lotus garlands, Lakshmi stands as a symbol of maternal benevolence. She is the universal mother, bestowing on her devotees plenty and contentment.

In an annual ceremony, ancient Indian rulers would go through a ritual of marrying Lakshmi, as Lokamata (mother of the world), to ensure fertility and good fortune. For the same reason, Sumerian kings annually went through a ceremony in which they married the fertility goddess INANNA.

The significance of the lotus cannot be overstated. It represents the female principle, the womb, procreation and fertility, life-giving waters, divinity, immortality, purity and spiritual strength, and the resting place of the enlightened.

See Love and Fertility, pp.106/107

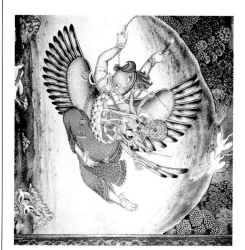

Vishnu and Lakshmi on the bird god Garuda

LEGBA

The Haitian god of the sun. His worshippers pray for protection against the evil spirits which roam the earth during the day.

Legba is a variant of the trickster god Legua from Dahomey, West Africa. *Hougans*, or mediums, brought across the Atlantic by slave traders, are thought to have transferred the legend to Haiti, along with many others, and Haitian Voodoo is now recognized as an offshoot of African belief.

Possession is a distinctive feature of Voodoo religion, and multiple possession occurs frequently. Legba appears as a ragged old man who controls the gate that opens to allow spirits possession of their devotees. He has dominion over the spirits of the day, whereas during the night the moon man Carrefow holds sway.

In cult rituals today his songs are sung first, because Legba's function is to "open the way" for the other gods to come and possess their devotees.

He is often equated with SATAN, an association originally made by missionaries in West Africa. The saints and symbols of Christianity have fused with Voodoo mythology to a bewildering degree. The Christian crucifix, for example, is used alongside Voodoo fertility symbols.

Legba's sacred animal is the dog, which he uses as a messenger.

A symbol used in Haitian Voodoo rituals

LEVIATHAN

The Hebrew sea serpent, which lives in the deep. The name literally means "coiled".

The myth of this serpent derived immediately from the Canaanite Lotan, a seven-headed monster which was slain by the goddess ANAT. She was the wife of EL, the equivalent of the Hebrew god Yahweh. Originally, though, the concept of Leviathan came from the Mesopotamian chaos-dragon TIAMAT.

Leviathan appears in the apocryphal Book of Enoch as an immense creature which inhabits "the abyss over the fountains of the waters". Though he was considered the creation and plaything of Yahweh, it was believed that in the last days Leviathan would challenge even the angels. In the Book of Job, Yahweh describes Leviathan's power vividly: "He esteemeth iron as straw, and brass as rotten wood . . . He maketh the deep to boil like a pot."

In medieval Christianity, Leviathan was identified with hell, whose entrance was often shown as a gigantic maw.

See Serpents, p.115

The serpent Leviathan, after Hans Baldung, 1515

SEE ALSO LOTAN, YAHWEH

LEZA

The supreme deity and remote sky god of several Bantu-speaking peoples of southern Africa.

According to the Kaonde people, Leza tried to prevent any harm from entering the world. In the beginning, he entrusted three calabashes to a honeybird with the instruction that he should take them to the first human beings, but only allow them to open two of them. These two calabashes contained seeds. The third calabash was not to be opened until Leza himself came down to earth. Then he himself would decide what should happen to its contents.

However, on his way to mankind, the honeybird became so curious about the calabashes that he opened all three. Two contained the promised seeds while the third held death, sickness and all kinds of wild animals and dangerous reptiles.

Leza found that he was unable to recapture the unpleasant contents, and so, for the first time, men had to build shelters for their protection.

A tradition preserved by the Basubiya, another Bantu people, relates how Leza taught mankind the correct procedure for his worship, then ascended into the sky on a spider's web. When the first people dared to follow the god, the thread broke and they crashed back down to earth. Thereafter, Leza remained aloof from human affairs, although the Basubiya sometimes say that a shooting star means that the god is considering his return.

LHA-MO

A terrifying demon in Tibetan Buddhism, derived from the destructive aspect of Devi, the mother goddess of the Hindu faith.

Lha-mo is envisaged as a horrible woman wearing the flayed skins of human victims. She is surrounded by flames and rides a mule, the saddle of which is made from the skin of her own son. Moreover, Lha-mo delights in the taste of human flesh and blood, which she drinks out of her favourite cup – a human skull.

The Tibetans blame Lha-mo for the arrival of disease and say that she directs the demons who inflict fatal illnesses upon mankind. In order to prevent this from happening, Lha-mo is worshipped for seven days at the end of each year. Usually, she is offered a cake containing the fat of a black goat, blood, wine, dough and butter. To tempt her appetite, the cake is made in the shape of a human skull.

Lha-mo's cruelty is always stressed. Unlike her prototype, the Hindu goddess DEVI, she shows no trace of compassion. It seems that Kali, the manifestation of Devi's destructive side, became overemphasized during Lha-mo's evolution. Yet even in Kali there is a reminder of personal salvation, for the goddess also blesses her devotees and points the way to spiritual fulfilment.

The harshness of the Tibetan landscape may have been a factor in the fearsome transformation of Lha-mo, since destruction always appears to be close at hand. This sense of desolation has also carried over into Tibetan methods of disposing of the dead. Corpses are gutted, the flesh is left for birds of prey and the bones are ground to dust.

See Death, p.91 and Demons, pp.126/127

SEE ALSO KALI

LOA

The creator deity in the Marshall Islands of the northern Pacific Ocean. He is the equivalent of the Tahitian god Ta'aroa.

In the beginning, Loa is said to have dwelt alone in the primeval sea and, for a countless period of time, he was content with this situation. However, Loa began to feel uneasy and, eventually, the sensation developed into loneliness and boredom.

To cope with this unpleasant feeling, the god distracted himself with games of creation. First he raised reefs and sandbanks, then he made plants and birds and, finally, he stationed a god at each of the cardinal points. Thinking that he had done enough, Loa relaxed and watched the new world. Then, to his surprise, the first man and woman, Wulleb and Lejman, suddenly emerged from his leg.

Once again Loa was happy to observe creation from a distance. However, before long, Wulleb was killed by his children and, frightened by such violence, Loa rushed away. But one of his legs produced more men, including the hero Edao.

Like OLOFAT, his counterpart in the neighbouring Caroline Islands, Edao experienced a series of adventures, including a trip to heaven in order to meet his divine ancestor Loa. In his concern about his own mortality, he is not unlike the Sumerian hero GILGAMESH.

According to another version of the creation story, Wulleb and Lejman were two worms living in a shell. Mankind is supposed to have descended from these creatures.

See Creation, p.135

SEE ALSO EDAO, LEJMAN, WULLEB

LOKI

The trickster god of Germanic mythology and a frequent companion of the great gods Thor and Odin. Although Loki's pranks caused the gods endless trouble, he was also the one who rescued them from the results of their own folly.

At first, Loki was an attractive character and frequently helped the gods. Once he prevented a giant from carrying off the beautiful goddess Freya, ODIN's first wife. Freya had been promised to a builder in payment for constructing a new wall at Asgard, the city of the gods.

The gods thought the task was impossible, not realizing that the builder was a giant in disguise and would be helped by a marvellous mare. When Loki found this out, he transformed himself into a dashing stallion, beguiled the mare, and so prevented the giant from receiving his prize. Moreover, the mare bore Loki a fantastic eight-legged stallion called Sleipnir, which Loki gave to Odin.

As time went by, Loki became increasingly deceitful and eventually so bitter at the gods' obvious dislike of him that he triggered Ragnarok, "the twilight of the gods", by arranging the death of BALDER, Odin's second son.

Loki was jealous of Balder and, on discovering that he could be harmed only by mistletoe, he persuaded the blind god Hodr to throw the plant at him. Balder died and, by refusing to mourn him, Loki prevented his release from the underworld. Too late, the gods realized that in Loki they had tolerated the growth of evil.

Sigyn, Loki's third wife, had two sons, Narve and Vali. To punish Loki for causing Balder's death, the gods turned Vali into a wolf and set him upon Narve. Narve's entrails were then used to bind Loki in a cave, where Sigyn stood by him.

The advent of "a wind age, a wolf age" was to be announced by the wolf Fenrir and the sea serpent Jormungandr, both the dreadful issue of Loki's second marriage to the giantess Angurbodi. Fenrir swallowed the sun and bit the moon, while Jormungandr, or the Midgard Snake, stirred up the ocean depths and blew up clouds of poison over the earth and sky.

In Germanic mythology the world was not everlasting nor were the gods looked upon as immortals. Just as the cycle of creation started with a world awash with the blood of Ymir, the first giant, so the final scene was a battlefield on the immense plain of Vigrid, where the gods were predestined to die. The forces of evil were mustered there under the command of Loki and Hrymir, chief of the frost giants, and against this host marched the gods and their followers, in full knowledge of the impending bloodbath.

The battle to end all battles raged amid towering flames; the world-tree YGGDRASIL shook in terror and one by one the gods fell. However, it was thought that after the catastrophe the earth would rise green again from the ashes and an idyllic age would emerge.

Loki is probably a personification of forest fire, one of the most destructive agencies known to ancient peoples. His name is related to the word "flame", his first wife's name, Glut, to "glow" and his daughters' names, Esia and Einmyria, to "ember" and "ashes".

See Trickster Gods, pp.78/79, Last Days, p.122 and Giants, p.159

Loki bound in chains to punish his wrongdoing

SEE ALSO ANGURBODI, ASGARD, FENRIR, FREYA, HODR, HRYMIR, JORMUNGANDR, NARVE, RAGNAROK, SIGYN, SLEIPNIR, VALI, VIGRID, YMIR

Last days

At the end of the world, it is believed that cataclysmic events will take place. But this event, also thought of in many traditions as the result of divine judgement, does not necessarily imply complete destruction. Following Ragnarok, the twilight of the gods in Germanic mythology, a new world was expected to rise from the ashes soon afterward.

At Armageddon, so the Bible's Book of Revelation predicts, there will be a battle between the forces of good and evil in the present-day state of Israel.

In Christian belief the realm of Satan (left) should be redundant in the last days, but the predicted fate of its inhabitants remains unknown.

In Hindu cosmology, cycles of creation and destruction alternate in an almost endless stream of time. Between them, Vishnu (above) rests.

LUGH

A prominent deity in the old Irish sagas, Lugh was a sun god, known for his handsome countenance as well as his skills in the arts and crafts. He saved the Tuatha De Danaan, "the peoples of the goddess Dana", from the evil Fomorii people.

Lugh was the grandson of the underworld god Balor, the most formidable of the Fomorii – evil, misshapen, violent people who dwelt in darkness, perhaps beneath the sea. A prophecy told how Balor would be slain by his grandson and so, to prevent this happening, Balor had his daughter Ethlinn locked away in a crystal tower. However, Cian, the son of the medicine god Dian Cecht, disguised himself as a woman and managed to enter the tower and sleep with her.

When Balor heard that Ethlinn had given birth to a son, he had the infant thrown into the sea to drown. However, a druidess rescued the child and MANANNAN, the god of the seas, fostered him. He became known as Lugh Lamhfada (long hand). He was also called Lonnbemnech (of mighty blows) and Samildanach (of many gifts). Like ODIN, his symbols include the raven and the spear.

According to some sagas, Lugh was raised by Cian's brother, the smith god Goibhniu – an appropriate foster-parent for a deity who was skilled in the arts and crafts. The technical assistance of both Goibhniu and Lugh was invaluable to the Tuatha De Danaan during their struggle with the Fomorii.

On reaching manhood, Lugh presented himself at the court of Nuada, the ruler of the Tuatha De Danaan. Since he was an expert warrior with the sling and spear, and a master craftsman, Lugh was made welcome.

During the second battle of Magh Tuireadh, Nuada fell under Balor's evil eye. This had such a malevolent gaze that it destroyed whoever looked at it. However, with the help of a magic stone ball, which pierced through the eye's drooping lid, Lugh killed Balor, thereby fulfilling the prophecy and defeating the Fomorii once and for all.

Lugh became king of the Tuatha De Danaan in Nuada's stead, but his reign was a short one. Ireland was divided between three different rulers, and the fortunes of the Tuatha De Danaan declined.

Lugh continued to go into battle, however. In the saga known as *The Cattleraid of Cuailgne*, he comes to the aid of his wearying son, Cuchulainn, sometimes called the hound of Ulster. Cuchulainn's mother was Dechtire, the mortal wife of an Ulster chieftain.

Legend recounts how, on swallowing a fly which flew into her cup at her wedding feast, Dechtire fell into a deep sleep. Lugh appeared to her in a dream as a handsome man and commanded her to take fifty handmaidens and follow him. He changed all the women into birds and they flew to an enchanted place. Three years later, the flock of birds returned to Ulster and changed back into Dechtire and her handmaidens. Shortly afterward, Dechtire gave birth to Cuchulainn, whom she persuaded her husband to accept as his own.

Lugh's final intervention on the battlefield is dated to the late second century, when he showed himself to Conn, a king of Ireland, in a magical mist and prophesied victory for his house over several generations.

The Tuatha De Danaan were finally defeated by a fresh wave of invaders led by Mil. They retreated underground to occupy hillocks and mounds allotted to them by DAGDA, the father of the gods, and were slowly transformed into the fairies of folk belief. The sun god Lugh eventually became the craftsman Lugh Chromain (little stooping Lugh) or, when anglicized, the leprechaun.

Lugh was probably identical with the Welsh Lleu and the Gallic Lugos, who gave his name to such modern towns as Lyon, Laon and Leyden. In Roman Britain, the town of Luguballium, which today is Carlisle, was named after him.

The story of the Greek god PERSEUS is similar to that of Lugh in that Perseus slew the gorgon whose gaze turned all who met it to stone.

The feast of Lugh, or Lughnasadh, was one of four major pre-Christian festivals which was later taken over by Christianity as Lammas, or the feast of first fruits.

See Craftsmen and Smith Gods, p.154

Leprechauns, a derivation from the Irish god Lugh

SEE ALSO BALOR, CIAN, DIAN-CECHT, ETHLINN, FOMORII, GOIBHNIU, NUADA, TUATHA DE DANAAN

MAHAVIRA

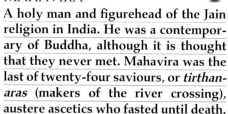

A holy man and figurehead of the Jain religion in India. He was a contemporary of Buddha, although it is thought that they never met. Mahavira was the last of twenty-four saviours, or *tirthanaras* (makers of the river crossing), austere ascetics who fasted until death.

Mahavira was born in about 540 BC to aristocratic parents. At his birth, the gods descended from heaven and the demons showered fruit, jewels, flowers, nectar and sandalwood on his father's palace. His childhood was distinguished by great feats which earned him the title Mahavira (Great Hero).

In adulthood, however, Mahavira led the life of an ordinary man, in that he married and had a child. But when his parents died he decided to follow his ascetic inclinations. At the age of thirty-two he gave away his personal possessions, left his wife and child and, like BUDDHA, became a wandering monk. His decision to search for enlightenment was marked by the sky glowing like a lake covered in lotus flowers.

Mahavira's teachings, which form the basis of the Jain religion today, propose that the individual soul is free to make its escape from the round of reincarnation through a sustained act of self-renunciation. He regarded the soul as physically bound by the actions of previous lives, or *karma*.

The path to release from the cycle of rebirth, the spiritual ascension to a mystical plane at the top of the universe, therefore involves disentangling oneself from *karma*. This can be achieved only by strict penance and disciplined non-violent conduct. Jain monks, for example, wear a veil over the mouth, and even lay devotees are forbidden to drink water after sunset, lest some insect be swallowed. The Buddhist doctrine of non-violence, *ahimsa*, thus reaches an extreme in Jainism.

See Saviours, p.75

MANANNAN

Manannan Mac Lir was the hero of the Manxmen. A ninth-century commentator suggested that he was a skilled navigator from the Isle of Man but it is more likely that he was the son of Lir, lord of the ocean in Irish mythology.

A shape-changer and magician, Manannan usually appeared as a noble, handsome warrior. He could drive his chariot over the waves as if they were a plain and it was during one such jaunt that he met BRAN, who was two days into his voyage to the wonderful islands of the western ocean.

Manannan also possessed a magic coracle, the Wave-Sweeper, and a mantle and helmet of invisibility. He lived on Tir Tairnigiri or "the land of promise", a fabulous island offering a myriad of pleasures, and defended it by conjuring an armada from peascods (peapods), which he magnified to gigantic proportions.

Manannan is credited with looking after the Tuatha De Danaan (the peoples of the goddess Dana) when they were settling into the fairy mounds of Ireland. Apparently he protected these displaced gods in their old age. His concern for their welfare is not surprising for he had fostered their champion, the sun god LUGH, after Balor had thrown him into the sea.

Manannan's wife was Fand (pearl of beauty). Once she quarrelled with Manannan and he left her. During his absence, her residence was attacked by the evil and misshapen Fomorii. Fand sent for Lugh's son, the hero CUCHULAINN, to protect her, and promised him her love if he defeated her attackers. Informed of the marvels of her residence, Cuchulainn defeated Fand's enemies and became her lover, remaining with her a month before returning home to his mortal wife Emer in Ulster.

Fand and Cuchulainn continued to meet and eventually Emer decided to give up Cuchulainn to prove how much she loved him. However, Manannan, deciding he could no longer tolerate his wife's affair, returned and told Fand to choose between himself and Cuchulainn. Fand decided on Manannan, since Cuchulainn already had a wife, and Manannan shook his cloak between the lovers to ensure that they would never see each other again. Later, Cuchulainn and Emer were given draughts of forgetfulness by the druids.

Manannan had both human and divine sons. For some unknown reason, his divine son Gaiar was punished for a love affair with the goddess Becuma. As a penalty for loving Gaiar, Becuma was banished from her home on Tir Tairnigiri to the human world, where her presence caused infertility and untold misery.

The birth of Mongan, one of Manannan's human sons, closely resembles that of ARTHUR, who was conceived out of wedlock and brought up by a wizard. Manannan used his magic arts to seduce the queen of Ulster while her husband was away at war. When the child was born, Manannan looked after him on Tir Tairnigiri, returning Mongan to his mother when he reached manhood.

In due course, Mongan became king and a great warrior, inheriting his father's shape-changing abilities. Mongan is probably a historical figure who lived around the seventh century.

Manannan was the object of a cult which lasted into the nineteenth century. Supposedly, the god was buried outside Peel Castle on the Isle of Man and, every Midsummer Eve, the people who lived nearby would carry green meadowgrass to his grave in payment of rent to Mannan-beg-mac-y-Leir.

In Wales, Manannan is known as Manawyddan, which may be another rendering of Morgan Mywnoaur. Indeed, Morgan Mywnoaur owned a marvellous chariot, similar to Manannan's amphibious vehicle, which was regarded as one of the treasures of Britain. The others, which also had magic powers, included a sword, cauldron, suit of clothes, hounds, a drinking horn, whetstone, destiny stone, knife, harp, bottle and platter.

SEE ALSO BALOR, BECUMA, EMER, LIR, TUATHA DE DANAAN

MANGAR-KUNGER-KUNJA

The great lizard ancestor of the Aranda people of central Australia. His name means "flycatcher".

According to the Aranda, the world was originally covered by an ocean and only a few hills stood out above the water. On the shore of one of these primeval islands lived two underdeveloped beings known as Rella-manerinja (two grown together).

These semi-men were so primitive that they had closed eyes and ears, a small hole in place of a mouth, hands which could not open, and stiff arms and legs. For a long time, the pair lived without making any movement.

Then the level of the waters fell and the lizard Mangar-kunger-kunja crawled on to the dry land where he cut the unformed pair apart with a stone knife. Afterward he made openings so that each possessed fully formed eyes, nostrils, ears and mouth.

Having completed the first people, Mangar-kunger-kunja presented them with various gifts including the stone knife, the spear, the shield and the boomerang. He also gave them a stone talisman and initiated the rites of circumcision and subincision. His final gift was the marriage ceremony.

These events – the completion of man and the founding of society – took place in Alchera (Dreamtime). The Aranda say that natural features such as impressive rocks or waterholes mark the places where Mangar-kunger-kunja performed his great deeds. Moreover, the Aranda still hold the lizard sacred. The penalty for killing one is possession by a craving for sex so strong that it can drive the taboo-breaker insane.

Other aboriginal groups also have myths about incomplete men. The Kaitish people believe that two hawk-men flew down and finished off the process of creation. They also tell how the disobedient sons of a creator god were expelled from heaven and how, in order that they might survive on earth, their father threw after them everything now used by mankind.

See Creation, p.135

MANU

The Hindu Noah. In Hindu myth, Manu was the first man, from whom the Hindus today trace their descent, and he alone survived the deluge.

Manu, the ancestor of mankind, was in fact the seventh Manu belonging to a line of mythical figures, whose lives each lasted for 4,320,000 years.

According to one account, Manu discovered a tiny fish in the water he was brought to wash his hands with. The fish begged Manu to spare its life, saying "Preserve me, and I will preserve you." Manu asked "From what will you preserve me?", and the fish answered, "A flood will soon carry away all living things. I will save you from that."

So Manu put the fish in a pot for safe keeping. But it grew so rapidly that he was obliged to move it to a tank, then a lake, and at last, to the sea itself. Thereupon the fish said, "After so many years the flood will come; then build yourself a large ship and pay me homage, and when the waters rise, board the ship and I will save you."

Manu followed the fish's instructions: he constructed a vessel, and gathered together wise men, the seeds of plants, and all kinds of animals. When the water rose, the fish returned. Manu fastened the ship's rope to the fish, and it guided them through the buffeting sea.

Their journey was long and took them above the submerged peaks of the Himalaya Mountains. Then the fish told Manu to fasten his craft to a crag, and to let it go down with the subsiding waters.

Manu saw that the deluge had swept away all living things, other than those he had saved, and he started to feel lonely. He offered a sacrifice so that he might have a wife. (This was the first sacrifice and thus the ritual was founded.) Manu's wish was granted and he was given a wife. From their union sprang the generations of Manu, the Hindus of today.

In later Hindu myth, the fish was considered to be Matsya, an avatar of VISHNU.

See Flood, pp.110/111

MARA

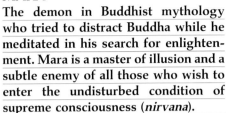

The demon in Buddhist mythology who tried to distract Buddha while he meditated in his search for enlightenment. Mara is a master of illusion and a subtle enemy of all those who wish to enter the undisturbed condition of supreme consciousness (*nirvana*).

The character of Mara developed from Kama, the Hindu god of love, who is addressed, among other things, as Depaka (inflamer), Mayi (deluder), and Mara (destroyer). This last aspect of Kama evolved in Buddhist myth into Mara the Devil, an embodiment of the powers of wickedness.

Mara recognized that BUDDHA's goodness threatened his dominion over evil. While Buddha sat in contemplation, immobile beneath a tree, Mara tried everything possible in order to disturb Buddha's single-minded concentration. He first sent his three beautiful daughters to sing and dance before him, then a band of devilish creatures, hideous and deformed, armed with dreadful weapons. Finally he hurled a fiery discus at Buddha's head. Throughout, Buddha remained unmoved and untouched by these forces.

Concerned to deny mankind enlightenment, to prevent people from escaping the round of reincarnation, Mara does his best to beguile the senses. Though he knows that Buddha has defeated him, Mara cherishes the hope that people will forget the correct path or, at least, that the souls of the wicked will become his captives.

See Demons, pp.126/127

The Buddhist demon, Mara

MARDUK

The chief god of Babylon, associated mainly with the creation of an ordered world out of the primeval chaos.

Marduk means "bull calf of the sun", although his father was the water god Ea. At first he was an agricultural deity, but his authority gradually included the moon, rain, justice, wisdom and battle.

In the Babylonian creation myth, the salt waters of the earth take the form of a she-dragon called TIAMAT. Tiamat was deeply resentful of the power of the other gods in the pantheon and vowed to destroy them. She gathered together a formidable army of monsters and faced the great gods one by one. However, none would meet her challenge.

Finally, the assembly of gods unanimously elected Marduk as their king and champion. They gave him the power to promote and demote gods, overlordship of all the temples, absolute command in battle, and the authority to pardon or kill captive enemies – if he could kill Tiamat.

Armed with bow and arrows, a mace, and a net to entangle the she-dragon, Marduk set lightning before him, filled himself with blazing light, and urged on his storm-chariot in a mighty rush of winds. A hurricane twisted the net around Tiamat, and when she opened her great mouth to swallow Marduk, he drove in a fierce wind. The blast of the wind forced her to keep her mouth open. The winds raged inside her stomach, distending her body. Marduk then fired an arrow which ripped through her and tore into her heart.

Having slain Tiamat, Marduk retrieved the tablets of destiny, which gave him control of the world. He hammered Tiamat's skull with his mace, severed her blood vessels and sliced her in half. One half he raised up to make the sky; the other half he used to make the earth.

Marduk then established the home of the gods in the sky, the stars and planets and their motions, the moon, time and the seasons. He took the blood of the enemy god Kingu and mixed it with some clay to create human beings.

The gods then rewarded Marduk with Babylon, which they built for him as his residence.

SEE ALSO EA, KINGU

Demons

The demons of mythology are personifications of the forces of evil, possibly with the power to punish wrongdoers. Demons may take a "human" form or be represented as animals or as monsters.

Kali's demonic face (below) is one aspect of Devi, the Hindu mother goddess. In this form she represents the world's natural processes of destruction, but when evil arises she becomes a warrior goddess and slays demons.

The idea of evil has been crystallized into Satan (above), the remorseless enemy of all that is good.

Witches, and others in league with evil, strike a note of terror – as this figure (right) from the demon-ridden island of Bali shows.

Two Oni, Japanese demons of disease, calamity and misfortune, which have sharp talons on hands and feet, are here being fought off by a sage (left).

MARS

As the Roman god of war, Mars was identified with Ares, the Greek war god. He was also associated with agriculture and particularly with the laurel tree.

Along with JUPITER, Mars was the favourite god of the Romans. His month, March, was very important since it heralded the rebirth of plant life and the season of wars and campaigns.

Originally Mars was closely identified with the pastoral deity Silvanus. Even after he became the great war god, something of this early association with agriculture remained.

Mars was conceived by JUNO without a mate. Annoyed that her husband Jupiter had produced MINERVA from his head without her aid, the goddess enlisted the help of Flora, the goddess of flowering and blossoming plants. Flora touched Juno with a magical herb and so helped to bring about the birth of Mars.

ROMULUS was perhaps the greatest gift Mars gave the Romans. Mars was said to have raped Rhea Silvia, a Vestal Virgin, while she drew water at a spring in his sacred grove. As a result, Rhea Silvia had twin sons, Romulus and Remus. When their birth became known, Rhea Silvia was condemned as a fallen priestess and imprisoned. Years later, however, her sons released her from captivity. Romulus founded the city of Rome shortly afterward.

Mars was believed to come to the aid of Romulus's descendants in times of crisis. On one occasion, a sacred shield fell from the sky and saved an army. The shield was thereafter kept in the Forum and was said to guarantee the continued existence of the Roman Empire.

The name of Mars was always invoked on the battlefield to strengthen the resolve of Roman soldiers. The horse races held in Rome in honour of the god were probably a survival of cavalry exercises.

Mars married a minor goddess called Nerio (strength). The meaning of the god's own name is not known.

See War, pp.94/95

SEE ALSO NERIO, REMUS, RHEA SILVIA, SILVANUS

MAUI

The trickster god and hero of Polynesian mythology. He resembled a miniature version of Heracles, but was endowed with magical powers.

In spite of his small stature, nothing frightened Maui. The twenty or so tales about his exploits reveal a determined, cunning hero, forever pitting himself against those who opposed his will.

When Maui was born, his mother Taranga wrapped him in a tuft of her hair and cast him into the sea, possibly because he was born prematurely. Saved by an observant ancestor, Maui was returned to the land and rejoined his family. As a result, his mother called him Maui-tiki-tiki-a-Taranga (Maui formed in the top knot of Taranga).

Maui's best-known exploit was his creation of the Pacific islands. With a magical hook, the hero fished up from the bottom of the sea the innumerable islands on which the Polynesians now live.

According to the Maoris of New Zealand, Maui caught the sun in a noose and beat it with his invincible weapon, the jawbone of an ancestress. The sun was so weak after the beating that it could only creep along its course, thus lengthening each day.

The Tongans say that the sky is sometimes dark because Maui used a poker to force the sky upward. When the hero was preparing an earth oven, his poker became stuck in the sky, then much lower than it is today, and so, to give himself more room to work comfortably, he simply pushed up the sky farther. The Hawaiians believe that this feat was intended to impress a woman.

Certainly, women fascinated Maui, and his mother seems to have encouraged the hero in his various affairs. Without such support, claim the inhabitants of the Tuamotu archipelago, Maui would never have dared attempt to satisfy the boundless desire of Hina, the wife of the monster eel Te Tuna. At first Te Tuna ignored the liaison, but the murmurings of other divinities eventually provoked him to challenge Maui.

The pair met on a beach in a tremendous storm and, as lightning flashed and thunder rolled, Maui and Te Tuna compared the size of their phalluses. Maui won, and so Hina confidently changed lovers. Later, when Te Tuna tried to take his wife back by force, the trickster hero's superior magic destroyed him. The Tuamotuans say that the first coconut tree grew from Te Tuna's buried head.

Two of the most popular tales about Maui focus entirely on his deceit. In one, he stole a hen from heaven in order to obtain fire since, according to the Polynesians, the secret of fire was guarded by a celestial chicken.

In the other popular adventure, the hero actually attempted to conquer death. Apparently, Maui found Hine-nui-te-po, the goddess of death, sleeping. He almost managed to pass through her body, but, at the last moment, the goddess was awakened by the twittering of birds and squeezed him to death. The Hawaiians say that Maui's blood made shrimps red and gave the rainbow its colours.

See Heroes, p.55 Trickster Gods, pp.78/79, and Creation, p.135,

MAWU-LIZA

The great god of the Fon peoples of Dahomey in West Africa. Originally, Mawu-Liza may have belonged to an enemy which the warlike Fon had vanquished.

The Fon have always regarded Mawu-Liza as a creator god, although an even older deity called Nana Buluku is still remembered. However, at the beginning of the present world, Mawu-Liza is said to have created both the gods of the sky and the gods of the earth. The creator god is also credited with shaping the universe from pre-existing material.

Mawu-Liza used his son, the smith god GU, as the divine tool, or instrument, in the process of creation. Gu is imagined as a stone handle from which a sharp blade projects, and he is believed to have shaped mankind from divine excrement.

The creator deity is conceived as both female (Mawu) and male (Liza), and the eternal union of these unseparated twins is regarded as the basis of universal order. (There is an exact parallel in AWONAWI-LONA, the male-female creator deity of the Zuni Indians of New Mexico and Arizona.) In maintaining the universe, Mawu-Liza is greatly aided by Da, a cosmic serpent. It is Da who turns the intentions of the creator god into action. Echoes of him are found in Haitian beliefs about a powerful sky serpent.

The Fon identify Mawu with the moon, night, fertility, motherhood, joy, gentleness and rest. Liza is associated with the sun, day, heat, power, work, war and strength.

See Serpents, p.115, Creation, p.135, and Craftsmen and Smith Gods, p.154

Maui cast into the sea by his mother Taranga

SEE ALSO HINE-NUI-TE-PO

SEE ALSO NANA BULUKU

MERLIN

The great wizard of Arthurian legend who probably derived from Myrddin, the sixth-century Welsh bard who became a wild man of the woods.

Merlin used his magic arts to bring together the couple who were to become ARTHUR's parents: Uther Pendragon, the English king, and Igraine, the Duchess of Cornwall. The seduction took place at Tintagel and Merlin accomplished it by tricking Igraine into believing that Uther Pendragon was her own husband. After the Duke of Cornwall died, Uther and Igraine were married.

Arthur was raised by Merlin, whose task was to prepare the child for a kingship greater than any previously known. Sometimes, Merlin is credited with creating Excalibur, the magic sword which proved Arthur's legitimacy. Fantastic weapons and vessels, such as the Grail itself, were commonplace in the Celtic mythology from which Arthurian legend derived. In the Welsh story, *The Spoils of Annwn*, Arthur and his followers raid the underworld in search of a cauldron which could provide bounty and restore life.

According to one tradition, Merlin built Stonehenge singlehanded. He is also believed to have created Arthur's Round Table, a possible copy of which still exists at Winchester in England.

Merlin was besotted with Nimue, one of the Lady of the Lake's damsels. However, Nimue merely encouraged Merlin's advances until "she had learned of him all manner that she desired". She then used the wizard's powers against him, thereby causing his downfall.

Having gleaned all Merlin's knowledge of magic, Nimue decided it was time to make her escape. So one day, when Merlin went beneath a great rock in order to show her a marvel, Nimue "wrought so there for him that he came never out for all the craft he could do. And so she departed and left Merlin". This end recalls Celtic belief in the trickery of fairies and the dangers of close associations with them.

See Seers and Magicians, pp.82/83

SEE ALSO HIAWATHA, IGRAINE, LADY OF THE LAKE, MORGAN LE FAY, NIMUE, TINTAGEL, UTHER PENDRAGON

MIDAS

The legendary king of Phrygia, a country fabled for its wealth. He was said to be a son of the goddess Cybele.

The most famous story about Midas concerns his ability to find wealth, a gift still referred to as "the Midas touch". The king once pleased DIONYSUS by returning the god's horselike companion, Silenus, to him after he had been captured drunk by country folk. Dionysus was so grateful that he offered Midas whatever he wished. Without pausing for thought, Midas asked Dionysus to allow everything he touched to be turned to gold.

At first, Midas was delighted with the results, but his joy soon turned to horror when he discovered that his food turned to gold whenever he took a bite. Dionysus took pity on him and sent him to purify himself in a certain river, the silt of which thereafter contained gold dust. The association of Midas with gold is not surprising because Phrygia and its neighbour, Lydia, were rich countries which issued the first coinage known to the ancient Greeks.

Silenus, formerly Dionysus's tutor, was renowned both for his practical knowledge and for his powers of prophecy. According to one version of the tale, Midas pumped wine into the water of a fountain at which Silenus drank in order to loosen his tongue. However, Midas received only cynical wisdom from the horse-man. When the king asked what was best for man, Silenus replied, "Not to be born, and next best to die in childbirth."

Another story about Midas concerns the rivalry between Apollo and PAN. When the king attended a musical contest between the two deities, he offended Apollo by saying that Pan was the better musician. As punishment, Apollo gave Midas the ears of an ass, making the king the laughing stock of his subjects.

SEE ALSO SILENUS

MIN

The Egyptian god of virility and generation. The Greeks identified him with Priapus, the son of Dionysus. Min was normally shown as a man with his penis erect and wearing a headdress with two tall plumes.

Min was one of the oldest and most popular gods in Egypt. He was the protector of nomads and hunters, and his domain was the western desert. He was also a god of fertility, whose cult was celebrated by settled cultivators during times of harvest.

In these celebrations, processions of priests would carry plants that were sacred to the god and the pharaoh would offer Min the first sheaf of corn and pay respect to a white bull, a sacred animal associated with him.

At a later time, Min's role became solely that of guardian of the traveller. His cult centre, at Coptos, was known as "caravan city", where traders set out for the desert frontiers. Games were held there in the name of the god – a unique feature in Egyptian religion.

Min, the Egyptian god of fertility

SEE ALSO PRIAPUS

MINERVA

The Roman goddess of handicrafts, identified with the Greek Athena.

Like ATHENA, who sprang from the head of ZEUS, Minerva was conceived by JUPITER without the aid of a mother. Her name may well be related to *mens* (thought).

Minerva was depicted sporting a helmet, shield and coat of mail. Although her worship was widespread in Italy, and probably of Etruscan origin, she only took on a warlike character at Rome, where she became a symbol of the city itself.

To some extent, Minerva's cult grew at the expense of the war god MARS. Moreover, in myth, when Jupiter's wife JUNO heard of the birth of Minerva, she was filled with anger and conceived Mars, who came to rival Jupiter himself.

See also Craftsmen and Smith Gods, p.154

Minerva, depicted in her warlike form

MINOS

Minos, the legendary king of Crete, was famed as a law-giver and appears in Greek mythology as lord of the seas. He was the son of Zeus and Europa.

EUROPA, the daughter of Agenor, King of Tyre, was carried across the sea to the island of Crete on the back of ZEUS, who was disguised as a bull. There, the Phoenician princess bore the god three sons: Minos, Rhadamanthys and Sarpedon, all of whom the Cretan king Asterius adopted when he married Europa.

After a dispute with his two brothers, Minos succeeded Asterius to the throne. The issue of the succession was settled when, having prayed for a divine sign, POSEIDON sent Minos a magnificent bull from the sea. However, because Minos neglected to sacrifice the bull, Poseidon cursed him, causing his wife, Pasiphae, to fall madly in love with the creature.

With the aid of the craftsman DAEDALUS, Pasiphae was able to satisfy her lust by hiding in a decoy cow. The Minotaur, a monster with a bull's head and a man's body, resulted from this strange union. To house it, Minos commissioned Daedalus to build a maze, the Labyrinth.

According to Athenian tradition, Minos insisted that each year nine boys and nine girls should be sent from Athens to the Labyrinth as food for the Minotaur. One year, the hero THESEUS was selected for sacrifice. However, he killed the beast and carried off Minos's daughter Ariadne who had helped him.

Daedalus, who was also involved in the plot, fled to Sicily with his son, Icarus, who died when the wax on his wings melted. Minos followed Daedalus to Sicily but the inventor avenged his son's death by arranging for boiling oil to kill the king when he took a bath at Kamikos.

Minos possessed a powerful navy, which made him a fearsome enemy. The unfavourable stories about him may have arisen from the wars he waged against rival kings on the Greek mainland. However, Minos governed Crete wisely.

SEE ALSO ARIADNE, ICARUS, MINOTAUR, PASIPHAE, RHADAMANTHYS, SARPEDON

MITHRA

The Iranian god of light and justice, and the guardian of the promised word. Although Mithra was worshipped by the Iranians in very early times, he was not introduced into the state religion of the Persian Empire until the reign of Artaxerxes I (456–425 BC).

For the ancient Iranians, Mithra was the light that preceded the sun when it rose, the god who dispelled darkness and saw all secrets. Originally, he and AHURA MAZDAH were the twin sky gods, creator-preservers of the cosmic order. Later, Ahura Mazdah became known as Ormazd, the supreme being and principle of goodness, and Mithra became his chief assistant. However, Mithra was still a very powerful deity. "When I created Mithra," Ormazd admitted, "I made him as worthy of veneration and reverence as I am myself."

The relationship of Ormazd and Mithra may have been similar to that of the Vedic sun god Mitra with VARUNA, the sky god of early Hindu mythology.

Apparently, at his birth, Mithra emerged from a rock armed with a knife and a torch. This doubtless explains why he was worshipped in rock sanctuaries and artificial caves. Having come to an agreement with the sun, Mithra attacked and killed the primeval bull, Geush Urvan. The slaughter may even have taken place at the sun's bidding. All kinds of animals and plants appeared from the corpse of the dead bull.

Mithra's violent aspect was particularly evident when he assumed the role of a war god. Wielding deadly arrows and a huge mace, he was the scourge of the battlefield. He also directed incurable diseases and a back-breaking boar at his enemies.

It was probably Mithra's guise as a war god which endeared him to the Roman legions. In the first century BC, when Rome expanded into West Asia, Mithra passed into Greco-Roman belief as the god Mithras.

The Mithraic mysteries that swept through the provinces of the Roman empire drew their greatest strength from the Iranian belief that Mithra had power over sorcerers. It was he, of all gods, who knew how to avert evil and keep at bay the darkness of AHRIMAN, the spirit of wickedness.

Seeing the afflictions suffered by mankind, Mithras came down to earth, where his birth was witnessed on 25 December by shepherds. After performing many good deeds on behalf of his followers, he held a last supper with the closest of them and returned to heaven.

At the end of the world, Mithras was expected to come again to judge resurrected mankind. Then, after a last battle with Ahriman, he would lead the chosen ones through a river of fire to eternal life. An inscription from the Walbrook temple in London tells how Mithras promised "life to wandering human beings". In order to prepare for this second coming, the devotees of Mithras underwent a graduated series of initiations.

Not surprisingly, the early Christians were extremely disturbed by a deity who bore such a close resemblance to JESUS. To add to their annoyance, the cult of Mithras was the most important pagan movement in the late Roman Empire. In the second century the historian Plutarch wrote that between Ormazd and Ahriman "is Mithras, whom the Persians call the Mediator. From him they learnt how to sacrifice votive offerings and thank offerings . . .".

The Mithraic rituals were held at night in underground sanctuaries, just as the Iranian Mithra was worshipped in caves. The initiation ritual bestowed immortality on the devotee, but the origin of its most famous part, the bull sacrifice, remains obscure. However, it seems not unlikely that aspects of it were borrowed from the cult of CYBELE.

See Saviours, p.75

MOIRAI

The three goddesses who decided the individual fates of the ancient Greeks. Moirai means "allotters".

The three Fates were Clotho (spinner), Lachesis (the drawing of lots) and Atropos (inevitable). The daughters of Nyx (night), the Moirai probably developed from a group of birth spirits, deities concerned with the future lives of babies. Thus their original purpose may have been to lay down the lot of each individual at birth.

Gradually, the Moirai acquired a wider role in Greek mythology, although the power of their decrees was by no means clear. Was ZEUS, as the king of gods and men, subject to them? Or could he alter what the Moirai decreed? On occasion, Zeus appears superior, but perhaps he is best seen as the hand of destiny rather than the power that decides its course.

The Moirai were envisaged as three old women, spinning out men's destinies like thread. Clotho drew them out, Lachesis measured their length, and Atropos cut them off. When the Moirai had arranged the time of death, the malevolent Keres appeared. These female spirits, with pointed claws and bloodstained cloaks, delivered the fatal blow and took their victims to the land of shadows.

See Fate and Punishment, p.143

The three Fates spinning men's destinies

SEE ALSO GEUSH URVAN, MITHRAS, MITRA

SEE ALSO NORNS

MOLOCH

The Canaanite deity associated with human sacrifice. The Hebrews derived "Moloch" from "Mlk", which means "master" or "king", but they added to it the connotation of a shameful or disgusting thing.

The Moloch of the Old Testament may have been the Baal-Hammon worshipped in the cities of Tyre and Carthage. His name means "the lord of the altar of incense". He was usually shown as an old man with ram's horns, holding a scythe.

A Roman writer tell us that in Carthage there was a bronze statue of Baal-Hammon with hands outstretched to receive young children, who were allowed to fall into a fire below. Recent excavations at Carthage confirm the custom of infant sacrifice to the god. By shedding blood, his devotees hoped to attain their ends, evade ill luck, and confound any spells cast upon them.

The Canaanite god Moloch

SEE BAAL-HAMMON

MULUNGU

The supreme but unusually remote god of the Nyamwezi people of Tanzania in East Africa.

Almost all African peoples believe in a powerful sky god, often referred to as the one who knows and sees all. According to the Ganda peoples of Uganda, the eye of god never blinks but keeps watch everywhere and at all times.

Similarly, the Nyamwezi believe that Mulungu is a deity who misses nothing. They call him Kube (the one who embraces all), and yet he is so distant that he cannot hear people's prayers. Instead, prayers are relayed to him through a chain of spirits, which rises up from the earth to an utterly remote heaven. He is also known as Limi (the sun) and Likubala (he who counts every step).

The remoteness of Mulungu forces the Nyamwezi to depend on mediums for communication. Even the very lowest in the hierarchy of spirits leading upward to the god can be addressed only by Nyamwezi medicine-men. As a result, there is a strong sense of loneliness in Nyamwezi mythology. Apparently, the first man rejected an offer of immortality on earth because the first woman advised him that death was certain to return them to the spirit world. Thus, death was seen as rescuing man from his isolation.

The idea of death as a door to a spirit kingdom is common among eastern and southern African peoples. Indeed, for the Nyamwezi, physical decay seems an almost welcome gift. As a result, they calmly accept the workings of an evil monster, armed with boxes containing disease and misfortune, and the scythe of death.

See Death, p.91

NANABOZHO

The trickster god of the Algonquin-speaking Indians of North America. His name, also spelt Manabozho, means "Big Rabbit".

North American Indians have always believed that every natural thing is inhabited by a mysterious power. For the Algonquins, the most widely spread of the native peoples and the first to come into contact with European settlers, Kici Manitou is the greatest of these in-dwelling powers. Kici Manitou made heaven, earth, people, animals and plants, but he left much of the work of creation to lesser deities such as Nanabozho.

One of Nanabozho's first gifts to mankind was the Mide, the most sacred of all ceremonies which was probably founded after the death of the god's brother.

Nanabozho was the eldest of quadruplets. He killed his youngest brother, possibly because the last-born was responsible for their mother's death. The third brother left to become a great sorcerer and so Nanabozho lived with the second until he was drowned by jealous deities. Inconsolable, Nanabozho attacked the murderers so violently that they were obliged to reveal to him the secrets of the sacred ceremony known as the Mide.

The powers of the Mide ceremony permitted the resurrection of the drowned brother and his appointment as chief of the underworld. Hence, human performers of the Mide believed that they gave Nanabozho comfort in his bereavement.

A secret order of initiates performed the Mide rite in a specially constructed oval lodge. Their knowledge encompassed magic and healing, the secrets of which Nanabozho was said to have revealed to them in order to prevent hunger and disease from overcoming his devotees.

However, one tribe after another outlawed the Mide, which suggests that the initiates used their god-given powers for evil purposes rather than good.

Nanabozho was probably not displeased by such trickery, for he was a particularly contradictory character whose greed and deceit often brought him to the point of disaster.

See Trickster Gods, pp.78/79

SEE ALSO KICI MANITOU

NAPI

Despite being the chief god and creator deity of the North American Blackfoot Indians, Napi displays many of the attributes of a trickster god in his dealings with mankind. His name means "old man".

Like NANABOZHO, the Algonquin trickster god, Napi is a curious mixture of contrasting qualities. At the creation of the world he appears as a thoughtful and wise sky father, but in other dealings with mankind he displays impishness, and even spite.

The Blackfoot, the most famous of the Algonquin-speaking tribes, are convinced of Napi's immortality. They say that he has withdrawn into the mountains, but has promised to return one day. Meanwhile, his place is occupied by Natos, the sun god.

One story surrounding Napi tells of a poor Indian who, together with his wife and two sons, scraped an existence by eating roots and berries. One night, the Indian had a dream in which a voice commanded him to obtain a giant spider-web and hang it across an animal trail to trap food.

The Indian did as he was told and was delighted to find deer and rabbits tangled in the web. His wife was pleased, too, but the Indian suspected that she had taken a lover while he was out at the trap since she had made a perfume from pine bark. However, he said nothing and continued to hunt with the web.

Eventually, he decided to send his wife out to the trap and, as soon as she was gone, he asked his sons where their mother went to gather wood. The boys pointed to a clump of dead trees, where the Indian discovered a nest of rattlesnakes.

Realizing that one of the serpents was his wife's lover, the Indian burned the clump. Then he gave his sons a magical stick, stone and piece of moss to protect themselves from their mother's anger. Finally, he stretched a web across the door of their lodge.

Escaping the smoke, the woman ran back to the lodge but was caught in the web. Only her head forced its way through the strands and it was so contorted with fury that her husband immediately chopped it off with his axe.

The headless body pursued the Indian, while the severed head rolled after the children. One of the boys threw down the magic stick which turned into a forest, but still the head came on, threatening to kill them. The other boy threw down the stone which turned into a mountain, but even this did not hinder the head. Finally, they threw down the piece of moss which turned into a river. Unable to stop, the head plunged into the water and drowned.

When the children returned home, another tribe had taken over their lodge and there was no sign of their father. Indeed, the Indian's fate, as the sun, was to be pursued forever across the sky by the moon, his decapitated wife, determined to avenge herself. One of the orphans was Napi, who went on to create the Blackfoot.

The Blackfoot also blamed a woman for the introduction of death. Having created the world, Napi made the first pair of human beings out of clay. One day, he introduced himself to them by a river and the woman asked him, "Will it always be like this?" Surprised, Napi replied, "I have not given any thought to that. Let us decide now. I will throw a piece of wood into the river. If it floats, when people die, in four days they will breathe again. If it sinks, then death will not last for four days but for all time."

Napi threw the stick into the river and it floated. However, the woman picked up a stone and said, "If it floats, there will be no death at all. But if it sinks, people must die." The stone sank. Napi said "You have chosen", and later, when the woman's baby died, she realized what she had done.

SEE ALSO NATOS

NAREAU

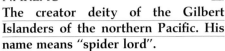

The creator deity of the Gilbert Islanders of the northern Pacific. His name means "spider lord".

The great myth of Nareau concerns the creation of the world. Tradition holds that Nareau was alone at the beginning of time. So, working with sand and water, Nareau created two primeval beings. From their union sprang the gods – Te Ikawai (the oldest), Nei Marena (the woman between), Te Nao (the wave), Na Kika (octopus lord), Ruki (the eel), and a multitude of others.

Nareau then asked the two primeval beings to add mankind to creation, and departed for heaven. Unfortunately, a dispute broke out between the two beings and their divine offspring, which resulted in the male member of the primeval pair being literally torn apart. His right eye was flung into the eastern sky and became the sun; his left eye, flung into the western sky, became the moon; his brains formed the stars; his flesh and bones became the islands and trees.

The octopus god Na Kika, the Gilbert Islanders say, demonstrated great skill during the formation of the numerous archipelagos in Micronesia. With his extra arms he could pull together vast quantities of stones and sand.

In this way the world was prepared for the first people, whom Nareau himself seems to have had to return from heaven to create.

See Creation, p.135

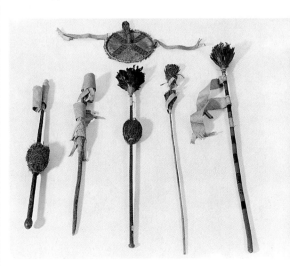

Canoe badges from the Gilbert Islands

SEE ALSO NA KIKA, TE IKAWAI, TE NAO

NAYENEZGANI

The chief hero of Navaho legend and protector of the world from the forces of destruction. His name means "slayer of evil gods".

Nayenezgani and his brother Tobadzistsini (child of water) patrol the world which the great god AHSONNUTLI created for the benefit of mankind. According to the Navaho Indians, who live in semi-arid New Mexico, the brothers deal with the periodic attacks of evil spirits, and are thus depicted as war gods.

Whereas Nayenezgani appears to derive his power from light, Tobadzistsini is a lord of water and darkness. One of the many legends surrounding these champions tells how, on the way to visit the sun god Tsohanoai, Nayenezgani noticed smoke rising from the ground. Looking closely, the brothers discovered that it came from an underground dwelling.

The brothers climbed down a smoke-blackened ladder and were greeted by Spider Woman, who told them of the dangers that faced them on their journey to the sun god. "Four perils, four places of danger await you," she warned. "Beware the rocks which crush, the sharp reeds which cut, the cacti which tear to pieces, and the boiling sands which overwhelm."

Spider Woman then gave the brothers two magic feathers and they continued on their way. After braving the four dangers, and surviving a couple of close scrapes, Nayenezgani and Tobadzistsini reached the sun god's house. There they were met by two silent young women, who wrapped them in a bundle and placed them on a shelf.

When the sun god returned home at the end of the day, he asked who had dared to visit in his absence. His wife tried to soothe him but, pulling the bundle from the shelf, Tsohanoai proceeded to test the strength of Nayenezgani and Tobadzistsini.

First of all, he hurled sharp spikes at them, but the brothers clutched Spider Woman's feathers and the cruel points failed to strike them. Then, the sun god tried to steam them in a great pot, but no matter how hot he made the fire, the water would not boil. Finally, Tsohanoai insisted that they smoke a pipe filled with poisonous herbs.

Unfortunately, Nayenezgani and Tobadzistsini had used up the feathers' magic powers during the previous two trials and, if Caterpillar had not come to their aid, they would have been poisoned. Caterpillar warned them of the danger and gave them magical stones to put in their mouths, which neutralized the poison.

At last, the sun god acknowledged their prowess and declared that they were his sons. Tsohanoai gave them powerful weapons with which they slew the enemies of the Navaho tribe and made safe the creation of the remote sky father Ahsonnutli.

See Heroes, p.55

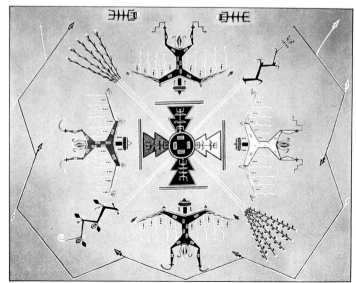

A Navaho sand painting depicting the sky spirits

SEE ALSO SPIDER WOMAN, TOBADZISTSINI, TSOHANOAI

NGEWO

The sky god and creator deity of the Mende people of Sierra Leone in West Africa.

Ngewo is regarded as the originator of all things, a belief evident in the Mende saying, "This is what god brought down to us long ago."

Ngewo no longer participates directly in earthly affairs and has become Leve (the high-up one). But he is believed to be present in natural phenomena. The rain, clouds, winds, plants and animals all behave according to the god's wishes.

However, the Mende believe that the spirits — genii and the souls of deceased ancestors — have direct contact with Ngewo. Propitiation of the spirits, as well as of Ngewo, is therefore considered to be immensely important, and the Mende often attribute bad luck or illness to the neglect of an ancestral spirit.

Sometimes, the genii, who take the form of beautiful women with smooth, fair skins, or bearded white men, act out of sheer spite, and attempt to take control of men. When this happens, the Mende believe that resolute action supported by magic is called for.

The distance which Ngewo has put between himself and people is explained in a myth. At first, the creator god told men to come to him for everything they needed. But they approached him so often that Ngewo said to himself, "If I stay near these people, they will wear me out with all their requests." To guard against this, Ngewo secretly built himself a house at the top of the sky and retreated to it while the first people were asleep. But this does not mean that Ngewo has deserted the earth, simply that he requires the world to be less dependent on him.

See Creation, p.135 and Natural Phenomena, p.138

Creation

The beginning of the world and the origins of humans are themes of all mythologies except those of North and South American Indians. Creation may be seen as a great event – as with the Pacific Islanders who envisaged the coming of a creator hero who formed the land, made humans and introduced plants.

On Easter Island, a bird god is believed to have laid a world egg, shown held up here by the island's bird man, who may represent the creator Make-make.

In China, the mountains (left) were thought to have been formed from the limbs of Panku, the original man who was born in the world, in a deathbed transformation. Humans descended from the fleas on his body.

The Polynesian hero Maui (above) pulled New Zealand from the ocean floor with a magic hook, but in his haste scattered the other islands over the Pacific.

In Hindu mythology, creation ebbs and flows on a vast scale, as Brahma (left), the progenitor of mankind and creator of the universe, sleeps and wakes. He is synonymous with Purusha, the first being, or cosmic man.

The Old Testament account of creation, that it comes from the hands of a great and powerful deity, is entirely within the West Asian tradition of ordering the world (see right).

NIMROD

In Hebrew mythology the wicked king of Shinar, and the builder of the Tower of Babel. His megalomaniac ambitions reached as far as planning a direct assault on heaven.

Apocryphal Hebrew texts tell of the power Nimrod derived from magical garments once worn by Adam and Eve, the ancestors of mankind. These clothes, made of skins, were said to be Yahweh's gifts to the couple, and possessed wonderful properties: animals recognized the authority of the person wearing them, and in battle they always secured the wearer victory.

Nimrod's success as a result of owning these clothes led his people to worship him as a god. However, even this adoration left Nimrod unsatisfied. He decided that nothing short of universal acclaim would be enough. So he ordered a tower to be built in Shinar high enough to be used to launch an attack on heaven. Arrows were shot into the clouds and fell back to the ground dripping with blood.

The situation for heaven was serious, and Yahweh had to do something about it. To prevent Nimrod adding yet more storeys to his tower and drawing even closer to heaven, Yahweh confounded the speech of the people of Shinar: when a man asked for a brick, he was handed mortar. Such misunderstanding soon caused strife, divided the people into hostile factions, and put an end to all building work. As a result of this, Nimrod's power was broken for ever.

The origin of the Nimrod myth is unknown, although recently fragments of a Sumerian story have been discovered which attribute the end of Sumerian civilization to ENKI's diversification of language.

It has also been suggested that the myth is a mixture of references to the great ziggurats on which the Mesopotamian gods were believed to live.

SEE ALSO ADAM, BABEL, EVE

NINHURSAGA

The Sumerian goddess of productivity and one of the main figures in the Sumerian pantheon. Her name means "lady of the stony ground", and she was associated with the goodness that can be reaped from the soil, even on the margins of the desert.

Ninhursaga had several forms: as Ninlil she was the wife of ENLIL; as Ninki she was the wife of ENKI and bore his children on the paradise island of Dilmun.

Originally Ninhursaga was probably the spirit of the stony tracks in the foothills of the Iranian mountains, or of the rocky edge of the Arabian desert. Her warlike son NINURTA, whose father was Enlil, was the thundercloud warrior and was credited with building Ninhursaga's mountainous domain and furnishing it with trees, plants, minerals and wildlife.

As a protector of wild creatures, Ninhursaga was distressed whenever animals were killed by hunters or captured and tamed. However, she was indifferent to the fate of any domesticated animal that might perish in her wilderness.

The only domesticated beasts for which Ninhursaga showed concern were cattle. This may have been because calves were born in the foothills that were her domain. Her emblem could be interpreted as the womb of a cow.

As a goddess of fertility, Ninhursaga's power over birth itself is clear. She nourished the Sumerian kings with her milk, thus giving them divinity. As the birth goddess Nintur, she is depicted suckling a baby. In one creation myth, Nintur was responsible for encouraging mankind to settle down in cities, and as "the lady who gives form", she decided the outcome of every birth.

See Love and Fertility, pp.106/107

SEE ALSO DILMUN, NINTUR

NINURTA

The Sumerian war god. Ninurta was associated with the thunderstorm and the spring flood. He was sometimes depicted as a lion-headed storm bird, when he was given the name Imdugud (heavy rain).

Ninurta was the son of ENLIL the air god, and NINHURSAGA the goddess of productivity. In early Sumerian myth, Ninurta first took the form of the bird Imdugud. The great span of his outstretched wings covering the sky was an excellent symbol for a roaring thundercloud. But the Sumerians came to feel that he ought to be given a human form as well.

The humanizing process was slow and uneven; at one time Imdugud grew a human body; at another, a human figure wore Imdugud's wings. But finally he assumed a wholly human form, as a charioteer, sometimes with Imdugud, his bird form, hitched in front of his team. Only on the battlefield did the lion-headed storm bird remain unchanged, possibly because its ferocious, powerful image was a useful weapon.

Ninurta's warlike character caused an uprising against him, in which all of nature, even the stones, took part. Some elements sided with him and others opposed him. Ninurta was victorious in the battle; he rewarded those who had supported him and cursed those who had fought him, which is why, for example, some stones are precious and others are not.

A legend tells of Ninurta's return from battle in his chariot, still all sound and fury. His father Enlil, no lover of noise, was obliged to send out a servant to tell his son to be quieter. Ninurta put away his weapons and stabled his horses, but his voice rose in excitement as he recounted his battle feats to his mother. A row between father and son was avoided only when Ninurta's barber hustled him away to his temple with the promise that he would dress the god's hair (hair was regarded as a sign of strength in West Asia).

See War, pp.94/95

NOAH

The biblical survivor of the flood which was sent to cleanse the earth of corruption. The story of this Hebrew patriarch is heavily influenced by earlier flood myths.

In Genesis, God made a conscious decision to destroy mankind. Grieving at the evil wickedness of the people he had created, he regretted ever having made them and vowed to wipe them from the face of the earth. This applied to animals as well. However, God regarded Noah as a just man and was prepared to save him.

God told Noah to build an ark and, with his wife and three sons, to gather a male and female of every animal into the ark. He then sent a flood to destroy life on earth. The deluge lasted for forty days and forty nights. When the rains stopped, Noah sent a dove to look for dry land. It returned bearing the branch of an olive tree in its beak and guided the ark to solid ground. The landing point of the ark is commonly believed to be on Mount Ararat in north-eastern Turkey.

After the flood, God sent the rainbow as a promise that he would not flood the earth again. He also told Noah to "be fruitful and multiply". Noah did so, and lived for three hundred and fifty years.

In Christian and Judaic myth, Noah's three sons Shem, Ham and Japheth were responsible for the spread of mankind around the world: Shem generated the Semites, Ham was the father of all dark-skinned peoples, and Japheth fathered the people of the north.

In West Asian mythology the flood story is very old. The GILGAMESH epic treats Utanapishtim as the hero of the flood, and other texts credit Atrahasis (or Ziusudra) with the timely building of a boat. Each of these men appears to gain eternal life as a reward for having saved all things from destruction. In Sumerian mythology, the god of the air ENLIL determined to reduce the noise produced by mankind by drowning all living things on earth. The water god ENKI advised a wise man, Atrahasis, to build a boat for all kinds of animals and his family, and thus life on earth survived.

See Flood, pp.110/111

SEE ALSO ATRAHASIS, HAM, UTANAPISHTIM, ZIUSUDRA

NTORO

The soul, in the traditional belief of the Ashanti people of Ghana.

The Ashanti believe that each person has a soul (*ntoro*). They also say that everyone possesses a tiny portion of the creator deity, a divine spark (*kra*). Whereas everyone has the same divine spark, the soul reflects individual character and the inheritance each of us owes to our parents.

This idea of a dual spirit – part divine, part human – is very old indeed. In earlier times the Ashanti were divided into groups according to the number of *ntoros* that were believed to exist.

Details of twelve distinct *ntoros* survive. These are described as the tough, the kind, the distinguished, the daring, the eccentric, the fanatical, the chaste, the pugnacious, the clever, the careful, the generous and the brave.

Each *ntoro* group had its own legends and favourite animals. For example, the clever group revered the snake. Once upon a time, the first pair of this *ntoro* group were unable to have children. Not only did they lack any desire to mate, but they were actually unaware of human reproduction. One day, a python asked them if they had any offspring and, on being informed they had not, told them that it would cause the woman to conceive.

The python sprayed the bellies of both the man and the woman with water, cast a spell and told them to return home and lie together. In due course, children were born. This is why members of the clever group bury a dead python whenever they encounter one.

Today, the Ashanti are less interested in *ntoro* groups, although the characteristics they possess are still used as a basis for describing human behaviour.

NUN

In Egyptian mythology, the personification of the primeval waters. Nun is portrayed as a man standing waist-deep in water, his arms raised to support the barque of the sun. All life was believed to have sprung from Nun.

In the creation myths or cosmologies of ancient Egypt, the origin of the universe lies in the watery chaos known as Nun. This endless, formless deep was there in the dark, at the beginning.

According to one creation myth, which originated in Hermopolis, the primeval waters contained four pairs: Nau and Naunet, Huh and Hauhet, Kuk and Kakuet, and Amun and Amaunet. These personifications of depth, infinity, darkness and invisibility had the heads of frogs and serpents, and were worshipped as deities. The four pairs swam and formed an egg in Nun. From the egg burst a bird of light, or, in some myths, a bird of air.

In Heliopolis, the sun god ATUM (who later became associated with RE) emerged out of Nun in the form of a hill or, in another version, appeared on a hill. Through a method of self-fertilization, Atum then gave birth to the first divine pair, the air god Shu and Tefnut the goddess of moisture. They in turn gave birth to the earth god Geb and the sky goddess NUT. From Geb and Nut sprang four children: the underworld deity OSIRIS, and his wife ISIS, the animal-headed SETH and his wife Nephthys.

See Creation, p.135

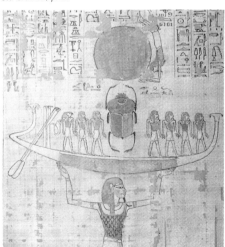

Nun, holding aloft the barque of the sun

SEE ALSO GEB, NEPHTHYS, SHU, TEFNUT

137

Natural phenomena

Gods have long been associated with the powerful and recurring wonders of nature – sunrise and sunset, thunder and lightning, frost and snow, earthquakes and volcanoes. And people everywhere have felt the need to propitiate the gods whose might controls these natural happenings, which may bring devastation or plenty in their wake.

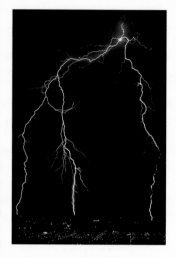

In Hawaii the volcano goddess Pele (left) enjoyed great respect, not least because the island group is a volcanic formation subject, even today, to regular, often unannounced, eruptions.

Lightning has everywhere been interpreted as divine wrath. In India it belongs to Indra, the sky's earliest ruler. For the Romans, the thunderbolt was the weapon of Jupiter.

For ancient Aztecs, storms were made by the rain god Tlaloc and his sky serpent, whose great belly contained all the waters of the heavens.

In ancient Greece, earthquakes were the handiwork of Poseidon, the turbulent sea god.

Re, the sun god of ancient Egypt, received great worship in the pantheon. Between sunrise and sunset, he was thought to make a daily journey across the sky in a barque, or boat.

NUT

The Egyptian goddess of the sky. In many representations she was shown with her body painted blue and encrusted with stars, bending over the body of her husband and brother Geb, the earth god.

In Egypt the sun's daily passage across the sky and disappearance at night gave rise to many myths.

In one, RE, the sun god, is angry at the marriage of Nut with her brother Geb, because he was not informed of the event, nor was his permission sought. So Re had the couple brutally separated by Shu, their father, and afterward decreed that Nut could not bear children in any month of the year.

But THOTH, the divine scribe, took pity on Nut. He devised a game of draughts to play with the moon whereby, if he won, the prize would be the moon's light. Thoth thus won enough light to make five new days, which were not on the official calendar. On each of these days Nut bore a child – OSIRIS, SETH, ISIS, Nephthys and (according to some myths) HORUS.

In another story, Re requested Nut to lift him up into the heavens to remove him from the world, which he found distasteful. Carrying him on her back, Nut raised herself, but the higher she reached, the dizzier she became. She would have toppled over and crashed to the ground if four gods had not steadied her legs, while Shu held up her belly. These gods became the four pillars of the sky, and Nut's body became the firmament, to which Re attached the stars.

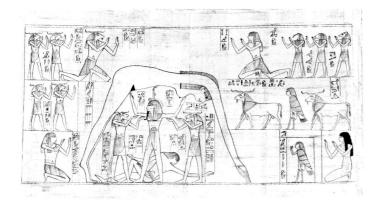

Nut arches over her husband Geb

SEE ALSO GEB, NEPHTHYS, SHU

NU'U

In Hawaiian mythology, the sole survivor of the deluge, which was sent to earth by the creator god Kane. Nu'u is therefore similar to the biblical Noah.

According to the Hawaiians, KANE once became so annoyed with human beings that he wiped out most of them with a great flood. The creator deity had already retired from earth and introduced death, but mankind's ingratitude continued to irk him. Unable to endure the situation any longer, he stirred up the clouds into a great storm that drowned the Hawaiian islands.

Only devout Nu'u escaped the deluge in a large boat with a house on top of it. Finding dry land on the summit of a mountain, Nu'u sacrificed food and drink to heaven, whereupon Kane descended on a rainbow and apologized to the good man. Although Kane was powerful, he never shared the bloodthirstiness of other Hawaiian deities. Because life was sacred to him, he never received human sacrifices.

The Banks Islanders of Melanesia tell a similar tale about the good-natured hero QAT. When a malevolent sea goddess drove the ocean upward, Qat built a canoe on high ground and awaited the flood.

The biblical flood story has clearly been entwined with both Melanesian and Polynesian legend, but there is reason to believe that the deluge myth existed in the Pacific before the arrival of Christian missionaries.

See Flood, pp.110/111

NUWA

The heroine of the Chinese flood myth and the mother of mankind.

In Chinese mythology, the great flood was caused by the tempestuous thunder god, a green-faced deity with large fins on his scaly back.

For an unknown reason, the thunder god was especially annoyed with one particular man who had two children, Nuwa (gourd girl) and Fuxi (gourd boy). Sensing a crisis was at hand, the man placed an iron cage in front of his house and stood patiently by its door with an iron fork in his hand.

In the midst of a frightful storm, the thunder god descended upon the house and threatened the man with an axe. However, the man remained composed and had the advantage of the thunder god who was beside himself with rage. Quickly, he bundled the god into the cage and shut the door fast.

The next day, the children were left to guard the thunder god while their father went to the market to buy spices in which to cook his captive. Before the man left, he instructed his children on no account to give the thunder god a drink.

So at first when the thunder god begged for a sip of water, the children refused. They were frightened to disobey their father. But the sad pleading of the thunder god eventually touched Nuwa's heart and she gave him some water. When she did so, the god burst out of the cage.

Before he returned to the sky, the thunder god gave Nuwa and Fuxi one of his teeth and told them to take shelter in the gourd that would grow from it. By the time their father returned from market, a tree had sprung up, bearing an enormous gourd. Realizing that the thunder god intended to take a swift revenge, the man built himself an iron boat.

Then catastrophe struck, with torrential rain and tearing winds. So the man boarded his iron boat and his children climbed into the gourd. When the waters rose to the door of heaven, the man banged on it, seeking entrance.

The king of heaven was so startled by the noise that he ordered the flood to cease. The waters receded at such an incredible rate that the man and his iron boat crashed down a thousand miles,

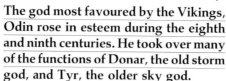

smashing to smithereens. Fortunately, the gourd was soft and only bruised the children when it bounced on the dry ground.

Because the deluge had drowned all the other inhabitants of the earth, Nuwa and Fuxi found themselves alone. For a long time, Nuwa resisted Fuxi's desire to marry her, but at last she consented and bore him a ball of flesh. When Fuxi chopped the ball into pieces with an axe, the wind scattered the fragments across the world as new people. Thus life began again.

See Flood, pp.110/111

In China, Nuwa is associated with floods

SEE ALSO FUXI

ODIN

The god most favoured by the Vikings, Odin rose in esteem during the eighth and ninth centuries. He took over many of the functions of Donar, the old storm god, and Tyr, the older sky god.

As a son of Bor, the father of the gods, Odin seems to have usurped Tyr's role as a creator deity. But, whereas Tyr was associated with law and justice, Odin was sometimes called Bileygr (shifty-eyed) and Glapsvidir (swift in deceit). Odin also eclipsed Donar and his successor THOR, the powerful gods of thunder. "Mighty as the other gods may be, still they all serve him as children do their father."

Like VARUNA, the Hindu sky god, Odin ruled through the use of magic. In his role as Sidfodr (giver of victories), he taught his favourite chieftains the spells of battle and instructed them how to draw up successful battle formations. Odin, sometimes Voden, Woden, Wotan, Votan or Wuotan, probably means furious. Certainly, the god inspired the frightful *berserkers*, maddened warriors who rushed naked into the midst of battle, frothing at the mouth and biting the edge of their shields.

As Valfodr (father of the slain), Odin adopted all the casualties of war. The Valkyries, Odin's special attendants, then took them to Valhalla (the hall of the slain) which was next to Odin's palace at Asgard, the city of heaven.

Although he was famous as a shape-changer, Odin was usually depicted as a vigorous man of about fifty, either with long curling hair, or bald with a long grey beard. When he wandered among mankind, he wore a large blue cloak and a wide brimmed hat to conceal his missing eye. His weapon was a spear called Gungnir. Made by dwarfs, it was infallible and so oaths were often taken on it. Odin also owned an eight-legged stallion, Sleipnir.

Odin's thirst for knowledge was insatiable. Two ravens, usually shown perched on his shoulders, gave him daily reports on the doings of gods, dwarfs, giants and men. His missing eye resulted from his pursuit of knowledge. He gave it to the giant Mimir in return for a drink from a well into which seeped knowledge from a root of YGGDRASIL, the world-tree.

Another time, Odin pierced himself with Gungnir and hung as a corpse on Yggdrasil in order to learn the secret of the runes. After nine days and nights, his self-sacrifice was sufficient to reveal the hidden knowledge, whereupon he cast off death and resumed his normal shape.

Mimir's well probably held the sacred water of destiny from which flowed happiness and misery, while Yggdrasil represented the tree of fate. Hence, Odin's two harrowing ordeals were probably intended both to make him superior to the course of events and to make him realize his fundamental lack of independence, his predetermined end at Ragnarok.

Perhaps Odin's special knowledge explains why he placed his judgement seat next to the well of Urd, where the Norns (Fates) tended one of Yggdrasil's roots. Their attention was part of a continuous tussle between the forces of evil and the forces of good within the world-tree. It was believed that when decay outran renewal, the branches would shudder, loosening the nine worlds and signalling doomsday.

Hanging was inextricably bound up with Odin worship, although sacrifice could also be offered with a spear or fire. The 2000-year-old naked man found preserved in Tollund bog in Jutland, in 1950, may have been hanged on a sacrificial gallows in memory of Odin's own ordeal on Yggdrasil.

Moreover, the devastating Viking raid in AD 842 on the French city of Nantes, which left thousands dead in its streets, was probably the fulfilment of a barbarous pledge to Odin Galgagramr (lord of the gallows), Geigudr (the dangling one) and Hangagud (the hanging god).

It seems paradoxical that Odin should have facilitated the northern movement of Christianity. The people who associated their bloodthirsty god with hanging were fascinated by the figure of JESUS, the gentle redeemer of mankind who was also nailed to a tree.

See War, pp.94/95 and Last Days, p.122

SEE ALSO ASGARD, GUNGNIR, MIMIR, NORNS, RAGNAROK, SLEIPNIR, TYR, URD, VALHALLA, VALKYRIES

Odin, the Norse god of war

ODYSSEUS

The legendary Greek hero and King of Ithaca, a small island in the Ionian Sea. He was known to the Romans as Ulysses.

Myth suggests that Odysseus was the illegitimate son of Sisyphus, the founder of the city of Corinth. This would certainly account for his quickwittedness, for Sisyphus was so intelligent that he successfully outwitted both Thanatos (death) and the king of the underworld, HADES.

Odysseus was, in fact, the brains behind the Greek siege of Troy. He had the idea of deceiving the Trojans by introducing into their city, in the guise of a religious offering, a wooden horse filled with Greek soldiers. When this strategem succeeded, the Greeks were at last able to end the war.

Because Odysseus offended the sea god POSEIDON, it took him ten years to return home. Among the strange places he visited were the land of the lotus-eaters (Lotophagi); the isle of the witch CIRCE, who tried to turn his crew into swine; the land of the cannibals (Laestrygones); the rocks occupied by the sweet-voiced Sirens; and the isle of the nymph Calypso, from which Odysseus alone escaped.

Disguised as a beggar, Odysseus finally arrived at his palace where a hundred suitors waited on Penelope, his faithful wife. Since, after twenty years, she could presume herself a widow, Odysseus suggested that she finally choose a second husband. So Penelope promised to marry the suitor capable of bending a mighty bow which belonged to Odysseus.

Having stripped the hall of weapons, Odysseus and his son Telemachus watched as each suitor in turn unsuccessfully attempted to string the bow. Then, to their astonishment, Odysseus, still disguised as a beggar, strung the bow, hit a target, and proceeded to massacre the suitors, aided only by two faithful servants and young Telemachus.

The final years of Odysseus's life are uncertain. He either lived quietly with Penelope in Ithaca or, according to one legend, was condemned to exile for the revenge he had taken.

See Heroes, p.55

SEE ALSO CALYPSO, LOTUS-EATERS, PENELOPE, SIRENS, SISYPHUS, TELEMACHUS, THANATOS

OEDIPUS

The infamous Greek prince who killed his father and married his mother, and the only man who solved the riddle of the Sphinx. His name means "swollen foot".

Oedipus's father, Laius, King of Thebes, was warned that he would be killed by any son his wife Jocasta bore him. Thus, when she gave birth to a boy, the king ordered that he be exposed on a mountainside. The child's feet were pierced and a shepherd was told to bind them with a cord.

However, the shepherd disobeyed his orders and instead gave the child to a peasant who passed him on to Polybus, King of Corinth. The childless ruler adopted the boy and, because his feet were swollen, called him Oedipus.

When Oedipus grew up he was taunted about his uncertain parentage. On inquiry, the oracle at Delphi told him that he would kill his father and marry his mother. Horrified, Oedipus immediately fled the court at Corinth, vowing never again to see Polybus and his wife, whom he assumed to be his parents.

On the road to Thebes, Oedipus encountered a stranger whom he slew in a quarrel over the right of way. The victim was Laius, his true father. Thus, unknown to Oedipus, the first part of the prophecy was fulfilled.

Oedipus then outwitted the SPHINX, a dangerous monster that was plaguing Thebes. As a result, he was offered the vacant throne and married his widowed mother, Jocasta. In time, Oedipus became aware that he had committed both patricide and incest. The discovery drove him first to blind himself, then to wander as an exile. Soon afterward, Jocasta hanged herself and Oedipus ended his days near Athens where he was secretly buried.

The Austrian psychoanalyst Sigmund Freud used the figure of Oedipus to illuminate one of his theories, the Oedipus complex.

See Fate and Punishment, p.143

SEE ALSO DELPHI, JOCASTA, LAIUS

OG

One of the mythical giants in Hebrew myth. Before the flood was sent to destroy creation, many giants lived on the earth. Og was the only one to outlive the flood waters that covered the "corrupt" earth.

Several reasons are given for Og's survival, the most obvious being his size – the deluge reached only to his ankles. Others suggest a relationship with NOAH.

Og was said to have perched on the roof of Noah's ark, and Noah fed him through a hatch. The giant may have offered himself as a slave or servant, a measure often adopted to ensure personal security in times of trouble. Whatever the arrangement, Noah must have found feeding Og far from easy, because he consumed a thousand oxen and a thousand barrels of liquid daily.

After the waters dried up, Og went his own way. In time, he fell in love with Sarah, the beautiful wife of Abraham. Og's jealousy was not expressed openly, nor were his plots against Abraham successful, but feelings between Og and the descendants of Abraham were hostile. This enmity was settled finally by Moses.

When Moses brought the Hebrew people out of Egypt into the land of Canaan, he was obliged to fight numerous campaigns. One of these was directed against the Amorite city of Edrei, over which Og ruled. The giant saw the encampment of Moses opposite his city and determined to strike the first blow. He lifted a mountain high above his head in order to crush the besieging force.

But Yahweh, Moses' god, prevented the disaster by unbalancing the mass of rock, and it fell heavily on Og's shoulders. When the giant struggled to throw off the mountain, his teeth grew into it, so that he could not see properly. Moses seized his opportunity, took an axe in both hands, jumped into the air and cut through the giant's ankles. Og toppled over, struck the ground with a roar, and died.

See Giants, p.159

SEE ALSO ABRAHAM, SARAH, YAHWEH

OGUN

The war god of the Yoruba of West Africa. He is closely associated with iron.

Ogun is the equivalent of GU, the smith god of the Fon people of Dahomey. But whereas Gu was originally thought of as a tool or a weapon made of solid stone from which projected a keen metal blade, Ogun was first and foremost an expert hunter.

According to the Yoruba, Ogun climbed down from heaven on a spider's web, an event which seems to have taken place before the process of creation was completed.

Ogun is not regarded as an evil deity and yet he can be undoubtedly harsh and fierce. His terrible nature is, in fact, simply an aspect of war itself, and the god will aid those who worship him. However, in the past, Ogun may have received human sacrifices. Even today, blacksmiths offer the god dogs in order to gain his goodwill.

See War, pp.94/95, and Craftsmen and Smith Gods, p.154

A sword used in the cult of Ogun, god of war

O-KUNI-NUSHI

The god of medicine and sorcery in the ancient Shinto tradition of Japan. He is credited with inventing therapeutic methods of healing.

During the travels he undertook in order to escape from the anger of his brothers, O-Kuni-Nushi (great land master) fell in love with and married Suseri-Hima, the daughter of the storm god SUSANOWO. Although the young lovers were very happy together, Susanowo was displeased by the marriage and subjected his son-in-law to a series of tests.

First, O-Kuni-Nushi was placed in a room full of poisonous snakes, but Suseri-Hima gave him a scarf which saved him. The next night, he slept in a room full of poisonous insects, but this time, too, Suseri-Hima had given him a scarf which provided complete protection. In desperation, Susanowo tried to engulf O-Kuni-Nushi in a grass fire, but a friendly mouse led him to an underground chamber in which he sheltered from the flames.

Susanowo began to feel more confident about O-Kuni-Nushi and decided not to test him again immediately. O-Kuni-Nushi saw his chance and, that night, tied all the storm god's hair to the beams of the house. He then made off with Suseri-Hima, together with Susanowo's magic bow and harp. Because Susanowo respected stealth, this trick seems to have reconciled the storm god to the marriage.

The mouse may have helped O-Kuni-Nushi in thanks for the medicine god's kindness to animals. Because of his generosity to a hare, cruelly tormented by his brothers, O-Kuni-Nushi had been advised by his mother to leave home. With Susanowo's bow, however, he was able to return and triumph over their wrath. With the consent of his father-in-law, O-Kuni-Nushi ruled over Izumo, a large province in central Japan.

See Seers and Magicians, pp.82/83 and Gods and Animals, p.103

Fate and punishment

In most mythologies divine retribution is inflicted on both heroes and ordinary mortals for their misdeeds. A serious crime might predestine successive generations of a family to punishment. This was the dreadful fate of the house of Atreus, in ancient Greece.

A temple dedicated to the goddess Nemesis lies in ruins north of Athens. She and the Erinyes, or Furies, were the avenging deities of Greek mythology.

Oedipus answers the riddle of the sphinx correctly, and survives this encounter. Thus he comes closer to fulfilling the dreadful prophecy that he would kill his father and marry his mother.

Eskimo shamans used a small wooden figure, called a tupilaq (below), to cast evil spells. Magic has been used for centuries to direct the flow of fate.

The whole range of reward and punishment, joy and sadness, freedom and fate are embodied in the Hindu god, Shiva. His hands bless and sustain, condemn and destroy.

Afterlife

The uncertainties of what may happen after death have always been a human preoccupation. The ancient Egyptians were so concerned about the afterlife that their religion was largely an attempt to gain access to the underworld kingdom of Osiris. Other peoples have placed the land of the dead on a cloud island in the sky or even beneath the sea, or have conceived of places such as heaven and hell.

The ancient Greeks were certain that ghosts dwelt in the underworld. In this medieval manuscript (left), they are shown dwelling with Hades and Persephone in a domain guarded by the three-headed dog Cerberus to prevent people from leaving.

Mictlan, the ancient Aztec underworld, is a place of relative ease, whose ruler Mictlantecuhtli (above) promised a welcome rest after the stress of life on earth.

The Papuan deity Hiyoyoa guarded the underworld, which lay beneath the sea. The souls of the dead were thought to work in the underwater gardens and, indeed, were witnessed there by ocean divers.

The funerary ceremony of the Australian aboriginal peoples, depicted on this bark painting, traces the path of the spirit after death, and re-enacts the events of a lifetime (right).

PAN

The Greek god of the pastures, Pan protected both sheep and goats. He originated in Arcadia, in central Greece.

The son of HERMES and the favourite of DIONYSUS, Pan was pictured with the horns and legs of a goat. At his birth, his mother was so shocked by his appearance that she fled, leaving her offspring to be raised by nymphs.

Pan means "feeder" and alludes to the god's care of the pasture. He was also responsible for the fertility of herds and flocks. His own wantonness was legendary, and was directed particularly toward nymphs. One nymph, Syrinx, changed herself into a reed-clump to escape his clutches. In revenge, Pan chopped down several reeds and made them into pan-pipes. He called the instrument a syrinx and played wonderful tunes upon it, beguiling still more nymphs, and women such as the moon goddess Selene.

Although Pan was usually playful, an irritable streak in his character could disrupt rural tranquillity. The god easily inspired a sudden groundless fright in both animals and men, hence the word "panic". When ZEUS overthrew his tyrannical father KRONOS, Pan helped him by creating confusion with blasts on a conch shell.

The Greek god Pan playing the syrinx

SEE ALSO SELENE, SYRINX

PANDORA

In Greek mythology, the woman who brought evil to mankind. She was introduced to earth by Zeus.

The smith god HEPHAISTOS made Pandora out of clay. ATHENA gave her life and her beauty was granted by APHRODITE. Quick-witted HERMES taught her guile and arranged for her marriage to Epimetheus, the brother of the Titan PROMETHEUS.

Whereas Zeus disliked people and did his best to harrass them, Prometheus offered them what protection he could. Zeus was so angry when Prometheus gave mankind fire that he became his sworn enemy and introduced Pandora to earth to plague the world with evils. Ignoring the warnings of Prometheus, Epimetheus married Pandora and accepted as her dowry a sealed jar of divine gifts.

It happened that the jar contained all the evils ever to beset the world. The only good thing in it was Hope, which lay at the very bottom. One day, against her husband's advice, Pandora opened the jar and released ruin into the world. According to another version of the myth, the jar contained everything that was good, and when the lid was raised, it all escaped.

Pandora's daughter Pyrrha married Deucalion, the Greek NOAH. When Zeus determined to destroy mankind on account of its wickedness, Deucalion and Pyrrha survived the great flood he sent by building a boat and stocking it with food.

See Flood, pp.110/111 and Fire, p.150

Pandora releases the world's evils

SEE ALSO DEUCALION, EPIMETHEUS

PANKU

In Chinese mythology, the gigantic primeval being from whose body the world was formed.

According to Chinese mythology, in the beginning there was nothing but darkness. The world was an enormous egg, its contents chaos.

Yet within the egg slumbered the giant Panku. At length, he awoke with a start in the darkness and cracked the shell with an axe. The lighter contents of the egg rose upward to form the sky, the heavier sank down and became the earth. But Panku was worried that they might converge again, so he pushed the sky up with his head and the earth down with his feet.

For thousands of years, Panku continued pushing sky and earth apart. Only when he was satisfied that his work was completed did the giant sink down and die. As Panku was dying, however, his body went through an amazing transformation. His breath became the winds and clouds, his voice thunder, his left eye the sun and his right eye the moon; his limbs became the mountains, his veins roads and paths, his flesh the soil in the fields, his skin vegetation, his hair the stars in the sky, his bones and teeth the minerals hidden in the earth, his sweat dew and rain. Indeed no part of the dead giant was without use, and even his fleas were the ancestors of the first men.

This late Chinese myth ultimately derives from the minority peoples living in the southwestern provinces. It is notable for the humble position assigned to mankind in the order of creation, a traditional Chinese point of view which is reflected in their landscape paintings where minute figures appear in vast panoramas of mountains, rivers and waterfalls, trees and lakes.

See Creation, p.135 and Giants, p.159

PAPA

The divine ancestress of the Hawaiian people. She was both the earth goddess and the queen of the underworld.

Papa means "flat" and it seems likely that the goddess was originally associated with the underwater foundations of the Hawaiian islands. Her full name was Papa-hanau-moku (the one from whom the land is born).

Certainly Papa was believed to be the mainstay of early life on the Hawaiian islands. She married Wakea, the first chieftain, bore him many children and showered his people with her blessings. However, when Wakea indulged in an incestuous relationship with their daughter, Papa was so furious that she left the earth and cursed mankind with death.

The divorce of Papa and Wakea was said to account not only for mortality, but also for the division of Hawaiian society into different classes. Indeed, one of Papa's abandoned children was fated to become the first slave.

Papa is also found in the Maori creation myth of New Zealand, where she is married to the sky god RANGI. In Hawaiian mythology, being married to the apparently mortal Wakea, she is much closer to human beings.

According to the Maoris, Rangi embraced Papa, thus trapping everything within the womb of the earth goddess. To remedy this situation, their son, Tane-mahuta, pushed them apart.

See Death, p.91 and Creation, p.135

Papa and Rangi pushed apart by Tane-mahuta

PERSEPHONE

The queen of the underworld in Greek mythology. She was the wife of Hades.

Persephone was the exceptionally beautiful daughter of ZEUS and DEMETER, the goddess of vegetation. In order to keep her safe, Demeter hid Persephone in Sicily, but the underworld god HADES discovered the hiding place.

Spying Persephone walking in the woods with her maids, Hades decided to abduct her. With the permission of his brother Zeus, he rose in his chariot from the earth, seized her, then disappeared beneath the ground again.

As the grief-stricken Demeter searched the earth for her lost daughter, the springs of fertility ran dry. Plants withered, animals ceased to mate and death stalked mankind.

Eventually, Zeus was obliged to reach a compromise with Demeter. They agreed that Persephone would spend one half of the year with her husband and the other half with her mother. The myth is an obvious parallel of that of APHRODITE and ADONIS.

Persephone accepted the role decreed by Zeus and was therefore worshipped as a goddess of generation and death. The Greeks themselves had no difficulty in espousing this ancient view of the ground as both the abode of the dead and the basis of life. As Kore (the maiden), Persephone was said to be the seedcorn buried in pits during the summer months before the autumn sowing.

See Death, p.91

SEE ALSO TANE-MAHUTA, WAKEA

SEE ALSO KORE

PERSEUS

The Greek hero who killed Medusa, chief of the three dreaded Gorgons.

A prophecy foretold how Danae, an Argive princess, would bear a son who would kill his grandfather, the king. To prevent this from happening, the king locked Danae in a bronze tower. But ZEUS, disguised as a golden shower, visited the princess in her prison and she gave birth to Perseus. Afterward, Zeus spirited away both mother and child.

Perseus was brought up in obscurity among fishermen but soon showed his worth by defending Danae from the advances of Polydectes, a local ruler. To rid himself of the hero, Polydectes ordered Perseus to fetch him the head of Medusa, whose features were so terrible that anyone who looked upon her was turned to stone.

Medusa was a Gorgon, with serpents instead of hair, golden wings, claws of bronze and glaring eyes. Because she had desecrated ATHENA's temple, the goddess gave Perseus a magic shield for his protection. And, as tokens of his admiration for the hero's courage, HERMES presented him with a cap of invisibility, a sharp sword and winged shoes.

Perseus was lucky enough to find the three Gorgons asleep. Nevertheless, because he would have been killed merely by glancing at Medusa directly, he approached the monster by looking at her reflection in his shield. Then he struck off Medusa's head and made his escape, helped by the cap of invisibility.

An alternative account relates that Athena decapitated Medusa and buried her head under the marketplace at Athens. Whatever the role of the hero in this adventure, Perseus went on to slay other monsters which harried mankind. He also accidentally killed his grandfather with a discus, thus fulfilling the prophecy.

See Heroes, p.55

SEE ALSO DANAE, GORGONS, MEDUSA, POLYDECTES

POSEIDON

The Greek god of seas and water. The Romans identified him with Neptune.

KRONOS had three sons: ZEUS, HADES and Poseidon. After overthrowing Kronos, who tyrannized over all his children, the sons divided the world between them. Poseidon became the ruler of the sea, a job he performed with considerable violence. The sea god's rages were terrifying, especially when he stirred up the waves with his magic trident, a gift from the CYCLOPES. He also caused earthquakes.

On one occasion, Poseidon even dared to dispute the supremacy of Zeus. With the aid of the goddesses HERA and ATHENA, Poseidon managed to bind him, but Zeus was eventually released by a hundred-armed giant summoned from the abyss of Tartarus.

Most of Poseidon's children inherited his violent temperament. His son Polyphemus, a Cyclops, was notable for eating some of the followers of ODYSSEUS. The Greek leader managed to escape only by blinding Polyphemus with the heated point of a stake, an injury for which Poseidon refused to forgive him.

In the works of the epic poet Homer, Poseidon is the implacable foe of the Trojans. This hostility arose from the dishonesty of the Trojan king, Laomendon, PRIAM's father. The king had agreed to give Apollo and Poseidon a certain sum of money for building the walls of Troy, but, when the task was completed, he refused to pay the gods. Although Apollo seems to have been content to send a plague upon the Trojans in punishment, Poseidon was not satisfied until Troy had been sacked by the Greeks.

Poseidon was believed to live in a palace beneath the Aegean Sea. He rode out from it in a chariot pulled by splendid seahorses.

See Natural Phenomena, p.138 and Giants, p.159

SEE ALSO LAOMENDON, NEPTUNE, POLYPHEMUS, TARTARUS

PRIAM

The aged king of Troy at the time of the legendary Trojan War, which seems to have occurred toward the close of the thirteenth century BC.

Priam was the son of Laomendon, whose ingratitude to Apollo and POSEIDON helped bring about the fatal conflict between the Greeks and Trojans. Laomendon refused to pay these gods the money he owed them for building the walls of Troy. In revenge, Poseidon helped the Greeks during their ten-year siege of the city, and did not rest until the city was sacked.

Priam was an honest ruler and brought great prosperity to his city. His principal wife was Hecabe, a Phrygian princess, and he had fifty sons, the most famous of whom were Hector, Paris and Troilus. One of his daughters, CASSANDRA, foretold the destruction of Troy, but Apollo had ensured that her prophecies would never be believed. Indeed, Cassandra was thought to be mad.

The chief myths surrounding Priam are to be found in Homer's *Iliad*, the epic story of the Trojan War. There he is shown as a kind and thoughtful king, whose honesty was acknowledged even by the Greek besiegers. The Greeks also admired Priam's courage in coming to ACHILLES to claim Hector's body, after his son had been killed in single combat with the Greek champion.

Priam's fate was that his city should be brought to ruin by his son, Paris, who eloped with HELEN, the wife of the Spartan king, Menelaus. APHRODITE, the goddess of love, aided Paris in his seduction, but it soon became clear to Priam that many deities were giving direct aid to the Greek expedition sent to rescue the Spartan queen. Helen's own sympathies during the long war were somewhat ambiguous, but Priam always showed her kindness.

Priam perished during the fall of Troy. He was killed by Pyrrhus, the son of Achilles.

SEE ALSO HECTOR, LAOMENDON, MENELAUS, PARIS, PYRRHUS, TROILUS

PROMETHEUS

The Greek fire god who was punished by Zeus for his kindness to humanity.

Prometheus means "forethought", while the name of his brother, Epimetheus, means "afterthought". Another brother was Atlas, who held up the sky. These Titans (giants), children of Iapetus and the nymph Themis, were hostile to ZEUS, who assumed control of the world after defeating his tyrannical father, KRONOS.

Prometheus helped Zeus in his struggle against Kronos but later rebelled against him because of his hostility toward people.

As well as being a fire god, Prometheus was a master craftsman. It was he, according to one tradition, who made the first men from clay he had found in Boeotia, in central Greece. For some reason, Zeus took a dislike to these creations. He decided to deprive them of the benefits of fire, and tried to starve them by demanding excessive numbers of animal offerings. However, Prometheus tricked Zeus by arranging for him to receive only the entrails of sacrificed animals rather than the meat. Zeus was enraged when he realized he had been outwitted, but he was even more furious when he discovered that Prometheus had restored fire to the world.

As a punishment, Prometheus was chained to a mountain peak and each day an eagle came to peck at his liver. Since Prometheus was immortal, though, his liver grew whole again each night. Despite warnings from Prometheus, who could see into the future, Epimetheus married PANDORA and accepted the sealed jar she brought from the gods as a dowry. Once opened, the jar introduced sorrows, diseases, and quarrels into the world.

Prometheus was finally released when he agreed to tell Zeus about the son who was destined to be his rival. HERACLES was sent to shoot the eagle and break the chains that bound the god.

See Fire, Craftsmen and Smith Gods, p.154 and Giants, p.168

SEE ALSO ATLAS, EPIMETHEUS, THEMIS

Fire

The significance of fire is both practical and spiritual. Without fire, it would have been impossible for human societies to progress. Fire embodied in godly form is seen as a symbol for the spiritual aspect of the universe, and revered as a cleanser and healer.

Tohil (above) was a Maya god of Mexico who brought with him the warmth of fire.

In Greece the volcanic island of Lemnos was associated with fire and the smith god Hephaistos.

For the ancient Greeks the bringer of fire was the giant Prometheus. He was punished by Zeus for passing such a valuable gift to mankind.

In ancient India, fire was the most sacred object of worship. Here, Agni, the fire god, is depicted with flames coming from each of his mouths.

PTAH

One of the most ancient of the Egyptian deities, whose cult centre was the city of Memphis. Ptah's importance rose with that of Memphis and he became patron of all arts and crafts.

Ptah was depicted as a mummified man with a shaven or bound head, holding a sceptre. At first he was probably a fertility god, like MIN – his name has connections with openings, including the womb.

In the third millennium BC, when Memphis became the capital of Egypt, the priests serving Ptah claimed that Ptah was an eternal god who manifested himself in many ways. It was believed that Ptah "created the gods, made their seats of worship, established their sacrifices, and fashioned their forms". Ptah became the protector of sacred and secular arts and crafts; he was the divine shaper, the moulder of all things.

Ptah was said to have performed great miracles. One of these relates how he saved the city of Pelusium from the Assyrians, led by Sennacherib. He instructed an army of rats to gnaw through the attackers' bowstrings and shield handles. Rendered defenceless, the Assyrians were forced to retreat.

In later times, when the influence of Memphis declined, Ptah was associated with other deities, especially those connected with the dead; he was then known as Ptah-Seker (Seker was the mummiform god of the dead at Memphis.) Ptah was also linked with OSIRIS, the god of the underworld. As Ptah-Seker-Osiris he often took the form of a bandy-legged dwarf.

One relationship of Ptah that remains obscure concerns the Apis bull, which was worshipped in a temple opposite his own. Every day at a fixed hour, the bull was let loose in the temple courtyard so that the future could be foretold from its behaviour. Apis bulls were normally allowed to die of old age – excavations have uncovered some 64 of them, all mummified. The bulls were believed to be an incarnation of Ptah.

As god of arts and crafts Ptah was identified by the Greeks with HEPHAISTOS, the smith god, and by the Romans with VULCAN.

SEE ALSO SEKER

PWYLL

The lord of Dyfed in Wales who changed places with Arawn, king of the underworld, for a year. The story of this strange exchange is the first tale in the Mabinogion, a collection of Welsh myths from the fourteenth century.

One day, while sitting on an enchanted mound, Pwyll saw a woman riding a white horse and sent his men to greet her. But no one could come close to her. The next time Pwyll sat on the mound and saw the woman, he tried to catch up with her himself but, until he addressed her as his love, he had no success.

A year later, Pwyll and the woman, Rhiannon, were married, and in due time a son was born, Gwri. However, one of Rhiannon's rejected suitors stole the child in revenge. The women charged with the child's safety were so afraid of Pwyll's anger that they framed Rhiannon. Blamed for devouring her own child, Rhiannon was condemned to sit at the gate of Pwyll's stronghold and tell strangers of her crime, then offer to carry them on her back into his hall.

Rhiannon's penance lasted for seven years, during which time Gwri was fostered by a distant chieftain who had found the infant one night in his stable.

When the news of Pwyll's loss finally reached the chieftain, Gwri was taken home as a man, although he was really aged only seven. Rhiannon's innocence was established and Gwri was renamed Pryderi (worry).

Pryderi grew up to be a warrior who fought with distinction in both Ireland and Wales. Arawn, King of Annwn (the abyss), turned to Pwyll when he was oppressed by Havgan, a fearsome fighter who could be overcome only by a single blow. If Havgan was struck a second time, he instantly revived. "Rid me of him and you shall have my friendship", said Arawn.

In order to accomplish this deed, Arawn and Pwyll changed places. When the time arrived for the contest, Pwyll met Havgan in the middle of a ford and delivered a mortal blow. Havgan begged Pwyll to finish him off with another blow, but Pwyll simply left his opponent to die. As a result of this service, Arawn and Pwyll became close allies and Dyfed prospered.

See Quests, p.64 and Death, p.91

QAT

The spirit hero of Banks Island in Melanesia. He gave the world its present shape and created its inhabitants.

According to Melanesian legend, Qat was neither a god nor a mortal but a spirit (*vui*). He was born when a stone burst asunder, releasing the fully formed hero.

Qat is said to have given shape to pre-existent matter and to have made the first pigs, trees and men. He also created night as a period of rest. Another creator, the spider spirit Marawa, introduced death. Qat carved people from wood and gave them life by beating a drum. Marawa, too, created people but buried them as soon as they showed signs of life. So death was brought into the world.

Qat and Marawa seem to have been friendly rivals rather than deadly enemies and on more than one occasion Marawa rescued Qat from a difficult situation. Nevertheless, Qat was always the more active of the two. He killed Qasavara, the cannibal spirit, and revived the corpses he discovered in the monster's food chest. Shortly after slaying Qasavara, the hero left the world by canoe.

The Banks Islanders believe that the best of everything was taken away from them when Qat departed. Until comparatively recently, they looked forward to his return.

See Creation, p.135

Tamate (ghost) mask from the New Hebrides

SEE ALSO MARAWA, QASAVARA

QUETZALCOATL

The snake-bird god or plumed serpent of Central America. He was a dying-and-rising god as well as a great king and bringer of civilization.

Quetzalcoatl's name combines "tail feather" with "serpent", signifying his complex nature. He is heaven and earth, light and darkness, life and death. A semi-legendary Toltec ruler, Quetzalcoatl was almost certainly a priest-king. It seems that, because he lapsed into drunkenness and sensuality, he faked his own death, left the Toltec capital and crossed the sea.

By 1200 the empire of the Toltecs, centred on the Mexican plateau, was in ruins, but memories lingered of a great ruler who had burned his palace, buried his treasures and sailed away, wearing his insignia of tail feathers. Later, in his *History of New Spain*, Bernardino de Sahagun wrote: "In the city of Tollan reigned for many years a king called Quetzalcoatl. He was a ruler of exceptional virtue, and the place of this king among the native people is like King Arthur among the English."

Quetzalcoatl may, indeed, have sailed away on a raft of serpents to an enchanted land, like ARTHUR. He may also have crossed the sea to the Yucatán peninsula and died there, perhaps burned phoenix-like on a pyre. Certainly, the Maya people who lived there recorded in 987 the coming of Kukulcan, "the feathered serpent", and the foundation of a new state.

The Aztecs, who ruled the Mexican plateau from the early fourteenth century, called themselves Quetzalcoatl's successors to justify their military state. But they exaggerated the Toltec practice of human sacrifice, making the cult of the plumed serpent one of the bloodiest in Central American Indian history.

At that time, the purpose of war was to take prisoners for sacrifice, since their blood was considered essential to the fertility of gods, plants and animals. Each year, the Aztecs sacrificed hundreds of captive warriors to Quetzalcoatl in order that the god might renew his strength and virtue.

The god Quetzalcoatl, like the ruler, was easily beguiled by strong drink. But in the god's case, it filled him with an uncontrollable longing for death, to which he finally succumbed, travelling over the ocean on a serpent to the land of the dead, *mictlan*. Indeed, Quetzalcoatl is sometimes represented as a joint deity with Mictlantecuhtli, the god of death.

Apparently, demons made Quetzalcoatl and his mother XOCHIQUETZAL drunk so that they would sleep together. Xochiquetzal was the goddess of flowering and fruitfulness, but she was also associated with the underworld.

The prophecy that one day the plumed serpent would return from the sea and claim his throne was exploited by the Spanish conqueror Hernando Cortés in 1519–21. The rumour of Quetzalcoatl's return so unsettled the Aztec ruler Montezuma that he loaded the temple of Mictlantecuhtli with gifts, including the skins of flayed men, and yearned for the peace of the god of death's kingdom.

See Serpents, p.115

Montezuma and Quetzalcoatl

SEE ALSO MICTLANTECUHTLI

RANGI

The sky god in the Maori myth of creation, Rangi tried to halt the development of the world, like his Greek equivalent, Ouranos. Rangi is also known as Raki.

The ancient Greeks and the Maoris of New Zealand have strikingly similar myths about the creation of the world. In the Greek version, Ouranos (sky) and Gaia (earth) were locked together in a continuous embrace. Their endless lovemaking was destructive, because it meant that Gaia's children could not escape from her womb. One of these unborn gods, KRONOS, solved the problem by emasculating Ouranos with a sharp sickle, which Gaia had provided. Then Kronos pushed his father up to form the sky.

In the Maori creation story, Rangi (sky) and Papa (earth) became inextricably entwined. When one of their sons suggested that the unborn children slay both parents, another son, Tane-mahuta, the deity of the forest, suggested it would be better to tear their parents apart.

Tane-mahuta simply pushed the sky upward with his head and the earth downward with his feet, and so separated the two without bloodshed. But one of the offspring, the storm god Tawhiri-ma-tea, sided with Rangi, and hurled storms and strong winds at his rebellious brothers. One by one they submitted to the storm god, except for Tu-matavenga, the warrior god. He turned on his cowardly brothers, and ate them all as a punishment for leaving him to fight the storm god on his own. Since Tu-matavenga was unable to kill and eat Tawhiri-ma-tea, he was obliged to leave the storm god in charge of the sky. Their long struggle, Maoris say, flooded the earth and created the islands of the Pacific Ocean.

Rangi is known under other names outside New Zealand. The inhabitants of the Tuamotu archipelago call him Rangi-Atea (Atea means light), the Hawaiians know him as Wakea, and the Tahitians as Tu Tumu (the source).

See Creation, p. 135

SEE ALSO ATEA, GAIA, OURANOS, TANE-MAHUTA, TAWHIRI-MA-TEA, TU-MATAVENGA, WAKEA

RASHNU

In ancient Iranian mythology, Rashnu was the judge of the dead, together with Mithra, the son of the supreme deity Ahura Mazdah.

The uprightness of Rashnu was his greatest quality. It was said that the golden scales on which he weighed the souls of the dead showed favour to no one. "Neither the good nor the bad, nor yet kings and princes. Not for a hair's breadth will he deviate, for he is no respecter of persons. He deals out impartial justice to the highest and the lowest."

Ancient Iranians believed that the soul remained for three days and nights beside the corpse, awaiting the decision of Rashnu. Once the stern judge had weighed all the evidence and reached a conclusion, the soul would be sent across a bridge which separated the living from the dead. The soul of a good person would be assisted in the difficult crossing by a fair maiden, who would lead him safely to heaven. But a damned soul would find the bridge as narrow as the edge of a razor and, unaided, would topple downward to a place of torment. There, demons welcomed the sinner with every kind of cruel punishment.

The judgement of Rashnu contrasts with that of OSIRIS in ancient Egypt. According to the Egyptians, it was possible for a soul to avert an unfavourable verdict as long as sufficient magical power had been mustered. For this reason, the scribe god THOTH evolved from being simply the recorder of judgement into both an advocate for the soul and a magician. The effectiveness of his intercession was thought to be reinforced by plentiful use of spells.

See Death, p.91 and Afterlife, p. 147

RE

The sun god of the ancient Egyptians (also known as Ra) and the most important member of the Egyptian pantheon. The name probably means "creator".

Despite his importance, Re had no great temples of his own, for the good reason that his worship was part of every other cult. Of the two principal gods who were worshipped in Egypt, Re and OSIRIS, the sun god was always paramount, although in the interests of personal salvation the underworld god had a massive following as well. The pharaohs styled themselves as the sons of Re.

The power of the sun clearly impressed the Egyptians. Its daily passage across the sky gave rise to a multiplicity of metaphors. At dawn the sun was regarded as a newborn child issuing forth from the womb of the sky goddess NUT, or as a calf being born from the great cow of the heavens. At midday, the sun was associated with a flying falcon, or a boat floating upon the blue sea of heaven. At dusk it was an old man who stepped down to the land of the dead, situated far below the western horizon.

The sun was sometimes an all-seeing eye, burning with judgement. But perhaps the most curious image was of a great scarab beetle which pushed the fiery ball of the sun before it, just as it rolls a ball of dung along the ground.

In the Heliopolitan myth of creation, as Atum, Re emerged from the primeval waters and, through an act of self-fertilization, brought forth the first divine pair – Shu, the god of air, and Tefnut, the goddess of moisture. From their union sprang the earth god Geb and the sky goddess NUT, the parents of OSIRIS, ISIS, SETH and Nephthys.

The arch-enemy of Re was the serpent Aapep (known by the Greeks as Apophis), who tried to attack him during the night, when the boat of the sun god sailed eastward through the underworld. Aapep was the Egyptian counterpart of the Babylonian chaos-dragon TIAMAT.

Magic was inextricably interwoven with Egyptian religion, and a spell was used in a ceremony to aid Re in his struggle with Aapep, who after sunrise even dared to raise stormclouds in the sky to shut out the light of the sun. The ritual involved the destruction of an effigy of Aapep, represented as a crocodile or a snake. This effigy was made of wax and Aapep's name was inscribed on it in green ink. It was then wrapped like a mummy in papyrus, insulted, chopped into pieces, and scattered on the ground.

In his dotage, Re was forced to give Isis a portion of his magical power by revealing his secret name (whoever knew the name owned the power of magic). He also commissioned the cow goddess HATHOR with the destruction of mankind.

See Natural Phenomena, p.138

The sun god Re crossing the sky

SEE ALSO AAPEP, NEPHTHYS

Craftsmen and smith gods

The ancients revered fire as one of the essential elements, along with earth, air and water. It was also prized for its power to advance crafts and technology, and as such became associated with a variety of gods. Fire and the forge were particularly important to the handling of metals.

The Celts revered metalwork and created some of the finest pieces known today, such as this gold buckle from the Sutton Hoo burial ground. Goibhniu was a Celtic chieftain god associated with metalwork.

Regin, the smith, here reforges a sword for Sigurd, a Scandinavian hero, who used it to kill the dragon Fafnir. He was eventually killed by Sigurd who suspected him of betrayal.

Mount Etna, so the Romans believed, was the place where Vulcan had his smithy. The sparks that flew from the forge were the eruptions from the volcano's fiery heart.

This neolithic passage grave on the Ridgeway in Oxfordshire, England, is known as Wayland's Smithy. The Celtic god Wayland was the greatest exponent of the smith's craft.

The powers of Ogun, the patron of smiths and metalworkers, and the god of war and of hunting, are celebrated in a ritual conducted by the Yoruba people of Nigeria.

ROMULUS

According to legend, Romulus founded Rome in 753 BC. His name simply means "Roman".

Romulus and his brother Remus were the twin sons of the war god MARS and a Vestal Virgin, Rhea Silvia. As a punishment for becoming pregnant, Rhea Silvia was imprisoned and her babies were set adrift in a small boat on the flooded Tiber. When the boat eventually came to ground in a muddy branch of the river, Mars' sacred animals, the she-wolf and the woodpecker, rescued the boys.

Faustulus, the royal herdsman, discovered the twins, took them home and, without telling anyone, he and his wife reared them. When they grew up, Romulus and Remus made their mark in local conflicts and eventually became so respected as warriors that many men agreed to live under their rule in a new city. This was to be Rome.

But at its foundation a bitter dispute erupted between the brothers, leaving Remus dead and his brother weeping over the corpse. Recovering from his grief, Romulus built the city and set about attracting settlers.

A shortage of women was ended by the so-called Rape of the Sabine Women. Enticed to Rome by a religious celebration, the women were made captive brides while their husbands and brothers were driven out of the city. In the ensuing war against the Sabine tribes, Romulus was aided by JUPITER, who encouraged the captive women to stand between the opposing armies and demand peace.

After reigning for forty years, Romulus suddenly disappeared. He was reviewing his army on the Campus Martius (the field of Mars) when a storm blew up and he vanished in a thundercloud.

See Founders, p.68

SEE ALSO FAUSTULUS, REMUS, RHEA SILVIA.

RUHANGA

The high god of the Banyoro people of Uganda, Ruhanga has always been looked upon as a kind of father.

According to the Banyoro, Ruhanga takes pleasure in sustaining his worshippers with good harvests, plenty of cattle, and a reliable supply of children. But the god also presides over disease, sickness and death. This less pleasant aspect of existence is accepted by the Banyoro as the inevitable price they have to pay for original disobedience.

Once, the dead could come back to life, although resurrection was denied to animals. All that was required for people to be reborn was for them to express joy during their life. But one day a woman refused to dress up in her best clothes and meet the newly risen, because her dog had just died. "Why should I go," she asked, "when my dog has gone?" Ruhanga heard this and said, "So people don't care what becomes of the dead. Let them never rise again then!"

The loss of power of resurrection among the Banyoro finds a parallel in the Germanic tale of BALDER's death. The underworld deity Hel was prepared to release Balder on condition that every creature should weep for him. All obliged – except the trickster god LOKI.

See Death, p.91

Cattle and children are granted by Ruhanga

SEE ALSO HEL

RUSTEM

An Iranian warrior and the hero of a tenth-century epic, *Shah-Nameh*. He is the counterpart of the Greek hero Heracles.

Rustem was the son of Zal, an Iranian noble and trusted adviser to the king. He inherited his father's skills as a counsellor, and excelled as a general.

His valour is celebrated in the many tales that have collected about his name. The wars in which he fought belong to the period when Iran was battling against the Indians in the east, the Turanians in the north, and the Semites in the west. Their setting is the Persian empire prior to its conquest by Alexander the Great of Macedonia, in 330 BC.

Not only was Rustem victorious over human foes, he showed equal prowess against a host of demons which attacked him throughout his life. When an especially powerful demon named Arzang succeeded in capturing and blinding the Iranian king, Rustem fought without rest against the magic of Arzang and his numerous supporters, until he was able to release the monarch. He even managed to restore the king's eyesight, by cutting out the heart of the leader of the northern demons and using that organ as medicine.

Neither waterless deserts nor towering mountains could deter Rustem in his pursuit of Iran's enemies. Whatever danger threatened the realm, Rustem rode to meet it on his trusty steed Rakush. In his loyal service to the throne Rustem might well have been the model for the Knights of the Round Table in the legends of the British King ARTHUR.

Only the treachery of the king himself, for whom Rustem had risked both life and limb, could cause the hero's death. Jealous of the fame Rustem increasingly enjoyed, the king ordered a pit to be dug and filled with sharp weapons. He then invited the hero to a hunt and lured him into the trap. Although his horse, Rakush, sensed the danger, Rustem urged him on, leading them both to death. Just before he died, however, Rustem succeeded in firing an arrow that killed the ungrateful ruler.

See Heroes, p.55

SEE ALSO ARZANG, RAKUSH, ROUND TABLE, ZAL

ST GEORGE

The patron saint of Britain and Portugal, who rose to prominence during the Crusades that took place between the eleventh and fourteenth centuries.

In 1222 the Council of Oxford decided that the saint's day should be kept as a national English festival. Shortly afterward St George was given a life history, and the myth of the dragon-slayer became firmly established. It is possible that he did exist, and lived in Palestine in the third century.

In his myth, which takes place in Libya, St George found that the local people were obliged to sacrifice a virgin each day by feeding her to a dragon. To relieve them of this horrific burden he slew the dragon with his lance and rescued the maiden, who was chained to a rock.

The saint seems to have derived some of his adventures from the Greek hero PERSEUS, and certainly this famous story would appear to be a direct borrowing from that hero's exploits.

Less well known is St George's power to fertilize barren women. According to ancient authors, barren women who visited the saint's shrines in northern Syria were magically impregnated by him.

Battles with dragons occur so often in West Asian mythology – from the examples of MARDUK and the Babylonian she-dragon TIAMAT – that it is not surprising that the theme has carried over into Christian legend. Even an animal lover like St David of Garesja was obliged to accept that the angels were right to strike down with a thunderbolt a dragon under his protection. He recognized that if the dragon were allowed to enter the sea, it would become a second LEVIATHAN.

See Heroes, p.55, Saviours, p.75

ST NICHOLAS

The patron saint of Russia and of sailors, thieves, children and virgins. St Nicholas found an American counterpart in Santa Claus.

According to Christian tradition, St Nicholas was the only son of devout parents who lived in Lycia, a Roman province in southern Asia Minor. When his parents died he gave away his inheritance to the poor. But, unlike St Anthony in nearby Egypt, St Nicholas did not choose to lead the life of a hermit in a desolate place. Instead he remained in society doing good works and showing, by his generosity, how a Christian should treat others.

St Nicholas is even credited with providing dowries for the daughters of poor families. His greatest gift, though, was when, as Bishop of Lycia, he persuaded a convoy of ships bound for Alexandria to unload their cargoes of grain, to feed the famine-stricken Lycians. He promised the sailors that if they performed this generous act, they would find the original quantity of grain in the ships' holds when they arrived at their destination. Following this miracle the sailors were converted to Christianity. Sailors remain his most devoted worshippers.

After his death in 342, his tomb became a place of pilgrimage, and many miracles were attributed to St Nicholas. The tomb itself was said to produce a miraculous oil with which serious diseases could be cured.

Santa Claus is a relatively modern development. It is the Dutch name for St Nicholas, and the present custom of exchanging gifts at Christmas seems to have begun among Dutch settlers in nineteenth-century New York State. He has since captured the modern imagination with his sleigh pulled by reindeer sailing high above the snowclad rooftops.

St Nicholas was removed from the calendar of saints of the Roman Catholic church in 1969.

SAOSHYANT

In Iranian mythology, the appearance of Saoshyant as a deliverer announced the last days, the coming of Frashkart (the final renewal). The god's name means "saviour".

According to Iranian mythology, the cycle of the world lasted twelve thousand years, comprising four three-thousand-year ages. The first three thousand years were the age of spiritual creation. Then AHRIMAN, the principle of evil, emerged from darkness and was dazzled by the light of AHURA MAZDAH (Ormazd), the principle of good. In the second age, Ormazd created the material world, but Ahriman declared war on the principle of good and sent a host of evil beings against all his creations, including mankind.

During the third age, the struggle between the principles of good and evil was intensified in an effort to dominate mankind, who descended from Gayomart, the first man. The third age closed with the appearance of the prophet Zoroaster, whose spirit was strengthened by drinking *haoma*, the counterpart of the *soma* juice of the Hindu gods.

The final age is that of Saoshyant, the saviour who will renew the world after three thousand years have passed. When this time arrives, a flood of molten metal will cover the earth and purify it. Finally, Ahriman will be destroyed in the last battle with Ormazd.

At Frashkart, both the living and the dead will have to endure a burning torrent which will purge them of their sins and enable them to return in joy to Ormazd. To the just, however, the torrent will seem like "warm milk".

Late Iranian mythology leaves the universality of Saoshyant's salvation uncertain, although the Sassanian kingdom (226–652) definitely leaned toward a final reconciliation between good and evil. Sometimes, the fate of Ahriman in the last days was thought to be imprisonment within the bowels of the earth, or, as with SATAN, removal from the world.

See Saviours, p.75 and Last Days, p.122

SEE ALSO ST ANTHONY

SEE ALSO GAYOMART, ORMAZD

SATAN

In the Old Testament, the word Satan originally meant adversary. However, from the third century BC onward, the Devil was developed as a separate entity in apocryphal literature. In Christianity he became the very embodiment of evil.

Satan, the prince of death, was often pictured as a handsome, sinister man, with horns on his forehead, a pointed tail and cloven hoofs.

He was held to have fallen from the heavenly kingdom as a result of his pride or envy. In the apocryphal Book of John the Evangelist, JESUS says of Satan, "My Father changed his appearance because of his pride, and the light was taken from him, and his face became unto a heated iron, and his face became wholly like that of a man: and he drew with his tail the third part of the angels of God, and was cast out from the seat of God and the stewardship of the heavens."

The same text reveals that, during a truce between the fallen angels and the heavenly host, Satan brought Adam and Eve into paradise. Once there, disguised as "a wicked serpent", he "seduced the angel that was in the form of a woman". As a result of this act of lust, men and women "were found having bodies of clay . . . and therefore were delivered unto death".

Other apocryphal works are more specific about Satan's hatred for Adam, whom Jesus says in the Gospel of Bartholomew was "the first-formed". The angels, the original "sons of God", were apparently down-graded to "messengers" after the arrival of mankind. Doubtless infuriated by this, the Devil refused to accept that Adam was made in "the image of God", which was tantamount to denying Yahweh's own divinity.

Although Hebrew and Christian demonology drew upon West Asian myth, Satan possessed neither the awesome power of the Babylonian chaos-dragon, TIAMAT, nor the implacability of AHRIMAN, the Iranian spirit of evil. Nevertheless, he was very real to early Christians. In the second century, the Greek convert Justin Martyr had no hesitation in using Jesus' name to subdue and cast out evil spirits.

The most famous of Satan's onslaughts on the faithful was the temptation of St Anthony, the founder of monasticism. In about 270, this young Egyptian farmer took literally Jesus' words, "Go, sell all ye have and give to the poor and follow me."

St Anthony withdrew to a desert where he lived a life of deprivation and exposed himself to martyrdom. The testing of his faith was left to Satan, who drew upon the entire resources of Hell in a manner similar to the attack of the demon MARA on BUDDHA. However, nothing disturbed Anthony's peace and purity of mind, and Satan was forced to admit defeat.

The apocryphal Gospel of Nicodemus describes Jesus' descent into the underworld and his release of the many souls held captive there. The gospel tells how, "suddenly Hell did quake, and the gates of death and the locks were broken small, and the bars of iron broken, and fell to the ground, and all things were laid open. And Satan remained in the midst and stood confused and cast down, and bound with a fetter about his feet."

Having rebuked the Devil for causing so much harm, Jesus placed a chain on his neck, bound his hands behind his back, and hurled him into a bottomless pit.

See Demons, pp.126/127

A medieval illustration of Satan

SEE ALSO ADAM, ST ANTHONY, YAHWEH

SATURN

An ancient Italian god of agriculture, identified by the Romans with the Greek god Kronos.

Saturn, like KRONOS, was regarded as the ruler of a distant Golden Age, when life was easy and peaceful. During this age, he had taught people how to till the fields and enjoy a civilized way of life.

As early as the fifth century BC Saturn's temple stood in the Forum at Rome and acted as the treasury. His festival, the Saturnalia, took place in December and lasted seven days. During the revels, people ate together and exchanged gifts at a public banquet in the Forum. At this time, slaves were also temporarily given their liberty.

As an agricultural deity, Saturn has more in common with a Greek goddess of agriculture, such as DEMETER, than with Kronos. His name may have derived from the Latin *satus*, meaning "sown". The Romans believed that Saturn arrived in Italy from Greece, where JUPITER had threatened to harm him. This is obviously an echo of the quarrel between Kronos and his son ZEUS.

The planet Saturn is named after the god, as is Saturday.

See Golden Ages, p.118

Saturn devouring his children

SEDNA

The myth of Sedna, Eskimo goddess of the underworld, sea and sea animals, is practically the sole Eskimo origin story. Also known as Arnaknagas, her hostility to mankind is shown in sudden storms.

Although Eskimo mythology does not explain the origin of mankind, Sedna is credited with peopling the sea while her father, Anguta, is held responsible for making the earth, sea and heavens.

Sedna is a one-eyed giantess, so hideous that only a medicine man (*angakoq*) can bear to look at her. Various tales describe her wild temper, her creation of animals and her dominion over the underworld, *adlivun* (those beneath us).

According to one tale, Sedna was an unmanageable child who would seize on flesh and eat it whenever possible. One night, she started to consume the limbs of her mother and father while they slept. They awoke in horror, restrained their ravenous daughter and, taking her far out to sea in a boat, cast her overboard. Sedna clung so strongly to the side of the boat, that her father had to chop off her fingers one by one to make her let go.

As the severed fingers touched the waves, they turned into whales, seals and shoals of fish. The fingerless Sedna then sank to the bottom of the sea where she now lives, keeping guard over the ungrateful dead who displeased her during her life. Numbered among these unpleasant beings are her own parents, who were devoured by sea animals when a storm overturned the boat from which they threw their daughter.

In another tale, Sedna is a reluctant bride who refused human suitors and instead favoured only a dog or a bird. Her enraged father discovered the tryst, killed the non-human lover, and immediately forced his erring daughter to accompany him home in his boat.

On the way back, a great storm blew up, and to lighten the boat Anguta threw Sedna overboard. As in the other tale, Sedna tried to hold on and lost her fingers which turned into sea creatures, while Anguta was drowned or eaten by sea animals when his boat sank.

Anguta had one three-fingered hand which he used to seize the dying and, like Sedna, one eye. The family deformity, and its connections with the dead, suggests that Sedna's descent to the bottom of the ocean was nothing more than an account of her enthronement as queen of the underworld. Anguta also occupies a part of Sedna's underworld house, where the mean-spirited live.

According to the Greenland Eskimos, the land of the dead is guarded by a huge dog and entered along a bridge as narrow as a knife edge. Nearby there is a wheel of ice and a huge, boiling cauldron of seals. Occasionally the spirits of the dead return to their villages, their ragged clothes flapping about them, terrorizing the living. The exact opposite of Sedna's underwater realm is *qudlivun*, the "happy land" in the sky, the home of all those who were generous or who had an unfortunate life during their time on earth.

See Natural Phenomena, p.138 and Afterlife, p.147

An Eskimo mask for propitiating hunting spirits

SEE ALSO ANGUTA

SEIDE

The "sacred stones" of the Lapps, who associated the peculiar shapes of these pieces of rock with the spirits of animals and men.

The Seide stones come in many different forms and sizes, worn by water and the weather rather than fashioned by human hands, and may even resemble human beings and animals. They were sometimes placed together deliberately to personify a family, and were used to predict the future or propitiated for assistance.

The Lapps also had wooden Seides, which were either tree stumps or wooden posts driven into the soil.

Several peoples of the extreme north of Europe possess a myth in which a great pole, or a rock, supports the world. The Samoyeds of Russia, for instance, have long believed that on peaks in the Ural Mountains certain stones act as bearers of the universe. For the Lapps it is the blood-sprinkled pole of Varalden-Olmai. This powerful deity rules over fertility and is the Lapp equivalent of FREY, the old Germanic god of sunshine, rain and fruitfulness. Another import in the pantheon of the Lapps was THOR, who became the thunder god.

Varalden-Olmai's pole clearly represents a merging of Germanic fertility rites with older traditions about the structure of the world.

Other examples of sky pillars are the evergreen tree by the temple at Uppsala and the Irminsul column destroyed by Charlemagne during his wars against the Saxons at Eresburg in 772.

See Natural Phenomena, p.138

SEKHMET

In Egyptian mythology, the lion-headed wife of Ptah, who was the chief god of Memphis. Sekhmet was a war goddess; her name literally means "powerful".

Sekhmet was usually associated with the destructive power of the sun, the solar eye that burns and judges. Whenever HATHOR the cow goddess became enraged, she was identified with Sekhmet. An example is the myth of Hathor's rampage on earth. RE, the sun god, was so angry at the lack of respect shown to him by mankind, that he ordered Hathor to devastate the earth. As Sekhmet, roaring and bloody-minded, Hathor followed the order so effectively that even Re had to put an end to the senseless slaughter.

A pitiless opponent on the battlefield, Sekhmet embodied the strength and bravery of the lion, expressing unbounded delight in the prey that fell to her. War was a matter of policy during the second millennium BC, when the Egyptian empire extended as far as present-day Syria, Palestine, Libya, Ethiopia and Sudan. In later times it must have seemed to the Egyptians that Sekhmet hunted with their enemies, for they fell victim in turn to the Assyrians, the Persians, the Greeks and the Romans.

Sometimes Sekhmet was merged with the cat-headed goddess Bastet, who was related to the moon. This connection was possibly linked to the way cats' eyes shine in the dark just as the moon does. Sekhmet and Bastet were both responsible for destroying the storm serpent Aapep with fire, when he dared to raise his huge head against Re.

Sekhmet and Bastet were closely linked with Mut, a vulture goddess and the wife of Amun-Re.

SEE ALSO AAPEP, BASTET, MENTHU, MUT

Giants

The idea of a giant race of men living at the beginning of time is widespread in mythology. Even the Old Testament says that before the flood "there were giants on earth in those days". Legend claims that the British Isles were once peopled by a race of giants.

The one-eyed Cyclopes are a type of giant in Greek mythology. To avoid being eaten by one of them, named Polyphemus, the wanderer Odysseus had to put out its eye (above).

A Germanic myth tells how the giant Baugi (left) drilled a hole through a mountain with an augur. He was trying to obtain the mead of poetry for Odin, god of inspiration.

The Biblical tale of how David slew the giant Goliath with a stone sling (below) was a favourite tale in the Middle Ages. This illustration from the breviary of Philip the Fair shows the entire episode.

SERAPIS

The state god of Egypt during the Macedonian occupation, from 305 to 30 BC. He was introduced by the first Greek ruler of Egypt, Ptolemy I Soter, "the saviour", who hoped to link the traditions of Egyptian and Greek mythology.

Serapis was portrayed as a man with curly hair and a beard, wearing a corn-measure on his head as a symbol of fertility. His association with the underworld was sometimes indicated by a dog at his feet.

The genesis of the god was supposed to have come from a dream experienced by Ptolemy, in which the king was directed to find a certain statue hidden at Sinope, in northern Asia Minor. The statue was found and identified as Serapis. It was housed in Alexandria, in a temple built especially for it, called the Serapeum. The temple towered above the city on a foundation one hundred steps high.

The establishment of Serapis was clearly a royal initiative aimed at linking Egyptian and Greek religious traditions. Perhaps Ptolemy also had in mind two events in the life of his distinguished predecessor, Alexander the Great. After Alexander had founded Alexandria in 331 BC, he crossed the Libyan desert to the oracle at Siwa, where he was hailed as the son of Amun, the national god of Egypt. But eight years later, when Alexander lay dying in Babylon, the only god that he invoked was Serapis. It has been plausibly argued that this Serapis was in fact a local Babylonian deity, but the utterance made the god's name famous everywhere.

In Egypt, Serapis absorbed aspects of Osir-Apis, "the dead bull Osiris". Apis was the sacred bull of Memphis and became an OSIRIS on its death. As Osir-Apis, Serapis drew strength as an underworld deity who was superior to fate. It was said that he could perform miraculous cures, a reputation which drew multitudes of sick pilgrims to Alexandria. He had tremendous influence as a healer among the Romans, until his cult was overshadowed by the goddess ISIS, the wife of Osiris. His great temple, the Serapeum, was destroyed by fire in 391 during a riot between Christians and pagans.

SEE ALSO APIS

SERMENYS

The long funeral feasts of the Balts, the old inhabitants of present-day Latvia and Lithuania in the Soviet Union.

In the thirteenth century, when Teutonic knights carried the Christian religion to Prussia and Lithuania, they were amazed at the elaborate attention paid by the Balts to the burial of the dead. It was the custom, when a person died, for relatives and friends to feast for a month or more. In order to delay the funeral itself, ice was used to preserve the corpse.

Although the Balts were converted to Christianity, their communal rites, which involved a whole neighbourhood, survived. They still exist in rural areas, although the details of the Baltic pantheon are lost. It would appear that the Balts once believed that souls were reincarnated in plants and animals. The lengthy wake must therefore have been intended to allow enough time for this transmigration to take place safely.

The chief deity of the Balts was Perkuons, the thunder god. There can be little doubt that he was related to the Germanic THOR, and Perenu, the Slavic sky god. It is unlikely, however, that the Balts saw Perkuons as a creator deity, this role being attributed to a shadowy and remote god who ruled over the world at the top of the sky.

According to Lithuanian folk tradition, a certain Perkunas once lived in a castle on the top of a mountain. He was a good ruler and was loved by his people. After his death he was taken to heaven, where his court now floats above the clouds. This may well be a tale about Perkuons, the old Balt god of thunder and lightning.

See Death, p.91, and Afterlife, p.147

SEE ALSO PERENU

SETH

The brother and enemy of Osiris, the Egyptian god of the underworld. Seth was a storm deity in Upper Egypt and was sometimes regarded as the incarnation of evil.

Seth took the form of an animal, possibly a donkey or a pig. He had long legs, long broad ears and a short upright tail.

In the mythical cycle that records the death and resurrection of OSIRIS, Seth plays the part of an implacable adversary. The motive for Seth's undying hatred of his brother was jealousy. Wanting to rule in his stead, Seth staged a coup and cast Osiris into the Nile, enclosed in a coffer.

When the goddess ISIS recovered the body, Seth cut it into fourteen pieces, which he scattered far and wide. Seth was so confident that it did not even bother him that his wife Nephthys deserted him to side with the bereaved Isis, along with most of the other gods.

It therefore came as a shock to Seth that the persistent Isis was able not only to gather the fragments of her husband and resurrect him but also conceive Osiris's son after his death. The son, HORUS, fought with Seth to avenge his father's death. The conflict between them was long, but ended with Seth's emasculation or death. Underlying the bitter struggle between Seth and Horus could be an historical rivalry between the two cults.

The Greeks compared Seth to TYPHON, the monster that challenged ZEUS.

Seth, the evil god of the Egyptian pantheon

SHENNONG

The ancient Chinese god of medicine, pharmacy and agriculture, who was credited with introducing new techniques and ideas that improved the life of the ancient Chinese people.

Shennong was an early ruler like HUANG DI, the Yellow Emperor. His gifts were all connected with good health: he taught the art of growing food, and revealed the medicinal properties of plants. Because he had a transparent stomach, Shennong was able to observe the effects on his body of all he ate and drank. One of his discoveries was the value of tea in thoroughly cleaning out the intestines and in this way aiding digestion.

Shennong's dedication to research actually led to his downfall: he died while investigating an unusual grass, which tore his intestines into pieces. His wife continued to contribute to early Chinese society by mastering sericulture (the breeding of silkworms). Later she became the goddess of housecrafts.

Shennong's preoccupation with medicine is typically Chinese; from ancient times they sought a natural way to long life, or even immortality. Many historical emperors worshipped Shennong as the deity of health. On a more practical level, they employed experts in dietary remedies in their palace kitchens.

SHIVA

One of the three supreme gods of the Hindu pantheon and a personification of the implacable powers of destruction. His male companions in the triad are Brahma and Vishnu.

In appearance, Shiva is fair of face, has four arms, four faces and three eyes. The third eye, in the centre of his forehead, possesses a fiery glance from which all created things shrink. It is usually represented by three horizontal lines, a mark worn by his devotees today.

Shiva wears the skin of a tiger and has a snake entwined around his neck, two creatures he defeated when they were sent against him by jealous demons. He is commonly shown seated in profound thought.

Shiva's neck is blue from drinking the poison of Vasuki, the serpent used by the gods and demons to produce AMRITA (the water of life). Had Shiva not swallowed the poisonous torrent, the world would have been destroyed. His mount is Nandi, a milk-white bull.

Shiva is a divine yogi, the arch-ascetic who sits alone on Mount Kailasa, high in the Himalayas. To test his devotions, or perhaps to disrupt them, INDRA the sky god ordered the love-god Kama to fire an arrow of desire at Shiva to rouse him from his timeless contemplation and draw his attention to his wife Parvati. When the flower-shaft found its mark and Shiva was shaken from his meditations, a lightning flash of anger broke from his middle eye, scorching Kama to cinders. Shiva agreed eventually to let the god of love be reborn, but insisted that he be recognized as the son of delusion (*maya*).

In his destructive aspect Shiva haunts cemeteries wearing serpents around his head and skulls around his neck. He is attended by a host of demons, terrifying in their lust for blood.

Yet Shiva's destructiveness is contained within a general scheme of personal salvation. When, as Nataraja (the lord of dance), he performs before Parvati, his divine steps are intended to relieve the sufferings of his followers. For the ways of the ascetic are believed to lead to self-knowledge and understanding.

Perhaps Shiva's greatest service to the world was the descent of the Ganges. Once, the sacred river washed only the sky, leaving the earth dry and dusty with the ashes of the dead. To put an end to the terrible drought, a sage sought to alter the river's course. But the river was so wide that the rush of water threatened disaster, until Shiva let it fall on his head and meander through his matted locks. Only then did it compose itself into seven smooth-flowing tributaries.

Shennong taught the Chinese herbal remedies

The Hindu god Shiva battles with a demon

SEE ALSO KAMA, NANDI, PARVATI, VASUKI, VRITRA

SIN

The Sumerian moon god, also called Suen, Nanna and Asimbabbar. The firstborn son of the air god Enlil, Sin was especially worshipped in the city of Ur, where his temple stood.

The name Sin seems to have referred to the crescent moon, Nanna to the full moon, and a third name, Asimbabbar, to the first glimmers of light at the beginning of each lunar cycle.

An eclipse of the moon was believed to be caused by the moon coming under attack from demons, who first won over the moon's two children, the fertility goddess INANNA and the god of the rainshower, Ishkur.

According to later Babylonian myth, the crisis was averted by MARDUK. Apparently, Sin's father, ENLIL, predicted the attack and warned the water god ENKI, who sent his son Marduk to the rescue. Ritual washing by Sumerian kings during a lunar eclipse was viewed as a symbolic purification of the moon.

Demonic attack was doubtless a legacy of the moon god's birth. The result of Enlil's rape of the grain goddess Ninlil, Nanna was born in the underworld after Ninlil had foolishly followed Enlil to the land of the dead, to which he was banished by the assembly of gods. Nanna was saved from death only by the substitution of an underworld spirit.

The marshes around the city of Ur were used as grazing land for cattle. Since Sin was worshipped in Ur, it is hardly surprising that he was held to be the protector of the cattle.

Sin had much in common with his son-in-law Dumuzi, who was the herdsman's god of fertility. Like Dumuzi, Sin ensured the fertility of the herds by raising the marsh waters and thus helping the growth of the grass they fed on.

It would appear that the rite of sacred marriage in the Dumuzi cult also formed part of the cult of Sin. In this rite the king assumed the identity of the god, while a priestess embodied the goddess. Certainly the high priestess of the moon god in Ur, who was chosen from the royal family, was considered to be Sin's spouse.

SEE ALSO DUMUZI, ISHKUR, NANNA, NINLIL

SPHINX

A fabulous creature in both Greek and Egyptian mythology. The Greek word sphinx means "the throttler".

The ancient Greeks viewed the Sphinx as a winged creature with a woman's head and a lion's body. The daughter of the many-headed monster TYPHON and the serpent Echidna, she was sent to earth by the goddess HERA to plague the city of Thebes in Boeotia. According to another version of the myth, the Sphinx was sent by Apollo after the people of Thebes neglected to perform the god's rites.

The Sphinx dwelt in a lonely place and preyed upon travellers, challenging them to answer a riddle. "What is the animal that has four feet in the morning, two feet at midday, and three feet at sunset?" she asked them. As long as no one answered her correctly the plague on Thebes would not be lifted. OEDIPUS, however, gave the correct answer: "You mean man who is at first a baby on all fours, then walks upright, and, when he is old, leans on a stick, as a third foot."

As soon as the Sphinx heard Oedipus answer her riddle, she threw herself into a chasm, killing herself.

In Egyptian mythology, the Sphinx was a guardian figure, the protector of the pyramids and the scourge of the enemies of RE, the sun god. The creature was envisaged as a recumbent lion with a human head, wearing the headdress of the pharaohs. This may have come about because the rock from which the Sphinx was carved at Giza suggested this shape.

See Serpents, p.115 and Fate and Punishment p.143

The Sphinx at Giza in Egypt

SEE ALSO ECHIDNA

SURYA

One of the oldest deities in the Hindu pantheon, Surya is the most distinct of early solar powers. He is the sun itself or the sun worshipped as a god.

Represented as a dark red man, with three eyes and four arms, Surya rides a chariot drawn by four or seven horses, driven by Aruna ("red" or "rosy"), the dawn. Two of his hands hold waterlilies, the third blesses, and with the fourth he encourages his worshippers. Sometimes he is called the son of heaven, Dyaus, and sometimes the son of Aditi (infinity).

In the ancient hymns of the *Rig Veda*, Aditi is the benevolent power visible beyond the sky, the vault of heaven with its clouds and stars. Of her eight sons, the one she cast from her was the sun, possibly because she could not be associated with a being responsible for the terrible heat that pours down on India during the dry season.

Surya's unbearable intensity recurs in a number of myths. When Surya married, his wife Sanjna (conscience) was so exhausted by the dazzling interest he took in her that she could not bear it and had to leave him. Before going away, she arranged for her handmaid to take her place.

Sanjna went to live in the forest in the form of a mare. But Surya soon missed her and, discovering her whereabouts, transformed himself into a horse and mated with her. As a result, Sanjna gave birth to the warrior Revanta and the two Aswins. The Aswins are ever young and handsome, bright with golden brilliance, swift as falcons, and the messengers of dawn.

To assist Sanjna in her domestic duties, her father, the great sage Viswakarma, placed Surya on his lathe and cut away an eighth of the sun god's brightness, trimming him in every part but his feet. This had the effect of making the god less hot and Sanjna cooler.

The fragments that were shaved off fell blazing to the earth, and from them Viswakarma fashioned the discus of VISHNU, the trident of SHIVA, and the weapons of other gods.

The other children whom Sanjna bore were MANU (the Hindu NOAH), the underworld god YAMA, and the goddess Yami, mistress of the Yamuna river.

Today Surya is worshipped in the states of Bihar and Tamilnad, where his benevolence is invoked for the healing of the sick. The symbol of the sun is also placed over shops, and stalls in open markets, in order to encourage good fortune.

Surya has a close counterpart in the Iranian god MITHRA, the focus of one of the most ancient sun cults. Indeed, Mitra is a title often given to Surya. Mitra was thought to dwell in the moon and care for the welfare of the world, hence Surya's title of Savitri (nourisher).

The two Aswins are the equivalent of CASTOR and Polydeuces in Greek mythology.

Surya, the Hindu sun god

SEE ALSO ADITI, ARUNA, ASWINS, SANJNA, YAMI

SUSANOWO

The turbulent storm god of Japanese Shinto mythology, a valiant but impetuous deity. Susanowo might be compared to the Greek god Heracles, whose divinely inspired anger drove the hero to a crime which could be expiated only by the Twelve Labours.

Even from the moment of his birth, Susanowo was cursed for his lack of grace. When the great ancestor IZANAGI was trying to wash away the polluting dust of the land of the gloom, which he had visited to see his dead wife, he cleared his nose so hard that the storm god was created. But Susanowo immediately grieved for Izanagi's wife, reminding him of his recent bereavement. With curses, Izanagi drove Susanowo away.

Susanowo proved an equal nuisance to his sister AMATERASU, the sun goddess, whom Izanagi made when he washed his left eye. For harassing her, Susanowo lost his beard, had his property confiscated and was banished by the gods. In exile, he began his wanderings and adventures.

At Izumo, in southern Japan, he met an old man and an old woman who were crying beside a girl. When Susanowo asked the reason for these tears, the old man told him that every year a serpent with eight heads had come and eaten one of his daughters. Seven had already been devoured, and now the great snake was coming to eat the last one. Susanowo told the old couple who he was, and asked them to give him the girl. They gladly consented.

Then Susanowo changed the girl into a comb which he pushed into his hair. He prepared eight large bowls filled to the brim with rice wine. When the monstrous serpent appeared, its senses were overwhelmed by the delicious smell of the wine, and without hesitation each of the eight heads bent to drink from the bowls.

The snake became drowsy and fell asleep. Susanowo attacked the serpent and cut open its belly. Inside he found a miraculous sword, a mirror and a jewel, articles which now form the insignia of the Imperial Family in Japan.

His other exploits involved conquering Korea, wiping out the plague, and planting the Pacific coast of Japan with trees.

TA'AROA

For the Tahitians, Ta'aroa was the supreme being and creator deity. They looked upon him as the author of life and death, who wielded absolute power.

In the beginning Ta'aroa, like the original Chinese giant PANKU, slept alone inside a cosmic egg until he was ready to start the process of creation. Then he cracked the shell and emerged. Although Ta'aroa was glad to have wakened, the emptiness and silence began to depress him, so he used one part of the egg to make the earth and another part the sky. Once he was satisfied with the world, he added everything that can now be found in it.

Another version of the story says that the body of Ta'aroa, like that of Panku, formed the raw material for the creation of the world.

The Tahitians regarded Ta'aroa as Rua-i-tupra (the source of growth), for out of his body the god built his own temple, which was called Roi-i-te-fatu-Ta'aroa (the resting place of the great lord). In 1769, on a visit to the island of Tahiti, the English explorer Captain Cook noted that "the general resemblance between this repository and the Ark of the Lord among the Jews is remarkable."

The Tahitians believed that Ta'aroa sent both blessings and disaster to the world. To appease him it was the custom to offer human sacrifices, *te avae roroa* (long-legged fish), in the belief that the god enjoyed the taste of flesh.

The creation myth of Ta'aroa is undoubtedly very old, but a rival account may exist in the story of a couple who took refuge from the primeval waters on a mountain top. On the other hand, this escape could be a legend about the flooding of the world. Ta'aroa is said to have become angry with mankind, so he raised the level of the sea, leaving only the scattered islands of the Pacific protruding above the water.

See Flood, p.110 and Creation, p.135

TANGAROA

In Polynesian mythology, Tangaroa (or Tangoloa) is the sea god, the deity responsible for all the fish and reptiles.

Tangaroa was one of the children of RANGI (sky) and PAPA (earth). His twin brother was Rongo, a deity whose interests covered both the ocean and the land. The children of Rangi and Papa were trapped in the womb of the earth goddess until Rangi was pushed upward by the forest god Tane-mahuta to form the sky. Inexplicably, Tawhiri-ma-tea, Tangaroa's elder brother, took offence at this action and sent storms to ravage land and water. The Maoris say that Tangaroa fled to the ocean so as to escape his brother's wrath.

A Tuamotuan legend about Tangaroa's travels recalls the titanic struggle between the sea god and the demon octopus Rogo-tumu-here. The fight occurred after Tangaroa's daughter-in-law was seized by Rogo-tumu-here as she was surfing. Tangaroa and his son Turi-a-faumea paddled their canoe to the lair of the demon octopus and, on a hook baited with sacred feathers, drew him up to the surface. In a desperate struggle, Tangaroa hacked off the demon's tentacles, then split open the head and pulled the girl from the dreadful creature's maw.

A rather odd myth about the creation of the moon blames its paleness on Tangaroa; it seems that the sea god kept the moon out of the sky too long, and it began to decompose.

In Hawaii, Tangaroa was called Kanaloa, and was associated with the squid. Kanaloa's vindictive nature finds a parallel in the story of a quarrel between the sea god and Tane-mahuta. Because Tane-mahuta had shown kindness to human beings by giving them the canoe, the spear and the fish-hook, Tangaroa took his revenge by drowning fishermen, flooding fields and eating away the shore. But this legend may simply be an explanation of Tangaroa's defence of his watery realm.

See Natural Phenomena, p.138

SEE ALSO KANALOA, TANE-MAHUTA, TAWHIRI-MA-TEA, TURI-A-FAUMEA

TANTALUS

The Lydian king who offended the Greek gods and was punished for eternity in the abyss of Tartarus.

The son of the Titaness Pluto (wealth) and ZEUS, Tantalus ruled the rich kingdom of Lydia. However Tantalus offended the gods, a crime which is variously recounted. Some say he betrayed secrets entrusted to him by Zeus, others believe that he stole the food of the gods. The best-known account describes his presumption in testing divine knowledge by serving the gods a dish of human flesh.

At a banquet for a group of gods, Tantalus included a course prepared from the corpse of Pelops, his son. The fare was recognized by all the divine guests, except DEMETER, who was lost in thought about her missing daughter PERSEPHONE. HERMES fetched the soul of Pelops back from the underworld and the gods restored him to life. Because Demeter had absentmindedly eaten part of his shoulder, she gave the prince an ivory replacement.

In punishment for offending the gods, Tantalus was imprisoned in Tartarus. Here he was kept perpetually hungry and thirsty while standing chin-deep in water with fruit hanging from branches just above his head. Whenever he tried to drink the water or eat the fruit, they receded from him, hence the word "tantalize".

See Fate and Punishment, p.143

Tantalus reaches for fruit

SEE ALSO PELOPS, PLUTO, TARTARUS

TARA

The great goddess of Tibetan Buddhism and the wife of the bodhisattva Avalokitesvara. Worship of Tara was once widespread in central, south and Southeast Asia.

In about 630, the Chinese pilgrim TRIPI-TAKA found an imposing shrine dedicated to the goddess at the great Buddhist centre of Nalanda, in northern India. Both Tara and AVALOKITESVARA were worshipped there as saviours of souls.

Her compassion is evident in many surviving texts. Tara was "the mistress of boats", the one who "was able to pacify the waters", and she had in her service female spirits who rescued the ship-wrecked. In the same way that Christian mariners have looked to the VIRGIN MARY as Stella Maris, Buddhist sailors have thrown themselves upon Tara's mercy.

Although the practical assistance the goddess gave to those in physical danger was important in her cult, the height of Tara worship was reached in contemplation, for above all else she assisted those who sought enlightenment. It was said that when the sea of knowledge was churned, Tara was born as the essence of wisdom. She was called Prajnaparamita (perfection of understanding) because she led her devotees across the river of experience to the shore of spiritual freedom.

Tara has a number of distinct forms in Tibet, where she is still worshipped. She is often shown seated on a lion, holding the sun in her hand, or as an elegant young woman holding a lotus, the flower holy to Hindus and Buddhists.

According to legend, the Tibetan peoples descend from Avalokitesvara and Tara. The cult of Tara seems, however, to have been introduced only during the reign of the first Tibetan king, Strong-btsan-sgam-po, who died in 650. When she married him, the king's Nepalese wife is known to have brought with her a sandalwood statue of the goddess.

·SEE ALSO STELLA MARIS

TARU

The Hittite weather god who slew the dragon Illuyankas. In AD 72, after the Romans had added the territory of Commagene to their province of Syria, the cult of Taru was transformed into that of Jupiter Dolichenus.

During the ascendancy of the Hittites in Asia Minor, in the second millennium BC, Taru was one of the names of the weather god. His position in the pantheon is hard to determine due to the fragmentary condition of the surviving religious texts, but the Illuyankas myth points up his importance.

Taru's victory over the dragon is comparable to that of the Babylonian god MARDUK over the chaos-dragon TIAMAT. However, whereas Marduk's success resides in his sheer power, Taru's depends more on trickery.

In the older version of the tale, Illuyankas defeated the weather god but was then caught out by the goddess Inaras. She prepared an enormous banquet and encouraged Illuyankas and his brood to eat and drink their fill. When they had done so, they were too fat to squeeze through the tunnel leading to their underground home. Hupasiyas, Inaras's mortal lover, then bound the dragons with a strong rope, whereupon Taru and the other gods fell upon them and overcame them.

According to the later version of the myth, the dragon vanquished Taru and took away his heart and eyes. In order to recover them, Taru begot a son whom he married to the daughter of Illuyankas. The son asked for the missing organs as a dowry and returned them to his father. Thus restored, Taru slew the dragon in a ferocious sea battle. He also killed his son, possibly because he had sided with his father-in-law.

Both stories relate to the West Asian theme of a dying-and-rising fertility god, for vegetation languished during the time that Taru was under the dragon's domination.

See Serpents, p.115

SEE ALSO HUPASIYAS, ILLUYANKAS, INARAS

TENGRI

The ancient sky god of the nomadic peoples of East Asia. He was looked upon as the creator of all things, visible and invisible.

Tengri (heaven) was once the supreme deity of both the Turks and the Mongol nomads living to the north of the Great Wall of China. He was the controller of destiny and the ruler of the world.

Like other northern peoples, the Mongols were deeply impressed by natural phenomena. Meteors were considered lucky, for whoever saw such a "crack in the sky" could at that moment ask a favour of Tengri. On the other hand, hail and thunderstorms meant bad luck. Because of a great hailstorm in 1246, medicine men (shamans) advised that the enthronement of Guyug, the grandson of Genghis Khan, should be postponed for nine days.

The sweeping victories of Genghis Khan were said to have been decreed by heaven, hence the anxiety over Tengri's display of unease in the form of hail on his grandson's becoming the khan. After the conversion of Kublai Khan (1260–94) to Buddhism, the goodwill of Tengri was of less importance, although many old folk-customs were tolerated and given new meanings. The power of the shamans declined, however.

Before the introduction of Buddhism to the peoples of the steppe, Tengri ruled alongside the earth goddess Itugen. While the sky god decreed events, Itugen ensured the fertility of people and cattle and protected the natural pastures over which the nomads herded their animals.

European accounts of visits to the Mongol court in Karakorum indicate that Tengri and Itugen were worshipped and propitiated with offerings of food and drink, and often also with human and animal sacrifice. The Mongols made idols of felt and believed that the spirits of the two deities dwelt in them.

See Natural Phenomena, p.138

TELIPINU

The Hittite deity of agriculture. Telipinu features in an epic cycle which celebrated the change of seasons. His cult centre was in the Anatolian uplands.

Son of the weather god TARU, Telipinu was in charge of the fertility of both animals and plants.

The epic cycle begins with Telipinu's angry withdrawal from the world. He went off in such haste that he put his right boot on his left foot and his left boot on his right foot.

As soon as Telipinu disappeared, a terrible blight struck the world and ruin faced both gods and men. Dust clouds rose up, trees withered, fields became parched, animals ceased to produce offspring. Famine and death stalked the land, littering the cities and countryside with corpses.

When an eagle sent out by the sun god failed to locate Telipinu, the mother goddess Hannahanna implored Taru to find the missing deity. Taru ranged the world, searching without avail, and finally gave up and sat down in despair.

Hannahanna then sent a bee to look for Telipinu, although the gods protested that so small a creature was unlikely to have any success when Taru, the chief deity, had been baffled. But the mother goddess brushed aside these objections and ordered the bee to sting the missing god when it found him. After a long search, the bee came across Telipinu, who was fast asleep in a meadow.

Stung on the hands and feet, Telipinu burst out in a second storm of anger, and continued the ravage of the land. It was not until Kamrusepas, the goddess of spells, or perhaps of healing, defused his fury by means of a magical ceremony, that he was persuaded to return. On the back of an eagle, he flew back to his temple and his duties. Only then did Telipinu end the dust storm, revive vegetation, and aid animal husbandry.

The discovery of a parallel myth about Telipinu's father Taru has encouraged the view that disappearance, or even temporary death, may have been a regular feature in the cults of Hittite gods.

SEE ALSO DUMUZI, HANNAHANNA, KAMRUSEPAS, TAMMUZ

TEZCATLIPOCA

The Aztec god of the summer sun, bringer of abundant harvests as well as drought and sterility. His name means "smoking mirror" and derives from the mirror made from black obsidian which sorcerers used to predict the future.

The Aztec conquerors of the Mexican plateau held Tezcatlipoca in the highest regard. He was identified with Itzli, the stone-knife god, since the Central Americans used obsidian to make spear points, hunting knives and axe blades as well as swords and sacrificial knives.

Obsidian's opposing qualities could well explain Tezcatlipoca's attributes. The sun god could be alternately kind and cruel: he enjoyed battle as much as the war god HUITZILOPOCHTLI; he collaborated with the earth goddess COATLICUE in nourishing mankind; and, in league with witches and demons, he took pleasure in the outrages of the night.

The Aztecs had several sun gods, of whom Tezcatlipoca was the most powerful. In common with other Aztec deities, he was thought to die each night, ossify, and return to the world each morning. It was also believed that he underwent an annual death and resurrection.

According to one Aztec legend, Tezcatlipoca passed the night wandering around with his head in his hand. Nervous people died on seeing him, but if anyone was brave enough to seize hold of him, the god would offer him wealth and invincible power if he was released before sunrise. However, the god did not fulfil his promise.

In Tenochtitlán, the Aztec capital, it was customary for a handsome youth to impersonate the god for a year, after which he would be killed with an obsidian knife and his heart offered to the sun.

It is hard to determine Tezcatlipoca's exact role in the Aztec pantheon. He was addressed as an omnipotent, invisible deity and was thought to be the arbiter of life and death. However, Ometechtli (dual lord), the bisexual creator, was more important than Tezcatlipoca.

See Natural Phenomena, p.138

Tezcatlipoca, the Aztec god of the summer sun   SEE ALSO OMETECHTLI

THESEUS

The legendary Greek hero and the champion of the Athenians.

The Athenians credited Theseus with numerous exploits, including the foundation of their own state. He accomplished this by unifying the laws and making the city of Athens the seat of government.

Above all, Theseus was celebrated for slaying the Minotaur, a monstrous bull-headed man. Each year, MINOS, the Cretan king, commanded the Athenians to send nine girls and nine boys to his palace at Knossos as food for the Minotaur, who dwelt there in the Labyrinth.

One year Theseus volunteered to go to Crete as a sacrificial victim, an offer which deeply upset his father Aegeus. Theseus calmed Aegeus by telling him to look out for the colour of his ship's sail on its return from Crete. If it had been changed from black to white, he would know that Theseus was still alive.

Assisted by Ariadne, Minos' daughter, who supplied him with a skein of thread, Theseus was able to escape from the Labyrinth after he had killed the brute. Some versions of the story say he killed the Minotaur with a sword, others say he did this with his bare hands.

Having fought his way back to the ship, Theseus escaped from Crete with Ariadne. For an unknown reason, the hero took the princess no farther than the island of Dia, probably Naxos. After several more stops, the ship headed for Athens, but Theseus was so pleased to be returning home that he forgot to change the sail. Aegeus saw the ship from a distance, assumed his son to be dead, and flung himself over a cliff.

After the funeral of Aegeus, Theseus became king and unified the Athenians into a single state.

Despite his position, Theseus continued his adventures, which included accompanying HERACLES on his expedition to the fierce female warriors, the Amazons. Eventually, various tragedies befell him and he retired to the palace of Lycomedes, King of Scyros. There, Lycomedes had Theseus killed.

See Heroes, p.55 and Founders, p.68

SEE ALSO AEGEUS, AMAZONS, ARIADNE, LYCOMEDES, MINOTAUR

THOR

After Odin, Thor was the most important Germanic deity. The god of thunderstorms and fertility he wielded a marvellous hammer called Mjolnir (the destroyer).

According to one tradition, Thor was ODIN's son, but it is more likely that he assumed the role of the old thunder god, Donar, whom Odin had overshadowed.

Thor was regarded as a generous deity, a gentle giant until provoked, whereupon he broke into tempestuous rages.

He was usually depicted as a tall, well-formed, muscular, red-haired man in his prime. His symbol was the hammer, a magic weapon that returned to his hand like a boomerang. When the hammer was red hot, the god wore an iron glove to protect himself. His strength was doubled by a magic belt and his chariot was drawn across the sky by two he-goats, Tann-gniortr (toothgrinder) and Tanngrisnr (toothgnasher). The thunderous noise of this vehicle derived partly from the collection of cauldrons which hung on its sides.

Thor's character is perhaps best shown in a legend from the *Thrymskirda*, a poem dating from about 900. It tells how the frost giants hid Thor's hammer and how Thrymr, their king, demanded the hand of the goddess Freya in exchange for it. The trickster god LOKI persuaded Thor to retrieve the hammer by travelling to the land of the giants disguised as Freya, with himself disguised as a maidservant.

Dressed as women, the two gods arrived for the wedding. At the nuptial feast, Thrymr was astonished to see the "bride" eat a whole ox, eight salmon, and all the dainties intended for the ladies, then wash everything down with three barrels of wine.

Cunning Loki explained this singular appetite by saying that Freya had been too excited to eat or drink before the marriage. When Thrymr took the hammer out, Thor grasped the weapon and laid low all the giants in attendance.

Loki also accompanied Thor on his famous journey to Jotunnheim (the land of the giants). There they encountered Skrymir (vast), a frost giant so enormous that the two gods inadvertently slept in the thumb of his empty glove, thinking it was a room. When Thor put on his magic belt

and attempted to smash the skull of the sleeping giant with his thunder hammer, Skrymir awoke, thinking that a leaf or twig had brushed his brow.

Later, Thor and Loki reached a city with battlements so high that they disappeared from view. Inside this strange city, the gods failed numerous contests, Thor himself being wrestled down by "an old, old woman". Only on the journey home did the disconcerted pair realize that both the giant and the city had been illusions, stupendous magical creations sent out by the frightened frost giants to baffle Thor.

At times, however, Thor enjoyed the company of giants, which suggests that he himself may once have been regarded as one. One legend tells of a fishing trip he took with the frost giant Hymir in the hope of hooking the sea serpent Jormungandr, the colossal offspring of Loki and the giantess Angurbodi. The serpent Jormungandr's writhings caused tempests and, though Thor made several attempts to kill the creature, he did not succeed until Ragnarok (the twilight of the gods). In that final battle, Thor was drowned in the venom which poured from the dying serpent.

See Natural Phenomena, p.138

The head of Thor's hammer, Mjolnir

SEE ALSO ANGURBODI, ASGARD, FREYA, HYMIR, JORMUNGANDR, RAGNAROK, SKRYMIR, TANNGNIORTR, THRYMR

THOTH

In Egyptian mythology, the divine scribe who recorded the weighing of souls when they entered the underworld. He was also associated with the moon, and worshipped as the patron of learning and the master of inventions. Thoth is sometimes referred to as Tehuti.

The chief god of Khmun, or Hermopolis, as it was called by the Greeks, Thoth was depicted as having the head of an ibis or a baboon. Although a latecomer to Khmun cosmology, Thoth was included in its creation myth.

The name "Khmun" derives from eight primeval frog- and snake-headed deities. It was believed that within NUN, the primeval waters, swam these eight deities, who personified infinity, darkness and all that is hidden. But to explain how the deities found themselves in the primeval waters, when nothing else existed, the Egyptians introduced Thoth as a creator. He hatched the cosmic egg and by his speech called into being the original four pairs of gods and goddesses.

Thoth is seldom depicted alone, but usually in a funeral group in tomb paintings, as the recorder of past deeds, both good and bad. Otherwise he appears at the judgement of the dead, reading the scales on which the heart of the deceased was weighed against the feather of truth, and recording the result. In the *Book of the Dead*, which was written over many centuries, Thoth took on a more active role in the funerary proceedings, and he was the one to whom the deceased turned for help in proving their innocence.

Thoth was the wise advocate who defended OSIRIS against the charges made by SETH, his brother and murderer. Since the gods who judged Osiris were regarded as sinister and hardly disposed to be merciful, it was thought necessary to supplement Osiris's claim of innocence by a plentiful use of magic. In the *Book of the Dead* a spell exists which was intended to secure Thoth's aid for the deceased.

Thoth remained a loyal supporter of Osiris after he had been killed by Seth. By his magic spells and effective speech, Thoth helped ISIS resurrect Osiris as lord of the underworld. He also aided the goddess in protecting her son HORUS, who she had conceived of the slain Osiris by magical means, reviving him for long enough for him to impregnate her. In the lengthy struggle between Seth and Horus, in which Seth tried to usurp Horus, Thoth eventually intervened and compelled the return of Horus's inheritance.

It is not surprising that Thoth acquired a reputation for the magical arts or that his priests claimed to have access to his books of magic in a crypt where the god had hidden them. Their spells were said to give the user dominion over natural forces, and even the gods themselves.

From Thoth the Greeks derived the mysterious Hermes Trismegistus, a clumsy translation of the Egyptian title "Thoth the very great". This shadowy figure was supposed to have been the author of works on astrology, magic and alchemy. The Greeks were so impressed by the antiquity of Egypt that they credited the country with the invention of ancient wisdom.

Thoth records the fate of the dead

TIAMAT

The Babylonian she-dragon of chaos. Tiamat represented the salt-water ocean, as opposed to the sweet waters of Abzu, an underground reservoir in ancient Mesopotamia.

In the creation epic *Enuma elish* (*When on high*), there is an account of what the universe was like before Tiamat died at the hands of MARDUK, and a new world order was created. At first, only mist swirled above the mingled waters of Abzu and Tiamat. But then, from the surface rose the first pair Lahmu and Lahamu, whose names probably mean "silt". This couple gave birth to the gods, who in time annoyed Abzu and Tiamat with their clamour. The water god Ea was able to subdue Abzu by magical means, and send him into a sleep which held the sweet waters motionless beneath the ground, but he lacked the power to oppose the will of Tiamat.

In despair, the assembly of gods turned to Ea's son Marduk. Because they were sure that no other god could face the she-dragon, they invested him with the absolute authority of heaven. The myth thus compares with that of DEVI who, in the form of Durga, was invested with the power of all the other gods to overcome the demon Mahisha. Armed with bow and arrows, a mace, and a great net, Marduk rode forth in his storm chariot to do battle with the terrible host of monsters that had been raised by Tiamat and her second husband Kingu. The latter was of little help to Tiamat, however. As soon as Kingu beheld Marduk his eyes clouded with terror and confusion seized his heart.

Tiamat was less alarmed by the champion of the gods, and she opened her jaws to swallow him. Seeing his opportunity, Marduk hurled a raging storm straight into her mouth, so that she could not close it, shot an arrow into her belly, and held her fast. Eventually, Tiamat died and her slayer could deal with the rest of his opponents. They tried to flee, but were caught in Marduk's net, and were disarmed. Marduk then took from Kingu the tablets of destiny, Tiamat's wedding present to him.

Having defeated his enemies and saved the gods, Marduk set about creating the universe from Tiamat's carcass. He smashed her skull and pulled her body apart; one section became heaven, the other the floor of the deep. From her pierced eyes flowed the great rivers, the Tigris and the Euphrates. The monstrous serpents in Tiamat's army were turned into statues, which decorated Ea's temple.

Only the fate of Kingu remained to be decided by the assembly of gods. Judged guilty of encouraging Tiamat, Kingu was killed and his blood used by Ea to create mankind, henceforth the drudges of the gods. Marduk then allotted specific duties to the gods and goddesses, the first of which was to build the great city of Babylon as his permanent home.

This is a paradoxical creation story in that the chaos monster, though slain and dismembered, remains the body of the world, while the blood of her mate is manifest in its inhabitants, mankind. West Asian mythology is full of malevolent serpentlike dragons, but their threatening behaviour is essentially a reworking of the old conflict between Marduk and Tiamat.

Tiamat – she-dragon of chaos

SEE ALSO EA, KINGU

TIRAWA

The great god of the Pawnee Indians, once the dominant group of Nebraska. Tirawa created the world and set the sun, moon and stars on course. He was a somewhat remote deity, given to outbursts of anger.

A Pawnee creation myth tells how Tirawa held a council in heaven and assigned tasks to the other gods present. The sun god was ordered to give light and warmth, the moon goddess sleep and rest during the night, and the stars were told to support the sky. He then gave certain stars command over the clouds, the wind and the rain, thereby ensuring that the earth remained fertile.

A boy resulted from the marriage of the sun and moon, and from that of the stars a girl. Tirawa placed these first human beings on earth and sent the gods down from heaven to instruct them in the arts of living. The young man learned of hunting, smoking and war, while the young woman mastered cultivation and cookery. The Pawnee Indians believe they were the descendants of this couple.

However, for an unknown reason, Tirawa destroyed his creation with a fire which raged unchecked until a deluge covered the earth. According to the Pawnee Indians, their ancestors emerged from a cave following the catastrophe. These survivors were an old man who carried a pipe, fire and a drum and his wife, who carried maize and pumpkin seeds. Together they reinstated civilization.

Death was introduced by accident. One of the lesser stars became jealous of the favours that Tirawa bestowed on a very bright star, particularly the large role he was allotted in the process of creation. Finding the sack of storms entrusted to the bright star hanging on a tree, the jealous star emptied its dreadful contents and sent deadly storms to earth. Thereafter, it was normal for living things to die.

See Death, p.91 and Creation, p. 135

TLALOC

The ancient rain god of Central America who, from his home on a mountain top, threw wind, rain, lightning arrows and terrible afflictions such as leprosy on to mankind. He was worshipped by the Toltecs and their successors, the Aztecs.

Tlaloc was portrayed as a black man with tusklike teeth, rings around his eyes and, often, with a scroll emerging from his mouth. Victims of his afflictions were admitted to his kingdom where they would never again suffer any need. This kingdom was called *Halocan*, the earthly paradise.

Tlaloc's wife Chalchihuitlicue (emerald lady) gave birth to a host of rain deities called *tlalocs*. A *tlaloc* was said to live in almost every hill and each year many children were sacrificed both to these minor gods and to Tlaloc himself.

In Tenochtitlán, the Aztecs' island-capital, priests prepared for Tlaloc's festival by buying infants for sacrifice from their mothers. If the mothers shed tears during the ritual slaughter, the worshippers rejoiced, saying that rain was sure to fall. As in other Aztec cults, the flesh of the sacrificial victims was eaten by the priests and the nobility, including the ruler.

Tlaloc's rain was not always beneficial. Whereas the Maya rain goddess IXCHEL possessed only one jug, Tlaloc owned four. However, Ixchel was always associated with death and destruction and her jug would empty the vials of her wrath on the earth. The water of Tlaloc's first jug, on the other hand, made plants grow; that of the second caused blight; that of the third brought frost; and that of the fourth total destruction. The Maya rain god Chac also corresponds to Tlaloc.

See Natural Phenomena, p.138

SEE ALSO CHAC, CHALCHIHUITLICUE

UKULAN-TOJON

The water spirit of the Yakuts, a Siberian people who live near Lake Baikal. They have always believed that the goodwill of Ukulan-Tojon is most essential to their security and health.

Ukulan-Tojon is a lord among spirits, for his authority extends over all the waters. In the past, sacrifices were made to him whenever water was involved. Indeed, the special respect accorded to water was noted by early European visitors to both Mongolia and Siberia. In Mongolia, sacrifices were made to effect a safe river crossing, while the unkempt appearance of the invaders of China can be attributed to their taboo on washing in running water.

At one time the peoples of Siberia and Mongolia believed in a world governed by spirits. Trees, mountains, rivers, lakes and animals all possessed spirits, and the decline and death of a person was said to be caused by the absence of a spirit in him or her. It was the task of the medicine-man (shaman) to mediate with this spirit world on behalf of his tribe. There is even a legend among the Bwiats, neighbours of the Yakuts, about a shaman bringing the souls of the dead back from the underworld.

See Natural Phenomena, p.138

Ukulan-Tojon was the Yakuts' water spirit

UNKULUNKULU

The supreme deity and sky god in the traditional religion of the Zulus of southern Africa, he was looked upon as the defender of a great warrior nation.

The Zulus have always regarded Unkulunkulu as an active deity, despite his great age. Like the Zulu armies in the past, the sky god would never tolerate any physical opposition. He was uGuqubadele (irresistible), uGobungquongqo (he who topples kings) and uMabonga-kutuk-izizwe-zonke (he who roars so that all nations are struck with terror). Yet the god was seen as the intelligence behind the universe and its guiding spirit.

According to the Zulu creation myth, Unkulunkulu evolved alone in emptiness, and once he had come into being, created the first men out of grass. Although the Zulus say that his ways are mysterious and unknown, they are certain of the moments when he intervenes on earth. When lightning strikes cattle, for instance, it is held that the sky god has slaughtered the animals to fill his larder.

As is common in traditional African belief, among the Zulus the advent of death is explained by a messenger myth. The tale makes Unkulunkulu indirectly responsible for man's loss of immortality by choosing the wrong creatures to deliver his messages. He sent a chameleon with the message of eternal life, and a lizard with the announcement of death. The chameleon was slow and stopped at a bush to eat so that the lizard arrived ahead of it. When the chameleon finally reached the first people, it was dismayed to discover that the lizard's message had been accepted by them as the correct one.

Unkulunkulu's answer to this unfortunate event was the institution of marriage so that brave warriors might father children. He also provided people with doctors for the treatment of disease and with fire to enable them to prepare food. Even the dead were embraced by the compassion of the god, for he provided them with a dwelling place in the sky. The Zulus say that the stars are the eyes of the dead looking down on the world; a similar idea exists among the Bushmen.

See Creation, p.135 and Natural Phenomena, p.138

URASHIMA

The Rip van Winkle of Japanese legend, Urashima was a young fisherman who married a sea maiden.

In the Japanese story, Urashima left human society to become the husband of a beautiful girl who lived in a palace beneath the waves. There Urashima led a blissful life until one day he was seized by a desire to see his parents once more.

To ensure the safe return of Urashima to the deep, his wife gave him a casket; provided it remained closed, he would be able to come back. When Urashima reached Japan, he was shocked to discover that centuries had passed, and in his despair he forgot his wife's instruction and opened the casket.

At once a puff of white smoke rose from it and drifted away toward the sea, while Urashima was shaken by a cold wind that turned him into an incredibly old man and then a corpse. Like the homesick sailor who sailed with the legendary explorer BRAN and turned to dust when he tried to return to Ireland, Urashima had discovered that without the help of magic a mortal could not inhabit different worlds. Another tale of a long journey is that of Maeldun who sailed in search of his father's murderers. However, Maeldun's youth was renewed by bathing in a natural lake. Today the shrine of Urashima stands on the coast of Tango.

Although Rip van Winkle only slept for twenty years, his return to society was also not altogether easy because of the profound changes that had taken place during his absence.

SEE ALSO MAELDUN, RIP VAN WINKLE

VAHAGN

The sun god and national deity of the ancient Armenians, whose pantheon was largely changed as a result of Iranian conquest. Vahagn could be said to symbolize the unending Armenian quest for freedom.

Vahagn was the most durable of the ancient Armenian gods. Not only did he survive the conquest of the homeland by Cyrus in the sixth century BC but he came to rival MITHRA in the conqueror's own pantheon. Like Mithra, Vahagn was always associated with light, and especially the sun. When he was born, "he had hair of fire, he had a beard of flame, and his eyes were suns." He was also the war god, upon whom soldiers called for strength in the thick of battle.

During the period when the ancient land of Armenia was troubled by invaders, Vahagn evolved into a national hero, although his exploits as a slayer of dragons may owe something to RUSTEM. This Iranian warrior was famous for his tireless battles against foreign foes, human and demonic. The Greeks identified Vahagn with HERACLES because of his heroic adventures.

According to Armenian tradition, Vahagn emerged spontaneously from a plant. Although the god was fierce and warlike in appearance, his youthfulness was always stressed by his worshippers.

See also War, pp.94/95

VARUNA

Possibly the most august deity in Vedic mythology, the ancient wisdom that underlies Hinduism. Varuna embodied the sky.

Often associated with SURYA, ruler of the sky during the day, Varuna was at one time the upholder of heaven and earth, the supreme deity to whom especial honour was due.

Varuna was said to possess infinite knowledge. He created the sun, hollowed out channels for the rivers, and saw that the ocean was never too full. Through his commands the moon kept its course and the stars remained in the firmament. Unlimited in power, Varuna controlled the destiny of mankind, sustaining life and offering protection from evil.

Varuna was called Pasabhrit (the noose carrier), because of the bonds or nooses with which he seized and punished those who dared to oppose his will. On the other hand, Varuna had a reputation for gentleness and a tendency to forgive even his confirmed opponents. He was also able to confer immortality, which he guarded carefully, together with YAMA, the god of death.

Although there is an obvious parallel with the Greek sky god Ouranos, Varuna does not have any special relationship with the earth, as Ouranos does with Gaia.

Relinquishing his cosmic duties to INDRA, Varuna became ruler of the seas and rivers. He was Kesa (lord of the waters); Variloma (watery hair); and Yadhapati (king of aquatic creatures). His cult no longer survives in India.

VASISHTHA

One of the most celebrated Hindu sages (*rishis*). These divinely inspired men composed the ancient Vedic hymns, which convey Aryan thought in symbolic language.

Legend records an intense rivalry between Vasishtha and Viswamitra, another *rishi*, which may reflect an early struggle for superiority among castes. Viswamitra's hundred sons were said to have been burned up by the breath of Vasishtha, following which Viswamitra engineered his revenge.

It happened that Saktri, the eldest son of Vasishtha, met a ruler called Kalmashapada on the road. The king ordered Saktri to get out of the way, but Saktri politely replied that the path was his, for a king must give way to a brahmin. The king then struck Saktri with a whip, and in reply Saktri cursed the king as a man-eater.

Observing this exchange, Viswamitra conjured a man-eating demon to take possession of Kalmashapada, who immediately devoured Saktri and his ninety-nine brothers. Vasishtha was so overcome with grief that he tried to kill himself, but without success.

Finally understanding that he could not die – even the alligators in a river rushed away in one hundred directions on his approach – Vasishtha returned to his hut. There he found the demented king waiting for him. Vasishtha exorcised the demon and delivered Kalmashapada from the curse he had endured for twelve years. As a result, the ruler acknowledged the respect due to brahmins.

Another tale relates the war over Vasishtha's marvellous possession, Nandini, "the cow of plenty", which had the power of granting him everything he desired. A great battle raged as Viswamitra's army fought the warriors that Nandini produced to support her master. Utterly defeated, Viswamitra had to leave his hundred sons dead on the battlefield and flee to the Himalayas.

Following another contest, Vasishtha and Viswamitra were finally reconciled – at the behest of the gods.

Gold patera with mythical beast

SEE ALSO MITRA

SEE ALSO VISWAMITRA

VIRACOCHA

The creator deity of the Incas, Viracocha, or Wiraqocha, was also a sun and storm god. He was extremely important in Peru even before the rise of the Inca empire in 1438.

Viracocha is said to have emerged from Lake Titicaca and made the sun, moon and stars. His name probably means "the lake of creation" and sometimes he was referred to as Illa (light) or Tici (the beginning). After setting the world in order, Viracocha created the Andean people by breathing life into statues. Like the AYAR, who founded the Inca dynasty, these first human beings were formed in caves.

Married to Mamacocha, the goddess of wind and rain, Viracocha was depicted as a bearded man, wearing the sun for a crown, holding thunderbolts in his hands, and weeping tears of rain. His sadness may have been caused by disappointment since one legend tells how, unhappy with his first creation, he swept the world with a flood, killing the first men, who were probably giants.

However, Viracocha made new and better men, again from stone. This time, to ensure that they developed correctly, he wandered among them, teaching them the rudiments of civilization and working miracles. His manifestation as a ragged and reviled beggar was unique for an all-powerful creator deity.

Along with Pachacamac (earthmaker) and Manco Capac, the first Inca ruler, Viracocha was sometimes regarded as a child of the sun god INTI. Nowadays, however, it is thought that the early Spanish commentators may have been mistaken in describing a multiplicity of Inca gods and that Viracocha and the other deities were in fact separate aspects of Inti, the one godhead. Their idea grew from the fact that Viracocha was worshipped in Cuzco's chief shrine, the Qorikancha or temple of the sun.

See Creation, p.135

SEE ALSO MANCO CAPAC, PACHACAMAC

VIRGIN MARY

In Christian tradition, the Mother of God, credited with a host of miracles.

Initially Mary was not honoured above other saints, but from the fourth century onward there was a marked growth in her worship. In 431 the Council of Ephesus, which met in a church supposed to contain her mortal remains, declared that she was "the Mother of God". Since then, the progress of her myth has been triumphant.

The period of the Virgin Mary's greatest importance was undoubtedly the Middle Ages. At that time, Mary gathered to her cult many of the attributes of the earth goddesses of earlier religions, and accumulated a whole array of miracles.

The Virgin always comforted those of the faithful who fell into deep despair. Once a poor knight sold his wife to SATAN for great riches, but the unfortunate woman sought refuge in a church and commended herself to Mary. In response to this cry for help, the Virgin went down to the underworld and forbade the Devil to hold anyone who invoked her name. Then she made the knight repent his greed before herself rewarding him with wealth.

So annoyed was Satan with this interference that he complained to heaven, without success.

The coronation of the Virgin Mary

VISHNU

A Hindu god who has risen to an almost supreme position in the Hindu pantheon. The root of his name, *vish*, means "to pervade", and he is regarded as a presence that permeates every thing. He is believed to have had ten chief incarnations in this world, in a variety of forms.

Vishnu is generally represented as a handsome youth, dark-blue in colour and dressed like an ancient king. In his four hands he carries a conch shell, a discus, a club and a lotus flower. His vehicle is the splendid sun bird Garuda who was the enemy of all serpents.

In his incarnations, or descents (*avatara*), a part of Vishnu's divine essence is manifested, in a human or supernatural form. An avatar is said to appear whenever there is an urgent need to counter some great evil influence in the world. The principal avatars of Vishnu are Matsya the fish, Kurma the turtle, Narasimha the man-lion, Varaha the boar, Vamana the dwarf, Parasurama, or "Rama with an axe", Rama, KRISHNA, BUDDHA, and Kalki, or the god "seated on a white horse".

In his incarnation as Matsya the fish, Vishnu warned MANU of the deluge, so that Manu could board a ship with the sages and "the seeds of all existing things" and so survive the flood. Matsya also came to the rescue of the sacred scriptures when they were stolen by the horse-headed demon HAYAGRIVA. This demon had taken advantage of the confusion brought about by the flood and stolen the scriptures from BRAHMA. Matsya killed Hayagriva and recovered the sacred texts.

Vishnu's second incarnation, Kurma the turtle, was called into action when INDRA requested Vishnu's aid in order to cope with the demons (*asuras*). To subdue the aggressors, a magical drink called AMRITA was produced, by churning the ocean with a mountain. Kurma supported the mountain on his shell, and it was turned by the gods and demons.

The third incarnation, Varaha the boar, was pitted in deadly combat against a ferocious giant named Hiranyaksha, "golden eye". The giant had dragged the earth down to the bottom of the sea, and to recover it, the boar had to fight the giant for a thousand years.

Another titanic struggle was fought by Narasimha the man-lion, Vishnu's fourth incarnation, against the giant's twin-brother Hiranyakasipu, "golden dress". By subjecting himself to incredible austerities Hiranyakasipu had obtained sovereignty of the world for a million years, during which he oppressed gods and men and even challenged the authority of Vishnu himself. When the arrogant giant struck a stone pillar in a temple and demanded to know if Vishnu was present in it, Narasimha came forth to vindicate the insulted god. After a protracted duel he tore Hiranyakasipu apart.

The fifth avatar of Vishnu is Vamana the dwarf. He appeared to counter the power of Bali, the demon king of the giants. Through his devotion and penance Bali defeated Indra, humbled the gods, and extended his rule over heaven, earth and the infernal regions.

In answer to the appeal of the gods, Vishnu was born as Vamana, and in due course presented himself before Bali to request a boon. He asked for ownership of the ground that he could cover in three steps. It was granted. At once, the dwarf stepped over heaven and earth in two strides. But then, out of respect for the demon king's generosity, he stopped short

and left him the infernal, underground regions, Patala.

As Parasurama, Vishnu used his axe to destroy Kartarirya, the arrogant thousand-armed king of the Himalayas. But as Rama, he is portrayed as a reluctant slayer of demons. The *Ramayana*, India's oldest epic, relates Rama's distaste for combat with a female demon. But when his beautiful wife Sita is kidnapped by the Sri Lankan demon king Ravana, Rama is stirred into action. Supported by a host of monkeys, led by the agile monkey god HANUMAN, Rama invades Sri Lanka, kills Ravana and frees Sita.

While the gods rejoiced in Ravana's destruction, Rama was suspicious of Sita's conduct when she was a prisoner. To prove her innocence she had to call a public witness to establish that her life had been faultless. Sita, whose name means "a furrow", was received by mother earth, who by opening up and taking her in proved Sita's goodness. Unable to endure life without Sita, the disconsolate Rama followed her into eternity by plunging into a river.

Of even greater renown is Vishnu's eighth incarnation, KRISHNA. This avatar has become so popular in India today that he has come to be regarded as a direct manifestation of Vishnu.

Because of the enormous success of Buddhist teachings in India, the brahmins chose to adopt Buddha as their own, rather than treat him as an adversary. Vishnu is said to have appeared as Buddha in order to encourage wicked men and demons to despise the Hindu scriptures, reject caste, deny the existence of gods and thereby to cause their own annihilation.

Kalki is a future incarnation of Vishnu whose task is the redemption of mankind from the evil of our present age.

Vishnu surrounded by his avatars

SEE ALSO GARUDA, HIRANYAKASIPU, HIRANYAKSHA, PATALA, RAVANA, SITA

WATI-KUTJARA

These two lizard men are the subject of many legendary cycles among the aboriginal peoples of central Australia.

Wati-kutjara (two men) lived on earth during the remote period known as Alchera (Dreamtime), when the ancestral spirits woke from their underground sleep and roamed the surface of the earth. Like other tribal ancestor spirits, as they travelled around, they created trees, plants and animals, as well as sacred objects in the landscape.

One of the lizard men was called Kurukadi after the white iguana, the other Mumba after the black iguana.

The chief myth about them concerns the saving of a group of women whom the moon man Kulu was pursuing. When Kulu refused to marry one of them and leave the others alone, the lizard men struck and wounded him with their magical boomerangs. Kulu died soon afterward either near a waterhole or a hillock. The paleness of the moon may be the result of this conflict.

The women saved by Wati-kutjara chose to leave the earth and become the cluster of stars called the Pleiades. The lizard men themselves are said to have become the constellation Gemini, whom the ancient Greeks associated with CASTOR and Polydeuces (known as Pollux to the Romans).

See Creation, p.135 and Natural Phenomena, p.138

Constellations in the night sky

SEE ALSO ALCHERA, POLYDEUCES

WAYLAND

The smith god of the Anglo-Saxon settlers of Britain. In the Icelandic *Eddas*, books on mythology dating from no later than the early thirteenth century, Wayland is known as Volund, the son of a giant.

Initially, Wayland learned his skills from Mimir, the giant who guarded the well of wisdom hidden under the world-tree YGG-DRASIL. Later, he learned more from two dwarfs. The swords Wayland forged had magical powers. He made one for the Aesir, ODIN's Germanic deities, and another for Beowulf, with which he slew the monster Grendel.

The *Eddas* tell how Wayland and his two brothers met three swan maidens by the shore of a lake and stayed with them until, seven years later, they flew away.

Distraught, the three brothers sought their lost loves, each taking a different path. Wayland soon ran into problems at the court of Nidud, who may have wanted to keep him prisoner to make use of his skills as a smith. Certainly, relations between the king and Wayland were strained, and reached the point of no return when the smith murdered Nidud's two younger sons and made drinking cups from their skulls, which he studded with precious jewels and mounted on silver.

While the smith may have killed the young men for daring to look at his treasures, nothing accounts for his seduction of their sister who simply brought him a ring to repair.

Memories of Wayland lingered on long after the Angles, Saxons and Jutes converted to Christianity. Alfred the Great (871–99) pointed out with satisfaction the passing away of pagan belief when he said, "Where are the bones of Wayland now, and who knows where they are?"

However, Alfred spoke too soon, for Wayland lived on in folk tradition almost to modern times. Indeed, when a neolithic passage grave called Wayland's Smithy, on The Ridgeway in Oxfordshire, England, was excavated in 1921, local people were not surprised to learn that iron bars formed part of the find.

See Craftsmen and Smith Gods, p.154

SEE ALSO AESIR, BEOWULF, GRENDEL, MIMIR, NIDUD

WELE

The supreme deity and sky god of the Abaluyia of Kenya, a northern group of Bantu peoples.

Wele (the high one) first made heaven and supported it on pillars. He then made two brothers, the sun and moon, who were supposed to assist him with the creation of the rest of the universe. But almost at once these two luminaries began to fight with each other.

First the moon knocked the sun out of the sky; in retaliation, the sun hurled the moon to earth and covered him with mud in order to reduce his brilliance. To end the bitter feud, Wele decreed that the brothers should never again appear in the sky together; since then the sun has shone in the daytime and the moon at night.

Wele next created the clouds, lightning, stars, rain, rainbows, hail and air. The creation of the earth followed, along with the first man, called Mwambu, and the first woman, Sela. Then Wele added the plants and animals.

According to the Abaluyia, the sun has taken a special interest in their welfare because of the beauty of an Abaluyian maiden. She refused steadfastly to marry any of the suitors who admired her good looks. Instead she was borne by a rope up to the sun, who had won her heart with a present of his rays, which she placed in a covered pot.

After several years of marriage and the birth of three sons, she asked her husband for permission to visit her parents. With her sons she descended to earth by means of the rope and was warmly welcomed. Great festivities followed, during which her father sacrificed many of his cows.

When she returned to the sun's house, she opened the pot containing the rays so that they could shine upon the earth. The result was astounding – the herds of the Abaluyia increased, and her father never again knew want.

See Creation, p.135 and Natural Phenomena, p.138

SEE ALSO MWAMBU, SELA

XIPETOTEC

The flayed deity of the Aztecs, Xipetotec was the god of agriculture and penitential torture. His name means "flayed lord".

The Aztecs, who ruled Mexico in the fourteenth and fifteenth centuries, feared that the gods would be unable to sustain the order of creation without an adequate flow of blood. They conducted wars specifically for the purpose of obtaining sacrificial victims. One of their favoured forms of human sacrifice was flaying. The skin of the victim was even donned by a priest of the god to whom the offering was being made.

This linking of pain with spiritual power explains why Aztecs worshipped Xipetotec, the "flayed lord", their great example of penitential torture and symbol of self-sacrifice and spiritual liberation. In imitation of his self-torture they readily lacerated their own bodies with cactus thorns and the sharp edges of reeds.

Perhaps because of his indifference to suffering, Xipetotec was held responsible for blindness, disease and insanity and was often identified with the war god HUITZILOPOCHTLI.

Xipetotec also had authority over planted corn, probably because maize loses its skin when the young shoot begins to burst forth, just as the god lost his. The link is made in an Aztec hymn addressed to the god: "It may be that you will fade and die, you the young corn stalk. A green jewel is your heart, but surely you will see gold. You will grow ripe, like a true warrior born."

The relationship of Xipetotec and COAT-LICUE, the Aztec earth goddess, may parallel that of the Greek deities Triptolemus and DEMETER. Triptolemus, though subservient to Demeter, was the active agent of fertility. Similarly, Xipetotec could have acted on behalf of the terrifying, snake-clad goddess, Coatlicue. The Aztecs regarded Coatlicue as the fierce owner of the soil, a deity to be placated with regular sacrifice.

Xipetotec also took an interest in the underworld and assisted the god of death, Mictlantecuhtli.

SEE ALSO MICTLANTECUHTLI, TRIPTOLEMUS

XOCHIQUETZAL

The Aztec goddess of flowers and fruits. With her brother Xochipilli, she ruled over beauty, love, happiness and youth. Her name means "feather flower".

Xochiquetzal and Mixcoatl, god of the chase, were the parents of the snake-bird god QUETZALCOATL. During the reign of Quetzalcoatl, Xochiquetzal covered the world with fruitfulness and beauty. However, in the tenth century, when Quetzalcoatl departed overseas, the goddess became less interested in human affairs.

Like the Celtic ARTHUR, Quetzalcoatl was believed to have gone to an undeath from which he was destined to return one day to reclaim his throne. This possibly explains Xochiquetzal's association with the underworld. During the elaborate festivals of the dead, the Aztecs offered her garlands of marigolds.

The Aztecs also regarded Xochiquetzal as the goddess of craftsmen and the moon. She was the companion of the sun god Tonatiuh in his youthful aspect. As the lady of the night, the moon goddess protected lovers, revellers and harlots. Whereas lovers invoked the goodwill of Xochiquetzal, those who served Tlazolteotl, goddess of pleasure, intoxication and death, were bent on a course of personal abasement and self-destruction.

Xochiquetzal was regarded as a sustainer of the family, the protectress of the marriage bond and the giver of children. Her strong association with fertility is emphasized by the fact that her brother Xochipilli appears to be her lover.

It is likely that Xochipilli was connected with the two deities of corn, the maize god Cinteotl and the flayed god XIPETOTEC. Certainly, a youthful joint deity, Xochipilli-Cinteotl, participated in the sacred ball games that marked the vernal equinox and were a popular part of many of their fertility festivals. Whenever a player scored during these games, the spectators cried, "He is a successful adulterer," probably referring to the illicit love of Xochipilli-Cinteotl and Xochiquetzal.

See Love and Fertility, pp.106/107

SEE ALSO CINTEOTL, MIXCOATL, TLAZOLTEOTL, TONATIUH, XOCHIPILLI

YAMA

The Hindu god of death. Originally he was conceived as the king of the departed spirits, although he later became a punisher of evil deeds. In the ancient hymns of the *Rig Veda* he is mentioned as a fierce deity.

Yama is the son of the sun god SURYA and Sanjna (conscience). He is the brother of MANU, the survivor of the deluge, and of the goddess Yami. Sometimes Yama and Yami are referred to as the first mortals, the first human pair. Yama is also described as "the first man that died, the first that left for the other world of the spirits. He it was who found out the way there, which can never be lost."

Yama's role as the chief of the dead, a friend rather than a foe, changed over time. He became the terrible punisher of human misdeeds, green in appearance, armed with a noose and a mace, and seated on a buffalo. Two insatiable dogs with four eyes and broad nostrils guarded his palace.

When a soul quits the body, it crosses the river Vaitarani to reach the land of the dead, and hastens past the guardian beasts to the judgement room. There the recorder Chitragupta reads out the account of the soul's deeds so that Yama may reach a verdict. The sentence will dispatch the soul to either a heavenly dwelling-place, one of the twenty-one hells, or back to the world of mankind, for rebirth.

Yama neither shared his authority with his sister Yami, in Hindu myth, nor relies on many assistants. Quite often, his two hounds wander the world to collect the souls of the dying. Otherwise, he uses the owl and the pigeon as his messengers.

In Chinese mythology, which received Yama via the Buddhist faith, the god of death Yanwang presides over ten courts and a bureaucracy which parallels the imperial one itself. Each court specializes in handling different crimes. The tortures reserved for serious offenders reflect the severity of traditional punishment: blasphemers have their tongues torn out, corrupt officials are compelled to swallow molten gold, and the utterly lost are thrown on beds of knives, plunged in boiling oil, crushed by heavy stones, or cut in half at the waist.

In China, Yama's kingdom merged with indigenous beliefs about the place of death, the Yellow Springs (*huangquan*). This dreary abode was not unlike our own world, and miners were always worried that they might break into it accidentally.

In Japan, Yama rules as Emma-o over a composite kingdom. His staff of eighteen generals and eighty thousand soldiers maintain strict discipline over the eight regions of fire and eight regions of ice it contains. But Emma-o judges men only, and leaves the task of deciding the fate of women to his sister.

Yama is not unlike the infernal Greek judge MINOS. Dante places Minos in the second cirle of hell and portrays him as the horrible and snarling reviewer of the offences of those souls who have been sent to "the abode of pain". Other elements in Yama's myth, which are reminiscent of the Greek underworld, are the ravenous guardian dogs, which have their Greek counterpart in the three-headed Cerberus, and the river crossing, which has a parallel in the Styx.

See Death, p.91

Yama, the god of death

SEE ALSO CERBERUS, SANJNA, STYX, YANWANG

MICROPEDIA

As a ready reference to the myriad myths and legends from all over the world, and to serve as an extension and elaboration of the other sections of the encyclopedia, this Micropedia consists of more than one thousand short entries alphabetically arranged. Most are names of characters, but some sacred places and subjects of myth and legend are also included.

The symbols above each entry relate to the culture with which they are associated, as elaborated in the first section of the book. Names in small capitals refer readers to the main entries in the A to Z section. Cross-references between Micropedia entries will be found using the Index.

A

Aapep The Egyptian serpent and enemy of RE, known usually by the Greek name of Apophis.

Aaron In the Old Testament, Aaron was the son of Abraham and elder brother of Moses. He possessed a magic rod which was capable of performing miracles, including the transformation of a road into a serpent. When Moses climbed Mount Sinai to speak to Yahweh, Aaron succumbed to the clamour of the people and made a golden calf for them to worship. On his return from the mountain, Moses discovered the Hebrews' idolatry, smashed the stone tablets on which the Ten Commandments were written, and burned the false idol. However, he managed to persuade Yahweh to spare Aaron's life and, thereafter, Aaron lived as a high priest of the Hebrews.

Abassi The sky god of the Efik people of Nigeria. He married Atai, who persuaded him to place the first man and woman on earth. However, Abassi was worried that these first human beings would threaten his authority, and so, to ensure his supremacy, he forbade them to work or to produce children. Nevertheless, before long the pair ignored these divine restrictions. Atai therefore visited death upon them and created discord among their children. The name Abassi means "god".

Abednego A biblical figure. In Hebrew and Christian mythology, Abednego, Shadrach and Meschach were the friends of DANIEL. Though captives, the four men rose to eminence at the court of Nebuchadnezzar, King of Babylon. However, being Hebrews, they refused to worship the king's

"image of gold" for which they were cast into a fiery furnace. To the astonishment of the king, the presence of a companion "like the Son of God" prevented the men from suffering injury.

Abel A shepherd who appears in the Bible. He was the second son of Adam and Eve and younger brother of Cain. Cain slew Abel because Yahweh preferred Abel's offering of lambs to Cain's offering of "the fruits of the earth". JESUS later called Abel the first martyr.

Abraham A biblical figure who founded the Hebrew people. He was the first patriarch, the husband of Sarah and the father of Isaac. Although he was raised in Ur, a city with many gods, Abraham became the father of monotheistic Judaism after Yahweh revealed himself to him. His devotion to the one Hebrew god was exhibited, above all, by his readiness to sacrifice his son, Isaac. Abraham instituted circumcision among the Hebrews. Moreover, through Abraham, Yahweh promised the Hebrews the land of Canaan. In Islamic tradition he is an ancestor, through Ishmael, of the Arabs.

Absalom In the Old Testament, the third son of King David. He plotted against his father and was killed by one of the king's men when his long hair became caught in a tree. On hearing the news, King David wept inconsolably.

Abuk The first woman in the mythology of the Dinka people of the Sudan. At first Abuk and her husband Garang were tiny clay figures who lived inside a pot. However, when the pot was opened, they grew larger and larger. The Dinka say that the great sky god allowed them to have one grain of corn each day but Abuk helped herself to more, thus

offending the deity. Abuk is the patron of women and is associated with produce, gardens and water. Her symbol is the snake.

Abzu The underground fresh waters in Mesopotamian mythology. On the instruction of his ancestor Utanapishtim, the hero GILGAMESH descended into Abzu in order to find a rejuvenating plant. Opposed to Abzu, or Apsu, was the chaos-dragon TIAMAT, who represented the tumultuous salt waters of the sea.

Acastus In Greek mythology, the king of Iolcus and son of Pelias, an Argonaut. Medea tricked Pelias's daughters into murdering their father and, in revenge, Acastus drove Medea and JASON, her lover, out of the land. Hippolyta, the wife of Acastus, falsely accused the hero Peleus of attempting to rape her and in the ensuing dispute Peleus killed Acastus.

Achelous In Greek mythology, the oldest of the river gods. Using his power as a shape-changer, Achelous turned into a bull and wrestled with HERACLES for the hand of Deianira, the hero's second wife. Achelous replaced the horn which Heracles broke off during the fight with that of a goat which had suckled ZEUS.

Acheron In Greek mythology Acheron was a river which led to the underworld, the realm of HADES. The bad-tempered boatman Charon ferried the dead across this river, or another known as the Styx, to the care of Hades. The fare was a coin known as an obol.

Achyuta In Hindu mythology, one of the names of the god VISHNU. It means "unfallen" and refers to the untarnished nature of the deity when he descends to the earth as an avatar.

Actaeon In Greek mythology, the mortal grandson of Apollo. Actaeon had the misfortune to surprise ARTEMIS, the virgin goddess of the chase, while she was bathing. In revenge, Artemis turned Actaeon into a stag and he was hunted down and killed by his own hounds.

Adad In Mesopotamian mythology, the god of rain. When ENLIL decided to punish mankind for the excessive noise made in cities, he instructed Adad to hold the rains back. But the people's prayers eventually weakened Adad's resolve and he released a torrent.

Adam The first man in the Bible. In Hebrew mythology, SATAN's fall from heaven is attributed to his jealousy of Adam. But Adam's importance in the Bible concerns his disobedience to Yahweh. By eating forbidden fruit, an apple from the tree of knowledge of good and evil, he committed original sin. He and his wife, Eve, were therefore cast out of the Garden of Eden.

Aditi In Hindu mythology, the boundless heaven as compared with the finite earth. Her name means "free" or "unbounded", and she is the mother of VISHNU.

Adroa The ambivalent creator god of the Lugbara people of Zaire and Uganda. He has two aspects: as the sky god, Adroa, he represents goodness; as the earth god, Adro, he represents evil. Usually invisible to mortals, Adro may reveal himself to those about to die. He has only half a body, with only one eye and one arm. His usual abode is a river.

Adu Ogyinae In the mythology of the Ashanti people of Ghana, the first man. He emerged through a hole in the earth's surface at the head of a small group of men and women, and he alone was unalarmed by the strange new sights that the earth presented. Two days later, Adu Ogyinae was killed by a falling tree, but the rest of the group survived to be the progenitors of the human race.

Aegeus In Greek mythology, the king of Athens and possibly father of THESEUS. Because the Athenians killed Androgeos, the son of MINOS, Aegeus was forced to send the Cretan king nine boys and nine girls every year as food for the monstrous Minotaur. Theseus set out under a black sail to rid Athens of this tribute, saying that he would return under a white sail if he were successful. He accomplished his mission, but forgot to change the sail. Aegeus, seeing a black sail on the returning ship, believed Theseus to be dead and threw himself down a precipice.

Aegir In Germanic mythology, the primeval sea god who preceded the Aesir and Vanir gods. He was the brother of LOKI and had nine daughters, the wave maidens. A fierce god, with fingers like claws, Aegir would appear on the surface of the sea to destroy ships.

Aegisthus In Greek mythology, the son of Thyestes by his daughter, Pelopia. Thyestes had been told by an oracle that he would be revenged on his brother Atreus, who had murdered his sons, only if he had a son by his own daughter. He therefore raped Pelopia, who later married Atreus without mentioning who she was or her pregnancy. Her child was Aegisthus. He was raised by Atreus, King of Mycenae, whom he killed to revenge the murder of his brothers. When Atreus's son and successor Agamemnon went to the Trojan War, his wife Clytemnestra became the lover of Aegisthus. Clytemnestra and Aegisthus murdered Agamemnon on his return from Troy, for which deed they in turn earned the vengeance of ORESTES, Agamemnon's son. The blood feud was ended by ATHENA, who persuaded the ERINYES (Furies) to accept the obligation of Orestes to avenge his father's death, even though in doing so he had to kill his own mother, Clytemnestra.

Aeolus In Greek mythology, the god of the winds. He lived on the floating island of Aeolia, where he kept the winds in a cave, inside a leather bag. When JUNO tried to stop the voyage of AENEAS to Italy, she persuaded Aeolus to release the winds from the bag.

Aesir One of the two races of gods in Germanic mythology, the other being the Vanir. The Aesir were led by ODIN and THOR, and included the trickster god LOKI among their ranks. Frequently at war with each other, the Aesir and the Vanir were eventually reconciled and hostages were exchanged. One such hostage was the Vanir god FREY.

Agamemnon In Greek mythology, the king of Mycenae and leader of the expedition against Troy, the city to which HELEN had been abducted. On his way to Troy Agamemnon's fleet was becalmed at Aulis, but he appeased ARTEMIS by sacrificing his daughter Iphigenia and was thus provided with a favourable wind. On his triumphant return to Greece, Agamemnon's wife, Clytemnestra, who had been tricked into sending Iphigenia to Aulis, had him stabbed to death by her lover Aegisthus.

Agdistis In the Phrygian myth of the castrated god ATTIS, he is a monster born of heavenly semen dropped to earth. Agdistis fell in love with Attis and disrupted his wedding to CYBELE. As a result, the grief-stricken Attis emasculated himself beneath a pine tree.

Only when he realized that his beloved was dying did Agdistis regret his behaviour, beseeching heaven to spare Attis's life. However, the request was not completely granted, for the soul of Attis passed away, leaving behind an uncorrupted body.

Agenor In Greek mythology, the king of Tyre and father of EUROPA. His son CADMUS founded the city of Thebes in central Greece.

Aglookik In Eskimo mythology, a spirit who directs hunters to game. He lives under the ice. In contrast, see the sinister sea goddess SEDNA.

Agunua In the mythology of the Solomon Islanders, a primeval serpent god, the creator of the first man and woman and of crops. The woman was made after the man, to do the cooking. The Solomon Islanders, in keeping with the widespread Oceanic belief in the existence of a coconut heaven, believe that the first coconut from every tree is sacred to Agunua.

Agwe The sea god of Voodoo belief in Haiti. His symbol is a sailing-boat and his dwelling-place a palace under the sea. Agwe is propitiated by generous gifts of food, which are cast into the waves.

Ahoeitu In Polynesian mythology, the legendary king and cultural hero of Tonga, whose name means "day has dawned". The mortal son of the sky god Eitumatupua by the worm Ilaheva, he climbed a tree to meet his father, who greeted him with joy. In jealousy, Ahoeitu's celestial brothers tore him to pieces, then cooked and ate him. Eitumatupua compelled them to vomit the pieces and, with the aid of magical herbs, recreated Ahoeitu.

Ahurani In Persian mythology, a water goddess who protected both standing water and rainfall. She was also the divine symbol of both health and prosperity.

Aigamuxa In Hottentot mythology, dreadful man-eating monsters who are encountered in deserts. Their eyes are set on their insteps, so that, in order to discover what is going on, they have to get down on their hands and knees and hold up one foot. This shortcoming enables their victim to escape.

Aine In Irish mythology, the goddess of love and fertility. Although she frequently took mortal lovers, Aine could prove to be vicious when men tried to force their unwanted attentions upon her. Ailill Olom (bare-ear), King of Munster, first lost his ear, then his life, for daring to pursue the goddess. Aine is sometimes identified with Morrigan, the chief war goddess.

Aiomum Kondi The chief dweller-on-high in the mythology of the Arawak Indians living in the Guianas. He twice punished his people for disobedience by destroying the earth, first by fire and then by water. However, he saved the good man Marerewana and his family from destruction.

Aiwel In the mythology of the Dinka people of the eastern Sudan, a cultural hero born of a woman by a water spirit. After his mother's death, Aiwel joined his father in a river, from where he returned as an ox called Longar. When famine devastated the land, he led the Dinka to a promised land across the river and gave them fishing spears.

Ajok The supreme god of the Lotuko people of Sudan. Usually a benevolent deity, his good nature nevertheless depended on prayers and sacrifices being constantly offered up to him. Although all-powerful, Ajok was not held responsible for bringing discord into the world. Instead, mankind created its own suffering, death being introduced into the world as a result of a family quarrel.

Ajysyt The mother goddess in the mythology of the Yakuts, a Turkic people living in Siberia. Her name means "birth-giver" and, from her heavenly dwelling-place, she visits every mother among her devotees at the time of childbirth, providing the soul of each newborn child.

Ala In the mythology of the Ibo people of Nigeria, the supreme mother goddess, daughter of the great god CHUKU. She is the ruler of the underworld, protectress of the harvest, and a fertility goddess for both men and animals.

Albion An ancient name for Britain, mentioned by Pytheas of Massilia in the fourth century BC. It is generally believed to be of Celtic origin, although the Romans assumed it to be a derivation of *albus* (white), taking it as a reference to the white cliffs of Dover.

Alcestis In Greek mythology, the daughter of Pelias, King of Iolcus. She was won in marriage by Admetus, who fulfilled her father's condition that her suitor should arrive in a chariot drawn by a wild boar and a lion. When Admetus was promised immortality by the gods if someone would die in his place, Alcestis sacrificed herself. There are two accounts of her escape from death. Either HERACLES defeated Thanatos (death) in a wrestling match, or PERSEPHONE, the queen of the underworld, was so touched by her devotion to her husband that she released her and reunited her with Admetus.

Alchera In the mythology of the Aranda people of central Australia, Alchera is "Dreamtime", the primeval time when the ancestors sang the world into existence and created thousands of men out of clay, one for each totemic species. As each ancestor travelled about the land, he left a trail of words and musical notes in his footsteps. These "dreaming lines" or "songlines" became, and remain, lines of communication between people joined together by ancient kinship.

The creator deities are believed to have returned to their underground resting places long ago. Since the earth was untouched at Dreamtime, it must remain so; to wound it is to wound humans.

Alcina In the legends of the Frankish emperor Charlemagne, a sexually alluring sea nymph, rather like the Greek witch CIRCE. Lovers who fell under Alcina's spell were changed into natural objects such as trees or waterfalls when she tired of them. Alcina's greatest lover, the hero Astolpho, was changed into a myrtle tree but was rescued by Melissa, who gave him her magic ring, thus breaking the spell. Astolpho then saw Alcina in her true old age and ugliness.

Alcmene In Greek mythology, the wife of Amphitryon, King of Tiryns. One night, she conceived Iphicles by Amphitryon and HERACLES by ZEUS, who stole into her bed in Amphitryon's form. When Alcmene died, Zeus sent HERMES to take her body from its coffin and bring it to the Elysian Fields. The stone which he left in place of her body was worshipped near Thebes.

Alfar In Germanic mythology, the elves (which are sometimes believed to include the dwarfs), who came from the flesh of the giant Ymir. The Lios Alfar, or white elves, lived in Alfhelm under the rule of Freya; the Svart Alfar, or dark elves, lived under the rule of the smith god WAYLAND. Whereas the former are benign and perform domestic chores, such as baking bread and brewing ale, the latter are essentially malevolent and may never show themselves in daylight.

Alfodr One of the titles of ODIN, chief of the Germanic gods. It means "father of the gods". His other titles include Fjolsvidr (wide in wisdom) and Oski (wish giver).

Alklha In Siberian mythology, a monster who eclipses the sun and the moon by swallowing them. The spots on the moon are the scars left by wounds he has inflicted. A similar legend is found among the people of China.

Altjira The pre-existing creator deity of the Aranda people of central Australia. While the Aranda have largely forgotten Altjira, as have other aboriginal people with similar myths, they look back with intense nostalgia to the later period of Alchera (Dreamtime). Then, the ancestral spirits rose from their slumbers beneath the ground and wandered the earth, instructing the first men in the arts of survival.

Aluluei In Micronesian mythology, the god of navigation. He was killed by his brothers, but his father restored him to life and gave him thousands of eyes with which to protect himself. The eyes are the stars, which guide seafarers.

Amaushumgalanna One of the names of Dumuzi, the dying-and-reviving husband of INANNA, the Sumerian goddess of fertility. Amaushumgalanna's name refers to the dates preserved in the storehouse, whereas that of Dumuzi is connected with animal husbandry. As Dumuzi-Amaushumgalanna, together they personified the agricultural wealth upon which the ancient cities of Mesopotamia were founded.

Amazons In Greek mythology, a nation of warrior women who lived in Asia Minor. They cut off one breast to facilitate the launching of spears and arrows and rode into battle on horseback. An Amazon was allowed to mate only after killing a man and, since the nation allowed no male members, could do so only with members of another tribe or race. Male offspring were killed, maimed or given to their fathers. The most prominent Amazon queen was Hippolyta, whom HERACLES killed during his ninth labour.

Amfortas In Celtic and Christian legend, the wounded fisher king who looked after the Holy Grail. Unable to mount a horse because of his wound, he was compelled to content himself with fishing. He could be healed only through the help of a knight who sought after the Grail.

Amida-nyorai In Japanese Buddhism, the "Buddha of Infinite Light". He is the equivalent of the Indian bodhisattva Amitabha. The realm of Amida-nyorai, an ambrosial grove with a lotus pond, angels' bells and the eternal singing of birds, is the paradise of "Pure Land", the highest celestial abode that the transient soul of a Buddhist can visit in its perpetual wandering. Whoever sincerely believes in the name of Amida-nyorai gains entry to this paradise which, against conventional Buddhist belief, has something of the air of a permanent resting place.

Amitabha In Buddhist mythology, one of the five bodhisattvas who emanated from the primeval BUDDHA, Adi-Buddha. Amitabha is the supreme being of the highest celestial abode, the "Pure Land".

Ammut In ancient Egypt, "the eater of the dead". Part crocodile, part lion and part hippopotamus, Ammut devoured the souls of those who were unworthy of immortality in the realm of OSIRIS.

Amphitrite In Greek mythology, a sea goddess. She was the reluctant wife of the sea god POSEIDON, who saw her dancing on the island of Naxos. His followers, the creatures of the sea, pleaded Poseidon's cause, and Amphitrite at last agreed to marry him. She was the mother of the sea god Triton.

Amphitryon In Greek mythology, the king of Tiryns and the grandson of PERSEUS. He accidentally killed his father-in-law Electryon, and, in alarm, fled with his wife Alcmene to Thebes. At Alcmene's bidding he went to battle to defeat Electryon's enemy, Pterelaos. On the night of his triumphant return, Alcmene conceived Iphicles by him, and on the same night she conceived HERACLES by ZEUS, who came to her disguised as Amphitryon.

Anat In Canaanite mythology, one of the names of ASTARTE, the mother goddess. Anat (lady of the mountain) was the wife of BAAL, the most active of the Canaanite gods. She bravely descended to the underworld to save her husband from death.

Anchises In Greek and Roman mythology, the mortal lover of APHRODITE, or Venus, who bore him AENEAS. To punish the Trojan Anchises for boasting about Aphrodite's admiration of his good looks, ZEUS struck him with a lightning bolt which lamed him. On the fall of Troy to the Greeks, Aeneas carried his father Anchises, on his back, to safety.

Andriambahomanana In the mythology of Madagascar, the first man. The supreme god waited until Andriambahomanana and his wife Andriamahilala had secured the future of mankind by producing numerous children and grandchildren, then asked them to choose their preferred form of death. Andriambahomanana chose to be turned into a banana plant, which quickly produces new shoots, whereas Andriamahilala chose to be sent to the moon. Thus, each month, the first woman dies, but the following month she is reborn.

Androcles A legendary hero of medieval Europe. He was a runaway slave who hid from his master in a cave, where he removed a thorn from the paw of a lion. He was captured and thrown into an arena with lions, but the beast that he had helped was there and protected him. The spectators, delighted by this display of gratitude, secured Androcles' release and freedom. The tale is a popular reworking of a Christian martyr story.

Andromache In Greek mythology, the wife of Hector, poignant in her mourning of his death. After Hector was slain at the seige of Troy, Andromache was carried off as a slave by Neptolemus, the son of the hero ACHILLES.

Andvari In Germanic mythology, a dwarf who lived in a waterfall. There, while in the form of a salmon, he was captured by the trickster god LOKI, disguised as a mortal. Loki freed Andvari in return for his gold, and later stole his ring. Andvari laid a curse on the ring so that anyone who possessed it would be destroyed. In Wagner's operas forming the Ring Cycle, Andvari is called Alberich.

Angakoq One of the names of an Eskimo shaman or medicine-man, the bearer of traditional lore and wisdom and the agent of communication with the spirit world. *Angakoqs* were commonly, but not exclusively, male. A shaman heals the sick, controls the weather and provides good hunting.

To be a shaman a person must acquire the protection of a guardian spirit (*tornaq*) which can assume the form of a human being, a bear or a stone. The most powerful of these *tornaqs* is the bear.

Angurbodi In Germanic mythology, the second wife of LOKI. She was a giantess of surpassing ugliness and was the mother of the underworld goddess Hel, the wolf Fenrir, and the sea serpent Jormungandr.

Angus The Irish god of love. He was the son of DAGDA, king of the gods, and the water goddess Boann. Dagda made Boann his mistress while her husband Elcmar was sent on a long journey. The spell cast on Elcmar made the nine months he was away from home seem like a day. Angus was called Mac Og (young son) because, Boann said, "Young is the son who was begotten and born on the same day." The god of love was handsome and was always accompanied by four birds.

Anguta In the mythology of many Eskimo people of North America, the one-eyed father of SEDNA, the deformed goddess of the underworld, sea and sea animals. Originally a creator deity, Anguta now rules *adlivun*, the land of the unhappy dead, with Sedna. There, each dead soul must sleep by Anguta's side for a year and be pinched by him.

Anna Perenna A Roman goddess, whose festival in early March provided an opportunity for merriment in the fields that bordered the Tiber. Anna Perenna seems to have been the deity of the year, although some Roman authors identified her with Anna, the sister of the Carthaginian queen, Dido. This princess had persuaded Dido to yield to her passion for AENEAS, the Trojan refugee.

Annency The spider and trickster hero in several West Indian mythologies. He derives from the West African ANANSI, and in some areas retains the same name. Noted for the cunning with which he gets the better of other animals and human beings, he is able to appear as either a spider or a man. The wealth of tales of his doings is retold at wakes, especially in Trinidad and Jamaica. In Haiti, he is called 'Ti Malice.

Annwn In Welsh legend, the underworld, ruled over by Arawn. It was from Annwn that ARTHUR's men stole a magic cauldron endowed with the power to restore life. The Christian myth of the Grail probably descended from the powers of this remarkable utensil.

Anshar In the Babylonian epic *Enuma Elish* (*When on high*), the god of the horizon. Anshar and Kishar are the second pair of deities, following Lahmu and Lahamu from the original waters. The epic presents the beginnings of the world as a watery chaos in which the fresh underground waters of Abzu mix creatively with the salt waters of TIAMAT. The names Lahmu and Lahamu suggest silt, while Anshar and Kishar refer to the horizon. From the union of Anshar and Kishar sprang the god of heaven. He was known both as Anu (Babylonian) and AN (Sumerian).

Antar In Arabian legend, a great warrior and poet. Antar had the hide of an elephant, which proved a useful protection in his frequent battles on behalf of distressed women. He also possessed a wonderful horse, Abjer, and an incredible sword, Djamy.

Antigone In Greek mythology, the daughter of OEDIPUS and his own mother, Jocasta. When Oedipus blinded himself after discovering he had committed incest, Antigone accompanied him during his exile in Attica. After her father's death, Antigone returned to Thebes, where her uncle, Creon, had her entombed alive for sprinkling earth on the unburied body of her rebellious brother Polynices. Creon was anxious to avoid personal responsibility for her death. In some versions, Antigone was rescued by Creon's son who sent her to live among shepherds.

Antiope According to the ancient Greeks, the beautiful daughter of Nycteus, a Theban nobleman. ZEUS, disguised as a satyr, lay with her and she bore him two sons, Amphion and Zethus. Nycteus ordered the infants to be exposed on a mountain to die, but they were saved by a shepherd. Antiope was given as a slave to Dirce, and remained in this lowly position until Amphion and Zethus grew up and learned of her true identity. They freed their mother and killed her cruel owner.

But DIONYSUS was offended by this action because of Dirce's devotion to his cult. He therefore drove Antiope mad and set her wandering through Greece. However, a certain Phocus cured her and made her his wife. There appears to have been some association between Antiope and the fertility of the earth, for people believed that they could ensure a good harvest by sprinkling her grave with soil.

Anu In Mesopotamian mythology, the name used by the Babylonians for AN, the Sumerian sky god.

Anunnaki The judges in the Mesopotamian underworld. The palace of the dead was imagined as a city ringed securely by seven walls, with seven gates set in them. Its rulers were Nergal and Ereshkigal. When INANNA, the Sumerian goddess of fertility, and ISHTAR, her Babylonian counterpart, descended to the underworld to revive their dead husbands, they were obliged to remove a garment at each gateway. But the seven Anunnaki were unimpressed by the persuasion of either goddess, and so they were both hung like dead meat on a hook.

Apis The Greek name for Hapi, the sacred bull in Egyptian mythology. He was sometimes called the son of PTAH, the creator deity of Memphis. The priests of several prominent Egyptian gods took part in the ceremonies associated with his cult.

Apollo In Greek mythology, Apollo and his twin, ARTEMIS, were born of ZEUS by Leto, the Titaness. He was associated with medicine, music, poetry and prophecy, and was also a protector of herds and flocks. His high moral and intellectual status gave him first rank as a nurturer of civilization. He was worshipped as the god of light. His sexual pursuits were rarely successful and indeed Daphne turned herself into a laurel tree to evade him. His chief oracular shrine was at Delphi, which, in some versions, he seized by killing the oracle's serpent protector, Python.

Apollyon According to Revelation, this was the angel who ruled over the damned in the bottomless pit of SATAN's kingdom. "In the Hebrew tongue", his name "is Abaddon, but in the Greek tongue . . . Apollyon". In later Christian mythology, this is also the name of the Devil.

Apophis The Greek name for Aapep, the serpent in Egyptian mythology who perpetually attacked RE, the sun god.

Apsu See Abzu.

Aqhat A legendary Canaanite king who seems to have been restored to life. Aqhat was expressly given by EL to Daniel, a local ruler, when he lacked a son and heir. One text refers to a quarrel with the goddess Anat (ASTARTE) over a supernatural bow, which led to Aqhat's murder. Rain then ceased to fall and vegetation languished. The end of this myth is unknown, although it is likely that Aqhat became a dying-and-rising god.

Arawn In the legends of Wales, the king of Annwn (the abyss). Arawn used the hero PWYLL to defeat his enemy, Havgan. However, the magic cauldron of Annwn was stolen by ARTHUR's men. It had the power to restore life.

Argo In Greek mythology, the fifty-oared longship which carried JASON and the Argonauts to Colchis in quest of the Golden Fleece. Its prow contained wood with magical qualities, a gift from the goddess ATHENA. The *Argo* ended its days in Corinth, where Jason met his death sitting under the rotting hulk.

Argonauts In Greek mythology, the band of heroes chosen by JASON to man the *Argo* and sail in search of the Golden Fleece.

Argus In Greek mythology, an enormous, powerful monster with many eyes. He was sometimes called Panoptes (all-seeing). When ZEUS tried to rape Io, an Argive princess, his wife HERA turned the girl into a white heifer and set Argus over her as her guardian. On the order of Zeus, however, HERMES slew Argus while he was sleeping, or Hera turned the monster into a peacock as he was about to expire. Although Hera still tried to deny her husband pleasure with Io by having the white heifer continually stung by a gadfly, Zeus eventually got his way. From Epaphus, Io's son by Zeus, the royal house of Argos traced its descent.

Ariadne In the Greek legend of THESEUS, the daughter of MINOS and Pasiphae, the king and queen of Crete. She fell in love with the hero Theseus and gave him the yarn that enabled him to find his way out of the Labyrinth after destroying the monstrous Minotaur.

The couple eloped, but on the voyage to Greece, Theseus abandoned Ariadne on what is probably the island of Naxos, where the god DIONYSUS consoled her. ZEUS granted her immortality and set her bridal crown in the heavens among the stars.

Arjuna In Hindu mythology, a semi-divine hero and the son of INDRA, the sky god. At the mighty battle of the Pandavas against the Kauravas, Arjuna's charioteer was KRISHNA, an incarnation of VISHNU. Krishna appeared in the great god's supreme form, as the "almighty prince of wisdom", and over-whelmed and frightened Arjuna.

Arsinoe An ancient Greek princess who was shut up in a chest by her brothers and then sold into slavery. She had protested when they slew Alcmaeon, her mad husband. The brothers also blamed Arsinoe for the murder.

Aruna In Hindu mythology, the god of dawn and charioteer of the sun. He was the son of Vinata and the sage Kasyapa. After lying with Kasyapa, Vinata laid two eggs. In her impatience, she broke one of them and discovered that the foetus was embryonic, with only the upper half developed. That embryo was Aruna, who cursed his mother and fled to the sky. Aruna means "rosy", but he is also called Rumra, "tawny". The ancient Greeks, on the other hand, imagined the dawn as a goddess named EOS. She was known to the Romans as Aurora.

Arunkulta The spirit of evil in the mythology of the Aranda, an aboriginal people living in central Australia. Their protector against the assaults of Arunkulta is MANGAR-KUNGER-KUNJA, the great lizard.

Aruru One of the names of the Mesopotamian goddess NINHURSAGA. It means "germ-loosener" and refers to her protection of the womb. After the foetus was fully developed and shaped, Aruru loosened it so that the processes which led up to the birth of a child could take place. The people of Uruk called upon her to create a companion for their king, GILGAMESH. In answer to their request, Arura made Enkidu, an enormously strong man.

Arzang In ancient Iranian legend, a demon, also called Arzend, who appears in the epic poem, *Shah Naman*. He was one of the many demons slain by the hero RUSTEM.

Asa The supreme deity of the Akamba people of Kenya. His name means "father". A benevolent god, Asa keeps watch over men and women and, whenever their efforts prove insufficient to overcome hardship or difficulties, he intervenes, providing both consolation and sustenance. Despite this merciful side to his nature, Asa is known as "the strong lord" and holds sway over the spirits. He is also called Mwatuangi (distributor), Mulungu (creator), and Mumbi (fashioner).

Ascanius In Roman mythology, the son of AENEAS and his first wife, Creusa. He escaped with his father and his grandfather, Anchises, from the sack of Troy by the Greeks. In Italy, he became the ruler of the city of Alba Longa.

Asgard In Germanic mythology, the home of the Aesir gods. Among its palaces was Valhalla, the vast banqueting hall where ODIN entertained slain warriors. Entrance to Asgard was gained by crossing the rainbow bridge named Bifrost, which was guarded by the watchman of the gods, HEIMDAL.

Asgardreia In Germanic legend, the wild hunt of ODIN, during which souls of the dead were released by a storm. An entry of 1127 in the *Anglo-Saxon Chronicle* relates how huntsmen were observed in the sky. They "were black, huge, and hideous, and rode on black horses and on black he-goats, and their hounds were jet black, with eyes like saucers, and horrible".

Asherah A Canaanite sea goddess, who appears to have been the wife of EL. However, this is not the only reading of the ancient inscriptions found at Ugarit. According to another interpretation, Asherah was the same goddess as Athirat, another name for ASTARTE, the mother goddess.

Asmodeus In the apocryphal tradition of the Bible, the demon of drunkenness and lust. In order to obtain Sarah, he slew seven of her husbands before being driven out of the land by the smell of burning fish which Sarah's suitor, Tobit, had prepared. Asmodeus was the son of a mortal woman and a fallen angel.

Asuras In Hindu mythology, *asura* (divine) originally referred to the supreme spirit as, in ancient Iranian belief, did Ahura in the name AHURA MAZDAH. Later, *asura* acquired an opposite meaning, so that the *asuras* are now the enemies of the gods. They are anti-gods or demons.

Aswins In Hindu mythology, the twin sons of the sun or sky. They are eternally young and handsome, and ride out before Aruna, the dawn. Aswins means "horsemen".

Atai In the mythology of the Efik people of Nigeria, the wife of the sky god Abassi. Abassi created the first man and woman and placed them on earth, commanding them neither to have children nor to work. The couple broke the commandments and to punish them Abassi sent Atai to inflict death upon the couple and sow discord among their children.

Atalanta In Greek mythology, a huntress renowned, like the goddess ARTEMIS, for her speed and daring. As a baby, she was abandoned to die but was raised by a she-bear and then a band of hunters. Having been warned by an oracle that marriage would bring unhappiness, she made her suitors race against her, forfeiting their lives if they lost. Eventually, Hippomenes won the race by dropping three golden apples during its course, each of which Atlanta stopped to recover, thus losing time.

When Hippomenes forgot to thank the love goddess APHRODITE for lending him the apples, both he and Atalanta were turned into leopards in punishment. The ancient Greeks believed that these animals did not mate.

Atar In Iranian mythology, the god of fire and the son of AHURA MAZDAH. He was the representative of the light of truth, the divine spark in man which signified Ahura Mazdah's presence. Atar fought the dragon Azhi Dahaka, who sought to extinguish the divine fire.

Ate In Greek mythology, the goddess of discord, wickedness and blind folly. She was the eldest daughter of ZEUS and Eris (strife). At the wedding of Peleus and Thetis, to which she had not been invited, Ate threw a golden apple inscribed with "for the fairest" into the crowd of merrymakers. Each of the goddesses claimed the apple, causing great discord. ZEUS refused to arbitrate their claims and charged Paris with the task. The dispute led to the Trojan War. Zeus cast Ate out of Olympus for her mischief.

Atea One of the names of the Polynesian sky god RANGI. It means "light". Rangi and PAPA (earth) were forcibly separated by their children at the beginning of creation.

Aten In ancient Egypt, the deity worshipped by the pharaoh Akhenaten as the universal and almost exclusive creator god. Aten was represented as the sun disc, whose rays brought life and beauty into the world. After the death of Akhenaten in 1350 BC, Tutankhamun returned Egyptian worship to AMUN, the ram-headed god of Thebes. As Amun-Re, this deity incorporated the power of RE.

Atlantis In European tradition, the legendary island that was destroyed by an earthquake. Mentioned by Plato, the Greek philosopher, the legend of Atlantis may have referred to the eruption of Thera (modern Santorini), in about 1500 BC.

Atlas In Greek mythology, the Titan who bore the sky on his shoulders. Originally, Atlas seems to have guarded the pillars holding up the heavens.

Atrahasis In Mesopotamian mythology, a good man who was saved from the deluge by the advice of the water god ENKI. In some versions of the myth he is called Ziusudra. The flood had been sent to earth by ENLIL, god of the air, because mankind made too much noise for him to sleep properly. Atrahasis was a forerunner of the biblical NOAH.

Atreus In Greek mythology, a king of Mycenae. He was the son of Pelops and father of Agamemnon and Menelaus. His brother Thyestes seduced Atreus's wife in order to obtain the golden ram that secured the throne for its possessor. In revenge, Atreus slew Thyestes's sons and served them up at a banquet. Thyestes then laid a curse on the house of Atreus, from which curse were born the tragic histories of Atreus's descendants, including Agamemnon, Electra and Iphigenia.

Audumla In Germanic mythology, the primeval cow, known as "the nourisher". She lived off the salt on rocks and, from one of the rocks she licked, produced the first man called Buri, or "the born one". The creation took three days: on the first day, a hair appeared where she licked, on the second, a head, and on the third, the whole man.

Augeas In Greek mythology, the king whose stables HERACLES cleaned out as one of his labours. These stables housed 3,000 sheep and oxen, including 12 sacred bulls, and had not been cleaned for 30 years. Augeas broke his promise to give Heracles one-tenth of his herd if the stables were cleaned in a day, and in revenge Heracles slew him.

Aurora The Roman equivalent of EOS, the Greek goddess of the dawn.

Avalon In Arthurian legend, the wonderful island to which ARTHUR was taken to be healed of his wounds. It was also the place of the blessed dead where, in some versions, Arthur exists as an immortal. The name Avalon is connected with apples.

Avatar The descent of a Hindu deity to earth in incarnate form. The god who most often becomes an avatar is VISHNU. The forms he has adopted include a boar, a turtle, a fish, a dwarf and a man.

Azhi Dahaka In Iranian mythology, the dragon who served the evil spirit AHRIMAN. When the hero Traetaona cut open Azhi Dahaka's breast with a sword, lizards, toads, snakes and scorpions poured out. The dragon was eventually chained to a mountain, from where he is prophesied to escape and wreak havoc on the earth until his defeat by a new hero, Keresaspa. Keresaspa's triumph will signal the birth of a new world.

Azra'il In the mythology of the Hausa-speaking people of Tunisia, the angel of death who introduced mortality to the world. However, in so doing, Azra'il did mankind a service, since before the introduction of death men and women had been forced to live for centuries. One virgin who died after 500 years was resurrected by Allah at the request of Moses. On returning from the grave, the virgin complained bitterly, saying that she was exhausted by life. Moses thus asked Allah to allow people to die sooner, and so Allah instructed Azra'il to limit the life of man to sixty or seventy years.

B

Baal-Hammon A Canaanite deity worshipped at Carthage. The name may mean "the lord of the altar of incense". The Greeks identified Baal-Hammon with KRONOS. He was, however, the Carthaginian counterpart of BAAL, the husband of Anat, an aspect of ASTARTE.

Baalzebub In the New Testament, another name for SATAN. He was sometimes believed to be Satan's chief assistant, and a development of BAAL. Baalzebub (lord of the flies) was probably a distortion of a Canaanite god's name meaning "lord of the house". Christianity inherited the Canaanite pantheon as its devil host.

Babel In the Old Testament, the city of NIMROD, a legendary ruler who challenged heaven by building a great tower. To thwart Nimrod, Yahweh made the people of Shinar speak in a variety of tongues, thus making it impossible for them to complete the tower. The diversity of languages in the world was said to stem from this event.

Bacabs In Maya mythology, the four giant brothers who supported the earth at its four corners and controlled the winds and the rain.

Bacchus The Roman equivalent of the god DIONYSUS.

Bachue In South American mythology, specifically that of the Chibcha Indians of Colombia, the mother goddess and protector of crops. Her name means "large-breasted". Bachue emerged from a sacred lake with a male infant after Chiminigaga, the creator god of the Chibcha people, had created light. She married the boy when he was six, bore the first human beings by him, and then returned with him to the sacred lake where they lived together as serpents.

Badger In the mythology of the Shoshonean Indians of North America, a hero animal who saved Dove and his children from the demon-monster DZOAVITS. When Dzoavits was pursuing Dove, Badger dug two holes in the ground, giving Dove and his children refuge in one of them and tricking Dzoavits into searching for them in the other. When Dzoavits disappeared down the wrong hole, Badger threw scalding rocks after him and sealed the entrance to the hole with a stone.

Bajang In southeast Asia, an evil spirit whose presence is said by Malay-speaking people to foretell catastrophe and sickness. He usually appears in the form of a polecat and is especially dangerous to children. However, in many versions, he can be enslaved by the master of a household, kept in a bamboo vessel and fed on eggs and milk. The master can then use his "familiar", a friendly spirit, to visit sickness on his enemies. But if he fails to feed him, the bajang will turn nasty and attack the master. The bajang can be handed down through generations.

Balaam A seer from the Bible who was asked by Balak, King of Moab, to curse the Hebrews. On the journey to Moab, the ass on which Balaam was riding saw an angel sent by Yahweh brandishing a sword and blocking his way forward. The angel was invisible to Balaam, who struck the ass for turning aside. The angel then appeared to Balaam, who confessed his sinfulness and was converted to the worship of Yahweh.

Balarama In Hindu mythology, the elder brother of KRISHNA, who was the eighth incarnation of VISHNU. It is believed that Vishnu took two hairs, a white and a black one, and that these became Balarama and Krishna. Even as a child, Balarama was able to slay demons. However, another Hindu tradition makes him the incarnation of the serpent Sesha. This creature has a thousand heads and provides the couch and canopy of Vishnu, while the great god sleeps during the intervals of creation. Whenever Sesha yawns, he causes an earthquake.

Balor In Irish mythology, the one-eyed god of death, and the most formidable of the Fomorii, a group of deities associated with evil and darkness. His one eye was poisoned by druids, when he saw these priests secretly making a draught of wisdom. Thereafter, he kept the lid of the eye half-closed. The eye possessed the power, when the lid was lifted by Balor's attendants, to kill enemies at a glance. Eventually, in battle, Balor's eye was destroyed by a magic stone, slung by the sun god LUGH, his grandson. Lugh then killed Balor and the Fomorii were routed at last.

Bamapana In Australian aboriginal mythology, specifically that of the northern Murngin tribe, a trickster, or madman, who violates customary taboos, notably that of tribal incest.

Bannik A Russian household spirit, usually encountered in the bath-house. He is an aged man, with a head too large for his body covered in unruly locks. A bannik can be kind or cruel, according to his mood. The traditional way to tame such a spirit is to leave some water for it to bathe in.

Banshee The English name for Bean Sidhe, the Irish fairy. The banshee descends from old Celtic gods who have gone underground. In country districts the wailing of the fairy is said to foretell the approach of death.

Basilisk One of the legendary beasts of Christian Europe, also known as the Cockatrice. It appeared in the shape of a small lizard or serpent. Its breath was so venomous that just the stench of it caused instant death, as did a mere glance from its eye. As a result, the creature lived apart from other beings in a self-created desert.

Bastet The cat goddess of ancient Egypt and the daughter of RE, the sun god. She was related to the moon, and the centre of her cult was the city of Bubastis, where a special necropolis housed mummified cats. But in some myths, Bastet takes on the destructive qualities of her counterpart, the lion-headed goddess SEKHMET. Both Bastet and Sekhmet were closely linked with the goddess Mut.

Baucis and Philemon In Greek mythology, the old Phrygian married couple who alone gave ZEUS and HERMES hospitality when they visited earth in order to test mankind. As a reward, Zeus transformed their humble dwelling into a temple, and they became its priest and priestess. When they died, they were turned into trees with intertwining branches.

Becuma In Irish mythology, a goddess who was banished to earth. She persuaded the high king, Conn, to take her as his wife, but she soon became jealous of his son, Art. The brave prince undertook a testing journey because of Becuma. Not only did he overcome the spell she had cast on him, but he also had her expelled from the court when he returned from his journey.

Bellerophon In Greek mythology, the son of Glaucus, King of Corinth. Originally named Hipponous, he was forced to change his name and go into exile after accidentally killing his brother. With the aid of his winged horse Pegasus, he successfully met the challenge of Iobates, King of Lycia, to destroy the Chimaera, the fire-breathing offspring of TYPHON. After a series of tests, Bellerophon was rewarded by being given Iobates' daughter in marriage. For attempting to ride Pegasus to the top of Mount Olympus, Bellerophon was flung down to earth by ZEUS, and spent the rest of his days wandering alone, blind and crippled. Unlike the hero HERACLES, Bellerophon failed to attain immortality.

Bellona A Roman war goddess, who may have been the deity of battle prior to the rise of MARS. As a result of a plea for victory that she answered in 296 BC, a temple dedicated to Bellona was built shortly afterward near the altar of Mars on the Capitoline hill.

Belshazzar He appears in the Bible and is the last Babylonian king. At Belshazzar's banquet, DANIEL interpreted the writing which appeared on the wall as foretelling doom. That night, Belshazzar was killed by Iranian forces in the sack of Babylon. The year was 539 BC.

Beowulf The Germanic hero of the seventh-century Anglo-Saxon epic, *Beowulf*. To rid the Danish king Hrothgar of the monster Grendel, the warrior Beowulf set a trap and in the fierce struggle tore off the creature's arm. Later, he slew Grendel's mother and cut off the head of the dying Grendel himself. It took four stout men to drag the monster's enormous head to the court of King Hrothgar.

Bergelmir In Germanic mythology, the only giant to escape being drowned in blood when ODIN slew Ymir, the chief frost giant. Bergelmir and his wife saved themselves by climbing into a boat made from a hollow tree trunk and so lived to beget the second race of frost giants.

Bertha In Germanic mythology, an Aesir goddess, usually identified with FRIGG. She lived in the hollow of a mountain and watched over the souls of unbaptized children. She also appeared as a "white lady" to foretell death.

Bes A popular household god in ancient Egypt, Bes was represented as a dwarf with a large bearded face, shaggy eyebrows, long hair, large projecting ears, a flat nose, and a protruding tongue. His arms were thick and long, his legs bowed, and he wore a tail. Bes was a benign deity – he protected children, slew poisonous snakes, helped at childbirth, and kept misfortune at bay. Bes was probably imported from what is now northern Sudan.

Bestla In Germanic mythology, the wife of BOR and mother of ODIN, Vili and Ve. Her father was Bolthor, one of the frost giants. In old Germanic society, there was a close relation between a man and his sister's son, so Bestla's brother would have been guardian to the young Odin.

Bhrigu In Hindu mythology, a renowned sage and possibly a son of BRAHMA. He was asked by the priests (brahmins) to discover which god most deserved their worship and, barred from seeing SHIVA (who was making love to his wife) and offended by Brahma's self-esteem, he declared that VISHNU was the only god worthy of worship. Bhrigu found Vishnu asleep and dared to stamp on the god's chest. But Vishnu said he was honoured by the sage's visit and thus won the contest in divine humility.

Bifrost In Germanic mythology, the rainbow bridge between Asgard, the home of the gods, and Mannheim, the world of men. It was doomed to break at Ragnarok (the twilight of the gods) under the weight of the frost giants. The bridge was guarded by HEIMDAL, who was charged with alerting the gods to the approach of the giants.

Big Owl In the mythology of the Apache Indians of North America, a cannibalistic monster, capable of transfixing his prey with a stare. He was destroyed by his brother.

Bishamon In the Buddhist mythology of Japan, one of the seven celestial guardians of the world, who brings good fortune and prosperity. He is also called Bishamon-tenno and is a god of war and riches. In 587, Prince Shotoku called upon his aid in fighting anti-Buddhist groups.

Blathnat An admirer of the Irish hero CUCHULAINN. She helped him find the secret entrance to her husband's stronghold by emptying milk into a stream which ran through it. Her pleasure was short-lived, however. As the triumphant Cuchulainn was carrying her away, a loyal retainer of her slain husband managed to kill Blathnat by dragging her over a precipice.

Bluebeard In medieval European legend, a villain who appears as a prince, wizard or merchant. He married seven wives in succession, each of whom he either killed or locked in a dungeon to feed on human flesh. The last of the wives killed Bluebeard or, in some versions, was rescued from him by a young hero.

Blue Jay In the mythology of the Mohawk Indians of North America, the agent of Sapling in his battle against the demon Tawiskaron. Tawiskaron's effort to build a bridge across which wild animals might pass to prey on human beings was foiled when Sapling sent the bird, Blue Jay, with a cricket's legs in his mouth, to terrify Tawiskaron into taking flight.

Bomazi According to the Bushongo people of Zaire, the father of their founder. One day, Bomazi announced to an old couple that they would have a child. In due course, the woman gave birth to a daughter whom Bomazi married. Together, they had five sons, two of whom were Woto and Moelo. When Woto grew up, he founded the Bushongo people.

Bona Dea An obscure Roman deity worshipped only by women. Her name means "the good goddess". She was associated with the serpent, and in her temple on the Aventine Hill in Rome there were many tame snakes. Her myth concerns the attempt made on her virginity by her own father, Faunus, the Roman equivalent of PAN.

Borak In Islamic mythology, a fabulous beast, part human and part animal, on whose back Muhammad rode on the night of his ascension into heaven. His name means "lightning".

Boreas In Greek mythology, the son of EOS and the god of the north wind. He was often contrasted with the gentle west wind, Zephyrus. During the Iranian invasion of Greece, Boreas assisted the Greeks in their defence by inflicting severe damage on the invaders' fleet at Artemisium in 480 BC.

Bragi The Germanic god of poetry and eloquence, and the son of ODIN. The trickster god LOKI called him "Bragi the bragger!" Bragi's wife, Idun, had charge of the golden apples of youth.

Brian In Irish mythology, one of the three sons of the goddess BRIGIT. As a punishment for slaying the father of LUGH, Brian and two of his brothers were required to fulfil eight labours. These included fetching three golden apples, a magic pigskin, a poisoned spear and a cooking spit which lay at the bottom of the sea. The myth thus has similarities with that of the labours of the Greek hero Heracles.

Britomaris In Greek mythology, an ancient Cretan goddess of the sea, wild places and chastity. She escaped the amorous pursuit of the Cretan king, MINOS, by jumping from a high rock into the sea, where, in some versions, she was rescued by ARTEMIS. Her name means "sweet maid". After the escape from Crete, Britomaris took up residence in a grove, sacred to Artemis, on the island of Aegina.

Brut The legendary founder of Britain. He was supposed to have been the great-grandson of AENEAS, the Trojan hero who settled in Italy. An oracle told Brut to found a new kingdom in the island situated north of Gaul (modern France). This he did with a select band of followers. In the conquest, they captured the last of the giants who once owned the island.

Brutus, Lucius Junius The legendary founder of the Roman Republic and the nephew of Tarquinius Superbus, the last Etruscan king of Rome.

When Sextus, the king's son, raped the wife of a prominent aristocrat, Brutus took an oath to end the tyranny of kings. In 509 BC, he led an armed rising in the city, and the people backed his idea of a republican government. Later in the same year, Brutus, as an elected magistrate, condemned his own two sons to death for joining a conspiracy to restore Tarquinius Superbus to the throne.

In acting so sternly on behalf of the common good, Brutus displayed the fortitude that Romans believed was their true national characteristic.

Bue The legendary hero of the Gilbert Islands. He was the son of a woman who had been magically impregnated by the sun god. Like the Polynesian hero MAUI, he had a whole series of adventures. But he was most remembered for the wisdom that he passed on to mankind. Bue taught people to build houses and canoes, how to cast spells, and how to dance.

Buga In Siberian mythology, and specifically that of the Tungus peoples, the creator god. He created the world and human beings out of iron, fire, clay and water. His name means "god".

Bumba The creator deity in the mythology of the Bushongo people of Zaire. At first, he lived alone in a universe without light and consisting solely of water. Then, one day, he was attacked by agonizing stomach pains and spat out the sun, moon and stars. Gradually, the sun dried up the water and the land began to emerge. Then Bumba vomited up eight living creatures: a beetle, a crocodile, an eagle, a fish, a goat, a heron, a leopard and a tortoise. Lastly, he created men and women and gave them laws and customs which he instructed them to follow.

Feeling satisfied with his creation, Bumba departed to his home in the sky. However, the creator deity continues to communicate with mankind through dreams and visions. He is believed to be a white being, shaped like a man.

Buri In Germanic mythology, the "born one". At the beginning of time, he emerged over three days from an icy rock licked by the primeval cow, Audumla. On the first day, a hair appeared, on the second, a head, and on the third, the whole man. Buri's son was BOR, who was himself the father of ODIN.

Buto A snake goddess of ancient Egypt, usually represented as a cobra. She may be winged or may wear a crown. Buto allied herself with the Egyptian goddess ISIS and helped her to protect her infant HORUS by removing him from the floating island of Chemnis.

Bylebog The Slavic deities Bylebog and Chernobog represented the two opposing forces of good and evil, creation and destruction. Bylebog means "white god" and Chernobog, "black god". Thus, Bylebog was a god of light and day, Chernobog of the shadows and night. Bylebog always helped travellers who lost their way in the dark forests, bestowed wealth and fertility, and helped with the harvest. With the introduction of Christianity to the western regions of the Slavonic world, Chernobog acquired many of the traits of SATAN.

C

Cacus In Roman mythology, a fire-breathing monster who lived in a cave on either the Palatine hill or the Aventine hill. The son of the smith god Vulcan, Cacus preyed on human beings who strayed within his grasp. When the hero HERACLES (Roman Hercules) was finishing his tenth labour, by driving the cattle of Geryon to Greece, he rested near the monster's cave. While Heracles slept, Cacus stole the herd and closed the entrance to the cave with a massive rock. Unable to shift the obstacle, Heracles tore the top from the hill, jumped into the cave from above and strangled Cacus. Then the hero dedicated an altar on the spot to JUPITER, sacrificing one of the cows to him.

Cain In the Bible, the eldest son of Adam and Eve. A tiller of the earth, he slew his brother Abel after Yahweh preferred Abel's offering of lambs to his of the fruits of the earth. In punishment, Cain was exiled. But the special mark which Yahweh placed on his forehead, now associated in the phrase "the mark of Cain" with the stigma attached to an outlaw, was placed there to protect Cain from others intent on avenging the murder.

Caishen The Chinese god of wealth. He is believed to based on an historical figure, Pi Kan, the uncle of the last Shang king. This was the ruler Di Xin, a cruel and oppressive man. When Pi Kan plucked up courage to reprove Di Xin for the dreadful state of affairs into which the kingdom had fallen, the king ordered his arrest. Consumed with anger, Di Xin exclaimed, "I hear the heart of a sage has seven holes", and had Pi Kan cut open to see if he were one. This murder took place just before the overthrow of the Shang dynasty in 1027 BC.

Calliope In Greek mythology, one of the nine Muses, that of epic poetry. She was the daughter of ZEUS and Mnemosyne and the mother of ORPHEUS, the marvellous musician. The name Calliope means "fair voice".

Callisto In Greek mythology, an Arcadian nymph, attendant upon ARTEMIS. For forsaking a vow of chastity and bearing a son to ZEUS, she was changed into a bear, in some versions, by Artemis. In other versions, Zeus's wife HERA transformed her, either to hide the adultery or to give vent to her jealousy. Zeus later set Callisto in the heavens as the constellation Ursa Major (Great Bear) and, alongside her, their son Arcas as the constellation Arcturus.

Calypso In Greek mythology, a goddess or nymph on whose island ODYSSEUS spent seven years, during his epic voyage home from the Trojan War. She bore him either one or two sons. When ZEUS commanded her to send him away, Calypso provided Odysseus with materials for a raft and with favourable winds. Calypso's island was called Ogygia, which means "the sea's navel". Her own name means "she who conceals".

Camelot The legendary site of ARTHUR's court and of the Round Table. It has been identified with places in Wales and Cornwall, although in the fifteenth century Sir Thomas Malory said it was Winchester. However, Camelot could have been a corruption of Camalodunum, the Roman name for Colchester in Essex.

Camilla In Roman mythology, a virgin huntress and warrior, the favourite of Diana, the counterpart of the Greek goddess ARTEMIS. She could move faster than the wind and she fought with one breast exposed in order to gain greater freedom with her bow arm. Camilla was killed while fighting with the Italian tribes against AENEAS. She was the daughter of Metabus, king of the Volsci.

Cardea One of the deities whom the Romans associated with the door. Limentinus guarded the threshold, Forculus the leaf of the door, and Cardea the hinges.

Cecrops In Greek mythology, a snake man, with the lower body of a serpent and the torso and head of a man. He was the first or second king of Attica, then known as Cecropia. When ATHENA and POSEIDON were in rivalry for possession of his kingdom, Cecrops decided that the goddess should have the worship of his subjects. He reached this decision because Athena made an olive tree grow on the Acropolis, whereas Poseidon could produce only a tiny spring. Cecrops also put an end to human sacrifice in Attica, and was the first ruler to acknowledge the supremacy of ZEUS.

Centaur In Greek mythology, a creature with the lower body of a horse and the torso and head of a man.

Centaurs were commonly lascivious, drunken followers of DIONYSUS, although some of them, notably Chiron, were teachers of men and nurturers of civilization. Chiron also instructed several of the gods, including Asclepius, and was particularly skilled in the use of herbs as natural remedies. The centaurs were the descendants of Centaurus, a son of Apollo, the god of prophecy, divination and the arts.

Cerberus In Greek mythology, the guardian of the gate to the underworld. A three-headed dog, he is usually shown with the tail of a serpent, but sometimes with the tail of a dragon.

Cerberus welcomed the newly dead to the realm of HADES, but his fierce howling and the stench of his breath frightened those dead who tried to escape to the world.

However, Cerberus did not welcome the living to the underworld. ORPHEUS had to charm him with music, and HERACLES had a terrific struggle to drag him to Tiryns in order to complete his last labour. By succeeding in this difficult task, Heracles staked his own claim to immortality.

Cerberus is said to have infected various herbs with his venom. These were gathered and used by magicians in the preparation of potions with which to perform evil spells.

Ceres The Roman goddess of vegetation and fruitfulness, especially of corn, and the equivalent of the Greek DEMETER. She wandered through the world, distributing grain and instructing men how to sow it. The word cereal derives from her name. The name of the annual festival devoted to her worship was known as Cerelia. Her cult on the Aventine hill of Rome was influenced by Greek practices from its beginning, in the early fifth century BC.

Chac In Central America, the Maya god of rain, lightning and thunder. He was thought of as four deities, each connected with a cardinal point and a colour: east/red, north/white, west/black and south/yellow. Although these four Chacs were portrayed with curling fangs and tears streaming from their eyes, they were kindly gods. The rain they sent from each of the four quarters brought fertility to the lands of the Maya. The Aztec equivalent was TLALOC.

Chalchihuitlicue In the mythology of the ancient Aztecs of Central America, a water goddess who was also the symbol of youthful beauty. QUETZALCOATL drove TLALOC, her husband, from the sky, where TEZCATLIPOCA had placed him and placed Chalchihuitlicue there instead. But she caused such floods that only those who turned themselves into fish survived. Chalchihuitlicue was portrayed as a river from which grew a prickly pear tree laden with fruit.

Chimaera In Greek mythology, a fabulous creature who breathed fire. He had the head of a lion, the body of a goat and a serpent's tail. Bellerophon, mounted on his flying horse Pegasus, killed Chimaera with an arrow. Chimaera was the offspring of TYPHON.

Chiron In Greek mythology, a centaur. Unlike most of the centaurs, Chiron was a sage, physician and teacher of men and gods, among them the heroes ACHILLES and HERACLES and the god ASCLEPIUS. He was skilled in the use of herbs and he applied his natural remedies with great effect. When Heracles accidentally wounded him, the pain was so great that Chiron yielded his immortality to PROMETHEUS and died. Several of Chiron's pupils accompanied JASON on his quest.

Chiuta The supreme deity of the Tumbuka people of Malawi, in southern Africa. His name means "the great bow in the heavens". Chiuta is looked upon as a self-created deity who sustains the world. His special gift is rain.

Chyavana In Hindu legend, a sage who regained his youth. He was the son of Bhrigu and the author of several hymns in the *Rig Veda*, the earliest religious document of India. According to one version of the legend, Chyavana's body became so shrivelled with age that the Aswins, twin sky gods, thought that they could easily seduce his wife, Sukanya. To their surprise, she not only remained faithful to her husband but also tricked them into renewing his youth.

At Chyavana's suggestion, Sukanya taunted the Aswins with being unimportant deities, and agreed to tell them in what way they were imperfect if they would make her husband young again. This they did by telling Chyavana to bathe in a certain pool. Sukanya then informed the Aswins that they were unimportant because they were not involved in a ceremony the other gods were performing at that time. Pleased with this information, they rushed away to join in. When at first INDRA refused to admit the Aswins, Chyavana conjured up an enormous monster. Fearful of the sage's wrath, Indra finally admitted the Aswins.

Cian In Irish mythology, the father of the sun god, LUGH. Cian's own father was Dian-Cecht, the god of medicine. It was prophesied that one-eyed Balor, the god of death, would die at the hand of his grandson. To stop this happening, Balor locked up his only daughter, Ethlinn, in a crystal tower, but Cian came to her, disguised as a woman. Their son, Lugh, killed Balor at the battle of Magh Tuireadh. Cian himself was slain by the three sons of Tuirenn, the husband of the goddess BRIGIT.

When he was approached by his enemies, Cian turned himself into a pig, but, recognizing the beast as magical, the enemies turned themselves into hounds and gave chase. Failing to capture Cian, they eventually assumed their human form again and stoned him to death. As a punishment, Lugh made the three sons of Tuirenn undertake a number of dangerous tasks.

Cincinnatus, Lucius Quinctius A legendary hero of the early Roman Republic, Cincinnatus is supposed to have saved his country from defeat in 458 BC. The tribe of the Aquei had cornered the Roman army, and the Senate elected Cincinnatus as dictator for six months in order to deal with the emergency. The deputation arrived to find the humble man working in his fields. Quickly washing himself and putting on his toga, Cincinnatus hastened to Rome, where he conscripted all men of military age. Resolute action dealt with the Aquei and saved the trapped army. Within fifteen days, Cincinnatus was able to resign his dictatorship and return to the obscurity of his farm.

Cinteotl The ancient Aztec god of maize. In Mexico, he was propitiated each spring by the spilling of blood upon reeds, which were then displayed on the doors of people's dwellings. Closely associated with Xochipilli, the flayed god of flowers and lord of souls, Cinteotl was a god whose beneficence ensured mankind a regular supply of food.

He was under the protection of the rain god TLALOC, and he had many female forms.

Clytemnestra In Greek mythology, the wife of Agamemnon, King of Mycenae, and mother of ORESTES, Chrysothemis, Electra and Iphigenia. With her lover, Aegisthus, she murdered Agamemnon on his return from the Trojan War, for which crime she was in turn murdered by Orestes. Clytemnestra was turned against her husband by his sacrifice of Iphigenia to ARTEMIS, in order to obtain a favourable wind to sail to Troy. Agamemnon had pretended to Clytemnestra that Iphigenia was being called to the expeditionary fleet to marry ACHILLES. Clytemnestra also killed CASSANDRA, whom her husband had brought back as a concubine from Troy.

Cockaigne In medieval European legend, a paradise of wealth and pleasure, particularly the pleasure of food and drink. A thirteenth-century English poem, *The Land of Cockaigne*, describes its houses and streets as being made from sugar and pastry. Cockaigne was often identified with London.

Coniraya The creator deity of the Huarochiri Indians of Peru. He was kindly disposed toward mankind, and intervened in daily affairs. But it is difficult now to understand the role Coniraya played in running the world, since with the rise of the Incas in the fifteenth century he was subordinated to the sun god INTI. There is even a legendary account of Coniraya's appearance before an Inca ruler in Cuzco. So powerful were the descendants of AYAR that all the other deities worshipped in Inca lands were allocated a lowly place in the official pantheon.

Conn A high king of Ireland. Before Conn's coronation, when he and his followers were engulfed in an enchanted mist, LUGH prophesied that his descendants would reign for generations. But life in the court of Conn was not without its troubles. The banished goddess Becuma wrought havoc there. She persuaded Conn to make her his wife, then alienated the king's affections from Art, the crown prince. Luckily for Conn, and Ireland, Art survived the perilous journey which Becuma imposed on him. He returned to court and had the cunning goddess sent into exile.

Coriolanus A legendary Roman soldier associated with a reactionary outlook. Only the pleas of his mother, Volumnia, dissuaded Coriolanus from attacking Rome when he considered the rights of the aristocracy to be endangered.

Coriolanus may originally have been a deity worshipped by the Volsci, an Italian people who were opposed to the Romans.

Coyolxauhqui The ancient Aztec goddess of the moon. Her name means "golden bells". She was killed by her brother HUITZILOPOCHTLI when he emerged from the womb of their mother, the earth goddess COATLICUE. Huitzilopochtli cut off Coyolxauhqui's head and threw it into the heavens to become the moon, aglow with the golden hue of her bells.

Cranaus A legendary king of Athens. He ruled after Cecrops, the snake-man who sprang from the soil. Although Cranaus also arose from the ground, he does not appear to have had a serpent's body. During his reign, ZEUS sent the flood, and Deucalion, the Greek NOAH, took refuge with Cranaus. After the waters subsided, Deucalion's son seems to have usurped the throne of Athens.

Creon In Greek mythology, the regent in Thebes after the death of its king, Laius, at the hands of OEDIPUS. He offered the throne, and marriage to the widowed queen Jocasta, to any man who could rid the city of the SPHINX. This Oedipus did. After a few years another plague visited Thebes, and the oracle at Delphi revealed that it was caused by wrongdoing. Oedipus had unwittingly killed his father and married his mother. Once again Creon had to assume power.

A bitter quarrel between Polynices and Eteocles, the sons of Oedipus, soon resulted in a war that left both of them dead. Creon buried Eteocles with honour, but forbade the same to Polynices, whose corpse was left to rot beyond the walls of Thebes. When Antigone, Oedipus's daughter, defied the ban, she was entombed alive by Creon for her disobedience.

Creusa The name of several figures in Greek and Roman mythology. It means "queen". One Creusa was a Corinthian princess loved by the hero JASON. When Jason tried to divorce his wife Medea in order to marry Creusa, Medea sent Creusa a poisoned wedding robe that burned her and her father to death. Medea was renowned for her magic arts. A second Creusa, first wife of AENEAS, was killed while fleeing from Troy.

Cupay In the mythology of the Inca people of Peru, Cupay or Supay was an evil spirit, the god of death. Child sacrifice may have been part of his cult.

Cymbeline In British legend, a king who reigned under the Romans for thirty-five years before handing over the throne to his son, Guidarius, who refused to pay tribute to the Romans. He derived from the historical Cunobeline, after whom the city of Camalodunum, or Colchester, in Essex is named.

D

Dagon A deity mentioned in the Old Testament. He was probably the sea god of the Philistines, a people who settled on the coast of Canaan in the twelfth century BC. Samson destroyed his temple at Gaza by pulling down its two middle pillars.

Dagon should not be confused with Dagan, who was a fertility god worshipped in both Canaan and Mesopotamia. King Hammurabi of Babylon (1792–50 BC) declared that he was the son of Dagan, as well as of SIN and MARDUK. The Canaanite god BAAL is also described as Dagan's son.

Dainichi-nyorai In Japanese Buddhism, the BUDDHA Mahavairocana (great illuminator). The sect's founder was Kobo-Daishi (774–835), who was initiated into its mysterious doctrines during a visit to China. Kobo-Daishi was buried alive, at his own request. His body is believed never to have rotted, but to be awaiting resurrection at the advent of the Buddha Mahavairocana.

Daityas The giant demons of Hindu mythology. They descended from Diti, the wife of the sage Kasyapa. In the balance of warring forces that makes up Hinduism, the Daityas are as necessary as the gods themselves. Together, they created AMRITA (the water of life) by churning up the ocean. Daityas are thus called *asuras*, non-gods or anti-gods.

Daksha In Hindu mythology, one of the ten sages (*rishis*). His name means "able" and suggests creativity. Daksha is the son of BRAHMA, and sprang from the god's right thumb. According to the

Mahabharata, an epic dating from the beginning of the first millennium, Daksha went through a rebirth as a result of a misunderstanding with SHIVA. This powerful god took offence when he made a sacrifice to VISHNU.

Uninvited and unpropitiated, Shiva stopped the ceremony violently and laid into the attendant deities and sages with devastating effect. INDRA was knocked flat, YAMA had his staff broken, the goddess Saraswati lost her nose, Mitra's eyes were gouged out, Pushan had his teeth punched down his throat, Bhrigu's beard was torn off, and Daksha lost his head. When humble apologies at last calmed Shiva down, it was found that Daksha's head had been thrown into the sacrificial fire. As a result, Shiva gave the sage the head of a ram in its place. Another version of this myth has the trident of Shiva fall on Vishnu's chest. The consequent fight between them is ended only by Brahma, who makes Shiva acknowledge Vishnu's power.

Damballa In the Voodoo mythology of Haiti, a powerful serpent deity. Damballa, or Damballa Wedo, is imagined as a great snake arching across the sky. His female counterpart, Ayida, is the rainbow and, entwined, they symbolize sexual unity. Like many Voodoo gods and goddesses, Damballa has been identified with a Christian figure, in his case St Patrick, who is said to have rid Ireland of all its serpents.

Dambhodbhava A legendary Hindu king who represents the vice of pride. Despite the advice of the brahmins in his court, Dambhodbhava decided to attack the sages Nara and Narayana. So he led his army to the mountain where they lived and ordered a charge. To the king's surprise, however, Nara turned a handful of straws into deadly missiles, which filled the sky. Realizing at last his own conceit, Dambhodbhava fell at Nara's feet and begged for peace.

Dana In Irish mythology, the mother goddess of the people of Dana, or Tuatha De Danaan. Also called Danu, she was the mother of DAGDA (the good god). After the defeat of the Tuatha De Danaan, Dagda found underground residences for them all.

Danae In Greek mythology, the mother of the hero PERSEUS by ZEUS. She was locked in a bronze chamber by her father, Acrisius, King of Argos, who had been warned by an oracle that his daughter would bring forth a son who would murder him. However, Zeus came to Danae in the form of a golden shower and their union produced a son. Afterward, Zeus spirited away both mother and child. Later, Polydectes fell in love with Danae, and to prevent Perseus from hindering his advances, he ordered Perseus to fetch the head of Medusa, a Gorgon. After Perseus had accomplished this, with the help of ATHENA, he killed Polydectes.

Daphne In Greek mythology, a mountain nymph who spurned men, but was loved by the god Apollo and the mortal Leucippus. Leucippus disguised himself as a nymph to woo her, but revealed his masculinity when bathing and was killed by the nymphs. Urged on by Eros, the god of love, Apollo then began his pursuit of Daphne. But, to escape him, she prayed to her father, the river Peneius, and he turned her into a laurel tree. However, Apollo then decreed that a laurel garland should be the sign of success in the arts.

Daphnis A legendary Sicilian shepherd whose indifference to love, like that of Daphne, is connected with the laurel. He was brought up by woodland nymphs and led a quiet life until he annoyed APHRODITE. What caused the love goddess to become so angry was Daphnis's boast that he could resist all the temptations of passion. Aphrodite made him fall desperately in love with Nais, a water nymph. Eventually, Nais took pity on Daphnis on the condition that he would remain eternally faithful to her. When a mortal woman desired the shepherd and gained her desire by making him drunk, Nais struck Daphnis blind. Later, he drowned in a river, his cries for help ignored by the water nymphs.

Daphnis and Chloe In Greek and Roman mythology, a goatherd and shepherdess, whose names mean, respectively, "laurel" and "young green shoot". Their youthful affection, nurtured in an idyllic pastoral setting, grows into a mature, faithful love. This Daphnis has no connection with the shepherd blinded by Nais.

David The biblical hero who killed the giant Goliath with a single stone from his slingshot. After cutting off the giant's head, he dragged it before Saul, the king of Israel. In medieval Christian belief, David was said to prefigure JESUS, his divine descendant. Thus, the slaying of Goliath was interpreted as a parallel of the temptation suffered by Jesus in the desert at the hands of SATAN.

Dazhbog The Slavic sun god. Son of the supreme deity Svarog (sky), Dazhbog, along with his brother Svarozich (fire), inherited his father's powers of creation. Dazhbog lived in a magnificent golden palace, from which he emerged each morning in a bejewelled chariot, pulled westward by a team of horses which breathed fire.

Dechtire In Irish mythology, the mother of the hero CUCHULAINN. She was wed to an Ulster chieftain but was turned into a bird and flew, together with fifty of her handmaidens, to an enchanted place where she lived with the sun god LUGH. She eventually returned home with their son. Her kind-hearted husband took her back and treated the boy as his own.

Deirdre In Irish mythology, the beautiful daughter of the Ulster lord Felim Mac Dall, the harper to the high king Conchobhar. Because it was prophesied by a druid that Deirdre would marry a king but bring death and sorrow to Ireland, the people of the land demanded her death. However, Conchobhar saved Deirdre by saying that he would bring her up until she was old enough to be his wife. In this way, no foreign king could marry her and cause trouble in Ireland.

But when the time came for her marriage to Conchobhar, Deirdre did not want to become the wife of an old man. Instead, her eyes fell on a handsome young warrior called Naoise, and she eloped with him to Scotland. As Conchobhar secretly desired Deirdre, messengers were sent to recall the lovers. On their return, the high king had Naoise killed, despite a promise of safe conduct, and forced Deirdre to marry him. She never smiled again. To avoid having to share her favours with a friend of Conchobhar, Deirdre finally dashed out her brains on a rock.

Delphi A town at the foot of Mount Parnassus. For the ancient Greeks, it was the site of Apollo's oracle. The oracular sayings, always equivocal, were delivered by a priestess seated on a golden tripod and were interpreted by a priest. The oracle had its origins in the worship of a pre-Greek earth goddess. A monstrous serpent called Python inhabited the place before the coming of Apollo. Serpents were associated with HERA, the quarrelsome wife of ZEUS, and Gaia (earth), the wife of Ouranos and the mother of KRONOS. In memory of the original ownership of Delphi, the priestess in Apollo's temple was always called Pythia.

Demong The Iban people of northern Borneo trace their descent from Bujang, a legendary hero who was born in a country near Mecca. After Bujang led the Ibans eastward to their present home, other warriors took charge of tribal affairs. One of these was Demong, the son of Entingi.

During the settlement of a certain river valley, Demong cemented good relations with the existing inhabitants by marrying Rinda, a local chieftain's daughter. She bore him several children, as did another local girl after Rinda's death. When he realized that his own end was approaching, Demong ordered a boundary stone to be set up to clearly mark the land the Iban people had settled. It is still standing today because whoever tries to move the stone hurts Demong and lays themselves open to his wrath. Stones that bleed are a notable feature of native legend in eastern Malaysia, and so they are treated with great respect.

Deng A sky god, and the creator ancestor of the Dinka people of eastern Sudan. Deng provides rain for plants to grow and ensures the fertility of cattle. His weapon is lightning. It is said that a person struck by lightning is taken straight to heaven. So no mourning takes place for the deceased. The Dinka blame the back-breaking toil of work on a greedy woman called Abuk. She annoyed Deng by hitting the sky with a very long pestle, when pounding more grain than she was entitled to. The result was a curse making the fruits of the earth harder to harvest.

Deucalion The ancient Greek equivalent of NOAH, and the son of PROMETHEUS. When ZEUS, to punish man for his irreverence, flooded the earth, Deucalion, warned by Prometheus of the impending catastrophe, took refuge with his wife, Pyrrha, in an ark, which survived the flood at the top of Mount Parnassus. When the waters receded, Deucalion and Pyrrha enquired of an oracle how they might repopulate the earth and were told to scatter the bones of their mother behind them. At first they refused to disturb the bones of the dead, but then it became clear that "mother" was the earth, and the "bones" stones, which became men and women.

Dhanvantari In Hindu mythology, the physician to the gods. He was born of the churning of the waters when the demons and the gods battled for possession of AMRITA, the water of life. He is also called Sudhapani, which means "carrying nectar in his hands".

Dharma In Hindu mythology, one of the ten ancient sages (*rishis*). He married thirteen daughters of the sage Daksha, who was the son of BRAHMA. The word *dharma* itself means duty, or justice. For Buddhists, on the other hand, *dharma* means the proper way of life for a follower of BUDDHA.

Dharmapalas The Buddhist protectors of the truth, or the *dharma*. There are eight such protectors, and in Tibet they take on particularly terrible forms. Their heads are broad, their teeth huge, their tongues protruding, and a third eye blazes in their foreheads. Dharmapalas waged eternal war against demons and MARA, the great enemy of BUDDHA in his search for enlightenment.

Dhyani-Bodhisattvas The five bodhisattvas (BUDDHAS-to-be) in the Mahayana tradition of Buddhism. their names are AVALOKITESVARA, Ratnapani, Samantabhadra, Vajrapani and Vishvapani.

Diana An ancient Italian goddess of the woodland, whom the Romans identified with the Greek ARTEMIS. She was the goddess of the moon and the forests and the protector of women in childbirth. A virgin goddess, she was worshipped in her temple in Rome, though the original centre of her cult was a sacred grove at Aricia. During the Middle Ages, Diana and the Titan HECATE were regarded as being leaders of the witches.

Dian-Cecht In Irish mythology, the god of medicine and healing, and the grandfather of the sun god LUGH. In his magic spring, he bathed dead and wounded warriors, restoring them to life and health. He appears in medieval Christian legend as an enchanter.

Dido To the Romans, the legendary queen of Carthage. She was the daughter of Mutto, King of Tyre, and the sister of Pygmalion. When the latter became king, he killed Dido's husband and she fled to Africa, where she founded and ruled over the city of Carthage.

When AENEAS was driven by storms on to the coast at Carthage, JUNO brought him and Dido together as lovers. However, at JUPITER's command, Aeneas departed from her and from Carthage, and the distraught Dido burned herself on a funeral pyre.

Even after her death Dido could not forgive his desertion, for when Aeneas descended to the underworld in order to consult his father's ghost, she turned away and fled from him.

Dies Irae In medieval Europe a preoccupation of many Christians was the imminent end of the world. The prospect of the second millennium, the coming of the year 1000, excited great concern, as did plagues, tempests, and earthquakes. Although the victory of good over evil was assured in the Last Judgement, there were many tribulations to be unleashed upon mankind before this final resolution, including the ANTICHRIST.

For that reason the Dies Irae (meaning "day of wrath") was to be a dreadful, though liberating, experience. As St Matthew's gospel plainly states: "For nation shall rise against nation, and kingdom against kingdom: and there shall be famines, and pestilences, and earthquakes, in diverse places. All these are the beginnings of sorrows", of "the abomination of desolation".

Di Jun In Chinese mythology, the great god of the eastern sky, whose house was situated at the top of an enormous tree. Nine of the ten sons born to Di Jun and his wife Xi He were shot down by the divine archer, YI.

Dilmun In Sumerian mythology, paradise, possibly Bahrain in the Persian Gulf. It originally lacked water but was transformed into a divine garden when ENKI, the god of fresh water, made his home there with NINHURSAGA. Neither sickness nor old age was known in Dilmun, an obvious parallel with the biblical Garden of Eden.

Dilwica The goddess of the hunt in Slavic, particularly Serbian, mythology. She may have derived from Diana, the Roman equivalent of ARTEMIS. Dilwica was always portrayed as a beautiful maiden and was usually shown riding through the forest on a swift steed and accompanied by her retinue.

Diomedes In Greek mythology, the king of Argos and a brave warrior at the siege of Troy. He entered the city in the wooden horse built at the suggestion of ODYSSEUS, and in the ensuing battle proved himself second only to ACHILLES in heroism. He was a favourite of ATHENA, especially for frightening ARES and wounding APHRODITE, both of whom sided with the Trojans. Helped by Athena, Diomedes was one of the few Greeks to have a safe and speedy voyage home after the sack of Troy.

Dives In medieval Christian legend, the name given to the "certain rich man" in Luke 16: 19–31, who refused to give Lazarus, a beggar at his door, the crumbs from his table. He went to hell, from where, in his torment of flames, he was able to see Lazarus, cradled in Abraham's bosom in heaven.

Dives is usually shown as the epitome of meanness, weighed down by his moneybag and tormented by SATAN.

Djanbun In the mythology of the Aboriginals of Australia, a man who turned into a platypus after blowing on a fire-stick in the effort to make its sparking end burst into flame. He failed, felt his mouth growing ever larger, jumped into a river and became a platypus. Aboriginals continue to warn against blowing too hard on a fire-stick.

Djanggawul In the mythology of the Aboriginals of northern Australia, three ancestral spirits, two sisters and a brother, who wandered the earth in the company of Bralbral. The two sisters, kept continually pregnant by their brother, populated the earth. Originally, the sisters had both male and female genitalia, but their brother cut off their male parts, thus securing the ascendancy of men in fertility rites.

E

Dolius In Greek mythology, the faithful servant of ODYSSEUS. His loyalty was put to the test on his master's return from Troy. Then Dolius and six of his sons helped Odysseus regain power in Ithaca. One son, Melanthius, and one daughter, Melantho, were killed for having sided with the suitors for the hand of Penelope, Odysseus's wife, during his absence.

Domovoi A house spirit in Slavic legend. He prefers to live near the stove, while his wife, Domovikha, commonly lives in the cellar. It is believed that these spirits have become benign through their close contact with mankind.

Donn An ancient Irish god of the dead, whose home was situated on an island off the southwest coast of Ireland. It would seem that he gave souls of the dead instructions as to their route to the underworld.

Dracula In Eastern European legend, the medieval Romanian tyrant called Vlad the Impaler. Though usually represented as a vampire, he appears in many stories simply as the heroic defender of his country against the Turks.

The idea of Dracula's interest in blood must have arisen from the lack of mercy he showed to his enemies. Once, a group of Turkish envoys refused to remove their turbans in his presence and so the terrifying Vlad had their turbans nailed to their heads.

The modern myth of Dracula stems from the novel of the same name by Bram Stoker.

Dragon In European mythology, a fire-breathing, reptilian beast, commonly represented as a huge monster with wings and a lashing tail. This tradition descends from the Mesopotamian chaos-dragon TIAMAT. In China, however, the dragon (*long*) is essentially a benevolent divinity and is held in high regard. He is the bringer of rain and lord of all the waters on earth. The dragon was associated with the emperor, a five-clawed *long* acting as the imperial insignia.

Dryads In Greek mythology, the woodland nymphs identified with trees. They were not immortal, as ORPHEUS discovered when his dryad wife Eurydice was bitten by a snake.

Duat In Egyptian mythology, the underworld. It was a valley in the sky, separated from the earth and the heavens by mountains, through which the sun-god RE passed each night after setting.

Dumuzi In Sumerian mythology, the dying-and-rising husband of INANNA, the fertility goddess. When Inanna visited the land of no return, (*kur-nu-gi-a*), she was not allowed to leave until she provided a substitute. Enraged that Dumuzi had not mourned for her, Inanna named him as the substitute and banished him to the underworld. Later he escaped, drawn forth by the ceremonial wailings of his worshippers. The myth of his death and resurrection reflects an emphasis on natural forces in Sumerian religion. It parallels the annual cycle of fertility and harvest.

Durvasas In Hindu mythology, a sage and incarnation of SHIVA. When INDRA refused his gift of a garland, Durvasas laid a curse of destruction on him. The curse so weakened Indra and the other gods that the demons seized the opportunity to challenge their ascendancy. The result was the battle for AMRITA, the water of life, which came from the churning of the ocean. The idea of creating amrita was suggested to the gods by VISHNU. The name Durvasas means "ill-clothed".

Dzelarhons The Haida Indians of the Pacific coast of North America regard Dzelarhons as an important animal deity. She is a frog goddess and her husband Kaiti a bear god.

Ea In Babylonian mythology, the god of fresh water. The equivalent of the Sumerian ENKI, he was the husband of Damkina and father of MARDUK, the chief god in the later Mesopotamian pantheon. Part fish and part human, he taught men the arts of agriculture and led them into the paths of reason and wisdom. He was, like Enki, one of a trinity of creator gods The other gods in the trinity were the sky god Anu and the air god ENLIL.

Echidna In Greek mythology, a female monster, half-human and half-serpent. Her name means "snake", and she was the wife of TYPHON, the monster who challenged ZEUS. She features in no major myths, but is important as the mother of the Hydra (which HERACLES killed), the SPHINX, Cerberus (the guardian dog of the underworld), and the Chimaera (which Bellerophon killed).

Echo In Greek mythology, a mountain nymph. Echo may have chattered ceaselessly to HERA to distract her from the adulterous pursuits of her husband ZEUS. Certainly, Hera was driven to remove Echo's power of speech, leaving her capable only of repeating what others said. In another version of the myth, Echo wasted away to an echoing voice when Narcissus rejected her love. Yet another version tells how PAN, one of her suitors, commanded shepherds to tear her apart when she spurned his advances, leaving only her voice.

Edao In the Micronesian mythology of the Marshall Islanders, an heroic adventurer and magician. He emerged from the leg of the creator god LOA, just as had

Wulleb and Lejman, the first man and woman. The adventures of Edao compare with those of OLOFAT, the chief Micronesian hero. In his concern about his immortality, Edao reveals himself as similar to the Sumerian hero GILGAMESH.

Efé In the mythology of the Pygmy people of Africa, the first man whom the sky god created on earth. After his creation, Efé went to heaven to be his creator's hunter. After a long absence, he reappeared on earth, but no one recognized him. Efé told mankind that the great god in the sky was alive and presented them with three of his celestial hunting spears.

Egeria In Roman mythology, a water nymph who protected unborn children. The legendary Numa, the second king of Rome, was said to have married Egeria and to have received from her instruction in religious and political matters. When Numa died, Egeria melted into tears and became a fountain.

Ehecatl In the mythology of the Aztec people of Central America, a god of the winds, an aspect of the snake-bird god QUETZALCOATL. He introduced sexual love to mankind by taking the maiden Mayahuel from the underworld and making love to her on earth. Where this took place, a beautiful tree with two strong branches sprang into life. The sound of the wind in trees was thereafter held by the Aztecs to represent Ehecatl's desire.

Einherjar In Germanic mythology, the slain warriors who dwelt with ODIN in Valhalla. They feasted on a boar which endlessly replenished itself, and drank from a never-empty barrel. Each day, they practised their skill as fighters, awaiting the end of time. Ragnarok, the last battle on the Vigrid plain, will witness their destruction, and that of the gods, in

a cataclysmic struggle between gods and men, giants and monsters. A similar sense of doom hung over the Vikings, and encouraged the crews of the longships to fight without concern for safety. Odin himself was said to inspire the terrible *berserkers*, maddened warriors who rushed naked and frothing at the mouth into the fray.

Ek Chuah In the Maya mythology of Central America, a fierce and violent god of war, distinguished for his one black-rimmed eye. His name means "black war chief". Ek Chuah was also the patron of merchants and, as such, was portrayed carrying a heavy sack of merchandise on his back.

Ekur The name of ENLIL's temple at Nippur, where the assembly of the gods occurred in ancient Mesopotamia. There, the gods decided on important matters and, in response to the threat posed by the chaos-dragon TIAMAT, they elected MARDUK as the divine champion. Before getting down to business the gods always fortified themselves with plenty of food and drink, however.

El Dorado The gilded king of Spanish legend concerning Central and South America. He appears in the sixteenth century, at the time when expeditions were sent in search of silver and gold. It was believed that El Dorado was himself covered in gold powder, and that his realm was a place of gold palaces and gold-paved streets. This garbled account of the Inca kings of Peru encouraged the Spaniards in their pursuit of wealth.

Two motives drove the conquerors of the New World – acquisitiveness and religious zeal. Many of the casualties suffered by the army of Hernando Cortés resulted from soldiers being overloaded with booty. They sank in the swamps surrounding Tenochtitlán, the Atzec capital.

Electra In Greek mythology, the daughter of Agamemnon and Clytemnestra. Her name means "amber". When Agamemnon, King of Mycenae, was murdered on his return from Troy by Clytemnestra and her lover Aegisthus, Electra arranged for ORESTES, her brother, to be sent safely into exile. Later, Orestes returned in order to avenge Agamemnon's death.

Elijah One of the outstanding prophets of the Old Testament. Elijah is chiefly associated with securing the worship of Yahweh against that of other Canaanite gods, and with denouncing idolatory. His battle of faith with BAAL ended in the death of that god's priests. At the end of his life, Elijah ascended bodily to heaven in a chariot of fire. In the New Testament, he appears with Moses at the transfiguration of JESUS.

El-lal A legendary hero of the mythology of the Tehuelche Indians of Patagonia. His father, wishing to eat him, tore him from his mother's womb. However, he was saved by Rat, who gave him refuge in his hole in the earth. El-lal eventually emerged from the hole and made himself ruler of the earth by means of his invention, the bow and arrow. He overcame a race of giant demons, killing the chief giant Goshy-e by turning himself into a gadfly and poisoning the giant's stomach with his sting. Having thus secured mankind's future, El-lal rose to the otherworld on the great wings of a swan.

Elysium In Greek and Roman mythology, the home of the happy and virtuous dead, identified with the Islands of the Blessed. The Champs Elysées in Paris are named after the Elysian Fields.

Emain Macha In Irish mythology, the seat of the kings of Ulster, situated near modern Armagh. The hero CUCHULAINN once circled the fortified town in his chariot, crying out for blood. His battle fury was tamed in a novel manner. A group of naked women from Emain Macha cooled down Cuchulainn in three vats of cold water.

Emer The wife of the Irish hero CUCHULAINN. She was the daughter of Forgall the Wily. Cuchulainn fell in love with the beautiful Emer on sight, but her father opposed the match. To win her hand, Cuchulainn had to undergo training as a warrior in Scotland. Even then, Forgall refused to let Emer marry, and he met his death while trying to deny Cuchulainn his desire. Although the hero got his own way at last, married life was far from easy for Emer, not least because so many women fell for Cuchulainn's charms.

Emma-O In Japanese Buddhism, the god of death, identified with the Chinese Yanwang. Both these gods derived from YAMA, the Hindu god of death, and were imported from India. Emma-O is a merciless judge who rules over Jigoku, the underworld. This realm is divided into eight hells of fire and eight of ice. A magic mirror assists Emma-O in detecting sin and therefore the correct abode of the sinner.

Endo Morito In medieval Japan, a legendary warrior who became a monk. He fell in love with Kesa and swore to kill all her family unless she assisted him in the murder of her husband and agreed to be his wife. Kesa told Endo to steal into her husband's room one night; he did so, cut off the head of the body, then discovered that it was Kesa dressed in her husband's night clothes. In penance for his deed, Endo became a monk and undertook great austerities.

Endymion In Greek mythology, the king of Elis. The moon goddess Selene fell in love with Endymion and bore him fifty daughters. Then, because she could not accept the idea of his death, she made him sleep for ever in a cave, eternally young and handsome. Alternatively, ZEUS, asked by Endymion for eternal youth, offered him a choice of immortality or eternal sleep, and Endymion chose the latter.

Enkidu In Mesopotamian mythology, the rival and friend of GILGAMESH, the semi-divine king of Uruk, an important Sumerian city. Enkidu was made by the goddess Aruru at the request of Gilgamesh's subjects, who were worn out by the king's energy. Because he was a natural man, born in the wild, Enkidu had authority over animals. However, Gilgamesh drew him into civilized living, fought him, and became his bosom friend. They remained loyal companions, wandering in search of adventure for the rest of Enkidu's life. The death of Enkidu set Gilgamesh on his quest for immortality. He travelled the world looking for his own ancestor Utanapishtim.

Epimetheus In Greek mythology, a Titan, the brother of PROMETHEUS and the husband of PANDORA, the first mortal woman. Pandora brought with her as a dowry a jar which it was forbidden to open. However, Epimetheus lifted the jar's lid, thereby letting all its gifts escape, in some versions, releasing all evils. Only Hope remained.

Epona In Celtic mythology, the goddess of horsemen and animals. Her name means "great mare". She is usually shown seated either on a horse, or on a throne with two foals eating from her lap. Grooms made shrines to her in stables, and her worship was widespread in the western provinces of Rome.

Ereshkigal In Mesopotamian mythology, the goddess of the underworld, and the sister of the fertility goddess INANNA. Ereshkigal ruled over *kur-nu-gi-a* (the land of no return). Inanna's descent into this realm of the dead, where she intended to assert her authority, ended in her own death. She was released only through the cunning of ENKI. He secretly revived her, but she was still bound to find someone to take her place. Inanna chose to volunteer her husband, Dumuzi.

Inanna's failure to exert overlordship in *kur-nu-gi-a* forced her to continue sharing power with Ereshkigal, and symbolizes the dualism of good and evil inherent in the Mesopotamian gods. It is our misfortune that this 5,000-year-old myth survives only in a fragmentary form.

Erichthonius In Greek mythology, an early king of Athens, portrayed as a man with legs of serpents or dragons. He was born of sperm dropped on the earth by HEPHAISTOS, when the smith god attempted to rape ATHENA. Athena placed Erichthonius in a basket which she gave to the daughters of Cecrops, the Athenian king, forbidding them to open it. They disobeyed Athena and were so frightened by Erichthonius's appearance that they were driven mad. Erichthonius invented the chariot so that he could conceal his deformed legs while in public. It is not unlikely that the invention myth reflects some improvement in the military capacity of Athens.

As regards the serpent nature of Erichthonius, this must refer to a pre-Greek cult of the mother goddess. The Athenians had originally spoken another language before adopting the Greek tongue. It is also clear that HERA, the wife of ZEUS, is a pre-Greek mother goddess. Cecrops, an early king of Athens, was also a snake man. Reverence for the serpent later became the basis for a law requiring citizens of Athens always to bury dead snakes.

Eros In Greek mythology, the youthful god of love, the equivalent of the Roman Amor (love) or Cupid (desire). Eros means sexual love. He has several birth myths. In some, he is a primeval god, born of Chaos and Gaia (earth); in others, he is the son of APHRODITE and ARES. It is clear that he antedates Aphrodite, so his adoption probably came about through the specialization of her own cult as the goddess of passionate love.

Eros is commonly represented as a winged youth with a bow and arrow. His arrow carries love into the heart of the person it strikes.

Erzulie The goddess of love in the Voodoo pantheon of Haiti. She is an ambivalent goddess, the sower of discord and envy and bringer of good health and prosperity. In her demonic aspect, she causes the people and animals that she possesses to twist themselves into grotesquely distorted shapes. As the benevolent goddess of love, she is lavish in her gifts, and is an opulently dressed and seductively scented figure. Sometimes, as Erzulie Ge-Rouge, she is shown weeping over the shortness of life and the passing of love.

Eshmun A Canaanite diety who suffered emasculation, and possibly death, at the hands of a passionate goddess named Astronoe. The cult of Eshmun has been found at Carthage, the great colony of Tyre in Africa. There, he was the god of healing, a Carthaginian equivalent of the Greek ASCLEPIUS. But it also seems likely that Eshmun was identical with ADONIS, the beloved of APHRODITE. The connection between Eshmun and Adonis would be obvious if Astronoe were discovered to be another name for ASTARTE, the Canaanite mother goddess. In Byblos, the temple of Astarte celebrated the annual death and resurrection of Adonis. His reappearance on earth was marked by the blooming of the red flower of the anemone.

Eshu In the mythology of the Yoruba people of Nigeria, a trickster intermediary between men and the gods. He speaks all languages and so is able to carry messages from the gods to mankind. He also delivers the sacrifices of mankind to the gods. He presides over, and instigates, the play of chance in human life.

Ethlinn In Irish mythology, the daughter of one-eyed Balor, the god of death, and the mother of LUGH. Having been told that his daughter would bear a son who would kill him, Balor imprisoned Ethlinn in a crystal tower so that she might never know a man. Cian, whose magic cow Balor had stolen, gained his revenge by disguising himself as a woman and stealing upon Ethlinn. She bore him three sons, two of whom Balor killed by drowning; the third, Lugh, escaped, and eventually killed Balor.

Etna A volcanic mountain on the east coast of Sicily, whose name is of uncertain origin. The Roman association of HEPHAISTOS, the Greek smith god, with their own Vulcan, led to the myth of Hephaistos's smithy being beneath Mount Etna. Another explanation of its volcanic activity was the imprisonment there of TYPHON. After a titanic struggle, this immortal monster was pinned down by ZEUS, who dropped the island of Sicily on top of him.

Euryclea In Greek mythology, the old nurse of ODYSSEUS, who recognized him on his return home from Troy. When she bathed his feet, an old scar on his leg gave away his identity. It was Euryclea's evidence that Odysseus used to decide on the execution of his wife's serving-women, after the massacre of her suitors. Those who had consorted with the suitors were put to death.

Eurydice In Greek mythology, a dryad and the wife of ORPHEUS. When Atistaeus, the son of Apollo, tried to rape her, she fled, was bitten by a snake and died. Orpheus descended into the realm of HADES to search for her and was promised that he could take her back to life on earth if he refrained from looking back at her while she followed him into the daylight. But Orpheus looked back and consequently lost Eurydice for ever.

Evander In ancient Greece, the original name for PAN or another Arcadian deity associated with him. For some unknown reason, Evander was transferred to Roman mythology as part of the story of AENEAS. Apparently Evander moved to Italy before the Trojan War. Already an old man on the arrival of Aeneas, he befriended the newcomer, and was a firm ally against hostile Italian tribes.

Eve In the Bible, the first woman on earth. The wife of Adam, she was created from one of his ribs. By allowing herself to be tempted by a serpent into handing Adam an apple from the tree of the knowledge of good and evil, she led Adam to commit the original sin of disobedience to Yahweh's command. Yahweh then banished Adam and Eve from the earthly paradise, the Garden of Eden.

Excalibur In Celtic legend, the magic sword which ARTHUR alone could pull from a stone. By accomplishing this feat, he revealed that he was the predestined King of Britain. When Arthur was mortally wounded, he commanded Sir Belevere to cast Excalibur into the sea, or a lake. When the knight did so at last, a hand rose from the water, grasped the sword and disappeared. Shortly afterward, three fairies took Arthur away in a boat to Avalon.

F

Fafnir In Germanic mythology, the dragon son of the farmer-magician Hredimar. When LOKI killed Fafnir's brother, Otter, he was made to fill the skin of the deceased with red gold in compensation. But a curse was placed on this treasure, with the result that Fafnir had to transform himself into a dragon to protect it. The hero Sigurd gained possession of the gold by killing Fafnir.

Faran A hero in the mythology of the Songhai people of West Africa. Faran owned a pond filled with rice plants, but each night the water spirit Zin-Kibaru played his guitar, persuading the fish to eat the rice. Faran decided that the only way to solve the problem was to fight the spirit. During the battle, both the spirit and the hero used magic to outwit each other. However, Faran's magic proved the stronger and Zin-Kibaru was conquered. He left all his magical instruments and spirit followers to Faran.

Farbauti In Germanic mythology, the giant who was the father of the trickster god LOKI. His mother was the giantess Laufey.

Faunus An Italian god of the countryside whom the Romans identified with the Greek PAN. Faunus was variously the grandson of SATURN and the descendant of MARS. He was revered by the Romans as a god of prophecy.

Faust In late European legend, the learned German magician Dr John Faustus, who sold his soul to SATAN. Although the story became famous in the sixteenth century, it derived from much earlier folklore. Faust made a pact with Satan, usually represented as Mephistopheles, by selling his soul in exchange for youth, wisdom and magical powers. One of the great beauties whom Faust was keen to meet was HELEN, the cause of the Trojan War.

Faustulus In Roman mythology, the royal herdsman who found the abandoned babies, ROMULUS and Remus, feeding on the milk of a she-wolf. He secretly raised the twin brothers, who became the founders of Rome.

Fengbo The Chinese god of the winds. He is usually portrayed as an old man with a beard, a cloak, and a cap. In his hands he holds a sack that contains the winds. Fengbo is in fact a high official of the celestial Ministry of Thunder, and follows the orders of Leigong (thunder god). Fengbo's own name means Wind Earl. Sometimes, he is replaced by his wife Feng Bobo.

Fenrir In Germanic mythology, a giant wolf, the offspring of LOKI, who was bound by the gods and will remain so until the end of the world. Then, at Ragnarok, Fenrir will swallow the sun and bite the moon, before dying in the general destruction.

Fides In Roman mythology, the goddess of honesty and public faith whose cult was instituted by Numa, the second king of Rome. Fides was portrayed as a white-clothed maiden, riding in a chariot. Her right hand is held open to symbolize both her candour and her good faith.

Fingal Another name for the Irish sage and warrior Finn Mac Cool, or Fionn Mac Cumhail. Fionn means "fair" and Fingal, "fair foreigner".

Finn Or Fionn Mac Cumhail. The legendary Irish hero, son of the captain of the Fianna, the royal bodyguard of the high kings of Ireland. Finn chose to study as a magician under a druid named Finegas. When the druid caught Fintan (the salmon of knowledge), he asked Finn to cook the fish for him. Finn burned his thumb on the flesh of the fish, sucked it, and so he, rather than Finegas, obtained wisdom. Later, Finn saved the palace of the high king from demonic attack and was made captain of the Fianna, since his father had already died.

The remainder of Finn's life comprised an heroic series of adventures, which encompassed love, fighting and sorcery. It was long believed that Finn was not dead but sleeping in a cave, ready to come to the aid of Ireland in the hour of her greatest need. This is an ancient Celtic idea that finds an echo in the "undeath" of ARTHUR, the British king.

Fintan In Irish mythology, the salmon of knowledge, which Finn Mac Cool tasted accidentally. He burnt his thumb on the flesh of the fish as he turned it on a spit. Once he sucked the thumb he became a sage. The ultimate source of wisdom were magic hazelnuts, which Fintan was supposed to have eaten.

Flora In Roman mythology, the goddess of flowering or blossoming plants. Flora touched JUNO with a herb so that the estranged wife of JUPITER could subsequently conceive the war god MARS.

Fomorii In Irish mythology, a misshapen and violent people who originally controlled the country. They were ruled over by the god of death, Balor, and probably lived beneath the sea. They were associated with darkness and the forces of evil, and were the enemies of the Tuatha De Danaan, the people of the mother goddess Dana. When Bres, a prince of the Fomorii, raised a host against the Tuatha De Danaan, he was defeated at the second battle of Magh Tuireadh.

Fortuna The Roman equivalent of the Greek goddess Tyche (luck). An ancient Italian goddess, originally of increase and fertility, Fortuna gradually came to be associated in Rome with the play of chance. That she showed no respect for class in her distribution of fortune is evident in her festival, held each June. Fortuna's festival was one of the very few occasions on which slaves could freely take part in the city's religious ceremonies.

During the Middle Ages in Europe, the idea of Fortune's Wheel became a very powerful legend. In Malory's *Morte d'Arthur*, published by Caxton in 1485, there is a graphic description of this wheel in a dream which visited ARTHUR, just before the fateful battle against Modred. The king dreamed that he sat on a chair tied fast to a wheel, beneath which was "a hideous deep black water, and therein were all manner of serpents, and worms, and wild beasts, foul and horrible."

Freya In Germanic mythology, a Vanir goddess of youth and sexual love. She was the sister of FREY and wife of Odur, the sun god. Her famous belt or necklace, called a *brisling*, was given to her by the dwarfs who made it in return for her making love to them.

Freya was sexually promiscuous with the gods, though she was supposed to have wept tears of amber and gold when Odur deserted her. She was capable of flying in the form of a falcon,

although her chariot was drawn by cats. Her day of worship, named after her, was Friday. After the reconciliation between the Aesir and the Vanir families of the gods, Freya became assimilated with FRIGG, the wife of ODIN.

Fugen-bosatsu In Japanese Buddhism, the bodhisattva (BUDDHA-to-be) Samantabhadra, who will be the last Buddha. He is commonly represented as a young man, seated on a white elephant with six tusks and holding a lotus flower. Fugen-bosatsu was of particular appeal to women in medieval Japan. In the thirteenth century, he appeared to a monk as a courtesan, thereby revealing that Buddhahood was potential in all human beings. Today, however, the bodhisattva is little worshipped.

Fuji Hime In Shinto legend, an immortal princess who lives on Fujiyama, the sacred mountain of Japan. She is able to make trees blossom and is traditionally represented with a sprig of wisteria in her hand. The troubles of medieval Japan were brought about by a revival of Shinto, the indigenous faith. Patriotic sects arose and taught that Japan was the chief of all nations, the centre of the world, and that Mount Fuji was the abode of Kunitokotachi, the supreme deity. Fuji Hime therefore became the guardian of the sacred mountain.

Fujiyama In Japanese mythology, the mountain where, according to patriotic sects of the sixteenth and seventeenth centuries, the supreme god Kunitokotachi lived. The sacred spirit of the mountain guarded the nation, and the mountain could be climbed only by someone who had undergone ritual purification. According to Shinto legend, Fujiyama is the abode of the immortal princess Fuji Hime.

Furies See ERINYES.

Futen In Japanese Buddhism, the god of the winds, who derived from the Hindu god of the winds, Vayu. He is represented as an old man with a flowing beard, carrying a banner which is unfurled by the winds.

Fuxi In the Chinese flood myth, the brother of NUWA. Together, they survived the deluge in a gourd provided by a grateful thunder god. Later on, their marriage repeopled the earth.

G

Gabriel An archangel who appears in the Bible as the messenger of Yahweh. He visits DANIEL twice, once to announce the return of the Hebrews from captivity in Babylon and once to explain the diversity of nations. Later, he presents himself to Mary to announce that she has conceived JESUS by the Holy Ghost. He is also the trumpeter who will sound the Last Judgement. In Islamic tradition, Gabriel (or Jibril) dictated the heavenly copy of the Koran to Muhammad.

Ga-gorib In the legends of the Hottentot people of southwestern Africa, a monster whose name means "thrower down". His habit was to sit at the edge of a great pit and invite passers-by to hurl stones at him. The stones always rebounded, killing whoever threw them and toppling the body into the pit. Ga-gorib was eventually destroyed by the hero HEITSI-EIBIB, who waited to throw his stone until the monster's gaze was averted, then struck him under the ear and tumbled him into the pit.

Gaia In Greek mythology, mother earth, the first-born child of Chaos. She was the mother of Ouranos (sky) and Pontus (sea). From her union with Ouranos, Gaia bore the first generation of the gods. These were the Titans, and included KRONOS and Rhea, the parents of ZEUS. She also gave birth to the CYCLOPES and the giants.

While Ouranos was mating with Gaia, Kronos dismembered him with a sickle which Gaia, infuriated with the passionate tyranny of her mate, had given him. Kronos thus eternally separated the sky from the earth. From the spilled semen and blood of Ouranos, Gaia gave birth to the ERINYRES (Furies), the nymphs, and further giants. According to some versions of the myth, Ouranos's genitals fell into the sea, where they engendered the love goddess APHRODITE, who rose from the foam.

When Kronos turned out to be as tyrannous as Ouranos, swallowing all his children, Gaia helped Rhea to hide his son Zeus on the island of Crete. Later, Zeus obliged Kronos to regurgitate his brothers and sisters, before imprisoning him with the other Titans in Tartarus.

The second generation of the gods, the Olympians, then ruled the world together. However, Gaia was not entirely pleased with this arrangement and she almost upset the new order by giving birth to the monster TYPHON. Only after a hard-fought struggle was Zeus able to win. This last conflict in Greek mythology strongly recalls the contest of the Hittite weather god TARU with the dragon Illuyankas. Both Zeus and Taru temporarily lost parts of their bodies.

Galahad An outstanding knight of the legendary Round Table, and the son of Sir Lancelot and Elaine. When Lancelot refused to marry Elaine, she used magic and assumed the form of Guinevere, the wife of ARTHUR, whom Lancelot loved. Although the son of a reluctant father, Sir Galahad was the purest and noblest knight in Christendom. He alone was deemed worthy enough to see the Holy Grail.

When Galahad sat in the Round Table's empty chair, which was reserved for whoever would successfully seek the Holy Grail, he remained unharmed, whereas all those who had previously dared to sit there had been swallowed up. Galahad therefore set out in quest of the Grail. After many adventures, he found it, then died and went to heaven, accompanied by a multitude of angels.

Galatea In Greek mythology, a sea nymph who lived off the island of Sicily and was the daughter of the sea god Nereus and Doris. She loved the beautiful youth Acis, the son of PAN and a river nymph, but was loved by the monstrous Polyphemus, who was one of the one-eyed CYCLOPES.

To remove his rival, Polyphemus killed Acis by crushing him under a huge rock. The blood of Acis was turned by the gods, or by Galatea herself, into the river that bears his name. However, one version of the legend does not include Acis, but instead has Galatea accept the suit of Polyphemus, who impresses her with his singing and piping.

Ganga In Hindu mythology, the name of the goddess of the Ganges, a sacred river. It is believed to spring from the toe of VISHNU. The river was brought down to earth by the prayers of the sage Bhagirathi, who used its waters to wash away the ashes of the dead. Because Ganga was unhappy to leave heaven, the river goddess threatened to cause a great flood which would have drowned all mankind.

To prevent this catastrophe from happening, SHIVA allowed the Ganges to flow first through his hair. This slowed it down and split it into seven quiet tributaries. As a result, Shiva gained the title of Ganga-dhara, which means "the upholder of the Ganges".

Ganymede In Greek mythology, the son of Tros, the founder of Troy. Ganymede was a beautiful youth whom ZEUS, disguised as an eagle, seduced and carried back to Olympus. There, to HERA's great anger, he remained Zeus's lover and became cup-bearer to the gods. To compensate Tros for the loss of his son, Zeus sent the messenger god HERMES to him with a gift of two immortal mares.

Gargantua The medieval European giant about whom François Rabelais (1483–1553) wove a legendary cycle of adventures. The name means "gullet" and refers to the inordinate appetite of the giant. His son was named Pantagruel (all-thirsty). MERLIN is credited with the creation of Gargantua, who easily dealt with the monster LEVIATHAN on one of his voyages of discovery.

Garm In Germanic mythology, the fierce hound chained in Gnipahellir, the cave at the entrance to the underworld. Garm is a parallel of the Greek Cerberus. Ragnarok will see him break loose and kill, and be killed by, the war god Tyr.

Garuda In Hindu mythology, a fabulous creature, half-man and half-bird, on which VISHNU flies. At his birth, Garuda was so brilliant that he was confused with the god of fire, AGNI. He is the king of all birds and the arch-enemy of the serpents. In one myth, he steals AMRITA, the water of life, which is recovered by INDRA only after a fierce contest in which Garuda smashes Indra's thunderbolt. A similar story is told about the Zu bird of Mesopotamian myth. Either the Zu bird or Imdugud, the lion-headed storm bird, stole the tablets of destiny from ENLIL. They were recovered by his son, the war god NINURTA.

Gauna In the mythology of the Bushmen of southwestern Africa, the chief of the spirits of the dead and the arch-enemy of the creator god KAANG. Less powerful than Kaang, Gauna, also called Gawa or Gawama, nevertheless eternally seeks to overcome him and to bring discord to the human world. Communal rites, especially a dance of exorcism, are performed to ward him off.

Gayomart In ancient Iranian mythology, the primeval man who, after existing for 3,000 years as a spirit, was created by AHURA MAZDAH. He was made mortal in the second great epoch of time, along with the primeval bull Geush Urvan. A cultural hero, he brought the arts of civilization into the world. From his seed grew a plant which produced the first human couple, Mashya and Mashyoi.

In the third great epoch, men suffered under the tyranny of the three-headed dragon Azhi Dahaka. Gayomart was eventually slain by AHRIMAN, the force of evil, at the prompting of the whore, Jeh. After Gayomart's death Mashya and Mashyoi accepted Ahriman's rule, for which sin they were condemned to exist in hell throughout eternity. Gayomart means "dying life".

Geb In Egyptian mythology, the earth god, the brother and husband of the sky goddess NUT and, like Nut, the offspring of Shu (air) and Tefnut (moisture). He is shown as a bearded man with a goose on his head, or as a goose. Geb and Nut gave birth to OSIRIS, ISIS, Nephthys and SETH. In some myths, the sun god RE, angry at Geb and Nut's marriage, separated them, thus forcing apart the earth and sky.

As an earth god, Geb was a provider of crops and a healer. But he also had an ominous aspect: it was feared that he might imprison the dead within him and thus keep them from life in the afterworld. His laughter, more probably his wailing for Nut, was believed to cause earthquakes. Geb was identified by the ancient Greeks with KRONOS.

Gefjon In Germanic mythology, a fertility goddess connected with the plough. She was a Vanir deity, but after the Vanir and Aesir gods combined forces, Gefjon married one of ODIN's sons. She bore him four giant sons, whom she turned into oxen to plough a vast tract of land. The land was then pushed out to sea and became the island of

Zeeland. This myth was connected with the custom in northern Europe of ploughing a token strip of land at the beginning of spring, before the fields were sown, to ensure fertility. Gefjon was one of Frigg's handmaidens and, like Frigg, knew all events in the present and future but was unable to affect them.

Genius In Roman mythology, a guardian spirit, equivalent to the Greek *daimon*, that presides over the birth of a person and controls his character and destiny. It means "the begetter". Reference is made to dual genii, one good, one evil. Every place, and indeed everything in nature, had its own genius or genii.

Gerda In Germanic mythology, a giantess, described in some versions as the most beautiful woman in the world. After resisting FREY's suit for a long time, despite his lavishing gifts on her, Gerda at last married him, having succumbed to the threats of his servant. It is thought that Gerda's name derives from the word for field.

In the myth of Frey's courtship, she is described as a glittering giantess, who filled the sky and the sea with bright light. Presumably, this refers to an ice-covered piece of ground, motionless beneath its weight of frozen snow. Once the sun had risen – Frey controlled both the rain and the sun – Gerda warmed up and her reluctance diminished. Accepting the embrace of Frey, Gerda became the goddess of the spring planting, a role she shared with Gefjon, ODIN's daughter-in-law.

Geryon In Greek mythology, a Spanish king with three heads and three bodies, joined at the waist. He owned a large herd of cattle, which was protected by a two-headed dog named Orthus, the offspring of the monster TYPHON. For his tenth labour, HERACLES had to steal the herd and take it to Greece, a task which he carried out after killing both Orthus and Geryon.

Geush Urvan In ancient Iranian mythology, the primeval bull, from whose corpse all kinds of plants and animals emerged. After living for 3,000 years, the bull was slain by MITHRA, according to most versions of the story, and went to heaven.

Giants Enormous men who occur throughout the mythologies of the world. The ancient Greeks called the giants "earth-born" because they were the offspring of Gaia, mother earth. They were usually of human shape, but had serpents' tails attached to their bodies. They were engendered by the blood of Ouranos, which fell on Gaia when he was emasculated with a sickle by his son KRONOS.

When ZEUS imprisoned Kronos and the other Titans in Tartarus, Gaia stirred up the giants to attack the gods who lived on Mount Olympus. In the great war that followed, Zeus was helped by HERACLES, POSEIDON and ATHENA. The hero Heracles was particularly valuable as an ally because the giants could not be killed by immortals. The killing of giants, on the other hand, proved no problem for Germanic gods such as ODIN and THOR – at least, not at first. Ragnarok, the battle at the end of time, is to be the revenge of the giants, although they are then destined to die in the final destruction, with the gods themselves.

Ginnungagap In Germanic mythology, the primeval void where the giant Ymir, the first of all living beings, was born. It lay between Muspellheim (the land of the fire giants), and Niflheim (the land of mist). After ODIN, and his two brothers Vili and Ve, slew Ymir and nearly all the other frost giants, they threw Ymir's body into the middle of Ginnungagap. Then, they used its various parts to create the world. From Ymir's skull, for instance, they made the sky.

Glaucus In Greek mythology, there are several figures who bear this name. One was a Lycian hero who fought against the Greeks during the Trojan War. Another, the son of Sisyphus, the founder of Corinth, was eaten alive by his own horses after he lost a chariot-race. The third Glaucus was a sea deity, who became immortal by eating a fish that swam near a magic herb. But the price he paid was to have the tail and fins of a fish.

The final Glaucus was the son of MINOS, King of Crete. His myth also concerns immortality. As a boy, Glaucus went missing in the palace of Minos at Knossos. When he was found drowned in a storage jar of honey, Minos insisted that his discoverer be shut in the store room with him.

While imprisoned, the unfortunate man noticed a snake approaching the body of Glaucus, and killed it. To his surprise, a second snake crept along to its dead mate with a herb in its mouth which it laid on the lifeless scales. Slowly, the snake revived and, seeing this miracle, the man placed the herb on Glaucus with equal success.

Godiva In English legend, the wife of Leofric, the eleventh-century earl of Mercia. When Godiva objected to the heavy taxation which Leofric had imposed on the people of Coventry, he agreed to rescind it if she would ride naked on a horse through the town's streets at midday. Godiva accepted the challenge, and everyone remained indoors or averted their gaze, except for a tailor, who was struck blind; he became known as "Peeping Tom".

Gog and Magog In British legend, two giants who were captured by the hero Brut and his companion Corineus. They were taken as slaves in chains to London. Occasionally, the two giants are combined into a single figure, Gogmagog, whose form can be seen today cut into the chalk hills near Cambridge.

Goga An old woman whom the Massim people of Papua believe was the original owner of fire. She was both a rain goddess and a fire goddess. When the first men stole a firebrand from her hearth, Goga sent a downpour to earth, but luckily a snake preserved the flame on its tail.

Goibhniu In Irish mythology, the smith who forged the weapons by which the Tuatha De Danaan overcame the Fomorii. Goibhniu slew Ruadan, a Fomorii spy, and was healed of the wounds he received in the fight by Dian-Cecht, the god of medicine.

Golden Fleece In the mythology of Greece, the magic fleece of the golden-winged ram who carried Phryxius and Helle in flight from their father, Athamas, the king of Boeotia. Athamas had vowed to kill Phryxius for allegedly bringing famine to the land. (In other versions, Phryxius was threatened by the jealous Ino, who was in love with him.) The ram flew to Colchis, but Helle fell into the sea on the way, at the place since known as the Hellespont or the Dardanelles.

At Colchis, Phryxius was welcomed by King Aeta; he then sacrificed the ram to ZEUS and hung the fleece in the grove of ARES. The ram was placed in the heavens as the constellation Aries. JASON and the Argonauts sailed from Greece in search of the fleece and, with the aid of Aeta's daughter, Medea, who fell in love with Jason, succeeded in recovering the fleece and bringing it back to Greece.

Golem An invented person, prominent in Jewish legends of the Middle Ages. One version of the story, set in Prague, makes Golem a defender of the Jews.

Gora-Daileng The Caroline Islanders of Micronesia believe that Gora-Daileng punishes the wicked after death. After burning them in a terribly hot furnace, he casts them into an endless river, from which none can return.

Gordian Knot In Greek and Roman mythology, the knot tied by the peasant Gordius, the father of MIDAS. The Phrygians hailed Gordius as a king, having been told by an oracle that the king who would save them would arrive in an ox cart. In gratitude, Gordius dedicated his cart to ZEUS and tied it to the yoke of the oxen with a knot so complex and so strong that no one was able to untie it. The legend grew that he who succeeded in untying the knot should rule over all Asia. Alexander the Great fulfilled the prophecy by cutting the knot with a sword.

Gorgons In Greek mythology, three monstrous sisters who had wings, sharp claws, and snakes for hair. Euryale and Stheno were immortal and could not die; Medusa, who was mortal, had her head cut off by the hero PERSEUS. All three, but especially Medusa, were so hideous that a mere glance from one of them could turn a person into stone.

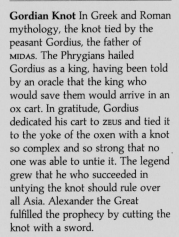

Grail One of the most widespread legends of medieval Christian Europe. The Sangreal, or Grail, was the chalice, cup or dish from which JESUS drank at the Last Supper. Its origin is sometimes said to be the emerald which SATAN dropped on his fall from heaven and which was later fashioned into a chalice.

Joseph of Arimathea used the Grail to gather some blood from Jesus' pierced side at the Crucifixion. Later, he brought it to England, where it was lost. The search for the Grail preoccupied the knights of the Round Table. But ARTHUR never saw it; only Sir Galahad, the son of Sir Lancelot, was allowed to find the Grail and ascend to heaven.

The custodian of the Grail was the Fisher King, who lay wounded and immobile, neither living nor dead. This undead god is clearly connected to Celtic mythology, with its wonderful cauldrons of rejuvenation.

Grendel In Anglo-Saxon legend, the sea monster and marauder of the borderlands against whom, at the behest of the Danish King Hrothgar, Beowulf prevailed in a wrestling match. Beowulf tore off one of Grendel's arms and later, when he found him on his death bed, cut off his head. Grendel's mother, also a monster, lived with Grendel under the North Sea. She, too, was slain by Beowulf.

Guecufu In the mythology of the Araucanian Indians of Chile, the spirit of evil. Guecufu was the eternal enemy of the supreme god GUINECHEN, and sent the deluge which flooded the earth. His allies, the lesser demons, bring earthquakes and assume animal forms to plague the earth, causing the destruction of crops by insects and disease, and eating the fish of the rivers.

Guinevere The legendary wife of ARTHUR, King of Britain. Arthur married Guinevere against the advice of the sage and magician MERLIN. Guinevere's adulterous love for Sir Lancelot destroyed the courtly values of the Round Table, weakening its unity.

However, according to Malory in his *Morte d'Arthur*, the collapse of the kingdom was brought about by a civil war between Arthur and his nephew Modred, rather than by Guinevere's indifidelity. Guinevere, whose name means "white ghost", passed her last days in a convent.

Gum Girl A character, also called Gum Doll or Gum Baby, who appears in the ANANSI legends of West Africa. The owner of a field whose crops were being stolen put the Gum Girl, an effigy covered in sticky gum, in the field in the hope of trapping the thief.

When Anansi came to the field he told the Gum Girl that he would kick her if she did not tell him who she was. When she remained silent, he kicked her, and his foot stuck to her. He then vowed to punch her if she did not release his foot, with the result that his hand also stuck to her. The farmer then appeared and gave Anansi a beating. The story of Gum Girl appears in several variants in many parts of the world. She is probably best known as the Tar Baby in the book *Uncle Remus*, by Joel Chandler Harris.

Gungnir The magic spear of ODIN, the one-eyed god of battle in Germanic mythology. It was forged by dwarfs and never missed the mark. Odin was called both the god of the spear and the hanged — the two ways in which men were sacrificed to him.

Gunnodoyak In the mythology of the Iroquois Indians of North America, the youthful assistant of the thunder spirit HINUN. He was a mortal whom Hinun took up to the skies. Here Hinun instructed him, gave him arms, and sent him back to earth to do battle against the serpent of the Great Lakes, which devoured mankind.

Gunnodoyak was unable to prevent the snake from swallowing him, but Hinun eventually killed it and, having resurrected Gunnodoyak, took him back to heaven. Afterward, the Great Lakes were at last safe from the snake's threat.

Gwydion A Welsh priest-king and magician, the son of Don the Enchanter. He was skilled in poetry and practised the arts of prophecy and divination.

Gwynn In Celtic mythology, a god of the underworld, the son of Nudd. He hunted men's souls and brought them to Annwn, the land of the dead, often with the aid of an owl, with whom he was traditionally represented. In later versions, he left the underworld to become chief of the Tylwyth Teg (Welsh fairies) and the Ellyllon (Welsh elves).

H

Hachiman In the Shinto mythology of Japan, a god of war who was also identified with the Buddhist faith. Although Hachiman served as a god of agriculture and protector of children, his chief role was acting as the guardian of the nation.

Hadad The Canaanite thunder god, the equivalent of the Mesopotamian Adad. He is sometimes called Ramman (thunder), a name recorded in the Old Testament as Rimmon. He appears to have been a dying-and-rising deity.

Hafaza In Islamic mythology, protective angels who guard people against the *djinn* (fallen angels, or devils). Every individual has four *hafaza*, two to watch over him during the day, two during the night. They keep a constant record of his good and evil actions. A person is most at risk at twilight and at dawn, when the *djinn* seek to establish their influence during the angels' changing of the guard.

Hahgwehdiyu In the mythology of the Iroquois Indians of North America, the creator god of goodness and light, the opposite of his brother Hahgwehdaetgah, the creator of evil. Hahgwehdiyu created the world by making his outstretched palm the sky, the head of his dead mother, Ataensic, the sun, and her breasts the moon and stars. By making her body the earth, he turned her from a sky goddess into an earth mother. To counter this creation, Hahgwehdaetgah sent hurricanes and earthquakes and created darkness; but he was defeated in a duel with his brother and banished to the underworld.

Hai-uri In the mythology of the Hottentots, a terrifying monster with one arm, one leg and one side. Despite these disabilities, Hai-uri can chase human beings with amazing agility, bounding over bushes in his pursuit. He is helped in his trouble-making by being only semi-visible.

Halirrhothius In Greek mythology, the son of POSEIDON and the nymph Euryte. He was murdered in Athens by ARES for raping the war god's daughter Alcippe. Ares was tried by POSEIDON in the court at Areopagus (the Hill of Ares) and was acquitted of his crime.

Ham In the Old Testament, the second son of NOAH, the others being Shem and Japheth. Along with his wife, brothers and sisters-in-law, he took refuge from the flood in Noah's ark. After the deluge subsided, Noah planted a vineyard and took to drink. One day, he cursed Ham for looking at his nakedness, whereas Shem and Japheth had walked backward to avoid offending him. Noah therefore promised that Yahweh would enlarge Japheth's stock and dwell in the tents of Shem, but that Canaan, Ham's son, should be their servant. Noah lived another 350 years after the flood, making him 950 years old when he died.

Hannahanna The mother goddess in the mythology of the Hittite people of Asia Minor. When TELIPINU, the god of agriculture, withdrew from the care of the world, thus bringing disease and famine to the land, Hannahanna sent a bee to sting him into action. The sting, however, merely enraged Telipinu and provoked him to flood the land. Telipinu was later restored to his duties by the healing powers of Kamrusepas, goddess of spells.

Hantu Pemburu In Malayan legend, the demon hunter who causes havoc on jungle tracks. Hantu Pemburu endlessly roams in search of a certain deer that he promised to bring home to his wife. The slaughtered animals he leaves behind him reflect his frustration at a hopeless quest.

Han Xiangzi One of the eight immortals of Daoism, the indigenous faith of China. He is usually portrayed playing a flute or floating on a log. One day, he attained immortality by falling from a peach tree, the symbol of eternal life. Daoist adepts were preoccupied with the pursuit of immortality and many attempts were made to produce an elixir of life.

Another immortal, Han Zhongli, is believed to have escaped death by taking such a draught. He is depicted as an old man without a care in the world.

Haoma In ancient Iranian mythology, the plant from which an intoxicating drink was brewed. *Haoma* is the equivalent of soma, the drink of the Hindu gods and brahmins and the elixir of life. The draught made from *haoma* was believed to render whoever drank it immune from disease and infection, and hence immortal. According to Iranian belief, AHURA MAZDAH allowed certain healing herbs, including *haoma*, to grow next to a sacred tree.

Haoma may take the form of a god, who is the son of Ahura Mazdah, the principle of good.

Hapi In ancient Egypt there were two gods who bore this name. One, a son of HORUS, was a mummified figure who protected the lungs of the dead.

The other deity called Hapi was the river god who sent the annual flooding of the Nile, and was hence a god of agriculture and prosperity. Sometimes identified with the Nile itself, he was really the personification only of the floods, and was therefore represented as either "little Hapi" or "big Hapi".

A well-fed god, with large breasts and a protruding paunch, Hapi was commonly represented with aquatic plants on his head. He lived in a cavern situated near the first cataract of the River Nile and presided over a retinue of crocodile gods and frog goddesses.

Hari-Hara A composite deity who drew together two of the greatest Hindu gods, VISHNU (Hari) and SHIVA (Hara). His name means "grower-remover": Hari denotes creation and growth, Hara destruction and death. Hari-Hara, whose right side is Shiva and whose left side is Vishnu, thus symbolizes the duality of the gods, who contain within themselves the opposing qualities of both light and darkness, good and evil.

In one myth, Shiva and Vishnu joined forces to counter the challenge to their ascendancy from the demon Guha. Having failed to overcome him individually, they were victorious when united as Hari-Hara. The composite deity was particularly revered in Cambodia, where the king was believed to be Vishnu incarnate.

Harimau Kramet The ghostly tigers of Malayan legend. They sprang from two domesticated cats belonging to a princess of Malacca. The reason for their savagery may be the cold-blooded character of their mistress, who was so cruel that she pricked her husband to death with a needle.

Harpies In Greek mythology, predatory monsters, the daughters of the sea god Thaumas and a sea nymph. Each had a vulture's body, wings and claws, and a woman's head. Insatiably hungry, they swooped down to snatch food from tables, fouling any scraps which remained with the stench of their breath, and were hence bringers of starvation and death. Their name means "snatchers".

Haumea The mysterious fertility goddess of Hawaiian mythology. Commonly identified with the mother goddess PAPA, Haumea was continually reborn and therefore able to bear children by her own offspring and their descendants. She was also associated with sacred fruit trees, which produced fruit at her command. Her magic stick populated the waters surrounding the Hawaiian islands with fish.

Hebe In Greek mythology, the goddess of youth and cup-bearer to the gods. She was the daughter of ZEUS and HERA and the wife of HERACLES, to whom she was given by Zeus when he was brought to Olympus as an immortal after completing his tremendous labours. Hebe is sometimes called Ganymeda, after Ganymede, with whom Zeus fell in love and who replaced Hebe as cup-bearer to the gods. Hebe means "youth".

Hector The greatest of the Trojan warriors who fought against the Greeks during the legendary Trojan War. He was the son of PRIAM and Hecuba, the king and queen of Troy, and the husband of Andromache. For slaying the youth Patroclus, the lover of ACHILLES, he was himself slain by the hero. Afterward, the body of Hector was dragged around the walls of Troy, behind the chariot of Achilles. Apollo had helped Hector in his duel with Achilles, but then ATHENA intervened and the outcome was a foregone conclusion. However, as the god of prophecy, Apollo gave the dying Hector the satisfaction of telling Achilles of his own imminent death.

Hecuba In Greek mythology, the second wife of PRIAM, King of Troy. Hecuba was the mother of, among others, Paris, Hector and CASSANDRA. She exposed her eldest son Paris at birth, having dreamed that he would bring harm to Troy. He was rescued and, as a young man, he abducted HELEN, thus causing the Trojan War. To save her youngest son Polydorus from the Greek attack, Hecuba sent him to Polymnestor, the king of Thrace.

After the defeat of the Trojans, Hecuba was taken captive by the Greeks and given into the charge of ODYSSEUS. When Odysseus visited Thrace, Hecuba learned that Polymnestor had murdered Polydorus. She therefore tricked the king into meeting her in a secret place, then tore out his eyes and murdered his children.

Hel In Germanic mythology, the goddess of death and ruler of Helheim (the underworld) and Niflheim (the land of mist). Hel was thrown into these cold regions by ODIN, who decreed that she would rule over those men who died of sickness or old age. She was the daughter of LOKI and the giantess Angurbodi, and the sister of the wolf Fenrir and the serpent Jormungandr.

Helheim In Germanic mythology, the underworld region ruled by Hel, from her palace Sleetcold. It is one of the worlds into which the branches of YGGDRASIL reach. Because LOKI would not weep for BALDER, the unfortunate deity was confined to Helheim after being killed by a spear made of mistletoe.

Helios In Greek mythology, the sun god, son of the Titan Hyperion, and Phoebus (shining).

Helios left his palace in the east in the morning and crossed the sky in a golden chariot drawn by four horses; he rested in his western palace in the evening and then sailed back to the east, via the river Oceanus, at night. His chief cult was at Rhodes, the island he was given by ZEUS in compensation for having been forgotten when the universe was shared out.

The one myth in which Helios plays a critical role is that of the war between the giants and the gods. By obeying Zeus's order to stay out of the sky, Helios prevented the earth goddess Gaia from growing a herb that would have made the giants immortal. As it was, they were vulnerable to heroes, like HERACLES.

Herakhty An ancient Egyptian god whose name means "Horus of the Horizon". When Horus was identified with the sun god RE, the name became Re-Herakhty. In this latter form, the deity appears as a man with the solar disc and a cobra. However, this Horus is an older solar deity and not HORUS, the son of OSIRIS. Herakhty represents the sun when rising and setting.

According to legend, when Tuthmosis IV (1425–1412 BC) was a prince, Re-Herakhty promised him that he would become pharaoh if he cleared away the sand that was submerging the Great Sphinx at Giza. The Sphinx was both the protector of the pyramids and the scourge of the enemies of Re.

Hercules The Roman version of the Greek hero HERACLES. His was probably the first foreign cult to be formally established in Rome, and his entire mythology was taken over by the Romans. Ritual was in the hands of a body of public slaves, and neither women nor dogs were allowed in his temple.

Hermaphroditos In Greek mythology, the son of HERMES and APHRODITE (hence his name). He was brought up in Phrygia. Later, in Caria, he spurned the love of Salmakis, a nymph who desired never to be separated from him. When Hermaphroditos swam in her pool, she merged with him physically and produced a being with both male and female characteristics, hence the word "hermaphrodite". Hermaphroditos was thus unlike his Phrygian fellow countryman ATTIS, who lost his sexuality by self-castration.

Hermodr In Germanic mythology, the messenger of the gods, and a son of ODIN. He was equivalent to the Greek HERMES, and, like Hermes, he carried the souls of the dead to the underworld. Odin sent him to recover BALDER from the underworld realm of Hel. To complete the journey as quickly as possible, Hermodr rode Sleipnir, his father's eight-legged horse.

Hero In Greek mythology, the lovers Hero and Leander lived across the Hellespont from each other. Because Hero was a priestess of APHRODITE, she was barred from marriage. So each night, Leander swam the Hellespont to be with her secretly. One stormy night, however, the winds blew out the torch that Hero used to guide Leander across the straits, and he drowned. When Hero saw his body on the shore, she committed suicide by jumping from a tower.

Herod In the New Testament, the wicked king of Palestine at the time of JESUS' birth. He sent the Magi to Bethlehem to find the infant Jesus so that he might slay him. He then ordered that all infants in Bethlehem under the age of two be slain. However, warned of the massacre of the innocents by an angel, Joseph fled with Jesus and Mary into Egypt before the king's murderous soldiers arrived in Bethlehem.

The tyrannous character of Herod is more clearly drawn in the apocryphal gospels than in the New Testament. His fate after death is graphically described in The Martyrdom of Matthew. The saint says, "But tell me, where is that ungodly Herod? He dwells in hell, where an unquenchable fire is prepared for him, as well as unending misery, boiling mire, and an unsleeping worm, because of the 3,000 children he killed."

Heru-pa-khret In Egyptian mythology, a manifestation, or aspect, of HORUS, the son of OSIRIS, as a child. He is usually shown being suckled by his mother ISIS, or sucking his own finger.

He is identified with RE, who emerged every morning as a child from the waters surrounding the earth. His equivalent in Greek mythology is Harpocrates.

Hesperides In Greek mythology, nymphs of the most westerly limits of the world, the daughters of Atlas and Hesperis, who personified the clouds made golden by the setting sun. They lived in a paradise where it was their duty, aided by the dragon Ladon, to guard a tree that bore golden apples.

The eleventh labour of HERACLES was to collect three of the apples. He succeeded either by slaying the dragon, or by holding up the sky for Atlas, while Atlas took the apples. Later, ATHENA arranged for their return to the guardian nymphs.

Hestia In Greek mythology, the goddess of the hearth, and, by extension, the home. She was the daughter of KRONOS and Rhea and the sister of ZEUS, HERA, POSEIDON, DEMETER and HADES. She was sworn to chastity and her fidelity to this vow is attested to by the fact that no tales about her exist. At the shrine of Vestia, her counterpart in Rome, an eternal flame was guarded by six Vestal Virgins. One of these, Rhea Silvia, was raped by the war god MARS; she gave birth to ROMULUS and Remus, the founders of the city of Rome.

Hiawatha The legendary sage of the Iroquois Indians of North America. He was an Onondaga chief who founded the League of Five Nations, also known as the Iroquois Confederacy, in the sixteenth century.

At first, the shaman Atotarho opposed the league's formation and killed Hiawatha's wife and daughter. This bloodthirsty magician had snakes instead of hair, and misshapen hands and feet. But the singing of the great Iroquois chiefs calmed his mind and restored his body to normal. Then, Atotarho and Hiawatha were reconciled and the five peoples united. These comprised the Cayuga, the Mohawk, the Oneida, the Onondaga and the Seneca.

Hine-nui-te-po In the mythology of the Maori people of New Zealand, the goddess of death. She was a specific variant of the more general Polynesian Hina, the lover of the hero and trickster god MAUI. Maui found Hine-nui-te-po sleeping and tried to pass through her body, but Hine-nui-te-po, awakened by birdsong, strangled him to death. As a consequence of Maui's defeat, men and women remained bound by mortality.

Hino In the mythology of the Iroquois Indians of North America, the god of thunder, husband of the rainbow. Hino's arrows of flame, shot from a giant bow, overcame the monstrous serpent in the Great Lakes, saving the world from flood. He has two habitual companions: the golden eagle Keneu, and Oshadagea, an eagle with a lake of dew on its back.

Hippolyta In Greek mythology, a queen of the Amazons, a nation of warrior-women. As one of his labours, HERACLES had to bring back her girdle to Tiryns. Either he did so by capturing Hippolyta, or Hippolyta generously gave Heracles the girdle, whereupon HERA, disguised as an Amazon, persuaded the Amazons that their queen was about to be carried off. They thus attacked Heracles, and in the conflict Heracles slew Hippolyta.

Hippolytus In Greek mythology, the son of THESEUS and the Amazon Antiope. He was a chaste and beautiful youth of the same age as Phaedra, who married Theseus after Antiope died. Phaedra conceived a passion for Hippolytus, who, being a devotee of the virgin goddess ARTEMIS, spurned her advances. In revenge, Phaedra convinced Theseus that Hippolytus had tried to rape her.

Theseus therefore asked his father, POSEIDON, to destroy Hippolytus. One day, when Hippolytus was being carried along the shore in his chariot, Poseidon sent a monster to rise from the waves. The monster so frightened Hippolytus's horses that they bolted, breaking the chariot into pieces and dragging Hippolytus to his death.

A Christian parallel exists with St Hippolytus, the protector of horses. He was converted to Christianity by St Lawrence and died a martyr for his faith, dragged to his death by wild horses.

Hino In the mythology of the Iroquois Indians of North America, the god of thunder, husband of the rainbow.

Hiranyakasipu In Hindu mythology, a demon who obtained from SHIVA dominion over the three realms of sky, air and earth for a million years. He was invulnerable to man, beast and all weapons, and was the special enemy of VISHNU. However, Prahlada, Hiranyakasipu's son, worshipped Vishnu, who protected him from his father's wrath. One day, Prahlada told his father that Vishnu was hiding in one of the pillars of his house, provoking Hiranyakasipu to strike the pillar. Vishnu then emerged from the pillar as the avatar Nara-simha, the man-lion, and tore the demon to pieces. Hiranyakasipu means "golden dress".

Hiranyaksha In Hindu mythology, a giant and the twin brother of Hiranyakasipu. Both of them were enemies of VISHNU. Hiranyaksha pulled the earth down to the bottom of the sea and kept it there for 1,000 years, the length of time it took Vishnu, as the avatar Varaha (the boar), to destroy him.

Hiyoyoa Among the Wagawaga people of Papua, the underworld situated beneath the sea. It is ruled by Tumudurere, a fair-skinned and smooth-haired deity. Unlike other realms of the dead, Hiyoyoa can be visited by the living provided that special precautions are taken. It is even said that plants have been brought back to earth from Tumudurere's garden.

Hkun Ai A legendary Burmese hero who married a beautiful dragon and fathered a great king. At first, Hkun Ai was happy with his wife because she had assumed human form. But he became uneasy at the time of the water festival, when she reverted to her serpentlike shape for a day.

At last, Hkun Ai decided to leave his dragon wife, but not before she had presented him with an egg.

From its shell emerged a son, whom he named Tung Hkam (golden dead leaves). Many years passed before Tung Hkam fell in love with a princess who lived on an island. However, the young man could not find a way to approach this girl until his own mother formed a bridge with her dragon back.

As in similar foundation myths found in both Cambodia and Laos, Tung Hkam went on to establish a powerful kingdom.

Hodr In Germanic mythology, the blind son of ODIN and FRIGG and twin brother of BALDER. When, one day, the gods were making sport by throwing weapons at the invulnerable Balder, LOKI tricked Hodr into throwing a spear of mistletoe, the one thing, as Loki knew, that would kill him. Balder died and could not be rescued from Hel, although it was prophesied that Hodr and Balder would be reunited in the new world that was to arise from the ashes of Ragnarok, the doom of the gods.

There is, however, another version of the relationship between Hodr and Balder. This tale suggests that whereas Hodr was virtuous, Balder was violent and lustful. Moreover, the instrument of Balder's death was not a mistletoe dart, but Hodr's sword. Later, Hodr himself was slain in revenge.

Holawaka The legendary messenger bird of the Galla people of Ethiopia. Holawaka was sent to advise the first men to slip off their skins when they grew old, so that they might become young again. On the way, the scatter-brained bird shared a meal with a snake. He told this creature how to slough its skin, but eventually let mankind know that death was its inevitable lot.

Holy Grail See Grail.

Horatius The Roman hero Horatius Cocles, who defended the only bridge over the Tiber when the Etruscans attempted to restore Tarquinius Superbus to the throne. He kept the enemy at bay with two other men. Then, having sent his companions to safety, Horatius remained facing the Etruscans until the wooden bridge was demolished behind him. Later he was able to swim across the river to safety.

Houris In Islamic mythology, black-eyed maidens who dwell in paradise and provide the blessed dead with sexual pleasure. Each man is given seventy-two *houris*, and each one's virginity is eternally renewed.

Hsien In Chinese Daoism, an immortal being who has partaken of the elixir of life.

There are three categories of *hsien*: celestial immortals or *tian hsien*, who inhabit the airy void; terrestrial immortals called *ti hsien*, who inhabit the mountains and forests of earth; and *shi chieh hsien*, the dead who slough off their bodies and are incorporeal immortals. The first person recorded to have become an immortal is HUANG DI.

Hunab The remote creator god of the ancient Maya people of Central America. He may have been the father of ITZAMNA, the moon god. Hunab, also called Hunab Ku (the single god), renewed the earth three times after having flooded it. Once he repopulated it with dwarfs, another time with an obscure race of "offenders" called *dzolob*, and the third time with the Maya people. The Mayas themselves are destined to be overcome by a fourth flood.

Hupasiyas In the Hittite mythology of Asia Minor, the mortal lover of Inaras, the goddess who helped to slay the dragon Illuyankas. After Inaras had made the dragon eat and drink until he was too distended to squeeze back into his home, Hupasiyas bound him with cords so that the weather god TARU might slay him. As a reward, Inaras built Hupasiyas a house, but told him never to look out of its windows in case he saw his mortal wife and children. When Hupasiyas disobeyed the command, Inaras killed him.

Hurakan In the Maya mythology of Central America, a creator god whose name means "one-legged". He dwelt in the mists hanging over the primeval flood, which he passed over in the form of the wind, ceaselessly repeating the word "earth" until the solid world rose from the seas. Other gods then peopled the earth with wooden beings into which they breathed life. However, Hurakan sent floods to destroy them, then created the ancestors of the Maya people. The relationship between Hurakan and Hunab is uncertain, since Maya records are incomplete. They may well be the same deity.

Hushedar The first saviour in ancient Iranian legend, and a son of the prophet Zoroaster. It was foretold that, at his miraculous virgin birth, the sun would stand still. Hushedar's birth was expected to bring peace for three years, before AHRIMAN reasserted his evil domination. The final saviour will be SAOSHYANT.

Huwawa In Mesopotamian mythology, the forester of ENLIL. By killing Huwawa, and the bull of heaven, GILGAMESH and Enkidu incurred Enlil's wrath. As a result of discussion in the assembly of the gods at Ekur, the temple of Enlil in Nippur, it was decided that in retribution Gilgamesh should lose his friend and companion Enkidu. The death of this mighty man set the distraught Gilgamesh on his personal quest for immortality.

It is difficult now to determine the significance of the terrible monster Huwawa. Like the bull of heaven, the divine, fire-breathing forester may simply have represented the will of the gods.

Hydra In Greek mythology, a monstrous water serpent, offspring of TYPHON and Echidna, which ravaged the country of Argos. When one of its many heads (traditionally nine) was cut off, two new ones grew in its place. HERACLES's second labour was to kill the beast. With the help of his servant Iolaus, he burned off all the heads and buried the central, immortal head under a rock. Hydra's venom was fatal and arrows dipped in it killed a number of heroes.

Hylas The principal Greek victim of the water nymphs. He was the son of Theodamus, the king of a pre-Greek people settled on the island of Euboea. HERACLES captured him because of his good looks. Although he became the hero's lover, and voyaged with him on the ship of the Argonauts, Hylas could not resist the endearments of the water nymphs. When sent to fetch water, he was pulled down into a pool and, despite the cries of Heracles from the shore, was never seen again.

Hymir In Germanic mythology, a sea giant whose name means "dark one". He was a constant irritant to THOR, who coveted Hymir's huge cauldron. In some versions of the myth, Tyr, Thor's ally, killed Hymir on an expedition to steal the cauldron. In others, Thor and Hymir went fishing together to land the water serpent Jormungandr, the dreadful offspring of LOKI. They caught it with the bait of a giant ox, but when Hymir saw the mighty serpent he was so frightened that he cut the line. Then, to escape the wrath of Thor, he jumped overboard and was drowned.

Hyperion In Greek mythology, an early sun god. The child of Ouranos (sky) and Gaia (earth), he fathered the sun (Helios), the moon (Selene) and the dawn (EOS). He was later supplanted, as was Helios, by the god Apollo.

Hypnos In Greek mythology, the god of sleep, equivalent to the Roman Somnus. His name means "sleep". He was the son of Nyx (night) and the brother of Thanatos (death). He lived in the underworld and never set eyes on the sun. However, at night he changed into a bird and brought sweet rest to mortals. His three sons – Morpheus, Phobetus and Phantasos – were, respectively, the bringers of dreams to humans, to animals, and to inanimate objects.

I

Iae In the mythology of the Mamaiuran Indians of Brazil, the god of the moon and the brother of the sun god KUAT. Together, the brothers stole light from Urubutsin, the vulture king of the birds.

Iblis In Islamic belief, the name for SATAN. Iblis was originally the angel Arazil, however. His name means "slanderer", and he was the father of the fallen angels, the *djinn*.

When Allah created Adam, the first man, out of clay, Arazil kicked him, fearing that men were to be raised above angels. Then, when Allah summoned the angels to praise his new creation, Arazil alone refused to attend. He was cast out of heaven and thereafter raised the *djinn* to continue the war against Allah by tempting human beings into sin.

Icarus In Greek mythology, the son of the craftsman and inventor DAEDALUS. Daedalus built wings of wax for himself and Icarus so that they might fly to freedom from the tyranny of MINOS of Crete, who held them in captivity. Icarus, ignoring his father's warnings, flew too close to the sun. As a result, his wings melted and he fell into the sea off the coast of Asia Minor and was drowned.

Idas In Greek mythology, the son of Aphareus and cousin of CASTOR and Polydeuces. On the wedding day of Idas and his brother Lynceus, the two brides were abducted by Castor and Polydeuces. After many years of enmity, Idas killed Castor, after waiting in ambush for him. ZEUS then killed Idas with a thunderbolt. Idas, Lynceus, Castor and Polydeuces were all hero figures and Argonauts.

Idomeneus In Greek mythology, a king of Crete and leader of Cretan forces in the Trojan War. On his return journey, Idomeneus encountered a violent storm and vowed to POSEIDON that, if he and his ship were delivered to safety, he would kill the first living thing that he met on dry land. The first living thing turned out to be his son, Idamente. Idomeneus had to fulfil his vow, but for the murder he was exiled to Italy.

Idun In Germanic mythology, the daughter-in-law of ODIN, the chief deity. She was the wife of Bragi, the god of poetry and eloquence. In her keeping were the coveted golden apples of youth.

Igraine The mother of ARTHUR, the legendary British king, and wife of Gorlois, lord of Tintagel Castle in Cornwall. She was loved by Uther Pendragon who, disguised as Gorlois, slept with her after laying siege to Tintagel and killing her husband. Uther and Igraine were brought together by the great wizard MERLIN, who effected Uther's disguise. When Arthur was born, Merlin brought him up in secret.

Iki-Haveve The Papuan cult connected with a divine cargo. It means "belly don't know" and describes the senselessness of those it has possessed since 1919.

The belief in a ship, and later a plane, manned by ancestral spirits derives from the teachings of a certain Evara. He said that a sacred cargo of plenty would be delivered to believers. Although the cult reached its peak before the end of 1923, its legacy is the modern cargo cult. Today, in parts of Papua, dummy runways, equipped with wooden control towers, still attempt to encourage the ancestors to touch down on earth in their marvellous aircraft.

Iku The god or spirit of death in the mythology of the Yoruba people of Nigeria.

Ilamatecuhtli Another name for COATLICUE, the earth goddess of the Aztecs of Mexico. It means "old goddess". Coatlicue was also called Tonantzin (mother), Tlatecutli (earth-toad-knife), and Itzapalotl (obsidian butterfly). As the first wife of Mixcoatl, the god of hunting, Ilamatecuhtli bore him seven sons, who went on to found the seven cities of the Nahuatl people. The myth suggests that Coatlicue absorbed the formerly independent cult of the "old goddess".

Ilé-Ifé In the mythology of the Yoruba people of Nigeria, the sacred city where the creation of the earth began and from where human beings dispersed all over the world. It is believed to be situated at the centre of the world. According to one myth, the supreme god sent a chameleon to examine earth. He decided that though it was wide enough, it was not dry enough. The earth was called Ifé (wide) and later Ilé (house) was added to its title to signify that it was the first home of every created thing.

Ilithyia The ancient Greek goddess of childbirth, whose own origins probably go back to pre-Greek Crete. In some versions she is the daughter of HERA and, on occasions, she appears as an aspect of the goddess. In Rome, Ilithyia was identified with JUNO.

Illuyankas The Hittite dragon, the equivalent of the Mesopotamian TIAMAT and the Hebrew LEVIATHAN, and the prototype for the Greek TYPHON. Illuyankas was slain by the weather god TARU, assisted by the goddess Inaras, who made the dragon drunk, and the mortal Hupasiyas, who bound him in cords. In some versions, Illuyankas survived this first assault and carried off Taru's eyes and heart. When Illuyankas's daughter married Taru's son, she was persuaded to restore the stolen organs as a dowry. Taru then succeeded in killing Illuyankas at last.

Ilya Muromets The legendary Russian hero who, until he reached the age of 33, was so feeble that he was unable to move. Then, two passing pilgrims gave him a draught of honey and he became all-powerful. Armed with a magic bow, he spent the rest of his life defending Christian Russia against unbelievers and invaders.

Imdugud In ancient Mesopotamia, a lion-headed storm bird identified with NINURTA, the Sumerian war god. The giant wings of Imdugud were believed to cover the skies with clouds. His name means "heavy rain", although it can also be read as "sling-stone". One myth relates how Imdugud became so unfriendly toward the gods that Ninurta had to fight the winged bird-lion in his mountain stronghold. This is a very curious episode because both of them were originally the same deity. While Imdugud had remained a gigantic storm bird, Ninurta had developed into a muscular hero similar to the Greek HERACLES.

Imilozi The ancestral spirits of the Zulu people of southern Africa. According to tradition, they whistle when they communicate with mankind, and indeed their name means "whistlers".

Inaras In the Hittite mythology of Asia Minor, the goddess who, with her mortal lover Hupasiyas, helped TARU to destroy the dragon Illuyankas. Apart from helping the weather god to slay monsters, Inaras seems to have acted as the protector of tradesmen.

Io In Greek mythology, the daughter of Inachus, the river deity and first king of Argos. ZEUS tried to rape Io, whereupon his wife HERA changed her into a white heifer and set the hundred-eyed monster Argus to watch over her. However, HERMES killed Argus while the monster was sleeping. Hera then sent a gadfly to torment Io, driving her across Europe to Asia, and then on to Egypt, thus preventing the attentions of Zeus.

The Bosphorus (cow-ford) was named after Io, since she crossed there. Eventually, Zeus restored Io to human form and she conceived Epaphus by him, from whom the royal house of Argos traced its descent. Alternatively, the god approached her as a cloud so that he would not be seen by Hera.

Iouskeha One of the twin trickster heroes of the Iroquois Indians of North America. Iouskeha was inclined to good, while his brother Tawiscaron preferred evil things. They fought a bloody fight for supremacy, which Iouskeha narrowly won. Thereafter, Tawiscaron was obliged to keep his bad actions within bounds.

Iphicles See Alcmene and Amphitryon.

Iphigenia The tragic Greek princess, who was the daughter of Agamemnon and Clytemnestra and the sister of ORESTES and Electra. When the Greek fleet was becalmed at Aulis on the way to Troy, ARTEMIS demanded the sacrifice of Iphigenia in return for providing a favourable wind.

To appease the goddess for an insult previously offered, Agamemnon agreed and tricked Clytemnestra into sending Iphigenia to Aulis on the pretext that she was to marry ACHILLES. In some versions of the myth, the sacrifice was made; in others, Artemis substituted a hind for Iphigenia at the last moment, and carried Iphigenia off to Tauris to be her high priestess.

Years later, when Orestes visited Tauris, and was himself threatened with being sacrificed to Artemis, Iphigenia saved his life by fleeing with him to Greece.

Iris In Greek mythology, the beautiful goddess of the rainbow and the messenger of ZEUS and HERA. Commonly represented as having wings, she could travel at great speed on her rainbow. Her special office was to unloose the souls of dying women from their bodies by cutting the thread of life. The iris of the eye derives its name from her association with the rainbow.

Irra A Mesopotamian god of plague and an equivalent of Namtar, the deity whom ENLIL used to threaten the noisy Sumerian cities. In this case Anu, the Babylonian version of the sky god AN, sent Irra as a punishment for rebellion against his commands. In another myth the plague god caused untold damage on earth during a visit of MARDUK to the underworld. His name is spelt either as Irra or as Erra.

Iruwa The generous sun god in the mythology of the Chaga people of Kenya. A man once decided to murder the sun in revenge for its having killed his two sons. Iruwa discovered the plot but, instead of being angry, he forgave the man and gave him riches, as well as sending him more sons.

Iseult In medieval Europe, the legendary love affair of Tristram and Iseult became associated with the tales of ARTHUR's knights. When Tristram travelled to Ireland, Iseult cured him of a terrible wound.

Ishkur In ancient Mesopotamia, the god of the rainshower. The Sumerians regarded him as a rather unimportant brother of INANNA, the fertility goddess. Possibly the idea of Abzu, the great reservoir of fresh water underground, led to Ishkur's neglect in comparison with Adad in Babylon and Hadad in Canaan. These later thunder gods played a more active role in mythology.

Italapas In North American Indian mythology, the name given to COYOTE by the Chinooks. Unlike other traditions, Coyote is not to them mischievous and unreliable but is a useful assistant to Ikanam, the creator deity.

Iwa The trickster and thief of Hawaiian legend. It is said that he began to steal while he was still in his mother's womb and, in a famous contest with other thieves, proved himself the master by stealing the contents of their houses while they were sleeping. He was also a champion canoeist, his magic paddle carrying him from one end of the Hawaiian archipelago to the other in only four strokes.

Ixion The first man to kill a kinsman, his father-in-law Eioneus, and thus the equivalent of the Hebrew Cain. Ixion was punished in the underworld by being tied to a fiery wheel.

Ixtab In the Maya mythology of Central America, the goddess of suicide. According to the Mayas, those who committed suicide or died by hanging, together with slain warriors, sacrificial victims, priests, and women who died in childbirth, went directly to eternal rest in paradise. It was Ixtab's function to gather them and take them there. She was commonly represented as hanging from a tree with a noose around her neck, her eyes closed in death and her flesh showing early signs of decomposition.

Ixtlilton In the Aztec mythology of Central America, the god of medicine. He kept healing potions made of black water (*tlital*) in jars which were housed in his temple. He devoted his attention above all to sick children.

Izanami In the Shinto mythology of Japan, the primeval creator goddess, the sister and wife of the creator god IZANAGI. With him, she created the first island, upon which they settled. But when Izanami gave birth to fire, she died and descended to the underworld. When Izanagi came to find her, he found her body rotting and fled from her in horror. Izanami tried to stop him from escaping, but he reached the opening and, having escaped, closed the gate to the underworld with a mighty rock. Izanami cursed him and promised to kill 1,000 people on earth every day.

J

Jacob In the Old Testament, one of the primary ancestors of the Hebrews. He was the son of Isaac and Rebecca and the younger twin of Esau. When Esau was hungry, Jacob forced him to sell him his birthright, as the elder son, for a "mess of pottage". Because Esau was a hairy man, Jacob clothed himself in goatskin and received the blessing of the blind Isaac, who was deceived by the way he felt.

Jacob then fled from the wrath of Esau to his uncle, Laban. On the way, he had a vision, or dream, of a ladder leading up to heaven, with angels ascending and descending it. In the vision, Yahweh spoke to Jacob, giving him and his descendants the land on which he was lying.

After serving Laban for 20 years, Jacob returned to the land of his fathers. On his journey home, he wrestled with an angel who, to gain release from Jacob's stranglehold, blessed him and named him Israel.

Janaka In Hindu mythology, an opponent of the brahmins and the father of Sita, the wife of Rama who was the seventh avatar of VISHNU. Janaka was a sage king who led a spotless life. He steadfastly refused to accept the hierarchical structure of the priesthood and therefore performed his own sacrifices to the gods without the intercession of priests. His stand is thought to have prepared the way for the mission of BUDDHA.

Jaras In Hindu mythology, the hunter who accidentally killed KRISHNA, the most popular avatar of the great god VISHNU. The accident occurred shortly after a drunken brawl in which Krishna's brother Balarama was killed. Jaras mistook the avatar for a deer and shot him in the foot, his vulnerable spot. Jaras means "old age".

Jarl One of the offspring of HEIMDAL, the watchman of the Germanic gods. By staying in turn with three mortal families – a slave household, a farm belonging to a free peasant, and the hall of a noble – he begat three sons. These were Thrall, an ugly man with a twisted back and enormous feet; Karl, a well-built countryman; and Jarl, an intelligent man with glowing eyes as grim as a snake. Jarl was the prototype of a Viking lord, a leader of the daring coastal raids.

Jataka The 547 "birth stories" of BUDDHA, which tell of his previous lives as bird, animal, man and god. Throughout these fascinating stories, the thread of rebirth that ended in the Buddha's own life and mission is celebrated and analysed. Virtues and vices are treated equally. In one incarnation, Buddha appears as a stray dog, which reveals to a king the innocence of a pack of wild dogs.

Job In the Old Testament, the victim of a contest between Yahweh and SATAN. Job was a devout man who enjoyed prosperity and the comfort of his family. Satan, believing that Job's faith would crumble if his prosperity were taken from him, persuaded Yahweh to test Job by sending pestilence upon him, destroying his family and afflicting him with a dreadful skin disease.

Job, refusing to believe that he had sinned and therefore not understanding his punishment, cursed the day that he was born and asked Yahweh why the innocent were made to suffer. Yahweh gave no answer but, at the last moment, Job accepted the unknowable and acknowledged his own lowliness.

Jocasta In Greek mythology, the wife of Laius, King of Thebes, and the mother of OEDIPUS. After Oedipus killed his father, as was foretold by the oracle at Delphi, he married Jocasta, knowing neither that the one was his father nor the other his mother. When Jocasta discovered that Oedipus was her son, she hanged herself.

Jok The creator god in the mythology of the Alur people of Uganda and Zaire. He was also known as Jok Odudu (god of birth). From him derives the word *djok*, the name given by the Alur to the ancestral spirits who inhabit the world as serpents or rocks. Jok is also the god of rain to whom sacrifices of goats are made in times of drought.

Jonah One of the minor prophets of the Old Testament. Sent to reform Nineveh, he sought to escape the mission by sailing for Tarsish, the Canaanite port, but was cast overboard by his crew for his disobedience. He was swallowed by a "Great Fish", a cousin of LEVIATHAN, and after three days was vomited up on dry land.

Repenting of his sin, Jonah went to Nineveh and warned the people that they must change their ways within 40 days or Yahweh would destroy the city. When the citizens of Nineveh at once repented, and Yahweh spared the city, Jonah was indignant. Later, however, Yahweh taught Jonah the meaning of mercy.

Jormungandr In Germanic mythology, a monstrous sea serpent fathered by LOKI. At Ragnarok, the day of the universal destruction, Jormungandr was destined to whip up the seas into a ferment, unloosing the ghastly ship of death *Naglfar*, and to spread clouds of poison throughout the world. THOR would kill Jormungandr, but would himself be drowned in its venom.

Joseph of Arimathea A New Testament figure who featured in numerous legends, especially those connected with the Grail. He stood near JESUS at the crucifixion and collected blood from his pierced side in a chalice, believed to be the Grail. He then carried the body of Jesus to his tomb in the Garden of Gethsemane and was later imprisoned. Here, he may have been sustained by Jesus' blood.

According to British legend, Joseph of Arimathea brought the Grail to Glastonbury. Its later disappearance was of prime concern to ARTHUR and the Knights of the Round Table, although only Sir Galahad was deemed worthy enough to see the Grail.

Joshua In the Old Testament, Moses' successor as the leader of "the chosen people". He led the invasion of Canaan, "the promised land", and captured the city of Jericho, whose walls, surprisingly, fell outward at the sound of Joshua's trumpets.

In another famous victory, Joshua ordered the sun to stand still so that the enemy could not not escape under cover of darkness. Joshua was perhaps fortunate in that the prophet Moses had already demolished the giant OG, who was an opponent of the Canaanites.

Jotunnheim In Germanic mythology, the realm of the frost giants. Situated under the first giant root of the world tree YGGDRASIL, Jotunnheim housed Mimir's well. The well, or spring, of Mimir was created by ODIN.

The wise Mimir was a giant sent by the Aesir deities to the Vanir deities as a hostage to ensure good conduct. When the Vanir cut off Mimir's head, Odin preserved it with herbs, put it in the spring and thereafter would visit it whenever he needed advice.

Juok The supreme god in the mythology of the Shilluk people of the Upper Nile. He provided the earth with crops and livestock and his breath sustains human life. In the beginning, he created the Nile to divide the world into two halves, earth and sky, traditionally represented as loaves. Juok's representative on earth is Nyikang, a legendary ancient king who intercedes with Juok on behalf of his Shilluk descendants.

Juturna An Italian water nymph beloved of JUPITER, who gave her power over springs. She was originally the daughter of a local ruler, but Jupiter made her immortal in compensation for losing her virginity. AENEAS slew Juturna's brother, Turnus, in single combat, although the nymph kept the two warriors apart for as long as fate allowed her to do so.

K

Kadaklan The thunder god in the mythology of the Tinguian people, who live in the mountainous interior of Luzon, the northernmost island of the Philippines. He lives in the sky and produces thunder by beating his drum. His faithful dog, Kimat, is the lightning that "bites" trees, houses and anything else that Kadaklan chooses. However, the thunder god receives less reverence than the ancestral spirits, whose goodwill the Tinguians are very concerned to retain.

Kae In Polynesian mythology, a wicked priest. At a banquet given by the sea god Tinirau, Kae fed on meat from his host's pet whale and was so delighted by it that he asked to be allowed to ride the whale home. Tinirau agreed, on condition that Kae dismounted when the water became too shallow for the whale to survive. However, Kae took the whale ashore and ate it. In revenge, Tinirau killed Kae and ate him. The Polynesians therefore use this myth to provide an account of the origin of cannibalism.

Kaitabha In Hindu mythology, a horrible demon who sprang from the ear of VISHNU while the god was asleep in an interval during creation. A companion demon was called Madhu. The ferocious pair tried to attack BRAHMA, who was also asleep, on the lotus growing from Vishnu's navel. But Vishnu awoke and killed both demons.

This curious myth doubtless draws attention to the preserving and restoring power of Vishnu, in contrast to the generally creative role of Brahma. Nevertheless, the demonic force of destruction was engendered in Vishnu's own ear, adding complexity to the story.

Kala Another name for YAMA, the Hindu god of death. It means "time". Yama is also called Kritanta (finisher), Samana (settler), and Pasi (noose-carrier).

Kali The most terrible and destructive aspect of the great Hindu goddess DEVI. The name now means "black one", although the original meaning is lost. Devi took the form of Kali when she was sent to earth in order that she might destroy a race of demons.

While on earth, Kali caused such devastation that countless men and women died. Only when she realized that she was standing on top of, and had killed, her husband SHIVA did she come to her senses. Consequently, she is usually represented as standing on the prostrate Shiva, who lies on a bed of lotus flowers. In two of her arms she holds a severed head and a sword, symbols of death; in the other two she holds the life symbols, a holy book and a string of prayer beads.

Kali is often shown wearing a necklace of skulls and a girdle of severed arms; her eyes are bloodshot and her tongue lolls bloodthirstily from her mouth.

Kalki In Hindu mythology, the last avatar of VISHNU. Kalki, the god "seated on a white horse", will not appear until the final days of destruction, at the end of the current age. Vishnu will then arrive riding on Kalki with a comet for a sword, and he will rid the world of all evil in a catastrophic destruction from which a new era of righteousness will arise.

Kalumba A creator god of the Lumba people of Zaire. Despite attempting to prevent it, he is responsible for allowing death into the world. He set a goat and a dog to watch over the highway along which Life and Death would pass, telling them to let Life go by, but stop Death. However, the goat wandered off while the dog was sleeping, and Death entered the world unhindered. The next day, the goat mistakenly captured Life.

Kama The brilliant Hindu god of love who was married to Rati, the goddess of sexual passion. Kama presides over the heavenly nymphs, the Apsaras, and, like the Greek Eros and the Roman Amor or Cupid, is represented with a bow (made of sugar-cane) and arrows (whose tips are made of sweetly-perfumed flowers).

The first-born of the gods, Kama embodies the primal desire of the universal mind. He was the cause of creation, the motive for original sin. His names include Dipaka (inflamer), Gritsa (sharp), MARA (destroyer), Mayi (deluder), Ragavrinta (stalk of passion), and Titha (fire).

Unlike other love gods, Kama is bodiless. This came about when Kama dared to disturb the contemplation of SHIVA. Although he inflamed Shiva with love for Sati, an aspect of DEVI, Kama was burned to cinders by the great god's third eye. Kama fired an arrow of desire at Shiva because INDRA, the sky god, wanted him to be roused from his timeless contemplation.

Kamrusepas In the Hittite mythology of Asia Minor, the goddess of spells and healing. When TELIPINU, the god of agriculture, forsook the earth, leaving it to famine and death, Kamrusepas used her magic arts to persuade him to return to his temple on the back of an eagle. Life and prosperity were then restored to the land.

Kanaloa The squid god of Hawaiian mythology. The demonic opponent of the creator god KANE, he is an evil-smelling god of darkness. Sometimes he is represented as a ruler of the land of the dead, but he is more commonly said to dwell on the same island as Kane. This paradisal land is situated in the clouds and called Kane-huna-moku (the hidden land of Kane).

Kanassa In the mythology of the Kuikuru Indians of Brazil, the creator god who brought fire to men. Like the Mamaiuran KUAT, he tricked the vulture king of the birds, who possessed fire, into his presence, then held him by the legs and forced him to send down an ember from the sky. Frogs tried to extinguish the ember, but a serpent helped Kanassa to carry it to safety. Kanassa's original attempt to derive fire from a firefly failed because he could not see in the primeval darkness. Thus, the fire may also be identified as light.

Kansa In Hindu mythology, the tyrannical king of Mathura. He had deposed his father, but he feared a prophecy that his sister's son would end his own rule. This turned out to be KRISHNA, the eighth avatar of the great god VISHNU.

Kapoo In the mythology of the Aboriginals of northern Australia, an ancestral kangaroo who gave cats their spots. When Jabbor, a cat, asked Kapoo to initiate him into the secrets of kangaroo rites, Kapoo refused. Then, when Jabbor prepared to fight, Kapoo and other kangaroos threw spears at him, leaving spots all over his body.

Karl In Germanic mythology, the ancestor of the countryman. He was the son of HEIMDAL, the watchman of the gods. When Heimdal visited earth, he created the three races of man: the slave (*thrall*), the free peasant (*karl*) and the noble (*jarl*).

Karttikeya The Hindu war god, the son of SHIVA. Identified with the planet Mars, six-headed Karttikeya was born for the purpose of destroying Taraka, a giant whose austerities had made him a rival of the gods. He is portrayed riding a peacock, and armed for battle with a bow and arrow.

Kasogana A rain goddess in the mythology of the Chaco Indians of the South American pampas. Although known as a sky spirit, Kasogana is said to appear on earth as an ant-eater. The creation of the world was followed by the separation of the first man and woman into two people. Originally, they were stuck together, but an ant-eater or a giant beetle pulled them apart.

Katonda The creator god and father of the sky gods in the mythology of the Buganda people of East Africa. He has numerous forms corresponding to his functions. Thus, as Kagingo he is "master of life", as Lugaba, "giver" and as Namuginga, "shaper of things". The final judge of men's lives, he intervenes in human history through his nature spirits, the *balubaale*, who control all events and phenomena on earth.

Kazikamuntu In the mythology of the Banyarwanda people of Ruanda, the first human being. He was created by IMANA, the supreme god, and had numerous children. However, when his sons reached manhood, they began to fight among themselves. This, say the Banyarwanda, is why men broke up into different tribes. Kazikamuntu means "root of man".

Keresaspa In ancient Iranian mythology, the hero destined to destroy the demon Azhi Dahaka with his magic club at the end of the world. One of his most famous battles was with the gigantic bird Kamak, whose huge wings prevented rain from reaching the earth. Keresaspa also destroyed the monster Gandarewa. The slaying of demons is a recurrent theme in ancient Iran, although the legendary hero RUSTEM was killed not by a demon but by his own king.

Keret In Canaanite mythology, the son of the creator god EL. He was a righteous king who lamented the death of his first wife and son. On El's instruction, he waged war on a neighbouring king, and found a second wife who bore him seven sons. The youngest, Yasib, was suckled by Athirat and Anat, both aspects of ASTARTE.

Later, when Keret became seriously ill, El healed him, but Yasib was keen to succeed his father as king, and therefore urged him to abdicate. Keret cursed Yasib, calling him the rebellious son of Astarte.

The clay tablets found at Ras Shamra, the ancient city of Ugarit, do not complete the story. But the implication is clear: as a king, Keret represents El on earth and is treated by the deity as his own son; in his impatience to rule, Yasib is challenging the will of heaven.

Khenti-Amentiu A funerary dog absorbed by OSIRIS, the Egyptian god of death, at Abydos. His name means "foremost of the westerners", and refers to the practice of burying the dead west of the Nile. The chief funerary dog deity was ANUBIS, who helped Osiris to judge the dead on their arrival in the underworld.

Khepra In ancient Egypt, a god who represented the rising sun. He was self-created, born of his own substance, and therefore an original creator deity. Khepra was portrayed either as a man with the head of a scarab beetle, or simply as a scarab beetle. He was often shown rolling a ball of dung along the ground to symbolize the movement of the sun across the sky.

The cult of Khepra was absorbed by RE, the sun god. According to one myth, Khepra's own semen produced Shu (air) and Tefnut (moisture). They in turn bore Geb (earth) and NUT (sky). From this pair descended OSIRIS, ISIS, SETH, and Nephthys, the attendant of Isis.

Khnum In Egyptian mythology, an ancient ram-headed creator god. He was believed to be the source of the Nile. His greatest deed was that of fashioning the bodies of the gods and men on a potter's wheel. His wife was the frog goddess Heqet. In later times, Khnum lost ground to RE, the sun god, and OSIRIS, the ruler of the dead.

Kholumulumo A fearsome monster in the mythology of the Sotho people of South Africa. He swallowed all human beings and all animals except for one pregnant woman who survived to give birth to a son, Moshanyana. Later, aided by the monster being so full with all it had eaten that it was unable to move, Moshanyana attacked and killed it. The hero then cut open Kholumulumo and released all the people and animals in its stomach.

So ungrateful were some of these people that they plotted Moshanyana's death. On the fourth attempt, they slew him.

Khonsu An ancient Egyptian moon god, the son of AMUN and Mut, the vulture goddess. As the moon, he was a wanderer who travelled across the sky in a boat. He was commonly represented as a young man, with a crescent moon supporting a full moon on his head; occasionally he was shown with a falcon's head. His ability to heal the sick drew many devotees to his temple at Thebes.

Khonvum The supreme deity of the Pygmy people of Africa. He made everything, including the Pygmies themselves, whom he created in the sky and then lowered down to earth. He also provided these hunter-gatherers of the forests with fruits and game. Each night, Khonvum is said to collect fragments of stars in a sack and throw them at the sun, thus renewing its energy. He communicates with mortals through animals, usually the chameleon.

Kibuka The dying war god of the Buganda people of Uganda. When the Bugandas went into battle, Kibuka would protect them by hiding in clouds above the action and shooting arrows down at the foe. One day, Kibuka slept with a woman who had been taken prisoner, despite having been forbidden to do so. As a result, he was mortally wounded in the next battle and died.

Kici Manitou In the mythology of the Algonquin Indians of North America, a creator god and supreme deity, who made all things and breathed the spirit of life into man. In some versions, when all around him was primeval water, Kici Manitou wandered about in search of the place where the earth would arise. A tortoise told him where soil could be found and water birds brought it to him in their beaks. From this, Kici Manitou then formed the earth and dried it in his sacred pipe.

Kingu In ancient Mesopotamia, the second husband of the chaos-dragon TIAMAT, whom he encouraged to attack the gods. In the ensuing battle, the Babylonian champion MARDUK slew Tiamat, took Kingu captive, and then killed him in the presence of Ea, the fresh-water god. Having already created the heavens and earth by splitting the corpse of Tiamat, Marduk created mankind from Kingu's blood.

Kintu In the mythology of the Buganda people of Uganda, Kintu was the first man and an immortal king. He was the representative on earth of the supreme god Katonda, to whom he occasionally spoke on the top of a mountain.

There are several accounts of how Kintu, together with his wife Nambi, brought death into the world. In one, Nambi was asked by her brother, Death, not to desert the sky, but was warned by her father, the sky god Gulu, not to return to the sky. Nevertheless, she did return, and when she went down to earth again, her brother followed her. Gulu then sent another of Nambi's brothers, Kaizuki, to wrestle with Death. He failed to vanquish Death, but forced him to hide in the underworld.

In another version, Kintu disobeyed Katonda by leaving a sack which the supreme god had given him unattended. Katonda therefore visited disease and death on the world.

Kitamba A legendary king of the Mbundu people of Angola. When his wife died, he forced all his subjects to join him in a period of mourning. No one was allowed to say a word or make the slightest noise. Not suprisingly, the Mbundu people were extremely put out by this and so, in the hope of putting an end to the situation, they decided that a doctor should dig down to the underworld to visit the king's wife.

Eventually, the doctor and his son reached the queen, who told them that it was impossible for her to return to the land of the living. Before they left, she gave the doctor a piece of jewellery to pass on to her husband. Once he had seen the armlet, Kitamba came to terms with the situation and put an end to the mourning.

Kiyohime The legendary murderess of a Japanese monk named Anchin, and a character in a No play. Overwhelmed with desire for the monk, Kiyohime chased Anchin into a Buddhist temple, where he hid under a great bell. As she approached his hiding place, the wooden supports holding up the bell collapsed, trapping Anchin inside its wide body. At once, Kiyohime turned from a young girl into a scaly monster, breathing fire. Her breath was so hot that the bell melted, burning Anchin and herself to death.

Ko Pala A legendary Burmese king who failed to satisfy his subjects and so was banished to an island, where he was left to die in a basket. However, reincarnated as a crab, he returned to the mainland and covered it in floods as retribution for his treatment.

Kore One of the titles, meaning "maiden", of PERSEPHONE, the ancient Greek queen of the underworld. In this aspect, Persephone was associated with her mother, the earth goddess DEMETER, and was worshipped as the power of growth within corn.

Kore's resurrection, her return from the underworld, took place when the seed corn germinated. The Athenians were ardent worshippers of Demeter, and the event was celebrated in an underground chamber at Eleusis, the cult centre of Demeter, south of Athens. The Eleusinian mysteries were among the most famous in the Greco-Roman world.

Kothar The Canaanite smith god and servant of EL, the father of the gods. Kothar made King Aqhat a bow made from twisted horns, shaped like a serpent, in gratitude for his hospitality. However, Anat (ASTARTE) stole the wonderful present and was so delighted with it that she offered Aqhat immortality in its exchange.

However, Aqhat had the presumption to refuse the offer and, with El's blessing, Anat killed him. But the bow fell into the waters, splintered and disappeared, whereupon disease and famine came upon the land.

Quite possibly, the myth was part of a longer cycle telling of Aqhat's death and resurrection. The role of Kothar himself in the drama remains uncertain.

Kraken In medieval legends of western Europe, a sea monster held responsible for shipwrecks and sinkings. He dragged ships down to the bottom of the ocean with his huge mile-long tentacles. The Kraken was an updated version of LEVIATHAN; the Hebrew sea serpent, which in turn derived from the Canaanite Lotan.

Kukulcan The Maya name for QUETZALCOATL, the snake-bird god of the Toltec people of ancient Central America. His name means "feathered serpent". He was worshipped at Chichén Itzá, a Toltec colony established in the Yucatan peninsula in about 980. He was said to have arrived from the west and founded a new kingdom at Chichén Itzá.

Kukumatz In the mythology of the Mohave Indians of North America, a creator deity and the twin brother of Tochipa. The offspring of earth and sky, the two brothers put the world in order and made the first people. However, they began to quarrel when one of them taught mankind the arts of civilized living. The dispute ended in a devastating flood, which killed almost everyone inhabiting the earth.

Kumush The legendary old man of the Modoc Indians of North America. A great shaman, Kumush took his daughter on a visit to the underworld, where he collected a great basket of bones. Once back in the sunlight, he selected bones to make the different tribes, although the Modocs were always his favourite people. Kumush then became a god and built a house for himself and his daughter in the sky.

Kunitokotachi In the Shinto mythology of Japan, the supreme primeval deity, who lives on Mount Fuji. He emerged from the primordial mire in the form of a reed, along with two subordinate deities, IZANAGI (male) and Izanami (female). Kunitokotachi means "eternal land ruler".

Kurma In Hindu mythology, the second avatar of VISHNU. He appeared in the form of a turtle and twice played important parts in cosmic events. First, he recovered objects lost in the great flooding of the earth; second, he helped the gods in their great battle with the demons for the AMRITA, or water of life. In the battle, known as the churning of the ocean, he acted as the pivot around which Mount Mandara spun to churn the waters.

Kururumany In the mythology of the Arawak Indians of the Orinoco Basin, a creator god who made male human beings. Females were made by his wife, Kulimina. After finishing his creation, Kururumany visited the world, saw with anger the corruption and wickedness of mankind, and took away its immortality.

Kururumany was subordinate to the supreme being Aluberi, an amorphous god, scarcely more than a first cause, who took no part in the creation nor in the subsequent events of the world.

Kvasir An ambiguous figure in Germanic mythology. He is described as a god and as a sage created from the spittle of the gods. Kvasir wandered the world giving instruction to men, until he was killed by two dwarfs who sought to take possession of his secret knowledge. His blood was mixed with honey to make the mead of poetry, which imparted wisdom and the gift of verse-making to those who drank it.

ODIN brought the mead back to Asgard, the home of the gods. He did this in the form of an eagle, with the wonderful liquid held in his mouth. The giant Suttung, who guarded the mead, chased after Odin in the guise of a second eagle, but failed to catch him. The triumphant Odin flew into Asgard and spat the mead into the waiting cups of the gods.

Kwannon The Japanese equivalent of KUANYIN, the goddess of mercy in Chinese Buddhism. The deity descends from the bodhisattva AVALOKITESVARA. In Japan, Kwannon appears as both a male and a female figure. Some representations of the deity possess 1,000 eyes, 11 heads, and occasionally even the head of a horse.

Kwatee A trickster god in the mythology of the Quinault Indians of North America. Also called Kivati, his name means "the one who changed things" and denotes his role as a creator god who, finding the earth ruled by gigantic animals, including COYOTE and Fox, prepared it for the first human beings. After making the first men and women from balls of sweat and grime which he rubbed off his own skin, he taught them how to use tools. His work accomplished, he retired to watch the sun sink over the horizon and then turned himself into a stone.

Kwoth According to the Nuer people of southern Sudan, the great spirit and creator deity. He willed the universe into existence and then looked after it, instituting the social order. Both homeless and bodiless, Kwoth makes himself known to people through natural phenomena. A benevolent deity, he looks after the poor and the unhappy. He acts according to his own will, but the Nuer accept whatever he does, trusting in his good nature.

L

Labyrinth In Greek mythology, the specially constructed home of the Minotaur at Knossos, the palace of MINOS in Crete. Its mazelike design was the work of DAEDALUS, who intended that those who entered the Minotaur's abode would have no difficulty in finding the monster, but would be unable to escape without receiving assistance.

The word labyrinth is pre-Greek in origin and its earliest meaning is unknown. However, it contains the idea of a difficult passage, a hard path to follow without a guiding thread, as the Athenian hero THESEUS discovered.

Lado In the mythology of the Slavs, the divine husband. Lado and his wife Lada personified marriage, pleasure and happiness. Later, under the influence of Christianity, Lada was equated with the VIRGIN MARY.

Lady of the Lake A Celtic enchantress who lived in a castle in the middle of a lake. She was identified with Nimue, the mistress of MERLIN, and she raised Sir Lancelot, who in some versions of the legend was given into her care by Merlin, in others, kidnapped by her. The Lady of the Lake also gave the magic sword Excalibur to ARTHUR and received it back from Sir Bedivere when Arthur died.

Laestrygones In Greek mythology, giant cannibals who inhabited a land of very short nights, commonly identified as Sicily. When ODYSSEUS landed there during his epic voyage, the giants sank all but one of his dozen ships and ate their crews.

Laius In Greek mythology, the king of Thebes and father of OEDIPUS. Warned by the oracle at Delphi that his son would kill him, Laius abstained from the bed of his wife Jocasta. Eventually, one night he returned home drunk, and Oedipus was conceived. Laius had the infant exposed on a mountain, but a shepherd gave him to Polybus, King of Corinth, who raised him to manhood. Later, Oedipus met his father, who was unknown to him, at a crossroads, quarrelled with him and killed him. Laius was buried at the site of the murder, at the foot of Mount Parnassus.

Lamia In Greek mythology, a being with a serpent's body and a woman's head. Before she took on this horrible shape, ZEUS made Lamia his mistress and she bore him a number of children whom jealous HERA cursed. As a result, Lamia devoured her own children, with the exception of the monster Scylla. Later, Lamia grew dreadful in appearance and became a child-killer, who sucked the blood of infants and ate their flesh.

Lancelot The most romantic member of the Round Table. He was raised by the Lady of the Lake and is thus sometimes called "Lancelot of the Lake". When he reached manhood, he was admitted to the Knights of the Round Table and became a champion of chivalry. However, Sir Lancelot was flawed by his love for ARTHUR's wife, Guinevere, and was thus prevented from approaching the Holy Grail.

The rivalry between Sir Lancelot and Arthur disturbed the unity of the Round Table, but it did not ruin the kingdom. Sir Lancelot left to seek his fortune abroad, and on his return he discovered that Arthur was dead and Guinevere a nun. He then gave up the profession of arms and became a hermit.

Laocoon In Greek mythology, the uncle of AENEAS and a priest of POSEIDON. In the last year of the Trojan War, he advised his fellow Trojans to refuse the gift of a wooden horse from the Greeks. He even hurled a spear at it, in an attempt to prevent it from being accepted.

While the Trojans considered Laocoon's words, he and his two sons were strangled by two gigantic serpents, an omen which the Trojans took to mean that his warning had been false. They therefore let the horse, with its hidden cargo of Greek soldiers, into the city, and Troy was doomed. From Laocoon's warning come Virgil's famous words, "Fear the Greeks, even when they bear gifts".

Laodice In Greek mythology, the most beautiful daughter of PRIAM, King of Troy. She fell in love with one of the Greek envoys who came to the city, demanding the return of HELEN to Sparta. On the fall of Troy, the ground opened and Laodice was swallowed up in the hole. Her name later came to be used for all women of high rank, and approximates to "princess".

Laomendon In Greek mythology, the faithless first king of Troy and the father of PRIAM. When he refused to pay Apollo and POSEIDON for building the walls of Troy, the two gods sent a sea monster to ravage the land, and warned Laomendon that catastrophe would be averted only if he sacrificed his daughter, Hesione. Laomendon then offered HERACLES two immortal stallions if he would save Hesione. Heracles killed the sea monster, but Laomendon would not give him the stallions. Heracles therefore killed Laomendon, and Priam became the second king of Troy.

Lao Zi The legendary Chinese sage who founded Daoism and opposed the philosophy of Confucius (551–479 BC). His name means "old philosopher". When the two met, Confucius is said to have been taken aback by Lao Zi's lifeless appearance, but the sage explained that this was due to his having "wandered among the unborn", a remark worthy of a shaman. Lao Zi disdained public office and ceremonial events, believing that truth could be found only through individual effort. He had no grave, a significant omission in ancestor-worshipping China. His final journey westward was explained as his preparation to become BUDDHA in India.

Leander See Hero.

Lear A legendary British king, most probably derived from the Celtic sea god (Lir in Irish, Llyr in Welsh). In his old age, Lear planned to parcel out his kingdom to his three daughters, according to the amount of love they professed to bear him. Goneril and Regan, the flatterers, were given all the land whereas Cordelia, who would not stoop to flattery, was cast out without a dowry. In some versions, Cordelia eventually inherited the kingdom and ruled over it for five years, before being imprisoned by her sisters' sons.

Lebe According to the Dogon people of Mali, the first ancestor to die. Through his death, mankind was given life. The great creator god Amma ordered Lebe to feign death and the ancestor's corpse was then buried with his head pointing northward. A serpent ancestor then swallowed him and afterward vomited stones in the pattern of a human body. The arrangement of stones was supposed to signify the nature of social relationships, especially marriage.

Leda In Greek mythology, an Aetolian princess. After being seduced by ZEUS, who appeared in the guise of a swan, she laid two eggs. One of the eggs produced CASTOR and Polydeuces, the other, according to some accounts, bore HELEN and, among others, Clytemnestra, ORESTES' mother.

Le-eyo The legendary ancestor of the Masai people of Kenya who lost the gift of immortality for his descendants. When a child died, the gods instructed him to say, "Man, die and return; moon, die and stay away". But, when next a child died, Le-eyo repeated the saying the wrong way round. When his own child died, though he repeated the formula correctly, it had lost its power. The moon therefore returns eternally, but man does not.

Lejman According to the Marshall Islanders, the first woman, whose partner was Wulleb, the first man. They emerged from the leg of the creator deity, LOA. Alternatively, Lejman and Wulleb were both worms who lived in a shell. When they raised the shell's upper half, they created the sky, leaving its lower half as the earth.

Lethe In Greek and Roman mythology, the river of forgetfulness, running through the underworld which HADES ruled. In some tales, new arrivals drank its water to induce sleep. In others, Lethe's waters of oblivion were drunk by souls destined to return to the world. They would thus forget the miseries of their previous existence and so be able to endure the miseries of their next life. In Dante's famous account of the afterlife, in the *Divine Comedy*, drinking the water of Lethe enables Christian souls to be freed from the memory of their past sins.

Leto In Greek mythology, the Titaness who bore the twins Apollo and ARTEMIS by ZEUS. Even though this happened prior to HERA's marriage to Zeus, Hera harried Leto, knowing that her children would be greater than her own. So, for many months, Leto wandered pregnant on earth because no land would accept her, fearing the wrath of Hera who had forbidden any place to receive the offspring. Hera also forbade Ilithyia, the goddess of childbirth, to attend Leto.

At last, after enduring days and nights of dreadful labour pangs, Leto gave birth to Apollo and Artemis on the floating island of Delos. Soon afterward, Apollo destroyed the terrible monster serpent Python.

Leve An alternative name for NGEWO, the sky god of the Mende people of Sierra Leone. His name means "the high-up one".

Libanza In the mythology of the Upoto people of the Congo, the sky god who wandered the earth, fighting and killing people and sometimes restoring them to life. Whereas Libanza lives in the eastern sky, his sister Ntsongo lives in the western sky. Libanza gathers the dead into the sky by sending a boat, the moon, around the earth to collect their souls. When Libanza ceases to hold up the sky, it will fall to earth and destroy the world.

Liber An old Italian god of the countryside, and especially wine, identified by the Romans with DIONYSUS. One legend credits Liber with the invention of Falernian wine, a favourite at Rome. Passing through a village in southern Italy, the god was once entertained by a peasant named Falernus. Nothing in the larder was denied Liber, although the household was too poor to provide wine. By magic, the grateful god filled the empty cups with red wine, over which Falernus eventually fell asleep. When he awoke, Liber had gone but the hillsides around the village were covered with grapevines.

Libertas In ancient Rome, a goddess who personified the personal liberty cherished by the citizens of that city. She was given a temple in 238 BC. Under the Roman emperors, she was believed to protect constitutional rights.

Lif In Germanic mythology, a mortal man. He and his wife Lifthrasir are to be the sole survivors of Ragnarok, the day of universal destruction, by being hidden in the world tree YGGDRASIL. Together, they will help to found a new world.

Lilith In the Old Testament, a female demon who disturbs rest at night. Her name means "storm goddess". She was supposed to be an earlier wife to Adam than Eve. For disobeying Adam, Lilith was exiled to the airy void. Whatever the foundation of this Hebrew legend, Lilith almost certainly derived from the Canaanite Lilitu, a female demon who harassed men.

Limbo In medieval Christian belief, the realm of the virtuous pagan dead and unbaptized infants. The inhabitants suffered no pain, but neither did they enjoy the bliss of heaven. The realm had its origin in the desire to find a place for the souls of those who had died before the coming of JESUS, and hence before the possibility of salvation. It was a necessary medieval invention to explain divine justice. The Christian damned went to hell, sinners to purgatory, and the blessed to heaven. However, before the Last Judgement took place, a home had to be found for worthy ancients.

Lir In Irish mythology, a sea god and the father of MANANNAN. He had four children by his first wife, Aobh, and, when she died, married her sister, Aoife. Aoife cultivated the affections of her four step-children, then turned them into swans. Lir cursed his children for their ingratitude (as did the British Lear) but, when he learned of Aoife's treachery, he returned them to mortal form. However, by then they were old and withered. Aoife was punished by being turned into a demon of the air. The Welsh sea god was named Llyr.

Lleu A legendary Welsh hero identified with LUGH, the Irish sun god. He was the son of Arianrhod by an unknown father and was born prematurely. Gwydion incubated and raised him, but each time he took the child to Arianrhod so that he might be given a name and weapons, his mother cursed him with namelessness and lack of arms.

Eventually, the youth won his name when, having shot a bird, his mother, not recognizing him through his disguise, cried out "Lleu" (one with a steady hand). Disguised as a bard, Lleu was armed by his mother when her castle was under assault from a phantom army which he himself had raised. Thereafter, Lleu proved himself a knight of great courage and virtue, a prototype of Sir Lancelot.

Lohengrin In medieval German legend, a knight of the Grail. The son of Parsifal, he was sent to Brabant to rescue the princess Else, who was accused of murdering her brother. He was carried to Brabant by a swan and was told that, as a keeper of the Grail, he must not reveal his name unless asked and, if asked, he must answer and then leave immediately. Else married him without knowing his name, but her curiosity eventually forced Lohengrin to reveal it. The swan then appeared and took Lohengrin away to the sacred mountain where the Grail was kept.

Long One of the mythical Chinese dragons, benevolent water gods who bring rain to replenish the earth. They can be as tiny as silkworms or large enough to blot out the sun. Their appearance is extraordinarily complex: they have stag's horns, a camel's head, the eyes of a demon, the ears of a bull, the whiskers of a cat, the neck of a snake, the scales of a fish, and the claws of an eagle.

The Chinese character for *long* appears on oracle bone inscriptions dating from the Shang dynasty (1650–1027 BC). Somewhat different in appearance is the *chi* dragon. It has neither horns nor scales, but it does possess a forked tail. Dragons are believed to have the pearl of wisdom in their mouths.

Lono In Hawaiian mythology, the god of the heavens. With Ku, an ancestral god, he helped the creator god KANE to make the world.

Lotan The Canaanite equivalent of LEVIATHAN. A swift serpent, he was killed by Anat (ASTARTE), or by BAAL when he overcame the sea god Yam. Mot, the god of death, taunted Baal with this easy slaughter when he invited him to come and eat at his table in the underworld. According to the Old Testament, Yahweh, "shall punish Leviathan the piercing serpent, even Leviathan that crooked serpent; and he shall slay the dragon that is in the sea". Lotan, on the other hand, is described as a coiled serpent with seven heads.

Lotophagi In Greek mythology, the lotus-eaters, a fabulous race of men who lived on the north coast of Africa and fed on the fruit of the lotus plant, which induced idleness and forgetfulness. When ODYSSEUS landed among the lotus-eaters, his crew ate the fruit and, forgetting their friends and homes, had to be dragged back to their ships.

Lotus-eaters See Lotophagi.

Lucan In Arthurian legend, the most trusted of King ARTHUR's friends. After Arthur was crowned, he became the king's butler, and was later admitted to the Round Table, although he never ceased to be a butler. In the war between Modred and Arthur, which brought doom to Camelot, Sir Lucan was mortally wounded while helping Sir Bedivere to carry the wounded Arthur from the battlefield.

Lucifer An alternative name for SATAN, in his aspect as the fallen angel. Originally, the name meant "morning star".

Lucretia In Roman legend, the wife of the nobleman Lucius Tarquinius Collatinus. Renowned for her virtue and fidelity, she was raped by Sextus, son of the reigning Etruscan king, Tarquinius Superbus. After telling her father and husband of the event, Lucretia took her own life. The crime so angered the Roman people that they drove the Tarquin family out of the city, abolished the monarchy and thus established the Roman Republic.

Ludd A Romano-British sea god, whose temple in Roman London was near St Paul's Cathedral. Ludgate Hill, the street leading to St Paul's, is named after him. He is credited with the foundation of London, which he preserved against three pestilences: the race of invaders – the Coranians – who knew every spoken tongue; a shriek, heard every May, that killed crops, animals and children and rendered women infertile; and two dragons.

Lugal-Dimmer-An-Ki-A The title bestowed on MARDUK, the city god of Babylon, after he had defeated TIAMAT. It means "king of the gods of heaven and earth". In voting for the new title, the assembly of the gods were emphasizing the importance of Tiamat's destruction. Under Marduk's control, the Mesopotamian pantheon was united under one leader and a new order came into existence. The first task that Marduk told the gods to perform was to build him a city – Babylon.

Lugalid One of the names of ENKI, the fresh-water god of the Sumerians. The name means "owner of the river" and refers to the life-sustaining role of the god in providing water to fructify the earth. The absence of rain in ancient Sumer led to the belief in a massive underground reservoir of fresh water, known as Abzu or Apsu. Enki drew his substance from this inexhaustible supply.

Lugeilan The sky god of the Caroline Islanders, who came down to earth and taught men the arts of agriculture, tattooing and hairdressing. His son, OLOFAT, was a trickster hero, who may have become the fire god, but who also used deceit and cunning to gain advantage over people. When Olofat was killed by the gods, Lugeilan revived him.

Lugulbanda The father of GILGAMESH, the ancient Mesopotamian hero. After killing the bull of heaven, which ISHTAR had sent against him, Gilgamesh presented its enormous horns to Lugulbanda as a votive offering. The entire population of Uruk crowded round to witness the ceremony.

Lugulbanda's area of authority as a god is unknown, although the presentation of the horns would suggest a connection with animals. However, he appears to have taken a special interest in kingship, for an inscription set up by the Sumerian ruler Shulgi (2046–2038 BC) mentions the protection he personally enjoyed from Lugulbanda and the cow goddess Ninsuna. The inscription also says that Shulgi regarded Gilgamesh as his brother and comrade.

Luonnotar In Finnish mythology, a creator goddess, the daughter of the air and maker of heaven and earth. She floated on the primeval waters for 700 years, until she mated with a bird and produced eggs. When the eggs hit the water, they shattered, the top parts forming heaven and the bottom parts, the earth. The egg yolks became the sun and the whites, the moon.

Luxing The Chinese god of salaries. With Fuxing and Shoulao he is one of a triad of gods concerned with good fortune. He is thought to have lived on earth before being deified and is depicted in human form, wearing the robes of a mandarin. He is also represented as a deer.

Lycaon In Greek and Roman mythology, the king of Arcadia, who was turned into a wolf. According to the Greeks, Lycaon's sons killed their brother, Nyctimus, and offered him in a soup to ZEUS, who was disguised as a beggar. Zeus restored Nyctimus to life, killed the brothers with a thunderbolt, and turned Lycaon into a wolf.

In the Roman version, JUPITER, who was visiting earth to discover whether reports of men's impiety were true, came to Lycaon's palace and announced himself as a god. The people prepared sacrifices to Jupiter, but Lycaon, to test the god's omniscience, killed a servant and served him to Jupiter in a soup. Jupiter then set fire to the palace with a flash of lightning and turned Lycaon into a wolf.

Lycomedes In Greek mythology, the king of Scyros. When THESEUS was out of favour in Athens, he took refuge with Lycomedes who, after receiving him cordially, eventually had him thrown from a cliff. The king seems to have feared that Theseus might usurp his throne. Lycomedes also gave refuge to ACHILLES when his mother, the sea nymph Thetis, knowing that Achilles was destined to die at Troy, dressed him as a girl and hid him among the women at Lycomedes' court. However, ODYSSEUS discovered Achilles there, and persuaded him to accompany him to Troy.

Lynceus See Idas.

Maat In ancient Egypt, the goddess of truth, or justice. She was the daughter of RE, the sun god, and was portrayed with an ostrich feather on her head. This "feather of truth" was used to weigh the virtue, or lack of virtue, which was found in souls at the judgement of the dead. The jackal-headed funerary god ANUBIS was given the task of holding the scales on which the measurement was made.

Mab The legendary Queen of the Fairies in Britain, a figure later replaced by Titania in folklore. Human beings occasionally wandered into her realm, which bordered on the earth. Mab may derive from Medb, a legendary queen of Connacht in Ireland. She was commonly represented as the midwife of fairies, due to her ability to bring dreams, the offspring of fairies, to life.

Maeldun In Irish mythology, a hero who undertook a fabulous voyage. Mael Dunn, or Maeldun, was the child of a nun whom Ailill raped. A lord of the Aran Isles, Ailill was killed by raiders.

When Maeldun eventually learned of his parentage, he went in search of his father's murderers. His voyage, which lasted three years and seven months, took him to many strange islands inhabited by giant ants, beautiful birds, monstrous dogs, demon horses, fire-like creatures, magic sheep, black weepers, and hermits.

On one particular island, Maeldun bathed in a sacred lake and renewed his youth. He faced many dangers and, when he finally found the murderers, he took no vengeance, in gratitude to the gods for delivering him safely back home to Ireland.

Maenads In Greek mythology, the female devotees of DIONYSUS. The name means "frenzied ones". In Roman mythology, they were known as *Bacchantes*, after Bacchus, the Roman equivalent of Dionysus. They lived in forests and mountains and dressed in animal skins and ivy leaves. By their dancing, they worked themselves into a frenzy that enabled them to tear animals apart with their bare hands. Such a fate also befell Pentheus, King of Thebes, when he slighted Dionysus.

The rending of flesh which commonly accompanied the frenzy of this god's devotees may have entered Greco-Roman worship from Asia Minor. It was a characteristic which worried the Roman authorities when the cults of Dionysus and CYBELE were first introduced into Italy.

Magi In the New Testament, the three Wise Men who told Herod of the birth of JESUS and were sent by him to discover the place where he lay. "Magus", the singular of Magi, is a word of ancient Iranian origin and apparently denotes a member of a priestly caste that was antecedent to, and continued into, the time of the prophet Zoroaster.

The three biblical kings were named Kaspar, Melchior and Balthazar. By following the star that appeared in the east, they found Jesus in a manger at Bethlehem and offered him gifts of gold (for kingship), frankincense (for the godhead) and myrrh (for the entombment). An angel warned them not to return to Herod, who sought to kill the infant Jesus, and they departed into their own lands.

Magna Mater The title that the Romans gave to CYBELE, the Phrygian goddess. It means "great mother". Her festival in Rome was celebrated on 4 April, when it was the custom of the rich to throw extravagant parties.

Mahaf In Egyptian mythology, the ferryman who steers the boat, called *meseket*, on which, each night, RE travels through the underground on his return to the east. The boat is protected from the monster Apophis by the serpent Mehen, who coils himself around it.

Mahendra One of the seven mountain ranges of southern India, and a name of INDRA, the Hindu god of the firmament. As a storm deity, Indra has long been associated with the clouds that collect around mountain tops. He is also called Vajrapani (of the thunderbolt hand), Divaspati (ruler of the atmosphere), and Meghavahana (carried on the clouds).

Mahisha In Hindu mythology, a colossal buffalo demon who, through incredible austerities, acquired sufficient strength to enable him to take control of the three worlds and threaten the gods. In response to this awesome challenge, the gods combined all their own powers and eventually created the great goddess DEVI.

As the ten-armed Durga, she went into battle against Mahisha and pierced him with her trident, provoking the demon to return to his original form, a 1,000-armed giant with 1,000 weapons. Then Durga seized Mahisha by his arms, lifted him into the air, threw him down to the ground, and killed him by driving an arrow into his breast. As a result of this victory, Devi gained the title Mahisha-mardini (destroyer of Mahisha). Durga means "the inaccessible".

Maia In Greek mythology, one of the Pleiades, the daughter of Atlas and the mother of HERMES by ZEUS. The name means "nurse".

Maid Marion In British legend, the lover of Robin Hood. In order to be with Robin, she disguised herself as a page and took her place among his merry band of outlaws. When she was discovered, she and Robin were married.

Maitreya In Indian Buddhism, the "enlightened one", or the BUDDHA who is yet to come. In the meantime, he dwells in his Tushita heaven, the apex of the sensual universe. In Chinese Buddhism, Maitreya's equivalent, Mi Lo, is a more elaborate and important figure than Maitreya is in Indian Buddhism. A fat, wrinkled figure, Mi Lo is popularly known as "the Laughing Buddha". In Japan, the equivalent figure is the Mirokubosatsu.

Malcandre In Egyptian mythology, a king of Byblos, an important Canaanite port. SETH, the brother and enemy of OSIRIS, had a chest made to Osiris's measurements and, at a banquet, offered it to whoever fitted inside it. When Osiris took his turn and climbed into the chest, the lid was immediately sealed and the chest thrown into the water at the mouth of the Nile to be carried away to the Mediterranean Sea. It washed ashore at Byblos in Phoenicia, and became enfolded in the trunk of a tree. Malcandre cut down the tree and used it as a pillar in a temple. ISIS recovered the chest from the pillar and so was reunited with her husband.

Malsum In the mythology of the Algonquin and Abnaki Indians of North America, the evil twin brother of the trickster and cultural hero GLOOSKAP. Determined to have a spectacular birth, Malsum killed his mother by forcing himself out of her armpit. He then created everything which he thought would inconvenience mankind, and made repeated attempts to kill his brother.

However, Glooskap killed Malsum with the only weapon that could end his charmed life, the root of a fern. Malsum thereafter lived in the underworld as a wolf, while Glooskap protected mankind from evil monsters and natural forces.

Mama Brigitte In the Voodoo mythology of Haiti, the female counterpart of GHEDE, the god of love and death. Her devotees worship her under her sacred trees, the elm or the weeping willow, and pray that she will inflict harm on their enemies. Like Ghede, Mama Brigitte guards dead bodies and converses with their souls as they journey to the underworld. Graves under her care are marked by piles of stones.

Mama Ocollo In the mythology of the Inca people of Peru, the sister-wife of the cultural hero Manco Capac; she is also known as Coya Mama. Both she and Manco Capac are children of the sun god INTI, who sent them to earth to save people by teaching them the arts of civilization. Alternatively, she was one of a group of four brothers and four sisters, and married the youngest brother, when the group founded the city of Cuzco and settled there. This myth is a variation on the founding of the royal Inca clan by the AYAR.

Mammon A Christian demon who represents the evils of wealth. He derived from JESUS' pronouncement that men "cannot serve God and mammon". The word means "worldly riches".

Manco Capac In one version of the legendary foundation of the royal Inca clan of Peru, the son of INTI, the sun god. One of the AYAR, Manco Capac was usually called Ayar Manco. Inti gave them a piece of gold and sent them to earth to assist uncivilized man, telling them

to settle wherever the gold sank into the ground. They thus came to found the city of Cuzco, where Manco Capac established his court and became the first king of the Incas.

Mani In the mythology of certain tribes of Indians in Brazil, a cultural hero who brought sustenance to his people by revealing the staff of life to them. He foretold that, one year after his death, the people would find a great treasure. In fulfilment of his prophecy, the people discovered the manioc plant, the staple diet of the Indians.

Manjusri In the Mahayana Buddhism of Nepal and Tibet, a bodhisattva, or BUDDHA-to-be, who receives worship as a divinity, like AVALOKITESVARA. He is regarded as the bringer of civilization to the Himalayas. In China, he is believed to be Buddha's missionary, who converted the Chinese to Buddhism. His function is to turn the wheel of the law (*dharma*). His symbols are the book of truth, the sword of wisdom and the blue lotus flower.

Manlius According to Roman legend, the commander of the garrison on the Capitol at the time of the Celtic sacking. He repulsed a night attack after being awakened by the cackling of the sacred geese. In 387 BC the Celts defeated the Roman army and set fire to the city, with the exception of the fortified area held by Manlius. This was crowded with the remaining inhabitants, apart from some elderly senators who resolutely stayed in their council chamber and awaited death dressed in their official robes.

Legend says the Celts broke in and, provoked by a senator who struck out at a warrior when he tried to stroke his beard, killed them where they sat. As a reward, Manlius was allowed to call himself Marcus Manlius Capitolinus.

Mannheim In Germanic mythology, the universe was imagined as divided into different lands, into all of which reached either the roots or branches of the world tree YGGDRASIL. These lands included Muspellheim, the land of the fire giants; Vannaheim, home to the Vanir deities such as FREY; Svartalfheim, the land of the dark elves; Ljosalfaheim, the land of the righteous; Mannheim or Midgard, the land of mankind; Helheim, the land of the dead ruled over by Hel; Jotunnheim, the land of the giants; Niflheim, the land of mist; and Godheim, or heaven, the site of the city of Asgard and the home of the Aesir, gods such as BALDER, LOKI, THOR and ODIN. Asgard was joined to Mannheim by Bifrost, the rainbow bridge, which HEIMDAL, the watchman of the gods, guarded.

Marawa In Melanesian mythology, especially that of the Banks Islands, a spider spirit, the friend and opponent of the other great spirit, the benevolent QAT. Though Marawa put every obstacle in the way of Qat's conquest of the sea, he also helped him to escape from difficult situations on several occasions. In some myths, Marawa represents death, or is portrayed as being the spirit who brings death into the world.

Marindi In Australian aboriginal belief, an ancestral dog, or dingo, whose blood turned the rocks red. This happened during Alchera (Dreamtime), when the lizard Adno-artina challenged Marindi to a fight. The cunning lizard persuaded Marindi to wait until evening, when he could see better. When at last the fight occurred, Adno-artina took a savage hold on Marindi's throat, killing the dog. The blood flowed out of the fatal wound and made the rocks red.

Maruts In Hindu mythology, storm gods fathered by Rudra, the early form of SHIVA. Maruts are armed with lightning arrows and thunderbolts. There are either twenty-seven or sixty of them. According to the *Ramayana*, the oldest epic of India, the Maruts were born from the broken womb of the goddess Didi after INDRA hurled a thunderbolt at her to prevent her from giving birth to too powerful a son. The goddess intended to remain pregnant for a century, before giving birth to a son who would confront Indra. Instead, the Maruts were formed from the shattered embryo.

Mati-Syra-Zemla In Russian legend, the earth goddess, whose name means "moist mother earth". She protected people from demons and disease, especially cholera. Virgins and widows used to dig up fields after midnight in order to release her spirit agents and allow them to disperse evil.

Matsya In Hindu mythology, the first avatar of VISHNU. He appeared in the form of a fish and saved MANU, the Indian NOAH, from drowning in the great flood, thus preserving human life. The deluge occurred during a cosmic night when BRAHMA, the great creator god, had his rest. The demon HAYAGRIVA took advantage of Brahma's sleep to steal the holy scriptures from his mouth. However, Matsya saved them.

Maya A very old and complex word even in ancient India. It means "delusion" and contains such ideas as self-deception, trickery, magic, and beguilement, to name but a few. In fact, *maya* denotes the world as perceived by the senses, and the workings of the mind itself. Medieval Hindu sages regarded it as the play of DEVI, the mother goddess. In Buddhism, however, *maya* was the means by which MARA attempted to deflect BUDDHA from his contemplations. Maya was also the mother of Buddha. Her dream of his birth amounted to a miraculous conception.

Medb In ancient Ireland, the legendary queen of Connacht. Medb's greed caused a bitter war between Connacht and Ulster. Only CUCHULAINN was powerful enough to fend off the forces of Connacht, though he, too, was eventually killed by Medb's sorcery. She was sexually ravenous, her lust so strong that her very appearance was said to drain men of their energy. She could be the prototype of Mab, the British Queen of the Fairies.

Medea In Greek mythology, a powerful witch or sorceress from Colchis. Medea fell in love with JASON, married him, and helped him to steal the Golden Fleece, which belonged to her father. After leaving Colchis with Jason, Medea bore him two children, Mermerus and Pheres. When Jason sought to abandon her and marry Creusa, a Corinthian princess, Medea revenged herself by poisoning Creusa's wedding gown so that it burned her to death. She may also have killed her own two children.

Medea then escaped to Athens in a magic chariot, drawn by winged serpents. There, she married Aegeus, the father or guardian of THESEUS, and gave birth to a son, Medus. When Theseus attempted to be recognized as the heir of Aegeus, Medea, anxious that Medus should be the heir, persuaded the king to send Theseus to Crete in order to fight the Minotaur. Once the Minotaur was dead, Aegeus accepted the claim of Theseus and Medea fled back to Colchis, where she succeeded in installing Medus as king.

Medusa In Greek mythology, the most famous of the three monstrous sisters, the Gorgons. She had snakes instead of hair and her face was so ugly that its appearance turned men to stone, and was thus often represented on Greek shields. ATHENA, whom Medusa had offended, sent PERSEUS to destroy her. He cut off her head, which he presented to Athena. Her blood gave rise to Chrysaor and the winged horse Pegasus. The other two Gorgons, Stheno (strength) and Euryale (wide-leaping) were immortal, unlike Medusa, whose name means "ruler".

Mehturt In ancient Egypt, a sky goddess who was portrayed as a cow and often identified with HATHOR. Her name means "great flood" and she was the celestial river, or canal, on which the sun god RE sailed in his boat.

Melampus A great Greek seer, who was able to foretell events by listening to the voices of animals. He acquired this singular gift as a result of grateful serpents licking his ears. Another gift of Melampus was the art of healing, which he used to cure the daughters of Proteus, the sea god, from madness.

Melqart A widely worshipped Canaanite god, whose chief temple was situated in Tyre. His name probably means "the king of the city". He was identified by the Greeks with the hero HERACLES, and it is not unlikely that the Pillars of Heracles were previously called the Pillars of Melqart.

Memnon The son of EOS, the Greek goddess of the dawn. His skin was said to be black because his mother spent so much time in the company of the sun god Helios. At Troy, Memnon fought on the side of his uncle, PRIAM, and brought a force of Ethiopians with him. He was killed by ACHILLES, but afterward ZEUS, at the request of EOS, resurrected Memnon and made him immortal. During the period of Roman dominion, a statue of the Egyptian ruler Nebmare Amenhotep III (1405–1367 BC), sited near the Valley of the Kings at Thebes, was visited by thousands of tourists because it talked. At daybreak, when Eos arose, a broken part of the statue made a distinct sound, which was interpreted as Memnon's cry to his mother. Memnon was believed to have led his brave Ethiopians past the same spot on the march to Troy.

Menelaus In Greek mythology, the King of Sparta, and husband of HELEN. He was the son of the cursed Atreus, and the younger brother of Agamemnon. When Menelaus was away on business, Paris abducted Helen and carried her off to Troy. Menelaus called upon the Greeks to go to war with him to recover his wife. After the defeat of the Trojans, he returned with Helen to Sparta, encountering many adventures on the way. The Spartan fleet suffered considerably because Menelaus had not appeased the gods of defeated Troy.

Menthu In Egyptian mythology, both a sun god and god of war. He was falcon-headed, like HORUS, and, when identified with the sun god RE, he was called Menthu-Re. Particularly fond of horses, Menthu's warlike aspect gained ascendancy in later times. As the Egyptian chariots bore down on the Hittites during the battle of Kadesh in 1286 BC, the pharaoh Ramesses II cried out that he was "like Menthu, shooting to the right and left".

Mephistopheles In medieval European legend, an agent or form of SATAN. Mephistopheles is principally associated with the legend of Faust, before whom he appears in many forms, some animal, some human, causing him great amusement. Finally, in the guise of a friar, Mephistopheles succeeds in persuading Faust to sign away his soul to him.

Mercury In Roman mythology, the god of trade or commerce and the messenger of the gods. The son of JUPITER, he is commonly identified as the Roman equivalent of the Greek god HERMES. However, although Hermes was also the gods' messenger, he was a more complex god than Mercury and had no association with trade. Mercury was especially associated with the corn trade. He was renowned for his great speed and the element mercury, or quicksilver, was named after him. Mercury's cult was formally established at Rome in the year 495 BC.

Mertseger An ancient Egyptian goddess with a serpent's head. She presided over the great necropolis at Thebes, where her touchiness caused visitors to pay her the greatest respect.

Meschach See Abednego.

Mesede In Melanesian mythology, a champion marksman whose bow burst into flames when it was drawn. Mesede saved Abele's son from the jaws of a crocodile and claimed as his reward Abele's daughters, who were then killed by Mesede's wife in a jealous rage. A magic drum was made from a daughter's head. It is used in the rites of several Melanesian peoples.

Meskhent In Egyptian mythology, the goddess who assisted in the delivery of babies and who played a part in assigning a destiny to each newborn child. She may have also stood by ANUBIS in OSIRIS's hall, the place where souls were weighed and judged. She was commonly represented as a tile, or brick, with a woman's head; the reason was that Egyptian women traditionally squatted on a brick during childbirth.

Mestra In Greek mythology, the daughter of Erysichthon, the impious king of Dotion in Thessaly. In punishment for defiling the sacred grove of DEMETER, the gods afflicted Erysichthon with insatiable hunger. In order to buy food, he sold everything that he owned, until he eventually put his daughter Mestra up for sale. POSEIDON, who was in love with Mestra, gave her the ability to change her shape, so that she always eluded her purchasers. When the ruse was discovered, and Erysichthon could no longer sell her, he started to devour his own flesh and died.

Methuselah A biblical figure, the son of Enoch and grandfather of NOAH. He fathered his first son, Lamech, when he was 187 years old and lived to the age of 969. He thus lived longer than any other person recorded in the Bible.

Metis A lover of ZEUS, the king of the gods in ancient Greece. Zeus persuaded Metis, a Titaness, to give KRONOS the drink that caused him to regurgitate his brothers and sisters. Zeus later swallowed Metis, in order to avoid having too powerful a daughter by her. In the event, ATHENA burst from Zeus's own head. Metis means "counsel".

Mictlantecuhtli The Aztec god of death and the ruler of the underworld (*mictlan*). His kingdom was a place of rest rather than of terror. Montezuma, the last Aztec emperor, presented Mictlantecuhtli with the skins of flayed men as a gift when, in 1519, he heard of the landing of the Spaniards under the command of Hernando Cortés. Clearly Montezuma believed the rumour that QUETZALCOATL had returned with the invaders, and his thoughts turned to the rest he would soon enjoy in the realm of the underworld.

Midgard In Germanic mythology, the land of mortals, which included Mannheim. It lay between Asgard, the home of the gods, and Jottunnheim, the home of the frost giants. It was created by ODIN and other gods from the body of the primeval giant Ymir, whose blood and sweat made the ocean, and whose skull, supported by four dwarfs, formed the arch of the heavens. Midgard was entirely surrounded by the serpent Jormungandr, also known as the Midgard Serpent or Snake.

Miletus The Greek youth who gave his name to the city of Miletus, founded by Sarpedon in Asia Minor. The love affair between Miletus and Sarpedon, which resulted in their banishment from Crete by a jealous MINOS, is simply a legendary account of the establishment of an important Greek settlement. Miletus possessed a powerful navy from its first years, a circumstance that would have worried Minos, the legendary king of the sea.

Mimir The wise Germanic giant who lost his head while held hostage by the Vanir deities. ODIN preserved Mimir's head with herbs, then gave it the power of speech, by means of a spell. It was placed by a spring near one of the roots of YGGDRASIL, the cosmic tree. When Odin needed advice, he would gallop to the spring on his eight-legged steed Sleipnir and converse with the head.

Min The ancient Egyptian god of reproduction, and an aspect of AMUN, the ram-headed god of Thebes. He was usually shown as a man wearing a two-plumed headdress, holding a sceptre in the form of a whip, and with an erect sexual member. He was an extremely popular deity.

Minawara One of the ancestral kangaroo men of the Nambutji people of central Australia. This aboriginal hero, along with his brother Multultu, emerged from a pile of rubbish left behind after a flood. Wandering from place to place, the brothers shaped the landscape, invented the spear, and started initiation rites.

Minotaur In Greek mythology, the monster with a bull's head and a man's body, who dwelt in the Labyrinth near the palace of MINOS. His name means "the bull of Minos", and refers to the creature's parentage: he was the offspring of Pasiphae, the wife of Minos, and a bull sent from the sea by POSEIDON. The craftsman DAEDALUS made a decoy cow, enabling Pasiphae to satisfy her desire. Daedalus also built the Labyrinth, into which the Athenian hero THESEUS stole to slay the Minotaur.

Minyas The legendary founder of Orchomenus, reputed to have been the richest city in ancient Greece. His wealth could not save him from disaster, however. One day, DIONYSUS visited his palace and drove his daughters mad. In a frenzy, they made a sacrifice of his grandson Hippasus.

Mirrimina In the mythology of the Murngin people of northern Australia, a waterhole. Its name means "rock python's back", since YURLUNYUR, the great copper python and ancestral snake spirit of the Murngin, lives in its waters. Waterholes are also important for the Kabi people of Queensland, whose chief god Dhakan, part fish and part man, lives in them. When he moves from one hole to another, he appears in the sky as a rainbow.

Mithras In Roman mythology, a development of the ancient Iranian god MITHRA, who himself was probably related to the Hindu sun god Mitra. The sacrifice of bulls to Mithras was cultivated by the soldiers of the Roman Empire, and hence spread as far north as Britain. It was believed to ensure prosperity in this world and bliss in the next.

As worship of pagan gods was drawing to a close in the Roman Empire, the cult of Mithras was very attractive to high-born traditionalists including the Emperor Julian. He worshipped him in a cave sanctuary in his palace at Constantinople and carried out many rituals.

Mitra One of the most ancient Hindu deities. A god of light, he was thought to care for the welfare of the world.

Mixcoatl In Aztec mythology, the cloud serpent and god of the chase. He was usually shown as a man with long hair and black eyes, and his body was covered with white stripes from top to bottom. Sometimes, as god of hunting, Mixcoatl was depicted with the features of a deer or a rabbit. He was married to COATLICUE, the earth goddess.

Mjolnir The magic hammer of THOR, the powerful son of ODIN. It was made for him by the dwarfs Brokk and Eitri. The properties of the hammer were remarkable: it was unbreakable and, like a boomerang, it returned to the hand however far it was thrown. It could also reduce itself in size so as to be hidden away in a pocket.

Alone of all weapons, Mjolnir could guard against the frost giants. When it was stolen by these enemies of the gods, the trickster god LOKI persuaded Thor to dress up as a bride and pretend to marry Thrymr, their king. As soon as Thor's fingers grasped the hammer once more, he brought it down so hard that it crushed the skull of Thrymr with a single blow. The sons of Thor, Modi and Magni, are to inherit Mjolnir in the new world that is to follow Ragnarok, the day of destruction.

Mnemosyne In Greek mythology, the daughter of the Titans Gaia and Ouranos (Uranus) and the mother of the Muses by ZEUS. Her name means "memory" and she was able to pass on her knowledge to her daughters.

Modred The cause of the disastrous civil war that ruined the Round Table of ARTHUR, the legendary King of Britain. Sir Modred's treachery led to the fatal engagement near Salisbury, where the flower of British chivalry perished and Arthur received a mortal wound.

The quarrel between Arthur and his nephew Modred may well echo an historic conflict. It is possible that in Arthur's time Britain comprised a number of small, independent kingdoms, firmly cemented together as allies whenever an external threat arose, but falling apart when it was removed during the long peace that the victories of the Knights of Round Table had secured. In his *History of Britain*, the ninth-century chronicler Nennius records, "Arthur and Modred perished together".

Mokos A goddess in Slavic mythology. During Lent, she passes the nights wandering from house to house disguised as a woman. She can be both benevolent and malevolent. Sometimes, she worries wool spinners, but at other times she will look after sheep and shear them herself. In an attempt to ensure her goodwill, strands of fleece are laid beside stoves at night.

Mongan In Irish mythology, a son of MANANNAN, the sea god. He was born in circumstances similar to those of ARTHUR. Mongan's generous nature almost cost him dear when an unscrupulous king made him promise to give him anything that was in his power. The king chose to take Mongan's wife. However, Mongan's shape-changing skills saved the day, since he persuaded the king to swap his wife for an old woman whom he had made to appear both young and beautiful.

Montezuma A god whose name was taken from the last emperor of the Aztecs. Despite bringing men the arts of civilization, Montezuma was also their scourge, playing endless tricks on them. He eventually retired to the underworld.

Morgan le Fay In British legend, the half-sister of ARTHUR. She was also identified with Nimue, the mistress of MERLIN. Most versions of Arthur's departure to Avalon have Morgan le Fay as the chief of the ladies who took the wounded king away. But Malory has Nimue in attendance also.

Morpheus In Greek mythology, the god of dreams, and the son of Hypnos, the god of sleep. The name of the hallucinatory drug morphine derives from him. Whereas Morpheus brought dreams to human beings, his two brothers, Phobetur and Phantasos, brought them to animals and inanimate objects. Morpheus means "shaper".

Morrigan The Irish goddess of war, who helped the Connacht queen Medb to slay CUCHULAINN. Her favourite shape was that of a crow or a raven.

Mot In Canaanite mythology, the god of death and infertility. The arch-enemy of BAAL, he was born of a primeval egg hatched from the union of air and chaos. When Baal, tired of Mot's authority, forbade him to visit any part of the earth but the desert, Mot replied by inviting Baal to the underworld. Baal dared not refuse the summons and so visited Mot's home, where he died. Outraged, Anat killed Mot, and Baal returned from the dead.

Mount Olympus See Olympus.

Moyna A legendary hero of the Dogon people of Mali. He invented the bull-roarer, a wooden object that creates an unusual sound when whirled at the end of a rope. Apparently, Moyna began to whirl the bull-roarer at a masked dance, which women were forbidden to attend. However, several women secretly looked on but, when they heard the sound of the bull roarer, ran away in terror.

Moyna told them that the sound was the voice of the Great Mask and that women and children must stay indoors when it was communicating with men, or it would destroy them. The secret of the bull-roarer was passed on to Moyna's sons. The hero told them to use it whenever an important person died because its sound was like that of the spirits of the dead. The bull-roarer is used in African secret societies and its sound frightens many people.

Muchalinda In Hindu mythology, a gigantic serpent spirit who lived in the shade of the Bo tree. When a storm approached, Muchalinda's great hood shielded the BUDDHA, who, deep in contemplation, remained ignorant of the weather. Thus, the Buddha was protected from the winds and rain. After seven days, the storm abated, whereupon Muchalinda uncoiled himself, changed into a young man and bowed to the Buddha.

Mukuru In the mythology of the Herero people of Namibia, the remote sky god. He exists alone, without any friends or family, and is a kindly deity. He sends life-giving rain to mankind, heals those who are ill, and looks after the old. Death is seen as a cause for happiness, since the dead are at last able to return home to this benevolent god in the sky.

Mummu In Mesopotamian mythology, the servant of Abzu, or Apsu, the enormous underground reservoir of fresh water. His name probably means "shape". According to the Babylonian creation epic, *Enuma Elish*, Abzu and Mummu once visited TIAMAT to conspire against the gods. However, the fresh-water god Ea, the equivalent of the Sumerian ENKI, cast a spell over Abzu and Mummu. While Abzu sank into an eternal sleep, Mummu was secured by having a string passed through his nose. The salt-water dragon Tiamat was less easily subdued, and in due course all the gods had to pool their resources in order that they might arm a champion, Ea's son, MARDUK.

Muses In Greek and Roman mythology, the goddesses of the arts, including music and literature. They were the daughters of ZEUS and the Titaness Mnemosyne (memory). Their interests were: Calliope, epic poetry; Clio, history; Euterpe, music; Terpsichore, lyric poetry and dance; Melpomene, tragedy; Thalia, comedy; Polymnia, mime; and Urania, astronomy.

Mushdama The ancient Mesopotamian god of architecture, and the close companion of Kulla, the god of bricks. Together, they were responsible for the erection of the artificial mountains of sun-dried bricks on which the temples of the gods stood. These ziggurats were the striking feature of cities in Sumer and Babylonia. They were so essential for a prosperous city that kings strove to out-build each other. The ultimate construction was the Tower of Babel, by means of which NIMROD hoped to be able to assault heaven itself.

Muspellheim In Germanic mythology, the realm of fire and heat that provided vital energy at the creation of the world. It was inhabited by the descendants of Muspell, the fire giant, and was guarded by Surt and his flaming sword, which will bring the fire of destruction to the gods at Ragnarok, the predestined day of final destruction.

Mut In ancient Egypt, the wife of Amun-Re, the ram-headed god of Thebes and the chief deity in the period of the New Kingdom (1567–1069 BC). Mut is portrayed either as a crowned woman or a vulture. The son of Amun and Mut was Khonsu, a god with great powers of healing. During the 21-day festival held for the Amun family, at the time of the Nile flood, the sacred barges of all three deities made their way to Luxor and back in great pomp.

Mwambu In the mythology of the Abaluyia people of Kenya, the first man, who lived with his wife Sela, the first woman. They were both made by the creator god WELE who gave the couple sunshine and rain, told them what food they could eat, and sent them male and female calves, and thus prosperity.

The couple lived in a house built on stilts so that, when dangerous monsters threatened them, they simply pulled up the ladder to their front door. The house was a miniature version of the creator god Wele's heavenly abode. In due course, Mwambu and Sela had several children who left their home and began to settle the earth.

Mwuetsi A god of the Makoni people of Zimbabwe, the first man and also the moon. Mwuetsi was made by the sky god Maori, then given a horn of potent *ngona* oil and sent to live at the bottom of a lake. He insisted on returning to earth, but found it void of all life. Then Maori gave Mwuetsi the maiden Massassi who created vegetation.

Morongo, another woman created by Maori, bore animals and children as a result of sleeping with Mwuetsi. But when Mwuetsi ignored the warning not to produce any more offspring, Morongo gave birth to lions, scorpions and snakes. Morongo then preferred the snake to her husband, and when Mwuetsi forced himself on her, the snake bit him. He sickened, as did the animals and plants. Eventually Mwuetsi's children learned that their father should not return to the lake and so buried him in the ground.

Mylitta According to the Greek historian Herodotus, a Babylonian goddess identified with APHRODITE. Herodotus was outraged by the custom whereby, once in her life, every woman in Babylon had to sit in the temple of ISHTAR and offer herself to any man who asked for her in the name of Mylitta. The goddess seems to have taken a special interest in childbirth.

Myrmidons In Greek mythology, soldiers who fought under ACHILLES in the Trojan War. Their name means "ant-men", and is derived from the myth in which Aeceus, King of Aegina, prayed to ZEUS to increase the population of his kingdom, whereupon Zeus transformed ants into warriors. Due to the Myrmidons' high reputation, on account of their fierce loyalty, the name is now used to describe people who carry out orders with unquestioning and ruthless thoroughness.

Myrrha In Greek mythology, a princess who fell in love with her father, Cinyras, King of Cyprus. Myrrha's nurse arranged for her to disguise herself and sleep with her father. When the king discovered the truth, he attempted to kill Myrrha, who fled to the land of Sabaea. There, she turned into a myrtle tree, the resin of which produces the fragrance myrrh. Ten months later, the tree bore ADONIS.

N

Na Atibu According to the Gilbert Islanders, the god who died so that mankind might live. NAREAU, the spider god, created Na Atibu and his female companion Nei Teukez from water and sand, then left them to create the world.

From Na Atibu's spine grew the sacred tree *kai-n-tiku-aba*, in the branches of which lived men and women, the fruit of the tree. When one of them, Kouri-aba, shook the tree in anger because excrement had fallen on him, the people fell to earth and were scattered. Thus, sorrow came into the world.

Na Atibu and Nei Teukez also gave birth to the gods. Na Atibu allowed one of them, Nareau the younger, to tear him apart so that his eyes might be used to bring light to the world. The right eye was placed in the eastern sky as the sun, the left eye in the western sky as the moon; his brains formed the stars and his flesh and bones the islands and trees.

Nacien A British hermit who delivered a critical message, via a damsel, to Sir Lancelot. According to Malory's *Le Morte d'Arthur*, Nacien told him that he was no longer the best knight in the world. Because of his secret love for Guinevere, ARTHUR's queen, Sir Lancelot agreed with the judgement. He was therefore surprised when the damsel told him that the Grail would feed his guests.

This miracle occurred on the very same evening, although no one present could see the Grail. However, Lancelot's house was filled "with good odours, and every knight had such meats and drinks as he best loved in the world". As a result of this visitation, many knights swore to search for the Grail, but only Sir Galahad, the son of Sir Lancelot, was blessed with a complete vision, which he experienced due to his purity. The Grail was believed to be the vessel used by JESUS at the Last Supper.

Nagas In Hindu mythology, water gods, or spirits, with human heads and serpent bodies. They form the retinue of the serpent Sesha and inhabit opulent and bejewelled subaquatic palaces. Sesha, who has 1,000 heads, forms the couch of VISHNU, when the great god sleeps during the intervals in creation. The serpent Muchalinda, on the other hand, shielded the BUDDHA from a week-long tempest when he was in contemplation. In Southeast Asia, local serpent princesses married Indian priests or warriors to establish dynasties there.

Naglfer In Germanic mythology, the horrific ship made from the nail clippings of the dead. It was destined to carry the frost giants to the final battle against the gods at Ragnarok. To put off the evil hour, it was customary for Germanic peoples to ensure that their dead went out of the world with their nails cut.

Naiads See Nymphs.

Najara In the aboriginal mythology of western Australia, a wicked spirit whose whistling tempts young boys away from their people, and who then induces them to forget their language and traditions. His whistling is heard in the grass.

Na-Kaa In the mythology of the Gilbert Islanders of Micronesia, one of the two primeval creator gods, the other of whom was his brother Tabakea (first of all). They were created in darkness from heaven which, feeling lonely, rubbed itself against earth. Na-Kaa watched over the sacred tree that only women were allowed to touch. One day, when he was off his guard, men touched the tree and, in his anger, Na-Kaa decided to bring death into the world. Thereafter, he guarded the gateway to paradise, catching in his net sinners who were forbidden entrance to the realm of eternal life.

Na Kika In Micronesian mythology, specifically that of the Gilbert Islands, the octopus god, son of the primeval creator gods Na Atibu and Nei Teukez. His many arms proved indispensable in making the archipelagos of the Pacific. They enabled him to pull vast quantities of sand and stone together to build the islands in preparation for the creation of men and women by NAREAU the younger, who was also known as Te Kikinto (mischief-maker).

Nama In Siberian mythology, an Altaic hero who built the ark which preserved him, his family, and animals from the great flood. Although he is similar to NOAH, Nama was also the god of the underworld and acted as the intercessor between men and the supreme god.

Nammu In Mesopotamian mythology, the mother of ENKI, the fresh-water god. At the beginning of time, when the gods had to toil to gain their livelihood, they appealed to Nammu for assistance. In response, Nammu asked her son to create mankind in order to relieve the gods of the burden of work. So, using clay, Enki made the first people.

However, Enki's wife, NINHURSAGA, boasted that she could easily spoil creation by changing the shape of people at will. Enki told her that, no matter what she made, a place could always be found for anything that was created. Thus, Enki placed all Ninhursaga's misshapen creatures, which included the giant, the cripple and the infertile, in human society.

Nammu may have been an aspect of Abzu, the reservoir of fresh water beneath the earth, or the marshlands at the mouth of the Euphrates and Tigris, where new land was constantly being created by the silt of these great rivers. The Nammu myth is of Sumerian origin.

Namtar The ancient Mesopotamian god of plague. His name means "fate", and recalls the wonder of early men at the sudden assault of fatal diseases. When ENLIL wished to destroy mankind because of the noise made by the cities, he sent Namtar to earth. However, the plague god was abashed at the number of offerings made to him, and he was too embarrassed to appear before the people.

Nana The earth goddess of the Yoruba people of Nigeria. Her husband is Obaluwaye, the earth god. The cult of Nana was gradually transferred through the slave trade to Brazil, where her name is spelt Nanan.

Nana Buluku In the mythology of the Fon people of Dahomey, the primeval creator god, the androgynous begetter of MAWU-LIZA, who created the universe. Because Nana Buluku is so remote, scarcely more than a first cause, the Fon people worship Mawu-Liza as the supreme deity.

Nanda In Buddhist mythology, the name of the woman who fed BUDDHA after he gave up self-mortification. Afterward he is said successfully to have chosen contemplation as the path to enlightenment.

Nandi In Hindu mythology, a sacred white bull, the guardian of all four-legged creatures, and the sentry at the four corners of the world. He is also SHIVA's mount, and is commonly represented with one leg bent, poised to move. He is frequently found guarding the entrances to temples.

Nanna In Germanic mythology, the goddess of flowers and vegetation and the wife of BALDER. When Balder was slain by Hodr, Nanna was so grief-stricken that she chose to die with him on his funeral pyre and accompany him to Hel. When Hermodr's mission to rescue Balder from Hel proved unsuccessful, Nanna elected to remain in the underworld with her husband.

Nanna In Sumerian mythology, the moon god. He was the son of ENLIL, the air god, and Ninlil, the grain goddess whom Enlil raped. For his crime, Enlil was banished to the underworld, where Ninlil followed him so that he could witness the birth of Nanna. Enlil somehow managed to effect Nanna's escape from the underworld so that he could light up the evening sky. In surviving hymns, Nanna is described as "a fierce young bull, thick of horns, perfect of limbs, with a beautiful beard of blue". The eclipse of the moon was explained in ancient Sumer as the work of demons, and kings took part in rites intended to secure Nanna's safety.

Narayana One of the names of BRAHMA, the creator deity of the Hindu pantheon. He is known as Narayana because his movement first stirred the primeval waters (*nara*). Later, VISHNU acquired the same title when he slept on Sesha, the 1,000-headed serpent king, during the intervals of creation.

Narcissus In Greek mythology, a beautiful youth who spurned all offers of love, including that of Echo. In punishment for his aloofness, the gods made him fall in love with his own image, reflected in a pool of water. Unable to possess the image, he pined away and, at his death, possibly through suicide, was changed into a flower, the narcissus.

Narve In Germanic mythology, the son of LOKI by his faithful wife, Sigyn. BALDER had to remain in the underworld because Loki refused to shed a tear for him and so THOR imprisoned the trickster god in a cave. Since Narve had already been eaten by his brother Vali, whom the gods had turned into a wolf, THOR used his entrails as rope. He bound Loki by the shoulders and the legs, and as soon as the knots were tied, the entrails became as hard as stone.

Natos The sun deity of the Blackfoot Indians of North America. His wife, Kokomikeis, was the moon deity and their children were the stars, all of whom, except Apisuahts, the morning star, were killed by pelicans.

Nefertem In Egyptian mythology, the god of the lotus flower from which, in some texts, the sun god RE emerged each morning. Many parents are attributed to him, most commonly PTAH and SEKHMET, the lion-headed goddess. Nefertem is usually portrayed as a bearded man with the headdress of a lotus, from which rise two tall plumes.

Nehebkau An ancient Egyptian deity in the form of a serpent with human arms and legs. He was the loyal servant of RE, the sun god. Quite possibly, Nehebkau was at first a snake that threatened the dead, but later he developed into a force for good.

Neith An ancient Egyptian goddess who came to be associated, like the cow goddess HATHOR, with creation myths. It was at one time believed that she wove the world into existence with her shuttle. Her cult centre was at Sais in Lower Egypt.

Nemesis In Greek mythology, the goddess of retribution. The agent of vengeance, and hence the embodiment of the gods' anger, she was associated above all with punishing mortals who succumbed to *hubris*, or pride. For instance, she pursued Agamemnon when he showed too great a pride in the Greeks' victory over the Trojans.

Nemesis had a fiery aspect and was commonly represented with a balance in one hand and a whip or an axe in the other. She was unsuccessfully pursued by ZEUS. Possibly, the catastrophe of the Trojan War caused some ancient writers to suggest that Nemesis, rather than Leda, was HELEN's mother.

Nemglan The ancient bird god of Ireland. His children were wonderful birds, but if threatened with violence, they turned into armed warriors. His wife was Mess Buachalla, a princess secretly raised by a cowherd. The father of the princess had wanted a son so much that he had ordered her to be exposed to the elements.

Neoptolemus In Greek mythology, the son of ACHILLES. He was also called Pyrrhus. In the Trojan War, he was one of the Greeks concealed in the wooden horse, the stratagem devised by ODYSSEUS to gain entry to Troy. During the subsequent sack of the city, Neoptolemus displayed both bravery and cruelty. He killed PRIAM at the altar of ZEUS and threw Hector's son Astyanax from the city wall.

After the war was over, Neoptolemus took Hector's widow,

Andromache, to his kingdom of Epirus, but deserted her for Hesione. He was murdered at Delphi after desecrating the shrine there. An alternative tradition says that Neoptolemus was killed by ORESTES.

Nephthys In Egyptian mythology, a funerary goddess, the daughter of NUT and Geb and the sister of OSIRIS, SETH and ISIS. She appears as a woman. Although she was the wife of Seth, Nephthys deserted him and had a son, ANUBIS, by Osiris, whom Seth later murdered. Nephthys means "the lady of the castle".

Neptune In Roman mythology, the god of water, hence identified with the Greek POSEIDON. However, compared to Poseidon, Neptune is a relatively unimportant god. He was commonly represented seated in a large seashell drawn by seahorses.

Nereids See Nymphs.

Nereus In Greek mythology, an older sea god than POSEIDON. He was the son of Pontus (sea) and Gaia (earth). In order to obtain the golden apples of the Hesperides, HERACLES surprised Nereus and obtained from him the location of the sacred garden. In the process the hero had to hang onto the sea god through a series of miraculous shape changes.

Nergal In Babylonian mythology, a god of war who led the gods in battle. More importantly, he was the god of death, the husband of Ereshkigal, the goddess of the underworld and the sister of INANNA. When Ereshkigal summoned him to her presence for having remained seated in the presence of one of her envoys, he threatened to cut her throat with a knife. However, she stopped him by

offering herself to him and promising him sovereignty over the realm of the dead. Thereafter, Nergal ruled the underworld.

In another version of the myth, Ereshkigal vowed to make the earth infertile if Nergal did not come to her bed. Nergal was identified with Erra, the deity responsible for civil and military disorder.

Nerio In Roman mythology, a minor goddess who was believed to have married the god of war, MARS. Her name means "strength".

Nessus In Greek mythology, a centaur which Heracles encountered during his second labour. Deianira, the second wife of HERACLES, was afraid that her husband would desert her. On the instruction of Nessus, she dipped one of Heracles' shirts in Nessus's blood, believing it to be a love potion to revive Heracles' interest in her. Instead, it killed the hero.

Nestor The elder statesman of the ancient Greeks during the Trojan War. He was renowned for his eloquence and wisdom and was said to have lived to a great age. He managed to return safely home to Pylos from Troy because he left before ATHENA blew up the great storm which wrecked the ships of many other Greek leaders. He seems to have died quietly at Pylos.

Ngunza According to the Mbundu people of Angola, a legendary hero who captured Death. While away from home, Ngunza dreamed that his brother had died and, on returning, his mother told him that her son had indeed been taken away by Death.

Ngunza decided to capture Death, who pleaded to be released, saying that human beings brought death upon themselves. Ngunza insisted on being shown that this was the case and so Death took him to his home. There, Ngunza found his brother enjoying a happier life than he had experienced on earth, and so he returned alone to the land of the living.

Eventually, Death sought out Ngunza himself, but the hero resisted him, until Death was forced to throw an axe at him, turning him into a spirit.

Nibelungs In Germanic mythology, the light dwarfs, or elves, who lived in the underworld kingdom of Nibelheim, or Alfheim. There they hoarded a vast treasure of gold. They were followers of the hero Sigurd, or Siegfried, for whom they made a magic gold ring.

Nidhoggr In Germanic mythology, the dragon who lived near the lowest region of Niflheim, at the foot of the world tree YGGDRASIL, and chewed at its roots. In his underworld domain, Nidhoggr also fed on corpses. His name means "corpse tearer".

Nidud In Germanic mythology, a king who kidnapped the smith god WAYLAND, whom he accused of stealing his wealth. Wayland killed two of Nidud's sons, possibly because they had dared to look at his treasures. He cut off their heads, decorated them with jewels, and returned them to Nidud. Wayland also appears to have seduced the daughter of the king.

Nike In ancient Greece, the winged goddess of victory, who fought on the side of the gods against the Titans. She was the inspirer of athletes and musicians in their various contests.

The Roman equivalent, Victoria, took on a more serious and warlike role, being associated with the cults of JUPITER and MARS. In 29 BC, Victoria's most famous altar was placed in the chamber of the Senate by Augustus, the first Roman emperor. During the imperial period, the goddess was worshipped by soldiers. One of the last great generals of Rome, the Vandal Stilicho who served Honorius, the emperor of Rome from AD 393 to 423, restored her altar.

Nimue The legendary Celtic enchantress whom MERLIN fell in love with when he came upon her in the woods. She is sometimes identified with the Lady of the Lake, but is otherwise believed to be one of her damsels. In response to her pleas, Merlin revealed his magic skills to her, and she used the power she acquired to trap him.

Ninazu A husband of Ereshkigal, the Mesopotamian goddess of the underworld. He was the brother-in-law of INANNA, the fertility goddess who dared to visit the underworld. Ninazu was conceived in the underworld by ENLIL and the grain goddess Ninlil. Enlil had been sent there by the assembly of the gods in punishment for raping Ninlil. However, Ninlil followed Enlil to the underworld in order to give birth in his presence. Once there, she and Enlil mated again, in order to find a substitute for their son Nanna, the moon god.

According to other Sumerian myths, Ninazu was the son of Ereshkigal. He certainly appears to have been an independent-minded deity. On one occasion, he released from the underworld a god called Damu, who had authority over the sap in trees and bushes each spring.

Ningishzida A Mesopotamian deity who has various duties in a number of Sumerian epics. In one, he acts as the gatekeeper of AN, the sky god; in another, his duties involve acting as an officer in the underworld; in a third epic, he helps Gudea, King of Lagash, to build a temple. Apparently, in about 2139 BC, Ningishzida appeared to Gudea in a dream and told him how to prepare the temple's foundation.

Ninlil The Mesopotamian grain goddess whom ENLIL raped near the city of Nippur. Their child was Nanna, the moon god.

Ninshubur In ancient Mesopotamia, a messenger goddess who played an important role in the sacred marriage rite. Kingship was regarded from Sumerian times onward as a gift from heaven, and its divine nature was celebrated annually in the marriage of the king to the love goddess INANNA. Ninshubur brought the royal bridegroom to the divine bride, who was probably impersonated by a high priestess. As the handmaiden of Inanna, Ninshubur went to see ENLIL at Nippur and pleaded for help when her mistress was trapped in the underworld. In the end, it was only ENKI who provided Ninshubur with useful assistance.

Ninsuna A Mesopotamian cow goddess whose name means "lady of the wild cows". While in the shape of a woman, she bore the Sumerian king of Lagash, Gudea (2142–2122 BC). She is also called the mother of Dumuzi, INANNA's husband, and of the hero GILGAMESH.

Nintur One of the titles used by NINHURSAGA, the Sumerian mother goddess and the model for all Mesopotamian earth goddesses. It means "the lady who gives form" and refers to Ninhursaga's role as a birth goddess. As Nintur, she was shown carrying the midwife's pail of water. Without the permission of the air god ENLIL, she could not let a new-born child die, however.

Njinyi In the mythology of the Bamum people of Cameroon, the creator god, whose name means "the one who is everywhere". He created strong and healthy men and women, and was dismayed to see them breathless, wooden and stiff. He therefore asked Death if he were responsible. Death answered that he was not, but that people wished to die. He took Njinyi, disguised as a banana skin, to witness people pass, complaining of life and asking for death. Each one that did so died immediately, and Njinyi walked away saddened.

Njord In Germanic mythology, the god of sea and winds and father of FREY and Freya. He was originally a Vanir god, but visited Asgard, the home of the Aesir gods, where he fell in love with the frost giantess Skadi, who had come in search of a husband. Skadi liked the icy mountains of Jotunnheim, the land of the giants, but Njord was not impressed, and so they returned after their honeymoon to Asgard. When Skadi found it just as intolerable, they agreed to spend three nights in one place, followed by three in the other; hence the establishment of the seasons.

Norns In Germanic mythology, the three goddesses of destiny: Urd (the past), Verdandi (the present), and Skuld (the future). They were thought of as spinners who held the threads of destiny in their hands. They lived by a fountain in the shade of the world tree YGGDRASIL. Each day they sprinkled the tree with water to ensure that it would not wither.

The Anglo-Saxon settlers of Britain knew the Norns as the Wyrd. They appear in Shakespeare's Macbeth as the weird sisters, or three witches, who tell the future King of Scotland his destiny.

Nuada The legendary high king of Ireland for whom LUGH did service. Nuada was the ruler of the Tuatha De Danaan, the followers of the goddess Dana. He was disqualified from kingship for having lost a hand in battle. However, the medicine god Dian-Cecht made him a silver replacement, which gave rise to his nickname of Airgetlamh (silver-handed).

Nudimmud The son of AN, the Mesopotamian god of heaven, and another name for ENKI, the fresh-water god. An divided the domination of the world between his two sons, Enki and the air god ENLIL. Both of these deities were acknowledged to be more active than An. They eventually became more powerful, too. Nudimmud means "the shaper".

Numa Pompilius The second legendary king of Rome who was believed to have come to the throne in 715 BC. He instituted the worship of JANUS and recruited the first Vestal Virgins to attend the sacred hearth of Vestia, the Roman equivalent of Hestia, daughter of KRONOS.

Nummo In the mythology of the Dogon people of Mali, the primeval man and woman, twin offspring produced by Amma, the supreme god, when he mated with earth. They were serpentlike creatures, with forked tongues and red eyes. Later on, the Nummo helped Amma to create mankind.

Nyame The creator god of the Ashanti people of Ghana. His name means "the shining one" and he is shown as either the moon or the sun. He is armed with lightning, known as god's axes. In the hope of averting Nyame's wrath, stone axes are placed by doorways with special offerings to the god.

Nymphs In Greek mythology, young women divided into a number of groups according to their association with natural phenomena. The most famous groups were the Naiads (nymphs of rivers, lakes and fountains), the Nereids (nymphs of the sea), the Oreads (nymphs of the mountains), and the Oceanids (daughters of Oceanos, the encircling ocean). Nymphs were neither deities nor immortal, although they had a long lifespan. They frequently fell in love with mortals, but they were a special target for ZEUS and the other gods.

Nyx The ancient Greek goddess of the night. She was considered to be among the first deities, having emerged from Chaos with the earth goddess Gaia. Nyx's offspring included Thanatos (death), Hypnos (sleep), Oizys (pain), Nemesis (retribution), and Eris (strife).

Nzambi According to the Bakongo people of Angola, a creator god. A self-existent deity, he is identified both with the sky and the earth. Other African tribes call him Nyambe, Nzame or Njambi. As Nyambe, he is the supreme god, possibly a solar deity, who created animals and people; as Nzame, he is believed to have created the world, but to have departed to the heavens long ago. The Lele people, who call him Njambi, credit him with having given the tropical forest and all the animals therein, to mankind. The spirits who live in the forest are also under Njambi's rule. They influence hunting and fertility.

O

Oberon In medieval European legend, the Fairy King. He was sometimes identified with Andvari, the wealthy dwarf of Germanic mythology. In the French romance, *Huon de Bordeaux*, in which he first appears, he is the son of Julius Caesar and Morgan le Fay and is given the power of insight into men's thoughts, as well as the ability to transport himself to any place instantaneously.

Oceanus In Greek mythology, a sea god, the Titan son of Gaia and Ouranos and the father of all the water gods and nymphs, except POSEIDON. He was represented as a kindly old man with a long beard and the horns of a bull. Oceanus was also the personification of the river of the same name that encircled the earth. All rivers were believed to flow from it, just as the sun and moon rose from, and sank into, it.

This early Greek idea of an encircling sea probably originated from Egypt and Mesopotamia, whose cosmologies pictured the earth floating like a raft on the primeval waters. Even Thales, the Greek philosopher of the sixth century BC, held that water was the first principle from which everything is fashioned and takes its life-giving force. Tethys, the wife of Oceanus, also gave birth to the rivers of the underworld, including the Styx (abomination).

Odrorir In Germanic mythology, the sacred cauldron of the dwarfs. It contained a wonderful mead, which was a mixture of honey and the blood of the wise Kvasir. It imbued whoever drank it with wisdom, the knowledge of spells, and poetic inspiration. ODIN stole it for the gods. The name Odrorir means "heart stirrer".

Oeax In Greek mythology, the brother of Palamedes, whom Agamemnon wrongly condemned to death at Troy. In his bitterness over this miscarriage of justice, Oeax went to Clytemnestra at Mycenae and told her that her husband Agamemnon was returning home with a Trojan concubine, CASSANDRA. In revenge, Clytemnestra took Aegisthus as her lover and plotted the death of Agamemnon. Oeax was also instrumental in having ORESTES banished after he had avenged Agamemnon's murder.

Oenopion The son of the Greek god DIONYSUS and Ariadne, the runaway daughter of MINOS, King of Crete. Oenopion mastered the art of growing the vine on the island, and later turned Chios, his own island, into a leading producer of wine. He promised the hand of his daughter Merope to the giant Orion, but went back on his word. Oenopion means "wine-drinker".

Ogma The Irish god of oratory and literature. The son of DAGDA, he was credited with the invention of writing. Ogma slew the Fomorii leader Indech at the second battle of Magh Tuireadh. Afterward, he claimed as spoils a magic sword called Orna. The miraculous weapon was able to tell its owner of the deeds it had performed.

Ogoun The Voodoo warrior hero of Haiti, a figure derived from the Nigerian OGUN. He is the god of fire, as well as a healer, teacher and magician. His devotees never offer him water, but always rum, which they pour on the ground and then set alight in order to produce Ogoun's sacred colour, red. If the god wants a drink while he is in possession of a devotee, he will shout, "My testicles are cold!"

Oisin The legendary bard of Ireland and the son of Finn Mac Cool. Oisin, also known as Ossian, was both a poet and a warrior. He fell in love with Niamh, a daughter of the sea god MANANNAN, and she took him to a fabulous island in the eastern ocean. Niamh bore him several children, but Oisin yearned to return to Ireland. She lent him her magic horse and warned her husband not to dismount, because three centuries had passed. In the event, Oisin fell from the horse and turned into an old man. However, St Patrick is said to have bid him a warm welcome.

Okonorote In the mythology of the Warrau Indians of Guiana, a hunter hero who lived in the sky and who founded the Warrau people. When an arrow which he shot fell through a hole in the sky, he climbed down an enormous tree and discovered the earth. He returned to the sky and told his companions to follow him to earth. Once there, they were prevented from climbing back to the sky because the hole was blocked by a fat woman. The sky god Kononatoo declined to make a second entrance to heaven because, while on earth, the Warrau girls had misbehaved, mating with serpent spirits.

Olokun In the mythology of the Yoruba people of Nigeria, a deity whose name means "owner of the sea". Trying to contest supremacy with Olorun, the sky god, Olokun accepted a challenge in which each of them would wear his finest attire and be judged by the Yoruba people. Olorun cleverly turned up for the contest as a chameleon and so matched whatever Olokun wore. Olokun confessed that he was outwitted and the ascendancy of Olorun was confirmed.

Olorun The head of the Yoruban pantheon, which contains 1,700 deities. He is known as Olofin-Orun (lord of heaven) and Olodumare (almighty). His name means "owner". A sky god, Olorun created the universe, appointed day and night, arranged the seasons, and fixed the destiny of men.

Whenever misfortune befalls a bad person, the Yoruba say that "he is under the lash of Olorun". At first, men did not die. They grew to an immense size, after which they shrank into feeble old people. Because there were so many of them creeping around, men prayed to Olorun, begging him to free them from too long a life, and in this way the ancients died.

Olympus In Greek and Roman mythology, the home of the gods. They inhabited its peaks, which were hidden from mortal sight by clouds. At nearly 3,000 metres (9,000 feet) above sea level, Mount Olympus is the highest mountain in the whole of Greece.

Olympus was presided over by ZEUS (JUPITER in Roman mythology) and his wife HERA (JUNO). With them lived Zeus's brother POSEIDON (Neptune), and his sisters DEMETER (Ceres) and Hestia (Vestia). HADES, the other brother of Zeus and the ruler of the underworld, rarely visited the place. With the seven children of Zeus, these comprised the twelve Olympian gods, successors to the rule of the Titans.

The children of Zeus were APHRODITE (Venus), Apollo (Apollo), ARES (MARS), ARTEMIS (Diana), ATHENA (MINERVA), HEPHAISTOS (Vulcan) and HERMES (Mercury). In some myths, Hestia resigns her place to make way for DIONYSUS (Bacchus). Sometimes, Aphrodite is held to be the daughter of Ouranos, having grown in the sea, created from his severed member.

Ometechtli In the Aztec mythology of Central America, the supreme, omniscient and transcendent god, whose name means "dual lord". He existed beyond time and space and was the source of all life. He was both male and female, or neither, and was the perfect expression of all dualities, including chaos and order, good and evil, light and darkness, motion and rest.

Oni In the Shinto mythology of Japan, flying demons who bring disease and misfortune. They are human in form, but have three eyes, three horns and three claws on each foot. They swoop down to steal the souls of people who are about to die. Buddhist monks, who perform annual Oni-expelling rites (Oni-yaraki), are thought to be the scourges of the demons.

Onyankopon The creator deity of the Ashanti people of Ghana. He is a sky god who controls all the spirits that inhabit the gods, ancestors and inanimate objects such as trees. A remote deity, Onyankopon lives in the sky, driven there from earth by an old woman who kept hitting him with her pestle while pounding yams. His name means "the great one".

Ops The Roman goddess of abundance, sometimes identified as the wife of SATURN. The word "opulence" comes from her name.

Orchomenus A fabulously rich Greek city during the period of the Trojan War. It was situated in Boeotia and founded by the legendary King Minyas. It was inhabited by the Minyans who were a semi-historical people around whom grew the earliest legends of the Argonauts.

Orcus One of the names used by the Romans for HADES, the Greek god of the underworld. Its meaning is uncertain, however. Dis was another name that the Greeks used to translate Pluton (rich), a title sometimes given to Hades.

Like the Greeks, the Romans regarded the ruler of the underworld as a grim deity, coldly collecting the souls of the dead without any concern for the individual, but they never considered him as unjust, or evil, like SATAN.

Orion In Greek mythology, a giant hunter who was renowned for his good looks. He was blinded by the King of Chios for raping his daughter Merope, but was guided by an assistant of HEPHAISTOS to the nearby island of Lemnos, where EOS, the dawn goddess, restored his sight to him.

Later, when Orion dared to approach ARTEMIS, the goddess of the chase, he fell victim to her cruel nature and she mercilessly killed him. He was subsequently placed in the sky as the constellation Orion, the hunter.

Ormazd In ancient Iranian mythology, the shortened name of AHURA MAZDA, the god of light and wisdom. Ormazd was the foe of evil AHRIMAN, the god of darkness. In Sassassian times (226–641), Ormazd and Ahriman were both said to have been the descendants of Zurvan Akarana, whose name means "eternity".

Oro In Polynesian mythology, the Tahitian god of war and son of the creator god, TA'AROA, and Hina-tu-a-ta (Hina of the land). He delighted in bloodshed and battle and demanded human sacrifices. In times of peace, he was called Oro-i-te-tea-moe (Oro with his spear laid down).

Ossa A mountain peak in Thessaly, in northern Greece. When the Titans sought to reach Mount Olympus and attack the gods, they piled Mount Ossa upon Mount Pelion (in some versions, the other way around) and hurled rocks and burning trees at ZEUS. The rocks that fell back to land formed the earth's mountains; those that fell in the ocean formed the islands.

Otshirvani In Siberian mythology, a god of light, the enemy of evil. He was sent by the supreme god to do battle against Losy, a giant snake who spat venom all over the world, killing mortals and animals. Otshirvani turned himself into a fabulous bird called Garide, seized Losy in his claws, and whirled him around the world mountain, Sumer, until his brains were dashed against the rocks.

Ouranos In Greek mythology, Ouranos, or Uranus, and Gaia were the two primeval gods of the sky and earth. They were passionate, unceasing lovers, and Ouranos so enveloped Gaia that her children were all imprisoned within her womb. One of these children, KRONOS, therefore acquired a mighty sickle and emasculated Ouranos, thus separating the sky from the earth. From the blood that flowed from the wound, Gaia conceived the Titans and the ERINYES (Furies).

In another version, Ouranos's severed member fell into the ocean, where it engendered APHRODITE. Thereafter, Ouranos was overshadowed by Kronos, who ruled the universe until he in turn was deposed by ZEUS.

P

Pachacamac An ancient creator deity of Peru. The Incas adopted his cult, and his name appears in the title of several rulers. When he created the first man and woman, he failed to give them food and the man died; the sun then made the woman fertile, but Pachacamac killed the son she bore and cut him into pieces, from which grew fruit and vegetables. Unable to catch the woman's second son, Wichama, Pachacamac killed the woman instead. In revenge, Wichama then drove Pachacamac into the sea.

Pachamama The earth goddess of the Incas of ancient Peru. Her worship survives today, while Indian Christians have also absorbed her into their religion as the VIRGIN MARY. Llamas were sacrificed to her.

Paeon An ancient Greek god of healing, who cured HADES of a wound inflicted by HERACLES when the hero stole Cerberus, the three-headed watchdog of the underworld. Hades made one of his rare visits to Mount Olympus for the treatment.

Paka'a The Hawaiian god of the winds, credited like the Greek craftsman DAEDALUS with the invention of the sail. He was one of the lesser deities and grew from the spittle of KANE, the great god of creation and generation.

Palici In Greek mythology, the twin gods of Sicily. Their name means "coming again" and refers to their mother the nymph Etna, a pool that regularly gave off natural gas. Her lover was HEPHAISTOS.

Palinurus In Greek and Roman mythology, the helmsman of AENEAS, the hero who led the Trojan refugees to Italy. He was drowned off the Sicilian coast in a storm sent by JUNO. When Aeneas met his ghost in the underworld, he promised Palinurus a proper burial on the recovery of his body.

Panacea The daughter of ASCLEPIUS, the ancient Greek god of healing. Her name means "cure-all".

Pandarus In Greek and Roman mythology, the go-between of the Trojan lovers Troilus and Cressida. Hence the word "pander".

Parasurama The sixth avatar of the great Hindu god VISHNU. The name means "Rama with the axe". He was incarnated as the son of Dasaratha, the king of Ayodhya in northern India. His purpose was to destroy Kartarirya, the arrogant thousand-armed king of the Himalayas.

Parijata In Hindu mythology, the tree that was produced when the gods and the demons churned the ocean to prepare AMRITA, the water of life. The tree perfumed the world with its blossoms and was eventually placed in INDRA's heaven.

Paris In Greek mythology, the son of King PRIAM of Troy and Hecuba, and the brother of Hector and CASSANDRA. Because it was prophesied that Paris would bring about the fall of Troy, the child was abandoned by his father on a mountain to die. However, he was discovered and raised by shepherds.

When Paris returned to Troy as a young man, ZEUS asked him who of APHRODITE, ARTEMIS and HERA should be awarded the golden apple as the fairest of the goddesses. Paris chose Aphrodite who, in return, promised him the most beautiful woman in the world. She then took Paris to Sparta to WOO HELEN, the beautiful wife of King Menelaus. When the Spartan ruler was away from home, Helen and Paris eloped to Troy, so starting the Trojan War.

During the siege of Troy, Paris killed ACHILLES by lodging a poisonous arrow in his heel, and was himself slain by Philoctetes, one of Helen's suitors before her marriage to Menelaus.

Parnassus The legendary home of the Muses in ancient Greece. The mountain was also sacred to Apollo, whose oracle was at nearby Delphi, and DIONYSUS. The boat of Deucalion, the Greek NOAH, came to rest on Mount Parnassus during the deluge sent to earth by ZEUS.

Parvati One of the names of DEVI, the wife of SHIVA and mother of the elephant-headed god of wisdom GANESA. Her name means "the mountaineer". In his aspect as Nataraja (king of dancers), Shiva would perform a cosmic dance before Parvati in order to relieve the sufferings of his followers. When Shiva reproached Parvati for her dark skin, she hid herself in the forest and took up an ascetic life. To comfort her and reward her for her austerities, BRAHMA gave her a golden skin, thus transforming her into Gauri, the emanation of Devi as the "yellow" or "brilliant" one.

Pasiphae In Greek mythology, the daughter of the god Helios, and wife of King MINOS of Crete. When Minos refused to sacrifice a white bull which POSEIDON had given him, the sea god punished him by making Pasiphae desire the animal. DAEDALUS made a decoy cow, into which she fitted in order that she might satisfy her passion. The offspring of the union was the monstrous Minotaur.

Patala In Hindu mythology, the infernal underworld realm of the serpents (*nagas*). The sage Narada visited Patala and on his return to INDRA's heaven reported on its luxury and pleasure.

Patroclus In Greek mythology, the lover and constant friend of ACHILLES. When, during the Trojan War, Achilles sulked in his tent rather than fight, Patroclus disguised himself in his armour and led the Myrmidons into battle. He was slain by Hector, whom Achilles then killed in revenge. After the death of Achilles, his ashes were mixed with those of Patroclus.

Pegasus The winged horse of Greek mythology, born of the blood which flowed from the head of the Gorgon Medusa when it was cut off by PERSEUS. Bellerophon, the Corinthian hero, rode Pegasus in his famous victory over the Chimaera, the fire-breathing son of TYPHON.

Pele A Hawaiian fire goddess associated with lava. After wandering the Pacific for many years, she made her home in Hawaii, where liquid poured from her head over the dry land. She lives in the Kilauea crater and is a fierce, wrathful goddess who turns men and animals to stone.

Peleus In Greek mythology, an Argonaut and the son of Aeacus, King of Aegina. He was the husband of the sea nymph Thetis and the father of ACHILLES. Because of a misunderstanding between husband and wife, when Thetis was attempting to make Achilles immortal by the use of fire, she left Peleus and returned to the sea. Uncertain as to his own ability as a parent, Peleus entrusted the upbringing of Achilles to the centaur Chiron. After the death of Achilles at Troy, Thetis came and took a distraught Peleus to live with her in the sea.

Pellinore In the legend of the Round Table, the ally of ARTHUR and the king who brought Nimue to Camelot, where she enchanted MERLIN. King Pellinore does not play a major role at Arthur's court.

Pelops In Greek mythology, the son of TANTALUS and Dione, the daughter of Atlas. Tantalus served Pelops as a stew at a banquet he gave for the gods. However, the gods, recognizing the food, put it back in the cauldron and restored Pelops to life. Because DEMETER had thoughtlessly eaten his shoulder, she replaced it with one made of ivory. Pelops journeyed to Elis in the Peloponnese (the Isle of Pelops), where he won by violence the hand of Hippodamia, a local princess. They had a large family, including the three sons Epidaurus, Sicyon and Troezen.

Pemba A legendary hero of the Bambara people of Nigeria. They believe that the wood spirit Pemba once descended from the sky and sought to govern the world. Because as a tree he grew thorns, Pemba lost his wife and in time became the victim of Faro, a water spirit who uprooted him. Thereafter, say the Bambaras, Faro controlled the world.

Penates In ancient Rome, the household gods who protected the larder. Theirs was the central cult of every Roman household and offerings were made to images of the Penates before meals.

Penelope The symbol of wifely faithfulness in ancient Greece. She remained true to ODYSSEUS, despite being left alone while her husband fought at Troy and during his ten-year voyage home from there. Beset by suitors during his absence, she reluctantly agreed to choose another husband, but only when she had finished her father-in-law's shroud. However, each night she unravelled what she had woven by day. When her ruse was discovered, she promised to marry the hero who could bend Odysseus's bow. None could perform the feat save a beggar, who revealed himself as the long-awaited Odysseus.

Pentheus In Greek mythology, a Theban king who slighted DIONYSUS when the god visited his city. Pentheus may have thrown Dionysus into prison. He was torn to pieces by the god's female devotees while spying on their secret rites. His own mother, Agave, took the lead in this frenzied action, mistaking Pentheus for a wild beast. In the *Bacchae*, written by the Greek playwright Euripides, Agave gradually awakes to the horror of her son's end. Pentheus was not the only ruler who was forced to suffer the wrath of Dionysus.

Perceval A legendary British Knight of the Round Table, who went in quest of the Grail, the vessel used by JESUS at the Last Supper. He is usually associated with the Germanic hero Parsifal. Sir Perceval was brought up in the forest and was untrained in the arts of chivalry. Nevertheless, he arrived at ARTHUR's court and made such an impression with his sincerity that he became a member of the Round Table. According to some versions of the tale, Sir Perceval may have been allowed to see the Grail. However, unlike Sir Galahad, he never went up to heaven as a result of his blessed vision.

Perenu The ancient thunder god of the Slavs, including the Russians. A creator deity as well as a war god, Perenu was identified with the Germanic THOR and the oak tree, with which his name is connected. He was usually represented carrying an axe, and sometimes a hammer, as the symbol of thunder.

Phaedra An ancient Greek princess, the daughter of MINOS and Pasiphae, the king and queen of Crete. Some years after the killing of the Minotaur, and the disappearance of her sister Ariadne, Phaedra was married to the Athenian king THESEUS by her brother, who had succeeded Minos. However, Phaedra fell deeply in love with Hippolytus, the son of Theseus by a previous wife.

When Phaedra realized that Hippolytus was outraged by her passion for him, she denounced him to Theseus, saying that he had tried to rape her. Then, Phaedra hanged herself. Her violent end was probably connected with the curse of POSEIDON, whom Minos had offended by neglecting to sacrifice the bull the god had sent him from the waves. The curse had previously made Phaedra's mother, Pasiphae, conceive the monstrous Minotaur.

Phaeton The son of the Greek sun god Helios. When Phaeton tried to drive his father's fiery chariot, he was unable to control its powerful steeds, and the vehicle burned the Milky Way across the sky. Then, it plunged earthward and created the Libyan desert. ZEUS was obliged to send a flood in order to prevent the whole earth from catching fire. According to some versions, he killed Phaeton with a thunderbolt.

Philemon See Baucis and Philemon.

Philoctetes The legendary Greek hero who agreed to light the pyre on which HERACLES lay dying. In exchange, Philoctetes received the bow and arrows of Heracles. The arrows never missed their mark and so the weapons would have helped him in the Trojan War. Certainly, they kept him alive when, at the suggestion of ODYSSEUS, he was left on the island of Lemnos because he suffered from a poisonous wound that would not heal. Philoctetes was eventually healed by a physician.

Phobos In Greek mythology, the god of panic on the battlefield. He was the son of APHRODITE by ARES and was attendant on his father. Deimos, the god of fear, was his brother. The other Greek deity who caused panic was PAN.

Phoebe In Greek mythology, the daughter of Ouranos (sky) and Gaia (earth). She was the grandmother of Apollo and ARTEMIS. The name Phoebe (bright) was also one of the titles of the Roman goddess of the moon, Diana, the equivalent of the Greek ARTEMIS.

Phoenix In ancient Egypt, a fabulous bird that was reborn from its own ashes. The Greek historian Herodotus claimed that he saw it at Heliopolis, in the sixth century BC. The phoenix was thought to represent the sun which, as RE, disappeared as an old man each night and appeared as a child every following morning.

Picus According to the Romans, he was an ancient Italian king and the son of SATURN. He also had the powers of prophecy.

Pillan In the mythology of the Araucanian Indians of Chile, the god of thunder and death who introduced blight and disease but also gave the Araucanians fire. He also gathers the souls of heroes slain in battle. He is subordinate to GUINECHEN, but equal to Guecufu, the evil flood god.

Pleiades In Greek mythology, the seven daughters of Atlas and the nymph Pleione. They were so distressed by the death of one of their number that they committed suicide. ZEUS then placed them in the sky as a cluster of seven stars. One of them, Merope, is fainter than the other stars because she was consumed with shame for having once loved a mere mortal.

Pluto In ancient Greece, another name for HADES, the god of the underworld. It was considered unlucky to utter the name of Hades and so, instead, he was often referred to using euphemistic titles such as Pluton (the rich). Pluto was also the name of the Titaness wife of ZEUS.

Polong The Malayan and Indonesian flying demon, created from the blood of a murdered man and kept by its owner, on whose blood it feeds. The owner can command his *polong* to attack his enemies, who as a result tear their clothing, go blind, and eventually lose consciousness. Spells are extensively used to give protection from such attacks.

Polydectes In Greek mythology, a king of Seriphos. He fell in love with Danae and, in order to prevent her son PERSEUS from standing in the way of his desires, sent him on a mission to collect the head of Medusa, a Gorgon. Polydectes thought the task was impossible to accomplish, but Perseus succeeded. When the king did not believe that Perseus had triumphed over the Medusa, the hero killed him.

Polydeuces See CASTOR.

Polydorus In Greek mythology, the youngest son of PRIAM, King of Troy. He was slain by ACHILLES, an event that roused his brother Hector to fury. An alternative tradition, however, says that Priam sent Polydorus away from Troy because of his tender age. He died at the hands of the Thracian ruler who was supposed to foster him.

Polynices One of the sons of the ancient Greek matricide OEDIPUS. When Oedipus went into exile, Polynices and his brother Eteocles became joint rulers of Thebes. The two brothers killed each other in a quarrel and their uncle, Creon, decreed that only Eteocles' body should receive burial. The body of Polynices was thrown outside the city walls.

Polyphemus In Greek mythology, a Cyclops and the shepherd son of POSEIDON. He lived on the island of Sicily, where he imprisoned ODYSSEUS and his crew in a cave. To escape, Odysseus made Polyphemus drunk, blinded him and left next morning, strapped to the underside of one of his sheep. However, the Cyclops almost managed to sink the ship of Odysseus by hurling a gigantic rock into the sea.

Pomona The Roman goddess of the orchard. Her name means "fruit". She was the reluctant mistress of Vertumnus, an Etruscan god of uncertain authority.

Pontiac A legendary Ottawa chief who in the 1760s tried to unite the Indian peoples living near the Great Lakes in an alliance against the incoming European settlers. In order to gain support for this war of liberation, Pontiac told a story about a Delaware brave who had dreamed of meeting the sky god on a beautiful mountain. "Red-coated men have come to trouble your lands," the deity said. "Drive them away. Wage war against them. Send them back to the lands I have made for them." Among the North American Indians, spirits have often communicated with warriors in dreams, giving them advice.

Poshaiyankayo In the mythology of the Pueblo Zuni Indians of North America, the wisest of men, born in one of the four wombs created by the earth mother Awitelin Tsta and the sky father Apoyan Tachi. Poshaiyankayo forced himself upward from the primordial slime in which the wombs were encased until he came to daylight. On the shores of the great ocean, he begged the great god AWONAWILONA (all-container) to release creation. The deity agreed, and the sun drew forth the other beings who were ready for life. Poshaiyankayo then founded the Pueblo Zuni people.

Prester John The hero in a potent European legend of the Middle Ages. He was believed to be a devout Christian ruler of a wealthy African kingdom. The germ of this idea must have been the continued resistance of the state of Axum to Moslem pressure. In 1493 Pedro de Covilhao, a Portuguese envoy, arrived in Ethiopia, the stronghold of Axum, hoping to forge an alliance against Islam. Although the legendary kingdom of Prester John really existed, it was a disappointment to the Portuguese, for surrounded by enemies, the Christian Ethiopians could not hope to lead a glorious crusade.

Priapus A fertility god of Greece and Rome, whose statues adorned gardens. Priapus was the son of APHRODITE and DIONYSUS, or possibly HERMES. He was usually represented as a dwarflike creature with a large, erect member. Priapus was often invoked as protection against the evil eye, and paintings of him have been found in several buildings at Herculaneum, the Roman city buried by the eruption of Vesuvius in 79.

Procrustes A notorious scoundrel in ancient Greece. He placed his victims, usually passing strangers, on an iron bed. If their legs were too long for the bed, he cut them off; if they were too short, he stretched them. He was killed by THESEUS, who made him lie in his own bed. The name Procrustes means "stretcher".

Proteus A minor sea god in ancient Greece, whose name means "old man of the sea". He was the son of POSEIDON and tended his father's sea herds. Able to assume any form or shape at will, Proteus was impossible to catch unless he was found having his afternoon sleep, when he could be bound in cords. According to one late legend, Proteus substituted a spirit in the shape of HELEN to be Paris's companion during the Trojan War. The real Helen remained safely hidden in an Egyptian cave, from which her husband Menelaus finally collected her.

Pryderi In Welsh legend, the son of PWYLL and Rhiannon. He was snatched from his cot by one of Rhiannon's rejected suitors and brought up by a chieftain, who discovered the infant in his stable when one of his colts was seized by a great arm. Called Gwri (golden hair), his parents renamed him Pryderi (worry) when he was finally restored to them. He eventually succeeded his father as lord of Dyfed.

Psyche In Greek mythology, a beautiful maiden loved by Eros, the adopted son of APHRODITE. Although Eros visited her every night, he always vanished at daybreak. Since he was immortal, he forbade her to look upon him, or know who he was. However, curiosity got the better of Psyche, and one night she lit a lamp and looked at Eros when he was asleep. However, she also dropped hot oil on him from the lamp, and Eros woke and fled in pain. Although Psyche went in search of her immortal lover, Aphrodite continuously thwarted the couple, until at last Psyche and Eros were reunited and married.

Ptah-Seker-Osiris A composite deity of ancient Egypt concerned with funerary practice. Seker was portrayed as a man with a falcon's head and swathed with grave linen, like the bearded OSIRIS, ruler of the underworld. PTAH was always shown as the shaven-headed smith god, the equivalent of the Greek HEPHAISTOS. The composite deity, however, was quite different: he appeared as a bandy-legged dwarf, clean-shaven, with a scarab-beetle upon his head.

Puarata In the Maori mythology of New Zealand, a malevolent sorcerer who owned a magical wooden head which he shared with another sorcerer, Tautohito. The head was

kept in a stronghold and anyone who dared approach it was bewitched. However, the power of Puarata and Tautohito was overthrown when the benevolent sorcerer HAKAWAU approached the stronghold in the company of a single companion and, by repeating incantations, remained unharmed.

Puca The mischievous spirits of Irish mythology. They were imps and delighted in causing confusion. They were also called Pooka.

Pu Hsien A legendary Chinese sage who protected the holy Buddhist mountain of Emei, in Sichuan province. He derives from the bodhisattva Samantabhadra, the source of "divine compassion" (*bhadra*), who is worshipped as Fugen-bosatsu in Japan. The mountain is the subject of the first guidebook ever to be published in China, directing Buddhist pilgrims to all its mythological features. It was published in 1887 and entitled *An Illustrated Guide to Mount Emei*.

Pundjel In Australian aboriginal mythology, a creator god who made the first human beings, two men, from clay and bark. One was fair-skinned, one dark-skinned. They were given wives who were discovered emerging from the muddy waters by Pundjel's brother, Pallian. In due time, the wives bore children, but Pundjel and Pallian cut them into small pieces because they proved to be evil. The pieces were scattered by winds and became the founders of the aboriginal peoples of northern Australia.

Puramdara One of the titles of INDRA, the king of the gods in the *Rig Veda*, the oldest religious document of India. It means "destroyer of cities" and may refer to the Aryan destruction of the Indus Valley cities around 1700 BC.

Purgatory A medieval European legend, which received the official sanction of the Roman Catholic Church in 1245. It claimed that purgatory was the region beyond the grave, inhabited by souls destined for heaven. It was a place of purification, where all sins had to be repented. Prayers were (and still are) said for the souls of the dead stranded there.

Pushan The toothless god of the Hindu pantheon, whose worshippers offer him gruel and cooked, ground foods. Pushan lost his teeth at the sacrifice of Daksha, the sage and son of BRAHMA. Daksha forgot to show sufficient respect to SHIVA at this ceremony for VISHNU, and the annoyed god attacked the worshippers with devastating effect. INDRA was sent sprawling and Pushan had his teeth punched down his throat. As a deity, Pushan protects cattle and generally helps country folk.

Pygmalion A legendary Greek king of Cyprus who fell in love with the statue of an ideal woman, carved at his request. When he asked APHRODITE for a woman of equal beauty, the goddess brought the statue to life. Pygmalion married the woman, whom he may have called Galatea.

Pyrrhus See Neoptolemus.

Python The serpent that inhabited the ancient Greek site of Delphi until it was slaughtered by the god of prophecy, Apollo. It was believed to have been female. In memory of Python, Apollo's priestess at Delphi was called Pythia.

Q

Qasavara In the Melanesian mythology of Banks Island, a cannibalistic monster spirit. He ate QAT's brothers while they were gathering fruit and was slain by Qat, who found their bones in Qasavara's food chest. The brothers were restored to life by Qat, who blew through a reed and bade the bones, if they were his brothers, to laugh.

Qebehsenuf In Egyptian mythology, one of the four sons of HORUS. A falcon-headed god, swathed in grave linen, he was associated with funerary rites. He was one of four gods whose duty it was to watch over the Canopic jars of the dead and to guard the four corners of the sarcophagus. Qebehsenuf's jar contained embalmed intestines.

Qetesh In ancient Egypt, a fertility goddess imported from Canaan. She was shown without clothes, holding flowers and standing on the back of a lion. Qetesh was usually associated with the Egyptian cow goddess HATHOR.

Quirinus An Italian god, probably of Sabine origin, who was associated with MARS. He gave his name to the Quirinal hill in Rome. From its beginning, the city sited there comprised a mixture of peoples – the Etruscans, the Sabines and the Latins.

R

Rabbit In the mythology of many North American Indians, especially of the southeastern United States, a prominent trickster hero, and the main character in many tales. He dupes mortals and other animals but also appears frequently as a benefactor to mankind, bringing fire to the world from the ocean.

Radha In Hindu mythology, the wife of the cowherd Ayanagosha and the lover of KRISHNA, the most popular avatar of VISHNU. Ayanagosha's sister told him of Radha's adultery, but when he went in search of Radha and Krishna, he found his wife with a goddess, whose form Krishna had assumed.

In some versions of the myth, Radha herself is regarded as an incarnation of LAKSHMI, the goddess of good fortune and the divine wife of Vishnu. According to this version of the Radha and Krishna romance, Lakshmi willed herself to be born as the beautiful village girl because she could not bear leaving her lord.

Radin A leader of the Iban people of northern Borneo. He was troubled by a hungry ghost after winning a battle at a place called Betong. To deal with the intruder, who brought smallpox to his tribe, Radin hid in a roll of matting one night and jumped out and sliced through the ghost with his sword. He heard something fall to the ground and, the next morning, found that a carving of a sacred bird, the hornbill, had been cut to pieces. By this sign, Radin realized that he could not hope to contend with such powerful forces, and so the tribe left Betong and moved elsewhere. The ghost did not trouble Radin again.

Ragnarok In Germanic mythology, the battle at the end of time between gods and men, giants and monsters. It is to be both an end and a beginning, since out of the destruction will come hope in the form of Lif (life) and Lifthrasir (eager for life), two human survivors who will create a new world. Hodr and BALDER will also return from the underworld to found a new heaven. Ragnarok cannot be avoided, even though HEIMDAL keeps watch for the march of the frost giants.

Quite possibly, the myth of a last great fight on the Vigrid plain drew its dramatic strength from the encroachment of Christianity on the old world of the Germanic gods. Already, ODIN's sacred trees in Frisia were being cut down by Christian missionaries, among them St Boniface (674–754).

Rahu A Hindu demon who causes eclipses of the sun and moon. During the churning of the ocean, the battle between the gods and demons for possession of the AMRITA (water of life), Rahu sipped a little of the sacred water. The sun and the moon told VISHNU what Rahu had done, and the god cut him into pieces. But because the demon had become immortal, he was unassailable. The head was placed in the heavens, where it constantly chases the sun and moon, causing an eclipse whenever it swallows one of them. Rahu is therefore now called Abhrapisacha, (demon of the sky).

Raktavija A Hindu demon of gigantic size, whom DEVI, manifested as Kali, eventually succeeded in slaying. When she set out to destroy him, Kali was able to kill his soldiers, but whenever she struck Raktavija, a thousand more giants sprang from each drop of his blood. The goddess was therefore forced to drink all his blood.

Rakush The steed of the Iranian hero RUSTEM. The king, envious of Rustem's exploits, dug a pit filled with sharp spears in Rustem's hunting ground in order to trap him. Rakush, scenting the trap, tried to pull up, but Rustem spurred him onward and both rider and horse died of the wounds they received. The hero managed to kill the king with an arrow before he died.

Rama In Hindu mythology, the seventh and, after KRISHNA, most popular avatar of VISHNU. Helped by the monkey HANUMAN and an army of monkeys, Rama overcame the powers of darkness in the form of the demon king Ravana. The invasion of Sri Lanka, Ravana's stronghold, was accomplished with the greatest difficulties. Only the versatility of Hanuman paved the way to victory.

The celebrations were spoilt by the disappearance of Sita, Rama's wife. Because Rama was suspicious about what had happened to her during her captivity in Sri Lanka, Sita was forced to ask the earth to bear witness to her purity. It did so, and then the ground opened and Sita (a furrow) was swallowed up. Unable to endure life without his wife, Rama drowned himself.

Ran The wife of the Germanic sea god Aegir. She loved to drag drowning men down with a net.

Rati The Hindu goddess of love and motherhood. Her name means "erotic desire". She appears as a huge-breasted goddess, who sneers at and taunts mortals who follow an ascetic way of life. Rati is particularly revered on the island of Bali, the only part of Indonesia to cling to the Hindu faith. She is the wife of Kama, the god of love, and her titles include Raga-lata (vine of love), Mayarati (deceiver), and Kelikila (shameless).

Ratovoantany The earth god of Madagascar, whose name means "self-created". Apparently, he grew out of the ground like a plant, unaided by the sky god ZANAHARY, who had made the earth, but had left it desolate. Zanahary visited Ratovoantany and found him making men out of clay, but unable to give them life. Zanahary offered to breathe life into them on condition that he could take them back to heaven. Ratovoantany objected to this and so it was agreed that Zanahary would have men's souls when they died and Ratovoantany their bodies.

Ravana In Hindu mythology, the demon king of Sri Lanka and lord of all Rakshasa demons. He was of immense size and his body was scarred with the marks of divine weapons, including INDRA's thunderbolt and VISHNU's discus. None of these blows had really hurt Ravana, who ignored every law and greedily took whatever appealed to his fancy. Because the demon king was so proud, Vishnu declared that he should be humbled. The god therefore adopted human form and, as the avatar Rama, he managed to slay Ravana with the aid of the monkey god HANUMAN.

Raven The chief servant of Sha-lana, the creator god of the Haida Indians of British Columbia in Canada. When Sha-lana tired of Raven's services, he threw him out of heaven. At first, the bird did not know what to do, but then he flapped his wings to make land rise from the primeval ocean. He later made people from clam shells and, finally, he stole a sun and a fire stick from heaven. Sha-lana ignored all Raven's work.

Re-Herakhty In Egyptian
mythology, the sun god RE at dawn
and dusk. Herakhty was Horus,
another solar deity, and not HORUS,
son of OSIRIS, the god of the
underworld. See Herakhty.

Remus In Roman mythology, the
twin brother of ROMULUS and, with
him, a legendary founder of Rome.
He was killed by Romulus in a
quarrel over precedence. Since the
brothers could not agree which of
them should take the lead in their
work, they let an omen decide.
According to the number of birds
each brother saw in the sky, the
outcome would be determined.
Remus observed six vultures, but
Romulus observed twice as many
and claimed precedence. Remus
nursed his jealousy and, when later
he taunted his brother about the
walls he was building, Romulus
struck him down with a spade. But
at his brother's funeral, Romulus
was overcome by grief.

Renenutet An ancient Egyptian
snake goddess, who protected the
harvest and the pharaoh. Her name
is connected with the idea of
nursing and raising children, and she
was often represented as the
embodiment of divine motherhood.
At the judgement of the dead, in
the great hall of OSIRIS, Renenutet
was always present at the weighing
of good and evil.

Resheph A Canaanite plague god,
the equivalent of the Mesopotamian
Namtar. Resheph could also be
invoked for healing, which suggests
that he may have had authority
over both health and illness. He was
usually portrayed with a shield,
spear and axe. In Egypt, he was
known as the war god Reshpu.

Rhadamanthys In Greek
mythology, the son of ZEUS and
EUROPA and the brother of MINOS,
King of Crete. When the time came
for him to die, Zeus sent him to
Elysium, possibly because of the
reputation he had gained for
learning and fairmindedness when
he ruled over several Aegean
islands. Rhadamanthys is a pre-
Greek word of uncertain meaning.

Rhea In Greek mythology, the
daughter of Ouranos (sky) and the
wife of KRONOS, by whom she bore
ZEUS. Kronos was given to eating
his offspring, so when Rhea was
pregnant with Zeus she went to a
secret cave in Crete to give birth to
him. She then gave Kronos a stone
in swaddling clothes, which he
devoured, believing it to be Zeus.
Rhea was also the mother of
POSEIDON, HADES, Hestia, HERA and
DEMETER, all of whom Kronos
devoured. When Zeus grew up, he
freed his brothers and sisters and
overthrew the rule of his tyrannous
father. Rhea was sometimes
identified with the Phrygian mother
goddess CYBELE.

Rhea Silvia In Roman mythology,
a Vestal Virgin who was raped by
MARS and gave birth to ROMULUS
and Remus, the legendary founders
of Rome. Her two sons were set
adrift on the Tiber, but were later
saved and suckled by a she-wolf, an
animal sacred to Mars.

Rhiannon In Welsh legend, the
wife of PWYLL and the mother of
Pryderi. Her name means "great
queen". Falsely accused of killing
her son, Rhiannon was compelled to
do penance by sitting at the gate of
Pwyll's stronghold and telling
strangers of her crime, then offering
to carry them on her back into his
hall. When, after seven years,
Pryderi was restored to his parents,
Rhiannon was released from her
punishment.

It is likely that Rhiannon was
originally a Celtic goddess
associated with horses, since Pryderi
was found in a stable after his
disappearance from Pwyll's house.

Rimmon See Adad.

Rip van Winkle The legendary
American hero of Washington
Irving's *The Sketch Book*. On a
ramble in the Catskill Mountains, he
met a gathering of dwarfs and, after
drinking the beverage they offered
him, fell asleep for twenty years.
When he awoke, he discovered that
his wife was dead and that the
American colonies had thrown off
servitude to Great Britain and
become the United States.

The idea of a journey, or a sleep,
that consumes a large number of
years is common to many myths
and legends. However, the
experience of Rip van Winkle
hardly compares with that of the
Irish heroes Oisin and BRAN, who
each used up a massive 300 years in
their travels.

Robin Hood The legendary outlaw
of Britain in the Middle Ages. His
band of archers was believed to
have lived in Sherwood Forest in
Nottinghamshire, although some
people thought the hideout was
located in Barnsdale, Yorkshire.

The most famous members of the
band were Friar Tuck, Little John
and Maid Marion, Robin's lover.
What made Robin Hood so
attractive was his policy toward
wealth: he stole from the rich to
give to the poor.

Robin escaped capture by killing
Sir Guy of Gisborne, sent in pursuit
of him, and disguising himself in the
knight's clothes to dupe the Sheriff
of Nottingham.

Rokola The Fijian carpenter god
who, on the arrival of Christianity,
was identified with NOAH. The
heresy prefigured the cargo cults of
Papua, but by 1900 it had ended.
Today, Rokola is remembered as a
legendary builder of boats.

Roland The Frankish hero of
Roncesvalles, where his men slew
100,000 Saracens. When his forces
were reduced to fifty, a fresh
phalanx of Saracens suddenly
appeared from over the mountains.
Only then did honour permit
Roland to blow on his ivory horn,
Olivant, in order to summon
Charlemagne to his assistance.

The sound of the horn was so
shrill that it killed birds in the sky,
split the horn itself in two, and
caused the Saracens to retreat in
alarm. But by the time Charlemagne
arrived, Roland had died of his
battle wounds.

The actual encounter that gave
rise to this legend occurred in
AD 778 when the Basques
annihilated the rearguard of
Charlemagne's army, which was
withdrawing after a campaign in
Spain. The eleventh-century
Chanson de Roland tells the story in
epic fashion.

235

Round Table The legendary table at which ARTHUR's knights sat. It was circular in shape so that the knights could feel that they were all gathered equally about one board, none being "able to boast that he was exalted above his fellow". MERLIN made the Round Table as a copy of the table used by JESUS at the Last Supper.

One seat at the table was always empty, and any knight who wished to seek the Grail had to sit there before setting out on his quest. If he remained unharmed by the experience, he was proved worthy of seeing the Grail. In most versions of the story, only Sir Galahad succeeded in doing so.

Ruadan In Irish mythology, a warrior hero of the Fomorii. The son of Bres and BRIGIT, he fought at the second battle of Magh Tuireadh and was sent to spy on the Tuatha De Danaan. He wounded the smith Goibhniu but was himself slain by the spear that Goibhniu was making at the time.

Rudra An ancient Hindu deity who appears in the *Rig Veda*, the great collection of early hymns. His name means "howler". A terrible god of storms, Rudra was sometimes associated with the destructive aspect of AGNI, the god of fire. Later texts say that he was born of BRAHMA's anger, emerging from the god's forehead. Rudra brought with him disease and calamity as well as health. He eventually came to be identified with SHIVA, a god whose name does not appear in the *Rig Veda*. Shiva's other destructive titles were Aghora (horrible), Hara (seizer), and Urga (fierce).

As Bhairava (the joyous devourer), Shiva, with a necklace of skulls and with serpents twined around his head, haunts burial places. In his train are imps and demons.

Rugaba The Ankole people of Uganda look upon Rugaba as a powerful creator deity. A sky god, he is called Mukameiguru (the ruler of heaven). Rugaba's concern for mankind is shown in the effort he makes to sustain everyday existence. The Ankole say that his "smile brings life".

Rusalkai Legendary Slavic water spirits, amphibious maidens who live half the year in water, half in the forest. They are said to be the souls of girls who died on their wedding night or, alternatively, those of unbaptized girls. Some of them are demonic, luring young men to a watery grave with their songs. Others are benevolent and bless people they meet.

S

Sabazius A Phrygian god who rose to fame as a saviour god in the century before the birth of JESUS. Usually identifed with DIONYSUS, he was also called ZEUS–Sabazius because of his power over thunder and lightning. His other symbols included the bull, the serpent, the lizard, corn, and the plough. Sabazius was portrayed as a countryman wearing a Phrygian cap on his head.

St Anthony In Christian legend, the patron saint of basket-weavers, who was celebrated for overcoming SATAN. In about 270, when he was twenty years old, he retired to the Egyptian desert. He had responded to the call of JESUS, "Go and sell that thou hast, and give to the poor, and thou shalt have treasure in heaven: and come and follow me." In the desert, where St Anthony lived as a hermit, Satan sent temptations and torments against him. He resisted and thus a colony of hermits gathered around him; in this way Christian monasticism was established.

St Brendan In Christian legend, the sixth-century patron saint of travellers and seafarers. With other saints, he travelled in a skin-covered boat to an earthly paradise in the western ocean. He was the last of a distinguished line of Irish voyagers that included BRAN.

St Brigit An Irish saint, legendary for her generosity. She was the despair of her father until he realized her saintliness. Clearly, she derives from BRIGIT, the goddess of fertility. St Brigit was said to have died at Kildare in 523.

St Christopher The Christian patron of travellers, possibly of Canaanite provenance. He is traditionally represented as a man of prodigious stature, fording a river with the aid of a staff. The saint's interest in Christianity was aroused when he noticed that the king he served made the sign of the cross at the mention of SATAN. He therefore went in search of Satan and joined his retinue. When he discovered that Satan trembled at the mere sight of a wayside cross, Christopher went to find JESUS, whom, he learned, the symbol represented.

However, the fasting and prayer of the Christian hermit's life did not suit Christopher at all and so he decided to serve Jesus in a more practical way, by carrying on his shoulders all who wished to cross a certain river. One day, Christopher carried a child across the river, and was surprised by his weight. The child turned out to be Jesus. Although officially removed from the Catholic calendar of saints in 1969, Christopher is still popular.

St Florian In early Christian legend, the fourth-century patron saint of brewers, coopers and chimney sweeps. He was also one of the patron saints of Poland and Austria. Many miracles were attributed to him, notably the quenching of a town fire with a single jugful of water. His protection was sought against fire, floods and famine. Florian appears to have been a Roman soldier who, because he was a Christian, came to suffer martyrdom by drowning.

St Giles In Christian legend, a seventh-century saint, born of royal blood in Athens. He was the patron saint of blacksmiths, beggars and cripples and had great healing power. On one occasion, his cloak made a lame man walk again, and on another his prayers removed the deadly venom of a serpent from a man. St Giles was one of the most popular saints of the Middle Ages.

St Hippolytus The patron saint of horses. He was a guard in the prison where St Lawrence was kept. Converted to Christianity by the saint, he dared to help bury St Lawrence after his martyrdom. It cost St Hippolytus his own life, for he was tied by the feet to untamed horses and dragged along the ground until he died.

St Ignatius The enthusiastic Christian martyr from Syria. In 107 he was devoured by lions in Rome so that only his large bones remained in the Colosseum. These were secretly collected by Christians living in the city and kept as holy relics. Thus St Ignatius became the legendary model for martyrdom. St Ignatius firmly believed that JESUS was about to return to reclaim the faithful. "These are the last times", he is believed to have told his followers just before he died.

St Louis The saintly king of France, who died in AD 1270. St Louis was a successful soldier, a crusader and a legislator. His holiness became evident when he washed the feet of lepers. But this act of penance did not stop him from introducing laws which forbade the unemployed and lepers from living in towns. Apart from being subject to prohibitions in the Middle Ages, lepers often became scapegoats in times of calamity. After the great famine of 1315–18, they were persecuted, along with Jews, for supposedly poisoning the wells of France.

St Patrick The legendary fourth-century patron saint of Ireland who converted the people of Ulster, then those of other parts of Ireland, to Christianity. He was renowned for working miracles, above all for ridding Ireland of snakes. He drove them all into the sea, except for one serpent, who refused to leave. St Patrick therefore built a box in which the serpent could rest, and the serpent, to prove that it was too small, entered it. St Patrick at once sealed the box and then threw it into the sea.

St Patrick's kindness to people was almost as famous as St Brigit's (BRIGIT), and he comforted Oisin when the bard returned to Ireland from the western ocean as a blind old man.

St Romanus A medieval French saint whose power over madness and demonic possession was legendary. His best-known exploit was the destruction of a dragon, which preyed on Christians in the countryside around Rouen. The saint bravely entered the dragon's lair and threw a net over its head. Later, the country folk burned the monster alive.

St Veronica The patron saint of drapers. Medieval legend in Europe said that she was healed by touching the garment of JESUS. Afterward St Veronica asked St Luke to paint her healer's portrait on a piece of cloth. When she was dissatisfied with the likeness, Christ himself wiped his face on the cloth in order to produce a proper portrait. Through the ages the cloth was the source of miraculous cures.

Sakhar A demon who impersonated Solomon, King of Israel. When Solomon went into the desert to atone for making an idolatrous image of the dead father of a concubine, Sakhar appeared before another concubine in Solomon's form. He took Solomon's magic ring from her and thus gained power over his kingdom. After forty days, Sakhar flew away and threw the ring into the sea. Solomon later recovered it from the stomach of a fish. He then caught Sakhar, weighed him down with a stone, and cast him into the sea.

Sakyamuni In ancient India, an important title of the BUDDHA. It means "the silent sage of the Sakya clan", and thus draws attention to the Buddha's aspect as a prophet, his silence and the ineffability of his message. Sakyamuni's chief shrine is now at Lhasa, the capital of Tibet.

Samantabhadra The final incarnation of a bodhisattva (BUDDHA-to-be) on earth. His name denotes his divine compassion (*bhadra*) in the service of enlightening wisdom (*samanta*). According to the Mahayana tradition, the wisdom of Buddha will take many centuries to spread across the nations of the world. In Japan, however, Samantabhadra has already appeared as Fugen-bosatsu.

Sampati The son of Garuda, the bird who served as a mount for VISHNU, the great Hindu god. When Vishnu was incarnated as Rama, Sampati proved to be a staunch ally.

Samson In the Old Testament, a special protégé of Yahweh and the legendary strong man who slaughtered the Philistines. An angel told his mother that he was never to drink alcohol and that his hair should never be cut. Samson's long hair endowed him with superhuman strength. But he revealed the secret of his strength to Delilah, a Philistine woman, who cut off his hair while he was sleeping. As a result, the Philistines were able to blind Samson and chain him in the great temple of BAAL at Gaza. However Samson's hair grew again, and he recovered strength. He then took revenge by pulling down the temple and slaying many of the Philistines. But Samson himself died in the superhuman effort.

Sandhya In Hindu mythology, a daughter of BRAHMA, the creator deity. According to one late text, Brahma once pursued Sandhya but she changed herself into a deer. The great god then assumed the form of a stag and chased her through the sky. Apparently, the chase ended when SHIVA shot an arrow at the stag and thereby succeeded in bringing Brahma to his senses.

Sani In Hindu mythology, the planet SATURN, born of the sun god SURYA and Chhaya (shade), and the mistress given to Surya by his wife, who was named Sanjna.

Sanjna In Hindu mythology, the wife of the sun god SURYA. Her name means "conscience". She was also called Dyumayi (brilliant) and Mahavirya (powerful). Because she could not bear the intense heat of her husband, she sent him a shade in the form of a mistress, Chhaya, who bore Surya three children. Sanjna was eventually reconciled to Surya, after her father had trimmed away some of her husband's flames on a lathe.

Sankara One of the names of SHIVA, the great Hindu god. It means "auspicious".

Saphon The mountain home of the Canaanite gods, equivalent to the Greek Olympus. It stood to the north of the ancient city of Ugarit, in western Syria. EL, the father of the gods, lived there, and afterward BAAL and all the other Canaanite gods were also its inhabitants.

Saphon has obvious connections with Mount Zion, the home of Yahweh, which is described in the Psalms as, "the city of our God, in the mountain of his holiness . . . on the sides of the north".

Sarah In the Old Testament, the wife of Abraham. After being barren until late in her life, Yahweh made her fertile and she gave birth to a son in her old age. By divine command he was named Isaac, which means "laughter", because Sarah had laughed at the idea of bearing a child at the age of ninety.

After Isaac's birth, Sarah drove Hagar, her handmaid and Abraham's concubine, into the desert, along with Hagar's son, Ishmael. Sarah is said to be buried at Hebron.

Saraswati In the *Rig Veda*, the early collection of Hindu hymns, one of three sacred rivers (the others being the Ganges and the Jumna). Saraswati means "watery". She may have also acted as Vach, the goddess of eloquence. In later times, Saraswati became the wife of BRAHMA, the protector of the *Rig Veda* and the god of creation.

Sarpedon Two Greek heroes bear the name of Sarpedon. The first was the son of ZEUS and EUROPA, and the brother of Rhadamanthys and MINOS. After a quarrel with Minos, the king of Crete, Sarpedon left the island and established the city of Miletus in Asia Minor. The second hero was a Lycian warrior, who led a force to Troy in order to help PRIAM against the Greeks. He was slain by Patroclus, the lover of the hero ACHILLES.

Sati The wife of the great Hindu god SHIVA and an aspect of DEVI, the mother goddess. She died for Shiva's sake by setting fire to herself, and thereby established the precedent for the custom of *suttee*, by which in earlier times a widow took her life by throwing herself on her husband's burning funeral pyre.

Satyrs The wild creatures of the woodlands in Greek mythology, and the companions of DIONYSUS. They were half-men and half-horse, and their lascivious nature was notorious.

Saul In the Old Testament, the first king of Israel, anointed by the prophet Samuel and chosen by Yahweh to liberate his people from the Philistines. His reign was a long battle against the Philistines and, in his mind, against his rival David, especially after the people shouted that Saul had slain his thousands, but David his ten thousands.

On the night before his final battle against the Philistines, at Mount Gilboa Saul visited the witch of Endor, who invoked the spirit of the dead Samuel and prophesied that Saul would die the next day. The prophecy came true: Saul was severely injured by arrow wounds and, fearing capture and humiliation, fell on his sword. His sons Jonathan, Abinadas and Malchishua were killed outright. The Philistines then cut off their heads.

Scathach A renowned female warrior who trained the legendary Irish hero CUCHULAINN. Her school was on the Isle of Skye. Uathach, the daughter of Scathach, became Cuchulainn's mistress after he slew her lover.

Scylla In Greek mythology, a sea monster who lived in the Straits of Messina. Originally, Scylla was a nymph, but CIRCE turned her into a six-headed monster. She made her lair in a cave opposite the whirlpool of Charybdis and preyed on passing sailors, including some of the crew of ODYSSEUS's ship.

Sebek In Egyptian mythology, the crocodile god of lakes and rivers. He was commonly represented with a solar disc on his head. Sometimes he combined with RE to form the composite god Sebek-Re. His cult centre was Fayum, where he splashed in a pool from which his devotees drank sacred draughts.

Seker An ancient Egyptian funerary god who protected the necropolis of Memphis. He was portrayed as a man wrapped in grave linen, with a falcon's head. Identified with PTAH and OSIRIS, Seker eventually merged with the former as an underworld deity. It is likely that Seker, like Osiris, was connected with fertility.

Sela In the mythology of the Abaluyia people of Kenya, the first woman. She and her husband Mwambu were both made by the creator god WELE. The couple lived together in a house raised on stilts.

Selene The ancient Greek goddess of the moon, who was known to the Romans as Luna. She bore ZEUS two daughters and put her mortal admirer Endymion to sleep for ever in a cave. She was later absorbed into ARTEMIS.

Semargl The god of the family and of barley in Slavic mythology. He was also worshipped by certain Russians. It is possible that Semargl once comprised two gods, one called Sem and the other Rgl.

Semele In Greek mythology, the daughter of Cadmus, founder of Thebes. A beautiful maiden, she was seduced by ZEUS, who appeared in the guise of a mortal. HERA, jealous of her husband's lovers, persuaded Semele to ask Zeus to appear before her in the full strength and glory of his immortal being. When he did so, Semele was consumed by the heat of his lightning; before she expired, Zeus snatched DIONYSUS from her womb and protected him from the flames by hiding him in his thigh. Semele is not a Greek name and could be of Phrygian origin.

Serqet The ancient Egyptian scorpion goddess, a funerary deity concerned with the protection of embalmed entrails. She was the companion of ISIS.

Sesha In Hindu mythology, a serpent deity and the king of the water spirits, or Nagas. He has 1,000 heads and is called Ananta (endless). During the intervals of creation, VISHNU uses Sesha as a floating couch on which to sleep.

Sessrumnir In Germanic mythology, the hall of Freya, the fertility goddess. It stood near ODIN's hall in Asgard, the home of the gods. So well built was this spacious hall that the trickster god LOKI had the greatest difficulty in breaking into it in order to steal Freya's magic necklace. He was forced to shrink to the size of a needle and then wriggle through a tiny crack in a door. To retrieve the necklace, Odin told Freya that she must stir up a war between two kings on earth, then resurrect the dead who fell in battle. Both Odin and Freya had a close interest in the slain.

Shadrach See Abednego.

Shamash In ancient Mesopotamia, a deity concerned with justice Shamash was a sun god and his attendants were Kittu (truth) and Mesharu (righteousness). His relation to Utu, the brother of INANNA, is obscure. Utu was also looked upon as the guardian of justice, the impartial judge of the actions of gods and men. In Babylon, the symbol for Shamash was the solar disc with a four-pointed star inside it. The god was usually portrayed as a ruler seated on a throne.

Shango In the mythology of the Yoruba people of Nigeria, the god of thunder and storms. Originally a ruler on earth, Shango was deified after he fled into the wilderness to escape his enemies and hanged himself from a tree. His followers continued to revere him and prayed for fire to destroy his enemies. When fire did come, devastating the land, even Shango's enemies came to believe that he had taken up residence in the sky as a god.

Sheol In the Old Testament, the subterranean realm where the dead resided as shadows. Rather than being a place of punishment, it was the resting place of everyone who died.

The Christian underworld, hell, derives its name from Hel, the Germanic goddess of the unhappy dead. The clearest expression of the idea of hell is found in *The Divine Comedy* of Dante, who describes in great detail the punishment accorded to each type of sinner. Dante places SATAN at the bottom, held upside down in a block of ice.

Sheol, on the other hand, was simply a dim, hopeless place. It was not unlike the Sumerian underworld, which the ghost of Enkidu described to GILGAMESH as "a house of dust".

Shouxing The Chinese god of longevity. He was originally a sage who ate magic peaches and gained a lifespan of 1,000 years. Shouxing is portrayed as an old man carrying two peaches and riding on a deer. In Japan, he is known as Tobosaku.

Shu The ancient Egyptian god of sunlight and air. In the creation myth, he and Tefnut (moisture), his sister and wife, were the first divine couple created by Atum. They in turn gave birth to the earth god Geb and the sky goddess NUT. Shu supported the sky with his arms.

Sibyl In Greek and Roman mythology, a divinely inspired prophetess. There were as many as ten Sibyls, and their oracles were in widely separated parts of the Mediterranean world. The most famous Roman prophetess was the Cumaean Sibyl, who offered her sacred books to Tarquinius Superbus, the last king of Rome. Because he mocked her, she kept burning the books until he agreed to her price, by which time the original nine had been reduced to three. These so-called Sibylline books were preserved on the Capitol in Rome; they were destroyed by fire in 83 BC. Long before all this happened, the Cumaean Sibyl had escorted AENEAS to the underworld.

Sidhe In Irish mythology, the hills under which the Tuatha De Danaan fled following the collapse of their power. They are the equivalent of the British Land of Faery.

Sigurd In Germanic mythology, a warrior hero who led the Volsungs, a family to whom ODIN had shown special favours. He possessed the magic gold ring made by the dwarfs, who had a hoard of treasure. This ring was able to increase the wealth of its owner, but led to Sigurd's downfall after it was cursed by LOKI.

Sigurd's name means "victory-peace", and in some versions he is called Siegfried. He was the husband of Gudrun and slew the dragon Fafnir.

Sigyn In Germanic mythology, the faithful wife of the trickster god LOKI. She remained constant to him despite all his evil mischief-making. When he was imprisoned in a cave, doomed to eternal punishment, Sigyn sat by him and caught in a bowl the venom of a snake that was meant to drop on him. Each time she emptied the bowl, the earth shook with Loki's shudders, as venom splashed his face. Sigyn and Loki are obliged to remain in the cave until Ragnarok, the final battle at the end of the world.

Silenus In Greek mythology, the elderly companion of DIONYSUS. Like the other *sileni*, he had the hind parts of a goat and the tail of a donkey. Silenus, who was habitually drunk and rode on a hump-backed donkey, was given long ears by the god Apollo. However, his donkey is said to have helped the gods in their battles against the giants, who were frightened by its hideous braying. Despite his love of wine, Silenus was renowned for his wisdom as well as his ability to foretell the future.

Silvanus An Italian woodland god, whom the Romans connected with MARS. They also identified him with PAN, the goatlike god of the Greeks. His name means "of the forest".

Sinon At Troy, a Greek who pretended to be a deserter. According to the Roman poet Virgil, Sinon told the Trojans a false tale about the building of the wooden horse. Once it was inside the city, he let out the Greek warriors hidden in its hollow belly. The fate of Troy was sealed because nobody would heed CASSANDRA's warning about the danger of admitting the wooden horse.

Sirens In Greek mythology, huge birds with women's heads who lived on an island off the coast of Sicily. By their sweet singing, they lured seafarers on to dangerous rocks. Curious, ODYSSEUS escaped them by blocking his crewmen's ears with wax and tying himself to the mast. He was the only man ever to hear their song and live. The Argonauts were saved from the Sirens by the musician ORPHEUS, who drowned their singing.

Sisyphus In Greek mythology, the founder of Corinth who was condemned by ZEUS to eternal punishment in the underworld. Sisyphus was made to roll a boulder continually up a hill. Each time he nearly reached the top, his strength failed, and the boulder rolled down the hill again. The other notable victim of punishment in ancient Greece was TANTALUS, who dared to serve his son Pelops to the gods in a stew.

Sita The wife of the Hindu god VISHNU in his incarnation as Rama. Her name means "furrow". She was captured by the demon Ravana, who held her prisoner in Sri Lanka. When Rama recovered Sita, with the help of the monkey god HANUMAN, he doubted her faithfulness to him. She proved her innocence by the ancient method of stating that all her life she had been true to her *dharma*, or duty. Simply by stating the fact, Sita was proved innocent, and the earth opened up to engulf her. Rama drowned himself shortly afterward.

Skadi In Germanic mythology, a frost giantess, married to Njord, a Vanir deity. Whereas Skadi liked to live at her father's home of Thrymheim, where she hunted in the cold of the mountains, Njord preferred the warmth of Asgard, where he had met Skadi. They therefore spent three nights in one place, followed by three in the other; hence the seasons.

Skirnir In Germanic mythology, a favourite and servant of the great god FREY. His name means "the one who makes things shine", and he acted as the go-between for Frey during the god's courtship of the giantess Gerda.

Skrymir In Germanic mythology, an immense frost giant whom THOR and LOKI encountered on a visit to Jotunnheim, the land of the giants. He was so large that the tired travellers were able to sleep in the thumb of his glove. Moreover, when Thor hammered on his skull, Skrymir merely thought that he had been grazed by a leaf. When Thor and Loki were on their way home, they suddenly realized that Skrymir was a great magician, who had conjured up illusions simply to mystify them.

Sleipnir In Germanic mythology, the eight-legged steed belonging to ODIN. It carried Hermodr on his mission to the underworld, from which he returned with the message that BALDER would be released from the underworld only if every living thing in the world wept for him. LOKI refused to comply.

Solomon An Old Testament king who was renowned for his wisdom. Many of his judgements have become proverbial, especially his pronouncement on the case of the two women, each of whom bore a child on the same night. One of the children died and each woman claimed the surviving child as her own. When Solomon suggested cutting the child in two, so that each woman could have half, one of the women agreed to the proposal. Solomon therefore knew that the other woman was the mother. By building the first temple at Jerusalem, Solomon made the city the chief among the cities of Israel.

Soma In Hindu mythology, an intoxicating drink and the equivalent of the ancient Iranian *haoma*. Soma is also the god of the moon, later thought to be the divine storehouse of the drink. As the moon wanes, so it is said, the gods consume its immortal properties.

Spartoi In Greek mythology, the "sown men" who grew from the teeth of a dragon at Thebes. After CADMUS had slain the loathsome creature, ATHENA advised him to sow half of its teeth in the ground. Immediately there sprang up a harvest of armed men, whom Cadmus overcame by setting them to fight one another. Five survived and became the ancestors of the leading Theban families.

Spider Woman In the mythology of the Navaho Indians of North America, a benevolent creature who helped NAYENEZGANI and Tobadzistsini to defeat the powers of evil. While travelling to the home of their father, the sun god Tsohanoai, the two brothers climbed down a hole and met the Spider Woman, called Naste Estsan. She warned the brothers of four dangers which lay ahead of them and gave them two magic feathers. One of these feathers would enable them to defeat their enemies, the other would preserve their lives.

Stella Maris In Christian mythology, one of the titles of the VIRGIN MARY, meaning "star of the sea". Apart from the obvious role as a saviour of shipwrecked sailors, Stella Maris is also a guide for the soul on its voyage across life's difficult waters. TARA, the great Buddhist goddess of Tibet, offers help to her worshippers in a similar way.

Stentor An ancient Greek herald with a voice equal to that of fifty men. However, he died as a result of injury sustained in a shouting contest against HERMES.

Sterope One of the seven daughters of Atlas, the Pleiades, whom the ancient Greeks believed held up the sky. She was made by ZEUS, as were her sisters.

Stribog The Slavic god of the winds. Although he was the chief deity, there were several other wind gods, such as Varpulis, who caused the sound of storms; Erisvorsh, the god of the "holy tempest"; and Vikhor, who held sway over whirlwinds.

Styx In Greek mythology, a river that encircled the underworld of HADES nine times. The dead were ferried across it by Charon, a bad-tempered old boatman. He demanded a fee and so the dead were buried with a coin, known as an obol, in their mouths. Styx (abomination) was the daughter of Oceanus and Tethys. ZEUS made the gods swear solemn oaths in the name of the river, and any god who broke his oath was forced to drink of its waters, which were so foul that it deprived him of voice and breath for nine years.

Suen In ancient Mesopotamia, an older name for SIN, the Sumerian moon god. He was the offspring of the air god ENLIL. The name may mean "the crescent moon".

Sugriva In Hindu mythology, a monkey king who was advised by HANUMAN, the monkey god. Sugriva and Hanuman helped Rama (an avatar of VISHNU) to overcome the demon Ravana, who ruled Sri Lanka.

Surabhi In Hindu mythology, the "cow of plenty", who has the power to grant wishes. She belongs to the sage VASISHTHA, whose own name means "most wealthy". Surabhi is also called Nandini, since she is the mother of the bull Nandi, SHIVA's mount. She appeared out of the milky waves during the churning of the ocean, and was the first sign to the gods that they were winning the battle against the demons for the possession of the AMRITA, or water of life.

Surasa In Hindu mythology, a female demon who tried to swallow HANUMAN, the monkey god, when he crossed to Sri Lanka to do battle with the demon king Ravana. Hanuman outwitted her by greatly elongating his body, forcing Surasa to do the same to her mouth, and then instantly becoming as small as a thumb, shooting through her head and escaping through her ear. Once on Sri Lanka, Hanuman greased his own tail and set it on fire. It caused chaos among Ravana's forces and burnt down the capital of the demon king.

Surt In Germanic mythology, a giant who will set fire to everything at Ragnarok, the end of the world. Then, Surt will throw fire in every direction, like a volcano.

Svantovit A Slavic war god, worshipped above all by the Balts. He may have been the father of the sun god Dazhbog and the fire god Svarogich. He was portrayed as a four-faced god who held a horn of wine. When the horn was full, a year of prosperity lay ahead, when less than full, a year of death and famine. He was propitiated by the annual sacrifice of a captive Christian. Each of his temples was guarded by more than 100 men. In 1168, the Danish king Valdemar destroyed the chief temple of Svantovit in Arkona.

Svarogich The fire god in Slavic mythology. His father was Svarog, or Svantovit, the war god, and his brother was Dazhbog, the sun god. Svarogich had the ability to prophesy events, and human sacrifices were made to him. He was portrayed wearing a helmet in the shape of a bird and with the image of a bison's head on his breast.

Svartalfheim In Germanic mythology, the underground home of the dark elves. No clear distinction was ever drawn between the dark elves and the dwarfs: both toiled away in workshops below ground. They were usually associated with smith gods, including the Anglo-Saxon WAYLAND in Britain.

Syrinx In Greek mythology, the name of the pipes played by the goat-like god PAN. Pan pursued a nymph called Syrinx who, being a devotee of ARTEMIS, spurned him. Syrinx's friends, the water nymphs, turned her into a reed plant just as Pan finally embraced her. Pan blew upon the reeds and produced such an affecting and plaintive melody that he made a set of pipes from them in memory of Syrinx.

T

Taburimai In the mythology of the Gilbert Islanders of Micronesia, a semi-divine ancestor. He was the son of Bakoa and Neg Nguiriki, and the brother of the shark spirit Teanoi. Because Taburimai had a strange human shape, Teanoi sought to kill him, but Bakoa sent him away to Samoa. There, Taburamai married a woman and settled down. Their son, Te-ariki-n-tarawa, an adventurous young man, took as his wife a tree goddess and begat the human race.

Tages In Roman mythology, an Etruscan sage. He was unearthed by a ploughman near Tarquinia, a city to the north of Rome. A child with the grey hair of wisdom, Tages was received by the twelve rulers of the twelve Etruscan cities, to whom he imparted his knowledge. When his mission was accomplished, he returned to the soil.

Taliesin The Welsh wizard and bard, whose name means "radiant brow". By accident, he swallowed three drops of the magic brew in the cauldron of Ceridwen, a powerful witch. As a result, Taliesin knew the secrets of the past, the present, and the future. Ceridwen pursued him relentlessly because of the theft.

Talos In Greek mythology, a man of brass made by the smith god HEPHAISTOS, and given to EUROPA by ZEUS as a guardian for the island of Crete. When strangers appeared, he would glow red-hot and take them in a fatal embrace. He also hurled rocks at the Argonauts when they attempted to land on Crete, but he was killed by one of them, Poeas, with an arrow.

Tammuz In Babylonian and Assyrian mythology, the god of crops and vegetation and the husband of the love goddess ISHTAR. His great love for Ishtar, and his death, caused by Ishtar's offering him to the underworld in her place, made him a cult figure among women, who lamented him at an annual seven-day festival marked by wailing and self-laceration. Tammuz is the equivalent of Dumuzi, the dying-and-rising husband of INANNA, the Sumerian love goddess.

Tane-mahuta In Maori mythology, the lord of the forests and the equivalent of the Hawaiian KANE. The son of RANGI (sky) and PAPA (earth), he separated his parents, simply pushing the sky up with his head and the earth down with his feet, thus dividing the heavens from the earth without bloodshed. After mating with various objects to produce trees, streams and reptiles, he longed for human children and created a woman out of clay. He married her and by her begat the Polynesian people. He has always been regarded as the personification of goodness.

Tangaloa In Polynesian mythology, an alternative name for the creator deity TA'AROA. On Tahiti he is called Rua-i-tupra (source of growth), while the Hawaiians have identifed him with the squid god Kanaloa. In all instances, the deity shows an evil side to his nature when angry.

Tanit The Canaanite moon goddess, who was worshipped as Tinit at Carthage, the great colony of Tyre in Africa. She represents a special form of ASTARTE, the mother goddess and the wife of BAAL. In Egypt, Tanit was sometimes given horns and identified with the cow goddess HATHOR.

Tanngniortr and Tanngrisnr In Germanic mythology, two he-goats whose names mean "toothgrinder" and "toothgnasher". They drew THOR's chariot across the sky.

Tano In the mythology of the Akan people of Togoland, the son of the supreme god and the brother of Bia. Because he was a disobedient son, Tano's father intended him to receive the desert lands of the earth. However, Tano disguised himself as Bia, presented himself to his father, and in error received the fertile lands.

Tapeia A legendary Roman girl of uncertain fame. She was killed by the Sabines when she opened the gate of the Capitoline fortress to them. What is not clear from the legend is whether the Sabines killed Tapeia after realizing that she had played a trick on them, having made them surrender their shields to her. The Romans themselves could not settle the uncertainty surrounding Tapeia's death, although traitors were thrown from the Tapeian Rock.

Tarchon In Roman mythology, the leader of the Etruscans on their journey to Italy. A famine in Lydia caused the migration and settlement of Tuscany, named after the Etruscans. Tarchon helped the Trojans under AENEAS settle on the banks of the River Tiber.

Tarquin A "recreant knight" of the Round Table of ARTHUR. He held several fellow knights captive until they were freed by Sir Lancelot. Finding a copper vessel suspended from a tree, Sir Lancelot struck it with his sword and brought Sir Tarquin to battle. In the struggle that ensued, Sir Tarquin fell mortally wounded.

Tarquinius Sextus In Roman legend, the man who caused the abolition of the monarchy. The youngest son of Tarquinius Superbus, an Etruscan ruler of Rome, his rape of Lucretia provoked a rebellion. This wife of a leading Roman stabbed herself to death, after extracting from her husband and her father a promise of revenge.

Tartarus In Greek mythology, the abyss of the underworld where the souls of the most wicked dead were afflicted with eternal torment. Among the inhabitants of Tartarus were KRONOS, the Titans, Ixion, Sisyphus and TANTALUS.

Tauret An ancient Egyptian hippopotamus goddess, the guardian of childbirth and protector of children. She was commonly represented with large, hanging breasts, the limbs of a lion and tail of a crocodile. Her ferocious appearance frightened away malevolent spirits at times of childbirth.

Tautohito In Maori mythology, a sorcerer who shared a magic wooden head with his fellow sorcerer, Puarata. They were both overcome by the magic of HAKAWAU.

Tawhiri-ma-tea In Maori mythology, the storm god and the son of RANGI (sky) and PAPA (earth). He sided with his father when his brothers and sisters tried to part their parents. Although Tawhiri-ma-tea whipped up mighty winds, thunderstorms and hurricanes, which uprooted trees and inundated the land, Rangi and Papa were separated. However, Tawhiri-ma-tea was not vanquished, but continued to be the enemy of men on land and at sea.

Tawiskaron In North American Indian mythology, an evil spirit who always tried to help wild beasts prey on mankind. According to the Mohawks, Tawiskaron did this by setting up a magic bridge from the sky to the earth.

Tefnut The ancient Egyptian goddess of moisture. She and her brother-husband Shu (air) were the begetters of both the earth god Geb and the sky goddess NUT. Tefnut helped Shu to hold up the sky and, each morning, she welcomed the sun, a circumstance that led to her association with RE. She was commonly represented as a woman with a lion's head surmounted by a solar disc.

Te Ikawai According to the Gilbert Islanders of Micronesia, one of the great gods born of Na Atibu and Nei Teukez. His name means "the eldest". The whole process of creation was started by NAREAU the elder, the spider spirit.

Telemachus In Greek mythology, the son of ODYSSEUS and Penelope. Left at home when Odysseus went to the Trojan War, he eventually went in search of his father under the protection of the goddess ATHENA. Telemachus failed to find him, but he returned to Ithaca in time to witness the slaughter of Penelope's suitors by Odysseus.

Temazcateci The ancient Aztec goddess of the bath. Her image was shown above the entrance to the hot baths favoured in Tenochtitlán. She may have been seen as a cleanser of physical and spiritual impurity.

Te Nao According to the Gilbert Islanders, one of the gods born of Na Atibu and Nei Teukez. His name means "the wave". Other deities who sprang from this pair include Na Kika (octopus lord), Ruki (eel), and Nareau the younger.

Tenes In Greek mythology, the son of Cycnus, King of Colonae near Troy, and his first wife, Procleia. Cycnus's second wife, Phylonome, desired Tenes and, when he spurned her advances, slandered him to his father. Cycnus put Tenes and his sister Hemithea in a chest and cast them into the sea. They were rescued by POSEIDON and taken to the island of Tenedos, where Tenes became king. When Cycnus discovered his wife's baseness, he murdered her and then joined Tenes in Tenedos.

Both father and son fought against the Greeks in the Trojan War and were slain by ACHILLES. Since Tenes also claimed to be the offspring of the god Apollo, the action of the Greek hero may have been foolhardy. One source says that, when Paris shot Achilles with his bow, Apollo guided the poisoned arrow.

Tengu Japanese trickster spirits with long beaks; hence their name which means "long nose". They are mischievous rather than malevolent, unlike the Oni.

Teucer According to the ancient Greeks, the first king of Troy. His daughter married the immigrant leader Dardanus, who inherited the kingdom on Teucer's death. PRIAM was the last descendant of Teucer to rule Troy.

Thanatos In Greek mythology, the personification of death. He was the twin brother of Hypnos (sleep) and the son of Nyx (night) and Erebus (darkness), or of Nyx alone. In Thessaly, the hero HERACLES once beat Thanatos in a wrestling match.

Thaumus An ancient Greek sea deity whose name means "wonder". He was said to be the father of the Harpies, ravenous bird-women that had wings.

Themis The mother of PROMETHEUS, the ancient Greek god of fire. She was a wise Titaness, well versed in oracles and laws, and hence the personification of virtue and justice. The second lover of ZEUS, she bore him the Horae (Hours) and the MOIRAI (Fates).

Thetis The immortal mother of the ancient Greek hero ACHILLES. She was a sea nymph beloved by both POSEIDON and ZEUS. Since it was prophesied that her son would outshine his father, Zeus made Thetis marry a mortal king, Peleus of Phthia.

Thetis burned her first six sons in order to ascertain whether they had inherited her own immortality. Her seventh son was Achilles, who was rescued from the flames by Peleus and given to the centaur Chiron to be raised by him. Thetis dipped Achilles in the river Styx to make him invulnerable; but where she held him by the heel, the waters did not touch him, and the heel therefore remained his weak spot. Achilles was killed at Troy when a poisoned arrow struck his heel.

Thrall See Jarl.

Thrymr In Germanic mythology, a frost giant who stole THOR's hammer and hid it deep in the ground. He promised to return it on condition that Freya became his wife. When, understandably, Freya refused, Thor was persuaded by LOKI to visit Thrymr, disguised as the goddess. At the banquet which Thrymr gave for his intended bride, he was astonished to see her consume vast quantities of food and drink. Loki explained that excitement at the forthcoming nuptials had left her unable to eat until then. When Thrymr produced the hammer, Thor grabbed it, slaughtered all the giants at the table with it, and departed for home with Loki.

Thunor The Anglo-Saxon name for THOR, the powerful son of ODIN, and a leading Germanic god. Place names in England that recall Thunor are Thundersfield in Surrey and Thundridge in Hertfordshire.

Tiberinus A son of JANUS, the Roman god of beginnings, or a descendant of AENEAS. As a result of his death, on or near the Tiber, the river was renamed after Tiberinus.

Tintagel The place where ARTHUR, the legendary King of Britain, was conceived. It was the stronghold of a Cornish lord, whose wife Arthur's father loved.

Tirawahat In North American Indian mythology, the creator deity of the Pawnees. Storms have always been looked upon as his messengers.

Tiresias The great blind seer of ancient Greece, who hailed from Thebes. According to one myth, he was blinded by the goddess ATHENA when he espied her bathing nude, and was then given the gift of prophecy by her in compensation. In another myth, he settled a dispute between ZEUS and HERA by saying that women enjoyed sexual pleasure more than men. Hera blinded him for siding with Zeus, who rewarded Tiresias with a long life and the power of prophecy.

When ODYSSEUS was about to visit the underworld in order to consult Tiresias, CIRCE told him that neither HADES nor PERSEPHONE had been able to dull the seer's inner vision. "For though he is dead," she noted, "he alone has a mind to reason with. The rest are mere shadows flitting to and fro."

On reaching the edge of the underworld, Odysseus performed rites to attract Tiresias. Having "cut the throats of sheep over a trench so that the dark blood poured in", the voyager "sat on guard, sword in hand, and prevented any feckless ghosts from approaching the blood before Tiresias came."

Tishtrya An ancient Iranian god of water, whether in clouds, lakes or the sea. Tishtrya was an ally of AHURA MAZDAH in the struggle against the dark forces of evil under AHRIMAN.

Titans In Greek mythology, the race of giants who ruled the universe before KRONOS, their leader, was overthrown by ZEUS. They were the offspring of Ouranos (sky) and Gaia (earth). The war between Zeus and Kronos lasted for ten years. It ended when Zeus released the CYCLOPES and Hectanochires (100-armed giants) from Tartarus and, with their aid, overcame Kronos. Zeus then condemned Kronos to eternal torment in Tartarus.

Tithonus The mortal lover of EOS, the ancient Greek dawn goddess. She asked ZEUS to grant Tithonus immortality, but forgot to ask that he might also have eternal youth. Tithonus therefore grew older and older, and more and more withered. When he pleaded that he might be released from immortality, Eos turned him into a cicada, an insect that sheds its shell.

Tiw The Anglo-Saxon for Tyr, the Germanic war god and son of ODIN. The village of Tuesley in Surrey, England, preserves his name.

Tlazolteotl In the Aztec mythology of Central America, the goddess of pleasure, intoxication and death. Her name means "dirty lady", and she was associated with witchcraft and the sexual passions. When a certain man let it be known that he wished to become a favourite of the gods, they tested his virtue by sending him Tlazolteotl. He succumbed to her enchantments and tried to embrace her. The gods therefore cut off his head and turned him into a scorpion.

Tobadzistsini In the mythology of the Navaho Indians of North America, a war god and the brother of NAYENEZGANI. Together, the brothers had countless adventures as they went about the world doing battle against the forces of evil.

To-Karvuvu According to the New Britain Islanders, one of the first two men, the other being his brother, TO-KABINANA. Whereas everything that To-Kabinana turned his hand to came out well, To-Karvuvu was a bungler, incapable of avoiding mishaps. Thus, To-Karvuvu symbolizes evil whereas his brother embodies good.

Tonatiuh In the Aztec mythology of Central America, the fourth in a series of sun gods. He was the ruler of a paradise called Tollan, where he received the souls of dead warriors and of women who died in childbirth. Offerings of human hearts and blood were made to him regularly. It was believed by the ancient Aztecs that Tonatiuh needed this sacrifice to maintain his strength, which was being used up all the time to support the universe.

Tonenili The rain god of the Navaho Indians of Arizona. Rather like COYOTE, he enjoys playing tricks on mankind, but never those that lead to a disaster. His name means "water sprinkler".

Triptolemus A young god who served DEMETER, an ancient Greek earth goddess. He transmitted her gift of corn and agriculture to the nations of the world. Triptolemus was born at Eleusis, the cult centre of Demeter to the south of Athens. He was usually portrayed as a handsome youth riding in a serpent-chariot and surrounded by male and female attendants. Sometimes he is shown carrying a wheatsheaf.

Tristram In the Middle Ages, Tristram and Iseult were two legendary lovers. He was the nephew of Mark, King of Cornwall, and she was the daughter of the king of Ireland. There are several versions of their legend. In one of them, Tristram was cured of a wound by the beautiful Iseult and told his uncle of her. Mark then sent Tristram to Ireland to make suit to Iseult on his behalf. But on the voyage back, the two unknowingly drank a magic potion prepared by Iseult's mother that turned them into lovers. Unable to free themselves of their passion, they were doomed to die tragic deaths.

Triton A minor Greek sea deity, the son of POSEIDON. He was a creature with a human head and torso, but with the fins and tail of a fish. Whenever he wished to calm the waves, he blew on a conch shell. Pallas, a daughter of Triton, was associated with ATHENA.

Troilus In Greek mythology, one of the sons of PRIAM, King of Troy. He was killed by ACHILLES in the Trojan War. The story of his love for Cressida became very popular in Europe in the Middle Ages. Troilus loved Cressida, who swore to be faithful to him when she was exchanged for a Trojan prisoner of war. In the Greek camp, where her father was a traitor, she fell in love with Diomedes. To end his sorrow, Troilus died willingly in the fray.

Troy For the ancient Greeks and Romans, the legendary seat of PRIAM. To this city HELEN was abducted by Paris, an action that brought about the Trojan War. After the Greek sack of Troy, AENEAS led a band of refugees to Italy where they became the forerunners of the Roman people. What was probably the historical site of the city was discovered in Turkey in 1873 by Heinrich Schliemann (1822–90).

Tsohanoai The sun god of the Navaho Indians of North America. He is human in form and carries the sun on his back across the sky. At night, the sun hangs on a peg on the wall of Tsohanoai's house.

Tsuki-Yomi In Japan, the Shinto god of the moon. After IZANAGI closed the entrance to the underworld with a massive stone, he washed himself in the sea in order to rid himself of all association with death. While he was washing his face, Tsuki-Yomi escaped from his left eye; the sun goddess AMATERASU emerged from his right eye.

Tuage A mortal woman loved by MANANNAN, the Irish sea god. But this passion was unfulfilled because the druid sent by Manannan to bring her to him let Tuage drown. For this incompetence the druid himself was drowned.

Tuamutef In ancient Egypt, one of the four sons of HORUS, all of whom were responsible for guarding the embalmed entrails of the deceased. During mummification, internal organs were removed, wrapped in linen and placed in what came to be known as Canopic jars; the jar containing the stomach was protected by Tuamutef. The other three mummiform sons of Horus were responsible for the intestines (the falcon-headed Qebehsenuf), the lungs (the ape-headed Hapi) and the liver (the human-headed Imsety). Tuamutef appears with the head of a jackal and is consequently associated with ANUBIS.

Tuatha De Danaan In Irish mythology, the people who conquered the Fomorii and replaced them as rulers of Ireland. They were believed to have come to Ireland from a northern country where they had great cities. The descendants of the goddess Dana, they ruled until they were overthrown by the Milesians, after which they retired to an underground realm. They were gods of light and the greatest among them was the sun god LUGH.

Tu-matavenga In Maori mythology, a war god and one of the children of RANGI (sky) and PAPA (earth). Rangi and Papa were so tightly coupled that their children could not break out from the darkness of the womb. One brother, the storm god Tawhiri-ma-tea, sided with Rangi, but Tu-matavenga stood up to, and eventually overcame, him. However, the storm god was left in charge of the sky.

Turi-a-faumea One of the children of TANGAROA, the Polynesian god of fish and reptiles, and Faumea, a mysterious fertility goddess. When Tangaroa's daughter-in-law was seized by the octopus demon Rogo-tumu-here, he and Turi-a-faumea rescued her, pulling the monster to the surface of the water and hacking off its tentacles. This encounter compares with that of THOR and Hymir fishing for the sea serpent Jormungandr.

Turnus In Roman mythology, an Italian prince who fought a duel with AENEAS in order to decide who should marry Lavinia, the daughter of Latimus, King of Latium. Turnus was betrothed to Lavinia, but the engagement was broken on the arrival of the Trojans. The love goddess Venus helped Aeneas to win Lavinia's hand.

Turquoise Woman In the mythology of the Navaho Indians of North America, an important goddess. She lived with her sister, White Shell Woman, at a time when the earth was inhabited by monsters. Turquoise Woman and White Shell Woman lost a contest with the Corn Maidens in which the prize was to become the wife of the Navaho deity, Monster-Slayer.

Twashtri The divine artisan of Hindu mythology; the equal of the Greek HEPHAISTOS and the Roman Vulcan. He makes useful objects for the gods, including INDRA's thunderbolts. Twashtri also imparts generative power and bestows children on mankind.

Tyndareus In Greek mythology, the king of Sparta and husband of Leda. On the night that Leda was seduced by ZEUS, who appeared in the form of a swan, she also slept with her husband. On that night, possibly CASTOR and Polydeuces, HELEN and Clytemnestra were all conceived. The exact parentage of each child was a matter of intense discussion in ancient Greece.

Tyr A Germanic war god, usually associated with law and justice. Tyr sacrificed one of his hands so that the wolf Fenrir could be bound by the gods.

U

Uathach A Scottish mistress of CUCHULAINN, the legendary Irish hero. When she served him food, Cuchulainn forgot his strength and broke her finger. Uathach's scream brought her lover to the room, where Cuchulainn quickly killed him. However, the girl soon forgot her distress and fell in love with the powerful Irishman.

Ueuecoyotl The ancient Aztec version of COYOTE. The name means "very old coyote". The Aztecs blamed Ueuecoyotl for causing unnecessary diversions from war, such as sexual passion.

Uke-mochi In the Shinto mythology of Japan, an agricultural spirit and food goddess, married to INARI, the god of rice. When the moon god Tsuki-yomi visited Uke-mochi, he was splendidly fed, for Uke-mochi filled the seas with fish, the mountains with game, and the fields with rice. But this abundance of food had come from Uke-mochi's mouth, which so displeased Tsuki-yomi that he killed her. However, her corpse gave birth to more food in the form of crops and cattle.

Ukko In northern Europe, the ancient sky god of the Finns. Sometimes called Pauanne (thunder), he restored fire to mankind after an evil spirit stole it from the earth. Ukko did this by sending down a thunderbolt from the sky, which a fish swallowed. The hero Vainamoinen caught the fish and found the fire in its belly.

Ulanji In the mythology of the Binbinga Aboriginals of northern Australia, one of many ancestral snakes. Ulanji once climbed rocks to bite off the heads of flying foxes. In circumcision rites to initiate young men into manhood, Binbinga youths are told that they give their foreskins to Ulanji.

Ulgan In the mythology of the Altaic Tartars of Siberia, another name for the supreme creator god Yryn-ai-tojon, who made the world by placing a disc on an expanse of water. Three fish support the disc and their sudden movements cause earthquakes.

When there was still primeval water everywhere, a piece of mud floating on the waves told Ulgan that it was the spirit of evil and that it lived on the ground underneath the water. Ulgan named the spirit, the first man, ERLIK, then asked for some of this earth, and from it he formed the continents. Thus, the forces of good and evil cooperated in the formation of the world.

Ull The Germanic god of archery and skiing. The name means "brilliant". He was always invoked in duels.

Uma In Hindu mythology, one of the titles of the great goddess DEVI, meaning "light". Uma spent long periods of ascetic denial on the mountain peaks of the Himalayas, thereby gaining the attention and favour of her husband SHIVA, the divine yogi.

Unicorn In European mythology, a fabulous beast with the hind parts of a deer, the tail of a lion, and the torso and head of a horse. It derived its name from its single horn which, when dipped in water, was thought to purify it from noxious substances. The unicorn loved innocence and purity, and hunters could catch it only by placing a virgin in its path, since the unicorn would always run to her, lie down at her feet and fall asleep. Medieval commentators on the Bible believed that the unicorn represents "JESUS conceived of the VIRGIN MARY".

Upuaut An ancient Egyptian wolf god, closely associated with ANUBIS. He helped to guide the dead to the hall of OSIRIS in the underworld.

Uranus Another form of Ouranos, the first sky god in ancient Greek mythology. He was born of Chaos. KRONOS separated him from Gaia (earth) in order to form the world.

Urd See Norns and Wyrd.

Ushas In Hindu mythology, the goddess of the dawn. She is kind and helpful, and is imagined as a willing young wife who is pleased to look after the home.

Utanapishtim In ancient Mesopotamia, one of the NOAH figures who survived the flood. He was an ancestor of GILGAMESH, King of Uruk. Warned of the coming inundation, Utanapishtim built an ark and filled it with gold and silver and living creatures of all kinds.

After seven days, the floods abated and Utanapishtim released a dove. When it returned, he released a swallow, which also returned. Finally, he released a raven, which did not return, signifying that it had found a resting place on dry land. The gods then blessed Utanapishtim and his wife and made them immortal. However, Utanapishtim was unable to pass on this divine gift to Gilgamesh, when the king visited him in search of immortality.

Uther Pendragon The father of ARTHUR, the legendary king of Britain. He fell in love with Igraine, the wife of the lord of Tintagel in Cornwall. With the help of MERLIN, he disguised himself as her husband and slept with Igraine. After the lord of Tintagel died, Uther Pendragon married Igraine. When Arthur was born, the child was given to Merlin, who brought him up in secrecy, and prepared him for kingship.

Utu In ancient Sumer, the original heartland of Mesopotamia, a righteous sun god who guarded justice. He was the judge of gods and men during the day, and at night he judged disputes among the dead in the underworld. The brother of INANNA, Utu refused to help her when she wanted to cut down a sacred tree and so GILGAMESH helped her instead. Utu made the ground swallow up everything fashioned from the tree's timber, because he disapproved of the excessive merriment in Uruk, Gilgamesh's city.

Uzume In the Shinto mythology of Japan, the goddess of laughter. When the sun goddess AMATERASU retreated into a cave, leaving the universe in darkness, the gods held a great feast to implore her to return. At the feast, Uzume's dancing and high spirits caused such laughter that the air was filled with deafening noise and the heavens shook, inducing a curious Amaterasu to leave her hiding place and bring light back to the world.

V

Vafthrudnir In Germanic mythology, a wise frost giant who was tricked by ODIN in a test of knowledge, and who paid with his life. The final words Vafthrudnir spoke were: "You will always be wiser and wisest." For Odin had already died on YGGDRASIL, the world tree, in order to be reborn with wisdom.

Vainamoinen The great legendary hero of the Finns. He invented music, poetry and spells. When threatened by his enemies, Vainamoinen used to escape on the back of a giant eagle. Usually the hero is portrayed as a strong old man with a white beard.

Valfodr One of the titles of ODIN, chief of the Germanic gods. It means "father of the slain". The Vikings believed that the heroic dead were gathered in Valhalla, Odin's hall.

Valhalla In Germanic mythology, ODIN's hall in Asgard. The home of warriors slain in battle, its walls were made of shields and its roof of spears. Entrance to it was via the gate of death, Valgrind. In Asgard, the slain heroes fight each other every day, while they wait for Ragnarok, the battle at the end of time. However, they are restored to health each evening by the meat of the boar Saehrimnir.

Vali In Germanic mythology, the son of LOKI and Sigyn. To punish Loki for causing BALDER's death, the gods turned Vali into a wolf and set him upon his brother Narve. Loki was then bound by Narve's entrails.

Valkyries In Germanic mythology, the maidens sent by ODIN to every battle in order to choose which warriors should be slain and brought to Valhalla. Their name means "chooser of the fallen". They rode on horses and the light reflected from their shields produced the Aurora Borealis, or Northern Lights. In some myths, they were able to turn themselves into ravens and wolves. When at Valhalla, they would bring horns of ale to the Einherjar (slain warriors).

Vanir A race of Germanic fertility gods and goddesses, essentially peaceful and benevolent. They were ruled by Njord and his children, FREY and Freya, and subscribed to an ideal beauty. They were originally the enemies of the warlike Aesir gods. However, the two races were eventually reconciled. Over a period of time, the Vanir were assimilated into the Aesir. The Vanir home was called Vannaheim.

Varuni The Hindu goddess of wine, notable for her rolling eyes. She was born during the churning of the ocean, emerging from the milky sea after the sacred cow, Surabhi. She is also called Mada (intoxication).

Vasuki In Hindu mythology, a great snake who wrapped himself around Mount Mandara and was used as a rope with which to spin the mountain, thereby producing the churning of the ocean from which AMRITA, the water of life, emerged. The gods pulled Vasuki by the tail, the demons pulled him by the head, and the effort so damaged him that venom poured from his weakened jaws. According to one version of the myth, the venom would have destroyed all living creatures had not the god SHIVA drunk it all up.

Vayu The Hindu god of the wind. In the *Rig Veda*, the ancient collection of hymns, he is associated with INDRA, the god of the firmament. Vaya is often described as Indra's charioteer. His other names are Sadagata (ever-moving) and Gandhavaha (bearer of perfumes).

Ve In Germanic mythology, one of the three original gods begotten by the primeval giants BOR and Bestla. With his brothers ODIN and Vili, he destroyed the giants and established the rule of the gods.

Venus In Roman mythology, the goddess of spring and love who was identified with the Greek APHRODITE. She was the wife of Vulcan and, by MARS, the mother of Cupid. She was sometimes represented as having been born in the sea, and her chariot, a scallop shell, was drawn by dolphins or swans. Originally, she must have been an Italian goddess with authority over ploughed land and gardens. Venus helped AENEAS throughout his life.

Verginia A legendary Roman maiden slain by her own father to save her from the lust of a corrupt official, Appius Claudius. A close parallel to the Lucretia story, the sacrifice was believed to have led in 449 BC to the overthrow of an aristocratic tyranny.

Vestia The Roman goddess of the hearth, identified with the Greek Hestia. At Rome, she was considered to be the protectress of the nation, and was worshipped by the Vestal Virgins. Her shrine was a small round temple in the Forum, the ruins of which are still visible.

Vigrid In Germanic mythology, the plain near Asgard where the gods and giants are to fight the battle that will destroy the world.

Vili A brother of ODIN, the Germanic war god. See Ve.

Viswamitra In Hindu mythology, a celebrated sage and the enemy of VASISHTHA, another wise man. Viswamitra rose to fame by the singular strength of his self-discipline. He had 100 sons.

Vodyanik The Slavic water spirit who usually appears as an old man with a fat belly, wearing a reed cap and a belt of rushes. He can be benevolent or malevolent, depending on his mood. In a mischievous mood, he surprises fishermen and overturns their boats; he may also drown bathers.

Volos The god of beasts and domestic flocks in Slavic mythology. Until the nineteenth century he was also worshipped in some parts of Russia. Volos had both demonic and benevolent aspects, the latter being assimilated into the legendary character of St Blaise, the third-century patron of physicians. Volos is called Vlas or Vlassy in Russia, and in Lithuania he is called Ganyklos.

Vor In Germanic mythology, the goddess from whom nothing could be hidden. She was invoked by defendants at trials.

Vritra In the collection of Hindu hymns called the *Rig Veda*, the demonic and destructive serpent who causes drought. He was so huge that his head reached the sky and his coils enveloped the mountains. When he challenged his enemy INDRA to a battle, he initially engulfed the god in his mouth. However, the gods gagged Vritra, enabling Indra to jump out of his mouth and kill him with his thunderbolt, liberating creation.

Vulcan The Roman smith god who was associated with all kinds of fire. He was the equivalent of the Greek HEPHAISTOS. On his forge beneath Mount Etna, Vulcan produced thunderbolts for JUPITER. Vulcan was a popular deity in Ostia, the port of Rome, possibly in recognition of the industry situated there.

W X

Wakea A legendary Hawaiian chief who married the earth goddess PAPA. The difference in status between Wakea and Papa is the origin of class division among the Hawaiian people. Their quarrel over their daughter, Ho'choku-ka-lani, with whom Wakea had an incestuous affair, led to their separation and the introduction of death into the world.

Wakonda The "great power above" of the Sioux Indians of North America. He has always been looked upon as the source of all wisdom and power, a generous deity who sustains the world and enlightens the shaman. The Dakota Indians also worship Wakonda, but as a mighty bird of thunder.

Watauineiwa The benevolent deity worshipped by the Yahgan tribe of Tierra del Fuego, at the southern tip of South America. His name means "most ancient one" and he sustains the world, which he made for the Yahgan tribe.

Wepwawet A funerary god with a dog's body. He was associated with OSIRIS, the ruler of the Egyptian underworld. His name means "the opener of ways".

Wihio In the mythology of the Cheyenne Indians of North America, a trickster who persuaded a coyote to beg for food with him. They disguised themselves as a mother and baby, but Wihio refused to give the coyote any of the booty. When the coyote threatened to reveal their deception, Wihio threw him into a lake.

William Tell The legendary Swiss hero who led his country against Austria. The Austrian governor Gessler ordered Tell to shoot at an apple placed on his son's head. Tell hit the apple with his first arrow. He then told Gessler that, if his first arrow had slain his son, his second would have killed Gessler. He was imprisoned for his impudence but, after his release, he ambushed and killed Gessler and initiated a rising which is supposed to have led to national independence.

Winpe In the mythology of the Algonquin Indians of North America, a terrible sorcerer and an opponent of GLOOSKAP. One day, he stole Glooskap's family and carried them off in a canoe. However, Glooskap pursued Winpe on the back of a great fish and overcame his magic. The sorcerer fell dead to the ground, like a mighty pine tree.

Woden The Anglo-Saxon name for ODIN, the leading Germanic deity. Apart from Wednesday, the day of the week named for him, place names in England, such as Wednesfield (Woden's plain) and Wednesbury (Woden's stronghold), derive from his name.

Wonomi In the mythology of the Maidu Indians of North America, the sky god and supreme father, whose name means "no death". He was also called Kodo-yapeu (world creator), Kodo-yanpe (world namer) and Kodo-yeponi (world chief). He ruled over all things until he was overthrown by COYOTE, for whom the people abandoned Wonomi.

Wotan In Germanic mythology, another name for ODIN, the one-eyed god of battle, magic, inspiration, and the glorious dead.

Wulleb See Lejman.

Wyrd The name by which the Anglo-Saxons in Britain knew the Norns, the three Germanic goddesses of destiny. Urd (fate) was the one whose name gave rise to Wyrd. By Shakespeare's time, in the sixteenth century, they had become the Weird Sisters of *Macbeth*.

Xanthus One of the two immortal horses of the Greek hero Achilles. The other was called Balius. When, during the Trojan War, Xanthus warned Achilles of impending death, the ERINYES struck him dumb.

Xi He In Chinese mythology, the wife of Di Jun, the god of the eastern sky. Every morning, Xi He used to transport one of her ten sons to the edge of the sky so that, as the sun itself, he could take a path across the sky.

Eventually, nine of her sons had to be shot down by YI, the divine archer, because they insisted on appearing in the sky all together.

Xochipilli The flower god of the ancient Aztecs of Mexico. It was believed that four years after death, the soul of a brave warrior became a richly plumed bird. As the god of flowers, the flayed Xochipilli was the guardian of such spirits.

Xolotl A strange Aztec deity in the shape of a deformed dog, with feet which turned backward. He was supposed to push down the curtain of night. Xolotl had a burst eye, a token of the austerities he had personally endured. Self-torture and ritual killing were the two aspects of the Aztec religion of suffering.

Y Z

Yahweh The name of the god of Israel, preserved only in its four consonants, YHWH. Another Canaanite deity often compared with Yahweh is EL. Yahweh is also called Jehovah.

Yambe-akka In the mythology of the Lapps of Scandinavia, the goddess who presided over the underworld. Her name means "old woman of the dead" and her shaking hands caused earth tremors.

Yamm The Canaanite sea deity and the enemy of BAAL. Yamm was killed in their struggle, and Baal was declared king of the world. However, the surviving texts from ancient Ugarit do not provide a clear picture of this contest.

Yanauluha The great Pueblo Zuni shaman who led the first members of the tribe from underground caverns to the surface in North America. Yanauluha also taught the arts of civilization: agriculture, husbandry and good manners.

Yanwang The Chinese equivalent of YAMA, the Hindu god of death. His task is the enforcement of the law of retribution. This imported Buddhist deity has become mixed up in the Chinese mind with the ruler of the indigenous underworld, the Yellow Springs.

Yasoda The wife of the cowherd Nanda and the foster mother of KRISHNA, the incarnation of the great Hindu god VISHNU.

Ymir In Germanic mythology, the first giant, formed when the warm air blowing from Muspellheim (the land of fire giants) met the cold pouring off Niflheim, and created a sea called Ginnungagap from which he emerged. He was slain by ODIN, Vili and Ve, and from his body they created Midgard (middle region), which included Mannheim (the land of men). From his flesh, the ground was formed, from his bones, the mountains, from his teeth and jaw, the rocks and stones. His skull became the sky and was supported by four dwarfs, who themselves evolved from the maggots in Ymir's corpse. To protect Midgard from the remaining giants, Ymir's eyebrows were used to make an enormous wall.

Yuga An age of the world in Hindu cosmology. The four ages, Krita Yuga, Treta Yuga, Dwapara Yuga and Kali Yuga, the present one, are all preceded and followed by periods of twilight, each of which lasts one-tenth of a Yuga. During this time, BRAHMA sleeps. The calculation of the number of human years involved is astronomical.

Zagzagel In Hebrew folklore, an angel whose name means "divine splendour". He is not mentioned in the Bible but, according to Jewish tradition, he helped the archangels Michael and Gabriel to bury Moses.

Zal In ancient Iranian legend, the father of the hero RUSTEM. Zal was born with only one flaw, his white hair, but it proved enough for his father to abandon him to die on a mountain. He was rescued and cared for by the fabulous bird, Simurgh. When his father, repenting of his error, sought and found his son, Zal forgave him.

Zaoshen The Chinese kitchen god, the benevolent spirit of the hearth. He is still worshipped with offerings of meat, fruit and wine in an annual ceremony. His goodwill is considered important because he presents reports on each family to the heavenly powers.

Zephyrus The west wind, and the son of EOS, the Greek goddess of the dawn. He fell in love with Hyacinthus, a handsome young man, but the god Apollo had already won the youth's affections. Zephyrus took a cruel revenge, causing a discus that Apollo threw to strike the hand of Hyacinthus so that he died. Zephyrus was the father of the immortal horses owned by ACHILLES.

Ziusudra In Mesopotamian mythology, a cultural hero who preserved the human race by building an ark for his family and friends during a great flooding of the earth. This deluge was sent by ENLIL. He is thus the equivalent of the biblical NOAH.

Zu In Mesopotamian mythology, one of the names of a huge bird. Zu wished to have ultimate power and to gain it he sought to dispossess ENLIL of the tablets of fate, which controlled destiny. He stole the tablets from Enlil's great hall and went into hiding with them in the mountains. NINURTA, Enlil's warrior son, recovered them from Zu.

Zurvan Akarana A late development in ancient Iranian mythology meaning "infinite time", and said to have given rise to good and evil, AHURA MAZDAH and AHRIMAN. Eventually, however, good will triumph.

FURTHER READING

GENERAL

Breasted, J. H. *The Dawn of Conscience*, London, 1933.

Campbell, J. *The Hero with a Thousand Faces*, New York, 1949.

Day, M. S. *The Many Meanings of Myth*, London, 1984.

Eliade, M. *Patterns of Comparative Religion*, London, 1958.

Farmer, P. *Beginnings. Creation Myths of the World*, London, 1978.

Frazer, Sir J. G. *The Golden Bough. A Study in Magic and Religion*, London, 1922.

Gimbutas, M. *The Goddesses and Gods of Old Europe: 6500–3500 B.C. Myths and Images*, London, 1982.

James, O. E. *Myth and Ritual*, London, 1958.

Jung, C. *Man and His Symbols*, London, 1964.

Kirk, G. S. *Myth. Its Meaning and Functions in Ancient and Other Cultures*, Cambridge, 1970.

Marshak, A. *The Roots of Civilization. The Cognitive Beginnings of Man's First Art, Symbol and Notation*, New York, 1946.

EGYPT

Alfred, C. *The Egyptians*, London, 1961.

Budge, Sir E. A. W. *The Gods of the Egyptians, or Studies in Egyptian Mythology*, London, 1984.

Cerny, J. *Ancient Egyptian Religion*, London and New York, 1952.

Frankfort, H. *Ancient Egyptian Religion*, New York, 1948.

James, T. G. H. *Myths and Legends of Ancient Egypt*, New York, 1971.

Moret, A. *The Nile and Egyptian Civilization*, London, 1927.

Reford, D. B. *Akhenaten. The Heretic King*, Princeton, 1984.

Shorter, A. W. *The Egyptian Gods. A Handbook*, London, 1937.

Steindorff, G. *When Egypt Ruled the East*, Chicago, 1942.

MESOPOTAMIA

Gilgamesh, The Epic of, translated by N. K. Sandars, Harmondsworth and Baltimore, 1960.

Hallo, W. W. and **Simpson, W. K.** *The Ancient Near East*, London and New York, 1971.

Hooke, S. H. *Babylonian and Assyrian Religion*, London and New York, 1953.

Jacobsen, T. *The Treasures of Darkness: A History of Mesopotamian Religion*, London and New Haven, 1976.

James, E. O. *Ritual and Myth in the Ancient Near East*, London, 1958.

Kramer, S. N. *Sumerian Mythology*, revised edition, London and New York, 1961.

Oates, J. *Babylon*, London and New York, 1979.

Oppenheim, A. L. *Ancient Mesopotamia*, second edition, London and Chicago, 1977.

Postage, J. H. *The First Empires*, Oxford, 1977.

IRAN

Frye, R. N. *The Heritage of Persia*, London and Cleveland, 1963.

Huart, C. *Ancient Persia and Iranian Civilization*, London, 1927.

Moulton, J. H. *Early Zoroastrianism*, London, 1913.

Zaehner, R. *The Dawn and Twilight of Zoroastrianism*, London, 1961.

CANAAN (including Syria and Asia Minor)

Bermant, C. and **Weitzma, M.** *Ebla. An Archaeological Enigma*, London, 1979.

Driver, G. R. *Canaanite Myths and Legends*, Edinburgh, 1956.

Gurney, O. R. *The Hittites*, Harmondsworth, 1952.

Harden, D. B. *The Phoenicians*, London, 1962.

Kenyon, K. *Amorites and Canaanites*, London, 1966.

Pritchard, J. B. *Ancient Near Eastern Texts Relating to the Old Testament*, Princeton, 1950.

Ringgren, H. *Religions of the Ancient Near East*, translated by J. Sturdy, Philadelphia, 1972, London, 1973.

GREECE

Chadwick, J. *The Mycenean World*, Cambridge and New York, 1976.

Cotterell, A. *The Minoan World*, London and New York, 1979.

Farnell, L. R. *Greek Hero-Cults and Ideas of Immortality*, Oxford, 1921.

Godwin, J. *Mystery Religions in the Ancient World*, London, 1987.

Graves, R. *The Greek Myths*, Harmondsworth and New York, 1955.

Guthrie, W. K. C. *Orpheus and Greek Religion*, London, 1935.

Kerenyi, C. *The Gods of the Greeks*, translated by N. Cameron, London, 1981.

Martin, L. H. *Hellenistic Religions*, New York, 1989.

Willets, R. F. *Cretan Cults and Festivals*, London, 1962.

ROME

Altheim, F. *A History of Roman Religion*, translated by H. Mattingly, New York, 1962, London, 1963.

Grant, M. *Roman Myths*, London, 1971.

Ogilvie, R. M. *The Romans and Their Gods*, London, 1969.

Rose, H. J. *Ancient Roman Religion*, London, 1948.

Trump, D. H. *Central and Southern Italy before Rome*, London, 1966.

CELTIC AND CHRISTIAN EUROPE

Curtin, J. *Myths and Folk Tales of Ireland*, Boston, 1980.

Darrah, J. *The Real Camelot: Paganism and the Arthurian Romances*, London, 1981.

Dillon, M. *Irish Sagas*, Dublin, 1954.

Flower, R. *The Irish Tradition*, Oxford, 1947.

Gantz, J. *Early Irish Myths and Sagas*, London, 1981.

James, M. R. *The Apocryphal New Testament*, Oxford, 1924.

Le Goff, J. *The Birth of Purgatory*, London, 1985.

MacCulloch, J. A. *Medieval Faith and Fable*, London, 1932.

Mabinogion, The, translated by Jones, G. and Jones, T., London and New York, 1949.

Senior, M.(ed.) *Sir Thomas Malory's Tales of King Arthur*, London, 1980.

Squire, C. *Celtic Myths and Legends*, London, 1901.

NORTHERN EUROPE

Branston, B. *The Lost Gods of England*, London, 1957.

Chadwick, H. M. *The Cult of Odin*, London, 1899.

Colum, P. *The Children of Odin*, London, 1922.

Crossley-Holland, K. *The Norse Myths*, London, 1980.

Davison, H. R. E. *Scandinavian Mythology*, London, 1969.

Kirby, M. H. *The Vikings*, Oxford, 1977.

Mabie, H. W. *Norse Stones*, London, 1902.

Munch, P. A. *Norse Mythology*, translated by S. B. Hustredt, New York, 1927.

Thomas, E. *Norse Tales*, Oxford, 1912.

INDIA

Bhattacharji, S. *The Indian Theogony*, Cambridge, 1970.

Conze, E. *A Short History of Buddhism*, London, 1980.

Kramrisch, S. *The Hindu Temple*, Calcutta, 1946.

O'Flaherty, W. *The Hindu Myths*, Harmondsworth, 1965.

Renou, L. *Religions of Ancient India*, London, 1951.

Waddell, L. A. *Tibetan Buddhism*, New York, 1971.

Zimmer, H. *Philosophies of India*, New York, 1951.

CHINA

Ch'en, K. *Buddhism in China. A Historical Survey*, Princeton, 1964.

Cotterell, A. *The First Emperor of China*, London, 1981.

Christie, A. *Chinese Mythology*, London, 1983.

Creel, H. G. *Confucius and the Chinese Way*, London, 1960.

Wright, A. F. *Buddhism in Chinese History*, New Haven, 1959.

JAPAN

Anesaki, M. *History of Japanese Religion*, London, 1930.

Kitagawa, J. *Religion in Japanese History*, New York, 1966.

Piggott, J. *Japanese Mythology*, London, 1969.

Saunders, E. D. *Buddhism in Japan*, Philadelphia, 1964.

Varley, H. P. *Japanese Culture: A Short History*, New York, 1973.

SOUTHEAST ASIA

Chandler, D. P. *A History of Cambodia,* Boulder, 1973.

Cole, F. C. *The Peoples of Malaysia,* New York, 1945.

Ramseyer, U. *The Art and Culture of Bali,* Oxford, 1977.

Sandin, B. *The Sea Dayaks of Borneo before White Rajah Rule,* London, 1961.

Taylor, K. W. *The Birth of Vietnam,* Berkeley, 1983.

NORTH AMERICA

Barbeau, M. *Peaux-Rouges d'Amérique: Leurs moeurs, leurs coûtumes,* Montreal, 1965.

Burland, C. *North American Mythology,* London, 1965.

Carpenter, E. *Eskimo,* Toronto, 1959.

Clark, E. L. *Indian Legends of Canada,* Toronto, 1960.

Matthews, W. *Navaho Legend,* Boston, 1897.

Schmidt, W. *High Gods in North America,* Oxford, 1933.

Spence, L. *The Myths of the North American Indians,* London, 1914.

CENTRAL AMERICA

Burland, C. A. *The Gods of Mexico,* London, 1967.

Derek, M. *Divine Horsemen. Voodoo Gods of Haiti,* London, 1953.

Morley, S. G. *The Ancient Maya,* Stanford and London, 1946.

Thompson, J. E. S. *Maya History and Religion,* London, 1971.

Valiant, G. C. *Aztecs of Mexico. The Origin, Rise and Fall of the Aztec Nation,* New York, 1944.

Weaver, M. P. *The Aztecs, the Maya, and Their Predecessors,* London, 1972.

SOUTH AMERICA

Bingham, H. *Lost City of the Incas: the Story of Macchu Pichu and its Builders,* New York, 1948, London, 1981.

Boas, O. V.and **Boas,C. V.** *Xingu. The Indians and Their Myths,* London, 1974.

Hemming, J. *The Conquest of the Incas,* London and New York, 1970.

Lumbreras, L. G. *The Peoples and Cultures of Ancient Peru,* translated by B. J. Meggars, Washington, 1974.

Reichal-Dolmatoff, G. 1974. *Amazonian Cosmos. The Sexual and Religious Symbolism of the Tukano Indians,* Chicago, 1971.

AFRICA

Abrahamsson, H. *The Origin of Death. Studies in African Mythology,* Uppsala, 1951.

Brown, J. T. *Among the Bantu Nomads,* London, 1926.

Forde, D. *African Worlds. Studies in the Cosmological Ideas and Social Values of African Peoples,* Oxford, 1954.

Mbiti, J. *Concepts of God in Africa,* London, 1970.

Parrinder, G. *African Mythology,* London, 1961.

AUSTRALIA

Elkin, A. P. *The Australian Aborigines, How To Understand Them,* Sydney, 1938.

Massola, A. *Bunjil's Cave: Myths, Legends and Superstitions of the Aborigines of Southeast Australia,* Melbourne, 1968.

Parker, K. L. *Australian Legendary Tales,* London, 1978.

Reed, A. W. *Myths and Legends of Australia,* New York, 1965.

Roheim, G. *The Eternal Ones of the Dream,* New York, 1945.

Spencer, B. and **Gillen, F. J.** *The Native Tribes of Central Australia,* London, 1899.

OCEANIA

Alpers, A. *Legends of the South Seas: The World of the Polynesians Seen through Their Myths and Legends, Poetry and Art,* New York, 1920.

Beckuith, M. *Hawaiian Mythology,* Honolulu, 1970.

Christian, F. W. *The Caroline Islands. Travel in the Sea of the Little Islands,* London, 1899.

Codrington, R. H. *The Melanesians. Studies in their Anthropology and Folk Lore,* Oxford, 1891.

Gill, W. W. *Myths and Songs of the South Pacific,* London, 1876.

Grimble, Sir A. *Migrations, Myth and Magic from the Gilbert Islands. Early Writings arranged by R. Grimble,* London, 1972.

Stair, J. B. *Old Samoa,* London, 1897.

White, J. *The Ancient History of the Maori: His Mythology and Traditions,* Wellington, 1887.

INDEX

Bedivere, Sir 63
bees 166
Bellerophon *189*
Bellona *189*
Belshazzar 82, *189*
Beowulf *189*; and Grendel 176
Bercilak de Hautdesert 90
Bergelmir *189*
berserkers 140
Bertha *189*
Bes *189*
Bestla *189*
Bhagavad Gita 116
Bhairavi 84
Bhrigu *189*
Bifrost 97, *189*
Big Owl *189*
birth 11; Greek myths 22, 131
Bishamon *189*
Blathnat *189*
Bluebeard *189*
Blue Jay *189*
boars 54, 89; Erymanthian 100
Bobbi-bobbi 49, **71**
Bochica **71**
bodhisattvas 30, 38, 67, 74, 75;
   Chinese 74; female companions 35;
   ultimate 118
Bomazi *189*
Bona Dea *190*
Boniface, St 178
Book of Daniel 60, 82
Book of the Dead 11, 168
Book of Enoch 120
Book of Genesis 137
Book of History 178
Book of Job 120
Book of John the Evangelist 157
Book of Kells 27
Book of Revelation 60
boomerang 49, 71
Bor **71–2**; son of 140
Borak *190*
Boreas *190*
Borneo 39
Bragi *190*
Brahma 32, **72**, 161; aspects of 72;
   day/night of 30, 72; faces 72; and
   Ganesa 89; and Gautama 74; "mind-
   born sons" 72; sacred lotus 56;
   symbols 72; theft of Vedas 97
brahmins 30
Bran 64, **73**, 124
Brekyirihunuade 46
Brer Rabbit 78
Bresla 71
Brian *190*
Brigit **73**
Britomaris *190*
Brontes 80
Brut *190*
Brutus, Lucius Junius *190*
Buddha 30, 31, 37, 39, **74**, 75, 174;
   contemporary of 124; incarnations
   67, 74; Mara and 125, 157; son of
   118; and Tripitaka 170; "the way
   of" 37
Buddhism 30, 32; Chinese 34, 118;
   collection of the scriptures 170;
   doctrine of non-violence 124;
   introduced to Tibet 67; Japanese 36,
   37, 74; Southeast Asian 38
Bue *190*
buffalo: Kalyls' belief 109
buffalo-monster, Hindu 83
Buga *190*
   Bujang 39
bulls: An as 60; bath in blood of 80;
   Cretan cult of 22, 23; Egyptian 151,
   160; Iranian 130; Nandi 32, 161; of
   Poseidon 100, 130; primeval 56;
   Sumerian 92; Zeus as 88, 130
   see also Minotaur
bull sacrifice 131

Bumba *190*
Buri 71, *190*
Bushmen 47, 114
Butsudo 37
Bylebog *190*

C

Cacus *191*
Cadmus 20, 68, **76**; daughter of 84
Cagn 114
Cain *191*
Caishen *191*
Calliope *191*; son of 144
Callisto *191*; Artemis and 62
Calypso 141, *191*
Camelot *191*
Camilla *191*
canals, Sumerian guardian of 86
cannibal spirit, Melanesian 151
Cara 112
Cardea *191*
cargo cult 51
Carrefow 119
Cassandra **76**, 149
Castor **77**; Aboriginal equivalent 175;
   Hindu equivalent 163
castration cult 80; Greek 19; Hittite
   19; Roman 67
castration myths: Egyptian 160; Greek
   50, 61, 117, 152; Phrygian 67, 80
caterpillar 114, 134
cat-headed goddess 159
cat man, Karadjeri 69
cats 12
Cattleraid of Cuailgne 123
cauldrons, magic 27, 81
Cecrops *191*; daughters of 66
Celts 26; crosses 27
cemeteries, cats' 12; Egyptian
   protectress of 96
Centaurs 65, 101, 112, *191*
Central America 42
Cerberus 95, 146, *191*; Heracles and
   101; Hindu equivalent 177
Ceres *191*; Demeter identified with 83
Cerynitian hind 100
Chac 169, *192*
Chalchihuitlicue *192*; children 169
chameleon 46, 172
Chandi 84
chaos-dragon 57; Babylonian 15, 60,
   153, 157, 165, 168; Mesopotamian
   120
Charon 95
chariots: Huang Di's 104; Indra's 107;
   Morgan Mywnoaur's 124;
   Poseidon's 149; Surya's 163; Thor's
   167; Xi He's 178
Ch'in Shih-huang-ti 104
Chia 71
childbirth, Murngin beliefs 179
childbirth goddesses: Egyptian 103;
   Greek 100; Maya 110; Roman 113;
   Sumerian 136
Chimaera *192*
China 34; influence on Japan 36;
   influence on Vietnam 38; Shang
   beliefs 34; Xia dynasty 34, 178
Chineke 77
Chippewa Indians 40
Chiron 65, 112, *192*
Chiuta *192*
Christianity: medieval 27; and Voodoo
   119
Chuku **77**
Chyavana *192*
Cian 122, *192*
Cincinnatus, Lucius Quinctius *192*
Cinteotl 177, *192*
Circe **77**; mother of 97; and Odysseus
   141
circumcision, Karadjeri 69
cities/towns, deities of 6; Babylonian

16, 114; Canaanite 69; Egyptian
   168; Roman 114, 130; Sumerian 14
civilization beliefs: Admiralty Island
   114; Caroline Islands 114
civilization deities: Chinese 104; Inca
   108; Maya 109
Claudius, Emperor 80
Clotho 131
clouds: Germanic goddess of 89;
   Navaho myth 57; Papuan myth 85
Clytemnestra 88, *192*; and Aegisthus
   144; and Cassandra 76; son of 144
Coatlicue **78**, 104, 166; and Xipetotec
   176
Cockaigne *192*
coconut tree, Tuamotuan 128
compass points: Hindu guardians of
   56; Navaho myth 57
Confucius/Confucianism 34, 36
Coniraya *192*
Conn, King 123, *193*
constellations: Cancer 100; Gemini
   175; Leo 100; Pleiades 175
coracle, magic 124
Coriolanus *193*
Cortés, Hernando 42, 152
corn god, Aztec 78
corn goddess, Pueblo Indian 67
Coronis 65
cow: Cadmus and 76; Heitsi-Eibib's
   parent 98; Hindu sacred 59, 173;
   Germanic 71; Sumerian 136
cow goddess: Egyptian 96, 102, 153
Coyolxauhqui 104, *193*
Coyote 41, 78, **79**
craftsmen 154; Aztec goddess of 177;
   Celtic 81; Greek 81, 130, 150;
   Greek patroness of 66; Irish god
   123; Sumerian patron of 86
   see also smith gods, weavers
Cranaus *193*
Crane 85
creation deities: Abnaki Indian 93;
   Algonquin 132; Arawak Indian 44;
   Ashanti 127; Babylonian 126, 168;
   Blackfoot Indian 133; Bushmen 114;
   Chinese 111; Egyptian 137, 151;
   Fon 93, 128; Germanic 71–2; Gilbert
   Islands 133; Hawaiian 116, 139;
   Hindu 32, 72; Ibo 77; Inca 44, 174;
   Karadjeri 69; Maidu Indian 79;
   Marshall Islands 121; Maya 43, 109;
   Melanesian 151, 170; Mende 134;
   Pawnee Indian 169; Polynesian
   127–8; Shinto 111; Siberian 88;
   Solomon Islands 114; Sumerian 86;
   Tahitian 164; Viking 140; West
   African 90; Zuni Indian 57, 67
creation myths 135; Aranda 125;
   Babylonian 168; Bakairi 44; Chinese
   147; Egyptian 12; Eskimo 158;
   Haida 41; Heliopolitan 153; Hindu
   30; Iranian 156; Japanese 36;
   Madagascan 179; Malay 70; Maori
   148, 152; Mesopotamian 12; Toltec
   42; Zulu 172
creativity, Irish goddess of 73
cremation: Germanic 70; Hindu 30, 39
Creon *193*
Crete 20; religion 22
Creusa 54, *193*
criobolium 80
crows 27; Chinese myth 178
Cuchulainn 27, **79**, 90, 123; and Fand
   124; wife 124
Culann 79
culture heroes: Abnaki Indian 93;
   Chinese 34; Greek 76; Pueblo Indian
   67; Zuni Indian 67
Cumae 54
Cupay *193*
Cybele 19, 23, **80**; Canaanite
   counterpart 66; Demeter identified
   with 83; Egyptian equivalent 96;

Greek equivalent 61; lover 67; son
   of 129; Sumerian equivalent 106
Cyclopes **80**, 117, 159; death of 65;
   gift to Poseidon 149; Zeus and 179
Cymbeline *193*
Cyrus, Emperor 56

D

Da 128
Daedalus 81, 130
Dagda 26, **81**; and Tuatha De Danaan
   123; aspects 81; children 62, 73
Dagon *193*
Dainichi-nyorai *193*
daityas 97, *193*
Daksha *193*
Dambhodhava *193*
Damballa *193*
Dana *194*; alternative to 73; people of
   26, 122; son 81
Danae *194*; son of 149
Daniel **82**
Daniel, Bel, and the Snake 82
Daoism 34, 215
Daphne *194*
Daphnis *194*
Daphnis and Chloe *194*
Darius I, King 16, 82
David 159, *194*
David of Garesja, St 156
dawn goddesses: Germanic 97; Greek
   87; Iranian 130; Roman 87
Dazhbog *194*
dead: Banyoro beliefs 155; Bushmen
   beliefs 114; Eskimo beliefs 158;
   Canaanite food for 18; Greek escort
   of 101; Iranian customs/beliefs 153;
   Japanese consoler of 37; judgement
   of 37; Ptah and 151; Zulu belief 46,
   172
death 11, 100, 131, 151; Aboriginal
   beliefs 93; Balt rites 160; Bantu
   belief 120; Christian prince of 157;
   Dunsun beliefs 93; fasting to 32;
   Galla myth 102; Gilbert Island
   myths 51; Ibo beliefs 77;
   introduction of 44; Japanese beliefs
   36; Melanesian beliefs 151; New
   Hebridean beliefs 93; Nyamwezi
   beliefs 132; Pawnee beliefs 169;
   purification after 56; Solomon
   Islands beliefs 114; Sumerian
   mistress of 87
death and resurrection: Babylonian 19,
   53, 54; Irish myths 26; shamanistic
   40; Viking myths 28
   see also dying-and-rising gods
death goddesses: Germanic 70;
   Polynesian 128; Sumerian 105
death gods: Araucanian 95; Aztec 56,
   152; Banyarwanda 105; Banyoro
   155; Canaanite 18, 65, 69, 85;
   Chinese 177; Egyptian 11, 61, 145;
   Germanic 70; Greek 95, 141; Hindu
   177; Maya 56; Shinto 111; Vedic
   173; Voodoo 90
decay 11; Japanese beliefs 36
deceit, Iranian myth 16
Dechtire 79, 123, *194*
Deimos 61
Deirdre *194*
Delphi 76, 80, 83, 142, 144, *194*
Demeter **83**, 84, 117, 157; children
   148; cult centre 83; Isis identified
   with 109; and Pelops 164; and
   Persephone 95, 164; and
   Triptolemus 78, 176
Demong *194*
demons: Aztec 152; Canaanite 65;
   Buddhist 97, 125, 157; Hebrew 69;
   Hindu 59, 83, 97, 157, 174; Iranian
   155; Lotan 65; Mara 74; Rahu 59;

Gilgamesh 14, 64, 86, **92**, 102, 121, 137, 144; companion of 92; Ishtar and 108
gimokod 93
Gimokodan 93
Ginnungapap 71, *202*
Glaucus *202*
Glooskap 93
Glut 121
goblins, flesh-eating 56
Godheim 178
Godiva *62*
Gog and Magog *202*
Goga *202*
Goibhniu 122, 154, *202*
gold 129
golden age 118; Chinese 104; Greek 117; Roman 157
Golden Fleece 77, 112, *202*
Golem *202*
Goliath 159
good: Iranian god of 57; Sassanians and 156
good fortune/luck: Hindu goddess of 119
Gora-Daileng *203*
Gordian Knot *203*
Gorgons 123, *203*; Medusa 149
Gospel of Bartholomew 157
Gospel of Nicodemus 27, 113, 157
Gospel of Pseudo-Matthew 113
Grail 27, 64, 129, *203*; guardianship of 63; Lancelot and 62; prototype 26
grain goddess, Sumerian 162
Greece 20–3; adoption of Asian beliefs 23; borrowed myths 20; and Roman pantheon 23, 25
Grendel 176, *203*
Gu 93, 128, 142
Guan Di **94**
guardian deities: Hindu 56; Roman 112
Guecufu 95, *203*
Guinechen **95**
Guinemapun 95
Guinevere, Queen 62, 90, *203*
Gullveig 89
Gum Girl 60, *203*
Gungnir 140, *203*
Gunnodoyak 101, *203*
Guyug 165
Gwri 151
Gwydion 62, *203*
Gwynn *203*

H

Hachiman *204*
Hadad *204*
Hades 22, 77, 85, **95**, 117, 146, 179; aspects of 95; Heracles and 101; and Kronos 149; Orpheus and 144; and Persephone 83; Sisyphus and 141; symbol of 80; wife of 148
Hafaza *204*
Hahgwehdiyu *204*
Haida Indians 41
Haile Selassie, Emperor 46
hai-uri *204*
Hakawau **96**
Halirrhothius 62, *204*
Halocan 169
Ham 137, *204*
handicrafts, Roman goddess of 130
Hannahanna *204*; and Telipinu 166
Hantu Pemburu *204*
Hanuman 34, 79, **96**; and Rama 175; magic stick 170
Han Xiangzi *204*
haoma 59, 156, *204*
Hapi *204*
Havgan 151
Hari-Hara *204*
Harimau Kramet *204*

harlots, Babylonian protectress of 108
harp, magic 81
Harpies 205
harvest gods: Aztec 104; Canaanite 85; Egyptian 59
Hathor **96**, 102; aspects of 96; Isis identified with 108; Re and 153; as Sekhmet 159
Haumea 205
Hawaii 50; beliefs 116, 139, 148
hawk-man 125
Hayagriva **97**, 174
headhunting, Irish 79
healing: Greek god of 65; Irish goddess of 73; Serapis and 160; Shinto beliefs 143
hearth/household goddesses: Germanic 89; Greek 206; Roman 25, 246
heaven: Canaanite lady of 66; entrances to 44; Germanic sentinel of 97; Navaho creator of 57; Sumerian personification of 60
Hebe 100, 205
Hebrews: and Athirat 66; in open revolt 82
Hecabe 149
Hecate **97**; aspects of 97; and Demeter 83
Hector 53, 58, 149, 205
Hecuba, Queen 205; daughter 76
Heimdal **97**
Heitsi-Eibib **98**
Hel 29, 205, 178; and Balder 70, 155
Helen 76, 77, **98**, 149; brothers of 77; as prize 61
Helheim 70, 178, 205
Helios 87, 205; children 77, 100; and Demeter 83
Hell: Christian 27; Leviathan identified with 120
Hephaistos 53, **98**, 100, 150; armour made by 58; and Athena 66; Egyptian equivalent 151; gifts for Hera 98; gift to Heracles 100; and Pandora 147; rival to 66; wife 61
Hera 21–2, 61, **100**, 117; and Artemis 62; children 62, 98; and Hermes 101; and Heracles 100, 101; Isis identified with 109; and Jason 112; and Poseidon 149; Roman equivalent 113; and Semele 84; and the Sphinx 162; and Zeus 179
Heracles 21, 59, **100**; and the Amazons 167; Armenian equivalent 173; Athena and 66; death of 101; Hera and 22; Iranian counterpart 155; labours of 20, 100, 163; Japanese counterpart 58, 163; and Jason 112; Polynesian equivalent 50, 127–8; and Prometheus 150; symbols of 20
Herakhty 102, 205
Hercules 205; *see also* Heracles
hermaphrodite gods, Navaho 57
Hermaphroditos 205
hermeia 101
Hermes **101**; Hindu counterpart 89; and the dead 95; and Odysseus 77; and Pandora 147; and Pelops 164; gift to Perseus 149; son 147; and Zeus 171
Hermes Trismegistus 168
Hermodr 205; and Balder 70
Hermopolis, cosmology of 59
Hero 205
Herod, King 113, *206*
Herodotus 16
heroes 55; Armenian 173; Arthurian 90; Athena and 66; Athenian 22; Banks Islands 139, 151; Celtic 27; Christian 156; Greek 20, 21, 53, 58, 59, 65, 76, 77, 100, 112, 141, 149, 167; Hottentot 98; Iban 39; Iranian

155; Irish 26, 79–80; Malay 70; Manx 124; Mesopotamian 14; Micronesian 144; Navaho 134; Polynesian 55; questing 64; Roman 24, 25; Scandinavian 154; Sioux/Dakota Indian 104; Trojan 54; twin 44; Sumerian 92
Herrera, Antonio de 42
Heru-pa-khret 102, *206*
Hesperides *206*; golden apples of 101
Hesiod: *Theogony* 21
Hestia 117, *206*
Hiawatha 83, 101, *206*
Hilaria 77
Hina 127–8
Hine-nui-te-po 55, *206*; Maui and 128
Hino *206*
Hinun **101**
Hippolyta *206*; belt of 100
Hippolytus *206*
Hiranyakasipu 175, *206*
Hiranyaksha 174, *206*
Hiranya-garbha 32
Hittites 18; defeat at Kadesh 59
Hiyoyoa 146, *206*
Hkun Ai *206*
Hodr 28, *207*; and Balder 70, 121
Holawaka 102, *207*
Holy Grail, *see* Grail
Homer 21; *Iliad* 53, 98, 149; *Odyssey* 77
Hope 147
Horatius Cocles 24, *207*
Horbehudet 102
horses: Buddhist protector of 97; of Eos 87; Frey's 89; Hindu myths 163; man-eating 100; Loki and 121; Rakush 155; Silenus 129; Sioux Indian belief 79; Sleipnir 70, 121, 140
Horus 10, **102**, 108, 139; aspects of 102; pharaoh identified with 11; and Seth 156, 160, 168; solar cult 102; symbols of 11, 102; wife/mother 96
"hound of Culann" 79
hound of Ulster 123
hougan 90, 119
Hou I 178
houris 207
housecrafts, Chinese goddess of 161
Hrymir 121
hsien 34, 104, *207*
Huang Di **104**
Huh/Hauhet 137
Huichol Indians 40
Huitzilopochtli 78, **104**, 166, 176; mother 78; symbols of 104
human sacrifice: Aztec 78, 104, 152, 166, 169, 176; Babylonian 60; Celtic 26; Canaanite deity of 132; Greek 144; Minoan 130, 167; Tahitian 164; Toltec 42; Viking 140
Hunab 43, 109, *207*
hunting 40, 103; Greek goddess of 62; Yoruba god of 154
Hurakan *207*
Hushedar *207*
Huwawa 92, *207*
Hvergelmir, well of 178
Hydra 100, *207*
Hyksos 59
Hylas *207*
Hymir *208*; and Thor 167
Hyperion *208*; daughter of 87
Hypnos *208*

I

Iae 119, *208*
Iapetus, children of 149
Ibn Fadlan 70
Iblis *208*

Icarus 81, 130, *208*; father 81
Ictinike **104**
Idas, Prince 77, *208*
Idomeneus *208*
Idun *208*
Igraine, Duchess 62, 129, *208*
Iki-Haveve *208*
Iku *208*
Ilamatecuhtli *208*
Ile-Ife *208*
Ilithyia 100, *208*
Illuyankas 171, *208*; and order 57; and Taru 165
Ilya Muromets *209*
Imana **105**
Imdugud 136, *209*
Imhotep **105**
Imilozi *209*
immortality: Agni and 56; depriving of 44; refusal of 53; Zheng and 34; *see also* dying-and-rising gods
Inanna **105–6**, 113, 119, 162; aspects of 106; Babylonian counterpart 108; Canaanite counterpart 66; Egyptian equivalent 96; Greek equivalent 61; Japanese counterpart 58
Inaras 165, *209*
Inari **107**
Incas 44; solar stone 68
India 30–3, 56, 107, 138; Indus civilization 30, 32
Indra **107**; and Agni 56; aspects of 32; Buddha as 74; and Durvasas 59; and Shiva 161; symbols of 32, 107; and Vishnu 174
inspiration, Germanic god of 71
Inti 44, 45, 68, 108, *209*; children of 174
Io *209*
invisibility: cap of 80, 149; helmet of 124; mantle of 124
Iolaus 100
Iouskeha *209*
Iphicles *209*
Iphigenia 144, *209*
Iran 16; as earthly paradise 56
Ireland: mythological cycles 26
Iris *209*
Irra *209*
irrigation: Canaanite god of 69; Chinese god of 178; Sumerian god of 86
Iruwa *209*
Isaiah 56
Iseult *209*
Ishkur 162, *209*
Ishtar 65, **108**; Canaanite counterpart 66; Egyptian equivalent 96; and Gilgamesh 92; Greek equivalent 61; husband 19; Ninlil identified as 65; Sumerian equivalent 106; and Tammuz 67
Isis 11, 23, **108**, 137, 139, 153; and Anubis 61; children 102, 108, 168; Demeter identified with 83; and embalming 13; and Hathor as 96; and Horus 168; and Osiris 108, 145, 160, 168; and Re 153; symbols of 108
Islam, Southeast Asian 38
islands: Arthurian 63; "of the blest" 34; of Calypso 141; Chinese immortals on 104; Circe's 77, 141; Dia 167; Dilmun 86; of Egyptian deities 10; Lemnos 98, 150; Sicily 171; Shinto beliefs 111; Tir Tairnigiri 124
Islands of Joy 73
Italapas *209*
Itherther **109**
Itugen 165
Itzamna **109**, 110
Itzli 166
Iwa *209*

255

Seker *238*; Ptah linked with 151
Sekhmet **159**
Sela *238*
Selene *238*; and Pan 147
Seleucids 16
Semargl *238*
Semele 84, *238*
Semites 14, 18
Serapeum 160
Serapis **160**
Sermenys **160**
"serpent skirt" 78
serpent kings: Buddhist 74; Greek 66
serpents: Aztec 43, 104, 138, 152;
   Babylonian 168; Chippewa 40;
   cosmic 31; Daniel and the sacred 82;
   of drought 107; Egyptian 12, 102,
   153; Fon 128; Germanic 29, 121,
   167; of the Great Lakes 101; Greek
   62, 76, 162; Haitian beliefs 128;
   Hebrew 120; Hindu 31, 117, 161;
   Malay 70; Maya 43, 109, 110;
   Mixcoatl 78; Murngin 179;
   Poseyemu identified with 67; raft of
   42, 152; Satan as 157; Shinto 163;
   Solomon Islands 114; water from 44
Serqet *238*
Sessrumnir *238*
Seth 10, 11, 108, 137, 139, 153, 156,
   160; and Anubis 61; and Horus
   168; and Osiris 61, 102, 108, 145,
   160, 168; wife of 137
shadow play, Indonesian 38
Shadrach 82, *238*
Sha-lana 41
Shang Di 34
Shah-Nameh 155
shaman/shamanism 40, 143; Japanese
   36
Shamash *239*
Shango *239*
Shapash 69
shape-changers: Bakairi Indian 44;
   Hindu 56; Manx 124; Navaho 57;
   North American 41
shark 103, 170; teeth of 50
sheep/lamb: bath in blood of 80; as
   messenger 77
Shem 137
Shennong 34, **161**
Sheol *239*
she-wolf 24, 68, 155
shield, magic 149
Shintoism 36; Floating Bridge of
   Heaven 111; household ceremonies
   37
Shiva 30, 32, 72, **161**; antecedents
   107; aspects of 32, 161; attributes
   161; and Brahma 72; and Ganesa 89;
   and the Ganges 161; and Kama 161;
   and Mahisha 83; Malay beliefs 70;
   phallus of 72; and rivers of poison
   59, 161; and Soma 59; son of 89;
   trident of 163; wife of 83–4, 161
Shotoku, Prince 36
Shouxing *239*
Shu 137, 139, 153, *239*
Shu Ching 178
Shun, Emperor 178
Sibyl 54, *239*
Siddhartha 74
Sidhe *239*
Sigurd *239*; and Fafnir 154
Sigyn 121, *239*
Silene 84, 87
Silenus 129, *239*
Silvanus 127, *239*
Sin **162**
Sinaa 171
Sinon *239*
Sirens 64, 141, *239*
Sir Gawain and the Green Knight 90
Sisyphus *230*; son of 141
Sita 96, 175, *240*

Skadi 89, *240*
Skidbladnir 89
Skirnir 89, *240*
sky: Babylonian belief 126; Chibcha/
   Muyscaya supporters of 71; Chinese
   immortals in 104; Egyptian beliefs
   139; Germanic supporters of 71;
   Greek belief 152; Tongan belief 127
sky goddesses: Egyptian 96, 108, 137,
   139, 152; Germanic 89; Japanese 58
sky gods: Abaluyia 176; African 132;
   Arawak Indian 44; Aranda 48; Bantu
   120; Blackfoot 133; Caroline Islands
   144; Chibcha/Muyscaya 71; Chinese
   178; East Asian nomads 165; Fon
   128; Greek 22, 50, 80, 95, 173, 179;
   Hindu 56, 59, 74, 107, 130, 138,
   140, 161; Iranian 130; Iroquois 101;
   malay 70; Maori 50, 148, 152;
   Mende 134; Navajo 134;
   Polynesian 164; Roman 114; Slavic
   160; Sumerian 60, 87; Vedic 173;
   Viking 140; Warrau Indian 44; Zulu
   46, 172
Skrymir 167, *240*
Sleipnir 70, 121, 140, *240*
smith gods 154; Anglo-Saxon 176;
   Canaanite 65, 86; Celtic 154; Fon
   93, 126, 142; Greek 53, 58, 61, 66,
   98, 100, 147, 150, 151; Icelandic
   176; Irish 79, 122; Roman 80, 151,
   154; Yoruba 154
smiths, Irish goddess of 73
snake-bird god, Toltec 42
snake-headed deities, Egyptian 168
snakes 44, 59, 104, 109; Aboriginal
   71; Admiralty Island myth 114;
   Asclepius and 65; Ashanti myths
   137; Bushmen traditions 47;
   Christian 113; Greek myths 76, 100;
   Iroquois 101; Karadjeri beliefs 69;
   sloughing of skin 92, 102; Sumerian
   92
   see also Midgard Snake; serpents
Snohomish Indians 41
Solomon *240*
Soma 32, 59, 107, *240*; Iranian
   counterpart 156
"Son of Heaven" 34
sorcerers: Chinese 34; Hottentot 98
   Maori 96; mirror of 166; Mithra and
   130; Shinto god of 143
souls: Ashanti beliefs 137; Egyptian
   belief 61, 145, 153, 168; Greek
   beliefs 146; Hindu beliefs 177;
   Iranian beliefs 153; Navaho myth
   57; Papuan belief 146; Siberian
   beliefs 77
   see also spirits
South America 44
Southeast Asia 38; cultural division 38
Spartoi *240*
Sphinx **162**; Oedipus and 142
Spider 60
spider spirit, Melanesian 151
Spider Woman 134, *240*
spirits: Banyarwanda beliefs 105;
   Bushmen leader of 114; Lapp beliefs
   158; Voodoo myth 119
Spoils of Annwyn 129
squid god, Hawaiian 116
Sri Ramakrishna 33
stars: Bushmen tradition 47, 172;
   Egyptian beliefs 139; Gilbert Islands
   belief 133; Hindu maker of 56; Rahu
   among 59; Zulu belief 172
   see also Pleiades
Stella Maris 165, *240*
Stentor *240*
sterility: Canaanite god of 69
Sterope 80, *240*
Stonehenge 129
stone-knife god, Aztec 166
Stribog *240*

storm gods: Canaanite 69; Chibcha/
   Muyscaya 71; Egyptian 160; Hindu
   32; Inca 174; Maori 50, 152;
   Mesopotamian 14; Shinto 111, 143,
   163; Viking 140
Stymphalian birds 100
Styx 53, 95, *240*
sudra 16
Suebi 28
Suen 162, *240*
Sugriva 96, *240*
suicide, Maya goddess of 110
Sumerians 14; Gates of God 136; idea
   of kingship 60
sun: Abaluyia beliefs 176; Blackfoot
   belief 133; Chinese beliefs 178;
   creation of 44; Egyptian beliefs 153,
   159; Germanic myth 121; Gilbert
   Islands belief 133; Hindu maker of
   56; Maori belief 127; set in place 44
sun-disc 12
sun goddesses: Shinto 36, 58, 111, 163
sun gods: Armenian 173; Aztec 166;
   Babylonian 60; Blackfoot 133; Celtic
   90; descendants of 44; Egyptian
   myths 12, 59, 96, 102, 108, 109,
   137, 138, 139, 153, 162; Greek 53,
   77, 83, 87, 100; Haitian 119; Hindu
   32, 56, 163, 177; Inca 44, 45, 68,
   108, 174; Irish 79, 81, 90, 122, 124;
   Mamaiuran Indian 119; Navaho 134;
   Papuan 85; Pawnee Indian 169;
   Scandinavian 89; Toltec sacrifices to
   42; Vedic 130
sunyata 30
supreme deities: Abaluyia 176; Akan
   46; Araucanian Indian 95; Assyrian
   14; Aztec 42, 43, 104; Babylonian
   14, 15, 53, 65, 126; Balt 160; Bantu
   120; Banyoro 155; Banyarwanda
   105; Blackfoot 133; Canaanite 18,
   66, 85; Chinese 34; Egyptian 59,
   145, 153; Fon 128; Greek 20, 21,
   179; Hebrew 85; Hindu 30, 32, 33,
   72, 83, 107, 161, 174; Ibo 77;
   Iranian 57, 130; Irish 73, 81; Jain
   124; Madagascan 179; Maya 109;
   Navaho 57; Nyamwezi 132; Pawnee
   169; Roman 114; Sumerian 53;
   Tahitian 164; Turk/Mongol 165;
   Vedic 173; Zulu 46, 172; Zuni 67
Surabhi 59, *241*
Surasa *241*; and Hanuman 96
Surt 241
Surya 56, *163*; son of 177; Varuna
   and 173
Susanowo 58, 111, **163**; daughter of
   143; and O-Kuni-Nushi 143
Suseri-Hima 143
Sutton Hoo burial 29, 154
Svantovit *241*
Svarogich 241
Svartalfheim 178, *241*
swans 57
swords 176; Frey's 89
Syrinx *241*; and Pan 147

T

Ta'aroa **164**; Marshall Island
   equivalent 121; names of 164
Taburimai 51, *241*
Tages *241*
Taliesin *241*
talisman 59
Talos 81, *241*
Tammuz 19, 53, 108, *241*; Germanic
   counterpart 70; and Ishtar 67, 92;
   original title 54
Tane-mahuta *241*; and Rangi 152, 164
Tangaroa 116, *164*, *241*; and Rogo-
   tumu-here 164
Tanit *241*
Tanngniortr and Tanngrisnr 167, *242*

Tano *242*
Tantalus **164**
Tapeia *242*
Tara 35, **165**; names of 165
Taranga 127–8
Tarchon *242*
Tarquin *242*
Tarquinius, Sextus *242*
Tarquinius Superbus 24
Tartarus *242*
Taru **165**; and Illuyankas 171; son of 166
Taueret 103, *242*
taurobolium 80
Tautohito 96, *242*
Tawhiri-ma-tea 50, *242*; and Rangi
   152; and Tane-mahuta 164
Tawiskaron *242*
tea 161
Te-ariki-n-tarawa 51
te avae roroa 164
Tefnut 137, 153, *242*
Te Ikawai 133, *242*
Telemachus 141, *242*
Telipinu **166**
Temazcateci *242*
temples: of Apollo 23; of Athena 21;
   city of 38; of Enlil 60; of Isis 108;
   Mesopotamian 14; Qorikancha 44;
   Parthenon 21; of Re 12; Roman
   Forum 25; of Saturn 157; of the Sun
   174; of Ta'aroa 164; of Vesta 25
Te Nao 133, *242*
Tenes, King 53, *242*
Tengri **165**
Tengu *242*
Te Tuna 127–8
Teucer *242*
Tezcatlipoca **166**
Thales 21
Thamuatz 109
Thanatos 100, *243*; Sisyphus and 141
Thaumus *243*
Theia 87
Themis *243*; children 150
Theseus 22, 23, **167**; and Ariadne
   167; and Helen 77; and Heracles
   167; and the Minotaur 81, 130, 167
Thetis 53, *243*
Thor 28, 29, 140, 158, **167**, 178; Balt
   equivalent 160; companion of 121;
   death of 121; and frost giants 167;
   and Jormungandr 167; lineage 29;
   mother of 89; symbols of 29, 167
Thora 114
Thoth 12, 61, 153, **168**; and Horus
   168; and Nut 139; and Osiris 168;
   and weighing of souls 145
Thrall 97, *243*
Thrymr *243*
Thrymskirda 167
thunder gods: Araucanian 95; Balt
   160; Chinese 139; Germanic 167;
   Guarani 170; Iroquois 101; Lapp
   158; Sumerian 136; Viking 29, 140
thunderbolts 32, 107, 138; Zeus and
   171
Thunor *243*
Tiamat 12, 15, 120, 126, 156, 157,
   168; and Antichrist 60; Egyptian
   equivalent 153; gift to Kingu 168;
   and order 57
Tiberinus 112, *243*
tigers 60
Tintagel *243*
Tirawa **169**
Tirawahat *243*
Tiresias 100, *243*; Odysseus and 77
tirthankaras 124
Tishtrya *243*
Tisiphone 88
Titans 19, 117, 150, 164, 179, *243*;
   Hindu equivalent 97
Tithonus *243*; Eos and 87
Tiw *243*

ACKNOWLEDGEMENTS

l=left; *r*=right; *t*=top; *c*=centre; *b*=bottom

1 The Bridgeman Art Library; 2/3 Anne de Henning/The John Hillelson Agency; 4/5 Axel Poignant Archive; 6/7 Lyle Lawson/APA Photo Agency; 8*l* Hutchison Library; 8*r* Aldus Archive; 9*tl* NASA/Science Photo Library; 9*r* British Museum/Michael Holford; 9*bl* British Museum/Werner Forman Archive; 10*t* Robert Harding Picture Library; 10*b* H. Veiller/Explorer; 11 Kelly Langley/Aspect Picture Library; 12/13 British Museum/Michael Holford; 13 Gilles Peress/Magnum Photos; 14 E.T. Archive; 14/15 William MacQuitty; 16 Ann and Bury Peerless; 16/17 Maroon/Zefa Picture Library; 17 Robert Harding Picture Library; 18 C.M. Dixon; 18/19*b* Gascoigne/Robert Harding Picture Library; 19 Hittite Museum, Ankara/E.T. Archive; 20 Sonia Halliday Photographs; 20/21 Bob Davis/Aspect Picture Library; 21*r* British Museum/Michael Holford; 22/23 Bob Davis/Aspect Picture Library; 23*t* C.M. Dixon; 23*c* Nobby Clark; 23*b* Damm/Zefa Picture Library; 24/25 A.J. Hartman/Susan Griggs Agency; 25*t* Adrian Evans/Hutchison Library; 25*b* British Museum/Michael Holford; 26*t* John Bulmer/Susan Griggs Agency; 26*b* Board of Trinity College, Dublin; 26/27 Birmingham City Art Gallery/The Bridgeman Art Library; 27 National Museum, Copenhagen/Werner Forman Archive; 28/29 Bryan and Cherry Alexander; 29*t* British Museum/Michael Holford; 30 Tweedie/Colorific; 30/31 Alain Thomas/Explorer; 31*l* Douglas Dickins; 31*r* Victoria and Albert Museum/Michael Holford; 32*t* William MacQuitty; 32*b* Robin Mayer/Colorific; 32/33 Ann and Bury Peerless; 34 Jean-Loup Gobert/Explorer; 35*t* Jean-Loup Gobert/Explorer; 35*b* Percival David Foundation; 36/37*r* Victoria and Albert Museum/Michael Holford; 37*t* Richard Kalvar/Magnum Photos; 37*b* Ernesto Bazan/Magnum Photos; 38 Jeremy Horner/Hutchison Library; 38/39 J. Alex Langley/Aspect Picture Library; 39*t* Burt Glinn/Magnum Photos; 39*b* Michael Macintyre/Hutchison Library; 40*t* Peter Newark's Western Americana; 40*b* Werner Forman Archive; 40/41 Bryan and Cherry Alexander; 42/43 Norman Owen Tomalin/Bruce Coleman; 43*t* Musée Guimet, Paris/Michael Holford; 43*b* British Museum/Werner Forman Archive; 45*t* Urs Kluyver/Zefa Picture Library; 45 Tony Morrison; 46 Bryan and Cherry Alexander; 46/47 Günter Ziesler; 47 Museum of Mankind/Michael Holford; 48/50 Axel Poignant Archive; 50/51 Axel Poignant Archive; 51 Tom Nebbia/Aspect Picture Library; 53 British Museum/Michael Holford; 55*t* British Museum/Michael Holford; 55*l* Bryan and Cherry Alexander; 55*r* F. Jack Jackson/Planet Earth Pictures; 55*b* British Museum/Michael Holford; 57 Wheelwright Museum/E.T. Archive; 58/59 Victoria and Albert Museum/Michael Holford; 60 Mary Evans Picture Library; 61/62 Pat Hodgson Library; 63 Janet and Colin Bord; 64*tl* Janet and Colin Bord; 64*tr* Louvre/photo Hubert Josse; 64*bl* British Museum/Michael Holford; 64*br* Bibliothèque de l'Arsenal/Giraudon; 65 British Museum/Michael Holford; 66*l* The Mansell Collection; 66*r* Hulton Deutsch Collection; 68*t* Robert Harding Picture Library; 68*tc* Palace of the Conservatori, Rome/C.M. Dixon; 68*bc* Sonia Halliday Photographs; 68*l* Tony Morrison; 68*br* G. Dagli Orti; 69 Louvre/Michael Holford; 70 Hulton Deutsch Collection; 71 Spectrum Colour Library; 72*l* Pat Hodgson Library; 72*r* Musée Guimet, Paris/Michael Holford; 73 National Galleries of Scotland; 74 C.M. Dixon; 75*tl* Dilip Mehta/Contact/Colorific; 75*tr* Spink and Son/The Bridgeman Art Library; 75*bl* Michael Holford; 75*bc* Richard Vogel/Wheeler Pictures; 75*br* Michael Holford; 76 Mary Evans Picture Library; 77 Ronald Sheridan/The Ancient Art and Architecture Collection; 78*t* Axel Poignant Archive; 78 National Film Archive; 78/79 Victoria and Albert Museum/C.M. Dixon; 79 Mary Evans Picture Library; 82 K. Kerth/Zefa Picture Library; 82/83 Walker Art Gallery, Liverpool; 83*t* National Film Archive; 83*b* Smithsonian Institution/E.T. Archive; 84*l* Victoria and Albert Museum; 84*r* Starfoto/Zefa Picture Library; 86 G. Dagli Orti; 87 The Mansell Collection; 88 Sonia Halliday Photographs; 90 Bodleian Library/E.T. Archive; 91*t* Ferdinand Anton; 91*c* Alain Thomas/Explorer; 91*bl* Chantal Regnault/Explorer; 91*br* Brian Shuel; 94*l* British Museum/C.M. Dixon; 94*r* Dr Jean Lorre/Science Photo Library; 94/95 Bodleian Library; 95 Victoria and Albert Museum/Michael Holford; 99*tl* G. Dagli Orti; 99*tr* E.T. Archive; 99*bl* Dr Georg Gerster/The John Hillelson Agency; 99*br* Victoria and Albert Museum/C.M. Dixon; 102 Pat Hodgson Library; 103*t* National Gallery, Melbourne/Robert Harding Picture Library; 103*c* Hutchison Library; 103*l* Collection André Breton/Michael Holford; 103*bc* Robert Harding Picture Library; 103*br* British Museum/Michael Holford; 105 Pat Hodgson Library; 106*t* Museum of Archaeology and Antiquities, Venice/ G. Dagli Orti; 106*b* Hughes/Spacecharts; 106/107 Victoria and Albert Museum/Michael Holford; 108*l* Werner Forman Archive; 107*r* Musée Guimet/Larousse; 108/109 Pat Hodgson Library; 112/114 The Mansell Collection; 117 Michael Holford; 118*r* Prado, Madrid/The Bridgeman Art Library; 118*tl* E.T. Archive; 118*bl* Ronald Sheridan/The Ancient Art and Architecture Collection; 119 C.M. Dixon; 110*l* Hutchison Library; 110*r* British Museum/Michael Holford; 111 Ann and Bury Peerless; 115*t* British Museum/Michael Holford; 115*c* Werner Forman Archive; 115*bl* Axel Poignant Archive; 115*br* E.T. Archive; 119 Chantal Regnault/Explorer; 120 Pat Hodgson Library; 121 Axel Poignant Archive; 122*t* City of York Art Gallery/The Bridgeman Art Library; 122*bl* Prado, Madrid/The Bridgeman Art Library; 122*br* National Gallery of Prague/Werner Forman Archive; 123 Mary Evans Picture Library; 125 Horniman Museum/ Michael Holford; 126 Victoria and Albert Museum/Michael Holford; 127*t* Pat Hodgson Library; 127*bl* British Museum/Michael Holford; 127*br* Museum of Mankind/Michael Holford; 129 The Facts on File Encyclopedia of World Mythology by Antony S. Mercatante; 130 The Mansell Collection; 131 The Tate Gallery/Aldus Archive; 132 Ronald Sheridan/The Ancient Art and Architecture Collection; 133 British Museum; 134 Wheelwright Museum/E.T. Archive; 135*t* Museum of Mankind/Michael Holford; 135*cl* Sally and Richard Greenhill; 135*bl* Musée Guimet/Michael Holford; 135*br* Vatican Museum and Galleries, Rome/The Bridgeman Art Library; 137 British Museum/Michael Holford; 138*t* British Museum/ Michael Holford; 138*cl* Soames Summerhays/Science Photo Library; 138*cr* Gordon Garradd/Science Photo Library; 138*bl* Steve McCutcheon/Frank Lane Picture Agency; 138*bc* Ferdinand Anton; 138*br* Robert Harding Picture Library; 139 Peter Clayton; 140 The Illustrated London News Picture Library; 141 Hulton Deutsch Collection; 142 British Museum; 143*t* G. Dagli Orti; 143*l* Giraudon/Aldus Archive; 143*bc* William Channing/Werner Forman Archive; 143*br* Victoria and Albert Museum/The Bridgeman Art Library; 144 Sonia Halliday Photographs; 145 British Museum/Michael Holford; 146*t* Bibliothèque Nationale, Paris/Aldus Archive; 146*cl* Ron and Valerie Taylor/Ardea; 146*cr* University Museum of Anthropology, Jallapa/Werner Forman Archive; 146*b* Axel Poignant Archive; 147*l* British Museum/Michael Holford; 147*r* The Mansell Collection; 148 Axel Poignant Archive; 150*t* Ferdinand Anton; 150*l* Konrad Helbig/Zefa; 150*r* Prado, Madrid/The Bridgeman Art Library; 150*b* Pat Hodgson Library; 151 Axel Poignant Archive; 153 Peter Clayton; 154*t* British Museum/Michael Holford; 154*cl* F. Troina/Granata/Planet Earth Pictures; 154*cr* C.M. Dixon; 154*bl* Janet and Colin Bord; 154*br* Hutchison Library; 155 Peter Carmichael/Aspect Picture Library; 158 Collection André Breton, Paris/Michael Holford; 159*c* Copenhagen Royal Library/Aldus Archive; 159*b* Bibliothèque Nationale, Paris/Robert Harding Picture Library; 160 British Museum; 161*l* Melanie Friend/Format; 161*r* Victoria and Albert Museum/C.M. Dixon; 162 Rosi Baumgartner/Explorer; 163 Pat Hodgson Library; 164 Mary Evans Picture Library; 166 Liverpool City Museum/Werner Forman Archive; 167 The Museum of National Antiquities, Stockholm/Weidenfeld and Nicolson archives; 168 British Museum; 169 The Mansell Collection; 170 Tony Morrison; 171 Hulton Deutsch Collection; 172 Howard Sochurek/The John Hillelson Agency; 173 History Museum, Sofia/E.T. Archive; 174 Pat Hodgson Library; 175*l* Victoria and Albert Museum; 175*r* © 1983 Royal Observatory, Edinburgh; 177 Pat Hodgson Library; 178 Rosi Baumgartner/Explorer; 179 Axel Poignant Archive.

Picture research: Anne-Marie Ehrlich and Pat Hodgson

Illustration and design: Tony de Saulles

Maps: Ed Stuart

All illustrations in the Micropedia from Dover Pictorial Archive Series